P9-DGB-084

Frommer's®
Chicago with Kids

4th Edition

by Laura Tiebert

Here's what the critics say about Frommer's:

"Amazingly easy to use. Very portable, very complete."
—BOOKLIST

"Detailed, accurate, and easy-to-read information
for all price ranges."
—GLAMOUR MAGAZINE

"Hotel information is close to encyclopedic."
—DES MOINES SUNDAY REGISTER

"Frommer's Guides have a way of giving you
a real feel for a place."
—KNIGHT RIDDER NEWSPAPERS

WILEY

Wiley Publishing, Inc.

ABOUT THE AUTHOR

Laura Tiebert is a freelance writer whose travels have taken her from the frozen tundra of Dawson City in Yukon Territory to the wide beaches of Muscat, Oman. A native Midwesterner, she lived in New York City for years before returning to Chicago. Today, she stays a bit closer to home in Wilmette, Illinois, where she lives with her husband, Andrew, and two young sons.

Published by:

WILEY PUBLISHING, INC.

111 River St.
Hoboken, NJ 07030-5774

ISBN 978-0-470-39324-6

Editor: William Travis
Production Editor: M. Faunette Johnston
Cartographer: Guy Ruggiero
Photo Editor: Richard Fox
Production by Wiley Indianapolis Composition Services
Front cover photo: The Loop Kapoor Sculpture Cloud: Children looking at their reflections
Back cover photo: Chicago skyline

For information on our other products and services or to obtain technical support, please contact our Customer Care Department within the U.S. at 877/762-2974, outside the U.S. at 317/572-3993 or fax 317/572-4002.

Wiley also publishes its books in a variety of electronic formats. Some content that appears in print may not be available in electronic formats.

Manufactured in the United States of America

5   4   3   2   1

CONTENTS

LIST OF MAPS	vi

1 HOW TO FEEL LIKE A CHICAGO FAMILY · 1

1 Favorite Chicago Family
Experiences...................2

2 The Best Hotel Bets 6

The Best Chicago Websites...........7

3 The Best Dining Bets 8

2 PLANNING A FAMILY TRIP TO CHICAGO · 12

1 Visitor Information 12

*Destination Chicago: Red
Alert Checklist*....................... 13

2 What to Pack......................14

Flying or Driving with Kids 15

3 Entry Requirements 15

*Cut to the Front of the Airport
Security Line as a Registered
Traveler* 17

4 When to Go.......................18

Kids' Favorite Chicago Events 19

5 Getting There 26

Air Travel Security Measures.........30

In-Flight Fun for Kids 36

Flying with Film & Video.............38

6 Money & Costs....................39

What Things Cost in Chicago 41

7 Health 41

8 Safety............................42

9 Sustainable Tourism..............43

It's Easy Being Green 44

10 Traveling Safely with Kids
in Chicago.......................44

*Frommers.com: The Complete
Travel Resource* 46

11 Staying Connected...............47

12 Getting to Know Chicago 48

A River Runs Through It 51

Neighborhoods in Brief..............52

*Frommer's Favorite Oh-So-
Chicago Experiences*................54

13 Getting Around 58

Sky Train: Chicago's El 62

14 Getting Kids Interested
in Chicago.......................65

3 SUGGESTED CHICAGO ITINERARIES · 66

1 The Best of Chicago in 1 Day......66

2 The Best of Chicago in 2 Days.....70

3 The Best of Chicago in 3 Days.....71

4 FAMILY-FRIENDLY ACCOMMODATIONS 73

Major Convention Dates............75

1 The Loop 75

2 South Loop 82

3 Near North & the
Magnificent Mile.................84

Making the Most of the
Concierge............................87

4 River North 97

5 The Gold Coast 100

6 Lincoln Park & the North Side ...101

5 FAMILY-FRIENDLY DINING 107

1 Restaurants by Cuisine 108

2 The Loop 111

Ethnic Dining near the Loop 114

Suburban Safaris....................121

3 West Loop 122

4 The Magnificent Mile & the
Gold Coast......................123

Dining Out in (Relative) Peace 124

5 River North 130

Breakfast & Brunch.................132

6 Lincoln Park.....................139

Dining Alfresco......................144

7 Wrigleyville & the North Side....148

8 Wicker Park/Bucktown 150

9 Only in Chicago.................154

6 EXPLORING CHICAGO WITH YOUR KIDS 156

1 Sights by Neighborhood........156

2 Kids' Top 10 Attractions 157

Do-It-Yourself Sightseeing..........166

Museum Free Days.................175

3 Best Views 175

4 More Chicago Museums 178

For Train Lovers 188

5 Best Rides.......................190

6 Historic Houses 191

The (Frank Lloyd) Wright Stuff......192

The Pride of Prairie Avenue.........196

7 Zoos............................196

8 Gardens & Conservatories.......199

9 Nature Centers..................200

10 Water Parks 201

11 Kid-Friendly Tours 201

7 NEIGHBORHOOD STROLLS 208

1 Near North/Magnificent Mile....208

Walk This Way: Chicago's
Underground Pedway 209

2 The Loop 209

3 The Gold Coast 211

4 Old Town 211

Chicago & the Great Black
Migration..........................212

5 Lincoln Park.....................214

6 Andersonville 214

7 Bucktown/Wicker Park 215

8 FOR THE ACTIVE FAMILY 216

1 Enjoying Chicago's Beaches 216

2 Green Chicago: City Parks 217

3 Playgrounds in the City Center... 222

4 Sports & Games................. 223

5 Indoor Playgrounds 229

6 Classes & Workshops............ 230

9 SHOPPING WITH YOUR KIDS 232

1 The Shopping Scene............ 232

2 Shopping A to Z 241

From Chicago with Love 246

10 ENTERTAINMENT FOR THE WHOLE FAMILY 253

Scoring the Elusive Ticket. 258

1 The Big Venues.................. 259

Going to the Show by El or Bus. 260

*If You Have a Sitter: The Music
Scene* 262

2 Seasonal Events................. 265

3 Theater 267

*A Brief Primer on Theater Etiquette
for Kids.* 269

4 Concerts......................... 270

*Chuckling the Night Away
at a Comedy Club* 272

5 Movies.......................... 274

6 Dance 275

7 Puppet Shows 276

8 Spectator Sports 277

9 Story Hours 280

10 Arcades......................... 280

11 SIDE TRIPS FROM CHICAGO 282

1 Indiana Dunes State Park........ 282

2 Kohl Children's Museum......... 283

3 Chicago Botanic Garden 285

4 DuPage Children's Museum 286

5 Wonder Works 287

6 Cuneo Museum & Gardens...... 288

APPENDIX: FAST FACTS, TOLL-FREE NUMBERS & WEBSITES 289

1 Fast Facts: Chicago.............. 289

2 Toll-Free Numbers & Websites... 295

INDEX 298

General Index.................... 298

Accommodations Index......... 307

Restaurant Index................. 308

LIST OF MAPS

Chicago & Vicinity 4

Chicago Neighborhoods 53

Downtown El & Subway Stations . . . 61

Suggested Chicago Itineraries 68

Central Chicago
Accommodations 76

Near North & River North
Accommodations 85

Lincoln Park & North Side
Accommodations 102

Central Chicago Dining 112

Dining in Lincoln Park &
Wrigleyville 140

Dining in Wicker Park/
Bucktown 151

Central Chicago Attractions 158

South Michigan Avenue &
Grant Park Attractions 161

Hyde Park Attractions 163

The Field Museum of Natural
History 164

The Loop Sculpture Tour 169

Museum of Science & Industry . . . 172

Oak Park Attractions 193

Lincoln Park Zoo 198

Grant Park 219

Lincoln Park 221

Magnificent Mile Shopping 233

Shopping in Wicker Park/
Bucktown 235

Entertainment in the Loop &
Magnificent Mile 254

Entertainment in Lincoln Park &
Wrigleyville 256

AN INVITATION TO THE READER

In researching this book, we discovered many wonderful places—hotels, restaurants, shops, and more. We're sure you'll find others. Please tell us about them, so we can share the information with your fellow travelers in upcoming editions. If you were disappointed with a recommendation, we'd love to know that, too. Please write to:

Frommer's Chicago with Kids, 4th Edition
Wiley Publishing, Inc. • 111 River St. • Hoboken, NJ 07030-5774

AN ADDITIONAL NOTE

Please be advised that travel information is subject to change at any time—and this is especially true of prices. We therefore suggest that you write or call ahead for confirmation when making your travel plans. The authors, editors, and publisher cannot be held responsible for the experiences of readers while traveling. Your safety is important to us, however, so we encourage you to stay alert and be aware of your surroundings. Keep a close eye on cameras, purses, and wallets, all favorite targets of thieves and pickpockets.

FROMMER'S STAR RATINGS, ICONS & ABBREVIATIONS

Every hotel, restaurant, and attraction listing in this guide has been ranked for quality, value, service, amenities, and special features using a **star-rating** system. In country, state, and regional guides, we also rate towns and regions to help you narrow down your choices and budget your time accordingly. Hotels and restaurants are rated on a scale of zero (recommended) to three stars (exceptional). Attractions, shopping, nightlife, towns, and regions are rated according to the following scale: zero stars (recommended), one star (highly recommended), two stars (very highly recommended), and three stars (must-see).

In addition to the star-rating system, we also use **six feature icons** that point you to the great deals, in-the-know advice, and unique experiences that separate travelers from tourists. Throughout the book, look for:

Finds	Special finds—those places only insiders know about
Fun Facts	Fun facts—details that make travelers more informed and their trips more fun
Moments	Special moments—those experiences that memories are made of
Overrated	Places or experiences not worth your time or money
Tips	Insider tips—great ways to save time and money
Value	Great values—where to get the best deals

The following **abbreviations** are used for credit cards:

AE	American Express	**DISC**	Discover	**V**	Visa
DC	Diners Club	**MC**	MasterCard		

FROMMERS.COM

Now that you have this guidebook to help you plan a great trip, visit our website at www.**frommers.com** for additional travel information on more than 4,000 destinations. We update features regularly to give you instant access to the most current trip-planning information available. At Frommers.com, you'll find scoops on the best airfares, lodging rates, and car rental bargains. You can even book your travel online through our reliable travel booking partners. Other popular features include:

- Online updates of our most popular guidebooks
- Vacation sweepstakes and contest giveaways
- Newsletters highlighting the hottest travel trends
- Podcasts, interactive maps, and up-to-the-minute events listings
- Opinionated blog entries by Arthur Frommer himself
- Online travel message boards with featured travel discussions

How to Feel Like a Chicago Family

What's the best part about visiting Chicago with your kids? On the positive side, Chicago is a big city. You'll find a rich diversity of cultures and languages and the opportunity to expose your kids to many different sights, sounds, and people. Free activities abound: Parks, a zoo, and the beach are a few of Chicago kids' favorite things—and they won't cost you a penny. Transportation is easy: Kids love the "El," carriage rides, trolley cars, and buses. And most activities are located around a compact city center—a brief bus or train ride from hotels on the Magnificent Mile, in River North, or the Loop will get you to any of the downtown museums or the Lincoln Park Zoo. You'll always find a coffee shop just around the corner, great restaurants and shopping, and miles of walkable terrain for you and your kids.

The negatives? Again, Chicago is a big city. Streets, shops, and museums can get crowded in the summer. Panhandlers can be a problem in certain congested downtown areas. Traffic can be hazardous—you'll need to be extra careful around busy intersections. (**Warning:** Cabs will not slow down for anyone—even families with kids.) The El is not always stroller-friendly and getting through the station onto the train can be challenging. You may find yourself having to walk up flights of stairs carrying the diaper bag, stroller, and more.

Is it worth it? Millions of visitors who flock to our city every year can't be wrong.

As I wrote the first edition of this book, my husband and I were preparing to welcome our first child. As I write the fourth edition, we are seasoned parents of two, and we've road-tested many of this new edition's suggestions for experiencing Chicago with kids. As we became part of the community of Chicago parents, many of them shared valuable been-there, done-that advice. I have those Chicago parents to thank for the wide variety of activities and opinions you'll find in these pages.

In this book I am working on three assumptions: One is that when you travel with kids, there has to be something in it for them. You can't expect kids to enjoy a vacation filled with adult activities. (In fact, take a kid into a fancy department store or to a fine French restaurant and the parents are unlikely to enjoy it either!) But while we want to keep the kids happy, the goal of this book is to find activities that offer something for parents and kids alike.

The second assumption is a preference for the simple over the complex. Take your 3-year-old to the zoo and she may wind up spending more time watching squirrels chase each other across the lawn than the big cats emerging from their dens. And that's okay. Later on, she'll appreciate the larger animals! In this book I emphasize some off-the-beaten track, simple (and often inexpensive) ideas for entertaining your kids. Many of these ideas have been contributed by a cadre of Chicago parents.

The third is that you will seek out activities that are unique to Chicago. Now, some people are comfortable going to Hard Rock Cafe or Six Flags because they have them in their own city—and their kids like that sort of predictability. More power to you—and those places are certainly listed in this guidebook. My focus, however, is on transportation, museums, and food that say "Chicago."

Insiders in the travel business sometimes whisper that Chicago is to the United States as Frankfurt, Germany, is to Europe: a hub for conventions, a business destination, but otherwise often considered flyover or airport layover territory. In this book I intend to demonstrate to even the most sophisticated travelers that Chicago is a worthy destination. This city can be a magical place for families, filled with new discoveries and favorite places you'll want to visit again and again over the years. Many of my friends recall annual trips to Chicago with great fondness. Colleen Moore's Fairy Castle at the Museum of Science and Industry, Buckingham Fountain's invigorating spray on a windy day—for this generation, Millennium Park's bedazzling "bean" sculpture and its fun-house reflections will become part of your family lore as well.

1 FAVORITE CHICAGO FAMILY EXPERIENCES

Chicago has made vast strides in beautifying the city and developing visitor-friendly attractions. Millennium Park, a world-class destination on 25 acres near Michigan Avenue and the Art Institute, is one of the city's biggest tourist attractions. The architectural highlight of the park is the Frank Gehry–designed Pritzker Music Pavilion, home of the free summer music concerts performed by the Grant Park Symphony Orchestra. Another popular attraction is the huge elliptical sculpture *Cloudgate* (immediately dubbed "the bean" by Chicagoans) by British artist Anish Kapoor—his first public work in the U.S. The dazzling $450-million park added to the already excellent facilities for families, including Museum Campus, now (in my humble opinion) the number-one collection of museums on one walkable campus in the country. The city created the campus by linking three great Chicago institutions—the Field Museum of Natural History, John G. Shedd Aquarium, and Adler Planetarium & Astronomy Museum—by rerouting major streets to make the area more pedestrian-friendly.

Chicago continues to work on its cultural institutions, many of which have launched fundraising drives to improve and enhance their facilities for visitors. Navy Pier was rehabilitated and opened in the mid-1990s, quickly becoming the city's number-one tourist destination. The

North Loop theater district has risen from a decades-long slumber. And the retail expansion along the city's fabled Magnificent Mile has yet to slow down. Is it any wonder that natives of the city have the reputation of never wanting to live anywhere else?

From the simple pleasures of summer baseball to the complexities of the world of science, here are my favorite Chicago experiences for families:

- **Encountering Jurassic Wonders:** Sue, the largest T-rex skeleton ever uncovered, has made the Field Museum her home. (Don't be taken aback by her intimidating presence in the museum's grand entry hall.) But don't be surprised if your kids are just as much in awe of the Field's many classic kid charmers: a life-size Egyptian tomb, rooms of glittering gemstones, the royal Cameroon palace from Africa, and hundreds of stuffed animals (not of the teddy bear variety) in their habitat. Beware of the Field's mesmerizing qualities on adults and kids alike: A friend of mine began meditating in an Indian tepee, only to open his eyes and find the museum closed! See p. 162.
- **Exploring Underwater Life:** Most kids have a fascination for life under the sea, and an afternoon watching dolphins frolic and colorful tropical fish swim

circles around a mammoth tank is sure to enthrall. John G. Shedd Aquarium, with its all-time-favorite dolphin show and precious beluga whales, is a surefire winner with kids. See p. 165.

- **Marveling at the Innovations of Science and Industry:** You can't go wrong at the Museum of Science and Industry, Chicago's perennial kids' favorite. Watch chicks hatch in an incubator. Catch an IMAX movie at the Henry Crown space theater. Step aboard a retired 727 United Airlines jetliner. Travel deep into a replica of a Southern Illinois coal mine. And explore the newly restored and always classic exhibit of a captured German U-boat. With so much to do, you might want to divide and conquer by spending a couple of afternoons here. See p. 170.

- **Taking to the Water from Navy Pier:** Chicago's number-one tourist attraction is home to another kids' favorite—the Chicago Children's Museum. Navy Pier is also the jumping-off point for many of the boat tours of Lake Michigan, so find a vessel that's your speed, from powerboats to tall-masted schooners, and take to the water! See p. 174.

- **Talking to the Animals:** Located within Chicago's famous lakefront park, the Lincoln Park Zoo is convenient, compact, and charming. And what's not to love about a place that's open 365 days a year and never charges a cent for admission? This, the nation's oldest zoo, is famous for its major collection of gorillas, who live in the newly rebuilt Great Ape House, which gives its residents more outdoor living space (and the ability to control the temperature in their habitat, believe it or not). The adjoining Farm-in-the-Zoo allows urban kids to wander a working farm and meet cows, pigs, horses, chicks, and goats. At Pritzker Children's Zoo, kids can watch otters play and pet tortoises. See p. 197.

- **Riding the "El":** *L* is not only the 12th letter of the alphabet, but also the greatest, least expensive entertainment your kids will enjoy in Chicago. Fares for the El (and for CTA buses) are $2, with an additional 25¢ for a transfer that allows CTA riders to make two transfers on the bus or El within 2 hours of receipt. Children 6 and under ride free, and those between the ages of 7 and 11 pay $1. Hop a southbound Brown Line elevated train toward the Loop, and watch the city unfold as the train crosses the Chicago River and screeches through downtown canyons. See "Kid-Friendly Tours," in chapter 6.

- **Cruising Chicago's Waterways:** A Chicago River cruise should be one of your first stops in our fair city. I didn't step aboard until I'd lived in the city for 2 years—and boy, did I miss out! Kids and adults alike will love the Chicago Architecture Foundation's river cruise. Or head to Navy Pier and hop on one of the myriad vessels that stand ready to chauffeur you around Lake Michigan. Whatever way you go, the best vantage point for viewing Chicago's world-renowned architecture is from the water. See "Kid Friendly Tours," in chapter 6.

- **Ogling Our Inland Ocean:** Chicago's magnificent lakefront is an emerald strand of parks and sand beaches, linked by running, walking, rollerblading, and biking trails. You'll appreciate the foresight of Chicago's forefathers even more when you compare our free and open public lakefront to that of other Great Lakes cities like Toronto, where much of the lakefront is used for industrial purposes or is privately owned. And at 22,300 square miles in size and reaching depths of 900 feet, our great lake will look more like the ocean to your kids. It's the only Great Lake that lies wholly in U.S. territory, and Chicago is blessed with 29 miles of lakefront for biking, 'blading, or simply being. So get

Chicago & Vicinity

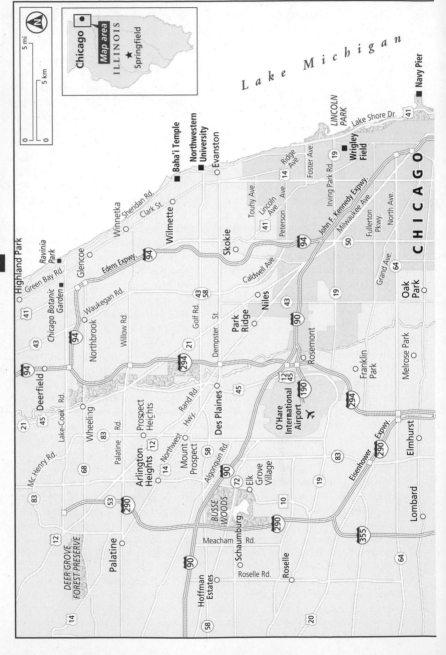

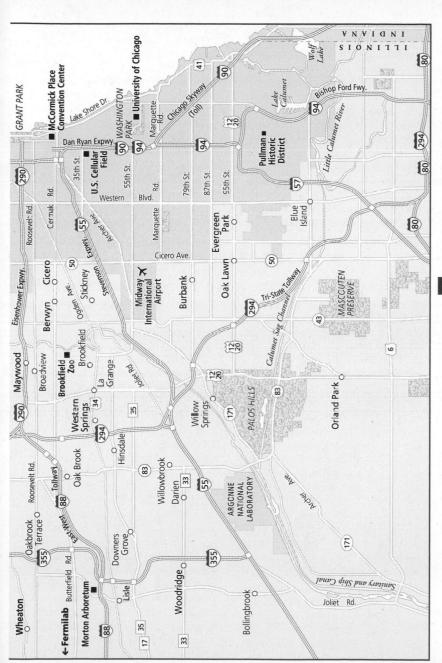

out there and enjoy the country's "third coast." See "Enjoying the 'Third Coast': Chicago's Beaches," in chapter 8.

- **Getting the Blues:** Even kids can get the blues, thanks to alcohol- and smoke-free nights at Blue Chicago (p. 270), one of the city's many fabled blues venues. The blues is the first original music of America and the basis for rock 'n' roll. It's an authentic piece of Chicago's heart and soul that you absolutely should not miss. If you want to learn more before your arrival in Chicago, read *Blues for Dummies,* written by the father-and-son team of Lonnie Brooks and Wayne Baker Brooks, two of Chicago's beloved blues musicians.

- **Rooting for the Home Team:** Win or lose (and sorry to say, historically speaking, it's usually lose—but as always, this may be our year!), an afternoon at Wrigley Field is a thrill for kids and adults alike. Even if the Cubbies aren't hitting them out of the park, hot dogs, peanuts in the shell, and a rousing rendition of "Take Me Out to the Ballgame" are sure to please. This most charming of major-league ballparks is a slice of Americana that you should not miss. One afternoon spent in the embrace of the Friendly Confines will have you hooked on the sheer magic of Wrigley Field. See p. 278.

2 THE BEST HOTEL BETS

Renovation, expansion, and new construction have been the name of the game in the Chicago lodging world for several years. From hip boutique hotels to huge facilities for convention-goers, plus a nice crop of family-friendly hotels, you'll find something to suit your needs. The downside: Room rates keep rising, making budget lodgings harder to find. On the luxury-hotel front, Trump International Hotel and Tower has opened to impressive reviews (and impressive prices), while the former House of Blues Hotel underwent a major renovation to become bohemian Hotel Sax. Family-friendly options abound, with mainstays like the family-owned Talbott Hotel offering large suites, some with multiple bathrooms. The hotel is ideally located near Michigan Avenue shopping (p. 93).

- **Most Family-Friendly:** With cribs, laundry service, free breakfast, and every room a suite, the **Embassy Suites Hotel Chicago—Downtown,** 600 N. State St. (© **800/362-2779**), or its sister hotel, **Embassy Suites Hotel Chicago—Downtown/Lakeshore,** 511 N. Columbus Dr. (© **312/836-5900**), are

ideal for families looking for a little more space than the typical hotel room provides. The in-room Nintendo, indoor pool, and location near a couple of popular kid-friendly venues—ESPN Zone and the Hard Rock Cafe—should keep Junior happy, too. (The Lakeshore hotel also has a wonderful location near Navy Pier and in a complex that includes a huge cinema and P.J. Clarke's restaurant.) See p. 97.

- **Newer Family-Friendly Hotel:** I always say that any hotel that's built recently is a good bet. New construction means fresh linens, fresh decor, updated heating and cooling systems—you get my drift. Although it's a couple of years old now, you'll still get all these benefits at the city's most recent family-friendly addition, **Four Points by Sheraton— Chicago Downtown/Magnificent Mile** (630 N. Rush St. (© **312/981-6600**), plus a great location just 1 block west of Michigan Avenue in the heart of the Magnificent Mile. There's also a pool, where you and the kids can unwind after a busy day of touring. See p. 95.

The Best Chicago Websites

The **World Wide Web** makes vacation planning simple. These Chicago-based sites provide up-to-date listings on everything from restaurants to walking tours.

- **www.choosechicago.com** is your best bet for comprehensive tourism information on hotels, special promotions, and citywide events from the Chicago Convention & Tourism Bureau (and ☎ **877/CHICAGO** [244-2246] also happens to be the phone number for the bureau's tourism information line).
- **www.metromix.com** is the *Chicago Tribune*'s entertainment-oriented site.
- **www.encyclopediaofchicago.com** is a collaboration between the New-berry Library and the Chicago Historical Society that is chock-full of fun facts and useful information about our city's history, architecture, and the lives of some of our city's famous and infamous personalities.
- **www.chicago.citysearch.com** offers reviews of restaurants, bars, shows, and shops.
- Two good general sites are **www.explorechicago.org** (Chicago Office of Tourism) and **www.enjoyillinois.com** (Illinois Bureau of Tourism).

- **Best Neighborhood Hotel:** Children 12 and under stay free at **Best Western Hawthorne Terrace Hotel,** 3434 N. Broadway (☎ **888/401-8781**). Rooms in this small hotel (just 59 rooms and junior suites) have refrigerators, microwaves, and irons. Best of all, parking is a bargain at $20 a day—about half the going rate at Chicago's downtown hotels. See p. 104.
- **Best Views:** This isn't an easy call. The astounding altitude offered by the **Trump International Plaza Hotel and Tower,** 401 N. Wabash (☎ **877/458-7867**), plus its riverside perch, make this hotel a strong new contender. But consider several other hotels for their mix of lake and city views: **Four Seasons Hotel Chicago** (p. 84), **The Drake** (p. 89), the **Ritz-Carlton Chicago** (p. 88), and **Park Hyatt Chicago** (p. 86).
- **When Hipness Is Important:** A hip hotel that's known for romance is using

its small size—and sense of whimsy—to cater to kids. **Hotel Burnham,** 1 W. Washington, at State Street (☎ **877/294-9712**), keeps wee ones entertained with special offers for tea at American Girl Place Cafe and deals at the museums and theaters. During holidays, you'll find special activities in the hotel lobby, including decorating gingerbread men at Christmas and hunting for eggs at Easter. Diaper bags, cribs, highchairs, changing tables, and more are available upon request. Rooms are clubby but glamorous, with plush beds, mahogany writing desks, and chaise longues—even the family pet is welcome. See p. 79.
- **When Price Is No Object:** The attention to detail, regal pampering, and well-connected concierges you will find at both the ultraluxe **Ritz-Carlton Chicago,** 160 E. Pearson St. (☎ **800/621-6906;** p. 88), and **Four Seasons Hotel Chicago,** 120 E. Delaware Place

(© 800/332-3442; p. 84), make them the hotels of choice for travelers who want to feel like royalty while in town. the **Peninsula Chicago,** 108 E. Superior St. (© 866/288-8889; p. 88), is also a major player on the luxury scene in Chicago.

- **When Price Is Your Main Object: Red Roof Inn Chicago Downtown,** 162 E. Ontario St. (© 800/733-7663; p. 97), offers a fabulous location for a bargain price. But the **Hampton Inn & Suites Chicago—Downtown,** 33 W. Illinois St. (© 800/HAMPTON [426-7866]; p. 99), gets bonus points for being a bargain stay, plus having a pool, which is not the case with many downtown chains.

- **Best Pool:** With its dazzling all-tile junior Olympic–size pool, constructed in 1929, the **InterContinental Chicago,** 505 N. Michigan Ave. (© 800/327-0200), takes this award easily. See p. 90.

- **Best Hotel Restaurant for Kids:** Go for **Atwood Cafe,** the stylish and funky

restaurant fronting State Street inside the **Hotel Burnham,** 1 W. Washington (© 877/294-9712). Amazingly, this eclectic restaurant with a grown-up sophistication welcomes kids and features a special kids' menu. See p. 111.

- **Tops for Teens:** For a bohemian boutique feel, the **Hotel Sax,** 333 N. Dearborn St. (© 800/235-6397), can't be beat, and its access to nearby House of Blues and 10pin Bowling Alley should score with teens, too. See p. 98. Teens might also enjoy the rock-'n'-roll attitude of the **Hard Rock Hotel Chicago,** 230 N. Michigan Ave. (© 866/966-5166), in the historic, distinctive, and recently renovated Carbon Carbide skyscraper. See p. 78.

- **Tops for Toddlers: Homewood Suites,** 40 E. Grand Ave. (© 800/CALL-HOME [225-5466]), offers cribs, highchairs, and babysitting services in a great location in River North—all great amenities for the toddling set. See p. 96.

3 THE BEST DINING BETS

With pizza and hot dogs among the city's signature dishes, Chicago is food heaven for kids. Before you run out and buy a case of antacids, however, take heart: Wonderful cuisine to please adults abounds, too. And I'm going to send you in that direction, right after I grab a garlic- and pepper-laden hot dog.

- **Best Views:** A location right on the Magnificent Mile means the observation deck of the **Hancock Observatory,** 875 N. Michigan Ave., is the ideal spot to get an up-close-and-personal view of the Magnificent Mile and its many high-rises. For lunch, visit the observatory's **Signature Room at the 95th** (© 312/787-9596), a sleek restaurant that serves a discounted lunch buffet for kids. On a clear day you can

see 50 miles and part of three surrounding states—Michigan, Indiana, and Wisconsin. (Moms and daughters, make sure to visit the women's restroom—it's got the best views in the restaurant!) See p. 175.

- **Best Ice Cream:** Since the 1920s, **Margie's Candies,** 1960 N. Western Ave., at Armitage Avenue in Bucktown (© 773/384-1035), has been serving up mammoth sundaes in conch shell–shaped dishes. You might still find family members manning the cash register. Don't miss the homemade hot fudge, real butterscotch, and caramel. The place hasn't changed much since 1940, and is stuffed with kitschy dolls, boxes of homemade candy, stuffed animals, and news clippings through the years. A second location, with a homey, retro decor, has opened in the North Center neighborhood at 1813 W. Montrose Ave. (© 773/348-0400). See p. 250.

- **Best Outdoor Eating:** Long tables and family-style dining reign in **Greektown,** making it a comfortable and fun destination for families and large groups; see "The West Loop," in chapter 5. At **Pegasus,** 130 S. Halsted St. (© 312/226-3377), a rooftop garden provides diners with a panoramic view of the Chicago skyline. The restaurant is so family- and large group–oriented, in fact, that when I called to make a reservation for a group of 10, the host replied, "Ten is not a big group!" See p. 115.

- **Most Kid-Friendly Service: Scoozi,** an Italian restaurant in River North at 410 W. Huron (© 312/943-5900), is a family favorite for its Sunday-afternoon pizza-making event that lets kids loose with tomato sauce and cheese to create their own pizzas (under the supervision of Scoozi chefs, who keep mess to a minimum and pop finished pizzas into the wood-burning oven). The evening is great for parents, too—they get a short break while their kids play chef to enjoy their meal and some grown-up conversation. Make a reservation, because your window of opportunity is small: The restaurant runs the program on Sunday only, from 5 to 6:30pm, and it's free for kids 11 and under. See p. 134.

- **Best Kids' Menu:** How many times have you seen the big three on kids' menus? Burgers, chicken fingers, and buttered noodles are great, but when you want to expand your horizons (just a little), head for **Wishbone,** 1001 Washington St., at Morgan Street (© 312/850-2663), or 3300 N. Lincoln Ave. (© 773/549-2663). You'll find a little Southern flair to the kids' menu, with hoppin' John (black-eyed

peas over rice), grilled ham, corn muffins, and home fries among the offerings. See p. 122.

- **Best Burgers:** The hamburger at **Mike Ditka's Restaurant,** 100 E. Chestnut St. (© 312/587-8989), tastes more like chopped steak and can easily feed two. Sports fans will be entertained by football memorabilia and Bears fans can relive the glory days of former Coach Mike Ditka, who owns the place. Take your kids to the main-level dining room, though, because the upstairs dining area is a little more adult-oriented, with live musical entertainment that tends toward Frank Sinatra favorites (and, often, bachelor parties dining in the adjacent private rooms). See p. 124.

- **Best Barbecue:** Old Town neighborhood institution **Twin Anchors Tavern** (1655 N. Sedgwick St., © 312/266-1616) is as unpretentious as its ribs are delicious. Tender baby back pork ribs and crispy onion rings are accompanied by coleslaw and dark rye bread. Kids will go for the burgers and the daily cheesecake special. Get there early and grab a red formica-topped table in the back room, away from the bar area. See p. 148.

- **Best Breakfast:** Although the restaurant is located in the young professional haven of Lincoln Park, parents report that the managers and staff at **Toast,** 746 W. Webster St., at Halsted Street (© 773/935-5600), are baby- and kid-crazy. The pancakes and waffles are pretty crazy, too: Stacks arrive covered in fruit, yogurt, powdered sugar, and more. Go for brunch starting at 8am on weekends. See p. 147.

- **Best Family-Style Dining: Maggiano's Little Italy,** 516 N. Clark St. (© 312/644-7700), is a mecca for Italian family-style dining. Heaping plates of pasta meant to be shared make Maggiano's a good choice for a budget-conscious family. In fact, everything on the menu is supersize. Most steaks are more than a pound, and the full pasta dishes weigh in at over 25 ounces. (You can also get half-portions, which are still plentiful.) You're expected to share dishes, pass things around, and try a little bit of everything. See p. 133.

- **Best Asian Food:** If you eat at **Big Bowl,** 6 E. Cedar St., at Rush Street (ℂ 312/640-8888), at the beginning of your visit to Chicago, I guarantee you will make a repeat visit before you leave. The food here is addictive. From noodle soups to pad Thai (try the tofu and veggie version), your kids will find tons to love here. Each child gets a small bowl of white rice, and crayons upon being seated. The restaurant bustles and kids will blend right in with the activity. Make sure to grab a handful of individually wrapped fortune cookies on your way out! See p. 128.

- **Best Hot Dog: Gold Coast Dogs,** 159 N. Wabash Ave. (ℂ 312/917-1677). This River North fast-food stand serves up the authentic item, meaning a Vienna All-Beef Frank slathered with mustard, green relish, chopped onion, sliced tomato, hot peppers, and celery salt. Your kids might be brave enough to ask for and receive ketchup, but as an adult, I wouldn't risk the disapproving, raised-eyebrow look you'll get from the counter staff. You can round out the meal with cheese fries, made from Idaho potatoes and topped with a generous glob of Wisconsin cheddar. See p. 155.

- **Best Pizza:** In the town where deep-dish pies were born, Chicagoans take their out-of-town relatives to either **The Original Gino's East of Chicago,** 633 N. Wells St. (ℂ 312/943-1124; p. 136), or **Lou Malnati's Pizzeria,** 439 N. Wells St. (ℂ 312/828-9800; p. 154), to taste the real thing: mouth-watering slabs of pizza loaded with fresh

ingredients atop delectably sweet crusts. Lou's fan base is so enamored that the restaurant has even instituted a popular overnight mail-order business to get expatriate Chicagoans with a deep-dish jones over the hump.

- **Best Fast Food:** Even though you're in the hometown of McDonald's, our vote goes to **foodlife** in Water Tower Place, 835 N. Michigan Ave. (ℂ 312/335-3663), a food court exemplar with everything from Asian noodles to pizza to smoothies. See p. 129.

- **Best Brunch:** Cajun and Southern cooking is in store for you at **Wishbone,** 1001 W. Washington Blvd. (ℂ 312/850-2663). Primitive art, bright colors, and a bustling crowd make this a great place for kids. A diverse crowd, from Harpo Studios employees (Oprah is headquartered right around the corner) to businesspeople in suits and ad agency types, frequent the place. For brunch, try the salmon cakes. See p. 122.

- **Best Girls' Day Out:** Can't help but notice those dark red bags that girls carry like badges of honor up and down Michigan Avenue? They come from **American Girl Place,** 835 N. Michigan Ave., on the first and second floors of Water Tower Place Mall (ℂ 877/247-5223), which also features a cafe. Call well in advance for breakfast, lunch, or afternoon tea reservations, or simply take your American girl and her doll to the store for a wardrobe makeover, a photo session, or a visit to the hair salon (dolls can even have their ears pierced here!). See p. 123.

- **Best Boys' Night Out:** What red-blooded American kid doesn't love baseball? Catch a ballgame at Wrigley Field or U.S. Cellular Field, then head downtown to **Harry Caray's,** 33 W. Kinzie St. (ℂ 312/828-0966), one of Chicago's most flamboyant eateries, filled with uniforms, helmets, cards, and photographs. Be sure to check out the bar—it measures 60 feet, 6 inches, the exact distance from the plate on the pitcher's mound to home plate in a major-league park. See p. 131.

- **Best Neighborhood Hangout: Stanley's Kitchen and Tap,** 1970 N. Lincoln Ave. (© **312/642-0007**), is a classic Lincoln Park restaurant with a family-friendly bent. There's a bar near the entrance, but the adjacent dining room, decorated with photos, quilts, bowling trophies, and children's drawings, feels like someone's family room. This popular family spot has a special kids' menu. On Saturday and Sunday from 11am to 4pm, there's an all-you-can-eat brunch buffet, featuring make-your-own omelets, build-your-own Belgian waffles, home-fried potatoes, fried chicken, and mashed potatoes. Daily specials are posted on the chalkboard out front. See p. 147.

- **Best Retro Diner:** Get back to the '70s at **Kitsch'n River North,** 600 W. Chicago Ave. (© **312/644-1500**), which features shag carpeting and one of the best kids' menus in the city (and Tang martinis for the grown-ups). Comfort foods like fried chicken and waffles, puff pastry pot pies, and green eggs and ham (the green is actually provided by spinach pesto) should keep the kids happy. If the weather's fine, sit on the large outdoor patio, enjoy a Twinkie tiramisu dessert, and imagine this huge riverside building as the former home of retailing giant Montgomery Ward. The original location, in the neighborhood of Roscoe Village, is smaller but just as kitschy and filled with families (2005 W. Roscoe St., © **773/248-7372**). See p. 137.

Planning a Family Trip to Chicago

Planning a trip is half the fun—and when kids are involved, planning is a chance to make them active participants in the upcoming family adventure. Ward off any potential kid meltdowns ("I didn't know we were going to do that!") by talking through the activities you all can enjoy. In this chapter we'll look at how to find up-to-date information on those activities, when to go, and how to get here.

1 VISITOR INFORMATION

SOURCES OF INFORMATION

The best source of information is the Chicago Convention and Tourism Bureau, which operates an information line at © **877/CHICAGO** (244-2246) and a very helpful and up-to-date website at **www.choosechicago.com**. The **Chicago Office of Tourism**, Chicago Cultural Center, 78 E. Washington St., Chicago, IL 60602 (© **312/744-2400** or TTY 312/744-2947; **www.explorechicago.org**), will mail you a packet of materials with information on upcoming events and attractions. The **Illinois Bureau of Tourism** (© **800/2CONNECT** [226-6632] or TTY 800/406-6418; **www.enjoyillinois.com**) will also send you a packet of information about Chicago and other Illinois destinations.

The number-one publication for families in the Chicago area is *Chicago Parent* (© **708/386-5555**), a monthly magazine that has won many awards as best regional parenting publication in the nation. Contact the magazine to request a copy of its June issue, which is the annual "Going Places" guide, a comprehensive listing of what to do with kids in the six-county metro area.

HELPFUL WEBSITES

Aside from official, government-run websites, some Chicago publications and other organizations have wonderful websites, some targeted to families. Check out *Chicago Parent* magazine's website, **www.chicagoparent.com**, prior to your visit, for a look at the calendar of events and excellent features on exploring Chicago with kids.

In addition, **www.gocitykids.com** provides a wealth of information, including current calendars of events for Chicago. You can search for activities, restaurants, and hotels, and see what's happening in specific neighborhoods.

Go to **http://chicago.citysearch.com** for the local edition of the national Citysearch, which has reviews of restaurants,

Destination Chicago: Red Alert Checklist

- If you're driving, do you have all the directions you need and detailed road maps? If you're flying, are you carrying a current, government-issued ID, such as a driver's license or passport?
- Do any theater, restaurant, or travel reservations need to be booked in advance?
- Did you make sure your favorite attraction is open, or verify the dates of any special events you plan to attend? Call ahead for opening and closing times.
- If you purchased traveler's checks, have you recorded the check numbers and stored the documentation separately from the checks?
- Did you stop the newspaper and mail delivery, and leave a set of keys with someone reliable?
- Did you pack your camera, bring along your charger, pack an extra set of camera batteries, and purchase enough film?
- Do you have a safe, accessible place to store money?
- Did you bring your ID cards that could entitle you to discounts, such as AAA and AARP cards, student IDs, and the like?
- Did you bring emergency drug prescriptions and extra glasses and/or contact lenses?
- Did you find out your daily ATM withdrawal limit?
- Do you have your credit card PINs? Is there a daily withdrawal limit on credit card cash advances?
- To check in at a kiosk with an e-ticket, do you have the credit card you bought your ticket with or a frequent-flier card?
- Did you leave a copy of your itinerary with someone at home?
- Do you have the measurements for those people you plan to buy clothes for on your trip?

bars, shops, and shows. For entertainment news, check out **www.centerstage.net**, or **www.metromix.com**, the *Chicago Tribune*'s entertainment-oriented site. Also check out **www.chireader.com**, the site of the *Chicago Reader*, the city's alternative weekly paper. For a blogger's view of the city, check out www.chicagoist.com.

Many of the city's performing arts groups sell tickets online through **www.ticketweb.com**, so you can reserve seats before leaving home.

Part of the City of Chicago's website, www.cityofchicago.org/Landmarks/, includes definitions of Chicago architectural styles, tour information, and maps.

PLANNING A FAMILY TRIP TO CHICAGO

2

WHAT TO PACK

As you have heard too many times already, Chicago's weather is changeable. So while I can give you general guidelines for packing for various seasons, always check out **www.weather.com** or **www.chicago tribune.com** for the long-range forecast. (Granted, in Chicago they seem to have it wrong at least half of the time, but it's better than a complete shot in the dark.) Ask yourself what you'd wear in your own city in this weather, and pack it. But leave some room in the suitcase, because you will undoubtedly buy items while traveling. In fact, one seasoned-traveler trick is to pack an empty nylon duffel bag in your suitcase. On the way home, you can stuff it with souvenirs and other Chicago loot.

Because you are apt to hit four seasons in just one Chicago day, here are some packing tips:

- **Pack a light sweater and jacket,** even for summer. The Windy City can get quite breezy, and that lake air has a chill at night. Theaters and restaurants can also overdo the air-conditioning, so a light sweater helps you ward off arctic chill.
- You are not too stylish to bring **practical headgear** to Chicago in the winter. Believe me, you will appreciate this advice later. When it gets cold in Chicago, no one goes without head covering.

- Pack **shorts** for a late-spring or early-fall trip as well as for summer. You can always pair them with a sweatshirt if it gets chilly.
- **Bring layers.** You can always stuff that jacket into your backpack, but if you skip it altogether, you may end up regretting it. This way, you'll be able to stay out all day without running back to your hotel for frequent wardrobe adjustments.

As far as dress codes go, unless you and your kids are planning a big night out, like at the Pump Room at the Omni Ambassador East Hotel, for example, you will be just fine in "nice casual" attire. For men, that means a dress shirt, sports jacket, and tie for the fanciest places. For women, a long skirt with boots and a nice sweater goes just about anywhere in the winter. In the summer you'll be comfortable in cool slacks and cotton tops with sandals. If you are planning a very special night out, check to see if the restaurant enforces a dress code. Otherwise, you might end up borrowing a less-than-attractive tie and jacket from the maitre d'. You'll find that people dress more conservatively here than in New York or Los Angeles, and as a traveler you can blend in easily with a suitcase full of the basics: khakis, jeans, shorts, sandals, boots, and sweaters.

 Tips **Quick ID**

Tie a colorful ribbon or piece of yarn around your luggage handle, or slap a distinctive sticker on the side of your bag. This makes it less likely that someone will mistakenly appropriate it. And if your luggage gets lost, it will be easier to find.

Flying or Driving with Kids

FOR A PLANE TRIP

When traveling with kids, consider packing the following in your carry-on bag:

- The number of diapers your child wears in a day, plus an extra three
- A changing pad in case the tiny restroom in the airplane has no pullout changing table
- A minimal number of toys—one coloring book and a stuffed animal will suffice, not 10 of each!
- Bottles for infants, sippy cups and snacks for toddlers
- A goodie bag with surprises, like a Discman with a CD of music or stories, books, or small plastic toys

For more comprehensive advice on flying with children, see "Getting There," later in this chapter, and pick up a copy of *Frommer's Fly Safe, Fly Smart,* by Sascha Segan (Wiley, 2002).

FOR A CAR TRIP

If you will be renting a car in Chicago, inquire about reserving a child safety seat; most major rental-car agencies have these available for a small fee (Avis, for example, charges $5 per day or $25 per week).

Driving to Chicago? Long-distance car travel with kids presents a completely different packing challenge. Pack the following to help your car trip go more smoothly:

- A cooler with drinks, snacks, fruits, and veggies.
- A flashlight to help locate items that have rolled under your seat for the 10th time in the last 5 minutes.
- Window shades for the sun.
- Audiotapes of stories or children's songs. Many parents put a TV/VCR in between the two front seats so kids can watch videos, which can be a great help for long stretches with nothing to do.

Other items to consider bringing include a first-aid kit, a box of wipes for cleanups, blankets, plastic bags for motion sickness, and a change of clothes. Always have a cellphone in case of emergencies

3 ENTRY REQUIREMENTS

PASSPORTS

New regulations issued by the Department of Homeland Security now require virtually every air traveler entering the U.S. to show a passport. As of January 23, 2007, all persons, including U.S. citizens, traveling by air between the United States and Canada, Mexico, Central and South America, the Caribbean, and Bermuda are required to present a valid passport. As of

January 31, 2008, U.S. and Canadian citizens entering the U. S. at land and sea ports of entry from within the Western Hemisphere will need to present government-issued proof of citizenship, such as a birth certificate, along with a government-issued photo ID, such as a driver's license. A passport is not required for U.S. or Canadian citizens entering by land or sea, but you are highly encouraged to carry one.

For information on how to obtain a passport, go to **"Passports"** in the **"Fast Facts"** section of the appendix (p. 293).

VISAS

The U.S. State Department has a **Visa Waiver Program (VWP)** allowing citizens of the following countries to enter the United States without a visa for stays of up to 90 days: Andorra, Australia, Austria, Belgium, Brunei, Denmark, Finland, France, Germany, Iceland, Ireland, Italy, Japan, Liechtenstein, Luxembourg, Monaco, the Netherlands, New Zealand, Norway, Portugal, San Marino, Singapore, Slovenia, Spain, Sweden, Switzerland, and the United Kingdom. (*Note:* This list was accurate at press time; for the most up-to-date list of countries in the VWP, consult www.travel.state.gov/visa.)

Even though a visa isn't necessary, in an effort to help U.S. officials check travelers against terror watch lists before they arrive at U.S. borders, as of January 12, 2009, visitors from VWP countries must register online before boarding a plane or a boat to the U.S. Travelers will complete an electronic application providing basic personal and travel eligibility information. The Department of Homeland Security recommends filling out the form at least 3 days before traveling. Authorizations will be valid for up to 2 years or until the traveler's passport expires, whichever comes first. Currently, there is no fee for the online application. Canadian citizens may enter the United States without visas; they will need to show passports (if traveling by air) and proof of residence, however. *Note:* Any passport issued on or after October 26, 2006, by a VWP country must be an **e-Passport** for VWP travelers to be eligible to enter the U.S. without a visa. Citizens of these nations also need to present a round-trip air or cruise ticket upon arrival. e-Passports contain computer chips capable of storing biometric information, such as the required digital photograph of the holder. (You can identify an e-Passport by the symbol on the bottom center cover of your passport.) If your passport doesn't have this feature, you can still travel without a visa if it is a valid passport issued before October 26, 2005, and includes a machine-readable zone, or between October 26, 2005, and October 25, 2006, and includes a digital photograph. For more information, go to **www.travel.state.gov/visa**.

Citizens of all other countries must have (1) a valid passport that expires at least 6 months later than the scheduled end of their visit to the U.S., and (2) a tourist visa. To obtain a visa, applicants must schedule an appointment with a U.S. consulate or embassy, fill out the application forms (available from www.travel.state.gov/visa), and pay a $131 fee. Wait times can be lengthy, so it's best to initiate the process as soon as possible.

As of January 2004, many international visitors traveling on visas to the United States will be photographed and fingerprinted on arrival at Customs in airports and on cruise ships in a program created by the Department of Homeland Security called **US-VISIT.** Exempt from the extra scrutiny are visitors entering by land or those who don't require a visa for short-term visits. For more information, go to the Homeland Security website at **www.dhs.gov/dhspublic**.

For specifics on how to get a visa, go to **"Visas"** in the **"Fast Facts"** section of the appendix (p. 294).

Cut to the Front of the Airport Security Line as a Registered Traveler

In 2003, the **Transportation Security Administration** (**TSA;** www.tsa.gov) approved a pilot program to help ease the time spent in line for airport security screenings. In exchange for information and a fee, persons can be prescreened as registered travelers, granting them a front-of-the-line position when they fly. The program is run through private firms—the largest and most well-known is Steven Brill's **Clear** (www.flyclear.com), and it works like this: Travelers complete an online application providing specific points of personal information including name, addresses for the previous 5 years, birth date, Social Security number, driver's license number, and a valid credit card (you're not charged the **$99 fee** until your application is approved). Print out the completed form and take it, along with proper ID, with you to an "enrollment station" (this can be found in more than 20 participating airports and in a growing number of American Express offices around the country, for example). It's at this point where it gets seemingly sci-fi. At the enrollment station, a Clear representative will record your biometrics necessary for clearance; in this case, your fingerprints and your irises will be digitally recorded.

Once your application has been screened against no-fly lists, outstanding warrants, and other security measures, you'll be issued a clear plastic card that holds a chip containing your information. Each time you fly through participating airports (and the numbers are steadily growing), go to the Clear Pass station located next to the standard TSA screening line. Here you'll insert your card into a slot and place your finger on a scanner to read your print—when the information matches up, you're cleared to cut to the front of the security line. You'll still have to follow all the procedures of the day like removing your shoes and walking through the X-ray machine, but Clear promises to cut 30 minutes off your wait time at the airport.

On a personal note: Each time I use my Clear Pass, my travel companions are still waiting to go through security while I'm already sitting down, reading the paper, and sipping my overpriced smoothie. Granted, registered traveler programs are not for the infrequent traveler, but for those of us who fly on a regular basis, it's a perk I'm willing to pay for.

—David A. Lytle

MEDICAL REQUIREMENTS

Unless you're arriving from an area known to be suffering from an epidemic (particularly cholera or yellow fever), inoculations or vaccinations are not required for entry into the United States.

CUSTOMS
What You Can Bring into the U.S.

Every visitor more than 21 years of age may bring in, free of duty, the following: (1) 1 liter of wine or hard liquor; (2) 200 cigarettes, 100 cigars (but not from Cuba), or 3 pounds of smoking tobacco; and (3) $100 worth of gifts. These exemptions are offered to travelers who spend at least 72 hours in the United States and who have not claimed them within the preceding 6 months. It is forbidden to bring into the country almost any meat products (including canned, fresh, and dried meat products such as bouillon, soup mixes, and so forth). Generally, condiments including vinegars, oils, spices, coffee, tea, and some cheeses and baked goods are permitted. Avoid rice products, as rice can often harbor insects. Bringing fruits and vegetables is not advised, though not prohibited. Customs will allow produce depending on where you got it and where you're going after you arrive in the U.S. Foreign tourists may carry in or out up to $10,000 in U.S. or foreign currency with no formalities; larger sums must be declared to U.S. Customs on entering or leaving, which includes filing form CM 4790. For details regarding U.S. Customs and Border Protection, consult your nearest U.S. embassy or consulate, or **U.S. Customs** (www.cbp. gov).

What You Can Take Home from Chicago

Canadian Citizens: For a clear summary of Canadian rules, write for the booklet *I Declare,* issued by the Canada Border Services Agency (✆ 800/461-9999 in Canada, or 204/983-3500; www.cbsa-asfc.gc. ca).

U.K. Citizens: For information, contact **HM Customs & Excise** at ✆ **0845/ 010-9000** (from outside the U.K., 020/ 8929-0152), or consult their website at **www.hmce.gov.uk**.

Australian Citizens: A helpful brochure available from Australian consulates or Customs offices is *Know Before You Go.* For more information, call the **Australian Customs Service** at ✆ **1300/363-263,** or log on to **www.customs.gov.au**.

New Zealand Citizens: Most questions are answered in a free pamphlet available at New Zealand consulates and Customs offices: *New Zealand Customs Guide for Travellers, Notice no. 4.* For more information, contact **New Zealand Customs,** The Customhouse, 17–21 Whitmore St., Box 2218, Wellington (✆ **04/473-6099** or 0800/428-786; www.customs.govt.nz).

4 WHEN TO GO

When should you go to Chicago? That depends on what kind of weather you like. Chicago has it all—heat and humidity, subzero temps, and wind, wind, wind. The city has a reputation for being really cold in the winter. In reality, it's about as cold as any other northern city. Maybe it's that wind that makes the cold seem more bitter. Still, most visitors prefer planning trips to Chicago in late spring through early fall. If you can't make it during prime time, err on the side of arriving later in fall rather than early in spring. Spring in Chicago can be notoriously late and fickle, but fall offers beautiful days that can extend to Thanksgiving.

Don't be afraid to try the off season: Museums are wide open, shops have sales (especially in Jan), and the streets aren't clogged with pedestrians. Chicago is definitely a four-season destination; its inhabitants are hardy enough to be out and about even in the depths of winter. As an added incentive to "off-season" travelers, hotel rates are rock-bottom during the winter.

One thing is certain: Whenever you decide to go, you should be prepared for changeable weather. Chicagoans like to joke that if you don't like the weather here, just wait an hour. One beautiful summer afternoon, I left my apartment in jeans and

	Jan	Feb	Mar	Apr	May	June	July	Aug	Sept	Oct	Nov	Dec
High °F	20.2	33.9	44.3	58.8	70.0	79.4	85.3	82.1	75.5	64.1	48.2	35.0
°C	–6.5	1.0	6.8	14.9	21.1	26.3	29.6	27.8	24.4	17.8	9.0	1.7
Low °F	13.6	18.1	27.6	38.8	48.1	57.7	62.7	61.7	53.9	42.0	31.4	20.3
°C	–10.2	–7.7	–2.4	3.8	8.9	14.3	17	16.5	12.2	5.6	–0.3	–6.5
Rainfall (in.)	1.6	1.3	2.6	3.7	3.2	4.1	3.6	3.5	3.4	2.3	2.1	2.1

a T-shirt, only to have to buy a sweatshirt downtown when the wind shifted and the temperature plummeted 15 degrees in 15 minutes. So even in July, make sure that you bring a light jacket or sweater. (And in the winter, however fashionable you are trying to be, don't think you can get by without a hat.)

For current conditions and **forecasts,** check www.chicagotribune.com and www. weather.com.

KIDS' FAVORITE CHICAGO EVENTS

Chicago is a festival city, with ethnic parades, food, music, art and flower fairs, and street celebrations packing the calendar. Particularly in the summer, it can be tough to choose among activities. In winter you'll have fewer choices, but some of the perennial favorites take place then.

To discover the latest and greatest special events in the city, ask the **Chicago Office of Tourism** (© 877/CHICAGO [244-2246]; **www.choosechicago.com**) or the **Illinois Bureau of Tourism** (© 800/2CONNECT [226-6632]; **www.enjoyillinois. com**) to mail you a copy of the *Chicago Visitor's Guide,* an excellent quarterly publication that surveys special events, including parades and street festivals, concerts and theatrical productions, and museum exhibitions. Also ask to be sent the latest materials produced by the **Mayor's Office of Special Events** (© 312/744-3315, or the Special Events Hot Line 312/744-3370, TTY 312/744-2964; www.cityofchicago.org/ specialevents), which keeps current with citywide and neighborhood festivals. You'll find food, music and flower fairs, garden walks, and more.

Remember that new events might be added every year, and that occasionally special events are discontinued or rescheduled. So, to avoid disappointment, be sure to telephone in advance or check the website of the sponsoring organization, the Chicago Office of Tourism, or the Mayor's Office of Special Events to verify dates, times, and locations.

JANUARY

Chicago Cubs Convention. Even though April and Opening Day seem (and are) very far away in January, Cubs fans dream of next season at this convention, the kickoff to spring training, which is held at the Hilton Chicago, 720 S. Michigan Ave. Players sign autographs and collectors buy, sell, and swap memorabilia. Call © 773/404-CUBS (404-2827) or go to **http://chicago. cubs.mlb.com** for more information. Mid-January.

Winter Delights. Throughout January and February, the city's Office of Tourism (© 877/CHICAGO [244-2246]; www.choosechicago.com) offers special travel deals to lure visitors during tourism's low season. Incentives include bargain-priced hotel packages, affordable prix-fixe dinners at downtown restaurants, and special music and theater performances. Families with cabin fever should seek great deals on hotels with pools—it's a great weekend away from the snow and cold. Early January through February.

Chicago Boat, RV & Outdoor Show, McCormick Place, 23rd Street and Lake Shore Drive (© **312/946-6200;** www. chicagoboatshow.com). This extravaganza has been a Chicago tradition for nearly 70 years. All the latest boats and recreational vehicles are on display, plus there's trout fishing, a climbing wall, boating-safety seminars, and big-time entertainment. Late January.

FEBRUARY

Chinese New Year Parade, Wentworth and Cermak streets (© **312/326-5320;** www.chicagochinatown.org). The twisting dragon is sure to please kids as it winds down the street at this annual celebration. Call to verify the date, which varies from year to year, depending on the lunar calendar (usually btw. Jan 21 and Feb 19).

Chicago Auto Show, McCormick Place, 23rd Street and Lake Shore Drive (© **630/495-2282;** www.chicagoauto show.com). More than a thousand cars and trucks, domestic and foreign, are on display at this show, a tradition since 1901. Kids can get behind the wheel of the latest models at this event, which draws nearly a million car owners or wannabe owners a year. Look for packages at hotels that include tickets. Mid-February.

International Cluster of Dog Shows, McCormick Place South, 23rd Street and South Lake Shore Drive (© **773/ 237-5100;** www.ikcdogshow.com). See canines great and small strut their stuff. They're all adorable, but only one can win Best in Show. More than 10,000 AKC (American Kennel Club) purebred dogs of all breeds heat up the competition. It's quite a scene, particularly in the poodle area, where you can see dogs getting their hair blow-dried until they look like canine rock stars. Third week in February.

MARCH

Spring Flower Shows. Spring is sprung a little earlier in the conservatories than it is outside in the real world, and thank goodness. See the lilies, daffodils, tulips, pansies, and other flowering perennials at **Lincoln Park Conservatory** (© **312/ 742-7737**) and **Garfield Park Conservatory** (© **312/746-5100**). Throughout March and April.

St. Patrick's Day Parade. Even the Chicago River puts on the green for St. Patrick's Day—it's actually dyed Kelly green for the occasion. The parade runs along Dearborn Street from Wacker Drive to Van Buren; the best place to view it is around Wacker and Dearborn. Saturday closest to March 17.

APRIL

Opening Day. Bundle up the kids and join the die-hard fans at the ballpark (and die-hard fans know to wear long underwear, so follow their lead). Optimism reigns supreme and fans hope again that this will be their season. And even if it's not, hot dogs and peanuts will take some of the edge off. For the Cubs, call © **773/404-CUBS** (404-2827) or visit **www.cubs.mlb.com**; for the White Sox, call © **312/674-1000** or visit **www.whitesox.mlb.com**. Early April.

MAY

Buckingham Fountain Color Light Show, in Grant Park, at Congress Parkway and Lake Shore Drive. The water and the ever-changing colored lights put on their show in the landmark fountain nightly until 11pm. May 1 through October 1.

The Ferris Wheel and Carousel at Navy Pier, 600 E. Grand Ave. (© **312/ 595-PIER** [595-7437]; www.navypier. com). Give your kids a bird's-eye view of Chicago from the Ferris wheel (those who are slightly less fond of heights can stay closer to earth on the carousel), when it starts spinning again after a long winter's sleep. From Memorial Day to Labor Day, Navy Pier also hosts twice-weekly fireworks shows Wednesday nights at 9:30pm and Saturday nights at 10:15pm. May through October.

Wright Plus Tour, at the Frank Lloyd Wright Home & Studio (© **708/848-1976;** www.wrightplus.org). Glimpse inside the brilliant mind of Frank Lloyd Wright on this annual tour, which features 10 buildings in Oak Park, including Frank Lloyd Wright's home and studio, the Unity Temple, and several other notable Oak Park buildings in both Prairie and Victorian styles. Tickets go on sale March 1 and can sell out within 6 weeks. Third Saturday in May.

JUNE

Ravinia Festival, Ravinia Park, in suburban Highland Park, north of Chicago (© **847/266-5100** for ticket reservations; www.ravinia.com). Summer wouldn't be summer without Ravinia, a Chicago tradition. Basically, it's an outdoor concert venue with a covered pavilion and plenty of lawn seating. Offerings range from classical to pop. Kids can enjoy a picnic on the lawn while parents revel in the music of the Chicago Symphony Orchestra. Pack a picnic, jump on the Metra commuter railroad, and join the crowds sitting under the stars on the lawn. *One warning:* Ravinia is so popular that many of the first-rate visiting orchestras, chamber ensembles, pop artists, and dance companies sell out in advance. June through September.

Chicago Blues Festival, Petrillo Music Shell, at Jackson and Columbus drives in Grant Park (© **312/744-3315**). The lineup looks better every year at this festival. Admission is free, but get there in the afternoon to stake out a spot on the lawn for the evening shows. You'll discover young up-and-coming blues stars (including some who are the offspring of blues greats, such as Shamekia Copeland, daughter of Johnny Copeland). A shuttle bus will take you from the park to blues clubs. Call for information. First week in June.

57th Street Art Fair, at 57th and Kimbark streets in Hyde Park (© **773/493-3247;** www.57thstreetartfair.org). This is the oldest juried art fair in the Midwest—in 2007, it celebrated its 60th anniversary. Kids will especially enjoy the arts and crafts projects and the fun rides. First weekend in June.

Chicago Gospel Festival, Petrillo Music Shell, at Jackson and Columbus drives in Grant Park (© **312/744-3315**). This is the largest outdoor, free-admission event of its kind. Blues may be the city's more famous musical export, but Chicago is also the birthplace of gospel music: Thomas Dorsey, the "father of gospel music," and the greatest gospel singer ever, Mahalia Jackson, were Southsiders. This 3-day festival offers music on three stages with more than 40 performances. Early June.

Printers Row Book Fair, on Dearborn Street from Congress to Polk (© **312/222-3986**). One of the largest free outdoor book fairs in the country, this weekend-long event features readings by children's-book authors, book signings, and panel discussions on everything from writing your first novel to finding an agent. Also on offer are more than 150 booksellers displaying new, used, and antiquarian books for sale; a poetry tent; and special activities for children. Early June.

Old Town Art Fair, historic Old Town neighborhood, at Lincoln Park West and Wisconsin Street (© **312/337-1938;** www.oldtowntriangle.com). Children's art activities abound at this fair; adults can appreciate the more than 200 painters, sculptors, and jewelry designers from the Midwest and around the country. The fair also features an art auction, a garden walk, and food and drink. Second weekend in June.

Wells Street Art Festival, Wells Street from North Avenue to Division Street (✆ **312/951-6106;** www.oldtown chicago.org). Held on the same weekend as the Old Town Art Fair, this arts fest is lots of fun, with 200 arts and crafts vendors, food, music, and carnival rides. Second weekend in June.

Andersonville Midsommarfest, along Clark Street from Foster to Balmoral avenues (✆ **773/728-2995).** You can relive the Scandinavian heritage of Andersonville, once Chicago's principal Swedish community. Parents rave about the Swedish American Museum's kids' exhibits; the treats at the Swedish Bakery, across the street from the museum, are not to be missed. Second weekend in June.

Puerto Rican Fest, Humboldt Park, Division Street and Sacramento Boulevard (✆ **773/292-1414;** www.pr paradechicago.com). One of Chicago's animated Latino street celebrations, this festival includes 5 days of live music, theater, games, food, and beverages. It peaks with a parade that wends its way from Wacker Drive and Dearborn Street to the West Side Puerto Rican enclave of Humboldt Park. Mid-June.

Jammin' at the Zoo, Lincoln Park Zoo, 2200 N. Cannon Dr., at Fullerton Parkway (✆ **312/742-2000;** www. lpzoo.com). Family fun is the emphasis at this concert; however, depending on the featured musical act (which could be rock, zydeco, or reggae music), you might find that singles are more dominant at this perfect date venue. The lovely lawn south of the zoo's Park Place Café is certainly one of the more

unusual outdoor venues in the city. The first of three summer concerts (ticket prices vary) is held in late June.

Grant Park Music Festival, Pritzker Music Pavilion, in Millennium Park (✆ **312/742-7638;** www.grantpark musicfestival.com). The free outdoor musical concerts in the park begin the last week in June and continue through August. If your kids are old enough to stay up past 10, call to find out about the movies in the park, shown outdoors on a large screen.

Taste of Chicago, Grant Park (✆ **312/ 744-3315**). The largest free outdoor food fest in the nation (according to the City of Chicago), "The Taste," as it's known to locals, can be hot, sweaty, and claustrophobic. If your kids are small or don't do well in crowds, avoid it. Going on a weekday morning will help you miss the heaviest crowds. Three-and-a-half million people eat their way through cheesecake, ribs, pizza, and more, all carted to food stands set up throughout the park by scores of Chicago restaurants. On the evening of July 3, things get pretty hairy when Chicago launches its Independence Day fireworks, and crowds are at their sweaty peak. Admission is free; you pay for the sampling, of course. Late June and the first week of July.

Chicago Country Music Festival, Petrillo Music Shell, at Jackson and Columbus drives in Grant Park (✆ **312/ 744-3315**), is less claustrophobic than Taste of Chicago and therefore more kid-friendly. And it's free! You'll see big-name entertainers of the country-and-western genre. Late June (during the first weekend of Taste of Chicago).

Gay & Lesbian Pride Parade, on Halsted Street, from Belmont Avenue to Broadway, south to Diversey Parkway, and east to Lincoln Park (✆ **773/348-8243;** www.chicagopridecalendar.org).

This parade is flamboyant and colorful, the culmination of a month of activities by Chicago's gay and lesbian community. The floats, marching units, and colorful characters will keep you entertained, so pick a spot on Broadway for the best view. Last Sunday in June.

Farmers markets open at two dozen sites all over the city at the end of the month and continue weekly through October. Downtown sites are Daley Plaza (every other Thurs) and Federal Plaza (every Tues). For other locations and times, call ℂ **312/744-3315.**

JULY

Independence Day Celebration (ℂ **312/744-3315**). Celebrated in Chicago on July 3, concerts and fireworks are the highlights of the festivities in Grant Park. The sight of fireworks exploding over and reflecting off of Lake Michigan is well worth braving the crowd. Take public transportation, or walk.

Irish-American Heritage Festival, Irish-American Heritage Center, 4626 N. Knox Ave., at Montrose Avenue (ℂ **773/282-7035**). If your kids are into Irish dancing, made famous by *Riverdance,* make sure to check out this festival, featuring Irish music, dance, food, readings, and children's entertainment. Second weekend in July.

Sheffield Garden Walk, starting at Sheffield and Webster avenues (ℂ **773/929-WALK** [929-9255]; www.sheffieldfestivals.org). One of Chicago's largest street parties, the Sheffield Garden Walk sounds a bit more refined than it actually is—but here's your chance to snoop into the lush backyards of Lincoln Park homeowners. There are also live bands, children's activities, and food and drink vendors on tap. Mid-July.

Chicago Yacht Club's Race to Mackinac Island (ℂ **312/861-7777;** www.chicagoyachtclub.org). Kids who love boats will get a kick out of watching the start of this 3-day competition. At Monroe Street Harbor, boats set sail on Saturday for the grandest of the inland water races. Mid-July.

Chicago SummerDance, cast side of South Michigan Avenue between Balbo and Harrison streets (ℂ **312/742-4007**). From July to early September, the city's Department of Cultural Affairs transforms a patch of Grant Park into a lighted outdoor dance venue on Thursday, Friday, and Saturday from 6 to 9:30pm, and Sunday from 4 to 7pm; ethnic dance lessons for kids are offered Saturday from 4 to 5pm. The 3,500-square-foot dance floor provides ample room for throwing down moves while live bands play music—from ballroom, jazz, klezmer, and country and western to samba, zydeco, blues, and soul. One-hour lessons are offered from 6 to 7pm. Free admission.

Taste of Lincoln Avenue, Lincoln Park, between Fullerton Avenue and Wellington Street (ℂ **773/868-3010;** www.wrightwoodneighbors.org). This is one of the largest and most popular of Chicago's many neighborhood street fairs; it features 50 bands performing music on five stages. Neighborhood restaurants staff the food stands, and there's also a kids' carnival. Third weekend in July.

Venetian Night, from Monroe Harbor to the Adler Planetarium (ℂ **312/744-3315**). Whimsical decorations on a carnival of illuminated boats make this a great kids' event. Fireworks and synchronized music by the Grant Park Symphony Orchestra complete the scene. Watch from the shoreline, or, if you can swing it, get onboard a friend's boat. Last Saturday in July.

Newberry Library Book Fair and Bughouse Square Debates, 69 W. Walton St. and Washington Square Park (© **312/255-3501;** www. newberry.org). For teens with an interest in history or a love of books, this fair will be a hit. At the fair, held over 4 days, Newberry Library sells tens of thousands of used books, most under $2. The highlight is soapbox orators re-creating the Bughouse Square Debates in Washington Square Park, just across the street. Late July.

AUGUST

Chicago Air & Water Show, North Avenue Beach (© **312/744-3315**). Kids love this hugely popular show, held on the lake at North Avenue Beach and overhead, where you'll see Stealth bombers, F-16s, and special appearances by the U.S. Air Force Thunderbirds and Navy Seals. Because the crowds are intense at North Avenue Beach, try grabbing a portable radio and hanging at Oak Street Beach, along the Gold Coast. Admission is free. Mid-August.

Viva! Chicago Latin Music Festival, Petrillo Music Shell, at Jackson and Columbus drives in Grant Park (© **312/744-3370**). Salsa, mambo, and the latest Latin rock groups hit the stage for this free festival. Last weekend in August.

SEPTEMBER

Boulevard Lakefront Bike Tour (Chicagoland Bicycle Federation; © **312/42-PEDAL** [427-3325]). This 10-mile leisurely tour especially for families lets you explore the city, from neighborhoods and the lakefront to Chicago's historic link of parks and boulevards. It starts and ends at the University of Chicago in Hyde Park, which hosts the annual Bike Expo, with vendors and entertainment, the same day. Mid-September.

Chicago Jazz Festival, Petrillo Music Shell, Jackson and Columbus drives in Grant Park (© **312/744-3315**). This festival features Chicago-style jazz, with several national headliners always on hand. The event is free; kids are welcome. First weekend in September.

Mexican Independence Day Parade, along Dearborn Street between Wacker Drive and Van Buren Street (© **312/744-3315**). Chicago is home to the nation's second-largest Mexican-American population, and that makes for a great parade. Another parade is held on the next day on 26th Street in the Little Village neighborhood (© **773/521-5387**). Mid-September.

World Music Festival Chicago, various locations around the city (© **312/742-1938;** www.cityofchicago.org/worldmusic). This relatively new and enormously popular festival is a major undertaking by the city's Department of Cultural Affairs. Call ahead for tickets, because many events sell out. The festival is held at venues around town—notably, the Chicago Cultural Center, Museum of Contemporary Art, Old Town School of Folk Music, and Hot House. You'll see top performers from Zimbabwe to Hungary to Sri Lanka performing traditional, contemporary, and fusion music. Shows are a mix of free and ticketed ($10 or less) events. Call for information and to receive updates on scheduled performances. Late September.

Celtic Fest Chicago, Petrillo Music Shell, Jackson and Columbus drives in Grant Park (© **312/744-3315**). The city's newest music festival celebrates the music and dance of Celtic traditions from around the world. Mid-September.

OCTOBER

Chicago Marathon (☎ 888/243-3344 or 312/904-9800; www.chicago marathon.com). Whether or not you or your kids are runners, cheering on the harriers is an uplifting experience. Sponsored by LaSalle Bank, Chicago's marathon is a major event on the international long-distance running circuit, with some of the world's top runners competing. It begins and ends in Grant Park, but can be viewed from any number of vantage points along the race route. Second Sunday in October.

Spooky Zoo Spectacular, Lincoln Park Zoo, 2200 N. Cannon Dr. at Fullerton Parkway (☎ 312/742-2000; www. lpzoo.com). Dress your tots in their Halloween finest for the free treats that are dispensed at various animal habitats. Bozo the Clown—himself a Chicago native—kicks things off with a parade through the zoo grounds. Late October.

NOVEMBER

The Big Top, United Center, 1901 W. Madison St. (☎ 312/455-4500); and the Allstate Arena, 6920 N. Mannheim Rd., Rosemont (☎ 847/635-6601). This is the month that Ringling Bros. and Barnum & Bailey comes to Chicago to set up its tent. Tickets are available from Ticketmaster (☎ 312/559-1212). Throughout November.

State Street Thanksgiving Parade (☎ 312/781-5681) is an annual event that takes place on Thanksgiving morning beginning at 8:30am. The parade marches up State Street, from Congress to Randolph.

Magnificent Mile Lights Festival (☎ 312/642-3570; www.gnmaa.com). Beginning at dusk, a colorful parade of Disney characters makes its way south along Michigan Avenue, from Oak Street to the Chicago River, with holiday lights being illuminated block by block as the procession passes. Carolers, elves, and minstrels appear with Santa along the avenue throughout the day and into the evening, and many of the retailers serve hot chocolate and other treats. Saturday before Thanksgiving.

Christmas Tree Lighting, Daley Center Plaza, in the Loop (☎ 312/744-3315). The switch is flipped on the day after Thanksgiving, around dusk.

Zoo Lights Festival, Lincoln Park Zoo, 2200 N. Cannon Dr. (☎ 312/742-2000). Colorful illuminated displays brighten long nights during the holidays. Another special tradition is the annual Caroling to the Animals, a day-long songfest on a Saturday early in the month. Late November through the first week in January.

DECEMBER

A Christmas Carol, Goodman Theatre, 170 N. Dearborn St. (☎ 312/443-3800; www.goodman-theatre.org). This is both a seasonal favorite and a Chicago institution; it's been performed for more than 2 decades. The show runs from around Thanksgiving to the end of December.

The Nutcracker, Joffrey Ballet of Chicago, Auditorium Theatre, 50 E. Congress Pkwy. The esteemed company performs its Victorian-American twist on this holiday classic. For tickets, call the Joffrey office at ☎ 312/739-0120; www.joffrey.com, or Ticketmaster (☎ 312/559-1212). The production runs for 3 weeks from late November to mid-December.

5 GETTING THERE

BY PLANE
The Major Airlines

Domestic carriers that fly regularly to O'Hare include **American** (© 800/433-7300; www.aa.com), **Continental** (© 800/525-0280; www.continental.com), **Delta** (© 800/221-1212; www.delta.com), **Northwest** (© 800/225-2525; www.nwa.com), **United** (© 800/241-6522; www.united.com) and discount offshoot **Ted** (© 800/CALL TED [225-5833]; www.flyted.com), and **US Airways** (© 800/428-4322; www.usairways.com). Commuter service is also provided by several regional airlines. Airlines that fly to Chicago's Midway Airport are **AirTran Airways** (© 800/247-8726; www.airtran.com), **America West** (© 800/235-9292; www.americawest.com), **Continental** (© 800/525-0280; www.continental.com), **Frontier** (© 800/432-1359; www.frontierairlines.com), **Northwest** (© 800/225-2525; www.nwa.com), and **Southwest** (© 800/435-9792; www.southwest.com). The toll-free numbers listed are for use in the United States and Canada.

Arriving at the Airport
IMMIGRATION & CUSTOMS CLEARANCE

International visitors arriving by air, no matter what the port of entry, should cultivate patience and resignation before setting foot on U.S. soil. U.S. airports have considerably beefed up security clearances in the years since the terrorist attacks of September 11, and clearing Customs and Immigration can take as long as 2 hours.

Long-Haul Flights: How to Stay Comfortable

- Your choice of airline and airplane will definitely affect your legroom. Find more details about U.S. airlines at **www.seatguru.com**. For international airlines, the research firm Skytrax has posted a list of average seat pitches at **www.airlinequality.com**.
- Emergency exit seats and bulkhead seats typically have the most legroom. Emergency exit seats are usually left unassigned until the day of a flight (to ensure that someone able-bodied fills the seats); it's worth checking in online at home (if the airline offers that option) or getting to the ticket counter early to snag one of these spots for a long flight. Many passengers find that bulkhead seating offers more legroom, but keep in mind that bulkhead seats have no storage space on the floor in front of you.

ⓘ Tips   Kids with Colds

It's more difficult for kids to make their ears pop during takeoff and landing than it is for adults. The eustachian tube is especially narrow in children; the passage is even tighter when mucous membranes are swollen. This can make ascent and descent especially painful—even dangerous—for a child with congested sinuses. If your little one is suffering from a cold or the flu, it's best to keep him grounded until he recuperates, if that's an option. If you must travel with your child as scheduled, give him an oral child's decongestant an hour before ascent and descent or administer a spray decongestant before and during takeoff and landing.

Tips Don't Stow It—Ship It

If ease of travel is your main concern and money is no object, you can ship your luggage and sports equipment with one of the growing number of luggage-service companies that pick up, track, and deliver your luggage (often through couriers such as Federal Express) with minimum hassle for you. Traveling luggage free may be ultraconvenient, but it's not cheap: One-way overnight shipping can cost from $100 to $200, depending on what you're sending. Still, for some people, especially the elderly or the infirm, it's a sensible solution to lugging heavy baggage. Specialists in door-to-door luggage delivery are **Virtual Bellhop** (✆ 877/235-5467; www.virtualbellhop.com), **SkyCap International** (✆ 877/775-9227; www.skycapinternational.com), **Luggage Express** (✆ 866/744-7224; www.usxpluggageexpress.com), and **Sports Express** (✆ 800/357-4174; www.sports express.com).

- To have two seats for yourself in a three-seat row, try for an aisle seat in a center section toward the back of coach. If you're traveling with a companion, book an aisle and a window seat. Middle seats are usually booked last, so chances are good you'll end up with three seats to yourselves. And in the event that a third passenger is assigned the middle seat, he or she will probably be more than happy to trade for a window or an aisle.

- To sleep, avoid the last row of any section or the row in front of an emergency exit, as these seats are the least likely to recline. Avoid seats near highly trafficked toilet areas. Avoid seats in the back of many jets—these can be narrower than those in the rest of coach. Or reserve a window seat so you can rest your head and avoid being bumped in the aisle.

- Get up, walk around, and stretch every 60 to 90 minutes to keep your blood flowing. This helps avoid **deep vein thrombosis,** or "economy-class syndrome." See the box "Avoiding 'Economy Class Syndrome,'" p. 42.

- Drink water before, during, and after your flight to combat the lack of humidity in airplane cabins. Avoid caffeine and alcohol, which will dehydrate you.

Flying for Less: Tips for Getting the Best Airfares

Airfares are a great example of capitalism at work: Passengers within the same airplane cabin rarely pay the same fare for their seats. Rather, each pays what the market will bear. Business travelers who need to purchase tickets at the last minute, change their itinerary at a moment's notice, or get home before the weekend pay the premium rate, known as the full fare. Passengers who can book their ticket long in advance, who don't mind staying over Saturday night, or who are willing to travel on a Tuesday, Wednesday, or Thursday after 7pm will pay a fraction of the full fare. On most flights, even the shortest hops, the full fare is close to $1,000, but a 7-day or 14-day advance purchase ticket is closer to $200 to $300. Here are a few other easy ways to save:

- Periodically, airlines lower prices on their most popular routes. Check your newspaper for advertised discounts, or

Tips **Coping with Jet Lag**

Jet lag is a pitfall of traveling across time zones. If you're flying north-south and you feel sluggish when you touch down, your symptoms will be the result of dehydration and the general stress of air travel. When you travel east-west or vice-versa, your body becomes confused about what time it is, and everything from your digestive system to your brain is knocked for a loop. Traveling east is more difficult on your internal clock than traveling west because most peoples' bodies are more inclined to stay up late than to fall asleep early.

Here are some tips for combating jet lag:

- **Reset your watch** to your destination time before you board the plane.
- **Drink lots of water** before, during, and after your flight. Avoid alcohol.
- **Exercise and sleep well** for a few days before your trip.
- If you have trouble sleeping on planes, **fly eastward on morning flights.**
- **Daylight** is the key to resetting your body clock. At the website for **Outside In** (www.bodyclock.com), you can get a customized plan of when to seek and avoid light.

call the airlines directly and ask if any **promotional rates** or special fares are available. You'll almost never see a sale during the peak summer vacation months of July and August, or during the Thanksgiving or Christmas seasons; in periods of low-volume travel, however, you should pay no more than $400 for a cross-country flight. If your schedule is flexible, ask if you can secure a cheaper fare by staying an extra day or by flying midweek. (Many airlines won't volunteer this information.) If you already hold a ticket when a sale breaks, it may even pay to exchange your ticket, but keep in mind you'll usually incur a change fee of as much as $100 to do so.

Note: The lowest-priced fares often are nonrefundable, require advance purchase of 1 to 3 weeks and a certain length of stay, and carry penalties for changing dates of travel.

- **Consolidators,** also known as bucket shops, are great sources for international tickets, although they usually can't beat Internet fares within North America. Start by looking in Sunday

newspaper travel sections; U.S. travelers should focus on the *New York Times, Los Angeles Times,* and *Miami Herald.* U.K. travelers should search in the *Independent,* the *Guardian,* or the *Observer. Beware:* Bucket shop tickets are usually nonrefundable or rigged with stiff cancellation penalties, often as high as 50% to 75% of the ticket price, and some put you on charter airlines, which may leave at inconvenient times and experience delays. Several reliable consolidators are worldwide and available online. **STA Travel** has been the world's lead consolidator for students since purchasing Council Travel, but their fares are competitive for travelers of all ages. **Flights.com** (© **800/TRAV-800** [872-8800]; www.flights.com) has excellent fares worldwide, particularly to Europe. They also have "local" websites in 12 countries. **FlyCheap** (© **800/FLY-CHEAP** [359-2432]; www.1800flycheap.com) has especially good fares to sunny destinations. **Air Tickets Direct** (© **800/778-3447**; www.airticketsdirect.com) is based in Montreal and leverages the currently weak Canadian dollar for low fares;

they also book trips to places that U.S. travel agents won't touch, such as Cuba.

- Search **the Internet** for cheap fares. Great last-minute deals are available through free weekly e-mail services provided directly by the airlines. Websites such as **Frommers.com** (www.frommers.com), **Travelocity** (www.travelocity.com), **Expedia** (www.expedia.com), **Qixo** (www.qixo.com), and **Orbitz** (www.orbitz.com) allow consumers to comparison-shop for airfares, access special bargains, book flights, and reserve hotel rooms and rental cars.

- Join a travel club such as **Moment's Notice** (© 718/234-6295; www.moments-notice.com) or **Travelers Advantage** (© 877/259-2691; www.travelersadvantage.com), which supply unsold tickets at discounted prices. You pay an annual membership fee to get the club's hot line number. Of course, you're limited to what's available, so you have to be flexible.

- Join **frequent-flier clubs**. It's best to accrue miles on one program, so you can rack up free flights and achieve elite status faster. But it makes sense to open as many accounts as possible, no matter how seldom you fly a particular airline. It's free, and you'll get the best choice of seats, faster response to phone inquiries, and prompter service if your luggage is stolen, if your flight is canceled or delayed, or if you want to change your seat.

Chicago's Airports

The one experience most Chicago visitors share is **O'Hare International Airport** (© 773/686-2200). O'Hare has long battled with Atlanta's Hartsfield for the title of the world's busiest airport. The airport reigns as a major hub for making connections worldwide. O'Hare has its own police force, zip code, medical center, cemetery, and chapel.

O'Hare is northwest of the city proper, about a 25- to 30-minute drive from downtown, depending, of course, on the traffic. A cab ride into the city will cost you about $30 to $35. You can also ask the taxi-stand attendant to arrange a shared ride for you, which will cost about $15 per person.

For $1.75, you can take the El (vernacular for the elevated train), which will efficiently get you downtown in about 40 minutes, regardless of traffic. Trains leave every 6 to 10 minutes during the day, and every half-hour in the evening and overnight. O'Hare also has outposts for every major car-rental company (see "Getting Around," later in this chapter, for details).

O'Hare has information booths in all five terminals, most located on the baggage level. The multilingual personnel, who are outfitted in red jackets, can assist travelers with everything from arranging ground transportation to getting information about local hotels. The booths also offer a plethora of useful tourism brochures. The booths, labeled AIRPORT INFORMATION, are open daily from 9am to 8pm.

On the opposite end of the city, the southwest side, is Chicago's other major airport, **Midway** (© 773/838-0600). A new terminal has eased considerable crowding problems and expanded the selection of restaurants and shops. Although it's smaller than O'Hare and fewer airlines have routes here, Midway is closer to the Loop and you may be able to get a cheaper fare flying into this airport. (Always check fares flying into both airports if you want to find the best deal.) The El Orange Line extends to Midway, so you can make it downtown in about half an hour for $1.75. Please note that the Orange Line stops operating each night at about 11:30pm and resumes service by 5am. Trains leave the station every 6 to 15 minutes. Most major car-rental companies have counters at Midway as well.

Air Travel Security Measures

In the wake of the terrorist attacks of September 11, 2001, the airline industry implemented sweeping security measures in airports. Although regulations vary from airline to airline, you can expedite the check-in process and alleviate airport stress by taking the following steps:

- **Arrive early.** Times vary from airport to airport, depending on their size. Figure on arriving for check-in anywhere from a minimum of an hour in advance to at least 2 hours before your scheduled flight.
- **Don't count on curbside check-in.** Some airlines and airports have stopped curbside check-in altogether, whereas others offer it on a limited basis. For up-to-date information, check with the individual airline.
- **Be sure to carry plenty of documentation.** An up-to-date, government-issued photo ID (federal, state, or local) is now required. You may need to show this at various checkpoints. With an e-ticket, you may be required to have with you printed confirmation of purchase, and perhaps even the credit card with which you bought your ticket. This varies from airline to airline, so call ahead to make sure you have the proper documentation.
- **Know what you can carry on—and what you can't.** Travelers in the United States are now limited to one carry-on bag, plus one personal bag (such as a purse or a briefcase). The **Transportation Security Administration (TSA)** has also issued a list of banned carry-on items; for more information, check the TSA website at www.tsa.gov. Your airline may have additional restrictions on carry-on items, so call ahead to avoid problems.
- **Prepare to be searched.** Expect spot-checks. Electronic items (such as a laptop or cellphone) should be readied for additional screening. Be prepared to place your jewelry, loose change, and any other metallic items on your person in bins before you go through security.
- **It's no joke.** If anyone asks you security-related questions, don't be flip. The agents will not hesitate to call security.

You can find the latest information on both airports at the city's Department of Aviation website: **www.ohare.com**.

Airport Transfers

Continental Airport Express (© 800/ 654-7871 or 312/454-7800; www.airport express.com) serves most first-class hotels in Chicago with its blue-and-white Airport Express vans; ticket counters are located at both airports near the baggage claim (outside Customs at the international terminal at O'Hare). For transportation to the airport, reserve a spot from one of the hotels (check with the bell captain). The cost is $21 one-way ($39 round-trip) to or from O'Hare and $16 one-way ($30 round-trip) to or from Midway. The shuttles operate from 6am to 11:30pm. For limo service from either O'Hare or Midway, call **Carey Limousine of Chicago** (© 773/769-0009; www.ecarey. com) or **Chicago Limousine Services** (© 312/726-1035). Depending on the number of passengers and whether you opt for a sedan or a stretch limo, the service will cost about $100 to $150, including gratuity and tax.

With 1 week's notice, **CTA Paratransit** offers door-to-door lift services to and from O'Hare for travelers with disabilities. Visitors must be registered with a similar program in their home city. For information, call © 312/432-7025 or TTY 312/917-1338.

Safe Seats for Kids

The practice of allowing children younger than 2 to ride for free on a parent's lap may be prohibited by the time you read this. At press time the FAA was writing a rule that would require all children under 40 pounds to have their own tickets and be secured in a child seat.

All the major American airlines except Delta now offer discounted infant tickets for children 2 years of age or younger, to make it more affordable for you to reserve a separate adjacent seat for your baby and a restraining device.

(Most airlines require that an infant be 2 weeks old to travel—bring a birth certificate. American and Continental only require that the child be 7 days old. Alaska lets babies fly as soon as they're born.)

For now, if a seat adjacent to yours is available, your lap child can sit there free of charge. When you check in, ask if the flight is crowded. If it isn't, explain your situation to the agent and ask if you can reserve two seats—or simply move to two empty adjacent seats once the plane is boarded. You might want to shop around before you buy your ticket and deliberately book a flight that's not very busy. Ask the reservationist which flights tend to be most full and avoid those. Only one extra child is allowed in each row, however, due to the limited number of oxygen masks.

On flights overseas a lap fare usually costs 10% of the parent's ticket price. Children who meet the airline's age limit (which ranges from 11 to 15 years old) can purchase international fares at 50% to 75% of the lowest coach fare in certain markets. Some of the foreign carriers make even greater allowances for children.

Children riding for free will usually not be granted any baggage allowance.

All airlines offer child meals if requested in advance. Ticketed babies can get "infant meals" on America West, Delta, and US Airways, and all major airlines except Alaska and Southwest will warm bottles on request.

Child Seats: They're a Must

According to *Consumer Reports Travel Letter,* the National Transportation Safety Board says that, since 1991, the deaths of five children and injuries to four could have been prevented had the children been sitting in restraint systems during their flights. Even in the event of moderate turbulence, children sitting on a parent's lap can be thrust forward and injured. When you consider that a commercial aircraft hits a significant amount of turbulence at least once a day on average, you'd do well to think about investing in a safety seat.

The FAA recommends that children under 20 pounds ride in a rear-facing child-restraint system, and says children who weigh 20 to 40 pounds should sit in a forward-facing child-restraint system.

(Fun Facts) O'Hare, Oh My

Chicago's O'Hare International Airport comes in second place (after Hartsfield-Jackson Atlanta International Airport) as the busiest airport in the world. Approximately 970,000 planes take off and land at O'Hare each year, generating about 500,000 jobs for the region. O'Hare is completely self-supporting, requiring no local taxpayer dollars to keep it going.

The Custody Trap

Because of concern about parental abductions, special requirements exist for children flying to many foreign countries, including Mexico. If they're with one parent, they must bring a notarized consent document from the other parent—even if the missing parent is the one waving goodbye at the airport! A decree of sole custody or parental death certificate will also do. Minors traveling alone to these countries must bring either two consent forms, a decree of sole custody and one consent form, or applicable death certificates. Ask your airline what's required when you book the ticket.

Children over 40 pounds should sit in a regular seat and wear a seat belt.

All child seats manufactured after 1985 are certified for airline use, but make sure your chair will fit in an airline seat—it must be less than 16 inches wide. You may not use booster seats or seatless vests or harness systems. Safety seats must be placed in window seats—except in exit rows, where they are prohibited, so as not to block the passage of other travelers in the case of an emergency.

The airlines themselves should carry child safety seats onboard. Unfortunately, most don't. To make matters worse, over-zealous flight attendants have been known to try to keep safety seats off planes. One traveler recounts in the November 2001 issue of *Consumer Reports Travel Letter* how a Southwest attendant attempted to block use of a seat because the red label certifying it as safe for airline use had flaked off. That traveler won her case by bringing the owner's manual and appealing to the pilot—you should do the same.

Getting safety seats on an international flight may be even more difficult. Ask to make sure you can use your safety seat when you book a flight on a foreign airline.

Until the new FAA rule comes into effect, if you can't afford the expense of a separate ticket, book a ticket toward the back of the plane at a time when air travel is likely to be slowest—and the seat next to you is most likely to be empty. The reservationist should also be able to recommend the best (meaning the least busy) time for you to fly.

Children Traveling Solo

Although individual airline policies differ (check with the specific airline for details), for the most part children ages 5 to 11 pay the regular adult fare and can travel alone as unaccompanied minors on domestic flights only with an escort from the airlines—a flight attendant who seats the child, usually near the galley, where the flight crew is stationed; watches over the child during the flight; and escorts the child to the appropriate connecting gate or to the adult who will be picking up the child. Unaccompanied minors typically board first and disembark last.

On domestic flights, the service costs between $30 and $75, depending on the airline and whether the child will have to change planes. On all the major airlines, several children traveling together from the same family will have to pay only one fee.

Unaccompanied children are never left alone; escorts stay with them until turning them over to an escort on the connecting flight or to a designated guardian. Airlines require attending adults to furnish a name, address, and government-issued photo ID. The adult who drops the child off at the airport must then designate the name and address of the adult who is authorized to pick the child up. At the destination city, the airline will not release the child to anyone but the authorized adult, after receiving a signature and seeing a photo ID.

Children ages 5 to 7 generally may travel unaccompanied on nonstop flights only; in other words, they're not allowed to change planes for connecting flights at that age. (Northwest and Delta allow all children to travel on connecting flights.) Children ages 8 to 11 may make connecting flights with an escort, with the exception of Southwest and America West, which do not allow any unaccompanied child under the age of 12 to take a connecting flight. America West's policy is relatively new, started in 2001 after two embarrassing incidents in which the airline sent one child to the wrong destination and neglected to tell a parent about another child's flight delay.

Children over the age of 12 are considered adults and may travel without an escort on every major carrier but Northwest, which requires escorts until age 14. They still qualify for assistance from the airline for the extra fee. Southwest is the only airline that does not allow children to use the escort service once they are able to fly without one, at age 12.

Because airlines want to avoid the responsibility of having to shepherd children overnight, minors are usually not allowed to take the last connecting flight of the day, when the risk of missed connections is greatest. Minors are usually not allowed to travel on standby, and they must have confirmed reservations.

On connecting flights, ask when you book if the child will be flying on more than one airline. (With the new airline alliances, your child may end up on a Northwest aircraft, even though you booked the flight through Continental.) If so, make sure you know each airline's policy for unaccompanied minors. Once you receive the ticket, review it yourself to make sure the city of origin and the destination are accurate. Review the ticket carefully with your child and explain simply how it works.

If you're booking a flight for your child, the airlines will request your name, telephone number, and address—along with the name, number, and address of the guardian who will meet your child at the destination city. An adult guardian must accompany the child to the gate or plane, furnish reasonable proof that another adult will meet the child at the final destination, and remain at the airport until the plane is in the air. The accompanying adult at the destination will have to sign a release form and furnish government-issued photo identification, such as a license or passport. If a child is unusually big or small, it's wise to bring a birth certificate to the airport as proof of age.

Solo Minors on International Flights

Major carriers' policies for minors traveling alone are basically the same for both domestic and international travel, although fees are higher on international flights. Children may be prohibited from boarding an international flight under poor weather conditions that could require that the plane be rerouted.

Parents should seriously consider using European airlines for international trips because of the extra services they provide for kids. British Airways has a toy chest on its planes, and Virgin Atlantic treats kids like royalty, with special entertainment channels, toys, and treats.

If you're booking a ticket for a minor on an international flight, you should call the consulate of the destination country to find out about visas and other special entry requirements.

Minor Orientation

With stricter security measures at airports, parents must now get a pass from the ticket agent for permission to escort their children to the departure gate. (Adults picking up unaccompanied minors at arrival gates also need this permission slip.) If your child has never flown before, it makes sense to show up at the airport a little early to wander around, watch other planes take off and land, and prepare your child in advance for how flight is going to feel. Be sure to discuss the danger of talking to strangers—even if you have had the same discussion before. You will be allowed to escort your child to the gate, but not onto the plane.

Some airlines allow unaccompanied minors to board first, so the flight crew has more time to meet the child, orient the child to the location of bathrooms and emergency exits, store carry-ons, review safety procedures, and—kids love this part—introduce the child to the cockpit crew. Make sure minors understand that they should contact an attendant in case of any type of problem—from sickness to a malfunctioning headset to a bothersome neighbor. If you can't make it all the way on to the plane, be sure to introduce your child to the gate attendant and ensure that the child will receive help boarding if necessary.

Some airlines offer special meals for children, such as hamburgers, hot dogs, or peanut butter sandwiches, which must be ordered in advance, when you make the reservation. It's still wise to send your child off with a bagged lunch, snack, and drinks. Also pack books and other entertainment in a carry-on and make sure your child knows how to get at them onboard the plane.

Make sure your child has cash and knows how to make a collect phone call. In one place, record your child's name, your own name, address, and phone number, along with the names and phone number of your child's hosts at the final destination. Review the information with your child and place it in a safe purse, pocket, or neck pouch. Be sure, however,

that your child knows not to share this information with strangers—not even a friendly neighbor in the cabin.

If your child is taking medication, it may be wise to postpone the trip unless you are certain your child is responsible for self-administering dosages properly. Flight attendants are not allowed to administer drugs to minors.

Easing Travel with the Tots in Tow

Several books on the market have tips to help you travel with kids. Most concentrate on the U.S., but two, *Family Travel & Resorts: The Complete Guide* (Lanier Publishing International; $19.95) and *How to Take Great Trips with Your Kids* (The Harvard Common Press; $9.95), are full of good general advice that can apply to travel anywhere. Another reliable tome, with a worldwide focus, is *Adventuring with Children* (Foghorn Press; $14.95).

Family Travel Times (📞 888/822-4FTT [822-4388]; www.familytraveltimes. com) is an excellent online newsletter updated twice monthly. Subscriptions are $39 a year, $49 for 2 years. Sample articles are available on the newsletter's website.

If you plan carefully, you can actually make it fun to travel with kids:

- If you're traveling with children, you'll save yourself a good bit of aggravation by **reserving a seat in the bulkhead** row. You'll have more legroom, and your children will be able to spread out and play on the floor underfoot. You're also more likely to find sympathetic company in the bulkhead area, as families with children tend to be seated there.

- Be sure to **pack items for your children in your carry-on luggage.** In case you're forced to check one of your carry-ons, consolidate the children's things in one bag or in your purse. When you're deciding what to bring, ready yourself for the worst: long, unexpected delays without food, bathrooms without changing tables, airline meals that feature your children's least favorite dishes.

- Have **a long talk with your children** before you depart for your trip. If they've never flown before, explain to them what to expect. If they're old enough, you may even want to describe how flight works and how air travel is even safer than riding in a car. Explain to your kids the importance of good behavior in the air—how their own safety can depend upon their being quiet and staying in their seats during the trip.
- **Pay extra careful attention to the safety instructions** before takeoff. Consult the safety chart behind the seat in front of you and show it to your children. Be sure you know how to operate the oxygen masks, as you will be expected to secure yours first and then help your children with theirs. Be especially mindful of the location of emergency exits. Before takeoff, plot out an evacuation strategy for you and your children in your mind's eye.
- Ask the flight attendant **if the plane has any special safety equipment for children.** Make a member of the crew aware of any medical problems your children have that could manifest during flight.
- **Be sure you've slept sufficiently** for your trip. If you fall asleep in the air and your child manages to break away, there are all sorts of sharp objects that could cause injury. Especially during mealtimes, it's dangerous for a child to be crawling or walking around the cabin unaccompanied by an adult.
- **Be sure your child's seat belt remains fastened properly,** and try to reserve the seat closest to the aisle for yourself. This will make it harder for your children to wander off—in case, for instance, you're taking the red-eye or a long flight overseas and you do happen

to nod off. You will also protect your child from jostling passersby and falling objects—in the rare but entirely possible instance that an overhead bin pops open.

In the event of an accident, unrestrained children often don't make it—even when the parent does. Experience has shown that it's impossible for a parent to hold onto a child in the event of a crash, and children often die of impact injuries.

For the same reason, sudden turbulence is also a danger to a child who is not buckled into his own seat belt or seat restraint. According to *Consumer Reports Travel Letter,* the most common flying injuries result when unanticipated turbulence strikes and hurtles passengers from their seats. (See "Child Seats: They're a Must," above, for suggestions regarding FAA-promoted child-restraint systems.)

- **Try to sit near the lavatory,** though not so close that your children are jostled by the crowds that tend to gather there. Consolidate trips there as much as possible.
- Try to **accompany children to the lavatory.** They can be easily bumped and possibly injured as they make their way down tight aisles. It's especially dangerous for children to wander while flight attendants are blocking passage with their service carts. On crowded flights, the flight crew may need as much as an hour to serve dinner. It's wise to encourage your kids to use the restroom as you see the attendants preparing to serve.
- Be sure to **bring clean, self-containing compact toys.** Leave electronic games at home. They can interfere with the aircraft navigational system, and their noisiness, however lulling to children's ears, will surely not win the favor of your adult neighbors. Magnetic checker sets, on the other hand, are a perfect

In-Flight Fun for Kids

With one of these children's game books onboard, even the longest plane ride will go faster.

Great Games for Kids on the Go: Over 240 Travel Games to Play on Trains, Planes, and Automobiles
by Penny Warner
Retail price: $12.95
Ages 4 to 8
   This book is full of entertaining educational games to help your kids while away the miles. Each game is highly engaging and entertaining and requires few materials and very little space.

Brain Quest for the Car: 1,100 Questions and Answers All About America
by Sharon Gold
Retail price: $10.95
Ages 7 to 12
   This book features cards with questions about American geography, culture, and customs.

Vacation Fun Mad Libs: World's Greatest Party Game
by Roger Price
Retail price: $3.99
Ages 8 and up
   As suggested by the title, this book is chock-full of Mad Libs. Your kids will want to keep playing even after you've touched down.

distraction, and small coloring books and crayons also work well, as do card games like Go Fish.

Visit the library before you leave home and check out children's books about flying or airplane travel. Geography-related books and coloring books that include their departure point and destination will also help engage them during air travel.

A Walkman with a few favorite recordings will also come in handy—especially if you throw in some sleepy-time tunes. By all means, don't leave home without a favorite blanket or stuffed animal—especially if it's your kid's best friend at bedtime.

- Some airlines **serve children's meals first.** When you board, ask a flight attendant if this is possible, especially if your children are very young or seated toward the back of the plane. After all, if your kids have a happy flight experience, everyone else in the cabin is more likely to as well.

- You'll certainly be grateful to yourself for **packing tidy snacks** like rolled dried fruit, which are much less sticky and wet and more compact and packable than actual fruit. Blueberry or raisin bagels also make for a neat, healthy sweet and yield fewer crumbs than cookies or cakes. Ginger snaps, crisp and not as crumbly as softer cookies, will also help curb mild cases of motion sickness. And don't forget to stash a few resealable plastic bags in your purse. They'll prove invaluable for storing everything from half-eaten crackers and fruit to checker pieces and Matchbox cars.

- **Juice or cookies** will not only keep them distracted during ascent and descent—often the scariest parts of flight for a child—but also help their little ears pop as cabin air pressure shifts rapidly. Juice (paper cartons travel best) will also keep them swallowing and help them to stay properly hydrated. Avoid giving young children gum or hard candies, since sudden turbulence may cause them to choke.
- If your children are very young, **bring pacifiers.** The act of sucking will keep their ears clear. By the same logic, take-off and landing are the perfect times for feedings. Your kids will be distracted from the deafening cabin noise, and their ears will pop more easily. If your schedule won't allow this, try placing drops of water on an infant's tongue, to facilitate swallowing. Don't forget to pack bottles and extra milk or formula as well, as these are unavailable on most aircraft. Many airlines prohibit flight attendants from preparing formula, so it's best to pack your baby's food premixed.

Tasteless: Dealing with Airline Food

Most airlines have cut back on food service recently—and even if you do get a "meal" on a domestic flight, it's likely to be a limp turkey sandwich. Your best bet is to brown-bag homemade sandwiches. Unlike fruit, for example, they have no leftover parts to throw away, and you won't have to tussle with airport security over silverware. But if you insist on eating economy-class cuisine, here are some tips:

- **Order a special meal.** Most airlines allow coach-class passengers to order from a range of special meals, including low-fat, low-cholesterol, vegetarian, and children's meals (usually a hamburger or hot dog). These meals aren't necessarily fresher than the standard ones, but at least you'll know what's in them. Call

your airline 2 days before your flight to secure your meal. Then double-check when you check in.
- **Become a vegetarian.** Dieticians and frequent fliers say vegetarian and vegan meals are often better than standard airline fare. Vegan meals skip cheese and sweets, leading to a healthier but more spartan platter.
- **Fly a tasty airline.** The Zagat organization rates airline food annually. For 2001, Midwest Express had the best economy-class meals (including fresh chocolate-chip cookies and real plates), while America West rated the worst of the airlines that actually serve meals (think that aforementioned turkey sandwich).

In general, coach-class passengers now get meals only on flights crossing two-thirds of the country or more; everyone else gets peanuts or other minibags of snacks. (Continental and Alaska are welcome exceptions, but "meals" on Continental flights under $3^{1}/_{2}$ hours are of the dreaded turkey sandwich variety.)

Most low-fare airlines generally serve only snacks (except for Midwest Express), even on cross-country flights. But some offer better snacks than others. Southwest offers a nonyummy bag of salted peanuts. But jetBlue serves up classy blue potato chips, and Frontier goes even further with chicken wraps and specialty bagels.

The Economy-Class Meal Policies of Major Airlines

- **Alaska:** Food served on flights of 2 hours or more. Breakfast 6 to 8:30am; lunch 10:30am to 1:30pm; dinner 4 to 7pm.
- **America West:** Food served only on flights between the East Coast and Phoenix. Breakfast 6 to 9am; lunch 11am to 1pm; dinner 5 to 7pm.
- **American:** Food served only on non-stop, transcontinental flights. Breakfast 5 to 8:30am; lunch noon to 1pm; dinner 5:30 to 7pm.

Flying with Film & Video

Never pack film—developed or undeveloped—in checked bags, as the new, more powerful scanners in U.S. airports can fog film. The film you carry with you can be damaged by scanners as well. X-ray damage is cumulative; the faster the film and the more times you put it through a scanner, the more likely the damage. Film under 800 ASA is usually safe for up to five scans. If you're taking your film through additional scans, U.S. regulations permit you to demand hand inspections. In international airports, you're at the mercy of airport officials. On international flights, store your film in transparent baggies, so you can remove it easily before you go through scanners. Keep in mind that airports are not the only places where your camera may be scanned: Highly trafficked attractions are X-raying visitors' bags with increasing frequency.

Most photo supply stores sell protective pouches designed to block damaging X-rays. The pouches fit both film and loaded cameras. They should protect your film in checked baggage, but they also may raise alarms and result in a hand inspection.

You'll have little to worry about if you are traveling with **digital cameras.** Unlike film, which is sensitive to light, the digital camera and storage cards are not affected by airport X-rays, according to Nikon. Still, if you plan to travel extensively, you may want to play it safe and hand-carry your digital equipment or ask that it be inspected by hand.

Carry-on scanners will not damage **videotape** in video cameras, but the magnetic fields emitted by the walk-through security gateways and hand-held inspection wands will. Always place your loaded camcorder on the screening conveyor belt or have it hand-inspected. Be sure your batteries are charged, as you may be required to turn the device on to ensure that it's what it appears to be.

- **Continental:** Food served on flights of 2 hours or more. Breakfast 7 to 9am; lunch 11am to 1pm; dinner 5 to 7pm.
- **Delta:** Food served only on flights of more than 1,750 miles. Breakfast 5 to 8:30am; lunch noon to 1pm; dinner 6:30 to 7:30pm.
- **Northwest:** Food served only on flights between Detroit/Minneapolis/Memphis and the West Coast. Breakfast 6 to 9:45am; lunch 11am to 1:15pm; dinner 4:30 to 7:15pm.
- **United:** Food served only on flights of more than 1,635 miles. Breakfast 5 to 9:59am; lunch 11am to 1:29pm; dinner 4:50 to 7:29pm.

- **US Airways:** Food served only on nonstop, transcontinental flights. Breakfast 6 to 10am; lunch 11am to 1pm; dinner 4 to 7pm.

BY CAR

Chicago is served by interstate highways from all major points on the compass. I-80 and I-90 approach from the east, crossing the northern sector of Illinois, with I-90 splitting off and emptying into Chicago via the Skyway and the Dan Ryan Expressway. From here, I-90 runs through Wisconsin, following a northern route to Seattle. I-55 snakes up the Mississippi Valley from the vicinity of New Orleans and enters Chicago from the west along the Stevenson Expressway, and in the opposite direction it provides an outlet to the Southwest. I-57 originates in southern Illinois and forms part of the interstate linkage to Florida and the South, connecting within Chicago on the west leg of the Dan Ryan. I-94 links Detroit with Chicago, arriving on the Calumet Expressway and leaving the city via the Kennedy Expressway en route to the Northwest.

Here are a few approximate driving distances in miles to Chicago: from **Milwaukee,** 92; from **St. Louis,** 297; from **Detroit,** 286; from **Denver,** 1,011; from **Atlanta,** 716; from **Washington, D.C.,** 715; from **New York City,** 821; and from **Los Angeles,** 2,034.

BY TRAIN

Rail passenger service, although it may never approach the grandeur of its heyday, has made enormous advances in service, comfort, and efficiency since the creation of Amtrak in 1971. As in the past, but on a reduced scale, Chicago remains the hub of the national passenger rail system. Traveling great distances by train is certainly not the quickest way to go, nor always the most convenient. But many travelers still prefer it to flying or driving.

For tickets, consult your travel agent or call **Amtrak** (© **800/USA-RAIL** [872-7245]; www.amtrak.com). Ask the reservations agent to send you Amtrak's useful travel planner, with information on train accommodations and package tours.

When you arrive in Chicago, the train will pull into **Union Station** at 210 S. Canal, between Adams and Jackson streets (© **312/655-2385**). Bus nos. 1, 60, 125, 151, and 156 all stop at the station, which is just west across the river from the Loop. The nearest El stop is at Clinton Street and Congress Parkway (on the Blue Line), which is a fair walk away, especially when you're carrying luggage.

BY BUS

The **Greyhound Bus Station** in Chicago is at 630 W. Harrison (© **800/231-2222** travel information; www.greyhound.com), not far from Union Station. Several city buses (nos. 60, 125, 156, and 157) pass in front of the terminal building, and the nearest El stop is at Clinton Street and Congress Parkway on the Blue Line.

6 MONEY & COSTS

ATMS

ATMs in Chicago are linked to a national network that most likely includes your bank at home. **Cirrus** (© **800/424-7787;** www.mastercard.com) and **PLUS** (© **800/843-7587;** www.visa.com) are the two most popular networks; check the back of your ATM card to see which network your bank belongs to. Use the toll-free numbers to locate ATMs in Chicago. When you ask for directions to an ATM, Chicagoans may point you to the nearest "Cash Station," our local term (Cash Station is the biggest ATM network in the city); almost every machine labeled "Cash Station" is part of the Cirrus or PLUS network.

Be sure to check your daily withdrawal limit before you leave for your trip. And note that many banks have begun to impose a fee for transactions, and that fee can be higher for international transactions (up to $5) than for domestic ones (rarely more than $2). In addition, your own bank may also charge you a fee for using ATMs from other banks. To compare banks' ATM fees, use www.bankrate.com. Visitors from outside the U.S. should also find out whether their bank assesses a 1% to 3% fee on charges incurred abroad.

(Tips) Small Change

Make sure you're carrying some small bills or loose change. Petty cash will come in handy for tipping and public transportation. Consider keeping the change separate from your larger bills so that it's readily accessible and you'll be less of a target for theft.

CREDIT CARDS

Credit cards are the most widely used form of payment in the United States: **Visa** (Barclaycard in Britain), **MasterCard** (EuroCard in Europe, Access in Britain, Chargex in Canada), **American Express, Diners Club,** and **Discover.** They also provide a convenient record of all your expenses, and offer relatively good exchange rates. You can withdraw cash advances from your credit cards at banks or ATMs, but high fees make credit card cash advances a pricey way to get cash.

It's highly recommended that you travel with at least one major credit card. You must have one to rent a car, and hotels and airlines usually require a credit card imprint as a deposit against expenses.

ATM cards with major credit card backing, known as **"debit cards,"** are now a commonly acceptable form of payment in most stores and restaurants. Debit cards draw money directly from your checking account. Some stores enable you to receive cash back on your debit card purchases as well. The same is true at most U.S. post offices.

These days everyone pays with plastic, even for the smallest purchase. So go ahead and use your card for a cup of coffee and a bagel—few merchants will bat an eye. You can use just about any credit card here; one that might be more popular around Chicago than in other parts of the country is Discover.

TRAVELER'S CHECKS

Though credit cards and debit cards are more often used, traveler's checks are still widely accepted in the U.S. Foreign visitors should make sure that traveler's checks are denominated in U.S. dollars; foreign-currency checks are often difficult to exchange. In Chicago, you should have no trouble using them at most hotels and downtown restaurants (places that are used to accommodate international visitors), but they may not be accepted at smaller businesses in the city's residential neighborhoods.

You can buy traveler's checks at most banks. Most are offered in denominations of $20, $50, $100, $500, and sometimes $1,000. Generally, you'll pay a service charge ranging from 1% to 4%.

The most popular traveler's checks are offered by **American Express** (© **800/807-6233;** 800/221-7282 for cardholders—this number accepts collect calls, offers service in several foreign languages, and exempts AmEx gold and platinum cardholders from the 1% fee); **Visa** (© **800/732-1322;** AAA members can obtain Visa checks for a $9.95 fee—for checks up to $1,500—at most AAA offices or by calling 866/339-3378); and **Master-Card** (© **800/223-9920**).

Be sure to keep a copy of the traveler's checks' serial numbers separate from your checks in the event that they are stolen or lost. You'll get a refund faster if you know the numbers.

Another option is the new **prepaid traveler's check cards,** reloadable cards that work much like debit cards but aren't linked to your checking account. The **American Express Travelers Cheque Card,** for example, requires a minimum

What Things Cost in Chicago	US$	UK£
Cab from O'Hare Airport to downtown hotel	40.00	20.20
Cab from Midway Airport to downtown hotel	30.00	15.15
Shuttle from O'Hare to downtown hotel	25.00	12.60
Shuttle from Midway to downtown hotel	20.00	10.10
Subway or bus ride	2.00	1.00
Transfer (good for two additional rides)	25¢	15p
Ticket to John Hancock Center Observatory	11 adults, 6.50 kids	5.55 adults, 3.25 kids
Ticket to Sears Tower Skydeck	12 adults, 8.50 kids	6.05 adults, 4.30 kids
Hot dog at Gold Coast Dogs	2.40	1.20
Movie ticket	9.50 adults, 6.50 kids	4.80 adults, 5.55 kids
20-ounce soft drink at drug or convenience store	1.29	65p
16-ounce apple juice	1.39	70p
Weekday *Chicago Tribune*	50¢	25p
Weekday *Chicago Sun-Times*	50¢	25p
Package of Pampers at drugstore	12.99	6.55
32-ounce bottle prepared Similac formula	4.99	2.50

deposit ($300), sets a maximum balance ($2,750), and has a one-time issuance fee of $15. You can withdraw money from an ATM ($2.50 per transaction, not including bank fees), and the funds can be purchased in dollars, euros, or pounds. If you lose the card, your available funds will be refunded within 24 hours.

WHAT TO DO IF YOUR WALLET IS LOST OR STOLEN

Almost every credit card company has an emergency toll-free number that you can call if your wallet or purse is lost or stolen. A representative may be able to wire you a cash advance off your credit card immediately and, in many places, can deliver an emergency credit card in a day or two. The **toll-free information directory** will provide the issuing bank's toll-free number if you dial ℭ 800/555-1212. **Citicorp Visa's** U.S. emergency number is ℭ 800/336-8472. **American Express** cardholders and traveler's check holders should call ℭ 800/221-7282 for all money emergencies. **MasterCard** holders should call ℭ 800/307-7309. If you do carry traveler's checks, be sure to keep a record of their serial numbers, separate from the checks, of course, so that you're guaranteed a refund in just such an emergency.

7 HEALTH

STAYING HEALTHY

You won't need to take any unusual precautions when traveling to Chicago. The regular assortment of antacids, antidiarrheals, and some acetaminophen or ibuprofen for headaches should suffice. Lake

Avoiding "Economy Class Syndrome"

Deep vein thrombosis, or as it's known in the world of flying, "economy class syndrome," is a blood clot that develops in a deep vein. It's a potentially deadly condition that can be caused by sitting in cramped conditions—such as an airplane cabin—for too long. During a flight (especially a long-haul flight), get up, walk around, and stretch your legs every 60 to 90 minutes to keep your blood flowing. Other preventive measures include frequent flexing of the legs while sitting, drinking lots of water, and avoiding alcohol and sleeping pills. If you have a history of deep vein thrombosis, heart disease, or other condition that puts you at high risk, some experts recommend wearing compression stockings or taking anticoagulants when you fly; always ask your physician about the best course for you. Symptoms of deep vein thrombosis include leg pain or swelling, or even shortness of breath.

Michigan rarely gets rough enough to advise bringing motion sickness medication for boat tours; however, if you or your kids are particularly susceptible, or if you're planning a long fishing excursion, you may want to add some to your bag.

Pack prescription medications in your carry-on luggage, and keep them in their original containers. Also bring along copies of your prescriptions in case you lose your pills or run out. And don't forget sunglasses and an extra pair of contact lenses or prescription glasses.

Where to Go If You Get Sick Away from Home

In downtown Chicago, the most centrally located hospital is **Northwestern Memorial Hospital,** 251 E. Huron St. (*©* **312/ 926-2000**), just east of Michigan Avenue. Their physician referral service is *©* **312/ 926-8000.** The emergency department is at 250 E. Erie St., near Fairbanks Court (*©* **312/926-5188**).

8 SAFETY

Chicago has all the crime problems of any urban center, so use your common sense and stay cautious and alert. At night you might want to stick to well-lighted streets along the Magnificent Mile, River North, Gold Coast, and Lincoln Park (stay out of the park proper after dark, though), which are all high-traffic areas late into the night. Don't walk alone at night, and avoid wandering down dark residential streets, even those that seem perfectly safe. Muggings can—and do—happen anywhere.

After dark, you might want to avoid neighborhoods such as Hyde Park, Wicker Park (beyond the busy intersection

of Milwaukee, Damen, and North aves.), and Pilsen, which border areas with more troublesome reputations. You can also ask the concierge at your hotel or an agent at the tourist visitor center for recommendations about visiting a particular area of the city.

The El is generally quite safe, even at night, although some of the downtown stations can feel eerily deserted late in the evening. When you're traveling with kids, I always recommend that when in doubt, spring for a taxi. Buses are a safe option, too, especially nos. 146 and 151, which pick up along North Michigan Avenue and State Street and connect to the North Side via Lincoln Park.

Blue-and-white police cars are a common sight, and officers also patrol by bicycle downtown and along the lakefront and by horseback at special events and parades. There are police stations in busy nightlife areas, such as the 18th District station at Chicago Avenue and LaSalle Street in the hopping restaurant-and-entertainment mecca of River North, and the 24th District station (known as Town Hall) at Addison and Halsted streets, near the busy strip of sports bars and nightclubs in Wrigleyville.

9 SUSTAINABLE TOURISM

Sustainable tourism is conscientious travel. It means being careful with the environments you explore, and respecting the communities you visit. Two overlapping components of sustainable travel are **ecotourism** and **ethical tourism.** The **International Ecotourism Society** (TIES) defines ecotourism as responsible travel to natural areas that conserves the environment and improves the well-being of local people. TIES suggests that ecotourists follow these principles:

- Minimize environmental impact.
- Build environmental and cultural awareness and respect.
- Provide positive experiences for both visitors and hosts.
- Provide direct financial benefits for conservation and for local people.
- Raise sensitivity to host countries' political, environmental, and social climates.
- Support international human rights and labor agreements.

You can find some eco-friendly travel tips and statistics, as well as touring companies and associations—listed by destination under "Travel Choice"—at the **TIES** website, www.ecotourism.org. Also check out **Ecotravel.com**, which lets you search for sustainable touring companies in several categories (water-based, land-based, spiritually oriented, and so on).

While much of the focus of eco-tourism is about reducing impacts on the natural environment, ethical tourism concentrates on ways to preserve and enhance local economies and communities, regardless of location. You can embrace ethical tourism by staying at a locally owned hotel or shopping at a store that employs local workers and sells locally produced goods.

Responsible Travel (www.responsible travel.com) is a great source of sustainable travel ideas; the site is run by a spokesperson for ethical tourism in the travel industry. **Sustainable Travel International** (www.sustainabletravelinternational.org) promotes ethical tourism practices, and manages an extensive directory of sustainable properties and tour operators around the world.

In the U.K., **Tourism Concern** (www. tourismconcern.org.uk) works to reduce social and environmental problems connected to tourism. The **Association of Independent Tour Operators (AITO)** (www.aito.co.uk) is a group of specialist operators leading the field in making holidays sustainable.

Volunteer travel has become increasingly popular among those who want to venture beyond the standard group-tour experience to learn languages, interact with locals, and make a positive difference while on vacation. Volunteer travel usually doesn't require special skills—just a willingness to work hard—and programs vary in length from a few days to a number of weeks. Some programs provide free housing and food, but many require volunteers to pay for travel expenses, which can add up quickly.

Tips **It's Easy Being Green**

Here are a few simple ways you can help conserve fuel and energy when you travel:

- Each time you take a flight or drive a car greenhouse gases release into the atmosphere. You can help neutralize this danger to the planet through "carbon offsetting"—paying someone to invest your money in programs that reduce your greenhouse gas emissions by the same amount you've added. Before buying carbon offset credits, just make sure that you're using a reputable company, one with a proven program that invests in renewable energy. Reliable carbon offset companies include **Carbonfund** (www.carbonfund.org), **TerraPass** (www.terrapass.org), and **Carbon Neutral** (www.carbonneutral.org).
- Whenever possible, choose nonstop flights; they generally require less fuel than indirect flights that stop and take off again. Try to fly during the day—some scientists estimate that nighttime flights are twice as harmful to the environment. And pack light—each 15 pounds of luggage on a 5,000-mile flight adds up to 50 pounds of carbon dioxide emitted.
- Where you stay during your travels can have a major environmental impact. To determine the green credentials of a property, ask about trash disposal and recycling, water conservation, and energy use; also question if sustainable materials were used in the construction of the property. The website

For general info on volunteer travel, visit **www.volunteerabroad.org** and **www.idealist.org**. Before you commit to a volunteer program, it's important to make sure any money you're giving is truly going back to the local community, and that

the work you'll be doing will be a good fit for you. **Volunteer International** (www.volunteerinternational.org) has a helpful list of questions to ask to determine the intentions and the nature of a volunteer program.

10 TRAVELING SAFELY WITH KIDS IN CHICAGO

The easiest way to stay safe in Chicago is to **hold hands with your kids.** It's safe and fun, without being overly protective. Keep your kids close and within eyeshot, and be extra careful around busy intersections. Cabs will not slow down for anyone—even families with kids. Do not cross anywhere but at traffic lights (it sounds obvious, but I've seen parents with strollers crossing in the middle of busy streets). Again, drivers won't stop for you

in the city just because you have a stroller. Stay on major streets and avoid construction sites.

Visitors should steer clear of situations where kids could get lost in a crowd. At the ballpark, at the end of the game, wait until most of the crowd files out so kids can go at their own pace. Remember, Michigan Avenue and major attractions can get crowded in the summer. **Make contingency plans for reuniting,** even

www.greenhotels.com recommends green-rated member hotels around the world that fulfill the company's stringent environmental requirements. Also consult **www.environmentallyfriendlyhotels.com** for more green accommodation ratings.

- At hotels, request that your sheets and towels not be changed daily. (Many hotels already have programs like this in place.) Turn off the lights and air-conditioner (or heater) when you leave your room.
- Use public transport where possible—trains, buses and even taxis are more energy-efficient forms of transport than driving. Even better is to walk or cycle; you'll produce zero emissions and stay fit and healthy on your travels.
- If renting a car is necessary, ask the rental agent for a hybrid, or rent the most fuel-efficient car available. You'll use less gas and save money at the tank.
- Eat at locally owned and operated restaurants that use produce grown in the area. This contributes to the local economy and cuts down on greenhouse gas emissions by supporting restaurants where the food is not flown or trucked in across long distances. Visit **Sustain Lane** (www.sustainlane. org) to find sustainable eating and drinking choices around the U.S.; also check out **www.eatwellguide.org** for tips on eating sustainably in the U.S. and Canada.

in the most ordinary situations. Start at the information desk at whatever attraction you're visiting, and make a plan to meet there in case you and your kids get split up.

Another tip is to **use public transportation.** If you are driving in to the city, park in a central location and walk or take the El or bus. Don't plan on taking a cab with small children unless you want to carry a car seat with you. Some parents find trains to be easier with children than buses because you can roll strollers right onto trains, and you don't have to stand on a busy street corner as you would if waiting for the bus.

Finally, **travel light** and avoid being overburdened or distracted by too much gear. Carry water, juice, and snacks (downtown, you will pay a ton to buy these items). Also, be prepared for a lack of chain fast-food outlets. When visiting major attractions, you may be able to avoid taking a stroller because most places rent them. If you do feel the need to bring a stroller, make sure it's light and narrow—some of the sturdy but wide strollers are hard to maneuver through city crowds and narrow store aisles.

Several books on the market offer additional tips to help you travel with kids. *How to Take Great Trips with Your Kids* (The Harvard Common Press; $9.95) is full of good general advice that can apply to travel anywhere. *Family Travel Times* (C **888/822-4FTT** [822-4388]; www.familytraveltimes.com) is an excellent online newsletter updated twice monthly. Subscriptions are $39 a year, $49 for 2 years. Sample articles are available on the newsletter's website. Other recommended family travel Internet sites include **Family Travel Forum** (www.familytravelforum. com), a comprehensive site that offers

Frommers.com: The Complete Travel Resource

It should go without saying, but we highly recommend **Frommers.com,** voted Best Travel Site by *PC Magazine.* We think you'll find our expert advice and tips; independent reviews of hotels, restaurants, attractions, and preferred shopping and nightlife venues; vacation giveaways; and an online booking tool indispensable before, during, and after your travels. We publish the complete contents of more than 128 travel guides in our **Destinations** section, covering nearly 3,800 places worldwide to help you plan your trip. Each weekday, we publish original articles reporting on **Deals and News** via our free **Frommers. com Newsletter** to help you save time and money and travel smarter. We're betting you'll find our new **Events** listings (http://events.frommers.com) an invaluable resource; it's an up-to-the-minute roster of what's happening in cities everywhere—including concerts, festivals, lectures, and more. We've also added weekly **Podcasts, interactive maps,** and hundreds of new images across the site. Check out our **Travel Talk** area, featuring **Message Boards** where you can join in conversations with thousands of fellow Frommer's travelers and post your trip report once you return.

customized trip planning; **Family Travel Network** (www.familytravelnetwork.com), an award-winning site that provides travel features, deals, and tips; and **Family Travel Files** (www.thefamilytravelfiles.com), which has an online magazine and a directory of off-the-beaten-path tours and tour operators for families.

PLANNING YOUR OUTINGS

Planning a day of touring a city with kids is a little like mapping out a military campaign: You should have a list of sights to hit, and a precise idea of how you will get from one activity to the next, leaving time in between for potty breaks and snack stops. If you plan carefully and center all your days' activities in close proximity, you can save yourself a lot of wasted transit time.

Prime areas for families include the **Magnificent Mile,** with the John Hancock Center, American Girl Place, The Apple Store, Niketown, and other shopping destinations; **Streeterville,** home of Navy Pier and the Museum of Contemporary Art; **River North,** with lots of chain establishments, including ESPN Zone, Hard Rock Cafe, Rock 'n' Roll McDonald's, The Rainforest Café, and Ed Debevic's; **Lincoln Park,** with the park, zoo, and botanical gardens; **Museum Campus,** with four museums within walking distance of each other; and **Hyde Park,** home to the Museum of Science and Industry.

FINDING A RESTROOM

The number-one tip for visitors from Chicago parents: Know where the nearest restroom is at all times! First order of business: Always use the bathroom at your hotel before you leave, and stop in the restroom before you leave any museum or restaurant. Failing that, key restrooms in prime locations include **900 N. Michigan Avenue mall,** on the second and fifth floors; **John Hancock Center,** in the lower level; **Water Tower Place;** and **Nordstrom,** in the Shops at North Bridge mall on Michigan Avenue, just south of the Chicago River. Most **Starbucks** coffee shops have restrooms—just ask the barista for the key. **Barnes & Noble** and **Borders** bookstores typically have bathrooms near the children's section. Major hotel lobbies are also good bets. Most restaurants will take pity on a distressed child, so just ask; some store owners may do the same. If you are really concerned about mapping out nearby bathrooms, there's even a website dedicated to the topic. The Bathroom Diaries (www.thebathroomdiaries.com) lists 10,000 bathrooms around the world, everywhere from Cambodia to Antarctica, with a focus on the U.S. Readers rank

bathrooms according to cleanliness, safety, and aesthetic beauty (believe it or not!).

NURSING MOMS & INFANTS

Chicago is like any other city—it's made up of all kinds of people. While most people will see a nursing mom and look the other way, some might stare rudely. If you need to breast-feed an infant, you'll probably feel most comfortable in women's lounges in major department stores (**Nordstrom** is best).

11 STAYING CONNECTED

TELEPHONES

Generally, hotel surcharges on long-distance and local calls are astronomical, so you're better off using your **cellphone** or a **public pay telephone.** Many convenience groceries and packaging services sell **prepaid calling cards** in denominations up to $50; for international visitors, these can be the least expensive way to call home. Many public pay phones at airports now accept American Express, MasterCard, and Visa credit cards. **Local calls** made from pay phones in most locales cost 50¢ (no pennies, please).

Most long-distance and international calls can be dialed directly from any phone. **For calls within the United States and to Canada,** dial 1 followed by the area code and the seven-digit number. **For other international calls,** dial 011 followed by the country code, city code, and number you are calling.

Calls to area codes **800, 888, 877,** and **866** are toll-free. However, calls to area codes **700** and **900** (chat lines, bulletin boards, "dating" services, and so on) can be very expensive—usually a charge of 95¢ to $3 or more per minute, and they sometimes have minimum charges that can run as high as $15 or more.

For **reversed-charge or collect calls,** and for person-to-person calls, dial the number 0 and then the area code and number; an operator will come on the line, and you should specify whether you are calling collect, person-to-person, or both. If your operator-assisted call is international, ask for the overseas operator.

For **local directory assistance** ("information"), dial 411; for long-distance information, dial 1, then the appropriate area code, and 555-1212.

CELLPHONES

Just because your cellphone works at home doesn't mean it'll work everywhere in the U.S. (thanks to our nation's fragmented cellphone system). It's a good bet that your phone will work in major cities, but take a look at your wireless company's coverage map on its website before heading out; T-Mobile, Sprint, and Nextel are particularly weak in rural areas. If you need to stay in touch at a destination where you know your phone won't work, **rent** a phone that does from **InTouch USA** (© **800/872-7626;** www.intouchglobal. com) or a rental-car location, but be aware that you'll pay $1 a minute or more for airtime.

> **(Tips)** **Hey, Google, did you get my text message?**
>
> It's bound to happen: The day you leave this guidebook back at the hotel for an unencumbered stroll through [neighborhood in your destination], you'll forget the address of the lunch spot you had earmarked. If you're traveling with a mobile device, send a text message to ℂ **46645 (GOOGL)** for a lightning-fast response. For instance, type "carnegie deli new york" and within 10 seconds you'll receive a text message with the address and phone number. This nifty trick works in a range of search categories: Look up weather ("weather philadelphia"), language translations ("translate goodbye in spanish"), currency conversions ("10 usd in pounds"), movie times ("harry potter 60605"), and more. If your search results are off, be more specific ("the abbey gay bar west hollywood"). For more tips and search options, see www.google.com/intl/en_us/mobile/sms. Regular text message charges apply.

If you're not from the U.S., you'll be appalled at the poor reach of our **GSM (Global System for Mobile Communications) wireless network,** which is used by much of the rest of the world. Your phone will probably work in most major U.S. cities; it definitely won't work in many rural areas. To see where GSM phones work in the U.S., check out www.t-mobile.com/coverage/national_popup.asp. And you may or may not be able to send SMS (text messaging) home.

INTERNET/E-MAIL
Without Your Own Computer

To find cybercafes in your destination, check **www.cybercaptive.com** and **www.cybercafe.com**.

Most major airports have **Internet kiosks** that provide basic Web access for a per-minute fee that's usually higher than cybercafe prices. Check out copy shops like **Kinko's** (FedEx Office), which offer computer stations with fully loaded software (as well as Wi-Fi).

With Your Own Computer

More and more hotels, resorts, airports, cafes, and retailers are going Wi-Fi (wireless fidelity), becoming "hotspots" that offer free high-speed Wi-Fi access or charge a small fee for usage. Wi-Fi is even found in campgrounds, RV parks, and entire towns. Most laptops sold today have built-in wireless capability. To find public Wi-Fi hotspots at your destination, go to **www.jiwire.com**; its Hotspot Finder holds the world's largest directory of public wireless hotspots.

For dial-up access, most business-class hotels in the U.S. offer dataports for laptop modems, and a few thousand hotels in the U.S. and Europe now offer free high-speed Internet access.

Wherever you go, bring a **connection kit** of the right power and phone adapters, a spare phone cord, and a spare Ethernet network cable—or find out whether your hotel supplies them to guests.

For information on electrical currency conversions, see "Electricity," in the "Fast Facts" section of the appendix.

12 GETTING TO KNOW CHICAGO

The best advice on orienting yourself on Chicago's streets? Look for our inland ocean. Whenever you spot Lake Michigan dead ahead, you are facing east. Another directional no-brainer? If you are on the Magnificent Mile, or in the Loop, look up. The tallest building around is that black glass behemoth, the Sears Tower, and it's to the south. The orderly configuration of Chicago's streets and the excellent public transportation system make this city more accessible than most of the world's other large cities.

VISITOR INFORMATION

The **Chicago Convention and Tourism Bureau** runs a toll-free visitor hot line (© **877/CHICAGO** [244-2246] or TTY 866/710-0294; www.choosechicago.com) and operates two visitor information centers staffed with people who can answer questions. Stop here to stock up on brochures on area attractions, including materials on everything from museums and city landmarks to lakefront biking maps and even fishing spots. The main visitor center, located in the Loop and convenient to many places that you'll likely be visiting, is on the first floor of the **Chicago Cultural Center,** 78 E. Washington St. (at Michigan Ave.). The center has a phone that you can use to make hotel reservations, and several couches and a cafe where you can study maps and plan your itinerary. The center is open Monday through Friday from 10am to 6pm, Saturday from 10am to 5pm, and Sunday from 11am to 5pm; it's closed on holidays.

A second, smaller center is located in the heart of the city's shopping district, in the old pumping station at Michigan and Chicago avenues. Recently renamed the **Chicago Water Works Visitor Center,** its entrance is on the Pearson Street side of the building, across from the Water Tower Place mall. It's open daily 7:30am to 7pm. This location has the added draw of housing a location of Hot Tix, which sells both half-price day-of-performance and full-price tickets to many theater productions around the city, as well as a gift shop and a Chicago Flat Sammies restaurant. Part of

the building has been converted into a theater, including a small cabaret space for tourist-oriented shows and a larger playhouse for the acclaimed Lookingglass Theatre.

The **Illinois Bureau of Tourism** (© **800/2CONNECT** [226-6632] or TTY 800/406-6418; www.enjoyillinois. com) can provide general and specific information 24 hours a day. Many of the bureau's brochures can be ordered online or picked up at the Water Works Visitor Center (see above).

INFORMATION BY TELEPHONE The **Mayor's Office of Special Events** operates a recorded hot line (© **312/744-3370** or TTY 312/744-2964; www.cityofchicago. org), which lists current special events, festivals, and parades occurring throughout the city.

PUBLICATIONS Pick up a free copy of *Chicago Parent* magazine at any bookstore, public library, park district building, or children's specialty shop. You will also find copies in newspaper vending boxes on Michigan Avenue. Each issue includes a daily calendar of events and a museum page that keeps readers abreast of new openings of interest to kids. Each June, the magazine publishes its annual *Going Places* guide. Call the magazine's offices in Oak Park at © **708/386-5555** to order one.

Chicago's major daily newspapers are the *Tribune* and the *Sun-Times.* Both have cultural listings, including movies, theaters, and live music, not to mention reviews of the latest restaurants that are sure to have appeared in the city since this guidebook went to press. The Friday editions of both papers contain special pull-out sections with more detailed, up-to-date information on special events happening over the weekend. The *Tribune* also publishes *Red Eye,* a weekday tabloid aimed at younger readers with a mix of "lite" news items, entertainment news, and quirky features.

(Value) Insider Tours—for Free!

Want your kids to see the city from a native's point of view? **Chicago Greeter,** a program run by the Chicago Office of Tourism, matches tourists with local Chicagoans who serve as volunteer guides. Visitors can request a specific neighborhood or theme (everything from Polish heritage sites to Chicago movie locations), and a greeter gives a free 2- to 4-hour tour. (Greeters won't escort groups of more than six people.) Kids of all ages are welcome (bringing newborns on the tours, however, is discouraged). When you call, please specify that you will be using a stroller so that your guide can plan accordingly for accessing public transportation. Chicago Greeter offers a special "Kids Activities" tour that includes Navy Pier. Other popular family tours include Lincoln Park Zoo and the Shedd Aquarium (see the website or call for details). Specific requests for these kid-friendly tours should be made at least a week in advance, but "InstaGreeters" are also available on a first-come, first-served basis, for 60-minute walking visits, at the Chicago Cultural Center, 77 E. Randolph St., from 10am to 4pm Friday through Sunday. For details, call ℂ **312/744-8000** or visit www.chicagogreeter. com. Millennium Park Greeter service originates from the Millennium Park Welcome Center (201 E. Randolph St.) and offers a free walking tour of the 24.5-acre park.

Chicago magazine is an upscale monthly with good restaurant listings. Even better for short-term visitors is the weekly magazine *Time Out Chicago,* which lists just about everything going on around town during the week, from art openings to theater performances. For a look at the city's beautiful people, pick up *CS* (formerly *Chicago Social*), a glossy monthly magazine filled with photos from charity galas and ads for high-priced local boutiques.

In a class by itself is the *Chicago Reader* (ℂ **312/828-0350;** www.chicagoreader. com), a free weekly that is an invaluable source of entertainment listings, classifieds, and well-written articles on contemporary issues of interest in Chicago. Published every Thursday (except the last week of Dec), the weekly has a wide distribution downtown and on the North Side; it is available in many retail stores, in building lobbies, and at the paper's offices, 11 E. Illinois St., by about noon on Thursday.

Another free weekly, *New City* (ℂ **312/ 243-8786;** www.newcitychicago.com), also publishes excellent comprehensive listings of entertainment options. Appealing to a slightly younger audience than the *Reader, New City* has an editorial tone tending toward the edgy and irreverent. Published every Wednesday, it's available in the same neighborhoods and locations as the *Reader.*

Most Chicago hotels stock their rooms or lobbies with at least one informational magazine, such as *Where Chicago,* that lists the city's entertainment, shopping, and dining locales.

CITY LAYOUT

The **Chicago River** forms a Y that divides the city into its three geographic zones: North Side, South Side, and West Side (Lake Michigan is where the East Side would be). The downtown financial district is called **the Loop.** The city's key shopping street is **North Michigan Avenue,** also known as the **Magnificent Mile**

(Michigan Ave. is home to 600 stores!). In addition to department stores and vertical malls, this stretch of property north of the river houses many of the city's most elegant hotels. North and south of this downtown zone, Chicago stretches along 29 miles of Lake Michigan shoreline that is, by and large, free of commercial development, reserved for public use as green space and parkland from one end of town to the other.

Chicago proper today has 3 million inhabitants living in an area about two-thirds the size of New York City; another 5 million make the suburbs their home. The villages north of Chicago now stretch in an unbroken mass nearly to the Wisconsin border; the city's western suburbs extend 30 miles to Naperville, one of the fastest-growing towns in the nation over the past 2 decades. A total of 59 million people now live within a day's drive of Chicago. The real signature of Chicago, however, is found between the suburbs and the Loop, where a colorful patchwork quilt of residential neighborhoods gives the city a character all its own.

FINDING AN ADDRESS Having been a part of the Northwest Territory, Chicago is laid out in a **grid system,** with the streets neatly lined up as if on a giant piece of graph paper. Because the city itself isn't rectangular (it's rather elongated), the shape is a bit irregular, but the perpendicular pattern remains. Easing movement through the city are a half-dozen or so major diagonal thoroughfares.

Point zero is at the downtown intersection of State and Madison streets. **State Street** divides east and west addresses, and **Madison Street** divides north and south addresses. From here, Chicago's highly

---

(Fun Facts) A River Runs Through It

The Chicago River remains one of the most visible of the city's major physical features. It's spanned by more movable bridges (52 at last count) than any city in the world. An almost-mystical moment occurs downtown when all the bridges spanning the main and south branches—connecting the Loop to both the near West Side and the near North Side—are raised, allowing for the passage of some ship or barge or contingent of high-masted sailboats. The Chicago River has long outlived the critical commercial function that it once performed. Most of the remaining millworks that still occupy its banks no longer depend on the river alone for the transport of their materials, raw and finished. The river's main function today is to serve as a fluvial conduit for sewage, which, owing to an engineering feat that reversed its flow inland in 1900, no longer pollutes the waters of Lake Michigan. Recently, Chicagoans have begun to discover another role for the river—a leisure resource, providing short cruises on its water, park areas, cafes, and public art installations on its banks, and the beginnings of a riverside bike path that connects to the lakefront route near Wacker Drive. Actually, today's developers aren't the first to wonder why the river couldn't be Chicago's Seine. A look at the early-20th-century Beaux Arts balustrades lining the river along Wacker Drive, complete with comfortably spaced benches—as well as Parisian-style bridge houses—shows that Chicago-based architect Daniel Burnham knew full well what a treasure the city had.

predictable addressing system begins. Making use of this grid, it is relatively easy to plot the distance in miles between any two points in the city.

All of Chicago's principal north-south and east-west arteries are spaced by increments of 400 in the addressing system—regardless of the number of smaller streets nestled between them. And each addition or subtraction of 400 numbers to an address is equivalent to a half-mile. Thus, starting at point zero on Madison Street and traveling north along State Street for 1 mile, you will come to 800 N. State St., which intersects Chicago Avenue. Continue uptown for another half-mile and you arrive at the 1200 block of North State Street at Division Street. And so it goes, right to the city line, with suburban Evanston at the 7600 block north, 9¹/₂ miles from point zero.

The same rule applies when you're traveling south, or east to west. Thus, heading west from State Street along Madison Street, Halsted Street—at 800 W. Madison St.—is a mile's distance, while Racine Avenue, at the 1200 block of West Madison Street, is 1¹/₂ miles from the center. Madison Street then continues westward

to Chicago's boundary with the near suburb of Oak Park along Austin Avenue, which, at 6000 W. Madison, is approximately 7¹/₂ miles from point zero.

The key to understanding the grid is that the side of any square formed by the principal avenues (noted in dark or red ink on most maps) represents a distance of half a mile in any direction. Understanding how Chicago's grid system works is of particular importance to those visitors who want to do a lot of walking in the city's many neighborhoods and who want to plot in advance the distances involved in trekking from one locale to another.

The other ingeniously convenient aspect of the grid is that every major road uses the same numerical system. In other words, the cross street (Division St.) at 1200 N. Lake Shore Dr. is the same as at 1200 N. Clark St., which is the same as at 1200 N. LaSalle St., and so on.

STREET MAPS Maps are available at the city's visitor information centers at the **Chicago Cultural Center** and the **Chicago Water Works Visitor Center** (see "Visitor Information," near the beginning of this chapter).

NEIGHBORHOODS IN BRIEF

THE LOOP & VICINITY

Downtown In the case of Chicago, downtown means the Loop. The Loop refers literally to a core of primarily commercial, governmental, and cultural buildings contained within a corral of elevated train tracks. However, greater downtown Chicago overflows these confines and is bounded by the Chicago River to the north and west, by Michigan Avenue to the east, and by Roosevelt Avenue to the south. The main attractions for families in the Loop are Millennium Park, the Art Institute, the Cultural Center, and the Harold Washington Library. If you are

catching a show, you'll find the revitalized theater district in the North Loop. Macy's on State Street, famous for its window decorations during the holidays, anchors a strip of retail shopping.

THE NORTH SIDE

Near North/Magnificent Mile North Michigan Avenue is known as the Magnificent Mile, from the bridge spanning the Chicago River to its northern tip at Oak Street. Many of the city's best hotels, shops, and restaurants are to be found on and around elegant North Michigan Avenue. The area stretching east of Michigan Avenue to the lake is also sometimes referred to as

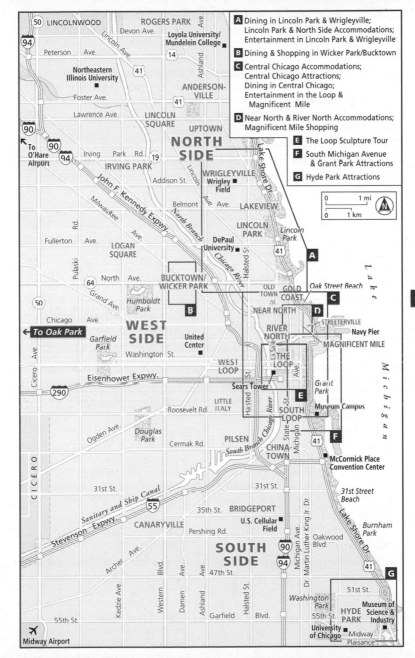

A Dining in Lincoln Park & Wrigleyville;
Lincoln Park & North Side Accommodations;
Entertainment in Lincoln Park & Wrigleyville

B Dining & Shopping in Wicker Park/Bucktown

C Central Chicago Accommodations;
Central Chicago Attractions;
Dining in Central Chicago;
Entertainment in the Loop &
Magnificent Mile

D Near North & River North Accommodations;
Magnificent Mile Shopping

E The Loop Sculpture Tour

F South Michigan Avenue
& Grant Park Attractions

G Hyde Park Attractions

0   1 mi
0   1 km

(Moments) **Frommer's Favorite Oh-So-Chicago Experiences**

- **Strolling the Lakefront.** Chicagoans use the lakefront in every possible way: for walking, rollerblading, biking, running, swimming, picnicking, and playing volleyball. Summers on the lakefront can get a little crowded, but that's part of the fun. Even in winter, you can see hardy souls out for a run while waves crash onto the shoreline. Most activity takes place around Oak Street Beach and North Avenue Beach.

- **Sightseeing on the Chicago River and Lake Michigan.** By far the best way to scope out the city is by taking a boat tour. Getting onto the water gives you a fresh perspective on a city that grew up around a lake and a river. Options include dinner cruises, speedboats, architectural tours, water taxis, and tall ships. See "Kid-Friendly Tours," in chapter 6, for suggestions.

- **Cheering the Cubbies.** Wrigley Field is not to be missed. In fact, Chicagoans regularly play hooky to hang out in the bleachers on a perfect summer afternoon. Eat a hot dog. Exercise your lungs during the singing of "Take Me Out to the Ball Game." I'm sure you'll leave agreeing with me that Wrigley Field is the most charming ballpark in America.

- **Riding the El.** The noisy, dirty El (Chicago's elevated train), which blocks sunlight from the streets beneath its tracks, is a quintessential part of Chicago. Even if you have nowhere in particular to go, hop on the El and ride around the Loop. The Brown Line heading south takes you on an up-close-and-personal view of Chicago's financial center. See "Getting Around," below, for more on riding the El. Also see the box "Sky Train: Chicago's El" for more on the history of the trains (p. 62).

"Streeterville"—the legacy of George Wellington "Cap" Streeter, an eccentric, bankrupt showman who staked out 200 acres of self-created landfill here about a century ago after his steamship had run aground on the shore, and then declared himself "governor" of the "District of Lake Michigan." True story.

River North Just to the west of the Mag Mile's zone of high life and sophistication is an old warehouse district called River North. It's also the site of most chain restaurants that cater to the kid set. Over the past 15 to 20 years, the area has experienced a rebirth as one of the city's most vital commercial districts, and today it is filled with many of the city's hottest restaurants, nightspots, art galleries, and loft dwellings. Several large-scale residential loft-conversion developments have lately been sprouting on its western and southwestern fringes.

The Gold Coast Some of Chicago's most desirable real estate and historic architecture are found along Lake Shore Drive, between Oak Street and North Avenue and along the adjacent side streets. Despite trendy little pockets of real estate popping up elsewhere, the moneyed class still prefers to live by the lake. This residential area doesn't offer much for kids, but it does have beautiful scenic streets for walking. On the

- **Getting the Blues.** This most American of music forms is venerated by Chicagoans, who keep the blues alive nightly in the city's clubs. Chicago-style blues is what most people think of when you mention live blues played in a nightclub setting. Catching a blues act is a great way for grown-ups to spend a night out on the town (see the box "If You Have a Sitter: The Music Scene" in chapter 10).

- **Discovering Wonders at Chicago's Museums.** Generations of Chicagoans recall permanent exhibits at Chicago museums with nostalgia. I remember Colleen Moore's Fairy Castle at the Museum of Science and Industry—the most fantastic dollhouse you'll ever see. My brother will never forget the Model Railway at the same museum. Whatever your family's fancy, you can find an exhibit about it somewhere among the Adler Planetarium & Astronomy Museum, Field Museum of Natural History, Art Institute of Chicago, Museum of Science and Industry, John G. Shedd Aquarium, or Museum of Contemporary Art.

   And don't miss out on Chicago's Museum Campus—a landscaped 57-acre area with terraced gardens and broad walkways that's home to the Field Museum of Natural History, John G. Shedd Aquarium, and the Adler Planetarium & Astronomy Museum. In my humble opinion, the Museum Campus is the most impressive collection of museums in the most beautiful setting anywhere in the country.

   For more on Chicago's museums, see chapter 6.

neighborhood's western edge, the northern stretch of State Street just south of Division Street has, in recent years, developed into a thriving zone of restaurants, bars, and nightclubs.

Old Town West of LaSalle Street, principally on North Wells Street between Division Street and North Avenue, is the nightlife district of Old Town. On Wells Street, and a few blocks east and a few blocks west on North Avenue, you'll find plenty of families and strollers during the day. This area was a hippie haven in the 1960s and 1970s, but in recent years its residential areas have been rapidly gentrified as Cabrini

Green, America's most notorious housing project, has finally fallen to the wrecking ball. Old Town's biggest claim to fame, the legendary Second City comedy club, has served up the lighter side of life to Chicagoans for more than 30 years.

Lincoln Park Chicago's most popular residential neighborhood is fashionable Lincoln Park. The neighborhood is notable for visiting families because it is bordered on the east by the huge park of the same name, which is home to two major museums and one of the nation's oldest zoos (established in 1868). The trapezoid formed by Clark

Street, Armitage Avenue, Halsted Street, and Diversey Parkway also contains many of Chicago's most happening bars, restaurants, retail stores, music clubs, and off-Loop theaters—including the nationally acclaimed Steppenwolf Theatre Company.

Lakeview & Wrigleyville Wrigleyville is the name given to the neighborhood in the vicinity of Wrigley Field—home of the Chicago Cubs—at Sheffield Avenue and Addison Street. Many homesteaders have moved into these areas in recent years, and a slew of nightclubs and restaurants have followed in their wake. Midway up the city's North Side is a one-time blue-collar, now mainstream middle-class and bohemian quarter called Lakeview. It has become the neighborhood of choice for many gays and lesbians, recent college graduates, and a growing number of residents priced out of Lincoln Park. The main thoroughfare is Belmont Avenue, between Broadway and Sheffield Avenue.

Uptown & Andersonville Uptown, along the lake and about as far north as Foster Avenue, is where the latest wave of immigrants—including internal migrants from Appalachia and the Native American reservations—has settled. Vietnamese and Chinese immigrants have transformed Argyle Street between Broadway and Sheridan Road into a teeming market for fresh meat, fish, and all kinds of exotic vegetables. Slightly to the north and west is the old Scandinavian neighborhood of Andersonville, whose main drag is Clark Street, between Foster and Bryn Mawr avenues. This neighborhood is friendly to families, with the feel of a small Midwestern village, albeit one with an eclectic mix of Middle Eastern restaurants, a distinct cluster of women-owned businesses, and a burgeoning gay and lesbian community. You'll find Ann Sather restaurant, the Swedish-American Museum, the Swedish Bakery, and Women and Children First, a great bookstore.

Lincoln Square Families flock to Old Town School of Folk Music's theater and education center, a beautiful restoration of a former library building, in this neighborhood west of Andersonville and slightly to the south, where Lincoln, Western, and Lawrence avenues intersect. Lincoln Square was the home to Chicago's once-vast German-American community. Lincoln Square is hopping with hot restaurants and chic shops as the surrounding leafy residential streets are now experiencing an influx of white middle-class families.

Rogers Park Rogers Park, which begins at Devon Avenue, is on the northern fringes of the city bordering suburban Evanston. Its western half has been a Jewish neighborhood for decades. The eastern half, dominated by Loyola University's lakefront campus, has become the most cosmopolitan enclave in the entire city: Asians, East Indians, Russian Jews, and German Americans live side by side with African Americans and the ethnically mixed student population drawn to the Catholic university. Much of Rogers Park has a neo-hippie ambience, but the western stretch of Devon Avenue is a Midwestern slice of Calcutta, settled by Indians who've transformed the street into a veritable restaurant row of tandoori chicken and curry-flavored dishes.

THE WEST SIDE

West Loop Also known as the Near West Side, the neighborhood just across the Chicago River from the Loop is the city's newest gentrification target, as old warehouses and once-vacant lots are transformed into trendy condos. The stretch of Randolph Street just west of

Hwy. 90/94 and the surrounding blocks are known as "Restaurant Row" for the many dining spots that cluster there. Nearby, on Halsted Street between Adams and Monroe streets, is Chicago's old "Greek Town," still the Greek culinary center of the city. Much of the old Italian neighborhood in this vicinity was the victim of urban renewal, but remnants still survive on Taylor Street; the same is true for a few old delis and shops on Maxwell Street, dating from the turn of the 20th century, when a large Jewish community lived in the area.

Bucktown/Wicker Park Centered near the confluence of North, Damen, and Milwaukee avenues, where the Art Deco Northwest Tower is the tallest thing for miles, this resurgent area is said to be home to the third-largest concentration of artists in the country. Over the past century, the area has hosted waves of German, Polish, and, most recently, Spanish-speaking immigrants (not to mention writer Nelson Algren). In recent years, it has morphed into a bastion of hot new restaurants, alternative culture, and loft-dwelling yuppies surfing the gentrification wave that's washing over this still-somewhat-gritty neighborhood.

THE SOUTH SIDE

South Loop The generically rechristened South Loop area was Chicago's original "Gold Coast" in the late 19th century, with Prairie Avenue (now a historic district) as its most exclusive address. But in the wake of the 1893 World's Columbian Exposition in Hyde Park, and continuing through the Prohibition era of the 1920s, the area was infamous for its Levee vice district, home to gambling and prostitution, some of the most corrupt politicians in Chicago history, and Al Capone's headquarters at the old Lexington Hotel.

However, in recent years, its prospects have turned around. The South Loop—stretching from Harrison Street's historic Printers Row south to Cermak Road (where Chinatown begins), and from Lake Shore Drive west to the south branch of the Chicago River—is one of the fastest-growing residential neighborhoods in the city.

Pilsen Originally home to the nation's largest settlement of Bohemian-Americans, Pilsen (which derives its name from a city in Bohemia) was for decades the principal entry point in Chicago for immigrants of every ethnic stripe. Centered at Halsted and 18th streets just southwest of the Loop, it is now the second-largest Mexican-American community in the United States. One of the city's most vibrant and colorful neighborhoods, Pilsen has been happily invaded by the outdoor mural movement launched years earlier in Mexico, and it has a profusion of authentic taquerías and bakeries. The neighborhood's annual Day of the Dead celebration, which begins in September, is an elaborate festival that runs for 8 weeks. The artistic spirit that permeates the community isn't confined to Latin American art. In recent years a diverse group of artists, drawn partly by the availability of loft space in Pilsen, have nurtured a small but thriving artists' colony.

Bridgeport & Canaryville Bridgeport, whose main intersection is 35th and Halsted streets, has been the neighborhood of two Mayor Daleys, father and son (the son moved not too long ago to the new Central Station development in the South Loop area). After the old Comiskey Park was torn down, the Chicago White Sox stayed in Bridgeport, inaugurating their new stadium there. Nearby Canaryville, just south and west, is typical of the "back of the yard," blue-collar neighborhoods that once surrounded the Chicago Stockyards. Neither area offers much to the typical visitor; in fact, "outsiders" aren't all that welcome.

Hyde Park Hyde Park's main attraction for families is the world-famous Museum of Science and Industry. Hyde Park is like an independent village within the confines of Chicago, right off Lake Michigan and roughly a 30-minute train ride from the Loop. The main drag is 57th Street, and the University of Chicago—with all its attendant shops and restaurants—is the neighborhood's principal tenant. The most successful racially integrated community in the city, Hyde Park is an oasis of furious intellectual activity and liberalism that, ironically, is hemmed in on all sides by neighborhoods suffering some of the highest crime rates in Chicago.

13 GETTING AROUND

The best way to tour Chicago is by walking its streets. Fortunately, it's also one of the easiest ways to get around with kids. But when walking is not practical—such as when moving between distant neighborhoods or getting around on cold winter days—Chicago's public train and bus systems are efficient modes of transportation. In fact, they may be the least expensive way of entertaining your child while visiting the city.

BY PUBLIC TRANSPORTATION

The **Chicago Transit Authority (CTA)** operates an extensive system of trains and buses throughout the city of Chicago. The sturdy system carries about 1.5 million passengers a day. Subways and elevated trains (known as the El) are generally safe and reliable, although it's advisable to avoid long rides through unfamiliar neighborhoods late at night.

The bus and the El each have pros and cons when traveling with kids. Parents with infants might prefer the El, since carrying a baby and a stroller up the bus steps (then paying the fare and finding a seat as the bus lurches into traffic) requires strength, coordination, and nerves of steel. Until your child can climb up steps, the easy-on, easy-off advantage of the El makes it the better choice (in spite of the fact that you might have to carry your stroller up and down stairs to reach the train platform).

Fares for the bus, subway, and El are $2, with an additional 25¢ for a transfer that allows CTA riders to make two transfers on the bus or El within 2 hours of receipt. Children 6 and under ride free, and those between the ages of 7 and 11 pay $1 (15¢ for transfers). Seniors can also receive the reduced fare if they have the appropriate reduced-fare permit (call ☎ 312/836-7000 for details on how to obtain one, although this is probably not a realistic option for a short-term visitor).

However, if you purchase a Chicago Card (the CTA's credit card–sized fare cards that automatically deduct the exact fare each time you take a ride), the cost per ride is less—$1.75 per ride. The reusable cards can be purchased with a preset value already stored, or riders can obtain cards at vending machines located at all CTA train stations and charge them with whatever amount they choose (a minimum of $2 and up to $100). If within 2 hours of your first ride you transfer to a bus or the El, the turnstiles at the El stations and the fare boxes on buses will automatically deduct from your card just the cost of a transfer (25¢). If you make a second transfer within 2 hours, it's free. The same card can be recharged continuously.

(Tips) Ticket to Ride

Visitors may consider buying a **Visitor Pass,** which works like a fare card and allows individual users unlimited rides on the El and CTA buses over a 24-hour period. The 1-day cards cost $5 and are sold at airports, hotels, museums, Hot Tix outlets, transportation hubs, and Chicago Office of Tourism visitor information centers. You can also buy them in advance online at www.transitchicago.com or by calling ✆ **888/YOUR-CTA** (968-7282). Also available now are 2-, 3-, and 5-day passes (they cost $9, $12, and $18, respectively). Although the passes save you the trouble of feeding the fare machines yourself, remember that they're economical only if you plan to make at least three distinct trips at least 2 or more hours apart. (You get two additional transfers for an additional 25¢ on a regular fare.)

Fare cards can be used on buses, but you can't buy a card on the bus. If you get on the bus without a fare card, you'll have to pay $2 cash (either in coins or in dollar bills); the bus drivers cannot make change, so make sure that you've got the right amount before hopping onboard.

CTA INFORMATION The CTA operates a useful telephone information service (✆ 312/836-7000 or TTY 312/836-4949 from any area code in the city and suburbs) that functions daily from 5am to 1am. When you want to know how to get from where you are to where you want to go, call the CTA. Make sure that you specify any conditions you might require—the fastest route, for example, or the simplest (the route with the fewest transfers or the least amount of walking), and so forth. You can also check out the CTA's website at **www.transitchicago.com**. Excellent comprehensive CTA maps, which include both El and bus routes, are usually available at subway or El stations, or by calling the CTA. The CTA also has added a toll-free customer service hot line (✆ **888/YOUR-CTA** [968-7282] or TTY 888/CTA-TTY1 [282-8891] Mon–Fri 7am–8pm, with voice mail operating afterhours) to field questions and feedback. Although the fare-box system has eliminated the need for ticket agents, agents are still available at some El stations to offer customer assistance.

BY THE EL & THE SUBWAY The rapid transit system operates seven major lines, which the CTA recently began identifying by color (although Chicagoans often still refer to them by their points of origin): the **Red Line** (also known as the Howard/Dan Ryan Line) runs north-south; the **Green Line** (also known as the Lake St. Line) runs west-south; the **Blue Line** (also known as the O'Hare Line) runs west-northwest to O'Hare Airport; the **Brown Line** (also known as the Ravenswood Line) runs in a northern zigzag route; the **Orange Line** runs southwest, serving Midway airport, and the **Pink Line** runs east-west from the loop, serving Cicero. The **Purple Line,** which runs on the same Loop elevated tracks as the Orange and Green lines, serves north suburban Evanston only during rush hour.

Study your CTA map carefully (there's one printed on the inside back cover of this guide) before boarding any train. Most trains run every 5 to 20 minutes, decreasing in frequency in the off-peak and overnight hours, but some stations close after work hours (as early as 8:30pm) and remain closed on Saturday, Sunday, and holidays. Only two lines operate 24

ⓣTips   Free Ride

During the summer, the city of Chicago operates kid-pleasing free trolleys daily between Michigan Avenue and the Museum Campus (site of the Adler Planetarium, the Field Museum of Natural History, and the Shedd Aquarium); the trolleys run only on weekends in the fall and spring. Free trolleys also run year-round between Navy Pier and the Grand/State Street El station on the Red Line. The trolleys are supposed to make stops every 30 minutes, but waits can be far longer during peak tourist season—and the trolleys aren't air-conditioned. If you get tired of waiting, remember that CTA public buses travel the same routes for only $2 per person.

hours a day. The CTA has posted timetables on the El platforms so that you can determine when the next train should arrive.

BY BUS   Chicago's comprehensive system of public buses means virtually every place in the city is within close walking distance of a bus stop. Other than on foot or bicycle, the best way to get around Chicago's warren of neighborhoods—the best way to actually see what's around you—is by riding a public bus. (The view from the elevated trains can be pretty dramatic, too; the difference is that on the trains you get the backyards, while on the bus you see the buildings' facades and the street life.) Look for the **blue-and-white signs** to locate bus stops, which are spaced about 2 blocks apart.

A few buses that are particularly handy for many visitors are the **no. 146 Marine/Michigan,** an express bus from Belmont Avenue on the North Side that cruises down North Lake Shore Drive (and through Lincoln Park during nonpeak times) to North Michigan Avenue, State Street, and the Grant Park museum campus; the **no. 151 Sheridan,** which passes through Lincoln Park en route to inner Lake Shore Drive and then travels along Michigan Avenue as far south as Adams Street, where it turns west into the Loop (and stops at Union Station); and the **no. 156 LaSalle,** which goes through Lincoln

Park and then into the Loop's financial district on LaSalle Street. If you need a bus that runs east-west, the **no. 66 Chicago** (Ave.) runs through the heart of the Magnificent Mile (a popular place to hop on is just west of Michigan Ave. at Chicago Ave.).

Pace buses (ⓒ **312/836-7000** from any Chicago area code, or 847/364-7223, Mon–Fri 8am–5pm; www.pacebus.com) cover the suburban zones that surround Chicago. They run every 20 to 30 minutes during rush hour, operating until midevening Monday through Friday and early evening on weekends. Suburban bus routes are marked no. 208 and above, and vehicles may be flagged down at intersections because few of the lines have bus stops that are marked.

BY COMMUTER TRAIN

If you plan to visit suburban destinations, your best public transportation bet is the **Metra** commuter railroad (ⓒ **312/322-6777** or TTY 312/322-6774 Mon–Fri 8am–5pm; at other times, call Regional Transportation Authority [RTA] at ⓒ 312/836-7000 or TTY 312/836-4949; www.metrarail.com). The Metra serves the six-county suburban area around Chicago with 12 train lines. Several terminals are located downtown, including **Union Station** at Adams and Canal streets, **LaSalle Street Station** at LaSalle and Van Buren streets, **Ogilvy Transportation Center**

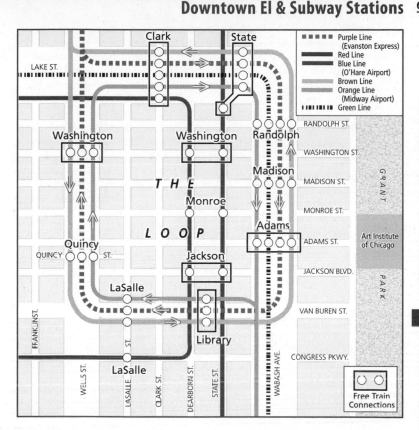

(formerly known as Northwestern Station and still referred to as such by many Chicagoans) at Madison and Canal streets, and **Randolph Street Station** at Randolph Street and Michigan Avenue.

To visit some of the most affluent suburbs in the country, take the **Union Pacific North Line** (previously known as the North Western train), which departs at the North Western Station, and select from among the following destinations: Kenilworth, Winnetka, Glencoe, Highland Park, and Lake Forest.

The **Metra Electric** (once known as the Illinois Central–Gulf Railroad, or the IC) runs close to Lake Michigan on a track that occupies some of the most valuable

real estate in Chicago. It will take you to Hyde Park. You can catch the Metra Electric in the Loop at the Randolph Street Station and at the Van Buren Street Station at Van Buren Street and Michigan Avenue (both of these stations are underground).

Commuter trains have graduated fare schedules based on the distance you ride. On weekends and holidays and during the summer, Metra offers a family discount that allows up to three children under age 12 to ride free when accompanying a paid adult. The commuter railroad also offers a $5 weekend pass for unlimited rides on Saturday and Sunday.

(Fun Facts) Sky Train: Chicago's El

It's a rare Hollywood film or TV series set in the Windy City that doesn't frame its stars against that most archetypal of Chicago images: the city's elevated train system, more commonly known as the **"El."** But the origin of the El has nothing to do with its celebrated gritty, rumbling, rail-screeching urban aesthetic.

Chicago made a miraculous recovery after the Great Fire of 1871—within 20 years, a sea of neighborhoods appeared on former prairies and swamps, and the downtown district overflowed with people, streetcars, wagons, horses, and horse droppings. The boom created two problems: It was hard to get downtown quickly in the pre-automobile era, and once you got downtown, it was impossible to actually move around.

So Chicago took to the sky, building a system of elevated trains 15 feet above all the madness. The South Side line (part of today's Green Line) was the first, opening in 1892 and running to 39th Street, about 5 miles south from downtown; the following year, the line was extended to Jackson Park, bringing commuters to the World's Fair. In 1893, the Lake Street line (also part of today's Green Line) began running to the West Side, and the Metropolitan West Side Elevated (part of today's Blue Line, serving the Northwest and West sides) opened in 1895.

The first El trains on the South Side and Lake Street lines were steam-powered, but the Metropolitan West Side Line debuted with a newfangled electric style of train. The cleaner, quieter trains were a hit, and the other El lines followed the West Side's lead. In 1896, the Lake Street Line started using electricity, and the South Side Line got wired in 1898. These lines were run by competing companies, and each line had its own terminal on the outskirts of downtown; so commuters still had to negotiate the traffic and the filth of downtown streets once they got off the train.

In 1895, the three El companies collaborated to build a set of tracks into and around the central business district that all the lines would then share. By 1897, the "Loop" was up and running, but it would take almost 100 years before the "El" would connect the whole city.

Chicago's El wasn't the nation's first. That honor belongs to New York City, which started running its elevated trains in 1867, 25 years before Chicago. But the New York El has almost disappeared, moving underground and turning into a subway early last century. With 289 miles of track, Chicago has the biggest El in the country, and the second-largest public transportation system.

BY TAXI

I don't recommend taking taxis with infants and very young children because unless the taxi is a new model, you may not be able to latch your car seat in the back. With older children, however, taxis are a pretty affordable way to get around the Loop and to get to the dining, shopping, and entertainment options found beyond downtown, such as on the near North Side, in Old Town and Lincoln

Park, and on the near West Side. But for longer distances, the fares will add up.

Taxis are easy to hail in the Loop, on the Magnificent Mile and the Gold Coast, in River North, and in Lincoln Park, but if you go much beyond these key areas, you might need to call. Cab companies include **Flash Cab** (*©* 773/561-1444), **Yellow Cab** (*©* 312/TAXI-CAB [829-4222]), and **Checker Cab** (*©* 312/CHECKER [243-2537]).

The meter in Chicago cabs currently starts at $2.25 and costs 20¢ for each 1/9 of a mile, and 20¢ for each 36 seconds of time elapsed, with a $1 surcharge for the first additional passenger, and 50¢ for each person after that.

BY CAR

Chicago is laid out so logically that it's relatively easy for visitors to get around the city by car. Although rush-hour traffic jams are just as frustrating as they are in other large U.S. cities, traffic runs fairly smoothly at most times of the day. The combination of wide streets and strategically spaced expressways makes for generally easy riding. But Chicagoans have learned to be prepared for unexpected delays; it seems that at least one major highway and several downtown streets are under repair throughout the spring and summer months. (Some say we have two seasons here: winter and construction.)

Diagonal corridors—such as Lincoln Avenue, Clark Street, and Milwaukee Avenue—slice through the grid pattern at key points in the city and shorten many a trip that would otherwise be tedious on the checkerboard surface of the Chicago streets. **Lake Shore Drive** (also known as the Outer Dr.) has to be one of the most scenic and useful urban thoroughfares anywhere. You can travel the length of the city (and beyond), never far from the Great Lake that is Chicago's most awesome natural feature.

DRIVING RULES One bizarre anomaly in the organization of Chicago's traffic is the occasional absence of signal lights off the principal avenues, notably in the River North and Streeterville neighborhoods. A block east or west of the Magnificent Mile (North Michigan Ave.)—one of the most traveled streets in the city—you will in some cases encounter only stop signs to control the flow of traffic. Once you've become accustomed to the system, it works very smoothly, with all—pedestrians and motorists alike—advancing in their proper turn.

Unless otherwise posted, a right turn on red is allowed after stopping and signaling.

PARKING Parking regulations are vigorously enforced throughout the city. Read signs carefully: The streets around Michigan Avenue have no-parking restrictions during rush hour—and believe me, your car will be towed immediately. Many neighborhoods have adopted resident-only parking that prohibits others from parking on their streets, usually after 6pm each day (even all day in a few areas, such as Old Town). The neighborhood around Wrigley Field is off-limits during Cubs night games, so look for yellow sidewalk signs alerting drivers during the dozen-and-a-half or so times the Cubs play under lights. You can park in resident-only permit zones if you're visiting a friend, who can provide you with a pass to stick on your windshield. Beware of tow zones, and, if visiting in winter, make note of curbside warnings regarding snow plowing.

A safe bet is valet parking, which most restaurants provide for around $10. Downtown you can also opt to park in a public garage, but you might have to pay the premium prices common in any metropolitan area. (Several garages connected with malls or other major attractions offer discounted parking with a validated ticket.)

The very best parking deal in the Loop is the **East Monroe Garage** (www.grant parkparking.com), which charges $13 for 12 hours or fewer (enter on Columbus Dr., 1 block east of Michigan Ave., btw. Monroe and Randolph sts.). Also relatively affordable and superconvenient are the remaining public parking lots underneath **Grant Park** (including **Grant Park South, Grant Park North,** and **Millennium Park** garages) with entrances at Michigan Avenue at Van Buren Street and Michigan Avenue at Madison Street. Parking varies for each garage, but some can cost up to $25 for an 8- to 24-hour stay. You'll find higher prices at most other downtown lots, including **McCormick Place Parking,** 2301 S. Lake Shore Dr. (© 312/791-7000); **Midcontinental Plaza Garage,** 55 E. Monroe St. (© 312/ 986-6821); and **Navy Pier Parking,** 600 E. Grand Ave. (© 312/595-7437).

CAR RENTAL Hertz (© 800/654-3131), **Avis** (© 800/831-2847), **National** (© 800/227-7368), and **Budget** (© 800/ 527-0700) all have offices at O'Hare Airport and at Midway Airport. Each company also has at least one office downtown: Hertz at 401 N. State St., Avis at 214 N. Clark St., National at 203 N. LaSalle St., and Budget at 714 S. Wabash St. Before you rent, please be aware that Chicago's sales tax on car rentals is a steep 20%.

BY BOAT

Boat transport is a great way to get around with kids. And boat traffic in Chicago has been stirring up a bigger wake recently. **Shoreline Sightseeing** (© 312/222-9328; shorelinesightseeing.com) ferries passengers on the Chicago River between Sears Tower, Michigan Avenue, Navy Pier, and Museum Campus for rates ranging from $3 to $13 for adults (depending on the distance of the trip) and $2 to $7 for kids. The **water taxis** operate daily Memorial Day to Labor Day from 10am to 6pm about every half-hour.

If you are staying in the suburbs and traveling to the Magnificent Mile, kids will love a ride on the Metra commuter train followed by a ride on a shuttle boat operated by **Wendella Commuter Boats** (© 312/337-1446; www.wendellaboats. com), which float daily April through October between a dock at Michigan Avenue, LaSalle/Clark Street, Madison Street, and Chinatown. The ride, which costs $2 each way (or $3 round-trip), takes about 10 minutes and is popular with both visitors and commuters. An all-day pass is $4. The service operates about every 20 minutes from 6:30am to 7pm.

BY BICYCLE

I wouldn't recommend trying to ride bicycles on the city streets with kids. Although the city of Chicago has earned kudos for its efforts to improve conditions for bicycling (designated bike lanes have been installed on stretches of Wells St., Roosevelt Rd., Elston Ave., and Halsted St.), it can still be rough trying to compete with cars and their drivers, who aren't always so willing to share the road. If you are determined to bike with your kids, though, you might want to take to the lakefront path or area parks. Make sure you wear a helmet at all times!

Bike Chicago (© 888/BIKE-WAY [245-3929] or © 312/729-1000; www. bikechicago.com) has four locations, including Navy Pier, Millennium Park, North Avenue Beach, and Foster Beach. The shops rent all sorts of bikes, including tandems and four-seater "quadcycles," baby seats, in-line skates, and Segways. Bikes rent for as little as $8 an hour or up to $40 a day (rates are $6 for kids' bikes, and $25 for the day). Helmets, pads, and locks are free. Hours vary by location (Millennium Park's location opens at 6:30am while Foster Beach's doesn't open until 11am), so check the website or call.

The **Chicagoland Bicycle Federation** (© 312/427-3325; www.biketraffic.org), a nonprofit advocacy group, is a good resource for bicyclists. The group publishes several bicycling maps with tips on recommended on-street routes and parkland routes, and a guide to safe cycling in the city.

14 GETTING KIDS INTERESTED IN CHICAGO

Kids will be most interested in your upcoming adventure when they have input into the activities you plan. Use this book to tell your kids about the great adventures awaiting them in Chicago—riding the El, climbing into a captured World War II U-boat at the Museum of Science and Industry, riding a high-speed elevator to see the sights from the John Hancock Center, or going to a McDonald's that's also a rock-'n'-roll museum.

Movie-wise, you can rent *Blues Brothers* (1979) and show Jake and Elmo jumping the bridge across the river and careening down the street under the El tracks. The movie features a classic multicar pileup in the center of downtown Daley Plaza. *Ferris Bueller's Day Off* (1985) is the ultimate teenage wish-fulfillment movie, set in Chicago and the suburbs. In fact, most of the John Hughes movies (*Pretty in Pink, Sixteen Candles,* and *The Breakfast Club*) are set in the Chicago area.

Children's books set in Chicago that will be readily available at your local library or bookstore include *Fair Weather,* by Richard Peck, in which a 19th-century farming family is turned upside down by a visit to Chicago for the 1893 World's Columbian Exposition; *Playoff Dreams,* by Fred Bowen, in which a boy attends a ballgame with his uncle at Wrigley Field and learns the story of the legendary Cubs player and Hall of Fame member Ernie Banks; and *The Dragon of Navy Pier,* by Kate Noble, in which Charlie, a young dragon on a carousel, comes alive one night and sets out to explore Navy Pier.

Show your kids photos of landmarks—Wrigley Field is a familiar sight to most of us. You might also find photos of Soldier Field, United Center (with its statue of Michael Jordan), the soaring John Hancock Center (with its girded black Xs crisscrossing all the way up the building), the Chicago Water Tower (the only building to survive the fire of 1871, allegedly started by Mrs. O'Leary's cow), Sears Tower, and the lakefront. Discuss the El trains and show kids photos of the elevated tracks. Show them the Chicago bridges that rise and lower, stopping traffic so boats can make their way to the lake. Tell them that the Chicago River that these bridges span runs from the lake (rather than into it, as most rivers do)—and about the engineering marvel that reversed its flow.

Suggested Chicago Itineraries

Chicago's sprawling nature means that reaching outlying neighborhoods and suburbs requires a fair amount of travel, but these itineraries aim to keep the walking and El- or taxi-riding to a minimum by keeping you near the city center—the Loop. When touring on your own, remember to bear in mind the travel time between sights or neighborhoods. The tours below seek to balance monumental architectural highlights with visits to the city's best museums and zoo. Along the way, you'll get intimate glimpses into what life as a Chicagoan might be and what makes Chicago run.

---

1 THE BEST OF CHICAGO IN 1 DAY

Capturing Chicago in 1 day means surveying the scene in the most efficient way possible—via our inland ocean, Lake Michigan, and its tributary, the Chicago River—and branching out from there to experience what I feel is Chicago's best museum for kids. Bring good walking shoes and as much energy as you can muster. This itinerary takes you on a tour boat (always a kid-pleaser), into the depths of the Museum of Science and Industry, and leaves you to explore the Magnificent Mile at leisure, with its glittering shops and restaurants and highly entertaining people-watching. *Start: Bus 151 to Michigan Avenue Bridge or Red Line to Grand/State, then head to the boat tour stop of your choice. Two of the most popular are Wendella Boats (on the northwest corner of the bridge) and the Chicago Architectural Foundation tours (on the southeast corner).*

---

❶ Boat Tours ★★★

Start the day with a boat tour of the Chicago River and Lake Michigan. Even if your kids are small, they'll love being on the water, while you marvel at our spectacular architecture. (Chicago is a showcase of modern architecture; for more on our best buildings, pick up *Frommer's Chicago.*) Some tours take you up and down the Chicago River, then through locks that release the boat into Lake Michigan. If you just want to get out on the water and don't care about a guided tour, hop on one of the water taxis that cruise from Ogilvy Transportation Center (many locals will refer to this train station

as "Northwestern Station") to Navy Pier, with stops at Wabash Street and Michigan Avenue, and more. At $2 a ride, it's the best deal on the river. See p. 204.

❷ Museum of Science and Industry ★★★

Back on land, head to the Museum of Science and Industry, the classic Chicago kids' attraction that never fails to enthrall. Don't miss seeing two of the all-time favorite exhibits—the *U-505* ★★ and **Coal Mine** ★. Best for older kids (the preschool set might be frightened by the darkness and cramped spaces), the *U-505* is a German submarine that was captured in 1944 and brought to the museum 10 years later. Your kids will undoubtedly join the legions who have been fascinated by the claustrophobic reality of underwater naval life. The full-scale Coal Mine, which dates back to 1934, now incorporates modern mining techniques into the exhibit. More low-tech—but fun for kids—are **The Farm** (where children can sit at the wheel of a giant combine) and the **chick hatchery** inside the exhibit **Genetics: Decoding Life.** Here, you can watch as tiny newborn chicks poke their way out of eggs. Girls (myself included) tend to love **Colleen Moore's Fairy Castle,** a lavishly decorated miniature palace filled with priceless treasures. (Yes, those are real diamonds and pearls in the chandeliers.) When you've worked up an appetite, you can visit the Food Court, which has an excellent selection of amazingly healthy and tasty choices—follow it up with a decadent stop at Finnegan's Ice Cream Parlor. See p. 170.

❸ The Art Institute ★★★

The Art Institute goes the extra mile to help kids get through a few hours here without even a hint of boredom. With the addition of the Modern Wing (it opens in spring 2009), there will be an even larger space for families. The Ryan Education Center, which covers the entire first floor of the east pavilion of the Modern Wing, is dedicated to kids, with its own galleries, studio space, and more. Even better is the fact that families can enter the space without paying admission to the museum—an amazing deal! Another kid favorite is the Thorne Miniature Rooms, with its tiny reproductions of furnished interiors from European and American history. See p. 178.

❹ Michigan Avenue Bridge

Walk north along Michigan Avenue and you'll come to this bridge, which spans the Chicago River. Stop here for a great photo op looking west to the newest addition to the city's skyline, the Trump International Tower and Hotel.

❺ The Magnificent Mile

The 14-block stretch of Michigan Avenue from the river to Oak Street, known as the "Magnificent Mile," is shopping central, a dense concentration of high-rise malls, designer boutiques, and practically every mass-market clothing brand. Restaurants also abound: One perennial kid-pleaser is **The Cheesecake Factory,** on the lower level of the John Hancock Center. Walk off that rich cheesecake with a stroll along Michigan Avenue, going north toward the **lakefront walking path.** Although you won't see the sun set over the lake (remember, the lake is always to the east), the colors can be spectacular anyway. (On the other side of the lake, those in Michigan and Indiana have the opposite view: They never see the sun rise over the lake, only set.) See p. 208.

❻ The Hancock Observatory ★★

The view from the top of Chicago's third-tallest building is enough to satisfy, but some high-tech additions are here to enhance your experience. "Talking telescopes" provide sound effects and narration in four languages; history walls illustrate the growth of the city; and the Skywalk open-air viewing deck—a "screened porch"—allows visitors to feel the rush of the wind at 1,000 feet. Kids can also check out the building's infrastructure on computers and find 80 Chicago attractions on virtual-reality television screens, or take a multimedia "sky tour." See p. 175.

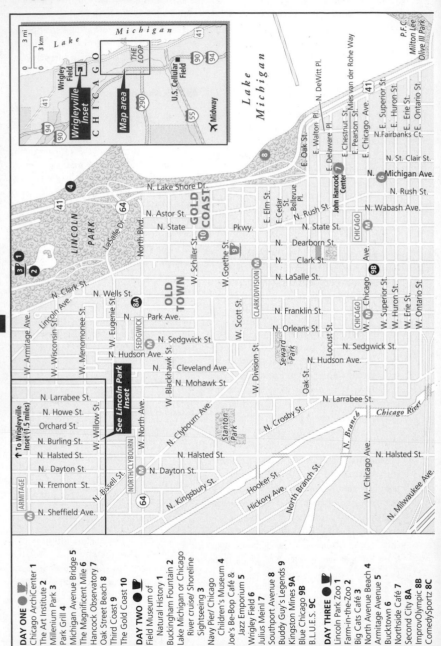

DAY ONE 🔴
Chicago ArchiCenter **1**
The Art Institute **2**
Millennium Park **3**
Park Grill **4**
Michigan Avenue Bridge **5**
The Magnificent Mile **6**
Hancock Observatory **7**
Oak Street Beach **8**
Third Coast **9**
The Gold Coast **10**

DAY TWO 🔵 📷
Field Museum of
    Natural History **1**
Buckingham Fountain **2**
Lake Michigan or Chicago
    River cruise/ Shoreline
    Sightseeing **3**
Navy Pier/ Chicago
    Children's Museum **4**
Joe's Be-Bop Café &
    Jazz Emporium **5**
Wrigley Field **6**
Julius Meinl **7**
Southport Avenue **8**
Buddy Guy's Legends **9**
Kingston Mines **9A**
Blue Chicago **9B**
B.L.U.E.S. **9C**

DAY THREE 🟢 📷
Lincoln Park Zoo **1**
Farm-in-the-Zoo **2**
Big Cats Café **3**
North Avenue Beach **4**
Armitage Avenue **5**
Bucktown **6**
Northside Café **7**
Second City **8A**
ImprovOlympic **8B**
ComedySportz **8C**

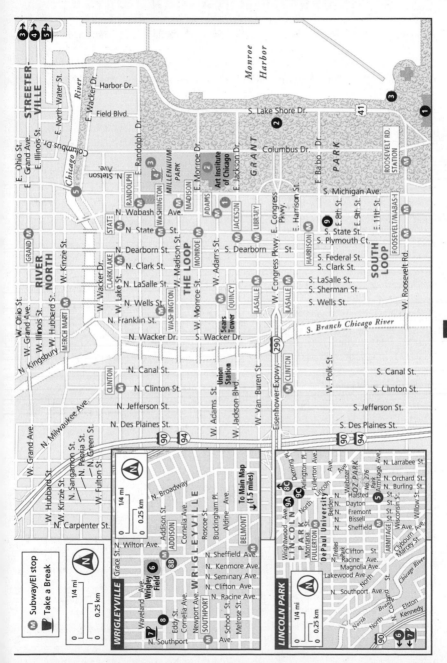

2 THE BEST OF CHICAGO IN 2 DAYS

Use your second day in Chicago to experience spectacular Millennium Park. Then head over to the country's largest aquarium, the Shedd Aquarium, and take in the dolphin show. Spend the evening cheering on the home team at one of America's venerable old ballparks, Wrigley Field. *Start: Red Line to Randolph/State or Bus 151 to Michigan and Randolph.*

❶ Millennium Park ★★★

Chicago's latest and greatest public project has proven to be a wonderfully interactive park for kids. Even the sculpture is interactive—the "bean" by Anish Kapoor is essentially a gigantic 3-D mirror with its reflective surface and house-of-mirrors qualities. At the Crown Fountain, another kid favorite, faces of Chicagoans are projected through the glass blocks and change at regular intervals—watch out, because water spews from their mouths when you least expect it. In warm weather, it's a wonderful place to take your shoes off and splash. The park's centerpiece is the Jay Pritzker Pavilion, with its Frank Gehry–designed ribbons of silver steel; the architect also designed the adjoining serpentine bridge. See p. 168.

PARK GRILL
Take a lunch break at the Park Grill (✆ **312/521-7275**; www.parkgrillchicago.com; daily 11am–10:30pm), an eatery overlooking the McCormick Tribune Plaza ice-skating rink. Next door to the grill, Park Café offers takeout picnic baskets, salads, and sandwiches. Parking is easy, too, with plentiful underground lots at the bargain rate of $12, one of the better deals in the city.

❷ Navy Pier ★

Yes, it's touristy. Yes, it's crowded. But Navy Pier is also full of energy—and if you stroll all the way to the end, you'll be rewarded with great views of downtown. Stopping at Navy Pier is pretty much mandatory when visiting Chicago with kids; there's a carousel and other carnival-type rides and lots of boats to admire, not to mention the Chicago Children's Museum. See p. 174.

JOE'S BE-BOP CAFE & JAZZ EMPORIUM
Owned by the same family that runs Jazz Showcase, one of the best jazz clubs in town, this Navy Pier cafe offers a fun atmosphere (with plenty of outdoor seating), Southern barbecue, and a great soundtrack. 600 E. Grand Ave. ✆ **312/595-5299**. See p. 273.

❸ John G. Shedd Aquarium ★★

First things first: Make sure you buy tickets for the dolphin show upon your arrival. While you wait for the show, walk around the **Caribbean Coral Reef** exhibit. This 90,000-gallon circular tank occupies the Beaux Arts–style central rotunda, entertaining spectators who press up against the glass to ogle divers feeding nurse sharks, barracudas, stingrays, and a hawksbill sea turtle.

The dolphin show takes place in the 3-million-gallon saltwater **Oceanarium ★★**, an indoor marine mammal pavilion that re-creates a Pacific Northwest coastal environment and also happens to be the largest of its kind in the world. **Soundings,** the restaurant inside the aquarium, has a spectacular view of Lake Michigan. See p. 165.

❹ Wrigley Field ★★★

In the evening, if the Cubs are in town, take the El uptown and catch a night game at **Wrigley Field.** Dine on hot dogs or bratwurst while you sip a beer and the kids polish off cotton candy and licorice whips, and cheer on the Cubs with the other perennially hopeful fans. See p. 278.

71

3 THE BEST OF CHICAGO IN 3 DAYS

Use your third day in Chicago to amble around the lovely grounds of one of the country's oldest (and, thankfully, still free of charge) zoos, or, if your kids are older, head to the Museum Campus to visit the Field Museum. End your day with an evening of theater at one of the North Loop Theater District's many restored historic theaters, or at Briar Street Theatre, home to Blue Man Group's popular show (but only for kids age 5 and over, please). *Start: Bus 151 to Lincoln Park Zoo.*

❶ Lincoln Park Zoo ★★★

This charming urban zoo is so compact that a tour of the various habitats takes all of 2 or 3 hours—a convenience factor even more enticing when you consider that the nation's oldest zoo (it was founded in 1868) stays open 365 days a year and is one of the last free zoos in the country. The star attraction is the lowland gorillas at the **Regenstein Center for African Apes** ★. The zoo has had remarkable success in breeding both gorillas and chimpanzees, and watching these ape families is mesmerizing. The popular **Sea Lion Pool** is home to harbor seals, gray seals, and California sea lions. Finish your visit with a ride (you'll pay a few dollars per rider, and the price is well worth it) on the gorgeous **Endangered Species Carousel.** See p. 197.

> ☕ **ZOO EATS**
> Between exhibits, stop for lunch at the **Park Place Café** food court, located in a historic building that originally was Chicago's first aquarium. Alternately, you can stop at **Big Cats Café**, a rooftop eatery in the Mahon Theobold Pavilion. It opens at 8am (1 hr. before the exhibits do) and serves fresh-baked muffins and scones, focaccia sandwiches, salads, and flatbreads.

❷ Farm-in-the-Zoo ★

Just south of the zoo, this re-creation of a working farm gets children in touch (literally) with animals. But the highlight for many little ones seems to be the giant John Deere tractor; you'll usually find a line of kids waiting to be hoisted up to sit behind the massive steering wheel. See p. 197.

❸ Oak Street Beach

Where Michigan Avenue merges into Lake Shore Drive at Oak Street, head down the underpass to get to Oak Street Beach, a curved stretch of sand that's a summertime hot spot. Bikers, skaters, and joggers fill the paths, while kids play in the sand. Think of it as Chicago's own miniresort getaway—but unless you're visiting us in the heat of June, July, or August, I wouldn't plan on swimming in the generally frigid water. See p. 168.

❹ The Field Museum of Natural History ★★★

You'll feel as though you've entered a truly grand place when you walk into the museum's massive Stanley Field Hall. Indeed, the Field Museum is one of those classic something-for-everyone institutions, with everything from animal dioramas to Sue, the largest *Tyrannosaurus rex* fossil ever discovered. The Field upped the ante for kids when it added the Crown

72

Family Playlab, where kids can dress up like a local animal and star in their own nature play, explore a pueblo home, or examine insects in amber. The Inside Ancient Egypt exhibit is more than just mummies: It's a complete re-creation of ancient daily life, including a marketplace, a royal barge, and religious shrines (with lots of hands-on activities for kids). The second-floor African and South Pacific exhibits are also worth a stop, with beautifully designed interactive displays that feel like movie sets. See p. 162.

⑤ Briar Street Theatre

The kid-pleasing **Blue Man Group,** at Briar Street Theatre in Lincoln Park, mixes percussion, performance art, mime, and rock 'n' roll. The three strangely endearing performers, whose faces and heads are covered in latex and blue paint, know how to get the audience involved. I dare you to find a kid who doesn't get a kick out of seeing the Blue Men stuff their faces (literally) with marshmallows. Of all the long-running hits in Chicago, this is the one to beat—and the best kid-pleaser in town. See p. 259.

Family-Friendly Accommodations

Downtown Chicago is packed with hotels, and the good news for families is that although most of the hotels are oriented to the city's convention trade, plenty cater to families. In fact, you won't have a problem finding midrange, family-friendly hotels in the most convenient neighborhoods, such as River North and even the Magnificent Mile, with the Red Roof Inn and Courtyard by Marriott Magnificent Mile taking their places near the luxury hotels. In the high-end market, a recent building boom has brought international players such as the Peninsula and Sofitel to the Midwest (and most recently, Mr. Donald Trump and his Trump International Hotel and Tower), but these wonderful hotels are not the kind that most families can afford. And though Chicago is not a city where luxury hotels have dibs on all the prime real estate, budget lodgings are becoming harder to find anywhere near downtown.

Because Chicago's hospitality industry caters first and foremost to the business traveler, hotels tend to empty out by Friday. Thus, hotels are sometimes willing to reduce prices on the weekends to push up their occupancy rate. (Keep in mind, though, that rooms are sometimes available at rock-bottom rates during conventions if a hotel is unable to book to capacity.) And many hotels known as "business hotels" have made efforts to add family-friendly amenities to entice families to stay the weekend. Still, the hotel industry has been so strong in Chicago in recent years that you won't find reservations agents as willing or able to wheel and deal as they once were.

Warning: You never know when a huge convention will gobble up all the desirable rooms in the city, even on a weekend. Check the convention schedule on p. 19, and make sure to book a room well in advance whenever you plan to visit.

If the city has a slow season, it's the depth of winter, when outsiders tend to shy away from the cold and the threat of being snowed in at O'Hare. Serious bargain hunters might choose to visit then. The **Chicago Convention & Tourism Bureau** usually offers a special promotion, "Winter Delights," from January to March. Call $\textcircled{C}$ **877/244-2246** for a brochure, or check out www.choosechicago. com. The promotion includes discounts on many of Chicago's leading hotels and restaurants.

Tip: If you'd like to watch your pennies but the idea of traveling in the dead of winter—and bundling the kids up 20 times a day as you pop in and out of attractions, restaurants, and your hotel—doesn't appeal to you, another option is to stay in a less expensive hotel during the week and move into swell digs for the weekend finale.

ACCESSIBILITY Most hotels are prepared to accommodate not only travelers with physical disabilities but also families traveling with children and the accompanying strollers and other equipment. You should, however, always inquire when you make reservations to make sure that the hotel can meet your particular needs.

RESERVE IN ADVANCE Whatever hotel or hotels you choose, regardless of season, making reservations well in advance will help ensure that you get the best rate available. I've provided toll-free phone numbers for all the hotels reviewed in this chapter, but you might find better rates by calling the hotel's reservations office directly. Most hotels have check-in times somewhere between 3 and 6pm; if you are going to be delayed, call ahead and reconfirm your reservation to prevent cancellation.

RESERVATION SERVICES For discounted rooms at more than 30 downtown hotels, try **Hot Rooms** (© **800/ 468-3500** or 773/468-7666; www.hot rooms.com). I've used this service and was very pleased to get a night in a top-rated downtown hotel for about half the regular price—and that was during the height of the busy summer season. The service is free, but if you cancel a reservation (and you must adhere to each individual hotel's cancellation policy), you're assessed a fee. Another source of information on reservations is the annual *Illinois Hotel-Motel Directory,* which also provides information about weekend packages. Call the **Illinois Bureau of Tourism** at © 800/2CON-NECT (226-6632) for a copy.

Chicago's Convention and Tourism Bureau's website, **www.choosechicago. com**, allows you to book hotels as well as complete weekend packages.

BED & BREAKFAST RESERVATIONS A centralized reservations service called **At Home Inn Chicago,** P.O. Box 14088, Chicago, IL 60614 (© **800/375-7084** or 312/640-1050; www.athomeinnchicago. com), lists more than 70 accommodations in Chicago. If you're of an adventurous bent, you'll find options ranging from high-rise and loft apartments to guest rooms carved from a former private club on the 40th floor of a Loop office building. Most lie within 3 miles of downtown (many are located in the Gold Coast, Old Town, and Lincoln Park) and will run you

$150 to $350 for apartments, and as low as $100 for guest rooms in private homes.

A group of local B&B owners has formed the **Chicago Bed and Breakfast Association,** with a website that links to various properties throughout the city: **www.chicago-bed-breakfast.com**.

Note: Most B&Bs require a minimum stay of 2 or 3 nights; also, many have restrictions on children. Some accept children only over age 10, for example, and others will not accept kids of any age. It's always wise to ask if children are welcome when making reservations.

LANDING THE BEST ROOM Somebody has to get the best room in the house; it might as well be you. You can start by joining the hotel's frequent-guest program, which may make you eligible for upgrades. A hotel-branded credit card usually gives its owner "silver" or "gold" status in frequent-guest programs for free. Always ask about corner rooms. They're often larger and quieter, with more windows and light, and they often cost the same as standard rooms. When you make your reservation, ask if the hotel is renovating; if it is, request a room away from the construction. Ask about nonsmoking rooms, rooms with views, rooms with twin, queen-, or king-size beds. If you're a light sleeper, request a quiet room away from vending machines, elevators, restaurants, bars, and discos. Ask for a room that has been most recently renovated or redecorated.

If you aren't happy with your room when you arrive, ask for another one. Most lodgings will be willing to accommodate you.

A NOTE ABOUT PRICES In this chapter I've divided hotels into four price categories: **Very Expensive** means double-occupancy rooms typically cost upwards of $400 per night; **Expensive** rooms, $200 and up to around $350 or $400; **Moderate,** less than $200 a night; and **Inexpensive,** less than $150.

Major Convention Dates

Listed below are Chicago's major (30,000 visitors or more) conventions for 2009, with projected attendance figures. Many of them take place here annually, around the same time each year. Plan ahead because hotel rooms and restaurant reservations can be hard to come by when the big shows are in town—and even if you snag a room, you'll be paying top price. Contact the **Chicago Convention and Tourism Bureau** (✆ **877/CHICAGO** [244-2246]; www.choosechicago.com) to double-check the latest info before you commit to your travel dates as convention schedules can change.

EVENT	2009 DATES	EXPECTED ATTENDANCE
International Home and Housewares Show	Mar 16–18	60,000
Kitchen/Bath Industry Show	Apr 11–13	60,000
National Restaurant Association Show	May 17–20	75,000
Neo-Con—World's Trade Fair	June 9–11	40,000
International Manufacturing Technology Show	Sept 8–13	90,000
Graph Expo	Oct 26–29	40,000
Radiological Society of North America	Nov 30–Dec 5	60,000

The rates given in this chapter are per night and do not include taxes, which are quite steep at 14.9%, or any discounts. Prices are always subject to availability and vary according to day of the week and seasonally. (The lower rates tend to be offered Jan–Mar and on nonholiday weekends.)

1 THE LOOP

Strictly speaking, "downtown" in Chicago means the Loop—the central business district, a 6×8-block rectangle enveloped by elevated tracks on all four sides. An outer circle beyond this literal loop of tracks is bounded on the north and west by the Chicago River and its south branch, forming an elbow on two sides; on the east by Michigan Avenue running along the edge of Millennium Park and Grant Park; and on the south by the Congress Expressway. Within these confines are the city's financial institutions, trading markets, and municipal government buildings, making for, as you might expect, quite a lot of hustle and bustle Monday through Friday. Come Saturday and Sunday, however, the Loop is pretty dead, despite the fact that it is also home to major music and theater venues and is near the Art Institute. On a nice day, it's easy to walk south from the Loop to the Museum Campus, home to the Field Museum of Natural History and John G. Shedd Aquarium.

For visitors who want a real "city" experience, the Loop offers dramatic urban vistas or skyscrapers and a feeling that you're in the center of weekday action. The Loop has an

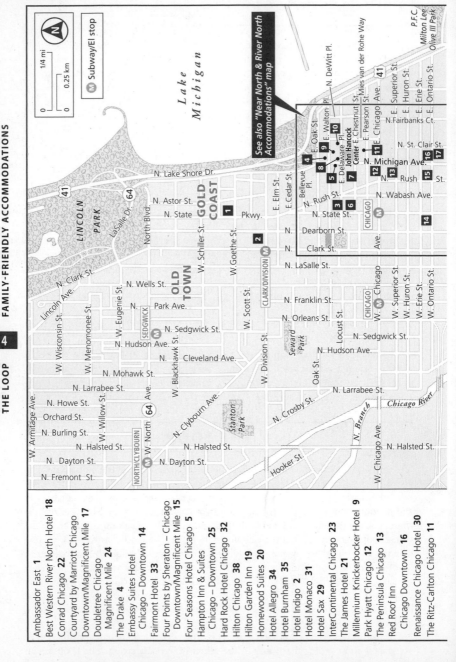

FAMILY-FRIENDLY ACCOMMODATIONS

THE LOOP

4

Ambassador East **1**
Best Western River North Hotel **18**
Conrad Chicago **22**
Courtyard by Marriott Chicago
  Downtown/Magnificent Mile **17**
Doubletree Chicago
  Magnificent Mile **24**
The Drake **4**
Embassy Suites Hotel
  Chicago – Downtown **14**
Fairmont Hotel **33**
Four Points by Sheraton – Chicago
  Downtown/Magnificent Mile **15**
Four Seasons Hotel Chicago **5**
Hampton Inn & Suites
  Chicago – Downtown **25**
Hard Rock Hotel Chicago **32**
Hilton Chicago **38**
Hilton Garden Inn **19**
Homewood Suites **20**
Hotel Allegro **34**
Hotel Burnham **35**
Hotel Indigo **2**
Hotel Monaco **31**
Hotel Sax **29**
InterContinental Chicago **23**
The James Hotel **21**
Millennium Knickerbocker Hotel **9**
Park Hyatt Chicago **12**
The Peninsula Chicago **13**
Red Roof Inn
  Chicago Downtown **16**
Renaissance Chicago Hotel **30**
The Ritz-Carlton Chicago **11**

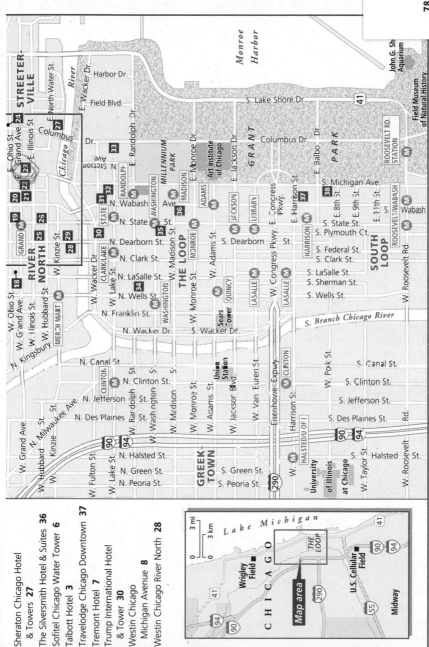

Sheraton Chicago Hotel
& Towers **27**

The Silversmith Hotel & Suites **36**

Sofitel Chicago Water Tower **6**

Talbott Hotel **3**

Travelodge Chicago Downtown **37**

Tremont Hotel **7**

Trump International Hotel
& Tower **30**

Westin Chicago
Michigan Avenue **8**

Westin Chicago River North **28**

interesting mix of grand hotels, such as the Fairmont, and brash new upstarts, most notably the hip triad run by the West Coast–based Kimpton Group: the Hotel Burnham, Hotel Monaco, and Hotel Allegro. Despite their differences, all offer undeniable convenience for families who prefer to be at the center of the city.

VERY EXPENSIVE

Fairmont Hotel ★★   The Fairmont is easily one of the city's most luxurious hotels, offering an array of deluxe amenities and services. This is the kind of place that regularly hosts high-level politicians and CEOs (but not rock stars). The overall effect is chic but a bit impersonal. The entrance looks out on anonymous office towers, and you're likely to wander the circular lobby a bit before finding the check-in desk. Still, families rave about the huge rooms and bend-over-backwards service; although families aren't the hotel's primary market, you will be made to feel more than welcome.

The large rooms are decorated in a comfortable, upscale style. (Ask for one with a lake view, although even the city view rooms offer some distance from neighboring offices.) The posh bathrooms feature extra large tubs, separate vanity areas, and swivel TVs. The windows even open (a rarity in high-rise hotels), so you can enjoy the breeze drifting off Lake Michigan. Suites have one or two bedrooms, a living room, a dining area, and a built-in bar—and all come with lake views. For $20 a day, guests can access Lakeshore Athletic Club without walking outside. The club has a pool, but unfortunately the club is open to children only after 2pm on Saturday and all day on Sunday. The hotel is connected to the city's underground pedway system (one of my favorite activities to do with kids), through which you can walk all the way to Macy's (formerly Marshall Field's) on State Street on inclement days without stepping outside.

200 N. Columbus Dr. (at Lake St.), Chicago, IL 60601. ✆ **800/526-2008** or 312/565-8000. Fax 312/856-1032. www.fairmont.com. 692 units. $129–$389 double; $229–$539 suite. Kids 17 and under stay free in parent's room. Rollaways $20/night; cribs free. AE, DC, DISC, MC, V. Valet parking $41 with in/out privileges. Subway/El: Red, Green, Orange, Brown, or Blue Line to State/Lake. Small pets accepted for a $25 fee. **Amenities:** Restaurant; lounge; access to nearby health club; business center; salon; 24-hr. room service; babysitting; laundry service; 24-hr. dry cleaning. *In room:* A/C, TV w/pay movies, CD player, fax, high-speed Internet access, minibar, hair dryer, iron.

EXPENSIVE

Hard Rock Hotel Chicago ★   The good news: This hotel is not located on top of the supertouristy Hard Rock Cafe, which is about a mile away in River North. In fact, the hotel is a relatively restrained rehab of one of the city's historic skyscrapers, the 40-story Carbide and Carbon Building. As you might expect, the theme here is music: Pop tunes echo through the lobby, TV monitors show videos, and glass cases display pop-star memorabilia. If your kids are in the age range that considers wearing a Hard Rock T-shirt from exotic locales a badge of honor, they may well get a kick from a stay here. But for the grown-ups in your crowd, the mix of old and new can be somewhat jarring. The black-and-gray lobby feels like a nightclub, but the marble-and-gold-trimmed elevator bank still says "high-rise office building." Don't expect too much rock-star attitude; to date, the Hard Rock appears to be populated by youngish business travelers and families. The guest rooms are neutral in decor with modern furnishings. The building's larger-than-average windows let in plenty of natural light. The so-called Hard Rock Rooms on the corners of each floor are larger than the standard double rooms and feature chaise longues for stretching out. Families might inquire about the suites, located in the tower at the top of the building, which come in various one- and two-bedroom configurations and allow an added layer of privacy (with only one or two suites per floor, you're separated from the masses).

The hotel's restaurant, China Bar & Grill, serves Asian fusion cuisine in a high-energy setting, and the lobby starts swinging after dark, when music gets going at the street-level bar, Base (open until 4am, it features live music and DJs most nights). And because the hotel actively courts rock bands who come through town on tour, you never know who you'll see stopping in for a drink.

230 N. Michigan Ave. (at Lake St.), Chicago, IL 60601. *C* **866/966-5166** or 312/345-1000. Fax 312/345-1012. www.hardrockhotelchicago.com. 381 units. $169–$349 double; from $1,500 suite. Weekend rates available. Kids 11 and under stay free in parent's room. No rollaways; cribs free. AE, DC, DISC, MC, V. Valet parking $39 with in/out privileges. Subway/El: Red or Blue Line to Lake. **Amenities:** Restaurant; bar; exercise room; concierge; business services; 24-hr. room service; same-day laundry service; dry cleaning. *In room:* A/C, TV w/DVD player and video games, CD player, free high-speed Internet access, minibar, coffeemaker, hair dryer, iron, safe.

Hotel Burnham ★★★   Here's my pick for Chicago's most distinctive hotel, one that took a historic location and jazzed it up with a dash of colorful modern style. This hip hotel uses its sense of whimsy to embrace, not exclude, families. Don't come to the Burnham if you're looking for extensive amenities—the lobby is tiny, as is the exercise room, and there's no pool. But it's my top choice for families in this price category, provided you book a suite, which will offer your family plenty of space.

The result of a brilliant restoration of the historic Reliance Building—one of the first skyscrapers ever built and a highly significant architectural treasure—this intimate boutique hotel (named for Daniel Burnham, whose firm designed the Reliance Building in 1895) is the work of the Kimpton Group, the trendsetting West Coast–based chain behind the Allegro and Monaco hotels (both reviewed later in this section). It occupies a prime spot in the heart of State Street, across from Macy's (formerly Marshall Field's) and 1 block south of the hopping North Loop theater district. The Burnham is a must for architecture buffs: Wherever possible, the restoration retains period elements—most obviously in the hallways, which recall the original office corridors with terrazzo tile floors, white marble wainscoting, mahogany door and window frames, and room numbers painted on the translucent glass doors.

Rooms are clubby but glamorous, with plush beds, mahogany writing desks, and chaise longues. The hotel's 19 suites feature a separate living room area and CD stereo systems. To keep wee ones entertained, ask the hotel for coloring books and crayons, games, and Super Nintendo. During holidays you'll find special activities in the hotel lobby, including decorating gingerbread men around Christmas and hunting for eggs at Easter. Diaper bags, cribs, high chairs, changing tables, and more are available upon request. And there's a turndown service with cookies and milk. The hotel's restaurant offers a children's menu. Ask the concierge for special offers for tea at American Girl Place Cafe and deals at the museums and theaters. And don't leave Fido at home: Pets are positively welcomed here. The hotel provides pet beds, treats, food and water bowls, and dog-walking services (and they'll even clean out your in-room kitty litter box!).

1 W. Washington (at State St.), Chicago, IL 60602. *C* **877/294-9712** or 312/782-1111. Fax 312/782-0899. www.burnhamhotel.com. 122 units. $179–$299 double; $229–$399 suite. Kids 17 and under stay free in parent's room. No rollaways; cribs free. AE, DC, DISC, MC, V. Valet parking $40 with in/out privileges. Subway: Red or Blue Line to Washington/State. Pets allowed. **Amenities:** Restaurant; small fitness room (and access to nearby health club); concierge; business services; 24-hr. room service; laundry service; dry cleaning. *In room:* A/C, TV, fax, dataport, free high-speed Internet access, minibar, hair dryer, iron.

Hotel Monaco ★★   This 14-story hotel deftly manages to straddle the line between fun and conservative. The stylish decor has a funky feel that adds to the hotel's playful spirit, which may be why it attracts a younger clientele, with an overall vibe that is laid-back and friendly rather than so-hip-it-hurts. (This is Chicago, after all, not New York.)

The plush, jewel-toned 1930s French Deco decor at the Kimpton Group's most upscale Chicago property infuses sizable rooms resembling theatrical set pieces; eclectic furnishings include deep-red headboards and green-striped walls, while the lobby—with its gold decorative accents and zebra-striped chairs—looks like a 1930s-era salon. Families will enjoy the suites, some of which adjoin rooms with two double beds. Rooms on the top three floors give you a vista of the Chicago River and surrounding skyscrapers. (If you're taller than average, you can request a Tall Room, with longer beds.) All rooms include "meditation stations"—comfy seats tucked into the larger-than-average windows, which are perfect for taking in the cityscape outside (ask for a river view). The cozy lobby is the spot for free morning coffee and an evening wine reception. You'll find the concierge happy to help with a list of kid-friendly attractions. And feel free to bring the family pet along—the hotel has welcomed every creature from parrots to poodles. Make sure to tell them about your pet when you make a reservation, as pet food and dog-walking services are available, too. (The Hotels Burnham and Allegro, sister hotels to the Monaco, offer similar services for traveling pets.)

225 N. Wabash Ave. (at Wacker Dr.), Chicago, IL 60601. ℂ **800/397-7661** or 312/960-8500. Fax 312/960-1883. www.monaco-chicago.com. 192 units. $169–$329 double; $279–$429 suite. Kids 17 and under stay free in parent's room. Rollaways and cribs free. AE, DC, DISC, MC, V. Valet parking $38 with in/out privileges. Subway/El: Brown, Green, or Orange Line to Randolph/Washington or Red Line to State/Lake. Pets allowed. **Amenities:** Restaurant (American); small fitness room (and access to nearby health club); concierge; business center; 24-hr. room service; in-room massage; babysitting; laundry service; dry cleaning. In room: A/C, TV w/pay movies, fax, high-speed Internet access, minibar, coffeemaker, hair dryer, iron, safe.

Renaissance Chicago Hotel ★★

The Renaissance is the most understated upscale hotel in the city, located at the top of State Street, just across the bridge from the Magnificent Mile and steps from the Loop's attractions. Although business travelers are the Renaissance's bread and butter, I was happy to discover that the hotel made a big effort to accommodate families traveling with children. One huge plus: A pool on the fourth floor is open from 6:30am to 10pm, with no restrictions on children's use. The hotel's restaurants offer kids' menus for breakfast, lunch, and dinner, serving everything from French toast to ravioli. PlayStation games on the television can keep kids entertained.

The hotel embraces its location with bay windows offering stunning views of the river and the towers of North Michigan Avenue. Standard double rooms include a small sitting area with an armchair and desk; families might prefer the deluxe doubles, which have much bigger bathrooms (some with separate showers and bathtubs) and two couches. Club-level rooms, located on the top four floors, are half a room larger and have their own concierge in a private lounge, where complimentary continental breakfast and evening hors d'oeuvres are served. Families often request connecting rooms, one of which has a king-size bed; the other, two queen-size beds. Request a river view for the best cityscape (corner suites also have excellent views of both the Chicago River and Lake Michigan).

1 W. Wacker Dr. (at State St.), Chicago, IL 60601. ℂ **800/HOTELS-1** (468-3571) or 312/372-7200. Fax 312/372-0093. www.marriott.com. 553 units. $199–$399 double; $249–$389 club-level double; suites from $500. Weekend rates available. Kids 11 and under stay free in parent's room. Rollaways free in Club Lounge rooms only; cribs free. AE, DC, DISC, MC, V. Valet parking $40 with in/out privileges. Subway/El: Brown Line to State/Lake, or Red Line to Washington/State. Small pets accepted. **Amenities:** Restaurant (American); lounge; indoor pool w/skylights; health club w/sauna and steam room; concierge; FedEx Office located in lobby; 24-hr. room service; babysitting; same-day laundry service and dry cleaning;

club-level rooms. *In room:* A/C, TV w/pay movies and PlayStation, CD player, high-speed Internet access, minibar, coffeemaker, hair dryer, iron.

The Silversmith Hotel & Suites ★ (Finds) You might call the Silversmith a hidden gem. The landmark building, designed by the celebrated firm of D. H. Burnham and Company, was built in 1897 to serve the jewelry and silver trade on Wabash Avenue, still known as Jeweler's Row. You'll be only a block south of Macy's (formerly Marshall Field's) on State Street. While the hotel isn't a traditional family hotel, it does provide cribs, babysitting service, and toys and games. Word about the Silversmith has been slow getting out (even many Loop office workers who pass by it every day don't know it's there), so it doesn't book up as quickly as other hotter spots. That's good news for families on vacation because it means that the hotel is more willing to make a deal on room rates. (The suites—perfect for families—often get discounted, I hear.) There is also more likely to be room at this inn during the busy convention season.

Rooms come in varying configurations, with 12-foot-high ceilings, 10-foot picture windows, handsome Frank Lloyd Wright–inspired wrought-iron fixtures, armoires, and homey bedding; bathrooms are generously sized. Because buildings surround this urban hotel, most rooms along the hotel's main corridor tend to be dark (with windows looking into neighboring office buildings). For a better—and quintessentially Chicago—view, get a room at the front on the fifth floor or higher, overlooking Wabash Avenue and the El tracks. In the evening stop by the lobby for a wine-and-cheese reception and complimentary desserts (including Eli's cheesecake, one of the city's signature sweet treats).

10 S. Wabash Ave. (at Madison St.), Chicago, IL 60603. © **312/372-7696.** Fax 312/372-7320. www.silversmith chicagohotel.com. 143 units. $179–$359 double; from $289 suite. Weekend rates available. Rollaways $25/night; cribs free. AE, DC, DISC, MC, V. Valet parking $30 with in/out privileges. Subway/El: Brown, Green, or Orange Line to Madison/Wabash; or Red Line to Washington/State. **Amenities:** Restaurant; lounge; tiny fitness room (w/access to nearby health club for $10/day); concierge; business center and secretarial services; limited room service; babysitting; laundry service; dry cleaning; club-level rooms. *In room:* A/C, TV w/pay movies, dataport, minibar, coffeemaker, hair dryer, iron, safe.

Swissôtel Chicago ★★ This sleek, modern hotel is all business and may therefore feel a bit icy to some families, but you won't believe the fantastic deals available when the business travelers clear out for the weekend and the atmosphere lightens up. The hotel's triangular design gives every room a panoramic vista of Lake Michigan, Grant Park, and/or the Chicago River. Spacious rooms let families spread out with separate sitting areas and warm contemporary furnishings. While business travelers appreciate the oversize desks, families dining in appreciate that the desk converts into a dining room table. Some rooms come equipped with CD players and high-speed and Wi-Fi Internet access. Families might request an executive suite, with wonderful 180-degree views, and separate sleeping areas.

Active parents will want to break a sweat in the lofty environs of the Penthouse Health Club and Spa, perched on the 42nd floor. And if you decide to splurge on a parents-only dinner out, make sure to book a table at the ultimate steak-and-lobster restaurant, the on-site outpost of New York's The Palm.

323 E. Wacker Dr., Chicago, IL 60601. © **888/737-9477** or 312/565-0565. Fax 312/565-0540. www.swissotel chicago.com. 632 units. $159–$409 double; $395–$2,500 suite. Rollaways $50/night; cribs free. AE, DC, DISC, MC, V. Valet parking $45 with in/out privileges. Subway/El: Red, Brown, Orange, or Green Line to Randolph. **Amenities:** 2 restaurants (steakhouse, American); lounge; penthouse fitness center w/indoor pool, spa, Jacuzzi, and sauna; concierge; business center w/extensive meeting services; 24-hr. room service; massage; babysitting; laundry service; 24-hr. dry cleaning; executive-level rooms. *In room:* A/C, TV w/pay movies, dataport, minibar, coffeemaker, hair dryer, iron.

MODERATE

Hotel Allegro ★ (Value)   For families in search of a fun, light-hearted vibe, the Kimpton Group's splashy Allegro is a good value. Although its published rates are similar to those of its sister properties, the Hotel Monaco and Hotel Burnham (both listed above), the Allegro is far larger and therefore more likely to offer special rates to fill space, especially on weekends and in the winter. Guests enter a lobby with plush, boldly colored furnishings. That whimsical first impression segues into the cheery, pink-walled guest rooms. Most rooms are small (without much space beyond the bed, an armoire, and one chair), but manage to feel cozy rather than cramped; the compact bathrooms, annoyingly, have only pedestal sinks—meaning minimal counter space for kids' toothbrushes and mom's makeup. Suites have separate bathrooms and foldout couches that come with robes and two-person Jacuzzi tubs. For a family of three or more, the hotel recommends a king suite with a Jacuzzi tub; the room includes a living room and separate bedroom with a king-size bed.

As befits a place where the doorman hums along to the tunes playing on speakers out front, the Allegro appeals to younger travelers. The hotel's restaurant, 312 Chicago, attracts nonguests in search of excellent Italian cuisine. There's no kids' menu, but the restaurant is accommodating to families. Like the other Kimpton Group hotels in Chicago, Hotel Allegro welcomes pets. If your family is in town to catch some theater, make sure to ask about the Allegro's access to exclusive seats for high-profile downtown shows and its special theater packages.

171 W. Randolph St. (at LaSalle St.), Chicago, IL 60601. (②) **800/643-1500** or 312/236-0123. Fax 312/236-0917. www.allegrochicago.com. 483 units. $149–$299 double; $225–$399 suite. Kids 17 and under stay free in parent's room. Rollaways free depending on room; cribs free. AE, DC, DISC, MC, V. Valet parking $30 with in/out privileges. Subway/El: All lines to Washington. Pets allowed. **Amenities:** Restaurant (northern Italian); lounge; exercise room (and access to nearby health club w/indoor pool for $10/day); concierge; business services; salon; limited room service; same-day laundry service; dry cleaning. *In room:* A/C, TV w/pay movies, free high-speed Internet access, minibar, coffeemaker, hair dryer, iron.

2 SOUTH LOOP

Unlike the area surrounding North Michigan Avenue—the "Mag Mile"—the South Loop is less about glamour and more about old Chicago. Running the length of Grant Park, South Michigan Avenue is ideal for a long city stroll, passing grand museums, imposing architecture, and the park's greenery and statuary. But although this stretch was once Chicago's most regal hotel row, it's certainly the worse for wear today. Over the past decade, however, the surrounding neighborhood has been revitalized, with the conversion of industrial buildings into loft apartments. Old-timers might complain about gentrification, but it's good news for visitors, who now find more restaurant options and livelier street life. For families, the proximity to Millennium Park, Grant Park, and State Street shopping makes the area attractive, particularly when summer music festivals or holiday shopping is on the agenda.

VERY EXPENSIVE

Hilton Chicago ★★   When it erupted onto Michigan Avenue in 1927, this massive brick-and-stone edifice billed itself as the largest hotel in the world. It certainly owns one of the most colorful histories of any Chicago hotel. Guests have included Queen Elizabeth, Emperor Hirohito, and every president since FDR. The classical-rococo public spaces—including the Versailles-inspired Grand Ballroom and Grand Stair Lobby—are magnificent, but the rest of the hotel is firmly entrenched in the present. The hotel is a solid choice for families: Children 17 and under stay free in their parent's room. There's plenty of space to wander, and it's close to all of the major museums and Grant Park (great for when the kids need to burn off some energy). Even better, there's a heated swimming pool and a fitness center with a whirlpool and sauna, all open to kids.

Some rooms are on the small side, but all are comfortable and warm; and many of the standard rooms have two bathrooms—great for families. Adjoining rooms are available; ask when you call for reservations. The views from those higher up facing Michigan Avenue offer a sweeping view of Grant Park and the lake. The hotel's Executive Level rooms offer a separate registration area, upgraded amenities (including robes), and a lounge serving complimentary continental breakfast and evening hors d'oeuvres (you'll pay about $75 above the standard rate for these rooms).

720 S. Michigan Ave. (at Balbo Dr.), Chicago, IL 60605. © 800/HILTONS [445-8667] or 312/922-4400. Fax 312/922-5240. www.hilton.com. 1,544 units. $129–$399 double; from $179 suite. Kids 18 and under stay free in parent's room. Rollaways $40/stay; cribs free. AE, DC, DISC, MC, V. Valet parking $45; self-parking $41. Subway/El: Red Line to Harrison/State. **Amenities:** 4 restaurants (cafe, American, steakhouse, Irish pub w/live music); 2 lounges; indoor pool; health club w/indoor track, hot tubs, sauna, and steam room; concierge; business center; 24-hr. room service; massage; babysitting; laundry service; 24-hr. dry cleaning. *In room:* A/C, TV w/pay movies, high-speed and Wi-Fi Internet access, minibar, coffeemaker, hair dryer, iron.

INEXPENSIVE

Travelodge Chicago Downtown (Value   You won't be reveling in luxury, but Travelodge promises and delivers neat, clean rooms at reasonable prices. The hotel's location near the Loop and Museum Campus is excellent: You are half a block from Grant Park and all the summer festivals, and only 4 blocks from the Field Museum. This 12-story hotel is one of few budget lodgings you'll find in the heart of the Loop. The hotel was built in 1925 as the Harrison Hotel, and for many years was one of the premier hotels in the city. Ever since Travelodge acquired the property, they've been promoting it as "a touch of old Chicago" and working to restore the property. To date, all guest rooms and the lobby have been renovated.

Families should request one of the "Sleepy Bear Den" rooms, which offer privacy for parents and for kids—but not too much privacy. The room is separated into two areas with an archway: On one side is a king-size bed for the parents, and on the other side is a double bed for the kids, specially decorated with whimsical curtains and bedding. Each side has its own television and VCR; the kids' side is stocked with children's movies. Also included are a microwave and refrigerator. Other rooms suitable for families offer two beds and two bathrooms. There's no pool, but two in-hotel restaurants cater to families: Chicago Carry-Out offers full breakfasts and sandwiches, and Charming Wok serves inexpensive Chinese fare from 11am to 11pm.

65 E. Harrison St. (at S. Wabash Ave.), Chicago, IL 60605. © 888/515-6375 or 312/427-8000. Fax 312/427-8261. www.travelodge.com. 250 units. $105–$165 double. Kids 17 and under stay free in parent's room. Rollaways $10/night; cribs free. AE, DC, DISC, MC, V. Indoor garage parking $15 car or small van, includes 1 in/out per day at no charge. Subway/El: Red Line to State/Harrison. **Amenities:** 2 restaurants. *In room:* A/C, TV w/pay movies, fax, dataport, minibar, coffeemaker, hair dryer, iron.

3 NEAR NORTH & THE MAGNIFICENT MILE

Along the Magnificent Mile—a stretch of Michigan Avenue running north of the Chicago River to Oak Street—you'll find most of the city's premium hotels. The location can't be beat.

VERY EXPENSIVE

Conrad Chicago ★★   Tucked into the back of Westfield North Bridge mall, the Conrad Chicago maintains a low profile. I'd recommend it for families seeking a luxurious option in the wintertime, thanks to the convenience of having a whole mall just a few steps away. You can get out without even bundling the kids up—an attractive proposition when it's icy outside. A quick elevator ride connects you with stores such as Nordstrom or the Lego Store or Chicago's Magnificent Meal food court, where you can grab anything from a Fluky's hot dog to Italian fare at Tuscany Cafe.

This property—part of the Hilton hotel group's new upscale "boutique" brand—is determined to compete with the city's more established luxury properties (with room rates to match). The overall vibe here is old-money classiness rather than new-money flashiness, from the lobby filled with dark wood furniture to the deep brown curtains in the tranquil guest rooms. Rooms here are a bit small (especially the least expensive ones on the north side), but the amenities are top-of-the-line: flatscreen TVs and Bose sound systems. High rollers will want to book one of the suites overlooking Michigan Avenue; a few even come with private terraces, something few hotels in this city can offer. The Conrad can't quite compete with the Park Hyatt or the Peninsula in the glamour department, but its cozy style should appeal to travelers looking for something a little more personal.

521 N. Rush St. (at Grand St.), Chicago, IL 60611. **①** **800/HILTONS** [445-8667] or 312/645-1500. Fax 312/645-1550. http://conradhotels1.hilton.com. 311 units. $325–$530 double; from $500 suite. Kids 11 and under stay free in parent's room. Rollaways and cribs free. AE, DC, DISC, MC, V. Valet parking $41 with in/out privileges. Subway/El: Red Line to Chicago/State. Pets accepted. **Amenities:** Restaurant (European bistro); bar; health club; concierge; business center; 24-hr. room service; in-room massage; babysitting; laundry service; same-day dry cleaning. *In room:* A/C, flatscreen TV w/pay movies and video games, CD player w/Bose sound system, high-speed Internet access, minibar, fridge, coffeemaker, hair dryer, iron, safe, turndown service.

Four Seasons Hotel Chicago ★★★   A fabulous pool and indulgences for kids make this hotel a thumbs up for families in search of luxury. Consistently voted one of the top hotels in the world by frequent travelers, the Four Seasons occupies a rarefied aerie between the 30th and 46th floors above the Mag Mile's most upscale vertical mall. The hotel has every conceivable luxury amenity, and in 2007 it underwent a $30-million renovation that changed its look from that of an English country manor to that of a sleek and modern getaway. The elegant rooms feature contemporary furnishings, subdued colors, and modern artworks, and each has windows that open to let in the fresh air. Bathrooms boast a lighted makeup mirror, oversize towels and robes, scales, and L'Occitane toiletries.

Kid-friendly services include child-size robes, tub amenities, board and video games, and a special room-service menu. The hotel has offered family packages, especially on weekends, which might include small gifts and discounts from kids' retailers. With the package, in the past, children 11 and under have been able to eat free from the kids' room-service menu—and receive a complimentary gift from the ice-cream man. Yes, it's

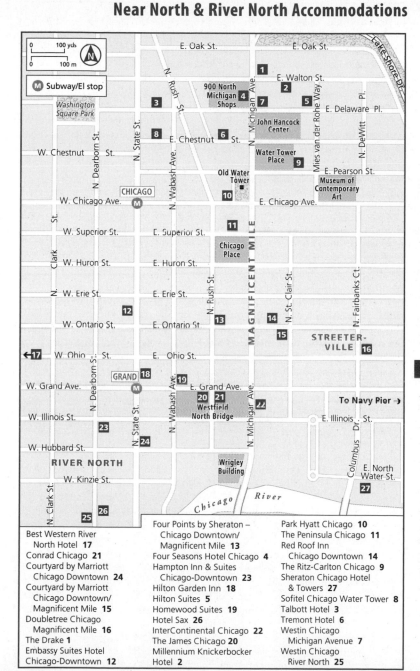

← 17

FAMILY-FRIENDLY ACCOMMODATIONS

4

NEAR NORTH & THE MAGNIFICENT MILE

Best Western River
  North Hotel **17**
Conrad Chicago **21**
Courtyard by Marriott
  Chicago Downtown **24**
Courtyard by Marriott
  Chicago Downtown/
  Magnificent Mile **15**
Doubletree Chicago
  Magnificent Mile **16**
The Drake **1**
Embassy Suites Hotel
Chicago-Downtown **12**

Four Points by Sheraton –
  Chicago Downtown/
  Magnificent Mile **13**
Four Seasons Hotel Chicago **4**
Hampton Inn & Suites
  Chicago-Downtown **23**
Hilton Garden Inn **18**
Hilton Suites **5**
Homewood Suites **19**
Hotel Sax **26**
InterContinental Chicago **22**
The James Chicago **20**
Millennium Knickerbocker
  Hotel **2**

Park Hyatt Chicago **10**
The Peninsula Chicago **11**
Red Roof Inn
  Chicago Downtown **14**
The Ritz-Carlton Chicago **9**
Sheraton Chicago Hotel
  & Towers **27**
Sofitel Chicago Water Tower **8**
Talbott Hotel **3**
Tremont Hotel **6**
Westin Chicago
  Michigan Avenue **7**
Westin Chicago
  River North **25**

true—as a special treat for wee ones, the hotel has an ice-cream man who will visit your room and let kids choose an ice cream and toppings, including Oreo pieces, gummy bears, M&Ms, sprinkles, freshly whipped cream, and chocolate sauce and caramel sauce. Most indulgent of all, however, are the twin beds—so soft that the hotel's gift shop sells about a hundred of them each year for $1,200 apiece.

An 18-foot-high white marble fountain marks the entrance to the opulent Seasons Restaurant (the hotel's other restaurant, the Café, offers kids' menus). I'd recommend that families make reservations for the Sunday brunch at Seasons, which takes place from 10:30am to 1:30pm. Children are welcome to join the fun in their own section of the restaurant, where a Harry Potter castle houses arts and crafts. The activities are supervised by a babysitter, and you can enjoy the best brunch in Chicago while your kids are within view. Kids can join you to eat, then run off to enjoy their own experience in the castle. *Bon appétit!*

120 E. Delaware Place (at Michigan Ave.), Chicago, IL 60611. ℭ **800/332-3442** or 312/280-8800. Fax 312/280-1748. www.fourseasons.com. 343 units. $495–$695 double; $735–$3,700 suite. Weekend rates from $385. Kids 17 and under stay free in parent's room. Rollaways and cribs free. AE, DC, DISC, MC, V. Valet parking $36 with in/out privileges; self-parking $30. Subway/El: Red Line to Chicago/State. Pets accepted. **Amenities:** 2 restaurants (New American, cafe); lounge; indoor pool (unrestricted access for kids); fitness center and spa; concierge; business center; 24-hr. room service; babysitting; laundry service; 24-hr. dry cleaning. *In room:* A/C, TV/DVD w/pay movies and video games, CD player, free high-speed Internet access, minibar, coffeemaker, hair dryer, iron, safe.

Park Hyatt Chicago ★★★   For those in search of chic modern luxury, the Park Hyatt is the coolest hotel in town (as long as money is no object). The hotel occupies one of the most desirable spots on North Michigan Avenue, overlooking Water Tower Square, and the best rooms are those that face east, overlooking the bustle of Michigan Avenue and the lake in the distance.

Luxury might be the watchword here, but the look is anything but stuffy: The lobby feels like a sleek modern art gallery. German painter Gerhard Richter's *Piazza del Duomo Milan* masterpiece is the visual centerpiece of the space, providing ample evidence of what visual treats lie in store for guests. Rooms feature Eames and Mies van der Rohe reproduction furniture and window banquettes with stunning city views. (Another plus: The windows actually open.) The bathrooms are especially wonderful: You can pull back a sliding cherrywood wall and enjoy a view of the city while you soak in the oversize tub.

Families often book connecting rooms, one with a king-size bed and one with two double beds. Every room has CD and DVD players with a flatscreen TV, and the concierge will loan from the hotel's library of DVDs (including kids' movies) at no cost. The health club is open only to those over 16, but the pool welcomes kids—and it's a stunner, with city views looking south and bronze-colored tiles. If you plan to spend significant time at American Girl Place, ask about the hotel's special package, which includes breakfast for two at the hotel, outfits for the doll, and a special turndown service—for your child's doll, too, of course. The hotel offers programs for children up to age 14, and in the past, that has included a backpack with a camera, maps, and coupons to redeem at the hotel, including a coupon for a tour of the behind-the-scenes workings of the hotel, which includes the kitchen (kids get a cookie and chef's hat), housekeeping, and more.

The crown jewel of the Park Hyatt is NoMI, a restaurant nestled on the seventh floor. Serving French-inspired cuisine and featuring an *Architectural Digest*–worthy interior, with an adjoining outdoor terrace, NoMI (an acronym for North Michigan) continues to receive stellar reviews. In the summer, you can sample appetizers and sip cocktails

Making the Most of the Concierge

Nearly all upscale hotels have concierges, and many smaller inns offer concierge services from the front desk. Too often, these people go underutilized by guests who don't know the full range of services concierges can provide. Beyond merely giving directions to Navy Pier, concierges are there to act as guests' problem solvers. The best ones take real pleasure in helping, and the more challenging the request, the better. When you're on vacation, why not truly relax, and let the concierge be your personal assistant during your stay?

House Cars: Upper-end hotels often have house cars available to drop off guests in the Loop or elsewhere within 5 miles of the hotel. Businesspeople use the service most, but any guest can enjoy this perk. If you want to take the kids to watch the White Sox play at U.S. Cellular Field, or you need a ride to a restaurant, request a house car through the concierge desk. There's usually no charge, but you may tip the driver at your discretion.

Restaurants: Every concierge will make dinner reservations for guests, and I recommend having the concierge phone ahead no matter where you are dining. If a restaurant is booked, the concierge may have more pull squeezing you in than you would on your own. But don't ask the concierge for any old restaurant recommendation. (I've been to some unremarkable, touristy places that way.) It's more effective to name two or three options and have the concierge tell you more about each one.

Other Services: You needn't limit requests to restaurant reservations. Concierges can also book cruises on Lake Michigan, car rentals, or even spa treatments—whatever requires a phone call. They can buy tickets to a sporting or entertainment venue or amend airline reservations.

Solutions: Did a child get sick? Head right to the concierge, who will make it a personal mission to ensure your kid is seen by a doctor as soon as possible. Concierges will also oblige less urgent requests, like reserving doggy day care or finding a last-minute gift. You don't even have to be checked into the hotel. You can fax and e-mail the concierge with your arrival date and particular request. If he or she does go beyond the call of duty, gratuities are always appreciated—although never expected.

while checking out the skyline from an outdoor terrace. Parents will want to book a sitter for an evening out here—it's far too chic to be kid-friendly.

800 N. Michigan Ave., Chicago, IL 60611. © **800/233-1234** or 312/335-1234. Fax 312/239-4000. www.parkchicago.hyatt.com. 198 units. $385–$525 double; $695–$3,000 suite. Kids 18 and under stay free in parent's room. No rollaways; cribs free. AE, DC, DISC, MC, V. Valet parking $42 with in/out privileges. Subway/El: Red Line to Chicago/State. **Amenities:** Restaurant (French/American); lounge; indoor pool; health club w/Jacuzzi and spa; concierge; business center w/computer technical support; 24-hr. room service; massage; babysitting; laundry service; 24-hr. dry cleaning. In room: A/C, TV w/DVD player and pay movies, CD player, free high-speed Internet access, minibar, coffeemaker, hair dryer, iron, safe, iPod connectivity.

The Peninsula Chicago ★★★ Taking design cues from the chain's flagship Hong Kong hotel, the Peninsula Chicago mixes an Art Deco sensibility with modern, top-of-the-line amenities. Service is practically a religion here. Rooms are average in size (except for the rather small "junior suites," which have living rooms that can comfortably seat only about four people). Rooms that are popular with families include suites with two double beds, or adjoining rooms that combine one room with a king-size bed and one with two double beds. The hotel's in-room technology is cutting edge: A small "command station" by every bed allows guests to control all the lights, TV, and room temperature without getting out from under the covers. The marble-filled bathrooms have separate shower stalls and tubs, spacious vanities, and another "command station" by the bathtub. Add in the flatscreen TVs, and you've got a classic hotel that's very much attuned to the present.

Kids' amenities include a treat upon arrival: milk and cookies (or popcorn and soda if they prefer). Rooms can be equipped with video games, DVDs, and a library of kids' movies—make sure to request them when you make your reservation. The bright, airy spa and fitness center fill the top two floors—check out the view from the outdoor deck. The spa has an Olympic-size pool, and one lane is always reserved for family swim. The 20th-floor health club is also open to children, with no restrictions. You can obtain child-care services through the concierge.

The sultry hotel bar—hidden from the lobby behind curved, leather-covered walls—is a top spot for a romantic evening with your mate. The Lobby is the best in-hotel restaurant bet for families, with a kids' menu. Don't miss breakfast at Pierre Gourmet, located just outside the hotel at the corner of Superior and Rush streets, for some of the best baked goods on the Magnificent Mile. The hotel's other restaurants, including the Avenue and Shanghai Terrace, do offer children's menus, but I'd recommend that the meal be an adults-only affair.

108 E. Superior St. (at Michigan Ave.), Chicago, IL 60611. ℂ 866/288-8889 or 312/337-2888. Fax 312/751-2888. http://chicago.peninsula.com. 339 units. $525–$650 double; $795–$7,500 suite. Kids 17 and under stay free in parent's room. Rollaways and cribs free. AE, DC, DISC, MC, V. Valet parking $45 with in/out privileges. Subway/El: Red Line to Chicago/State. Pets accepted. **Amenities:** 4 restaurants (contemporary, Asian, eclectic, and European bakery); bar; indoor pool w/outdoor deck; fitness center; spa; hot tub; sauna; concierge; business center; 24-hr. room service; in-room massage; babysitting; laundry service; same-day dry cleaning. *In room:* A/C, TV/DVD w/pay movies, fax, free Wi-Fi, minibar, fridge (upon request), coffeemaker, hair dryer, iron, safe.

The Ritz-Carlton Chicago ★★★ Perched high atop Water Tower Place, the Ritz-Carlton casts a soothing presence on guests as they're deposited into the airy 12th-floor lobby. Not surprisingly, the quality of the accommodations is of the highest caliber, although the standard rooms aren't very large. Doubles have space for a love seat and desk but not much more; the bathrooms are elegant but not huge. Suites are especially suited to families, with an additional living area furnished with a sofa and chair, a writing desk, a second TV, and a stereo. Lake views cost more but are spectacular (although in all the rooms, you're up high enough that you're not staring into surrounding condominium buildings). Families will find this luxury crash pad quite welcoming: Every child receives a gift and can borrow toys and games from a stash kept by the concierge. PlayStation and Nintendo are also available, and kids' food can be delivered by room service 24 hours a day.

Guests staying in suites are treated to a gratis wardrobe pressing upon arrival, personalized stationery, and fresh flowers. Service is the Ritz-Carlton's selling point, whether it's the "compcierge" who helps guests with computer problems or the allergy-sensitive rooms that are cleaned with special nonirritating products and come stocked with non-feather duvets and pillows, plus hypoallergenic bath products on request.

Whether or not you stay here, the Ritz-Carlton is an elegant place for afternoon tea, served at 2:30 and 4:30pm in the lobby. At one end of the lobby is the Greenhouse restaurant, designed with a glass roof and wall that seems to jut out over the city. The hotel's excellent Sunday brunch includes a special buffet for children replete with M&Ms, mac and cheese, chicken nuggets, and peanut-butter-and-jelly sandwiches.

160 E. Pearson St., Chicago, IL 60611. ℂ **800/621-6906** or 312/266-1000. Fax 312/266-1194. www.four seasons.com. 435 units. $495–$635 double; $710–$4,000 suite. Weekend rates from $385. Kids 17 and under stay free in parent's room. Rollaways and cribs free. AE, DC, DISC, MC, V. Valet parking $40 with in/out privileges; self-parking $32 with no in/out privileges. Subway/El: Red Line to Chicago/State. Pets accepted. **Amenities:** 2 restaurants (French, American); 2 lounges; indoor pool; health club w/spa, Jacuzzi, and sauna; children's programs; concierge; business center; 24-hr. room service; in-room massage; babysitting; laundry service; same-day dry cleaning; premier suites. *In room:* A/C, TV/VCR w/pay movies, CD player, high-speed Internet access, minibar, hair dryer, iron, safe.

Sofitel Chicago Water Tower ★★★   Whether or not you stay here, you'll quickly spot the Sofitel, thanks to its striking white stone-and-glass facade and geometric shape: A narrow prism tower rising from a square base. Located 1 block west of the Magnificent Mile, the Sofitel doesn't cater specifically to families, but service is so accommodating that you and your kids will be made to feel right at home. The place has a whimsical air that will appeal to kids: Luminescent floor tiles in the lobby change color in a never-ending light show. The overall feel of the hotel is European modern; most employees seem to hail from exotic French-speaking locales such as Morocco, giving the hotel an international flair that you won't find in most of Chicago's hotels. Foreign language magazines are scattered on tables throughout the lobby. The hotel's bright, stylish Café des Architects has become a favorite business lunch spot for locals.

Of the 415 rooms, 55 are suites that offer pullout sofas and striking views of the lake and city. (To comfortably fit a crib in the room, you'll want a suite.) Up to two children can stay in a room for no extra charge—try a suite or a standard room with two double beds. And speaking of beds, they're outfitted with fabulously fluffy and inviting duvets. Closets are spacious, and the bathtub is stocked with candles and fresh flowers. Babysitting services are available upon request, and little guests receive their own Sofitel teddy bear.

20 E. Chestnut St. (at Wabash St.), Chicago, IL 60611. ℂ **800/SOFITEL** (763-4835) or 312/324-4000. Fax 312/324-4026. www.sofitel.com. 415 units. $240–$555 double; $370–$685 suite. Kids 17 and under stay free in parent's room. No rollaways; cribs free. AE, DC, DISC, MC, V. Valet parking $40. Subway/El: Red Line to Chicago/State. Small pets accepted. **Amenities:** Restaurant (French cafe); bar; fitness center; concierge; business center; 24-hr. room service; babysitting; laundry service; same-day dry cleaning. *In room:* A/C, TV w/pay movies, high-speed Internet access, minibar, hair dryer, iron, safe.

EXPENSIVE

The Drake Hotel ★★★   If ever the term "grande dame" fit a hotel, it fits The Drake. Fronting East Lake Shore Drive with a prominent rooftop marquee that has a signature on the city's skyline, the landmark building opened in 1920 and soon became one of the city's finest hotels. Longtime Chicagoans still think of The Drake with possessive pride; it's our version of New York's Plaza or Paris's Ritz.

For all its old-time glamour, the hotel seems a bit dated when compared to gleaming newer upscale hotels such as the Park Hyatt or the Peninsula (both reviewed earlier in this chapter), but this, of course, is part of The Drake's charm. The Drake welcomes families, but the lack of a pool, game room, or other kid-friendly amenities (many of which its competitors offer) may be a negative. Still, plenty of families have made it a tradition to stay here.

Parents will be happy to know that the typical room is generous in size and furnished comfortably with a separate sitting area; some have two bathrooms. The lakeview rooms are lovely, and—no surprise—you'll pay more for them. Be forewarned that "city view" rooms on lower floors look out onto another building, so you'll probably be keeping your drapes shut.

Even if you don't stay at the hotel, take your older kids to the lavishly decorated Palm Court for afternoon tea, which is accompanied by a harpist. The hotel's restaurants include Drake Bros., an upscale restaurant with great views of the lake and Michigan Avenue; the Cape Cod Room, an old-time-style local favorite for seafood; and Coq d'Or, one of Chicago's most atmospheric piano bars. All of the restaurants have kids' menus.

140 E. Walton Place (at Michigan Ave.), Chicago, IL 60611. © **800/55-DRAKE** (553-7253) or 312/787-2200. Fax 312/787-1431. www.thedrakehotel.com. 535 units. $199–$425 double; $279–$495 executive floor; from $545 suite. Kids 18 and under stay free in parent's room. Rollaways and cribs free. AE, DC, DISC, MC, V. Valet parking $32 with in/out privileges. Subway/El: Red Line to Chicago/State. **Amenities:** 3 restaurants (American, steakhouse, seafood); 2 lounges; fitness center; concierge; business center; shopping arcade (including a Chanel boutique); barbershop; 24-hr. room service; in-room massage; babysitting; laundry service; 24-hr. dry cleaning; executive-level rooms. *In room:* A/C, TV w/pay movies, high-speed Internet access, minibar, coffeemaker, hair dryer, iron.

Hilton Suites Chicago/Magnificent Mile ★

This full-service all-suite hotel is a very good choice for families seeking something with a little less starch. Best of all is its location: just off the Mag Mile and next door to the Hancock Building and Water Tower Place. Suites might not be huge, but they're warm, inviting, and immaculate to boot. All include a separate living room (with pullout sofa) and bedroom. The price depends on bed size, floor (some have spectacular lake views), and furnishings. The hotel doesn't feel that different from other Hilton Suites properties, but that consistency might be just what some people are looking for.

The hotel's high spot—literally—is the fitness center on the 30th floor, with a pool that's surrounded by stunning views of Navy Pier and the Magnificent Mile; kids are welcome at both. (Stop by on a summer Wed or Sat evening for a great view of the fireworks at Navy Pier.) The hotel also is home to Mrs. Park's Tavern, a family-friendly place featuring creative American fare. The restaurant has a kids' menu and sidewalk seating that offers prime people-watching in the shadow of the John Hancock building.

198 E. Delaware Place, Chicago, IL 60611. © **800/HILTON1** (445-8661) or 312/664-1100. Fax 312/664-8627. www.hilton.com. 345 units. $159–$229 double. Kids 17 and under stay free in parent's room. No rollaways (sofa beds in every suite); cribs free. AE, DC, DISC, MC, V. Valet parking $50 with in/out privileges. Subway/El: Red Line to Chicago/State. **Amenities:** Restaurant; lounge; indoor pool; fitness room; hot tub; sauna; concierge; business center; 24-hr. room service; babysitting; laundry room; dry cleaning; free high-speed Internet access in public spaces. *In room:* A/C, TV w/pay movies, dataport, minibar, fridge, coffeemaker, hair dryer, iron.

InterContinental Chicago ★★

Newer hotels might get all the attention, but the InterContinental remains a sentimental favorite for many Chicagoans, ranking right up there with The Drake in our affections. Built as the Medinah Athletic Club in 1929, the building's original lobby features truly grand details: marble columns, hand-stenciled ceilings, and historic tapestries. The addition of a drab, impersonal modern tower in the 1960s added more rooms but gave the InterContinental a somewhat schizophrenic quality. A

2002 renovation integrated the two sides into a cohesive whole, giving the public spaces a more unified, upscale look.

A soaring, four-story rotunda, topped by a 50-foot-wide dome, serves as the entry point to the hotel, providing a suitably dramatic welcome. Guest rooms have two distinct identities, depending on location. Rooms in what's called the Main Building (the '60s addition) have an elegant, urban style, with lots of dark wood, deep yellow walls, and red velvet banquettes. The bathrooms feel brand-new but aren't particularly spacious, with small tubs. Rooms in the Historic Tower (the original building) have a more old-world feel: elaborately carved headboards, gold accents, and deep-red-and-cream drapes and bedding. The bathrooms, however, are completely modern; most come with both a tub and a separate, larger shower stall. (You'll pay about $50 more for rooms in the Historic Tower.)

While you're here, treat your kids to a swim in the city's best pool: The InterContinental's main claim to fame is the junior Olympic-size pool on the top floor. One of the first aboveground swimming pools ever built, it's decorated in a lavish "Venetian" style, with mosaics, marble columns, and painted tiles. Also be sure to ask about the family packages when making your reservation. In the past, the hotel has offered deals for families that include a backpack for your child, containing a T-shirt and other goodies, a coupon for a free in-room movie, and a 50% discount on all kids' meals in the hotel. Complimentary parking has been part of the package, as were complimentary milk and cookies at turndown time.

The hotel's restaurant, Zest, is the only street-level restaurant on Michigan Avenue, and it offers a kids' menu. (Try to grab a table by the front windows to enjoy the never-ending street scene.)

505 N. Michigan Ave. (at Grand Ave.), Chicago, IL 60611. © **800/327-0200** or 312/944-4100. Fax 312/944-1320. http://chicago.intercontinental.com. 790 units. $235–$350 double; from $500 suite. Kids 17 and under stay free in parent's room. Rollaways only in historic South tower $25/night; cribs free. AE, DC, DISC, MC, V. Valet parking $43 with in/out privileges. Subway/El: Red Line to Grand/State. **Amenities:** Restaurant (American); 2 lounges; indoor pool; fitness center w/sauna; concierge; business center; 24-hr. room service; massage; babysitting; laundry service; same-day dry cleaning. *In room:* A/C, TV w/pay movies, high-speed and Wi-Fi Internet access, minibar, coffeemaker, hair dryer, iron, safe.

The James Hotel ★★   One of the city's newest hotels (opened in 2006), the James brought a much-needed small luxury alternative to Chicago's hotel scene. Yes, you'll see more business travelers here than families, but well-heeled families in the know stay here, too (it's probably best for kids 8 and older). Cool and stylish, the hotel has a small lobby. Rooms are a tribute to modern minimalism: dark wood platform beds, leather cube stools, chocolate-colored carpeting, and slate-tiled bathrooms complete the decor. The hotel's strength is its amenities. There's a good chance your kids will hardly notice the decor when they see the 42-inch plasma television in the room. There's also Wi-Fi and a stereo with an iPod dock. A small spa and gym are located on the lower level. Parents should get a sitter and try the hotel's steakhouse, David Burke's Primehouse, and check out the nightlife at adjoining J Bar. One downside is the lack of views. Make sure to ask for a street view, and you'll be able to admire the famed Medinah Temple down the street; courtyard views are dismal. Families might want to inquire about the one-bedroom corner apartments that include a wet bar; they start at $329 per night. Loft rooms are 550 square feet in size and feature artwork by Chicago artists.

55 E. Ontario St. (at Wabash Ave.), Chicago, IL 60611. © **877/526-3755** or 312/337-1000. www.james hotels.com. 297 units (including 52 studios). $189–$529 double; $229–$569 studio; $289–$629 loft; $329–$669 apt; $1,400–$2,000 penthouse loft. Kids 11 and under stay free in parent's room. Rollaways

$30/night; cribs free. AE, DC, DISC, MC, V. Valet parking $42 with in/out privileges. Subway/El: Red Line to Grand/State. **Amenities:** Restaurant (steakhouse); adjoining bar/lounge; fitness center w/sauna and spa; concierge; 24-hr. room service; laundry; dry cleaning. *In room:* A/C, TV w/pay movies, stereo w/iPod/mp3-player dock, fax, Wi-Fi, minibar, coffeemaker, hair dryer, iron, safe.

Millennium Knickerbocker Hotel ★

Another historic hotel that's undergone a face-lift, the Knickerbocker looks spiffy from the lobby but retains a shabby-chic feel on the guest floors. The epitome of Jazz Age indulgence when built in 1927 as the Davis, the Knickerbocker has since undergone more transformations than Madonna. During the Capone era it was rumored to have shady underworld connections. In the 1970s Hugh Hefner turned it into the gaudy Playboy Towers and invited the leisure-suit set to a perpetual disco inferno on the hotel's famed illuminated ballroom floor. By the time the 1980s rolled around, the Knickerbocker had been through the wringer. A multimillion-dollar renovation in 2000 brought the hotel back to life, even if its past glamour has long since faded.

Weekends are popular with families, thanks to the hotel's superb location a block from Oak Street Beach and across the street from The Drake. You'll be in the heart of Magnificent Mile shopping, and walking distance from the American Girl Place.

The rooms aren't especially spacious, but they are warm and comfortable. Bathrooms are small but nicely done. ***One caveat:*** Views are often rather dismal, but you can catch a glimpse of the lake in all rooms ending in 14, and corner rooms (ending in 28) look onto Michigan Avenue. Families might consider staying on the executive level, which has rooms that include separate sitting areas with sofa beds, larger bathrooms, and upgraded bath amenities, including robes and slippers. If you tell the staff that you're traveling with kids, they will provide some family-friendly amenities such as milk and cookies at turndown. Pay-per-view movies always feature a children's program.

163 E. Walton Place (½ block east of Michigan Ave.), Chicago, IL 60611. © **800/621-8140** or 312/751-8100. Fax 312/751-9663. www.milleniumhotels.com. 305 units. $169–$299 double; $285–$1,000 suite. Kids 16 and under stay free in parent's room. Rollaways $20/night; cribs free. AE, DC, DISC, MC, V. Valet parking $40 with in/out privileges. Subway/El: Red Line to Chicago/State. **Amenities:** Restaurant (American); bar; exercise room; concierge; business center; 24-hr. room service; babysitting; laundry service; dry cleaning. *In room:* A/C, TV w/pay movies, high-speed Internet access, minibar, coffeemaker, hair dryer, iron, safe, turndown service.

Sheraton Chicago Hotel & Towers ★

Here's a beautifully situated hotel, perched on the riverfront with a view of the lake. You're only a short walk away from Navy Pier and steps from Michigan Avenue, with all its shopping and entertainment, and buses to whisk you to the Museum Campus. You're also close to walking paths along the river and lakefront, the Michigan Avenue Bridge, and a few blocks from Millennium Park.

You can request a room with views of the Chicago River, Lake Michigan, or the city skyline, and suites are available. The indoor pool and sun deck on the seventh floor has wraparound views; the pool has recently been renovated. There's a charge for using the fully equipped health club, with treadmills, Lifecycles, elliptical cross-trainers, life steps, and weight training, plus a sauna and massage therapy. If parents want to spend time on their own, babysitting services are available through the concierge.

The hotel has five restaurants and lounges, including Shula's Steakhouse. For families wanting a quick bite, there's also a snack bar and cafe.

301 E. North Water St., Chicago, IL 60611. © **877/242-2558** or 312/464-1000. Fax 312/464-9140. www.sheratonchicago.com. 1,209 units. $299 double; from $450 suite. Kids 17 and under stay free in parent's room. Rollaways $25/night; cribs free. AE, DC, DISC, MC, V. Valet parking $40 with in/out privileges. Bus:

151 to Michigan Ave. Bridge; walk east. **Amenities:** 3 restaurants and lounges; indoor pool; health club; **93**
sauna; business center; 24-hr. room service; massage. *In room:* A/C, TV w/video games, dataport, minibar,
coffeemaker, hair dryer, iron, safe.

Talbott Hotel ★★ (Finds)

The family-owned Talbott is a small, European-style gem that's one of the city's best small, independent hotels, and a fine choice for families. Constructed in the 1920s as an apartment building, the Talbott was converted to a hotel in 1989. That's great news for families, because the hotel has many suites with two bedrooms and two bathrooms, plus kitchen facilities. The location just off the Magnificent Mile is superb, and it's across the street from an upscale grocer, Goddess and Grocer, which makes it easy to pick up snacks and drinks to stock your kitchen. The hotel's wood-paneled lobby, decorated with leather sofas and velvety armchairs, two working fireplaces, tapestries, and numerous French horns used for fox hunts, is intimate and inviting. Kids' amenities are sparser here than at some larger hotels, but the homey, nonchain hotel atmosphere, large suites, availability of kitchens, and prime location make this one of my favorites for families.

Rooms are decorated in neutral tones, with furniture chosen for its residential feel, such as carved wooden desks, plus European linens and plasma TVs. They vary in size, so ask when making reservations. Suites and the hotel's king rooms entice with Jacuzzi tubs; suites have separate sitting areas with sofa beds and dining tables. The Talbott is not for families in need of extensive hotel facilities, but the cozy atmosphere and personal level of service appeal to visitors looking for the feeling of a small inn rather than a sprawling, corporate hotel.

20 E. Delaware Place (btw. Rush and State sts.), Chicago, IL 60611. (©) **800/TALBOTT** (825-2688) or 312/944-4970. Fax 312/944-7241. www.talbotthotel.com. 149 units. $169–$449 standard kings; $260–$671 suites. Kids 17 and under stay free in parent's room. Rollaways $20/night; cribs free. AE, DC, DISC, MC, V. Valet parking $40 with in/out privileges; self-parking $30. Subway/El: Red Line to Chicago/State. **Amenities:** Restaurant (Italian); lounge; complimentary access to nearby health club; concierge; business services; 24-hr. room service; laundry service; dry cleaning. *In room:* A/C; TV, high-speed and Wi-Fi Internet access, minibar, hair dryer, iron, safe.

Tremont Hotel

Slightly more upscale than the Talbott but with the same small, European-style feel, the Tremont caters mainly to adults. Suites are the only realistic family option, as most guest rooms tend to be on the small (or shall we say, "intimate") side. In fact, all rooms except the suites have only one bed and accommodate two people. Rooms in the Tremont House—a separate building next door—have kitchenettes. Suites are designed so one room includes a king-size bed with its own television, minibar, and bathroom. The adjoining living room includes a sofa bed, television, minibar, and bathroom. The cozy lobby with a fireplace sets the mood from the start. The furnishings are tasteful without being somber, and rooms are cheery, with yellow walls and large windows.

The steak-and-chops restaurant off the lobby, the memorabilia-filled Mike Ditka's Restaurant (p. 124), is co-owned by the legendary former Chicago Bears football coach.

100 E. Chestnut St. (1 block west of Michigan Ave.), Chicago, IL 60611. (©) **800/621-8133** or 312/751-1900. Fax 312/751-8650. www.tremontchicago.com. 130 units. $119–$279 double; $199–$299 suite. Kids 17 and under stay free in parent's room. No rollaways (most rooms are too small); cribs free. AE, DC, DISC, MC, V. Valet parking $40. Subway/El: Red Line to Chicago/State. **Amenities:** Restaurant; small exercise room (and access to nearby health club); concierge; business services; massage; babysitting; laundry service; dry cleaning. *In room:* A/C, TV/VCR, CD player, high-speed Internet access, minibar, coffeemaker, hair dryer, iron, safe.

MODERATE

Courtyard by Marriott Chicago Downtown Marriott's budget chain offers families good value in the heart of River North. You're a short walk from Michigan Avenue, the Loop, and the many theme restaurants of River North, including the ESPN Zone. The trolley to Navy Pier stops a block from the hotel (on State St.). Plus, you'll get access to an indoor pool, a fitness center (kids 12 and under must be supervised by an adult), a whirlpool, a sauna, and a sun deck. Guest rooms feature granite vanities, high-speed Internet access, and sofas, some with pullout beds. Rooms especially good for families include connecting rooms (both double-bedded and king-size) and suites which offer a bedroom plus a sitting room with a sofa bed. The 30 East Café and Lounge has a breakfast buffet (with a special price of $7 for kids), lunch, dinner, and room service. There's no kids' menu, but most kids will be able to find something they like among the kid-friendly, sandwich-and-soup options on the regular menu.

30 E. Hubbard St. (at State St.), Chicago, IL 60611. ✆ **800/321-2211** or 312/329-2500. Fax 312/329-0293. www.marriott.com. 337 units. $119–$209 double; $159–$400 suite. Kids 18 and under stay free in parent's room. Rollaways and cribs free. AE, DC, DISC, MC, V. Valet parking $33 with in/out privileges; self-parking $21. Subway/El: Red Line to Grand/State. **Amenities:** Restaurant; lounge; indoor pool; exercise room; concierge; room service; laundry service and self-service laundry. *In room:* A/C, TV w/pay movies, dataport, high-speed Internet access, coffeemaker, hair dryer, iron.

Courtyard by Marriott Chicago Downtown/Magnificent Mile A half-block east of the Magnificent Mile, this hotel is not the place to indulge in luxuries. However, it's a great choice for families, with a killer location plus that rarest of rarities in downtown hotels: a pool, on the 10th floor. There's even a large fitness room with great views. Rooms here are generally larger than those at the Courtyard's sister hotel in River North. Double rooms with two beds feature two queen-size beds (not two double beds, which is standard in the industry)—a nice option for families of four. King suites have a kitchen with a refrigerator and microwave, plus a pullout couch in the living area. Rooms offer city views, some of Michigan Avenue. Another family-friendly feature in the room design is the shower and bathtub area, which is separate from the vanity and dressing area, a plus when multiple people are trying to get ready in the morning. The lobby decor is Art Deco, and the room decor is pretty standard; but everything is clean and new. An American cafe, Viand Bar & Kitchen, is kid-friendly and also provides room service. And when mom and dad need a pick-me-up, they can get a cup of coffee from the Starbucks in the lobby.

165 E. Ontario St. (just east of Michigan Ave.), Chicago, IL 60611. ✆ **312/573-0800.** Fax 312/573-0573. www.marriott.com. 306 units. $249 double; $309 king suite. Kids 18 and under stay free in parent's room. Rollaways and cribs free. AE, DC, DISC, MC, V. Valet parking $35 with in/out privileges; self-parking $25 with no in/out privileges. Subway/El: Red Line to Grand/State. **Amenities:** Restaurant; lounge; indoor pool; exercise room; concierge; room service; laundry service and self-service laundry. *In room:* A/C, TV w/pay movies, dataport, coffeemaker, hair dryer, iron.

Doubletree Chicago—Magnificent Mile ★★ ⓥⓐⓛⓤⓔ The soaring modern atrium lobby is impressive, as is the location east of the Magnificent Mile and close to the Ohio Street Beach and Navy Pier. Although the public spaces have the impersonal feel of a conference center, the rooms are cheerily decorated, and the large windows allow sweeping city views from the upper floors. (I recommend the rooms on the north side of the building, which look toward the Hancock Building.) But it's the amenities that help this hotel stand out, making it one of the best values in the city.

Fitness devotees will delight in the fact that the hotel adjoins the Lakeshore Athletic Club, where guests may enjoy the extensive facilities free of charge (including an indoor pool, fitness classes, and a sauna); you don't even have to go outside to get there. The hotel also has its own spacious outdoor pool and sun deck; in the summer you can sit back and enjoy a drink at the outdoor bar. (Be forewarned, however, that the hotel fills up during summer vacation; book as far in advance as possible for July–Aug). Rooms on the two Priority Floors include upgraded amenities, a daily newspaper, and feather pillows.

The Doubletree is a good bet for the budget-conscious family, as kids 17 and under stay free in their parent's room. Leave the pay-per-view movies one night and head to the massive AMC theaters next door, where all 21 screens offer stadium seating.

300 E. Ohio St. (at Fairbanks Court), Chicago, IL 60611. ℭ **312/787-6100.** Fax 312/787-6259. www. doubletreemagmile.com. 500 units. $109–$270 double. Rollaways $20; cribs free. AE, DC, DISC, MC, V. Self-parking $38. Subway/El: Red Line to Grand. **Amenities:** 2 restaurants (American, cafe); bar; outdoor and indoor pools; complimentary access to nearby health club w/whirlpool and sauna; concierge; business center; 24-hr. room service; babysitting; laundry room; dry cleaning; executive-level rooms. *In room:* A/C, TV w/pay movies and video games, high-speed Internet access, coffeemaker, hair dryer, iron, safe.

Four Points by Sheraton   Chicago Downtown/Magnificent Mile ★   This

hotel's location puts you and your kids in the heart of the action—just 1 block west of the heart of Michigan Avenue, with its shopping and great restaurants. You'll also be a block from the stop for the no. 151 bus, which will whisk you south to Millennium Park and the Art Institute, or the no. 146, the express bus that goes to Museum Campus. Hotel staff is friendly and accommodating to families: If American Girl Place is on your list of things to do, the hotel will provide miniature beds for your little girl's dolls. Rooms feature whirlpool tubs and flatscreen TVs—some come equipped with refrigerators and microwaves, so make sure to ask about those amenities. Families might want to book a junior suite with two double beds, which also provides a separate sitting area. The pool and whirlpool area is bright and airy. Room service comes from Lawry's Prime Rib, the venerable steakhouse across the street. At press time, room rates were quite reasonable— I've heard as low as $160 for a junior suite in the high season—and self parking is only $28, a bargain compared to many Magnificent Mile hotels.

630 N. Rush St. (just west of Michigan Ave.), Chicago, IL 60611. ℭ **312/981-6600.** www.starwoodhotels. com. 226 units. $185 double; $215 junior suite; $245 king suite. Kids 14 and under stay free in parent's room. Rollaways $25; cribs free. AE, DC, DISC, MC, V. Self-parking $28 with no in/out privileges. Subway/ El: Red Line to Grand/State. **Amenities:** Snack bar; indoor pool and whirlpool; fitness room; room service. *In room:* A/C, TV w/pay movies, free Internet access, fridge, microwave, coffeemaker, hair dryer, iron.

Hilton Garden Inn ★   Although it might seem out of place in these urban climes,

this Hilton Garden Inn, located on prime real estate between North Michigan Avenue and the River North neighborhood, is every inch a big-city player. The hotel caters to business types, but families certainly won't feel out of place here: The building is adjacent to ESPN Zone, a Virgin Megastore, and the Shops at North Bridge mall. The hotel offers weekend packages for families, so ask for current deals when you call. The hotel doesn't have much personality—the lobby is strictly business and feels cold. What the place does have going for it—besides location—is a high-rise sensibility that should appeal to families looking for an urban experience. The ample rooms are located between the 13th and the 23rd floors. Views higher up, especially on the east side and from corner suites facing north and south, afford dramatic vistas of the cityscape and skyline. The hotel's six suites include a parlor area, wet bar, and dining table, with possible connections to adjacent rooms.

10 E. Grand Ave. (at State St.), Chicago, IL 60611. ✆ **800/HILTONS** (445-8667) or 312/595-0000. Fax 312/595-0955. www.hilton.com. 357 units. $169–$309 double; $400–$700 suite. Kids 18 and under stay free in parent's room. Rollaways $20/night; cribs free. AE, DC, DISC, MC, V. Valet parking $34 with in/out privileges; self-parking $20 with no in/out privileges. Subway/El: Red Line to Grand/State. **Amenities:** Restaurant; lounge; indoor pool; fitness center w/Jacuzzi and sauna; concierge; business center; limited room service; babysitting; laundry service; same-day dry cleaning. In room: A/C, TV w/pay movies, dataport, fridge, coffeemaker, hair dryer, iron.

Homewood Suites ★   An excellent choice for families, this hotel offers a handy location and fresh, clean rooms with some nice extras. Because all of the rooms are suites with full kitchens, you can prepare your own meals, and there's plenty of room in the suite for everyone to spread out. Housed just off the Mag Mile in a sleek tower above retail shops, offices, and a health club—and adjacent to ESPN Zone—the hotel's design aesthetic is best described as "Italian Renaissance meets Crate & Barrel." Distressed-leather sofas, Mediterranean stone tile, wrought-iron chandeliers, and beaded lampshades adorn its sixth-floor lobby.

Rooms—one- and two-bedroom suites and a handful of double-double suites, which can connect to king suites—feature velvet sofas that are all sleepers, and the beds have big, thick mattresses. Each comes with a dining room table that doubles as a workspace, and decent-size bathrooms. The hotel provides a complimentary buffet breakfast and beverages and hors d'oeuvres every evening; there is also a free grocery-shopping service and free access to an excellent health club next door.

40 E. Grand Ave. (at Wabash St.), Chicago, IL 60611. ✆ **800/CALL-HOME** (225-5466) or 312/644-2222. Fax 312/644-7777. www.homewoodsuiteschicago.com. 233 units. $109–$359 2-room suite. Kids 17 and under stay free in parent's room. Rollaways and cribs free. AE, DC, DISC, MC, V. Valet parking $35 with in/out privileges. Subway/El: Red Line to Grand/State. **Amenities:** Fitness room w/small pool and views of the city; concierge; business services; babysitting; laundry machines on all floors; dry cleaning. In room: A/C, TV w/pay movies, high-speed Internet access, kitchen, coffeemaker, hair dryer, iron.

Westin Chicago Michigan Avenue ★★   Located across the street from the John Hancock Center, this hotel is right on the Magnificent Mile, steps from Bloomingdale's and Water Tower Place. In past years the Westin looked a bit shabby, but renovations have spruced up the lobby, fitness center, and guest rooms. Rooms were recently renovated and feature a marble foyer, an expanded bathroom, and carpeting.

This hotel offers the Westin Kids Club for kids 12 and under. Other notable family amenities are the many baby and toddler accessories available to guests, from bottle warmers and cribs to night lights and electrical outlet covers. Kids are greeted with Westin Kids Club sports bottles or sippy cups, which are filled with complimentary beverages at meals. Also available are coloring books, bathtub toys, and a story line on the hotel phone that plays age-appropriate bedtime stories when you dial a four-digit number. The hotel restaurant will make sure kids' meals are ready when you arrive if you call in advance, and special menus are available through room service, too. Older kids can while away the hours with in-room PlayStations.

The Grill on the Alley, which serves American cuisine in a contemporary atmosphere, has been winning great reviews. You'll be comfortable bringing the kids here, and the kids' menu features pastas and burgers. A lobby cafe is a good stop for breakfast. The small fitness center is open to kids and includes free weights, treadmills, Lifecycles, and StairMasters, and men's and women's locker rooms feature saunas.

909 N. Michigan Ave., Chicago, IL 60611. ✆ **800/228-3000** or 312/943-7200. Fax 312/397-5580. www. thewestinmichiganavenue.com. 751 units. $179–$250 double; $600–$800 suite. Kids 18 and under stay free in parent's room. Rollaways $25/night; cribs free. AE, DC, DISC, MC, V. Valet parking $33 with in/out

INEXPENSIVE

Red Roof Inn Chicago Downtown ★ (Value)   This hotel is your best bet for the lowest-priced lodgings in downtown Chicago. The location is its main selling point: right off the Magnificent Mile (and within blocks of the Ritz-Carlton and Peninsula, where rooms will cost you at least four times as much). The guest rooms are stark and small (much like the off-the-highway Red Roof Inns), but the hotel makes continual efforts to update linens and room decor. Ask for a room facing Ontario Street, where you'll get western exposure and some natural light (rooms in other parts of the hotel look right into neighboring office buildings). For a family of three or four, go for the king suite, which has a sofa bed, microwave, and refrigerator. Room service is available through Coco Pazzo Café (p. 127), an excellent northern Italian restaurant around the corner from the hotel's front door.

162 E. Ontario St. (½ block east of Michigan Ave.), Chicago, IL 60611. (© **800/733-7663** or 312/787-3580. Fax 312/787-1299. www.redroof-chicago-downtown.com. 195 units. $100–$140 double; $110–$159 king suite. Kids 17 and under stay free in parent's room. No rollaways; cribs free. AE, DC, DISC, MC, V. Valet parking $28 with no in/out privileges. Subway/El: Red Line to Grand/State. **Amenities:** Business services; free morning coffee in lobby. *In room:* A/C, TV w/pay movies, dataport, hair dryer, iron.

---

4 RIVER NORTH

The name "River North" designates a vast area parallel to the Magnificent Mile. The zone is bounded by the river to the west and south, and roughly by Clark Street to the east and by Chicago Avenue to the north. The earthy red-brick buildings that characterize the area were once warehouses of various kinds and today form the core of Chicago's art-gallery district. The neighborhood also has spawned many of the city's trendiest restaurants. You'll find many of the city's family-friendly hotels here. That, coupled with the proximity of tourist draws such as the Hard Rock Cafe, Rainforest Café, and ESPN Zone, means River North is an area families should consider when booking a hotel.

EXPENSIVE

Embassy Suites Hotel Chicago—Downtown ★★   You might fancy yourself in Florida when you first set foot in this hotel, where a gushing waterfall and palm- and fern-lined landscaped ponds lie at the bottom of the huge central atrium. But you're not in the Tropics: You're in one of Chicago's most family-friendly hotels, even though it bills itself as a business hotel and does a healthy convention business. Accommodations are spacious enough for parents and kids: All guest rooms are suites, which have two rooms, consisting of a living room with a sleeper sofa, a round table, and four chairs; and a bedroom with either a king-size bed or two double beds. Guests staying on the VIP floor get nightly turndown service and in-room fax machines and robes. At one end of the atrium, the hotel serves a complimentary cooked-to-order breakfast and, at the other end, it supplies complimentary cocktails and snacks in the evening. And yes, there's a pool. On the weekends, step into the elevator and you'll find plenty of Chicago-area families with kids wrapped in towels making good use of the hotel as a weekend getaway.

Off the lobby is an excellent restaurant, Osteria Via Stato, and next door is a Starbucks outlet with outdoor seating.

Embassy Suites has a second downtown location at 511 N. Columbus Dr. (© **312/ 836-5900**), just a few blocks from Navy Pier. Highly recommended!

600 N. State St. (at W. Ohio St.), Chicago, IL 60610. © **800/EMBASSY** (362-2779) or 312/943-3800. Fax 312/943-7629. www.embassysuiteschicago.com. 366 units. $139–$279 king suite; $169–$319 double suite. Kids 17 and under stay free in parent's room. Few rollaways available, ask upon check-in (sofa beds in every suite); cribs free. AE, DC, DISC, MC, V. Valet parking $38 with in/out privileges. Subway/El: Red Line to Grand/State. **Amenities:** Restaurant (Italian); coffee bar; indoor pool; exercise room w/whirlpool; concierge; business center; limited room service; babysitting; laundry machines; dry cleaning. *In room:* A/C, TV w/pay movies and video games, high-speed Internet access, kitchenette, coffeemaker, hair dryer, iron.

Hotel Sax Chicago ★★

In 2007, a $17-million renovation transformed the former House of Blues Hotel into the new Hotel Sax Chicago, a luxury property with a bohemian boutique feel. While the lobby is certainly grand—with Italian marble floors and *trompe l'oeil* candelabras—the adjoining lounge, Crimson, goes for a Middle Eastern vibe, with exotic rugs, jewel-tone colors, and floor-to-ceiling screens and mirrors. This eclectic sensibility carries over to the guest rooms, which feature wingback chairs covered in snakeskin and side tables constructed entirely of mirrored panels. Despite the eye-catching decor, one of the hotel's biggest selling points remains its location in the entertainment-packed Marina Towers complex. Within steps of the hotel, you've got a bowling alley, a marina with boat rentals, the riverside Smith & Wollensky steakhouse (an outpost of the New York restaurant), the innovative Bin 36 wine bar and restaurant, and the House of Blues music hall and restaurant (p. 272; don't miss its gospel brunch on Sun).

333 N. Dearborn St. (at the river), Chicago, IL 60610. © **877/569-3742** or 312/245-0333. Fax 312/923-2444. www.hotelsaxchicago.com. 353 units. $269–$449 double; $629–$849 suite. Kids 18 and under stay free in parents' room. Rollaways $20/night; cribs free. AE, DC, DISC, MC, V. Valet parking $40 with in/out privileges. Subway/El: Brown Line to Clark/Lake, or Red Line to Grand. Pets accepted. **Amenities:** Lounge; access to Crunch fitness center for $15/day; concierge; business center; 24-hr. room service; babysitting; laundry service; same-day dry cleaning. *In room:* A/C, TV w/pay movies and video games, Wi-Fi, minibar, coffeemaker, hair dryer, iron, safe, multiline telephone.

Westin Chicago River North ★★★

Located on the northern bank of the Chicago River, the Westin River North has the personality of a business hotel but has made an effort to be family-friendly. Especially notable are the many baby and toddler accessories available to guests, from bottle warmers and cribs to night lights, jogging strollers, and electrical-outlet covers. Like the Westin Michigan Avenue (reviewed in the previous section), this hotel offers the Westin Kids Club for kids 12 and under. Kids are greeted with Westin Kids Club sports bottles or sippy cups, which are filled with complimentary beverages at meals. Other perks include coloring books, bathtub toys, and a story line on the hotel phone that plays age-appropriate bedtime stories when you dial a four-digit number. Kids' meals are available at the hotel restaurant with advance notice, and special menus are available through room service.

Rooms are handsome, and the whole hotel has a slight Japanese feel to it (years ago, it was the Japanese-owned Hotel Nikko), with a Zen rock garden at the rear of the lobby; the lobby's Hana Lounge also offers a sushi menu. Rooms are handsome, with furniture and artwork that give them a residential feel. For the best view, request a room facing south, overlooking the Chicago River. For those who feel like splurging, a suite on the

19th floor more than satisfies, with three enormous rooms, including a huge bathroom and a large window offering a side view of the river.

320 N. Dearborn St. (on the river), Chicago, IL 60610. ℭ 800/WESTIN1 (937-8461) or 312/744-1900. Fax 312/527-9650. www.westinchicago.com. 424 units. $199–$350 double; $400–$2,800 suite. Kids 18 and under stay free in parent's room. Rollaways $25/night; cribs free. AE, DC, DISC, MC, V. Valet parking $39 with in/out privileges; self-parking $16. Subway/El: Brown, Orange, or Green Line to State/Lake. **Amenities:** Restaurant (contemporary American); lounge; fitness center; concierge; business center; 24-hr. room service; babysitting; laundry service; same-day dry cleaning. *In room:* A/C, TV w/pay movies and video games, fax, high-speed Internet access, minibar, coffeemaker, hair dryer, iron, safe.

MODERATE

Best Western River North Hotel (Value)   This former motor lodge and cold-storage structure conceals a very attractive, sharply designed interior that scarcely resembles any Best Western in which you're likely to have spent the night. One of the few hotels located right in the midst of one of the busiest nightlife and restaurant zones in the city, it lies within easy walking distance of interesting boutiques and Chicago's art-gallery district. Rooms are spacious, and the bathrooms are spotless (though no-frills). One-room suites have a sitting area, while other suites have a separate bedroom; all suites come with a sleeper sofa (the Family Suite has two separate bedrooms and two bathrooms). A big selling point for families is the indoor pool, with an adjoining outdoor roof deck (a smallish fitness room looks out onto the pool). The Best Western's reasonable rates will appeal to families on a budget—and the almost-unheard-of free parking can add up to significant savings for anyone who drives here for a visit. There's a 2-night minimum for weekend stays May through October.

125 W. Ohio St. (at LaSalle St.), Chicago, IL 60610. ℭ **800/528-1234** or 312/467-0800. Fax 312/467-1665. www.rivernorthhotel.com. 150 units. $159–$199 double; $225–$295 suite. Kids 17 and under stay free in parent's room. Rollaways $10/night; cribs free. AE, DC, DISC, MC, V. Free parking for guests (1 car per room) with in/out privileges. Subway/El: Red Line to Grand/State. **Amenities:** Restaurant (pizzeria); lounge; indoor pool w/sun deck; exercise room; room service; laundry service; same-day dry cleaning. *In room:* A/C, TV w/pay movies and video games, high-speed and Wi-Fi Internet access, coffeemaker, hair dryer, iron, safe.

Hampton Inn & Suites Chicago—Downtown ★ (Value)   The Hampton, with its combination of rooms, two-room suites, and studios, is a smart choice for families. Kids will appreciate the indoor pool and in-room video games and VCRs after a busy day of sightseeing. You won't have far to go to find dinner: The Hard Rock Cafe and Rainforest Café are both a few blocks' walk away. Though built in 1998, the hotel still feels brand-new; the Prairie-style lobby and breakfast lounge give the place a tranquil feel. The rooms have an urban look, with dark wood furniture and plush duvets. Request a room overlooking Illinois or Dearborn streets if you crave natural light; most rooms don't offer much of a view. The standard rooms include a desk, an armchair and an ottoman; a studio has a microwave, sink and minifridge along one wall; and the apartment-style suites feature galley kitchens with fridges, microwaves, dishwashers, and cooking utensils, and a separate bedroom. Nice touches for families include a nightlight in the bathroom and clock radios with guides to local radio stations. You won't have to cook breakfast in your kitchenette—the hotel offers a complimentary breakfast buffet, with two hot items per day. Off the lobby is an Italian restaurant, and a second-floor skywalk connects to Ruth's Chris Steakhouse next door.

33 W. Illinois St. (at Dearborn St.), Chicago, IL 60610. ℭ **800/HAMPTON** (426-7866) or 312/832-0330. Fax 312/832-0333. www.hamptoninn.com. 230 units. $159–$199 double; $199–$309 suite. Kids 17 and under stay free in parent's room. Rollaways $10/night; cribs free. AE, DC, DISC, MC, V. Valet parking $38 with

in/out privileges. Subway/El: Red Line to Grand/State. **Amenities:** Restaurant (Italian); indoor pool w/ Jacuzzi and sun deck; exercise room w/sauna; business center; room service; laundry and dry-cleaning service. *In room:* A/C, TV w/pay movies and video games, high-speed Internet access, coffeemaker, hair dryer, iron, safe.

5 THE GOLD COAST

The Gold Coast begins approximately at Division Street and extends north to North Avenue, bounded on the west by Clark Street and on the east by the lake. The area encompasses a short strip of some of the city's priciest real estate along Lake Shore Drive. From the standpoint of social status, the streets clustered here are among the finest addresses in Chicago. It's a lovely neighborhood for a stroll among the graceful town houses and the several lavish mansions that remain relics from a glitzier past. The hotels here tend to be upscale without hitting the peak that some of the nearby Michigan Avenue hotels reach.

To locate these hotels, see the "Central Chicago Accommodations" map on p. 76.

EXPENSIVE

Ambassador East ★　The ring-a-ding glory days of the Ambassador East, when stars including Frank Sinatra, Humphrey Bogart, and Liza Minnelli shacked up here during layovers or touring stops in Chicago, are ancient history. But even though big-name celebs tend to ensconce themselves at the Peninsula or Park Hyatt these days, the Ambassador name still evokes images of high glamour in these parts. For the past 50 years, celebrities who have come to town to mingle with Chicago's Gold Coast society have done so most publicly from the revered Booth One in the ritzy Pump Room restaurant. Less pricey than the Peninsula or Park Hyatt, and located on a beautiful tree-lined street in the Gold Coast, the Ambassador East is a good choice for families looking for accommodations near, but not on, the Magnificent Mile.

The Ambassador still retains a sense of elegance, from the large floral arrangements in the lobby to the mahogany four-poster beds in the king-size rooms. Executive suites have separate sitting areas; celebrity suites (named for the stars who've crashed in them) come with a separate bedroom, two bathrooms, and a dining room. Most extravagant is the Presidential Suite, which has a canopied terrace, a marble fireplace and an oval dining room. One nod to modern times are the "Get Fit" rooms, which come with treadmills and a minibar stocked with healthy snacks.

1301 N. State Pkwy. (1 block north of Division St.), Chicago, IL 60610. ℂ **888/506-3471** or 312/787-7200. Fax 312/787-4760. www.theambassadoreasthotel.com. 285 units. $189–$299 double; from $400 suite. Kids 18 and under stay free in parent's room. Rollaways and cribs free. AE, DC, DISC, MC, V. Valet parking $34 with in/out privileges. Subway/El: Red Line to Clark/Division. **Amenities:** Restaurant (contemporary American); small fitness room; concierge; business center; 24-hr. room service; babysitting; 24-hr. laundry service; dry cleaning. *In room:* A/C, TV w/pay movies, high-speed Internet access, minibar, coffeemaker, hair dryer, iron, safe.

MODERATE

Hotel Indigo ★ (Finds　An accessible version of the boutique hotel concept, the Indigo is perfect for families with older kids looking for a cool (but not too edgy) alternative to the cookie-cutter chain hotel. The bright, beachy decor makes the place feel more like a tropical resort than an urban hotel; the small lobby has oversize Adirondack chairs

and walls painted in shades of blue, peach, and green, and pineapple-shaped chairs line
the bar.

But it's the guest rooms that really make an impact. Rather than the dark wood furniture and generic carpeting found in so many chain hotels, rooms here are light and bright with blonde hardwood floors and white wood furniture. Walls have splashes of bright color and giant photomurals of seashells, fruit, and other "relaxing" images. Because this is a conversion of an older property, room sizes vary. The king rooms on the north side of the building tend to be larger (with separate entry halls and sitting areas), but they also look out on neighboring buildings (and, in some cases, the fire escape). If you don't need a lot of room to spread out, the queen rooms (on the south side of the building) are small but have lovely views of downtown and plenty of natural light. Bathrooms have glass-walled shower stalls (no tubs, thus my recommendation that this hotel is best suited to families with older children only) and spa-style shower heads; they're fairly small, but have lots of storage space (multiple wall hooks and a granite storage ledge above the sink). There are also three suites, which have separate sitting rooms and working fireplaces.

Hotel Indigo won't overwhelm you with facilities; the hotel's restaurant and bar are both quite small, but there's a decent-size fitness room and—very unusual in a hotel of this size—a salon/spa with separate facial and massage treatment rooms. Though Hotel Indigo is tucked on a residential street, it's close to restaurants and shopping, and within walking distance of Michigan Avenue, Division Street, and Lincoln Park's many attractions. The surrounding neighborhood of elegant town houses makes a great place for a stroll—without the traffic and noise of other downtown neighborhoods.

1244 N. Dearborn St. (1 block north of Division St.), Chicago, IL 60610. © **866/2-INDIGO** (246-3446) or 312/787-4980. Fax 312/787-4069. www.goldcoastchicagohotel.com. 165 units. $169–$269 double. Kids 18 and under stay free in parents' room. Rollaways $20/night; cribs free. AE, DC, DISC, MC, V. Valet parking $35 with in/out privileges. Subway/El: Red Line to Clark/Division. Pets accepted. **Amenities:** Restaurant (American); lounge; exercise room; spa services; concierge; business center; room service; same-day dry cleaning. *In room:* A/C, TV w/pay movies and video games, high-speed and WI-FI Internet access, coffeemaker, hair dryer, iron, safe.

---

6 LINCOLN PARK & THE NORTH SIDE

If you prefer the feel of living amid real Chicagoans in a residential neighborhood, several options await you in Lincoln Park and farther north. Not only do these hotels tend to be more affordable than those closer to downtown, but they also provide a different vantage point from which to view Chicago. If you stay at the Majestic Hotel or the City Suites Hotel, for example, you can join the locals on a pedestrian pilgrimage to Wrigley Field for a Cubs game. The area is flush with restaurants, and public transportation via the El or buses is a snap.

EXPENSIVE

The Belden-Stratford ★ Finds   This north-side hotel is a great option for families who want to do as the natives do in a neighborhood atmosphere. Actually a condominium building that offers 25 hotel rooms, the two-story lobby feels grandly European, and paneled entry doors lead the way to airy rooms with 9-foot-high ceilings, crown molding, and plush carpeting. Rooms are large, the doorman greets you as if you were a resident, and Lincoln Park, where kids can run free, is across the street. You are right across from

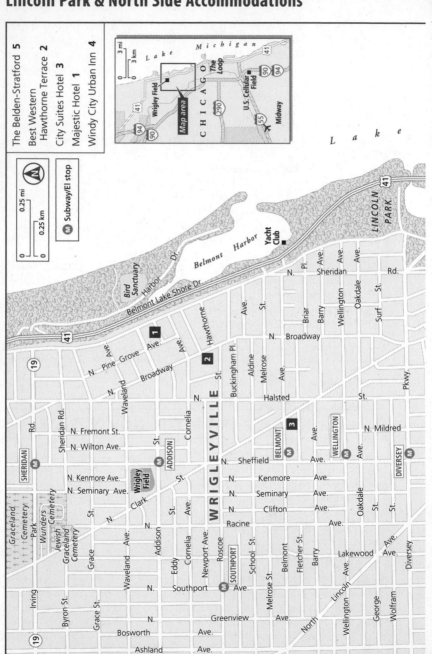

The Belden-Stratford **5**
Best Western
Hawthorne Terrace **2**
City Suites Hotel **3**
Majestic Hotel **1**
Windy City Urban Inn **4**

Ⓜ Subway/El stop

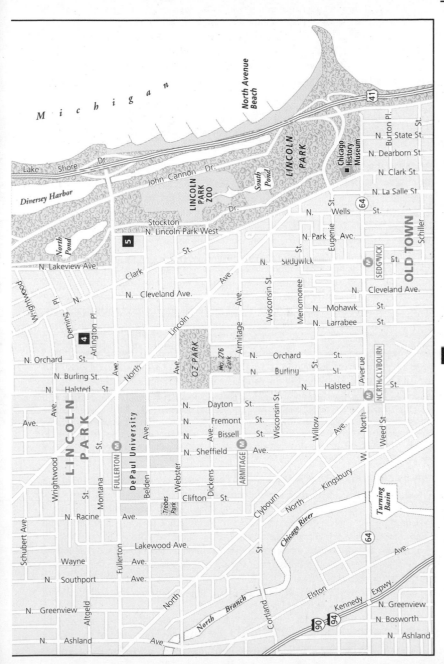

the Lincoln Park Zoo and the Conservatory, and steps from the lake and buses that will take you downtown in a matter of minutes.

Be sure to ask for a room with a park view so that you can watch runners pass and couples stroll. (Some rooms feature wraparound views with south, west, and east exposures.) Even though it's a condominium building, there's maid and valet service and a rooftop sun deck. One downside: Because the Belden-Stratford is not a full-service hotel, there's no room service or concierge.

2300 N. Lincoln Park W., Chicago, IL 60614. © **800/800-6261** or 773/281-2900. Fax 773/880-2039. www. beldenstratford.com. 25 units. $209–$299 double. Kids 17 and under stay free in parent's room. Rollaways $20/night; cribs free. AE, DC, DISC, MC, V. Valet parking $25 with in/out privileges. Subway/El: Red Line to Fullerton. **Amenities:** Fitness center; spa; salon; coin-op laundry. In room: A/C, TV; hair dryer and iron upon request.

MODERATE

Best Western Hawthorne Terrace ★ ⓥalue   A fantastic bargain for families who don't mind staying a bit north of the beaten track, this hotel offers plenty of space for a great price. Located in Lakeview—within walking distance of Wrigley Field, Lake Michigan, and the Lincoln Park walking and bike paths—the hotel is set back from busy Broadway Avenue, thanks to a charmingly landscaped terrace (a good spot to enjoy your complimentary continental breakfast when the weather's nice). Inside, the relatively large rooms—decorated in standard motel decor—won't win extra style points, but most are bright and cheery, with spotless bathrooms (another plus: many rooms have two windows, a bonus if you crave natural light). Junior suites provide a room with two double beds, and an adjoining living room with a pullout couch; families of four will fit comfortably in one of these suites, which can also accommodate a crib. The spacious "Whirlpool King" rooms come with whirlpool bathtubs, DVD players, pay-per-view movies, and great views out onto the street. The ground-level exercise room is especially welcoming, with large windows to let light in and a glass-enclosed hot tub. Best of all? Parking is a bargain at $20 a day—about half the going rate of most downtown hotels.

3434 N. Broadway (at Hawthorne Place), Chicago, IL 60657. © **888/401-8781** or 773/244-3434. Fax 773/ 244-3435. www.hawthorneterrace.com. 59 units. $149–$229 double and suites. Rates include continental breakfast. Kids 12 and under stay free in parent's room. Rollaways free (sofa beds provided in junior suites); cribs free. AE, DC, DISC, MC, V. Valet parking $20 with in/out privileges. Subway/El: Red Line to Belmont. **Amenities:** Exercise room w/hot tub and sauna; concierge; business services; same-day dry cleaning. In room: A/C, TV w/pay movies, free Wi-Fi, fridge, microwave, coffeemaker, hair dryer, iron.

Windy City Urban Inn ★★ ⒻInds   Children over the age of 10 are welcome at this grand 1886 home, located on a tranquil side street just blocks away from busy Clark Street and Lincoln Avenue—both chock-full of shops, restaurants, and bars. The inn is charming enough, but the true selling point of the Windy City Inn is hosts Andy and Mary Shaw. He's a well-known political reporter, and she has 20 years of experience in the Chicago bed-and-breakfast business. Together, they are excellent resources for anyone who wants to get beyond the usual tourist sites. Subtle Chicago touches give guests a distinctive experience: Blues and jazz play during the buffet breakfast, and local food favorites offered to guests include the famous cinnamon buns from Ann Sather's restaurant and beer from Goose Island Brewery.

The remodeled building has a more open feel than the typical Victorian home. The five rooms in the main house and three apartments in a coach house are each named after Chicago writers. Families should choose one of the two coach-house apartments that can sleep four: two in an upstairs bedroom and two on a bed that folds up against the wall. (Custom-made for the Shaws, these feature top-quality mattresses, making them much more comfortable than the Murphy beds of old.) These apartments have kitchens and are wonderfully cozy with their fireplaces and Jacuzzi tubs.

In good weather, guests are invited to eat breakfast on the back porch or in the garden between the main house and the coach house. There, you can sit back and imagine that you're living in your very own Chicago mansion—the type of home that many Chicagoans wish they could live in themselves.

607 W. Deming Place, Chicago, IL 60614. (C) **877/897-7091** or 773/248-7091. Fax 773/529-4183. www. windycityinn.com. 8 units. $125–$255 double; $175–$325 coach-house apts. Rates include buffet breakfast. Kids 10–18 stay free in parent's room (coach-house apts only). No rollaways or cribs. AE, DC, DISC, MC, V. Parking $6 in nearby lot with in/out privileges. Subway/El: Red Line to Fullerton. **Amenities:** Laundry machines. In room: A/C, TV, Wi-Fi, kitchenette.

INEXPENSIVE

City Suites Hotel (**Value**)   A few doors down from the El stop on Belmont Avenue, this charming small hotel has a 1930s Art Deco aesthetic, and feels more along the lines of an urban bed-and-breakfast than a big hotel. Most rooms are suites, with separate sitting rooms and bedrooms, all furnished with first-rate pieces and decorated in a homey and comfortable style. Families should ask about the king suite, with a king-size bed and sitting area with sofa bed; they can also accommodate a crib. The amenities are excellent for a hotel in this price range, including plush robes and complimentary continental breakfast. Families will be happy to know that fridges and microwaves are available upon request in suites.

A bonus—or drawback, depending on your point of view—is the hotel's neighborhood setting. Most rooms can be fairly noisy; those facing north overlook Belmont Avenue, where nightlife continues into the early-morning hours, and those facing west look right out over rumbling El tracks. On your way in and out of the hotel, you'll mingle with plenty of locals, from young professional families to gay couples to punks in full regalia. Blues bars, nightclubs, and restaurants abound hereabouts, making the City Suites a find for the bargain-minded and adventuresome. Room service is available from Ann Sather, a Swedish diner and neighborhood institution (p. 149).

933 W. Belmont Ave. (at Sheffield Ave.), Chicago, IL 60657. (C) **800/248-9108** or 773/404-3400. Fax 773/ 404-3405. www.cityinns.com. 45 units. $149–$249 double; $199–$409 suite. Rates include continental breakfast. Kids 12 and under stay free in parent's room. No rollaways (sofa beds in suites); cribs free. AE, DC, DISC, MC, V. Parking $22 in nearby lot with in/out privileges. Subway/El: Red Line to Belmont. **Amenities:** Free access to Bally's health club 5 blocks away; concierge; limited room service; laundry service; same-day dry cleaning. In room: A/C, TV, free Wi-Fi, hair dryer, iron.

Majestic Hotel ★★ (**Finds**)   Owned by the same group as the City Suites Hotel, the Majestic blends seamlessly into its residential neighborhood. Located on a charming tree-lined street (but convenient to the many restaurants and shops of Lincoln Park), the hotel welcomes kids with open arms. Guests receive a complimentary continental breakfast and afternoon cookies in the lobby. Some of the larger suites—the most appealing are those with sun porches—offer butler's pantries with a fridge, microwave, and wet bar. Families should ask about the two-room king suite, which includes a bedroom with king-size bed, a living room with a sofa bed, and a kitchenette with refrigerator and microwave. Other than the larger suites, many of the rooms are fairly dark because you're surrounded by apartment buildings on almost all sides. Avoid the claustrophobic single rooms with alley views. The hotel is ideally suited for enjoying the North Side and is only a short walk from both Wrigley Field and the lake.

528 W. Brompton St. (at Lake Shore Dr.), Chicago, IL 60657. © **800/727-5108** or 773/404-3499. Fax 773/404-3495. www.cityinns.com. 52 units. $99–$179 double; $129–$219 suite. Rates include continental breakfast. Kids 11 and under stay free in parent's room; age 12 and over, $10 per person. No rollaways (sofa beds in suites); cribs free. AE, DC, DISC, MC, V. Self-parking $22 in nearby garage with no in/out privileges. Subway/El: Red Line to Addison; walk several blocks east to Lake Shore Dr. and then 1 block south. **Amenities:** Free passes to nearby Bally's health club; secretarial services; limited room service; laundry service; same-day dry cleaning. In room: A/C, TV w/pay movies, free Wi-Fi, minibar, coffeemaker, hair dryer, iron.

Blcfst

Billy Goat Tavern
Ann Sathers → Cubsgov
Cinn. Rolls

Snacks
Russian Tea

Lunch

Dim Sum
Hot Daugs

Dinner (3)

Uno/ Lou Malnoti's
Ed Debevics
Atwood

Pilsen—Mexican

Family-Friendly Dining

Chicago has come into its own as a major dining destination, and that's not limited to the chic, see-and-be-seen spots. Plenty of options await families, too. In addition to those stylish restaurants, you'll find an amazing array of steakhouses, family-style Italian restaurants, and just about every kind of ethnic cuisine you could possibly crave. You'll be surprised at the number and range of restaurants that welcome kids in Chicago. Even restaurants that don't offer a specialized kids' menu often will provide half-size portions for children. Whether you're looking for a restaurant for your family's big night out or simply a no-frills spot to dig in, in this chapter you'll find places the locals go to when they want to eat well.

It's not easy to narrow down the list of impressive restaurants in this city. For a thorough listing of those budget-busting spots that routinely make national best-of lists (Charlie Trotter's, Alinea, and Moto come to mind), you should check out *Frommer's Chicago*. I've listed a few of these special-occasion restaurants in case you get a sitter, but the focus here is on places that have wonderful food at more palatable prices, such as the wine bar Avec (which has attracted a loyal following of local foodies), River North's Osteria Via Stato, and Bucktown's homey Hot Chocolate—all of which are attracting diners by focusing on simple preparations and a fuss-free ambience.

Chicago's ethnic restaurants appeal to any price range, and are a highlight of the city's dining scene. Affordable (and attitude-free) restaurants still thrive in the city's original immigrant neighborhoods—Greektown, Little Italy, and Chinatown. For more on ethnic food, see the "Ethnic Dining near the Loop" box on p. 114.

A NOTE ABOUT PRICES Unfortunately, Chicago is no longer the budget-dining destination it once was, but just because prices have risen doesn't mean that attitudes have. Restaurants in Chicago might have become trendy, but they're still friendly.

I've divided restaurants in this chapter into three price categories: **"Expensive"** indicates that most entrees run from $18 to $25 (and sometimes more); **"Moderate"** means that most entrees are $20 or less; and at an **"Inexpensive"** place, they cost $15 or less.

Whether you're looking for a restaurant where you can blow your dining budget for the month, or simply a no-frills spot to dig in, these are the places the locals go when they want to eat well. To find out more about restaurants that have opened since this book went to press, check out the *Chicago Tribune*'s entertainment website (**www.metromix.com**), the websites for the monthly magazine *Chicago* (**www.chicagomag.com**) and the weekly *Time Out Chicago* (**www.timeoutchicago.com**), and the entertainment/nightlife website **http://chicago.citysearch.com**.

Note to smokers: The Chicago City Council has banned smoking in all restaurants; those with a separate bar area can allow smoking, but only if they have installed an air-filtration system.

1 RESTAURANTS BY CUISINE

Alsatian

Brasserie Jo ★ (River North, $$$, p. 130)

American

American Girl Place Cafe ★★★ (Magnificent Mile & the Gold Coast, $$$, p. 123)

Ann Sather ★★ (Wrigleyville & the North Side, $, p. 149)

Café Brauer ★ (Lincoln Park, $, p. 143)

Carson's ★ (River North, $$, p. 131)

Charlie's Ale House on Navy Pier ★ (Magnificent Mile & the Gold Coast, Lincoln Park, $, p. 129)

Cheesecake Factory (Magnificent Mile & the Gold Coast, $$, p. 126)

Dave & Buster's (River North, $, p. 135)

ESPN Zone (Magnificent Mile & the Gold Coast, $$, p. 127)

Goose Island Brewing Company (Wrigleyville, $$, p. 148)

Hard Rock Cafe (River North, $, p. 137)

Harry Caray's ★★ (River North, $$$, p. 131)

Hot Chocolate ★ (Wicker Park/ Bucktown, $, p. 152)

Jack Melnick's Corner Tap (Magnificent Mile & the Gold Coast, $$, p. 127)

John Barleycorn (Lincoln Park, $, p. 146)

John's Place ★★★ (Lincoln Park, $, p. 146)

Kitsch'n River North ★ (River North, $, p. 137)

Mr. Beef ★ (River North, $, p. 138)

Northside Café ★ (Wicker Park/Buck-town, $, p. 153)

Oak Street Beachstro ★ (Magnificent Mile & the Gold Coast, $$$, p. 125)

Oak Tree ★ (Magnificent Mile & the Gold Coast, $, p. 130)

O'Brien's Restaurant (Lincoln Park, $$$, p. 139)

O'Donovan's (Wrigleyville & the North Side, $, p. 149)

Park Grill ★ (the Loop, $$$, p. 111)

Petterino's ★ (the Loop, $$$, p. 116)

Piece ★ (Wicker Park/Bucktown, $, p. 153)

Rainforest Café (River North, $, p. 139)

South Water Kitchen ★ (the Loop, $$, p. 118)

Stanley's ★★ (Lincoln Park, $, p. 147)

Toast ★ (Lincoln Park, $, p. 147)

Asian

Big Bowl ★ (Magnificent Mile & the Gold Coast, $, p. 128)

Flat Top Grill (Lincoln Park, $, p. 146)

Penny's Noodle Shop ★ (Wrigleyville & the North Side, $, p. 149)

Barbecue

Carson's ★ (River North, $$, p. 131)

Twin Anchors ★ (Lincoln Park, $, p. 148)

Bistro

Bistro 110 ★★ (Magnificent Mile & the Gold Coast, $$, p. 126)

Breakfast

Ann Sather ★★ (Wrigleyville & the North Side, $, p. 149)

Billy Goat Tavern ★ (Magnificent Mile & the Gold Coast, $, p. 128)

FAMILY-FRIENDLY DINING

5

RESTAURANTS BY CUISINE

Bourgeois Pig ★ (Lincoln Park, $, p. 143)

Corner Bakery (Magnificent Mile & the Gold Coast and citywide, $, p. 129)

House of Blues (River North, $$, p. 132)

Lou Mitchell's ★★ (the Loop, $, p. 120)

Oak Tree ★ (Magnificent Mile & the Gold Coast, $, p. 130)

Toast ★ (Lincoln Park, $, p. 147)

Uncommon Ground ★ (Wrigleyville & the North Side, $, p. 150)

Wishbone ★★★ (West Loop, $$, p. 122)

Burgers

Billy Goat Tavern ★ (Magnificent Mile & the Gold Coast, $, p. 128)

Ed Debevic's ★ (River North, $, p. 135)

Green Door Tavern (River North, $, p. 137)

John Barleycorn (Lincoln Park, $, p. 146)

Northside Café ★ (Wicker Park/Bucktown, $, p. 153)

Cajun/Creole

Heaven on Seven ★★ (the Loop, $, p. 119)

House of Blues (River North, $$, p. 132)

Wishbone ★★★ (West Loop, $$, p. 122)

Continental

Bistro 110 ★★ (Magnificent Mile & the Gold Coast, $$, p. 126)

Diner

Ed Debevic's ★ (River North, $, p. 135)

Heaven on Seven ★★ (the Loop, $, p. 119)

Lou Mitchell's ★★ (the Loop, $, p. 120)

Manny's Coffee Shop & Deli ★ (near the Loop, $, p. 120)

Nookies (Lincoln Park, $, p. 147)

Silver Cloud Bar & Grill ★ (Wicker Park/Bucktown, $, p. 153)

Eclectic

Atwood Cafe (the Loop, $$$, p. 111)

foodlife ★★ (Magnificent Mile & the Gold Coast, $, p. 129)

Jane's ★ (Wicker Park/Bucktown, $$, p. 152)

Oak Street Beachstro ★ (Magnificent Mile & the Gold Coast, $$$, p. 125)

Fondue

Geja's Café ★ (Lincoln Park, $$$, p. 139)

French

Brasserie Jo ★ (River North, $$$, p. 130)

La Creperie ★★ (Lincoln Park, $, p. 146)

Greek

Artopolis (Greektown, $, p. 115)

Athena (Greektown, $$, p. 115)

Costas (Greektown, $$, p. 115)

Greek Islands (Greektown, $$, p. 115)

Parthenon (Greektown, $$, p. 115)

Pegasus (Greektown, $$, p. 115)

Santorini (Greektown, $$, p. 115)

Hot Dogs

Fluky's (Magnificent Mile & the Gold Coast, $, p. 155)

Gold Coast Dogs (Magnificent Mile & the Gold Coast, $, p. 155)

Hot Doug's (Logan Square, $, p. 155)

Murphy's Red Hots (Wrigleyville, $, p. 155)

Portillo's (River North, $, p. 155)

Superdawg Drive-In (Far North Side, $, p. 155)

The Wieners Circle (Lincoln Park, $, p. 155)

Buca di Beppo (River North, $$, p. 131)

Club Lucky ★★ (Wicker Park/ Bucktown, $$, p. 152)

Coco Pazzo Café ★ (Magnificent Mile & the Gold Coast, $$, p. 127)

Harry Caray's ★★ (River North, $$$, p. 131)

La Cantina Enoteca (the Loop, $$, p. 117)

Leona's (Lincoln Park, $, p. 142)

Maggiano's ★ (River North, $$, p. 133)

Mia Francesca (Wrigleyville, $$, p. 149)

Osteria Via Stato ★★ (River North, $$, p. 134)

The Rosebud ★★ (near the Loop, $$, p. 118)

Scoozi ★ (River North, $$, p. 134)

Tufano's Vernon Park Tap (near the Loop, $, p. 121)

Tuscany ★ (near the Loop, $$$, p. 117)

The Village ★ (the Loop, $$, p. 118)

Vivere ★ (the Loop, $$, p. 119)

Japanese

Kabuki (Lincoln Park, $$, p. 142)

Mirai Sushi ★★ (Wicker Park/Bucktown, $$$, p. 151)

Ron of Japan (Magnificent Mile & the Gold Coast, $$$, p. 126)

Sai Café ★ (Lincoln Park, $$, p. 142)

Mexican

El Jardin (Lincoln Park, $, p. 142)

Frontera Grill & Topolobampo ★★★ (River North, $, p. 136)

Middle Eastern

Reza's ★★ (River North, $$, p. 134)

Noodles

Penny's Noodle Shop ★ (Wrigleyville & the North Side, $, p. 149)

Pizza

California Pizza Kitchen (Magnificent Mile & the Gold Coast, $, p. 128)

Chicago Pizza & Oven Grinder (Lincoln Park, $, p. 154)

Edwardo's (Magnificent Mile & the Gold Coast, South Loop, and Lincoln Park, $, p. 154)

Gino's East ★★ (River North, $, p. 136)

Leona's (River North, $$, p. 154)

Leona's Pizzeria (Wrigleyville, $, p. 142)

Lou Malnati's Pizzeria ★ (River North, $, p. 154)

Piece ★ (Wicker Park/Bucktown, $, p. 153)

Pizzeria Due (River North, $, p. 138)

Pizzeria Uno ★ (River North, $, p. 138)

Ranalli and Ryan's (Lincoln Park, $, p. 154)

Russian/Tea

Russian Tea Time ★★ (the Loop, $$$, p. 116)

Sandwiches

Bourgeois Pig ★ (Lincoln Park, $, p. 143)

Corner Bakery (Magnificent Mile & the Gold Coast and citywide, $, p. 129)

Potbelly Sandwich Works (the Loop, $, p. 120)

Uncommon Ground ★ (Wrigleyville & the North Side, $, p. 150)

Seafood

La Cantina Enoteca (the Loop, $$, p. 117)

Southern

House of Blues (River North, $$, p. 132)

Wishbone ★★★ (West Loop, $$, p. 122)

Southwestern

Bandera (Magnificent Mile & the
Gold Coast, $$$, p. 123)

Spanish/Tapas

Cafe Iberico ★★ (River North, $,
p. 135)

Steakhouse

Mike Ditka's Restaurant ★★ (Magnif-
icent Mile & the Gold Coast, $$$,
p. 124)

Swedish

Ann Sather ★★ (Wrigleyville & the
North Side, $, p. 149)

2 THE LOOP

Chicago's business power center isn't exactly attuned to family dining—what you'll find here are corporate types on expense accounts. (Because of the area's business orientation, keep in mind that some of the downtown eateries are closed on Sun.) But in case you're going for a parents'-night-out blowout meal, or looking for sandwiches for the kids after spending the day touring the Loop's many attractions, I've got you covered in this section. The good news: Just west of the Loop, Little Italy offers inexpensive ethnic dining.

EXPENSIVE

Atwood Cafe ECLECTIC   Colorful and offbeat, this stylish eatery in the Hotel Burnham provides enough fun for kids, and enough sophistication for adults, all while serving up a fresh take on American comfort food. Tuck your family into a cozy ban-quette in one of the room's nooks and crannies, and take in the bustle of State Street from the comfort of your own table. Executive chef Heather Terhune plays around with global influences (most notably Asian and Southwestern) in appetizers such as calamari with graham cracker coating; ahi tuna and salmon tartar; and warm pistachio-crusted goat-cheese salad with roasted beets, honey, and orange zest vinaigrette. Recent entree selec-tions included maple-grilled pork chops with three-cheese macaroni; braised lamb shank with lemon zest-mint pesto; and spinach tagliatelle with bacon, peas, and shrimp in a garlic cream sauce. In the winter, try one of the signature potpies. Adults won't want to miss the mussels in a garlicky tomato sauce with crusty, grilled homemade bread. Ter-hune began as a pastry chef, so desserts are a highlight on Atwood Cafe's menu. Seasonal fruit is the basis for cobblers, trifles, and pies. Kids will love the decadent banana and white chocolate bread pudding—if they manage to save room for dessert.

1 W. Washington St. (at State St.). © **312/368-1900.** www.atwoodcafe.com. Kids' menu, highchairs, boosters. Reservations recommended. Main courses $18–$26; kids' menu $10. AE, DC, DISC, MC, V. Mon-Fri 7–10am; Sat 8–10am; Sun 8am–3pm; Mon–Sat 11:30am–3:45pm; Sun–Thurs 4:30–10pm; Fri–Sat 5–11pm. Subway/El: Red Line to Washington/State.

Park Grill ★ AMERICAN   Location, location, location—it's what sets Park Grill apart from all the other upscale comfort-food restaurants in town. Set in the middle of Millennium Park, along Michigan Avenue and Randolph Street, Park Grill makes a great stop after your family's late-afternoon stroll or before a summer concert at the Pritzker Music Pavilion (this is a popular preshow dinner spot, so definitely make a reservation). The dining room is simple but welcoming, with floor-to-ceiling windows along one wall that look out onto the Michigan Avenue skyline (you won't, alas, get a view of the park). Your kids should find plenty to like on the menu, which highlights American favorites, some prepared simply (pot roast, rotisserie chicken, pork chops), and others featuring a

THE LOOP FAMILY-FRIENDLY DINING

5

American Girl Place Café **12**
Artopolis **55**
Athena **53**
Atwood Café **49**
Bandera **36**
Big Bowl **5**
Billy Goat Tavern **38**
Bistro 110 **11**
Brasserie Jo **41**
Buca di Beppo **44**
Café Iberico **23**
California Pizza Kitchen **14**
Carson's **18**
Charlie's Ale House on Navy Pier **30**
Cheesecake Factory **10**
Coco Pazzo Café **32**
Corner Bakery **4**
Costas **56**
Dave & Buster's **6**
Ed Debevic's **22**
Edwardo's **3**
ESPN Zone **35**
Fluky's **37**
Foodlife **13**
Frontera Grill & Topolobampo **40**
Geja's Café **1**
Gino's East **21**
Gold Coast Dogs **39**
Greek Islands **53**
Green Door Tavern **20**
Hard Rock Cafe **26**
Harry Caray's **42**
Heaven on Seven **48**
House of Blues **43**

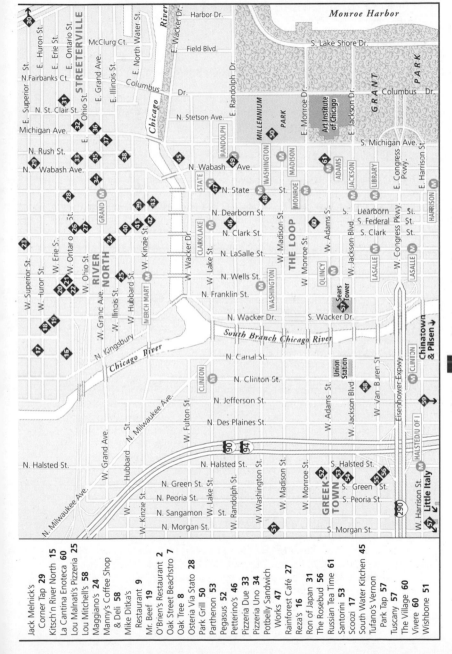

Jack Melnick's
  Corner Tap **29**
Kitsch'n River North **15**
La Cantina Enoteca **60**
Lou Malnati's Pizzeria **25**
Lou Mitchell's **58**
Maggiano's **24**
Manny's Coffee Shop
  & Deli **58**
Mike Ditka's
  Restaurant **9**
Mr. Beef **19**
O'Brien's Restaurant **2**
Oak Street Beachstro **7**
Oak Tree **8**
Osteria Via Stato **28**
Park Grill **50**
Parthenon **53**
Pegasus **52**
Petterino's **46**
Pizzeria Due **33**
Pizzeria Uno **34**
Potbelly Sandwich
  Works **47**
Rainforest Café **27**
Reza's **16**
Ron of Japan **31**
The Rosebud **56**
Russian Tea Time **61**
Santorini **53**
Scoozi **17**
South Water Kitchen **45**
Tufano's Vernon
  Park Tap **57**
Tuscany **57**
The Village **60**
Vivere **60**
Wishbone **51**

Ethnic Dining near the Loop

CHINATOWN

Chicago's Chinatown is about 20 blocks south of the Loop. The district is strung along two thoroughfares, Cermak Road and Wentworth Avenue as far south as 24th Place. Hailing a cab from the Loop is the easiest way to get here, but you can also drive and leave your car in the validated lot near the entrance to Chinatown, or take the Orange Line of the El to the Cermak stop, a well-lit station on the edge of the Chinatown commercial district.

The spacious, fairly elegant **Phoenix,** 2131 S. Archer Ave. (btw. Wentworth Ave. and Cermak Rd.; ② **312/328-0848**), has plenty of room for big tables of family or friends to enjoy the Cantonese (and some Szechuan) cuisine. A good sign: The place attracts lots of Chinatown locals. It's especially popular for dim sum brunch, so come early to avoid the wait. Late night, stop by the more casual **Saint's Alp Teahouse** downstairs (② **312/842-1886**), an outpost of the Hong Kong chain, which is open until midnight daily.

Penang, 2201 S. Wentworth Ave. (at Cermak Rd.; ② **312/326-6888**), serves mostly Malaysian dishes, but some lean toward Indian and Chinese (they've even added a sushi bar to complete the Pan-Asian experience). Sink your teeth into the *kambing rendang* (lamb curry in 11 spices) or the barbecued stingray wrapped in a banana leaf.

Open since 1927, **Won Kow,** 2237 S. Wentworth Ave. (btw. 22nd Place and Alexander St.; ② **312/842-7500**), is the oldest continually operating restaurant in Chinatown. You can enjoy dim sum in the mezzanine-level dining room from 9am to 3pm daily. Most of the items cost around $2. Other house specialties include Mongolian chicken and duck with seafood.

LITTLE ITALY

Convenient to most downtown locations, a few blocks' stretch of Taylor Street is home to a host of time-honored, traditional, hearty Italian restaurants. If you're staying in the Loop (an easy cab ride away), the area makes a good destination for dinner (I don't think it's worth a special trip if you're staying farther north—there are plenty of great Italian places elsewhere in the city).

Regulars return for the straightforward Italian favorites livened up with some adventurous specials at **Francesca's on Taylor,** 1400 W. Taylor St. (at Loomis St.; ② **312/829-2828**). I recommend the fish specials above the standard meat dishes. Other standouts include eggplant ravioli in a four-cheese sauce with a touch of tomato sauce and shaved parmigiana, as well as sautéed veal medallions with porcini mushrooms in cream sauce.

Expect to wait well beyond the time of your reservation at **Rosebud on Taylor,** 1500 W. Taylor St. (at Laflin St.; ② **312/942-1117**), but fear not—your hunger will be satisfied. Rosebud is known for enormous helpings of pasta, most of which lean toward heavy Italian-American favorites: deep-dish lasagna and a fettuccine Alfredo that defines the word "rich." I highly recommend any of the pastas served with vodka sauce. A newer location is near the Mag Mile at 720 N. Rush St. (② **312/266-6444**).

Tuscany, 1014 W. Taylor St. (btw. Morgan and Miller sts.; ✆ **312/829-1990**), is one of the most reliable Italian restaurants on Taylor Street. In contrast to the city's more fashionable Italian spots, family-owned Tuscany has the comfortable feel of a neighborhood restaurant. The menu features large portions of Tuscan pastas, pizzas, veal, chicken, and a risotto of the day. Specialties include anything cooked on the wood-burning grill and Tuscan sausage dishes. A second location is across from Wrigley Field at 3700 N. Clark St. (at Waveland Ave.; ✆ **773/404-7700**).

GREEKTOWN

A short cab ride from the Loop across the south branch of the Chicago River will take you to the city's Greektown, a row of moderately priced and inexpensive Greek restaurants clustered on Halsted Street between Van Buren and Washington streets. Many restaurants have wonderful outdoor seating and spectacular views of the city—plus, long tables of families and shouts of "Opa!" make quite a ruckus that will keep your kids entertained.

To be honest, there's not much here to distinguish one restaurant from the other: They're all standard Greek restaurants with similar looks and similar menus. That said, **Greek Islands,** 200 S. Halsted St. (at Adams St.; ✆ **312/782-9855**); **Santorini,** 800 W. Adams St. (at Halsted St.; ✆ **312/829-8820**); **Parthenon,** 314 S. Halsted St. (btw. Jackson and Van Buren sts.; ✆ **312/726-2407**); and **Costas,** 340 S. Halsted St. (btw. Jackson and Van Buren sts.; ✆ **312/263-0767**), are all good bets for gyros, Greek salads, shish kebabs, and the classic moussaka. On warm summer nights, opt for either **Athena,** 212 S. Halsted St. (btw. Adams and Jackson sts.; ✆ **312/655-0000**), which has a huge outdoor seating area, or **Pegasus,** 130 S. Halsted St. (btw. Monroe and Adams sts.; ✆ **312/226-3377**), with its rooftop patio serving drinks, appetizers, and desserts. Both have wonderful views of the Loop's skyline. **Artopolis,** 306 S. Halsted St. (at Jackson St.; ✆ **312/559-9000**), a more recent addition to the neighborhood, is a casual option offering up Greek and Mediterranean specialties, wood-oven pizzas, breads, and French pastries, all of them tasty.

PILSEN

Just south of the Loop and convenient to McCormick Place and Chinatown, Pilsen is a colorful blend of Mexican culture, artists and bohemians, and pricey new residential developments. The area's nascent restaurant scene is showing signs of life, but, for now, the local fare is decidedly casual.

Nuevo Leon, 1515 W. 18th St. (at Laflin St.; ✆ **312/421-1517**), is a popular Mexican restaurant serving the standard offerings. Across the street, **Playa Azul,** 1514 W. 18th St. (at Laflin St.; ✆ **312/421-2552**), serves authentic Mexican seafood dishes, salads, and soups.

On the more bohemian side, linger over a salad, sandwich, or refreshing fruit milkshake *(liquado)* at **Café Jumping Bean,** 1439 W. 18th St. (at Bishop St.; ✆ **312/455-0019**), or kick back with a cup of coffee at artsy **Café Mestizo,** 2123 S. Ashland Ave. (btw. 21st St. and Cermak Rd.; ✆ **312/942-0095**).

Tips **Chilling Out with an Italian Ice**

When in Little Italy, do as the Italians do: Cool off with an Italian ice. In a heat wave, **Mario's Italian Lemonade,** at 1068 W. Taylor St., has been the place to chill for 35 years. They're open from 11am to midnight from May to mid-September. Lemon is the most popular flavor, but piña colada, fruit cocktail, or chocolate might appeal to more adventurous kids.

more international twist, such as pappardelle pasta with littleneck clams, chorizo sausage, leeks, and basil. For lighter appetites, a number of salads and some thin-crust pizzas round out the menu. Lunch selections include a good mix of sandwiches—everything from Cajun chicken breast and barbecue beef to a smoked-salmon club and BLT with truffle mayonnaise—and a kids' menu includes the usual mac and cheese, spaghetti, chicken fingers, and more.

11 N. Michigan Ave. (at Madison St.). © **312/521-PARK.** Kids' menu, highchairs, boosters. Reservations recommended. Main courses $10–$21 lunch, $17–$41 dinner; kids' menu around $6. AE, DC, MC, V. Sun–Thurs 11am–10:30pm; Fri–Sat 11am–10:30pm. Subway/El: Red Line to Washington or Brown, Orange, Purple, or Green Line to Madison.

Petterino's ★ AMERICAN   Named for Arturo Petterino, maitre d' at the Pump Room in the days when it swarmed with celebrities, this restaurant re-creates the feeling of downtown dining in the 1940s and 1950s. Inside the Goodman Theatre building, Petterino's is a popular pre-theater option, so book a table in advance if you have to catch a show. Families will want to avoid the bar area, which does offer tables with great street views, but is often smoky. Go instead for the dining room, decorated in dark wood with red leather booths. The overall feel is relaxed rather than hyped-up. The straightforward menu is filled with classic American big-night-out favorites: veal chops, New York strip steak, slow-cooked beef brisket, and some fresh fish selections. Pastas include baked ravioli and fettuccine Alberto (a version of Alfredo with peas and prosciutto). Among the old-time appetizers, you'll find shrimp *de jonghe,* coated with garlic and bread crumbs, and an excellent tomato bisque soup. Kids can choose from half-orders of any of the pastas (the ravioli is a favorite), and the restaurant will make cheeseburgers, mashed potatoes, chicken sandwiches, and other kid favorites upon request. In keeping with the restaurant's entertainment connection, some dishes are named after local celebrities—a nicely done salad of chopped mixed greens and blue cheese is named for longtime *Sun-Times* columnist Irv Kupcinet. The lunch menu offers smaller versions of the dinner entrees, along with a good mix of salads and sandwiches.

150 N. Dearborn St. (at Randolph St.). © **312/422-0150.** www.leye.com. Highchairs, boosters. Reservations recommended. Main courses $9–$25 lunch, $10–$40 dinner; kids' menu about $10. AE, DC, DISC, MC, V. Mon–Thurs 11am–9pm; Fri 11am–11pm; Sat 11:30am–11pm; Sun 3–7pm. Subway/El: Red Line to Washington or Brown Line to State/Lake.

Russian Tea Time ★★ **Finds** RUSSIAN/TEA   Need a respite after touring the Art Institute of Chicago? Russian Tea Time is a popular spot, and is open the entire afternoon, making this the perfect stop for a midafternoon snack for your kids. This family-owned restaurant's extensive menu is like a tour through the cuisine of czarist Russia and the former Soviet republics (for Russian neophytes, all the dishes are well described). The atmosphere is old-world and cozy, with lots of woodwork and a friendly staff. Don't

worry about finding something your kids will like: There are plenty of options on the **117**
kids' menu, such as potato pancakes with applesauce, meatballs, and beef stroganoff.
Adults will want to start with blini with Russian caviar, or chilled smoked sturgeon; if
you can't decide, you can share a number of mixed appetizer platters. For main courses,
try the *kulebiaka* (meat pie with ground beef, cabbage, and onions); or roast pheasant
served with brandied prunes and a walnut, brandy, and pomegranate sauce.

77 E. Adams St. (btw. Michigan and Wabash aves.). ℭ 312/360-0000. www.russianteatime.com. Kids'
menu, highchairs, boosters. Reservations recommended. Main courses $15–$27; kids' menu about $6. AE,
DC, DISC, MC, V. Sun–Thurs 11am–9pm; Fri–Sat 11am–midnight (the restaurant sometimes closes earlier
during the summer months). Tea service daily 2:30–4:30pm. Subway/El: Brown, Purple, Green, or Orange
Line to Adams, or Red Line to Monroe or Jackson.

Tuscany ★ ITALIAN   Tuscany is one of the most reliable restaurants on Taylor Street,
which is Chicago's version of Little Italy, home to a host of time-honored, traditional,
hearty Italian restaurants. In contrast to the city's more fashionable Italian spots, family-
owned Tuscany has the comfortable feel of a neighborhood gathering place. Although the
food is of high enough quality to draw a fine-dining crowd, the unpretentious atmosphere
means you'll find big tables of families, so don't worry about disturbing the peace. As you
might expect, the extensive menu features the culinary fare of the Tuscany region, including
pastas, pizzas, veal, chicken, and a risotto of the day, and the portions are large. Specials
include anything cooked on the wood-burning grill and Tuscan sausage dishes. There's no
kids' menu, but half-orders are available. You'll find a second location in Wrigleyville, across
from Wrigley Field at 3700 N. Clark St. (at Waveland Ave.; ℭ 773/404-7700).

1014 W. Taylor St. (btw. Racine Ave. and Halsted St.). ℭ 312/829-1990. www.stefanirestaurants.com. Highchairs, boosters. Reservations recommended. Main courses $9–$27. AE, DC, DISC, MC, V. Mon–Fri 11am–
3:30pm; Mon–Thurs 5–11pm; Fri–Sat 5pm–midnight; Sun 2–9:30pm. Subway/El: Blue Line to Polk.

MODERATE

La Cantina Enoteca (Value ITALIAN/SEAFOOD   La Cantina is the most casual
and moderately priced of the three restaurants in the Italian Village. It makes the most
of its basement location by creating the feel of a wine cellar. During the day the restaurant attracts a daily regular clientele of lawyers, judges, and the like, many of whom eat
at the bar. During pre-theater dining hours, you'll find plenty of other families eating
here. Specializing in seafood, La Cantina offers at least five fresh varieties every day, plus
a fish soup appetizer, macaroni with scallops and shrimp in a garlic pesto sauce, and

---

Finds   The Italian Village

The building at 71 W. Monroe St. houses three separate Italian restaurants, collec-
tively known as the Italian Village, a downtown dining landmark. Each restaurant
has a unique take on Italian ambience and cooking; they also share an exemplary
wine cellar and fresh produce grown in a family garden. Each of the three restaurants in the Italian Village is detailed in this section. Families with young children
will be most comfortable at moderately priced La Cantina Enoteca; if you have
older kids, they might enjoy the atmospheric Village, designed to re-create a dining experience in the Italian countryside. Vivere is the most upscale of the three
restaurants.

seafood-filled ravioli. Nonseafood items include your basic pasta favorites (there are no surprises where the pasta is concerned—all the reliable standards are here) and some beef and veal dishes.

71 W. Monroe St. (btw. Clark and Dearborn sts.). ✆ **312/332-7005**. www.italianvillage-chicago.com. Sassy seats. Reservations recommended. Main courses $11–$25 lunch, $13–$32 dinner. AE, DC, DISC, MC, V. Mon–Fri 11:30am–4pm; Mon–Sat 5pm–midnight. Subway/El: Red or Blue Line to Monroe.

The Rosebud ★★ Ⓥ𝐚𝐥𝐮𝐞 ITALIAN   If you want a real Chicago dining experience, this is it: At Rosebud you'll be surrounded by locals, not tourists. The old-style, dark rooms are filled with families celebrating birthdays and older couples who have been coming here for years. If your kids are on the verge of a hunger meltdown, ask for some breadsticks to tide them over: You can expect to wait well beyond the time of your reservation. Rosebud is known for its enormous helpings of pasta, served up in massive white bowls. Expect to walk out with a doggie bag, or—even better—have your whole table share a few dishes. But the portions aren't just large, they're also delicious. Most pastas lean toward heavy Italian-American favorites: deep-dish lasagna and fettuccine Alfredo that defines the word "rich." But the menu has been hipped up with more modern takes on Italian cooking. Any of the pastas with vodka sauce are out of this world. Rosebud also offers pasta lovers five different *cavatelli* dishes, a house specialty, and a tempting selection of *secondi*—meat, fish, and poultry dishes.

If you don't feel like trekking to the original, Rosebud has another, trendier version just off the Mag Mile at 720 N. Rush St., at Superior Street (✆ **312/266-6444**).

1500 W. Taylor St. (1 block east of Ashland Ave.). ✆ **312/942-1117**. Highchairs, boosters. Reservations recommended, especially on Sat and Sun. Main courses $5.95–$13 lunch, $16–$30 dinner. AE, DC, DISC, MC, V. Mon–Thurs 11am–10:30pm; Fri 11am–11:30pm; Sat 5–11:30pm; Sun 4–10pm. Subway/El: Blue Line to Polk.

South Water Kitchen ★ AMERICAN   Although South Water Kitchen isn't breaking any new culinary ground, it deserves a mention as one of the few places in the Loop that welcomes kids while featuring food sophisticated enough for discerning moms and dads. The dining room evokes the spirit of an old-fashioned city saloon, and the menu goes the retro route as well. Entrees include modern twists on familiar favorites, including a grilled spiced pork tenderloin, with mac and cheese and sautéed spinach; 5-hour braised short ribs with garlic mashed potatoes; and a veal T-bone with sage bread pudding. The restaurant provides not only kids' menus but also games to keep the little ones occupied. Best of all, half the proceeds of all children's meals go to charity.

In the Hotel Monaco, 225 N. Wabash Ave. (at Wacker Dr.). ✆ **888/306-3507**. www.southwaterkitchen. com. Kids' menu, highchairs, boosters. Reservations accepted. Main courses $9–$19 lunch, $16–$26 dinner; kids' menu around $6. AE, DC, MC, V. Mon–Fri 7–10am and 11am–3pm; dinner 5–10pm nightly. Brunch 7am–2pm Sat–Sun. Subway/El: Red Line to State/Lake.

The Village ★ ITALIAN   Upstairs in the Italian Village is the Village, with its charming interpretation of alfresco dining in a small Italian town, complete with a midnight-blue ceiling, twinkling "stars," and banquettes tucked into private, cavelike little rooms. It's the kind of Pan-Chicago place where you might see one man in a tux and another in shorts. This is old-school Italian: eggplant parmigiana, a heavy fettuccine Alfredo that would send your cardiologist into fits, veal scaloppini, calves' liver, and, yes, even pizza. The food is good rather than great, but what sets the Village apart as a place for families is the bordering-on-corny faux-Italian atmosphere that will delight your kids, and an old-time waitstaff that somehow keeps up with the nonstop flow of patrons. The staff here are pros at handling pre-theater dining.

71 W. Monroe St. (btw. Clark and Dearborn sts.). (C) **312/332-7005**. www.italianvillage-chicago.com. Sassy seats. Reservations recommended (accepted for parties of 3 or more). Main courses (including salad) $9–$23 lunch, $13–$24 dinner. AE, DISC, MC, V. Mon–Thurs 11am–1am; Fri–Sat 11am–2am; Sun noon–midnight. Subway/El: Red or Blue Line to Monroe.

Vivere ★ ITALIAN   On the main floor of the Italian Village is Vivere, the Italian Village's take on gourmet cooking—and eye-catching design. The bold interior, with rich burgundies, textured walls, spiraling bronze sculptures, and fragmented mosaic floors, makes dining a theatrical experience. No spaghetti and meatballs here: The pasta dishes feature upscale ingredients, from the *pappardelle* with braised duck to the *agnolottini* filled with pheasant. Fresh fish is always on the menu (a recent entree selection was salmon with spiced carrot broth), along with a good selection of meats and game. Grilled venison medallions are served with foie gras ravioli, while roasted duck is accompanied by a potato terrine and sautéed spinach.

71 W. Monroe St. (btw. Clark and Dearborn sts.). (C) **312/332-4040**. www.italianvillage-chicago.com. Sassy seats. Reservations recommended. Main courses $13–$24 lunch, $16–$34 dinner. AE, DC, DISC, MC, V. Mon–Fri 11:30am–2:30pm; Mon–Thurs 5:30–10pm; Fri–Sat 5–11pm. Subway/El: Red or Blue Line to Monroe.

INEXPENSIVE

Heaven on Seven ★★ (Finds)   CAJUN/DINER   Kids will love the "every day is Mardi Gras" feel of this highly popular spot, a favorite of local office workers. Just check out the lunchtime crowd that packs the restaurant, located on the seventh floor of the Garland Building, across from Macy's. Chef/owner Jimmy Bannos's Cajun and Creole specialties come with a cup of soup, and include such Louisiana staples as red beans and rice, a catfish po' boy sandwich, and jambalaya. If your kids don't have a taste for Tabasco, the enormous coffee shop–style menu covers all the traditional essentials: grilled-cheese sandwiches, omelets, tuna—the works. Indulge in chocolate pecan pie or homemade rice pudding for dessert. Usually open only for breakfast and lunch, on the third Friday of the month, Heaven on Seven serves dinner from 5:30 to 9pm. Although the Loop original has the most character, a second Mardi Gras–infused location is found along the Mag Mile at 600 N. Michigan Ave. ((C) **312/280-7774**), adjacent to a cineplex; unlike the original location, it accepts reservations and credit cards and is open for dinner. I'd highly recommend the Mag Mile restaurant for kids, where you'll be in the company of many families.

111 N. Wabash Ave. (at Washington St.), 7th floor. (C) **312/263-6443**. www.heavenonseven.com. Kids' menu, highchairs, boosters. Reservations not accepted. Sandwiches $8–$12; main courses $10–$14; kids' menu around $6 (includes soda and an ice-cream sandwich). No credit cards. Mon–Fri 8:30am–5pm; Sat 10am–3pm; 3rd Fri of each month 5:30–9pm. Subway/El: Red Line to Washington/State.

(Moments)   **Watching the World Float By from Chicago's Riverwalk**

The outdoor cafes along the banks of the Chicago River's main branch, between Wabash Avenue and Wells Street, are run by restaurants that change from year to year. But food is almost an afterthought: Kids will thrill to the parade of schooners and speedboats cruising along the Chicago River on their way to Lake Michigan. Open seasonally.

Lou Mitchell's ★★ (**Finds**) BREAKFAST/DINER Lou Mitchell's is the genuine article and a Loop breakfast institution, located across the south branch of the Chicago River from the Loop, a block farther west than Union Station. A French food critic passing through Chicago rated Lou Mitchell's the number-one breakfast spot in America, home of the "five-star breakfast." Quirky touches bound to amuse kids are everywhere: If the waiter discovers you're from out of town, don't be surprised if a table flag of your home state or country is plopped down on your table.

Don't worry about the line to get in; female patrons get boxes of Milk Duds, and everyone gets free donut holes while waiting. Turnover is continuous and service efficiently attentive. If your kids are old enough, you might shorten the wait for a table by grabbing a counter seat. One specialty here is the airy omelets served in sizzling skillets; you'll double your pleasure (and cholesterol) with Mitchell's use of double-yolk eggs. Orders arrive with thick slabs of toasted Greek bread and homemade marmalade. You might also have the best bowl of oatmeal you've ever eaten—deliciously creamy. Orange juice and grapefruit juice are freshly squeezed. At the end of your meal, a small paper cup of vanilla soft-serve ice cream will be offered up, gratis. If you eat breakfast here, you'll likely be full enough to make it practically to dinner without even noticing that you missed a meal.

565 W. Jackson Blvd. (at Jefferson St.). (𝄐 **312/939-3111.** Highchairs, boosters. Reservations accepted for groups of 8 or more. Breakfast items $1.95–$6.95. No credit cards. Mon–Sat 5:30am–3pm; Sun 7am–3pm. Subway/El: Blue Line to Clinton.

Manny's Coffee Shop & Deli ★ (**Value**) DINER If your itinerary includes a trip back in time, make sure you visit Manny's, a South Side institution since 1942. Kid highlights include spaghetti, beef stew, rice pudding, German chocolate cake, and the occasional special, from franks and beans to chop suey. Adults can grab a tray and navigate the fast-moving line. Even if they go for more standard fare, kids will be awed by the carving station known for its enormous corned-beef sandwiches (about half a pound), Reubens, world-class hot pastrami, and steamship rounds the size of VW Beetles. Gruff yet friendly staff in paper hats take their métier seriously, and the effect—and the food— is absolutely reassuring. Seat yourself and snarf down knishes, borscht, liver and onions, meatloaf, tongue, and stewed prunes. Introduce your kids to the old-fashioned joys of cream soda and Green River.

1141 S. Jefferson St. (𝄐 **312/939-2855.** www.mannysdeli.com. Highchairs, boosters. Reservations not accepted. Main courses $4.95–$8.95. No credit cards. Mon–Sat 5am–4pm. Subway/El: Red Line to Roosevelt.

Potbelly Sandwich Works (**Value**) SANDWICHES Ask a Chicagoan where to go for a great sandwich, and she'll invariably point the way to Potbelly. Yes, there's a potbellied stove inside, as well as a player piano and other Old West saloon-type memorabilia, but go here for the mouthwatering made-to-order sandwiches. (That's basically the entire menu.) Prepared on homemade sub rolls stuffed with turkey, Italian meats, veggies, pizza ingredients, and more, and layered with lettuce, tomato, onion, pickles, and Italian seasonings, they're warmed in a countertop toaster oven. Even with all the fixin's, each is around $6. Tempting milkshakes keep the blender mighty busy, and a guitarist entertains over the lunch hour. Potbelly has nearly 20 other locations throughout the city, including one in The Shops at North Bridge, 520 N. Michigan Ave. ((𝄐 **312/527-5550**), that is convenient for Loop and Magnificent Mile sightseers and shoppers.

190 N. State St. (at Lake St.). (𝄐 **312/683-1234.** Highchairs, boosters. Reservations not accepted. Main courses under $9. No credit cards. Mon–Fri 10am–9pm; Sat 10am–7pm; Sun 11am–6pm. Subway/El: Red Line to State.

Tips **Suburban Safaris**

If you have access to a car, you'll want to explore suburban Chicago's highways and byways. These restaurants alone are worth a special trip:

- **Phil Smidt's,** 1205 N. Calumet Ave., Hammond, IN (© **800/376-4534**). Northwest Indiana is just a hop, skip, and jump across the Chicago Skyway (and close to the Indiana gambling boats). The fried perch dinners (all-you-can-eat, a boon for families with growing kids) will make your kids reconsider their preference for frozen fish sticks. For dessert, try the tart gooseberry pie. Closed on Monday.

- **White Fence Farm,** 1376 Joliet Rd., Romeoville, IL (© **630/739-1720;** www.whitefencefarm.com). For the best fried chicken north of the Mason-Dixon line, Chicagoans in the know head to White Fence Farm. And what better kid-pleaser than a fried chicken dinner with all the fixings?

- **Robinson's No. 1 Ribs,** 940 Madison St., Oak Park, IL (© **708/383-8452;** www.rib1.com). Backyard Chef Charlie Robinson parlayed a win in the late Chicago journalist Mike Royko's first annual rib cook-off into this large and extremely popular venue. After a day touring the Oak Park's architectural gems, go lowbrow and dive right in to a plate of smoky ribs slathered in a secret sauce made with 17 herbs and spices.

- **Hecky's Barbecue,** 1902 Green Bay Rd., Evanston, IL (© **847/492-1182;** www.heckys.com). When in Evanston, do as the locals do and indulge at this rib joint. Since the place isn't big on atmosphere (there is a dining room, two doors down the street, so you must pick up your food and go), the best plan is to get dinner to go, head back to your hotel, and dive in (don't skimp on the napkins). Other specialties include hot pork links, chicken, and turkey drumsticks. If your travel plans don't include a visit to Evanston, head to Hecky's new Chicago branch, at 1234 N. Halsted St. (© **312/377-7427**).

- **Homer's Ice Cream,** 1237 Green Bay Rd., Wilmette, IL (© **847/251-0477;** www.homersicecream.com). Homer's is the kind of place where you feel good about feeding your kids burgers and ice cream. And in fact, Homer's is all about the ice cream, which is the best I've had. (Adults should try the cappuccino chip; kids go for peppermint stick or mint chocolate chip.) Seasonal flavors might include pumpkin in the fall, and prairie berry and peach in the summer. The burgers, hot dogs, and chicken sandwiches are fresh and grilled to order. The red-and-white signage outside and matching decor inside evoke good old ice-cream-parlor fun. Homer's is a convenient stop after a tour of the North Shore and a welcome relief from the usual fast food.

Tufano's Vernon Park Tap ITALIAN   Taking the family to the United Center to catch a Chicago Bulls game? Here's a great spot to fortify your family for the evening ahead. Located on the eastern edge of Little Italy, Tufano's is a popular place that's been family-owned for 60 years—and it's attracted neighborhood regulars as well as celebrities and politicians. (Check out the wall of photos that includes everyone from Tommy Lasorda to Dolly Parton.) The bar is a Chicago classic, and the cuisine is Italian. The traditional pasta dishes, Tufano's lemon chicken with potatoes and orange roughy with broccoli are always good bets. On the weekends, go for the homemade ravioli and cavatelli. On Friday, regulars choose the seafood salad.

1073 W. Vernon Park Place. (C) **312/733-3393.** Highchairs, boosters. Reservations not accepted. Menu items $7–$13. Cash only. Tues–Thurs 11am–10pm; Fri 11am–11pm; Sat 4–11pm; Sun 3–9pm. Subway/El: Blue Line to UIC/Halsted.

3 WEST LOOP

Much of the stretch of Randolph Street just west of the Chicago River—once known as the Market District—is about the "scene." And when traveling with kids, making the scene ranks pretty low. But you might want to make a trip to the West Loop just to dine at **Wishbone** or to experience **Greektown,** filled with cheap eats and noisy, boisterous restaurants where kids blend right in. In general, though, the West Loop feels like a neighborhood in transition; it's home to some of the city's coolest restaurants and clubs, but not much else.

Transportation to the West Loop is easy—it's about a $7 cab ride from Michigan Avenue or a slightly longer trek by bus (no. 8 or 9) or El, with stops at Halsted and Lake, a block from Randolph Street's "restaurant row." The walk from the Loop is pleasant and secure in the daytime, but at night I'd take a taxi.

MODERATE

Wishbone ★★★ BREAKFAST/CAJUN/SOUTHERN   This Southern-style restaurant has much to recommend it for families. First, it's a homegrown restaurant, not a chain, with a casual ambience. Second, children can be kept busy looking at the large and surrealistic farm-life paintings on the walls. The food is diverse enough that both adults and kids can find something to their liking, but there's also a menu geared just to children. The sprawling, loft-style space is quirky enough to be fun (plenty of folk art), but still relaxed and attitude free.

Known for Southern food and big-appetite breakfasts, Wishbone's extensive, reasonably priced menu blends hearty, home-style choices with healthful and vegetarian items. Brunch is the 'Bone's claim to fame, when an eclectic crowd of bedheads packs in for the plump and tasty salmon cakes, omelets, and red eggs (a lovely mess of tortillas, black beans, cheese, scallions, ancho chile sauce, salsa, and sour cream). Brunch can be a mob scene, though, so to avoid a long wait, try lunch or dinner; offerings run from "yardbird" (charbroiled chicken with sweet red-pepper sauce) and blackened catfish to hoppin' John or hoppin' Jack (the vegetarian variation on the black-eyed-pea classic). Variety is Wishbone's strong point: Every entree comes with a choice of sides, so diners can mix and match to their hearts' content. The restaurant provides outdoor seating in nice weather.

There's a newer location at 3300 N. Lincoln Ave. ((C) **773/549-2663**), but the original location has more character.

1001 Washington St. (at Morgan St.). (C) **312/850-2663.** www.wishbonechicago.com. Kids' menu, highchairs, boosters. Reservations accepted, except for weekend brunch. Main courses $5–$10 breakfast and lunch, $6–$15 dinner; kids' menu around $7. AE, DC, DISC, MC, V. Mon–Fri 7am–3pm; Tues–Thurs 5–9pm; Fri–Sat 5–10pm; brunch Sat–Sun 8am–3pm.

A Taste of Poland

Chicago has long been a popular destination for Polish immigrants (currently, about one million Chicagoans claim Polish ancestry). It's somewhat mystifying, then, why they haven't made much of an impact on the city's dining scene. There are Polish restaurants here, but they tend to be small, casual, family-run affairs in residential neighborhoods far removed from the usual tourist attractions. If you'd like to try some hearty, stick-to-your-ribs Polish food, the best-known restaurant is **Red Apple** (Czerwone Jabluszko), 3121 N. Milwaukee Ave. ((*C*) **773/588-5781;** http://redapplebuffet.com). Dining here is strictly buffet, and the lineup includes Polish specialties such as pirogi (meat- or cheese-stuffed dumplings) and blintzes, as well as a huge selection of roast meats, salads, and bread (there's even fruit, should you feel nutrient-starved). Best of all is the price: $8.50 on weekdays and $9.50 on weekends for all you can eat.

4 THE MAGNIFICENT MILE & THE GOLD COAST

Yes, the Mag Mile is all about designer shopping—and designer eating—and you'll be pleasantly surprised to discover that plenty of those eateries welcome kids. In fact, a great many families who visit Chicago never stray far from the Magnificent Mile and the adjoining Gold Coast area. From the array of restaurants, shops, and pretty streets in the area, it's not hard to see why.

EXPENSIVE

American Girl Place Cafe ★★★ AMERICAN   Dining with dolly has never been done in a more appealing manner than at the cafe inside the American Girl Place store. Not to be sexist, but most boys will be less than thrilled about spending time here surrounded by girls, dolls, and dresses: It's really best for a girls' day out. With an eye-popping black, white, and red striped decor, the cafe has loads of kid appeal. The view of the Museum of Contemporary Art and surrounding street life from the second-floor cafe is wonderful. Parents and daughters can bond over lunch, dinner, or tea, and dolly (only of the American Girl species, of course) can join in, settled on a special booster seat. Treats on the menu include fresh cinnamon buns, quiche Lorraine, chicken Caesar salad, and tic-tac-toe pizza. Top your meal off with chocolate ice cream accompanied by a brownie heart, and homemade sugar cookies, and wash everything down with a pink lemonade or hot chocolate. American Girl Place is a prime destination for many families visiting Chicago, so plan well in advance to avoid disappointing the American girl in your life. The cafe recommends booking 8 to 12 weeks in advance.

835 N. Michigan Ave. (inside Water Tower Place mall). (*C*) **877/247-5223.** Highchairs, boosters. Reservations required. Prix-fixe menu (includes gratuity) lunch $17, tea $16, dinner $18. AE, DC, DISC, MC, V. Lunch seatings 11am and 12:30pm daily; tea seatings 2:30 and 4pm daily; dinner 5:30pm Mon–Thurs, 7:30pm Fri–Sat. Subway/El: Red Line to Chicago/State.

Bandera SOUTHWESTERN   The open-range ambience here is created by the chicken roasting over a hickory-burning fire. Some complain that the room even gets a

Dining Out in (Relative) Peace

- **Set the ground rules.** Before entering a restaurant, remind kids that you are going to a special place and that a few key rules apply, such as inside voices and good manners.
- **Bring entertainment.** Crayons, markers, paper, stickers, and so on will give your children something to do while awaiting their food. If the kids are old enough, bring postcards for them to write on.
- **Try word games.** "I Spy" is a good one. Another word game involves one person naming something in a category, such as food. The next person names a word in the same category that starts with the last letter of the previous word. (For example: orange, eggplant, tomato, onion. . . .)
- **Remember the value of conversation.** Talk with your kids about what you did during the day or what you have planned for the next one. That will help pass the time and encourage restaurant-appropriate behavior.
- **Decide who's "on duty."** Decide ahead of time which adult will have to interrupt his or her meal, should a child act up. Take turns at each meal.
- **Use timeouts.** If your normally polite child acts up, immediately and quietly take him or her outside. This will avoid embarrassment, and will be a lesson to the child. You shouldn't have to do this more than once or twice before your child gets the message.
- **Make exceptions.** Your child may normally drink milk with dinner. Permit him or her to have a Shirley Temple (7UP and grenadine with a cherry). This will make dinner out seem special.

bit too smoky from that open fire, but in the wintertime it gives Bandera a cozy, rustic Western feel. If your kids will eat cornbread and roasted chicken with mashed potatoes, they'll do fine here. Menu offerings include roasted prime rib, pork tenderloin with barbecue sauce, Western beef back ribs, and wood-roasted salmon. This is a national chain, so the restaurant might look awfully familiar; but a location on Michigan Avenue that affords views of the street life below makes this branch particularly well situated.

535 N. Michigan Ave. (C) **312/644-3524.** Kids' menu, highchairs, boosters. Main courses $15–$25; kids' menu $5–$10. AE, DC, MC, V. Mon–Thurs 11:30am–10pm; Fri–Sat 11:30am–11pm; Sun noon–10pm. Subway/El: Red Line to Grand. Bus: 151 and 157.

Mike Ditka's Restaurant ★★ STEAKHOUSE   For many Chicago football die-hards, the glory days of former coach "Iron" Mike Ditka, who led the Bears to victory in Super Bowl XX in 1985, are still alive and well. Football memorabilia lines the walls of this restaurant, filled with amber light and dark wood. Kids who are at all into the game might inadvertently get a little history lesson—even the Bears' 1985 victory, seemingly still fresh in the minds of Bears' fans who love to relive the glory days, probably qualifies as ancient history to your kids. Televisions in the posh bar allow patrons to simultane-ously sip Scotch and pray for "da Coach" to return. Upstairs, there's more dining space, often accompanied by live music (last time I was dining here, Ditka himself was at a

- **Use rewards and bribery.** Tell kids that if they behave well and eat their dinner, they'll get a special dessert.
- **Be flexible.** If the kids are tired, skip the appetizers or order food that is quick to prepare. If they've reached their limit, have one parent take them outside to stretch their legs or hunt down a dessert spot while the other parent pays the bill.
- **Slow down.** Before dinner, take them back to the hotel for a nap to rest up or to a playground to let loose some pent-up energy.
- **Eat early.** If you plan to eat at a more elegant restaurant or if it's the weekend, arrive early, before the restaurant gets full. (Plan a post-dinner walk or activity, such as strolling Navy Pier in summer or the John Hancock Center's Christmas tree in winter.)
- **Do lunch.** Some of the city's finer restaurants are open for lunch. Why not make lunch your special meal of the day? The ambience may be more kid-friendly, the prices lower, and your children better behaved. Then you can all have pizza for dinner, and you won't feel you've missed out.
- **Relax.** Chicagoans are very friendly, and most restaurants are delighted to have children dining with them.

table—yes, he makes regular appearances). The hamburger here (really, a chopped steak burger) is one of the best in the city and easily feeds two. Appetizers here are called "Kickoffs" and include a "Duck Cigar," a hand-rolled pastry with a hearty duck-and-mushroom filling, and a "Souper Bowl" of corn chowder. There are lots of salads, pastas, and seafood dishes to choose from, but why be a wimp? Go for the "Fullback Size" filet mignon with spinach and homemade onion rings, or "Da Pork Chop," surrounded by warm cinnamon apples and a green peppercorn sauce.

100 E. Chestnut St. (in the Tremont Hotel, btw. Michigan Ave. and Rush St.). ℂ **312/587-8989.** www. mikeditkaschicago.com. Kids' menu, highchairs, boosters. Main courses $10–$16 lunch; $15–$40 dinner; kids' menu around $8. AE, DC, DISC, MC, V. Mon–Thurs 7am–10pm; Fri–Sun 7am–11pm. Subway/El: Red Line to Chicago Ave.

Oak Street Beachstro ★ AMERICAN/ECLECTIC Could a location be more prime? Settled on the curve of Oak Street Beach, this bistro offers tables on the sand. (The cafe is open in warm weather only and opens in early May.) Take a dip in the lake with your family, then head up the beach for specialties such as the grilled salmon sandwich, Cobb salad, and salmon filet. Less exotic offerings such as salads, sandwiches, and pasta should please kids. For the grown-ups, beer and wine are available, and frozen drinks can be made sans alcohol for the kids. Outdoor seating provides some of the best people-watching around. Saturday and Sunday you'll find a breakfast buffet from 8 to 11:30am. Come at twilight and you'll be treated to a beautiful violet sky.

1001 N. Lake Shore Dr. (at Oak Street Beach). ℭ **312/915-4100.** Highchairs, boosters. Reservations accepted for parties of 6 or more only. Main courses $16–$25. AE, DC, DISC, MC, V. May–Oct (weather permitting) Mon–Fri 11am–10:30pm; Sat–Sun 8am–11:30pm. Subway/El: Red Line to Chicago. Bus: 145, 146, 147, or 151.

Ron of Japan JAPANESE   The heyday of teppanyaki dining (you know, Japanese chefs chopping and grilling at your table, with the accompanying flashing knives and flying shrimp tails) passed decades ago, but the show is still a kid-pleaser. Specialties include shrimp with egg-yolk sauce, filet mignon, prime rib served on a samurai sword, and Shogun dinner (lobster and steak). Grilled on an iron plate set into each table, the food is cut, seasoned, and served by chefs who dish up amazing flair as well as flavor. The restaurant has 14 such tables—larger ones accommodate up to 10 diners, the smaller ones, six or so. As knives and pepper shakers fly through the air, meats sizzle on the hot iron plate. Above each grill/table is a retractable hood that keeps smoke out of everyone's eyes.

230 E. Ontario St. ℭ **312/644-6500.** Kids' menu, highchairs, boosters. Reservations accepted for parties of 8 or more only. Main courses $15–$25; kids' menu $13–$15. AE, DC, DISC, MC, V. Mon–Thurs 5–9:30pm; Fri 5–10:30pm; Sat 5–10pm; Sun 4:30–9pm. Subway/El: Red Line to Chicago/State. Bus: 151 or 157.

MODERATE

Bistro 110 ★★ BISTRO/CONTINENTAL   Bistro 110 enjoys a prime location just half a block west of North Michigan Avenue. A neighborhood crowd gathers here for the bistro's changing weekly specials, posted on a chalkboard, where you can also check out the weather forecast and other local news. This popular spot opened in 1987, putting it on the cutting edge of the bistro-style dining trend. The restaurant is much larger than an authentic bistro would be, with plenty of hustle and bustle that helps families fit right in.

The menu covers a broad price range and several bistro classics, such as escargots in puff pastry, mussels in white-wine sauce, French onion soup, cassoulet, and steak au poivre. Chicago holds Bistro 110 dear for the roasted heads of garlic served with crusty bread and its wood-roasted meats and vegetables. (The wood-roasted items, including a delicious, savory half chicken and a bountiful roast vegetable plate, are among your best bets here—some of the other items can be inconsistent.) The kids' menu ranges from beef tenderloin to grilled cheese. Sunday brunch, complete with a jazz trio, is a good time to bring your kids. (Yes, the trio will visit your table and "serenade" you—rather loudly.) Brunch is extremely popular, so get there early to avoid a long wait.

110 E. Pearson St. (just west of Michigan Ave.). ℭ **312/266-3110.** www.levyrestaurants.com. Kids' menu, highchairs, boosters. Main courses $16–$30; kids' menu $6–$14. AE, DC, DISC, MC, V. Mon–Thurs 11:30am–10pm; Fri–Sat 11:30am–11pm; Sun 10:30am–10pm. Subway/El: Red Line to Chicago/State.

Cheesecake Factory AMERICAN   It really must take a factory to produce the 34 flavors of cheesecake offered here. While this restaurant is one of the usual "kid-friendly" suspects, a handy location on Michigan Avenue and the prospect of outdoor dining on the John Hancock Center Plaza make this better than your average chain dining experience. The restaurant is big and noisy, and be prepared for your name to be added to a long list when you arrive. (You'll be given a pager for the wait.) The odd decor, with copper-colored metal sculpted into aerodynamic shapes that overhang the entryways, gives kids plenty to gawk at while you wait.

Even picky eaters will find something to order on the enormous menu. There's no kids' menu, but the regular menu features chicken strips and mini cheeseburgers, among

other tot treats. Baja chicken tacos, barbecued ranch chicken salad, and avocado egg rolls
are a few of the items on the wide-ranging menu. And the cheesecake! Save room for
white chocolate raspberry truffle, chocolate peanut butter cookie dough, or, seasonally,
pumpkin cheesecake.

875 N. Michigan Ave. (in the plaza of the John Hancock Center). ✆ **312/337-1101.** Highchairs, boosters.
Main courses $8.95–$16. AE, DC, DISC, MC, V. Mon–Thurs 11:30am–11pm; Fri–Sat 11:30am–12:30am; Sun
10am–11:30pm. Subway/El: Red Line to Chicago/State.

Coco Pazzo Café ★ ITALIAN

Here's the perfect combination for families: food
sophisticated enough for grown-ups, simple enough for kids. An added plus is a scenic
sidewalk cafe for that rare perfect-weather day in Chicago. The cafe is the more casual
version of Coco Pazzo restaurant. The decor is colorful, with ceramic tile, wall murals,
and a copper-topped bar. Cuisine is rustic Tuscan and northern Italian. The menu
includes focaccia, thin-crust pizza, seafood, veal, chicken dishes, and pasta. For adults,
specialties include fish *cartoccio* (fresh fish in parchment paper), gnocchi with tomato and
basil, and tagliolini with wild mushrooms. Sunday brunch features a fixed-price menu
that varies every week.

636 N. St. Clair St. ✆ **312/664-2777.** Highchairs, boosters. Reservations recommended. Main courses
$9–$15. AE, DISC, V. Mon–Thurs 11:30am–10:30pm; Fri–Sat 11:30am–11pm; Sun 11:30am–10pm. Sub-
way/El: Red Line to Chicago. Bus: 3, 145, 146, 147, 151, or 157.

ESPN Zone AMERICAN

Kids will love it, but grown-ups prone to indigestion might
want to tread carefully. (Maybe you'll want to skip dining here and just hit the arcade?)
The frenetic activity inside this temple of televised athletics will likely please your kids
(and please you, too, if you have trouble keeping them entertained) but can be a bit
overwhelming. Every wall is covered with television screens or sports art, with a full-on
visual and audio assault on your senses. This massive 35,000-square-foot sports-themed
dining-and-entertainment complex features three components: the Studio Grill, designed
with replicas of studio sets from the cable networks' shows (including *SportsCenter*); the
Screening Room, a sports pub featuring a 16-foot screen and an armada of TV monitors
and radio sets carrying live broadcasts of games; and the Sports Arena, a gaming area with
interactive and competitive attractions. Good news for adults: The food here is better-
than-average tavern fare, including quite a few salads and upscale items such as a salmon
filet baked on cedar and served with steamed rice and grilled vegetables.

43 E. Ohio St. (at Wabash Ave.). ✆ **312/644-3776.** Kids' menu, highchairs, boosters. Main courses
$7.25–$20; kids' menu $5–$8. AE, DISC, MC, V. Sun–Thurs 11am–midnight; Fri–Sat 11am–1am. Subway/
El: Red Line to Grand.

Jack Melnick's Corner Tap AMERICAN

This casual neighborhood pub provides a
comfortable, welcoming, and fun environment—a local hangout where folks can "come
as they are." Specialties include burgers done seven ways, chopped salads, and home-style
specials such as barbecued ribs and chicken. A 50-foot old-fashioned bar is the epicenter
of Jack's, featuring an extensive bottle and tap beer selection from around the world,
"from Old Style to Newcastle." Patrons can catch just about any sporting event from
baseball to hockey on the 16 screens featuring DirecTV, or play a game of darts. The
dining room has always been one of my favorite spots on the Magnificent Mile, with a
screened-in porch area that lets in the lake breeze in the summer, and a stone fireplace
and deep booths that make for cozy dining in the wintertime. Desserts include apple pie,
banana cream pie, and a chocolate-chip-cookie skillet sundae. On Sunday catch brunch
from 11am to 4pm.

might cause an "Ewwwww!" reaction from your kids, but you'll likely be safe with tamer **129**
options such as barbecued chicken or plain cheese. Traditional meat-and-cheese pizzas
are also available, as are soups, salads, pasta dishes, and desserts. If all else fails, there's a
children's menu with pepperoni pizza; Caesar salad topped with cheddar goldfish crackers; buttered noodles; and brownies.

835 N. Michigan Ave. (Water Tower Place, 7th floor). © **312/787-7300.** Kids' menu, highchairs, boosters.
Reservations not accepted. Menu items $7–$10; kids' menu $5. AE, DC, DISC, MC, V. Mon–Sat 11am–
10pm; Sun noon–9pm. Subway/El: Red Line to Chicago/State.

Charlie's Ale House on Navy Pier ★ AMERICAN   One of several outdoor dining
options along Navy Pier, this outpost of the Lincoln Park restaurant wins for lip-smacking pub fare and a great location on the southern promenade overlooking the lakefront
and Loop skyline. It's a great vantage point for Wednesday- and Friday-night fireworks,
too. The Navy Pier location is handy for sightseers; kids will like the burgers, meatloaf,
and, maybe, the chicken potpie. The original location in Lincoln Park triumphs with a
wonderful beer garden, which is welcoming to families. (The restaurant says everyone is
welcome—except dogs!) It's spacious, surrounded by tall, ivy-covered brick walls, and
buzzing with activity and good vibes. The Lincoln Park restaurant is at 1224 W. Webster
Ave. (© **773/871-1440**); take the Red Line to Sheffield. A third location is at 5308 N.
Clark St. in Andersonville (© **773/751-0140**).

600 E. Grand Ave. © **312/595-1440.** Kids' menu, highchairs, boosters. Reservations accepted only for
parties of 15 or more. Main courses $11–$17; kids' menu $5. AE, DC, DISC, MC, V. Mon–Fri 11am–mid-
night; Sat–Sun 11am–1am. Subway/El: Red Line to Grand/State; transfer to Navy Pier's free trolley.

Corner Bakery BREAKFAST/SANDWICHES   In case of emergency hunger meltdown, it's a good idea to locate the nearest Corner Bakery ahead of time. A very popular
destination (and justifiably so), there are about 40 outlets in Chicago and its suburbs. It's
easy to get addicted to the coffee and sweets here: In fact, when my former office mates
and I counted up our visits each week, we decided to dub our local branch "Corner
Bankruptcy." Sandwiches, salads, fruit, and amazing baked-good desserts are highlights.
(Try the lemon bars dusted with powdered sugar, or the cream cheese brownie, or the
mini caramel Bundt cake—try anything!) The homemade chips sprinkled with Parmesan
are impossible to resist. Grilled panini with turkey, bacon, and cheese, or homemade mac
and cheese will appeal to kids. Some of the main locations include one in River North at
516 N. Clark St. (© **312/644-8100**), attached to Melman's Maggiano's Italian restaurant; and a location east of Michigan Avenue at 676 N. St. Clair St., at Erie Street
(© **312/266-2570**).

1121 N. State St. (at Cedar St.). © **312/787-1969.** Highchairs, boosters. Reservations not accepted. Menu
items $7–$10. AE, DC, DISC, MC, V. Mon–Thurs 7am–8:30pm; Fri–Sat 7am–9pm; Sun 7am–8pm. Subway/
El: Red Line to Clark/Division.

foodlife ★★ (Finds) ECLECTIC   Yes, another successful concept courtesy of Lettuce
Entertain You's Rich Melman: a food court with a healthy twist. Located on the mezza-
nine of Water Tower Place, just outside the entrance of the Mity Nice Grill, foodlife
consists of a dozen or so kiosks serving both ordinary and exotic specialties—a total of
700 different items. Four hundred seats are spread out cafe-style in a very pleasant environment under realistic boughs of artificial trees festooned with strings of lights in the
shapes of grapes and other fruits.

 The beauty of a food court, of course, is that it tries to offer something for everybody.
At foodlife the burger-and-pizza crowd will be satisfied, but so will vegetarians and diners

looking for, say, a low-fat Caesar salad. Diners here can also choose south-of-the-border dishes, an assortment of Asian fare, and veggie-oriented, low-fat fare. Special treats include the Miracle Juice Bar's fresh orange juice and raspberry fruit smoothie, as well as a host of healthy or gooey desserts, and, at a booth called Sacred Grounds, various espresso-based beverages. A lunch or a snack at foodlife is basically inexpensive, but the payment method (each diner receives an electronic card that records each purchase for a total payment upon exit) makes it easy to build up a big tab while holding a personal taste-testing session at each kiosk.

In Water Tower Place, 835 N. Michigan Ave. ✆ **312/335-3663.** Highchairs, boosters. Reservations not accepted. Most items $5–$10. AE, DC, DISC, MC, V. Mon–Thurs 11am–8pm; Fri–Sat 11am–9pm. Subway/El: Red Line to Chicago/State.

Oak Tree ★ AMERICAN/BREAKFAST   Tucked away on the sixth floor of the 900 N. Michigan indoor mall (home of Bloomingdale's), Oak Tree isn't exactly high-profile. But it's one of my favorite places for a meal during a day of Magnificent Mile touring. The cafe decor is bright and cheery (with nature-inspired murals to help you momentarily forget that you're inside a mall). If you can, get a table along the windows that look down on Michigan Avenue. Oak Tree's draw is the enormous, varied menu. You'll find something for everyone in the family: a large salad selection, Asian noodles, sandwiches that range from meatball to duck breast, Mexican quesadillas, and even blue-plate specials such as turkey hash or a patty melt. The breakfast menu is just as extensive. Oak Tree can get quite crowded at prime time, with hefty waits, so try to time your visit accordingly.

900 N. Michigan Ave., 6th floor. ✆ **312/751-1988.** Highchairs, boosters. Reservations not accepted. Main courses $9–$15. AE, DC, DISC, MC, V. Mon–Fri 7:30am–6:30pm; Sat–Sun 7:30am–5:30pm. Subway/El: Red Line to Chicago/State.

5 RIVER NORTH

Most families visiting Chicago will find themselves heading for dinner in River North at least once during their stay. The city's hot spot for family dining, River North offers an ever-growing, something-for-everyone array of restaurants—from fast food to theme and chain restaurants (plus some of the most fashionable dining destinations, so parents might want to hire a sitter one night and return for "date night"). Whether you seek a quick dog or burger, a casual French meal, or contemporary American fine dining, River North has it all.

EXPENSIVE

Brasserie Jo ★ ALSATIAN/FRENCH   Brasserie Jo, the casual dining destination from Jean Joho (whose upscale Everest restaurant is one of the city's longtime gourmet destinations), is a popular spot for convivial meals of robust fare in a Parisian, retro-chic setting. It's big and bustling enough to welcome kids, and once you explain that a croque-monsieur is really a toasted ham and cheese, your kids will find something wonderful on the menu. For the adults, following in the tradition of the classic Alsatian brasserie (meaning "brewery"), Brasserie Jo makes a malty house brew, and diners are welcome for a quick stop-in snack with a glass of wine or a full five-course meal.

You can order a hearty Alsatian *choucroute,* but the menu focuses more on casual French classics: Entrees are divided into seafood, steak, and a variety of bistro-style specialties (coq au vin, pork tenderloin ratatouille, rack of lamb), along with tartes, the Alsatians' version of thin-crust pizza. One house specialty that's worth a try is the "famous shrimp bag," a phyllo pastry filled with shrimp, mushrooms, and herb rice garnished with lobster sauce. Save room for dessert: The delightfully caramel-banana coupe is served in a tall glass, and might be the perfect sundae. Or try the rich chocolate mousse, which is served tableside from a massive silver bowl, then topped with fresh cream and shaved chocolate—just like in Paris.

59 W. Hubbard St. (btw. Dearborn and Clark sts.). ✆ 312/595-0800. www.brasseriejo.com. Kids' menu, highchairs, boosters. Reservations recommended. Main courses $18–$30; kids' menu $7–$9. AE, DC, DISC, MC, V. Mon–Thurs 5–10pm; Fri–Sat 5–11pm; Sun 4–9pm. Subway/El: Red Line to Grand, or Brown Line to Merchandise Mart.

Harry Caray's ★★ AMERICAN/ITALIAN   A shrine to the legendary Cubs play-by-play announcer, this landmark building near the Chicago River is a repository for the staggering collection of baseball memorabilia that Harry amassed, and it covers almost every square inch of the place. Even the bar is a nod to baseball: At 60 feet, 6 inches long, it's the distance from the pitcher's mound to home plate.

But you don't have to be a baseball lover to appreciate Harry's. The dining rooms have an old-Chicago feel that is comfortable and familiar, with high tin ceilings, exposed brick walls, and red-checked tablecloths. It would be easy to lump Harry's with other celebrity restaurants, but as one reviewer pointed out, the food is better than it has to be. The portions are enormous; unless you want leftovers for days, plan to share. Main courses run from traditional items such as pastas with red sauce to chicken Vesuvio, veal, and a variety of seafood choices. Harry's is also a good place to order big plates of meat: dry-aged steaks, lamb, veal, and pork chops. And from the list of side dishes, be sure to order the signature Vesuvio potatoes.

33 W. Kinzie St. (at Dearborn St.). ✆ 312/828-0966. www.harrycarays.com. Kids' menu, highchairs. Main courses $15–$40; kids' menu around $7. AE, DC, DISC, MC, V. Mon–Sat 11:30am–2:30pm; Mon–Thurs 5–10:30pm; Fri–Sat 5–11pm; Sun 11:30am–4pm (lunch bar only) and 4–10pm. Subway/El: Brown Line to Merchandise Mart, or Red Line to Grand.

MODERATE

Buca di Beppo ITALIAN   Always fantasized about being part of a wacky, extended Italian family? You'll feel you've found your home at this Italian-American restaurant (part of a national chain), which serves humongous family-style dishes. The restaurant is a loud, high-energy place with large groups of diners; its decor is eclectic, covered with garage-sale-type mementos gathered by the owners in Italy. You'll find plenty of Romanesque statues, red checkered tablecloths, and photos of famous and infamous Italians. Portions are huge—one order of chicken cacciatore serves up to five people; pizzas are measured in feet, not inches; and meatballs weigh a half-pound each. Even the smaller portions of pasta serve up to three people.

521 N. Rush St. ✆ 312/396-0001. Highchairs, boosters. Reservations not accepted, but you can call ahead to put your name on the list. Main courses $16–$25. AE, DC, DISC, MC, V. Mon–Thurs 11am–10pm; Fri–Sat 11am–11pm; Sun 11am–9pm. Subway/El: Brown Line to Wellington. Bus: 8.

Carson's ★ AMERICAN/BARBECUE   A true Chicago institution, Carson's calls itself "The Place for Ribs," and, boy, is it ever. The barbecue sauce is sweet and tangy, and the ribs are meaty. Included in the $20 price for a full slab of ribs are coleslaw and one of four types of potatoes (the most decadent are au gratin), plus right-out-of-the-oven rolls.

Breakfast & Brunch

NEAR THE LOOP & MAGNIFICENT MILE

You can get a good (and upscale) breakfast at one of the hotels near the Loop or Magnificent Mile. Favorites include the Café at the **Four Seasons Hotel,** 120 E. Delaware Place (© **312/280-8800**), and Drake Bros. Restaurant at **The Drake Hotel,** 140 E. Walton Place at Michigan Avenue (© **312/787-2200**).

A more informal choice in the Loop, overlooking the El tracks, is **Heaven on Seven** (p. 119), where the Cajun and Creole specialties supplement an enormous diner-style menu that has anything you could possibly desire.

For brunch with some soul, head to **House of Blues,** 329 N. Dearborn St., at Kinzie Street (© **312/527-2583**), for its popular Sunday gospel brunch. To guarantee seating, it's a good idea to book a spot 2 weeks in advance.

A local breakfast favorite since 1923 is **Lou Mitchell's,** 565 W. Jackson Blvd. (© **312/939-3111**), across the south branch of the Chicago River from the Loop, a block farther west than Union Station. You'll be greeted at the door with a basket of doughnut holes and Milk Duds so that you can nibble while waiting for a table.

For a Southern-style breakfast of spicy red eggs, cheese grits, or biscuits and gravy, head over to **Wishbone** (p. 122), a homespun dining hall in a warehouse district west of the Loop.

LINCOLN PARK & THE NORTH SIDE

Ann Sather (p. 149), famous for its homemade cinnamon rolls, is the perfect breakfast or brunch spot if you're heading up to Wrigleyville for a Cubs game or to Belmont Avenue for a day of antiquing.

The **Nookies** restaurants are Chicago favorites for all the standard morning fare. Locations include 2114 N. Halsted St., in Lincoln Park (© **773/327-1400**);

For dinner there's often a wait, but don't despair. In the bar area you'll find a heaping mound of some of the best chopped liver around and plenty of cocktail rye to go with it. (Kids who turn up their noses at chopped liver should start with a kiddie cocktail instead.) When you're seated at your table, tie on your plastic bib—and indulge. In case you don't eat ribs, Carson's also barbecues chicken, salmon, and pork chops, and the restaurant's steaks aren't bad either. But ribs are the house specialty, so make sure that at least someone in your group orders them. (The waitstaff will be shocked if you don't.) If by some remarkable feat you have room left after dinner, the candy-bar sundaes are a scrumptious finale to the meal. Carson's popularity has led to something of a factory mentality among management, which evidently feels the need to herd 'em in and out, but the servers are responsive to requests not to be hurried through the meal.

612 N. Wells St. (at Ontario St.). © **312/280-9200.** Kids' menu, highchairs, boosters. Reservations accepted only for groups of 6 or more. Main courses $8.95–$30; kids' menu $6–$14. AE, DC, DISC, MC, V. Mon–Thurs 11am–11pm; Fri 11am–12:30am; Sat noon–12:30am; Sun noon–11pm. Closed Thanksgiving. Subway/El: Red Line to Grand.

1748 N. Wells St., in Old Town (© **312/337-2454**); and 3334 N. Halsted St., in Lakeview (© **773/248-9888**).

Go to **Orange,** 3231 N. Clark St., at Belmont (© **773/549-4400**), for a fun twist on breakfast foods. Try the Green Eggs and Ham—eggs scrambled with pesto, tomatoes, mozzarella, and pancetta. There's a kids' menu, too, making this a popular choice for families. But a warning to all those with hungry kids (and parents): Come early or late; the line for a table winds outside during prime weekend brunch hours.

Lincoln Park's **Toast,** 746 W. Webster St., at Halsted Street (© **773/935-5600**), is homey yet slightly funky, and kids are encouraged to scribble away on the butcher block table coverings. Breakfast includes a twist on the usual diner fare. Pancakes come in all sorts of tempting varieties, from lemon/poppy seed drizzled with honey to the "pancake orgy" of a strawberry, mango, and banana-pecan pancake topped with granola, yogurt, and honey. Come early on weekends, though; by 10:30am or so, there's guaranteed to be a lengthy wait.

WICKER PARK/BUCKTOWN

The brightly colored **Bongo Room,** 1470 N. Milwaukee Ave. (btw. Evergreen Ave. and Honore St.; © **773/489-0690**), is a neighborhood gathering place for the hipsters of Wicker Park/Bucktown, but the restaurant's tasty, creative breakfasts have drawn partisans from all over the city who feel right at home stretching out the morning with a late breakfast. (*A caveat:* Don't bother trekking over here for weekend brunch, when you'll have to wait an hour or more for a table; it's much more pleasant eating here during the week.) The same owners also run **Room 12,** 1152 S. Wabash Ave. (btw. 11th St. and Roosevelt Rd.; © **312/291-0100**), in the South Loop; the food is just as good as at the Wicker Park restaurant, and it tends to be less crowded.

Maggiano's ★ ITALIAN A great pick for large groups, Maggiano's is a shrine to family-style Italian dining. Like many of its fellow Lettuce Entertain You restaurants, Maggiano's feels a bit contrived, with traditional Italian red-checkered tablecloths and old family portraits (which family, we'll never know), designed to create the feel of Little Italy throughout the nine separate dining rooms. Still, heaping plates of pasta meant to be shared make Maggiano's a good choice for a large and budget-conscious family. In fact, everything on the menu is supersize. Steaks are all more than a pound, and most pasta dishes weigh in over 25 ounces. You're expected to share dishes, pass things around, and try a little bit of everything. The menu is vast and features Italian pasta classics such as chicken and spinach manicotti, eggplant Parmesan, and meat or marinara lasagna, plus chicken, veal, steaks (try the Prime New York Steak al Forno Gorgonzola, a strip steak served with caramelized onions and melted Gorgonzola cheese), chops, and seafood. There's no kids' menu, but the kitchen will accommodate with smaller portions. Downstairs, a banquet room accommodates parties of 20 to 200. On holidays, Maggiano's has live music.

516 N. Clark St. ✆ **312/644-7700.** Highchairs, boosters. Main courses $11–$33. AE, DC, DISC, MC, V. Mon–Thurs 11:30am–10pm; Fri–Sat 11:30am–11pm; Sun noon–10pm. Subway/El: Brown Line to Merchandise Mart; Red Line to Grand. Bus: 22 or 65.

Osteria Via Stato ★★ (Finds) ITALIAN At Osteria Via Stato, the choices are plentiful, and the food is served family-style; so bring your brood and enjoy a real Italian feast. A set price of $36 buys you a full, European-style meal: a range of antipasto plates (smoked salmon, salami, warm focaccia, and more), two pasta dishes (served family-style), and a meat entree (the only dish you actually choose from the menu). Pastas are usually a mix of hearty and light; pappardelle with free-range chicken ragu might be served alongside gemelli with sage and brown butter. Entrees include halibut Milanese with lemon-herb breadcrumbs; braised pork shank with white beans and bacon; or chicken Mario, a simple chicken breast perfectly seared with butter and olive oil. If you want to keep things simple with drinks, ask for the "Just Bring Me Wine" program, which matches a glass of wine to each course at three different price levels (the most affordable level, $15, is a great deal). They'll bring you unlimited helpings of everything except the entrees, so come with an appetite. The kids' menu is adequate but nondescript, with hamburgers, chicken sandwiches, and pasta with marinara sauce. Lunch follows the same format, but there are fewer antipasti, and the entrees include salads and panini.

620 N. State St. (at Ontario St.). ✆ **312/642-8450.** www.leye.com. Kids' menu, highchairs, boosters. Reservations recommended. Set price $36 per person dinner, $20 lunch; kids' menu $8. AE, DC, DISC, MC, V. Mon–Sat 11:30am–2pm; Mon–Thurs 5–10pm; Fri–Sat 5–11pm; Sun 4–8:30pm (bar open later). Subway/El: Red Line to Grand.

Reza's ★★ (Value) MIDDLE EASTERN Whether your kids are already avid eaters of Middle Eastern food or you want to start exposing them to it, Reza's is a good option. With high ceilings and exposed brick, this warm and family-friendly restaurant is housed in a former microbrewery. Specialties include a deliciously rich chicken in pomegranate sauce, and kids might go for one of a variety of kebabs. Despite the menu's meat-heavy emphasis, there's a full selection of vegetarian options, too. The appetizer combo is a nice option for families; it includes hummus, stuffed grape leaves, tabbouleh, and other standbys nicely presented in a red lacquer bento box. Reza's has another location in Andersonville, at 5255 N. Clark St. (✆ **773/561-1898**), but the River North spot is the most convenient for visitors staying downtown.

432 W. Ontario St. (at Orleans St.). ✆ **312/664-4500.** Highchairs, boosters. Main courses $9.95–$17. AE, DC, DISC, MC, V. Sun–Sat 11am–midnight. Subway/El: Red Line to Grand.

Scoozi ★ ITALIAN Families should plan to visit Scoozi on Sunday evening, when the restaurant gives kids "make your own pizza" time from 4 to 5pm (free for children 11 and under). Chefs show kids how to make a pizza, then pop them in the wood-burning oven. Kids dine on their culinary masterworks, and you get a nice stretch of "adult time" at the table while your little chefs are at work.

Scoozi's sprawling loft space has been its home since 1986, the year it opened and began serving up authentic Italian cooking—a real pioneering effort at the time, complete with focaccia in its breadbaskets. Scoozi's menu is no longer unique, but Chicagoans return for its reliable lineup of Italian flavors. Appetizers include an antipasti bar (favorites are orzo with shrimp and wood-roasted mushrooms); deep-fried calamari with basil, aioli, and arrabbiata sauce (a spicy tomato sauce); or small pizzas, such as one smothered with garlic spinach, oven-roasted tomatoes, and goat cheese. Main courses include *petto di pollo* (grilled chicken breast with baby artichokes, red potatoes, and warm **135** coriander-seed vinaigrette); ravioli baked in a wood oven (smoked chicken, Taleggio cheese with smoked bacon, or artichoke); and *gnocchi con salsa rossa* (homemade potato dumplings in a tomato-basil cream). For dessert, head directly for the tiramisu.

410 W. Huron St. (at Orleans St.). (C) **312/943-5900.** Kids' menu, highchairs, boosters. Reservations recommended. Main courses $16–$25; kids' menu around $6. AE, DC, DISC, MC, V. Mon–Thurs 5:30–9pm; Fri 5:30–10pm; Sat 5–10pm; Sun 5–9pm. Subway/El: Red Line to Chicago.

INEXPENSIVE

Cafe Iberico ★★ SPANISH/TAPAS   Families should arrive early to ensure getting a table at this wildly popular tapas joint with a festive atmosphere. I'd recommend this place especially for older kids and teens with adventurous palates. (Get them to try *pulpo a la gallega*—the best fried octopus around!) Cafe Iberico gets very loud, especially on weekends; on weekdays, crowds begin pouring in at the end of the workday, so if you arrive around dinnertime, expect a wait. Put a dent in your appetite with a plate of *queso de cabra* (baked goat cheese with fresh tomato-basil sauce). When your waiter returns with the first dish, put in a second order for a round of both hot and cold tapas. Then continue to order as your hunger demands. The waiters are pleasant yet can get a little harried, so it sometimes takes some effort to flag them down. A few standout dishes are the vegetarian Spanish omelet, *patatas bravas* (spicy potatoes with tomato sauce), *pincho de pollo* (chicken brochette with caramelized onions and rice), and *pulpo y la plancha* (grilled octopus with potatoes and olive oil). There are a handful of entrees on the menu, and a few desserts in case you're still not sated.

739 N. LaSalle St. (btw. Chicago Ave. and Superior St.). (C) **312/573-1510.** Highchairs. Reservations accepted during the week for parties of 6 or more; reservations not accepted for Fri–Sat dinner. Tapas $4–$7; main courses $7–$10. DC, DISC, MC, V. Mon–Thurs 11am–11:30pm; Fri 11am–1:30am; Sat noon–1:30am; Sun noon–11pm. Subway/El: Red Line to Chicago/State, or Brown Line to Chicago.

Dave & Buster's AMERICAN   Good old-fashioned fun of the coin-operated variety means that you may have to tear your kids away from the games to get them to sit down for dinner. At the Chicago outpost of the Dallas-based mega entertainment and dining chain, you can combine casual dining and an evening's entertainment. (Don't send teens by themselves: Kids must be accompanied by an adult 25 years old or older.) The menu is expansive and features bar food, including pasta, burgers, steak, and ribs. Before you sit down to eat, let your kids burn off energy by getting lost in this neon-lit games emporium. You'll find 1950s-era carnival games, Vegas-style casino games, video games, and virtual reality tests. The main attraction is the glitzy Million Dollar Midway on the second level. Do your kids dream of being an Alpine ski racer or driving the Grand Prix? Video games on the Midway let them simulate the experience. Grown-ups might try a computerized version of blackjack or swing away at the indoor golf simulator, a "virtual" golf driving range that uses laser beams to calculate the ball's flight.

1024 N. Clark St. (C) **312/943-5151.** Kids' menu. Main courses $9–$20; kids' menu $3–$8. AE, DC, DISC, MC, V. Mon–Thurs 11am–1am; Fri–Sat 11:30am–2am; Sun 11:30am–midnight. Subway/El: Red Line to Clark/Division. Bus: 22, 36, or 70.

Ed Debevic's ★ BURGERS/DINER   "Eat at Ed's" is the call to action at this temple to America's hometown lunch-counter culture. Wherever you sit, in an upholstered banquette or booth or the lunch-counter stools, you'll be surrounded by 1950s nostalgia. Tunes such as "Duke of Earl" and other vintage oldies fill the air. Food specialties include pot roast, fountain drinks—and meatloaf. Ed Debevic's calls itself the place "where meatloaf is king." There's no kids' menu, but with the entire menu based on burgers and fries, who needs one? The 1950s-costumed waitstaff cracks gum at you and dishes out rude comments along with the food. And when the jukebox strikes up a song, don't be surprised if your waiter leaps onto the counter (or onto your table, if that's where he happens to be), to dance along. It's all a performance, but it works. One nice bonus is a good view of River North and the skyscrapers of the Loop to the south.

640 N. Wells St. Ⓒ 312/664-1707. Highchairs, boosters. Reservations accepted only for parties of 15 or more. All main courses under $10. AE, DC, DISC, V. Mon–Thurs 11am–9pm; Fri 11am–11pm; Sat 9am–11pm; Sun 9am–9pm. Subway/El: Brown Line to Franklin.

Frontera Grill & Topolobampo ★★★ MEXICAN   Owners Rick and Deann Groen Bayless, authors of the popular *Authentic Mexican: Regional Cooking from the Heart of Mexico,* are widely credited with bringing authentic Mexican regional cuisine to a wider audience. Their restaurant is the place to taste *real* Mexican food, so don't show up expecting a plate of nachos with processed-cheese topping. The building actually houses two restaurants: the casual Frontera Grill (plain wood tables, terra-cotta tile floor) and the fine-dining Topolobampo (white linen tablecloths, a more hushed environment). At both restaurants, the focus is on fresh, organic ingredients supplied by local artisanal farmers.

For families, I'd recommend the casual atmosphere of Frontera Grill, where the signature appetizer is the *sopes surtidos,* corn-tortilla "boats" with a sampler of fillings (chicken in red mole, black beans with homemade chorizo, and so on). The ever-changing entree list might include pork loin in a green mole sauce; smoked chicken breast smothered in a sauce of chiles, pumpkin seeds, and roasted garlic; or a classic *sopa de pan* ("bread soup" spiced up with almonds, raisins, grilled green onions, and zucchini). Yes, you can also get tacos (with fillings such as portobello mushrooms, duck, and catfish). The Baylesses up the ante at the adjacent Topolobampo, where both the ingredients and presentation are more upscale.

It can be tough to snag a table at Frontera during prime dining hours, so do what the locals do: Put your name on the list, order the kids some chips, and have a margarita while you wait in the lively, large bar area.

445 N. Clark St. (btw. Illinois and Hubbard sts.). Ⓒ 312/661-1434. www.fronterakitchens.com. Reservations accepted at Frontera Grill for parties of 5–10; accepted at Topolobampo for parties of 1–6. Frontera Grill main courses $21–$28. Topolobampo main courses $32–$38; chef's 5-course tasting menu $75 ($120 with wine pairings). AE, DC, DISC, MC, V. Frontera Grill Tues–Fri 11:30am–2:30pm; Sat 10:30am–2:30pm; Tues–Thurs 5–10pm; Fri–Sat 5–11pm. Topolobampo Tues 11:45am–2pm; Wed–Fri 11:30am–2pm; Tues–Thurs 5:30–9:30pm; Fri–Sat 5:30–10:30pm. Subway/El: Red Line to Grand.

Gino's East ★★ PIZZA   This famous Chicago pizzeria invites patrons to scrawl all over the graffiti-strewn booths. Waiting in the frigid cold (or sweltering heat) to get into Gino's at its former location just west of the Magnificent Mile used to be a Chicago tourist rite of passage. Now that the restaurant has moved into the vast space formerly occupied by Planet Hollywood, there are no more lines out front.

Many Chicagoans consider Gino's the quintessential deep-dish Chicago-style pizza. True to its reputation, the pizza is heavy (a small cheese pizza is enough for two), so work up an appetite before chowing down here. Specialty pizzas include the supreme, with layers of cheese, sausage, onions, green pepper, and mushrooms; and the vegetarian, with cheese, onions, peppers, asparagus, summer squash, zucchini, and eggplant. Gino's also offers salads, sandwiches, and pastas, but I've never seen anyone order them. If you want to take a pizza home on the plane, call a day in advance and Gino's will pack a special frozen pie for the trip.

Green Door Tavern BURGERS   The Green Door is a neighborhood refuge and a well-needed respite from the many trendy restaurants in River North. At lunch you'll find the advertising and graphic-design types who work in the neighborhood chowing on burgers in the unpretentious atmosphere. The restaurant's wood-frame building was put up temporarily after the 1871 fire, presumably just before the city ordinance that banned such construction inside the newly designated "fire zone." The place began as a grocery store with living quarters on the second floor, and evolved into a restaurant in 1921. Later a speak-easy was established in a downstairs room no longer open to the public. Apparently the original framing crew went light on the bracing timbers in a few places because the whole building leans to the right. About a decade ago a newly con-structed building across from the Green Door was consumed with fire and burned to the ground. Firefighters sprayed the Green Door, earning undying gratitude and an annual honorarium called the Golden Helmet Awards from the management.

There's no kids' menu, but regular menu items should please, including the hickory burger, the triple-decker grilled cheese, and the Texas chili. There are even a veggie burger and a turkey burger, and the menu includes some Cajun fare and pasta. Specials, includ-ing the Wednesday meatloaf offering, are posted daily.

678 N. Orleans St. (at Huron St.). (C) **312/664-5496.** Highchairs, boosters. Reservations accepted only for parties of 7 or more. Main courses $6.95–$12. MC, V. Mon–Fri 11:30am–2am; Sat 11:30am–3am; Sun noon–9pm. Subway/El: Brown Line to Chicago.

Hard Rock Cafe AMERICAN   Not just an eatery, Hard Rock Cafe is also one of Chicago's main tourist attractions. (Don't expect to find many locals or members of the over-30 age group here.) A regular rock-'n'-roll museum, you could easily spend hours here poring over the hundreds of drumsticks, concert photos, gold records, or auto-graphed guitars of your favorite artists, including the likes of Mick Fleetwood and George Harrison. (The most popular pieces are a guitar autographed by the members of Nirvana and a motor scooter used in the 1979 movie *Quadrophenia*, which was based on The Who's album.) The food is pretty standard fare, with fajitas and burgers as special-ties, plus a children's menu. But who comes here for the food? The round building has a circular bar decorated in a sports motif, with some nice touches: autographed bats by Ryne Sandberg, Mark Grace, Shawn Dunston, and Frank Thomas, among other ball-players. Interesting restaurant fact: The original Hard Rock Cafe was founded June 14, 1971, in London by Isaac Tigrett and Peter Morton, the son of Chicago restaurateur Arnold Morton of Morton's steakhouse fame. The Chicago location was opened 12 years later.

63 W. Ontario St. (C) **312/943-2252.** Kids' menu, highchairs, boosters. Main courses $8–$15; kids' menu $7. AE, DISC, V. Mon–Thurs 11am–11pm; Fri 11:30am–11:30pm; Sat 11am–midnight; Sun 11am–10pm. Subway/El: Red Line to State/Grand.

Kitsch'n River North ★ AMERICAN   This '70s-inspired diner features shag carpet-ing and one of the best kids' menus in the city (and Tang martinis for the grown-ups!). Comfort foods like fried chicken and waffles, puff pastry potpies, and green eggs and ham (the green is actually provided by spinach pesto) should keep the kids happy. If the weather's fine, sit on the large outdoor patio, enjoy a Twinkie tiramisu dessert, and imag-ine this huge riverside building as the former home of retailing giant Montgomery Ward.

Rocking & Rolling at the Golden Arches

The reality of traveling with kids means the occasional fast-food meal can be a real lifesaver. In McDonald's hometown (corporate headquarters is located in west suburban Oak Brook), I would be remiss in not mentioning the second-busiest franchise in the world. If you're going to go the fast-food route, head for the McDonald's at the corner of Grand Avenue and Clark Street, which was unveiled for the company's 50th anniversary in 2005. The gleaming, glass-enclosed building looks like something out of *The Jetsons,* and it's filled with stylish amenities that would look right at home in a luxury airport lounge. You can chow down while relaxing in a reproduction of Mies van der Rohe's famous Barcelona chair, check out the exhibit of collectible Happy Meal toys from inside a 1960s-style egg chair, or order a cappuccino and gelato at the upstairs cafe.

The original location, in the neighborhood of Roscoe Village, is smaller but just as kitschy and filled with families (2005 W. Roscoe St.; © 773/248-7372).

600 W. Chicago Ave. © 312/644-1500. Reservations not accepted. Main courses $9–$15; kids' menu under $5. AE, DISC, MC, V. Mon–Thurs 8am–7pm; Fri 8am–8pm; Sat–Sun 9am–3pm. Bus 66.

Mr. Beef ★ (Finds) AMERICAN   Mr. Beef doesn't have much atmosphere or seating room, but it's a much-loved Chicago institution. Squeeze in alongside the lunchtime regulars and enjoy the atmosphere (or lack thereof). Families with small children will be happier getting their sandwiches to go, as lack of space means Mr. Beef is not a highchair-friendly place. Its claim to fame is the classic Italian beef sandwich, the Chicago version of a Philly cheese steak. The Mr. Beef variety is made of sliced beef dipped in *jus,* piled high on a chewy bun, and topped with sweet or hot peppers. Heavy, filling, and *very* Chicago, Mr. Beef really hops during lunchtime, when dusty construction workers and suit-wearing businessmen crowd in for their meaty fix. While you're chowing down, check out the celebrity photos and newspaper clippings covering the walls and you'll see why this place is considered a local monument.

666 N. Orleans St. (at Erie St.). © 312/337-8500. Reservations not accepted. Sandwiches $6–$8.50. No credit cards. Mon–Fri 8am–5pm; Sat 10:30am–3:30pm. Subway/El: Red Line to Grand.

Pizzeria Uno ★ (Value) PIZZA   In 1943 Pizzeria Uno invented Chicago-style pizza, and many deep-dish aficionados still refuse to accept any imitations. Uno is now a nationwide chain, but this location is the original. You may eat in the restaurant itself on the basement level or, weather permitting, on the outdoor patio right off the sidewalk. Salads, sandwiches, and a house minestrone are also available, but, hey, the only reason to come here is for the pizza. As with Gino's East (see above), pizzas take about 45 minutes to make, so if the kids are starving, order an appetizer or a salad.

Uno was so successful that the owners opened **Pizzeria Due** in 1955 in a lovely gray-brick Victorian town house nearby at 619 N. Wabash Ave., at Ontario Street (© 312/943-2400). The menu is identical at both restaurants, although the space at Pizzeria Due is much larger, with more outdoor seating.

29 E. Ohio St. (at Wabash Ave.). © 312/321-1000. www.unos.com. Highchairs. Reservations not accepted Fri–Sat. Pizza $7–$22. AE, DC, DISC, MC, V. Mon–Fri 11am–1am; Sat 11:30am–2am; Sun 11:30am–11:30pm. Subway/El: Red Line to Grand.

Rainforest Café AMERICAN   This Minnesota-based chain bills itself as "a wild place to shop and eat." The restaurant strives to create the feel of a rainforest with the sounds of waterfalls, thunder and lightning, and wild animals echoing throughout the place. Check out the floor-to-ceiling aquarium tanks, and duck to avoid the swinging orangutans. The Mexican and Caribbean-inspired menu features salads, sandwiches, and a range of entrees that will please a family of picky eaters. The "chicken-fried chicken" is a bestseller, as is the "mojo bones" rib appetizer. The kids' menu features standard burgers, hot dogs, and mac and cheese. The restaurant also sponsors educational programs designed to bring awareness of the planet's dwindling rainforests.

605 N. Clark St. (at Ohio St.). © 312/787-1501. www.rainforestcafe.com. Kids' menu, highchairs, boosters. Reservations recommended. Main courses $9–$11; kids' menu $6–$8. AE, DC, DISC, V. Mon–Thurs 11am–9:30pm; Fri 11am–10:30pm; Sat 11am–11pm; Sun 11am–9pm. Subway/El: Red Line to State/ Grand.

6 LINCOLN PARK

Singles and upwardly mobile young families inhabit Lincoln Park, the neighborhood roughly defined by North Avenue on the south, Diversey Parkway on the north, the park on the east, and Clybourn Avenue on the west. No surprise, then, that the neighborhood has spawned a dense concentration of some of the city's best restaurants.

EXPENSIVE

Geja's Café ★ FONDUE   Are your kids over age 10? Can they sit through a 2-hour meal? If so, they will love Geja's (pronounced Gay *haz*), an all-fondue restaurant. For some diners, the dark rathskeller decor will be a welcome change from the slick, commercial trattorias and bistros common all over the city. The restaurant has single-handedly preserved the fondue experience in Chicago, providing a fun and welcome break from the ordinary mode of dining.

Choose the Prince Geja's combination dinner, the best Geja's has to offer. The meal begins with a Gruyère fondue appetizer, into which you dip apple wedges and chunks of dark bread. Next, a huge platter arrives, brimming with squares of beef tenderloin, lobster tails, chicken breast, scallops, and jumbo shrimp—all raw—and a caldron of boiling oil to cook them in—the reason only kids 10 and up are allowed! These delicacies are accompanied by a variety of raw vegetables, and eight different dipping sauces. When the flaming chocolate fondue arrives for dessert, with fresh fruit and pound cake for dipping and marshmallows for roasting, you'll want to beg for mercy. *One word of caution:* You have to work for your fondue—keeping track of how long each piece of meat has been cooking, and taking it out before it burns—so Geja's is not the best choice if you just want to sit back and be pampered.

340 W. Armitage Ave. (btw. Lincoln Ave. and Clark St.). © 773/281-9101. Reservations accepted every day except late Fri–Sat. 3-course dinners $20–$39. AE, DC, DISC, MC, V. Mon–Thurs 5–10pm; Fri 5–11:30pm; Sat 5pm–midnight; Sun 4:30–9:30pm. Subway/El: Brown Line to Armitage. Bus: 22.

O'Brien's Restaurant AMERICAN   From the looks of the interior, you'd expect O'Brien's to be a rather ordinary restaurant with that standard "Irish pub" feel—dark wood, brass, and hunter green feature prominently. But outdoors, you'll make an amazing discovery: the best alfresco dining in Old Town. And that's saying something, as you'll find multiple options up and down Wells Street. In good weather the chance to

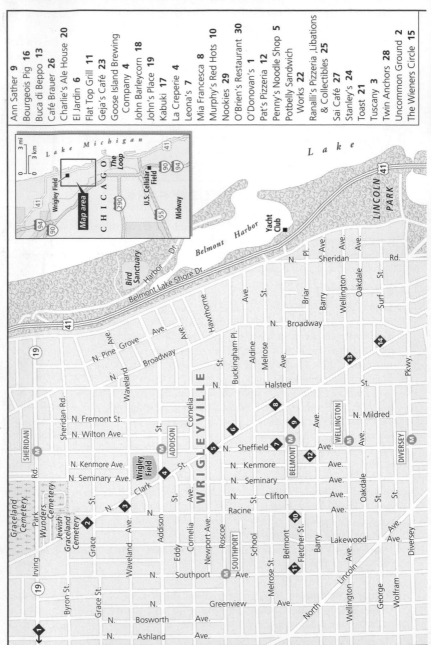

Ann Sather 9
Bourgeois Pig 16
Buca di Beppo 13
Café Brauer 26
Charlie's Ale House 20
El Jardin 6
Flat Top Grill 11
Geja's Café 23
Goose Island Brewing Company 4
John Barleycorn 18
John's Place 19
Kabuki 17
La Creperie 4
Leona's 7
Mia Francesca 8
Murphy's Red Hots 10
Nookies 29
O'Brien's Restaurant 30
O'Donovan's 1
Pat's Pizzeria 12
Penny's Noodle Shop 5
Potbelly Sandwich Works 22
Ranalli's Pizzeria, Libations & Collectibles 25
Sai Café 27
Stanley's 24
Toast 21
Tuscany 3
Twin Anchors 28
Uncommon Ground 2
The Wieners Circle 15

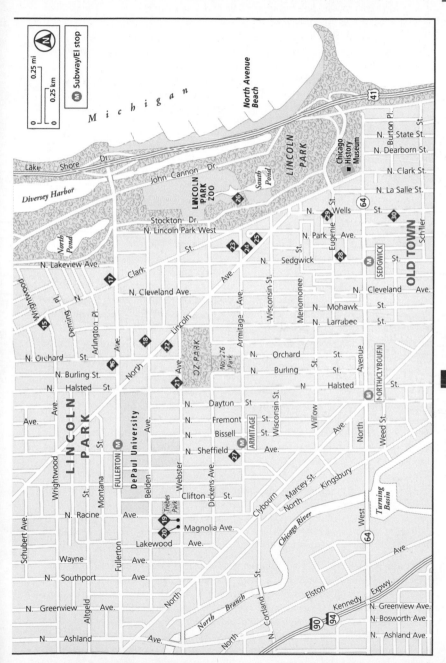

kick back outdoors with your kids can make for a much less stressful dinner—who cares if a few fries wind up on the patio bricks? The birds will thank you for it. The outdoor patio has teak-wood furniture, a gazebo bar in the center, and a mural of the owners' country club on a brick wall. Order the dressed-up chips, a house specialty. Rib-eye steak, Dover sole, and fish and chips are specialties. The bar has a nice assortment of micro-brews. Every night from 7pm to midnight, O'Brien's features live piano music.

1528 N. Wells St. (2 blocks south of North Ave.). ℰ 312/787-3131. Kids' menu, highchairs, boosters. Reservations recommended. Main courses $15–$25; kids' menu $5–$8. AE, DC, DISC, MC, V. Sun–Thurs 11am–10pm; Fri–Sat 11am–midnight. Subway/El: Brown Line to Sedgwick.

MODERATE

Kabuki JAPANESE   Parents appreciate the laid-back atmosphere at this no-frills sushi restaurant located just off of the busy intersection of Clark and Fullerton. The clientele is mostly Lincoln Park's young professionals, but the atmosphere is welcoming to all. The menu runs the gamut of Japanese foods—sushi, sashimi, tempura, teriyaki, and noo-dles—in an intimate, 55-seat dining room. Bonsai trees, brush paintings, and window screens decorate a dining room that is dominated by two highly trained sushi chefs from behind their 10-seat sushi bar. Those who want to sample sushi and try a little bit of everything should go for the 11-piece Kabuki combination. Timid beginners may also find a six-piece, cooked sushi platter a low-risk entree into the world of raw fish. For an appetizer, Kabuki recommends the *goma-ae,* a boiled spinach appetizer served cold in a sesame-and-peanut-butter sauce, although your kids might also get a kick out of peeling and eating a pile of salty *edamame* (soybeans cooked in the pod). When Kabuki over-flows, you can head to Kabuki II, just a few doors down at 2473 N. Clark. In Wrigleyville visit Kabuki III at 3647 N. Southport (ℰ 773/281-9155).

2407 N. Clark. ℰ 773/281-3131. Highchairs, boosters. Reservations recommended. Main courses $8–$15. AE, MC, V. Sun–Tues 4:30pm–midnight; Fri–Sat 4:30pm–1am. Closed Wed. Bus: 22 to Clark or 36 to Broadway.

Leona's ITALIAN/PIZZA   This Chicago-based home-style Italian food chain has a vast menu, good pizza, and budget-friendly prices. With 16 locations and still family-owned and -operated after 52 years, Leona's is a real Chicago restaurant success story. All food is fresh and made from scratch. Be prepared for huge portions and unusually warm and hospitable service in a very family-friendly setting. The menu (actually, it reads more like a book) runs the gamut and includes ribs, chicken wings, steak sandwiches, burgers, pasta, pizza (deep-dish or thin crust), and salads. If that's not enough, Leona's also has a children's menu featuring spaghetti marinara, chicken strips (fried, grilled, or barbecued), 6-inch pizzas, lasagna, fettuccine Alfredo, and more.

3215 N. Sheffield St. ℰ 773/327-8861. Kids' menu. Main courses $9–$25; kids' menu $5–$8. AE, DC, DISC, MC, V. Mon–Thurs 11am–11pm; Fri–Sat 11:30am–midnight; Sun noon–11pm. Subway/El: Brown Line to Merchandise Mart; Red Line to Grand. Bus: 22 or 65.

Sai Café ★ JAPANESE   Here's another good spot to start exposing your kids to the wonders of Japanese cuisine. Despite some upscale sushi bars surfacing in high-profile restaurant districts in the past few years, Lincoln Park's modest Sai Café remains the choice for Lincoln Park residents more interested in food than funky decor. More than 30 varieties of sushi are lovingly prepared and served with élan in this neighborhood setting just off chic Armitage Avenue. And of course, white rice, chicken teriyaki, and shrimp and vegetable tempura are always on the menu, should raw fish prove too daring for your kids. A la carte selections come by the piece or maki-mono style, which pairs

anything from tuna and avocado to flying-fish eggs and scallions, and then wraps it all
up in rice and a thin sheet of dried seaweed. Combo plates feature different meat, fish, and vegetables that can be dressed in tempura or teriyaki, or served sashimi-style. Sai Café also offers a large selection of noodle and rice dishes.

2010 N. Sheffield Ave. (at Armitage Ave.). ℭ **773/472-8080.** Highchairs, boosters. Main courses $16–$24 (a la carte sushi $3.75–$6.95 per piece). AE, DC, MC, V. Mon–Thurs 4:30–11pm; Fri–Sat 4:30pm–midnight; Sun 3:30–10pm. Subway: Brown Line to Armitage.

INEXPENSIVE

Bourgeois Pig ★ (Finds) BREAKFAST/SANDWICHES Eclectic antiques fill this brownstone that's become a mecca for DePaul University students and neighborhood families. Bookshelves are packed with literature, and the atmosphere is cluttered and comfy. The menu makes it clear that the Bourgeois Pig caters to an intellectual crowd: "The Sun Also Rises," "Hamlet," and "The Old Man and the Sea" are among the menu's 25 gourmet sandwiches. Kids will enjoy the "build your own sandwich" menu, and staff will accommodate kids' tastes with less-than-gourmet fare such as American cheese. Baked goods, including ginger molasses cookies, are homemade. The Pig always ranks high in surveys for best cup of coffee in Chicago, so don't miss one of the four varieties brewed daily, or one of a mind-bending array of espresso drinks. Juices, shakes, and root beer made here are also great bets. You'll feel comfortable bringing kids in, as there are often a couple sets of parents with strollers parked inside. Treat the kids to an ice cream for dessert.

738 W. Fullerton Pkwy. (at Burling). ℭ **773/883-5282.** Highchairs, boosters. Main courses under $10. AE, DISC, MC, V. Mon–Fri 6:30am–11pm; Sat–Sun 8am–11pm. Subway/El: Red or Brown Line to Fullerton. Bus: 8, 11, or 74.

Café Brauer ★ AMERICAN A postcard-perfect view of the skyscrapers on North Michigan Avenue, plus Lake Michigan and the greenery of Lincoln Park, makes this a step above the average microbrewery. Stop here for lunch during a tour of the park, and grab a sandwich, kebabs, or flatbread. (Brats and shrimp kebabs are among my favorites.) This pondside cafe is conveniently near the Lincoln Park Zoo and reopened its doors to the public in 1990 after a major restoration. The beer garden, full of flowers and greenery, is perfectly family-friendly.

2021 Stockton Dr. ℭ **312/742-2480.** Highchairs, boosters. Main courses under $8. AE, DC, DISC, MC, V. Mon–Sat 11am–8pm, Sun noon–8pm; winter hours for restaurant 11am–5pm daily; beer garden Thurs–Sun 11am–7pm. Bus: 151 or 156.

El Jardin MEXICAN The staff at this sometimes raucous and always fun restaurant loves to cater to kids. Because it's just 3 blocks south of Wrigley Field (that's where the "raucous" comes in), don't show up after a game unless you're prepared for a long wait. At other times you'll be able to walk right in and grab a table in one of the two main dining rooms, the sidewalk cafe, or the backyard garden. The solid Mexican fare should keep both kids and grown-ups happy. Kids might try tacos, enchiladas, burritos, grilled chicken, or carne asada. Little ones can try *sopa de fideo,* a simple noodle soup. Should you have a special occasion to celebrate, the staff will happily trot out a flan decorated with candles. Don't confuse this location with El Jardin Fiesta Cantina Bar, a bar/dance club located a few doors north on Clark Street. On Sunday, try the Fiesta Buffet, served from 11am to 3pm. The buffet includes about 20 items, including soups and egg, beef, chicken, and pork dishes for $9.95.

3335 N. Clark St. ℭ **773/528-6775.** Highchairs, boosters. Main courses $9–$15. AE, DC, DISC, V. Sun–Thurs 11am–10pm; Fri–Sat 11am–midnight. Subway/El: Red, Brown, or Purple Line to Belmont.

Dining Alfresco

Cocooned for 6 months of the year, with furnaces and electric blankets blazing, Chicagoans revel in the warm months of late spring, summer, and early autumn. For locals and visitors alike, dining alfresco is an ideal way to experience this multifaceted city. Be prepared to wait on a nice night; you'll be fighting a lot of other diners for a coveted outdoor table.

THE LOOP & VICINITY

Athena   212 S. Halsted St., between Adams and Jackson streets (✆ **312/655-0000**). This Greektown mainstay offers a stunning three-level outdoor seating area. It's paved with brick and landscaped with 30-foot trees, flower gardens, and even a waterfall. Best of all: an incredible view of the downtown skyline with the Sears Tower right in the middle.

Park Grill   11 N. Michigan Ave., at Madison Street (✆ **312/521-PARK** [521-7275]). Millennium Park's restaurant serves upscale versions of American comfort food with panoramic views of Michigan Avenue. In the summer, you can pick up a sandwich and grab a seat on the large patio (converted into an ice-skating rink come winter).

Rhapsody   65 E. Adams St., at Wabash Avenue (✆ **312/786-9911**). A tranquil oasis amid the Loop high-rises, Rhapsody's outdoor garden is my top pick for a romantic meal downtown.

MAGNIFICENT MILE & GOLD COAST

Charlie's Ale House at Navy Pier   600 E. Grand Ave., near the entrance to the Pier (✆ **312/595-1440**). One of several outdoor dining options along Navy Pier, this outpost of the Lincoln Park restaurant wins for lip-smacking pub fare and a great location on the southern promenade overlooking the lakefront and Loop skyline.

Le Colonial   937 N. Rush St., just south of Oak Street (✆ **312/255-0088**). This lovely French-Vietnamese restaurant, located in a vintage Gold Coast town house and evocative of 1920s Saigon, *does* have a sidewalk cafe, but you'd do better to reserve a table on the tiny second-floor porch, overlooking the street.

Oak Street Beachstro   1000 N. Lake Shore Dr., at Oak Street Beach (✆ **312/915-4100**). Suit up and head for this warm-weather-only beachfront cafe—literally on the sands of popular Oak Street Beach—which serves inventive cafe fare (fresh seafood, sandwiches, and pastas). Beer and wine are available.

Puck's at the MCA   220 E. Chicago Ave., at Fairbanks Court (✆ **312/397-4034**). This cafe—run by celebrity chef Wolfgang Puck—is tucked in the back of the Museum of Contemporary Art, where, from the terrace, you'll get a view of the museum's sculpture garden. (Restaurant-only patrons can bypass museum admission.) Take in the art, the fresh air, and a shrimp club sandwich, Chinois salad, or wood-grilled pizza.

RIVER NORTH

SushiSamba Rio   504 N. Wells St., at Illinois Street ((_C_) **312/595-2300**). For stunning nighttime views of the skyline—and some pretty stunning people—head to the rooftop deck of this Latin-Asian fusion spot. Canopied banquettes and flickering tea lights create a sultry atmosphere, along with a menu of specialty cocktails.

LINCOLN PARK

Charlie's Ale House   1224 W. Webster Ave., at Magnolia Avenue ((_C_) **773/871-1440**). A true neighborhood hangout, this Lincoln Park pub's wonderful beer garden is spacious and buzzing with activity and good vibes.

North Pond   2610 N. Cannon Dr., halfway between Diversey Parkway and Fullerton Avenue ((_C_) **773/477-5845**). Set on the banks of one of Lincoln Park's beautiful lagoons, the excellent North Pond serves upscale, fresh-as-can-be American cuisine in a romantic and sylvan setting. *One caveat:* Alcohol is not permitted on the outdoor patio.

O'Brien's Restaurant   1528 N. Wells St., 2 blocks south of North Avenue ((_C_) **312/787-3131**). Wells Street in Old Town is lined with several alfresco options, but the best belongs to O'Brien's, the unofficial nucleus of neighborhood life. The outdoor patio has teakwood furniture, a gazebo bar, and a mural of the owners' country club on a brick wall. Order the dressed-up chips, a house specialty.

WRIGLEYVILLE & VICINITY

Arco de Cuchilleros   3445 N. Halsted St., at Newport Avenue ((_C_) **773/296-6046**). Savvy Spanish tapas aficionados thumb their noses at trendy Cafe Iberico and Café Ba-Ba-Reeba!; the tapas and sangria at this lesser-known Wrigleyville restaurant can compete with the best of them. The intimate, leafy terrace out back glows with lantern light.

Moody's   5910 N. Broadway Ave., between Rosedale and Thorndale avenues ((_C_) **773/275-2696**). Moody's has been grilling some of the best burgers in Chicago for the past 30 years. It's ideal in winter for its dark, cozy dining room (warmed by a fireplace), but it's better still in summer for its awesome outdoor patio, a real hidden treasure.

WICKER PARK/BUCKTOWN

Northside Café   1635 N. Damen Ave., just north of North Avenue ((_C_) **773/384-3555**). On a sunny summer day, Northside seems like Wicker Park's town square, packed with an eclectic mix of locals catching up and checking out the scene. The entire front of the restaurant opens onto the street, making it relatively easy to get an "outdoor" table.

Flat Top Grill ASIAN   This create-your-own-stir-fry restaurant often has lines, but never fear, they move quickly. Kids love creating their own dishes, and if you've never been here before, you might want to follow the suggested recipes on the giant blackboards. Choose from more than 25 homemade sauces and 70 fresh ingredients including rice, noodles, seafood, chicken, beef, veggies, and sauces—all for one low price. Best yet, the price includes multiple visits to the food line (a lifesaver if your brilliant culinary combination has gone awry).

3200 N. Southport Ave. (just south of Belmont Ave.). ℂ **773/665-8100.** www.flattopgrill.com. Kids' menu, highchairs, boosters. Main courses lunch around $9, dinner around $12; kids' stir-fry (under age 11) $5. AE, DC, DISC, MC, V. Mon–Thurs 11:30am–10pm; Fri–Sat 11:30am–11pm; Sun 9am–10pm. Bus: 76.

John Barleycorn AMERICAN/BURGERS   Want to get a feel of what it's like to live in a Chicago neighborhood? Stop in to John Barleycorn, which has been a popular neighborhood pub and restaurant since the 1960s. There's a heavy emphasis on food here, so you won't feel like you're taking your kids to a bar. Located in a 19th-century building, the restaurant has that well-worn feel that makes you feel immediately at home. You won't find any pretensions here: Relax with a cold drink and a thick, juicy burger in the outdoor patio. The pub has a storied history, and reputedly served John Dillinger frequently when operating as a speak-easy in the 1920s. A collection of handmade ship models or a quick game of darts should entertain your kids while you're waiting for your food.

658 W. Belden Ave. ℂ **773/348-8899.** Highchairs, boosters. Reservations not accepted. All main courses under $8. AE, DISC, V. Mon–Fri 5pm–2am; Sat 3pm–3am; Sun 3pm–2am. Subway/El: Red Line to Fullerton.

John's Place ★★★ AMERICAN   This neighborhood favorite combines uncomplicated food with an inviting setting of exposed brick walls and hardwood floors. Families make up a fair share of the crowd at lunch, through the afternoon to early dinner. Although the place wasn't designed to attract kids, it's a natural for the sophisticated 30-something parents who populate the neighborhood and first came to John's while dating. The menu emphasizes vegetarian meals, organic foods, and salads. Some of the highlights of the menu are seafood enchiladas, barbecue-glazed pork tenderloin, and, of course, the burgers. The wild line-caught Alaskan salmon, which comes seared as a sandwich at lunchtime, is a knockout. On the weekend, health-conscious eaters will enjoy the free-range Amish chicken eggs served during brunch, and kids are sure to go for pumpkin pancakes and French toast. On a busy afternoon, all 25 of the restaurant's highchairs are put to use.

A second location is found in the Roscoe Village neighborhood, at 2132 W. Roscoe St. (ℂ **773/244-6430**).

1200 W. Webster Ave. ℂ **773/525-6670.** Kids' menu, highchairs, boosters. Reservations not accepted. All main courses under $8. AE, DISC, V. Tues–Thurs 11am–10pm; Fri 11am–11pm; Sat 8am–11pm; Sun 8am–9pm. Subway/El: Red Line to Fullerton.

La Creperie ★★ ⟨Finds⟩ FRENCH   Germain and Sara Roignant have run this intimate gem of a cafe since 1972, never straying from the reasonably priced crepes that draw repeat customers aplenty. (Hey, a crepe is just a pancake rolled up, right, kids?) The decor is heavy on '70s-era brown, but if you find the main dining room more dark than cozy, head to the back patio (enclosed in winter), which sparkles with strings of white lights. Onion soup, pâté, and escargots are all good starters, but the highlights here are the whole-wheat crepes—each prepared on a special grill that Germain imported from his native Brittany. Single-choice fillings include cheese, tomato, egg, or ham; tasty duets feature chicken and mushroom or broccoli and cheese. Beef bourguignon, coq au vin, or curried chicken are the more adventurous crepe combinations. Noncrepe offerings are few: orange roughy and steak frites. Don't leave without at least sharing one of the dessert crepes, which tuck anything from apples to ice cream within their warm folds. La Creperie is an especially great option if you're taking in a show at one of the nearby off-Loop theaters, such as Briar Street, where the popular Blue Man Group is in residence.

2845 N. Clark St. (½ block north of Diversey Pkwy.). © **773/528-9050.** www.lacreperieusa.com. Highchairs, boosters. Reservations accepted for groups of 6 or more only. Main courses $5–$14. AE, DC, DISC, MC, V. Tues–Fri 11:30am–11pm; Sat 11am–11pm; Sun 11am–9:30pm. Subway/El: Brown Line to Diversey.

Nookies DINER   This "chain" of three restaurants is a Chicago favorite for standard breakfast fare. On weekends you'll find Nookies packed with families and young professionals grabbing pancakes or an omelet after a late night out. This family-owned chain serves breakfast all day, plus soups, salads, and sandwiches. Tables and a lunch counter are available. Nookies has additional branches in Lincoln Park at 2114 N. Halsted St. (© **773/327-1400**), and in Lakeview at 3334 N. Halsted St. (© **773/248-9888**).

1748 N. Wells St. © **312/337-2454.** Highchairs, boosters. Reservations not accepted. All main courses under $8. Cash only. Mon–Sat 6:30am–10pm; Sun 6:30am–9pm. Subway/El: Brown Line to Sedgwick.

Stanley's ★★ AMERICAN   Here's another great neighborhood bar and restaurant that stands in the heart of Lincoln Park, normally the epicenter of the young and the restless, but instead caters to families. Stanley's front room is a bar with several booths, tall tables with old chrome and leather bar stools, satellite- and cable-fed TVs, and a jukebox. The adjacent dining room is an abrupt leap into the family den, decorated with photos, quilts, bowling trophies, and children's drawings. This popular family spot has a special kids' menu with corn dogs and PB&J. On Saturday and Sunday there's an all-you-can-eat brunch buffet, which includes make-your-own omelets, build-your-own Belgian waffles, home-fried potatoes, fried chicken, and mashed potatoes for $11. Daily specials are posted on the chalkboard out front.

1970 N. Lincoln Ave. © **312/642-0007.** Kids' menu, highchairs, boosters. Main courses $8–$15; kids' menu $4. Mon–Fri 11am–2pm; Sat 10am–3am; Sun 10am–2am. Bus: 11 or 73 to Armitage.

Toast ★ AMERICAN/BREAKFAST   Located in Lincoln Park, Toast is homey yet slightly funky—note the shelf of vintage toasters. Kids are welcome here: The crayons and butcher-block table coverings will keep them busy, and the staff has a reputation for being baby and kid crazy. Breakfast is served all day and includes a twist on the usual diner fare. Pancakes come in all sorts of tempting varieties, from lemon/poppy seed drizzled with honey to the "pancake orgy" of a strawberry, mango, and banana-pecan pancake topped with granola, yogurt, and honey. (Try it—it tastes even better than it looks!) The house specialty is French toast stuffed with mascarpone cheese and strawberry purée. If pancakes equal dessert for you, try one of the omelets or the breakfast burrito. On the side, you can order grilled chicken sausage, apple-wood smoked bacon, or, of course, a stack of toast. Fresh-squeezed orange juice and grapefruit juice are also available. The lunch menu includes a range of creative sandwiches, salads, and wraps. Toast has a second location at 2046 N. Damen Ave. (© **773/772-5600**).

746 W. Webster St. (at Halsted St.). © **773/935-5600.** Highchairs, boosters. Reservations not accepted. Breakfast $5–$10. AE, DC, DISC, MC, V. Tues–Fri 7am–4pm; Sat–Sun 8am–4pm. Subway/El: Red Line to Fullerton.

Twin Anchors ★ BARBECUE   Come early (around 5pm—later on, there's more of a bar scene) and experience this Old Town landmark; a fixture since the end of Prohibition, Twin Anchors manages to maintain the flavor of old Chicago. Actually, it also has a flavor of a supper club in northern Wisconsin, which is perhaps why so many transplanted small-town Midwesterners feel comfortable here. It's a friendly, family-owned pub with Frank Sinatra on the jukebox and on the walls. (He apparently hung out here on swings through town in the 1960s.) This totally unpretentious place has a long mahogany bar up front and a modest dining room in back with red Formica-topped tables crowded close. Of course, you don't need anything fancy when the ribs—the fall-off-the-bone variety—come this good. Even non–meat eaters may be swayed if they allow themselves one bite of the enormous slabs of tender baby back pork ribs. (Go for the zesty sauce.) Hamburgers will keep kids happy. Ribs and other entrees come with coleslaw and dark rye bread, plus your choice of baked potato, tasty fries, and the even-better crisp onion rings. For dessert, there's a daily cheesecake selection.

1655 N. Sedgwick St. (1 block north of North Ave.). ✆ **312/266-1616.** www.twinanchorsribs.com. Kids' menu, highchairs, boosters. Reservations not accepted. Main courses $9.95–$20; sandwiches $6.75–$8.75; kids' menu around $5. AE, DC, DISC, MC, V. Mon–Thurs 5–11pm; Fri 5pm–midnight; Sat noon–midnight; Sun noon–10:30pm. Subway/El: Brown Line to Sedgwick.

7 WRIGLEYVILLE & THE NORTH SIDE

Families visiting the area surrounding Wrigley Field will probably be in the neighborhood for that very reason—Wrigley Field. The area, however, has a long history of being a neighborhood of working-class families. Lately, it's gentrified as developers have built new town houses and apartments, and with that affluence has come a group of new, very popular restaurants spanning a range of culinary offerings and price ranges. Throughout the North Side you'll find a wealth of ethnic restaurants that allow diners to embark on further gastronomic globe-trotting.

MODERATE

Goose Island Brewing Company AMERICAN   Some of the best beer in Chicago is manufactured at this comfy, award-winning microbrewery, which features an enclosed beer garden that welcomes families (just avoid late nights or Cubs games during the playoffs!). In the course of a year, Goose Island produces about 100 varieties of lagers, ales, stouts, Pilsners, and porters that change with the seasons. But why include a beer-oriented joint in a book for kids? Because the food at the Goose is almost as good as the beer on tap, and the casual dining area attracts plenty of families, especially on the weekends.

The cut-above bar food includes burgers (including a killer, dragon-breath-inducing Stilton burger with roasted garlic), sandwiches (pulled pork, catfish po' boy, chicken Caesar), and some serious salads. Goose Island is also known for its addictive homemade potato chips, fresh-brewed root beer, and orange cream soda. The zero-attitude, come-as-you-are ambience is very refreshing for a lazy afternoon pit stop or a casual lunch or dinner.

3535 N. Clark St. ✆ **773/832-9040.** www.gooseisland.com. Kids' menu, highchairs, boosters. Reservations recommended on weekends. Sandwiches $8–$10; main courses $11–$17; kids' menu under $5. AE, DC, DISC, MC, V. Mon–Wed 4–11pm; Thurs 4pm–midnight; Fri 4pm–2am; Sat 11am–2am; Sun 11am–11pm. Subway/El: Red Line to Addison.

Mia Francesca ITALIAN   Though it's been open since 1992, Mia Francesca remains
a hot dining spot—one that has spawned more than 10 sister restaurants throughout the
city and suburbs. Its strict no-reservations policy used to mean weekend waits of up to 3
hours, but that's eased now that the reservation policy has been changed (that said,
families should definitely call in advance for a table). The restaurant's clean, modern take
on the Italian trattoria concept attracts lots of locals, and the affordable prices keep them
coming back. The food—unpretentious but never dull—includes a range of homemade
pastas, thin-crust pizzas, chicken, veal, and standout seafood (even if you don't usually
order fish in an Italian restaurant, it's worth trying here). Tables are packed close together,
so you can't help eavesdropping on your neighbors—and checking out their food.

You'll find mostly the same menu at three other Francesca's locations in the city: **Francesca's Forno,** 1576 N. Milwaukee Ave., in Wicker Park (© **773/770-0184**); **Francesca's on Taylor,** 1400 W. Taylor St., in Little Italy (© **312/829-2828**), and **Francesca's Bryn Mawr,** 1039 W. Bryn Mawr Ave., north of Wrigleyville (© **773/506-9261**). All
accept reservations, which are highly recommended on weekends.

3311 N. Clark St. (1½ blocks north of Belmont Ave.). © **773/281-3310.** www.miafrancesca.com. Reservations recommended. Main courses $13–$27. AE, MC, V. Sun–Thurs 5–10pm, Fri–Sat 5–11pm; Sat–Sun
11:30am–2pm. Subway/El: Brown or Red Line to Belmont.

INEXPENSIVE

Ann Sather ★★ AMERICAN/BREAKFAST/SWEDISH   A sign hanging by Ann
Sather's door bears the following inscription: ONCE ONE OF MANY NEIGHBORHOOD SWEDISH RESTAURANTS, ANN SATHER'S IS THE ONLY ONE THAT REMAINS. Ann Sather is a real
Chicago institution, where you can enjoy Swedish meatballs with buttered noodles and
brown gravy, or the Swedish sampler of duck breast with lingonberry glaze, meatball,
potato-sausage dumpling, sauerkraut, and brown beans. All meals are full dinners,
including appetizer, main course, vegetable, potato, and dessert. It's the sticky cinnamon
rolls served at breakfast, though, that make addicts out of diners. Weekend brunch here
can get frenzied (get here before 11am), but the people-watching is priceless: a cross section of gay and straight, young and old.

There are smaller cafes with similar menus in Lakeview at 3411 N. Broadway (© **773/305-0024**) and 3416 N. Southport Ave. (© **773/404-4475**).

929 W. Belmont Ave. (btw. Clark St. and Sheffield Ave.). © **773/348-2378.** www.annsather.com. Highchairs, boosters. Reservations accepted for parties of 6 or more only. Main courses $6–$12. AE, DC, MC, V.
Mon–Fri 7am–3pm; Sat–Sun 7am–4pm. Free parking with validation. Subway/El: Red Line to Belmont.

O'Donovan's ⓕⓘⓝⓓⓢ AMERICAN   This century-old neighborhood restaurant and
jovial pub has kept up the tradition that has thrilled kids for decades: Magicians who
perform tableside tricks on Saturday evenings. (To avoid the bar-oriented rush, come
early, at 5 or 6pm.) Although there's no kids' menu, ordering appetizers for the kids
works just as well. For adults, burgers are the thing, although options also include steaks,
chops, and seafood. As the night progresses, O'Donovan's draws a good mix of late-20-
something blue- and white-collar patrons with a healthy selection of microbrews. On
Sunday the expansive buffet features all-you-can-eat scrambled eggs, bacon, sausage,
carved ham, roast beef, waffles, omelets made to order, and biscuits and gravy.

2100 W. Irving Park Rd. © **773/478-2100.** Highchairs. Reservations not accepted. Main courses $6–$16.
AE, MC, V. Mon–Fri 11am–2am; Sat–Sun 11am–3am. Subway/El: Brown Line to Irving Park. Bus: 11 or 80.

Penny's Noodle Shop ★ ⓥⓐⓛⓤⓔ ASIAN/NOODLES   Predating many of Chicago's
Pan-Asian noodle shops, Penny's has kept its loyal following even as others have joined

FAMILY-FRIENDLY DINING

5

WRIGLEYVILLE & THE NORTH SIDE

the fray. Penny Chiarnopoulous, a Thai native, has assembled a concise menu of delectable dishes, all of them fresh and made to order—and at prices that will make you do a double take. The two dining rooms are clean and spare. The Thai spring roll, filled with seasoned tofu, cucumber, bean sprouts, and strips of cooked egg, makes a refreshing starter. Of course, noodles unite everything on the menu, so your main decision is choosing among noodles (crispy wide rice, rice vermicelli, Japanese udon, and so on) in a heaping bowl of soup or spread out on a plate. There are several barbecued pork and beef entrees, and plenty of options for vegetarians.

The original Penny's, tucked under the El tracks at 3400 N. Sheffield Ave., near Wrigley Field (① 773/281-8222), is small and often has long waits; you stand a better chance of scoring a table at the Diversey Avenue location (address below) or the one in Wicker Park, at 1542 N. Damen Ave. (① 773/394-0100). The original location is BYOB; the Diversey Avenue and Wicker Park locations have decent beer and wine lists.

950 W. Diversey Ave. (at Sheffield St.). ① **773/281-8448.** Highchairs, boosters. Reservations not accepted. Main courses $5–$8. MC, V. Sun–Thurs 11am–10pm; Fri–Sat 11am–10:30pm. Subway/El: Brown Line to Diversey.

Uncommon Ground ★ ⓕinds BREAKFAST/SANDWICHES A living-room atmosphere created by a wood-burning stove and artwork on the walls that rotates frequently (and is always available for purchase), Uncommon Ground is home to local artists, musicians, and writers. (Five nights a week, you can check out a performance in the back room by a local trying to make the big time—highly recommended for families with teens.) Thankfully for families, the atmosphere is 100% smoke free. Sit next to a window and watch the traffic cruise by on Clark and Grace streets while you indulge in steaming bowls of latte and hot chocolate and some of the yummy baked goods, or choose from the menu, which is heavy on breakfast foods like nutty oatmeal with bananas; the "uncommon" breakfast burrito; a croissant with ham, egg, and cheese; and granola piled with fresh fruit and yogurt. One can't-miss choice is the apple-pecan whole-wheat pancakes with cranberry-honey butter. Lunchtime means sandwiches, hummus platter, and a full bar (Thurs night is $4 martini night). Teens will get a kick out of the Midwest's alternative press on hand here, from the *Reader* to the *Onion,* for your reading pleasure.

3800 N. Clark St. (at Grace St.). ① **773/929-3680.** Kids' menu, highchairs, boosters. Main courses $9–$15; kids' menu $4–$9. AE, DC, DISC, MC, V. Mon–Fri 9am–2am; Sat–Sun 8am–2am. Subway/El: Red Line to Addison. Bus: 22.

8 WICKER PARK/BUCKTOWN

The booming Wicker Park/Bucktown area followed closely in the race to gentrification on the heels of Lincoln Park and Wrigleyville. First came the artists, photographers, and musicians, followed by armies of yuppies and young families, originally following the cheap rents and real estate, and later chasing the cachet that became attached to the neighborhood. Happily, what's now one of the city's hippest restaurant scenes includes a number of fun options for families. Get yourself to the nexus of activity at the intersection of North, Damen, and Milwaukee avenues, and you won't have to walk more than a couple of blocks in any direction to find a hot spot. Cab fare is within reason from downtown, or you can take the El's Blue Line to Damen Avenue.

EXPENSIVE

Mirai Sushi ★★ JAPANESE/SUSHI Blending a serious devotion to sushi and sake with a decidedly youthful, funky-chic ambience, Mirai is a hot destination for cold raw fish (though it serves other Japanese fare as well). You'd be surprised at how many city kids enjoy sushi, and kids are more than welcome here. If you're out on a date night, the futuristic second-floor sake lounge is the hippest place in town to slurp down sushi, chilled sakes, and "red ones," the house cocktail of vodka with passion fruit, lime, and cranberry juices. The bright main-floor dining room offers a comparatively traditional environment.

Fish is flown in daily for the sushi bar, where several chefs are hard at work master-crafting a lovely list of offerings—from the beginner sushi standards such as California rolls and *ebi* (boiled shrimp) to escalating classifications of tuna, three additional shrimp varieties, five types of salmon, a half-dozen varieties of fresh oysters, and a tantalizing list of four caviars (in addition to the four roes offered). The informative sake menu of about a dozen selections opens up a new world to diners accustomed to the generic carafe of heated sake.

2020 W. Division St. (at Damen Ave.). © **773/862-8500.** www.miraisushi.com. Reservations recommended. Sushi $2–$6 per piece. AE, DC, DISC, MC, V. Mon–Wed 5–10pm; Thurs–Sat 5–11pm. Upstairs lounge until 2am. Subway/El: Blue Line to Division.

MODERATE

Club Lucky ★★ Ⓥalue ITALIAN   Naugahyde banquettes, Formica-topped bar and tables, and Captain Video ceiling fixtures might seem retro to some, but everyone from young families to stylish couples find Club Lucky both an interesting scene and a good deal on good food. The scene here changes throughout the evening: Young families gradually give way to stylish couples posing with glasses of the restaurant's signature martinis. Prices are moderate, especially considering the generous family-style portions. The large calamari appetizer—"for two," the menu says—will almost certainly feed everyone in your family. The menu offers real Italian home-style cooking, such as *pasta e fagioli* (thick macaroni-and-bean soup—really a kind of stew); rigatoni with veal meatballs, steamed escarole, and melted slabs of mozzarella; and spicy grilled boneless pork chops served with peppers and roasted potatoes. There's no kids' menu, but the restaurant serves sides of pasta dishes and meatballs. The lunch menu includes about a dozen Italian sandwiches, such as scrambled eggs and pesto, meatball, and Italian sausage.

1824 W. Wabansia Ave. (1 block north of North Ave., btw. Damen and Ashland aves.). © **773/227-2300.** www.clubluckychicago.com. Highchairs, boosters. Reservations accepted for parties of 6 or more. Sandwiches $8–$11; main courses $10–$36. AE, DC, DISC, MC, V. Mon–Thurs 11:30am–11pm; Fri 11:30am–midnight; Sat 5pm–midnight; Sun 4–10pm; cocktail lounge open later. Subway/El: Blue Line to Damen.

Jane's ★ Ⓕinds ECLECTIC   Jane's has long been ignored by dining critics on the hunt for the next big thing—all the more reason to love this inconspicuous charmer. This does not, however, mean that snagging a table at Jane's is an easy feat. On the contrary; this is a hugely popular destination among Wicker Park/Bucktown habitués, who'd prefer to keep it a secret. It's a neighborhood-y place, and in the early evening, you'll find loads of young families with tots in tow.

More than anything else, it may be the cozy ambience that attracts diners. Jane's is ensconced in an old house that has been gutted and rehabbed to create an open, two-story space with just 16 tables. (In summer seven more are set up on an outside patio.) The menu offers piquant, upscale comfort food prepared simply and with loving care, including both meat (duck breast pan-seared with turnips and peaches; seared sea bass with mashed potatoes, arugula, caramelized pearl onions, and mushroom coulis) and vegetarian options, such as a goat cheese, tofu, and veggie burrito. The salads are standouts, especially the greens with pear, blue cheese, pecans, and balsamic vinaigrette.

1655 W. Cortland St. (1 block west of Ashland Ave.). © **773/862-5263.** www.janesrestaurant.com. Reservations recommended. Main courses $15–$25. MC, V. Sun–Thurs 5–10pm; Fri–Sat 5–11pm; Sat–Sun 10am–2:30pm. Subway/El: Blue Line to Damen.

INEXPENSIVE

Hot Chocolate AMERICAN ★   If you're looking for a special place to take your kids for a dessert, look no further than Hot Chocolate. A casual neighborhood spot, Hot Chocolate is the kind of place you can stop in for a brioche and coffee in the morning, a Kobe beefsteak sandwich at lunch, or a plate of glazed pork tenderloin in the evening. A kids' menu offers grilled cheese, peanut-butter-and-jelly sandwiches, and other customized dishes. However, desserts are the main event here. Many, including the apple-cider potpie and the banana napoleon, with layers of caramelized bananas, banana coffeecake, graham crackers, and a topping of banana ice cream, use seasonal fruit, but chocoholics can get their fill, too, with dishes such as the rich chocolate soufflé with **153** caramel ice cream or a flight of mini hot chocolates served with homemade marshmallows. The restaurant is stylish but warm, with lots of exposed wood and (not coincidentally) chocolate-brown upholstery. Come on a weekday (for a late lunch or early dinner) to avoid a wait.

1747 N. Damen Ave. (at Willow St.). © **773/489-1747.** Kids' menu, highchairs, boosters. Reservations not accepted. Main courses $10–$13 lunch; $12–$23 dinner. Kids' menu about $6. AE, MC, V. Tues–Fri 11am–3pm; Sat–Sun 10am–2pm; Tues–Wed and Sun 5:30–10pm; Thurs 5:30–11pm; Fri–Sat 5:30pm–midnight. Subway/El: Blue Line to Damen.

Northside Café ★ (Value AMERICAN/BURGERS I highly recommend this spot for high-quality cheap eats. Northside cooks up great burgers, sandwiches, and salads, all for $15 and less. This is strictly neighborhood dining, without attitude and little in the way of decor. The back dining room looks like a rec room from around 1973, complete with a fireplace, pinball machines, and a pool table. In nice weather Northside opens up its large patio for dining, and a sky-lit cover keeps it in use during the winter. You're sure to be entertained people-watching, as Northside attracts all sorts. During the week it's more of a neighborhood hangout, but on the weekends a touristy crowd from Lincoln Park and the suburbs moves in.

1635 N. Damen Ave. (at North and Milwaukee aves.). © **773/384-3555.** Highchairs, boosters. Reservations not accepted. Menu items $6–$15. AE, DC, DISC, MC, V. Sun–Fri 11:30am–2am; Sat 11am–3am. Subway/El: Blue Line to Damen.

Piece ★ AMERICAN/PIZZA Piece proves to deep-dish-loving Chicagoans that thin-crust pizza deserves respect. A casual, welcoming hangout, Piece makes a good lunch or early dinner stop for families, but later in the evening, it becomes a convivial scene full of young singles sipping one of the restaurant's seasonal microbrew beers. The large, airy dining room—a former garage that's been outfitted with dark wood tables and ceiling beams—is flooded with light from the expansive skylights overhead; even when it's crowded (as it gets on weekend evenings), the soaring space above keeps the place from feeling claustrophobic. A selection of salads and sandwiches on satisfyingly crusty bread is also available, but pizza in the style of New Haven, Connecticut (hometown of one of the owners), is the house specialty. Pick from three styles—plain (tomato sauce, Parmesan cheese, and garlic), red (tomato sauce and mozzarella), or white (olive oil, garlic, and mozzarella)—and add on your favorite toppings. Sausage and/or spinach works well with the plain or red, but the adventurous shouldn't miss the house specialty: clam and bacon on white pizza.

1927 W. North Ave. (at Milwaukee Ave.). © **773/772-4422.** www.piecechicago.com. Highchairs, boosters. Reservations accepted for groups of 10 or more. Pizza $11–$17. AE, DISC, MC, V. Mon–Thurs 11:30am–11pm; Fri–Sat 11:30am–12:30am; Sun 11am–10pm. Subway: Blue Line to Damen.

Silver Cloud Bar & Grill ★ DINER How can kids not feel at home here? Silver Cloud is one of few Chicago restaurants I know that has tater tots on the menu (and naturally, every time I eat here, I work my entire meal selection around this "side"). This Bucktown restaurant's motto is FOOD LIKE MOM WOULD MAKE IF SHE WAS GETTING PAID. Although the food isn't extraordinary, it should please kids. The grilled cheese is made with mozzarella, Monterey Jack, and cheddar on Italian bread and served with a bowl of Campbell's tomato soup. Other favorites are chicken potpie, pot roast, and even sloppy Joes. Retro desserts include s'mores and root beer floats. Roomy red leather booths are a hit with families. In good weather sit outside (the seating area is on the side street, so you avoid the noise of Damen Ave.). This place is not a tourist hot spot, so enjoy the people-watching—most customers are neighborhood folks. While Silver Cloud attracts a mix of families, couples, and groups of friends during the day and early-evening hours, it becomes more of a cocktail lounge at night. You might try the Sunday brunch, which is especially popular.

1700 N. Damen Ave. (at Wabansia St.). ✆ **773/489-6212.** www.silvercloudchicago.com. Highchairs, boosters. Reservations accepted. Main courses $6–$10 lunch, $10–$16 dinner. AE, DC, MC, V. Mon–Thurs 11:30am–11pm; Fri 11:30am–midnight; Sat–Sun 10am–midnight. Subway/El: Blue Line to Damen.

---

9 ONLY IN CHICAGO

Pizza-loving and hot dog–inhaling kids have it made in Chicago: We've turned them from fast food into art forms. Of course, Chicagoans have their own take on these all-American staples, so to have an authentic taste of Chicago, shun the thin-crust pizza and the ketchup as condiment of choice for hot dogs. Try them our way, and I guarantee you'll understand why Chicagoans are passionate about their dogs and pizza.

PIZZA

To the uninitiated: Chicago-style pizza, also known as deep-dish, is thick-crusted and often demands a knife and fork. The thin-crust variety favored in New York is also widely available; a third type, called stuffed, is similar to a pie, with a crust on both top and bottom. Many pizzerias serve both thick and thin, and some make all three kinds.

Three of Chicago's best gourmet deep-dish restaurants are **Pizzeria Uno** (p. 138), **Pizzeria Due** (p. 138), and **Gino's East** (p. 136). In River North **Lou Malnati's Pizzeria** ★, at 439 N. Wells St. (✆ **312/828-9800**), bakes both deep-dish and thin-crust pizza and even has a low-fat cheese option. **Edwardo's** is a local pizza chain that serves all three varieties, but with a wheat crust and all-natural ingredients. (Try the tasty spinach pizza, the specialty here.) It has several Chicago locations, including one in the Gold Coast, at 1212 N. Dearborn St., at Division Street (✆ **312/337-4490**); one in the South Loop, at 521 S. Dearborn St. (✆ **312/939-3366**); and one in Lincoln Park, at 2662 N. Halsted St. (✆ **773/871-3400**). Very near to the Lincoln Park Zoo is **Ranalli and Ryan's,** 1925 N. Lincoln Ave. (btw. Wisconsin St. and Armitage Ave.; ✆ **312/642-4700**), with its terrific open-air patio and an extensive selection of beers.

In Wrigleyville, just off Belmont Avenue, are **Leona's Pizzeria,** 3215 N. Sheffield Ave. (btw. Belmont Ave. and School St.; ✆ **773/327-8861**), which serves all three kinds of pizza. Leona's also has a location in Little Italy, at 1419 W. Taylor St. (btw. Bishop and Loomis sts.; ✆ **312/850-2222**).

For a unique take on the deep-dish phenomenon, try the "pizza potpie" at **Chicago Pizza & Oven Grinder,** 2121 N. Clark St., steps from Lincoln Park Zoo (btw. Webster and Dickens aves.; ✆ **773/248-2570**). The pizzas are baked in a bowl and then turned over when served, for a distinctive upside-down pizza experience. This neighborhood spot stays popular year after year, so plan on showing up early for dinner to avoid a wait.

HOT DOGS

Chicagoans like to think that they stand head and skewers above the rest of the world when it comes to hot dogs. The facades of Chicago's hot dog stands, as if by some unwritten convention, are all very colorful, with bright signs of red and yellow, exaggerated lettering, and comic illustrations of the wieners and fries. The classic Chicago hot dog includes a frankfurter by Vienna Beef (a local food processor and hallowed institution), heaps of chopped onions and relish so green it could be pop art, a slather of yellow mustard, pickle spears and fresh tomato wedges, a dash of celery salt, and, for good measure, two or three "sport" peppers, those thumb-shaped holy terrors that turn your mouth into its own bonfire.

Chicago is home to many standout hot dog stands and shops, but one, **Hot Doug's,** 3324 N. California Ave. (at Roscoe St.; ✆ **773/279-9550**), takes encased meats to a new level, featuring several gourmet sausages on a bun every day except Sunday (plan on standing in line no matter which day you show up—and it's always worth it). Hot Doug's also serves a great classic Chicago dog just like many other stands in town, including **Gold Coast Dogs,** 159 N. Wabash Ave., at Randolph Street (✆ **312/917-1677**), in the Loop just a block from Michigan Avenue. **Fluky's,** in The Shops at North Bridge mall at 520 N. Michigan Ave. (✆ **312/245-0702**), is part of a local chain that has been serving great hot dogs since the Great Depression (Dan Aykroyd and Jay Leno are fans). Especially popular with kids is **Portillo's,** at 100 W. Ontario St. (at Clark St.; ✆ **312/ 587-8910;** www.portillos.com), another local chain that specializes in hot dogs but also serves excellent pastas and salads (and top it off with a slice of their incredibly fudgy and decadent chocolate cake). **Murphy's Red Hots,** 1211 W. Belmont Ave. (✆ **773/935-2882**), is a neighborhood spot not too far from Wrigley Field. Besides hot dogs, Murphy's serves charbroiled Polish sausages, burgers, and tasty hand-cut fries. **The Wieners Circle,** in Lincoln Park at 2622 N. Clark St. (btw. Wrightwood Ave. and Drummond Place; ✆ 773/477-7444), is a favorite where rude order-takers are part of the shtick.

If you've got a car, head up to the legendary **Superdawg Drive-In,** 6363 N. Milwaukee (✆ **773/763-0660**), on the northwest side of the city. It's impossible to miss: Mr. and Mrs. Superdawg, in Tarzan and Jane tableaux, beckon the masses from the rooftop, their beady eyes pulsing an electric red. Maurie and Florrie Berman haven't changed a thing about their place—the city's last real drive-in, with its Order-Matic ordering system and female carhops on roller skates—since they opened for business in 1948. Their main attraction still arrives in a red 1950s-design enclosed box that declares on one side, YOUR SUPERDAWG LOUNGES INSIDE, CONTENTEDLY CUSHIONED IN SUPERFRIES.

Exploring Chicago with Your Kids

While Chicago has sights that top any world traveler's list (although fewer than New York or London), Chicago offers big family attractions, too. Part of Chicago's kid-friendliness comes from the location of our major museums, which sit within walking distance of beaches and miles of parks. Kids can learn in the morning and run free in the afternoon. Compared to some major cities, outdoor space is easy to find, thanks to miles of unimpeded lakefront. And as every parent knows, being outdoors is a welcome relief when kids need to let off steam.

Although crowds do pack the major museums on weekends and holidays, the crowdedness is not on the level of New York City on a similar day. Summer is prime time here: Families flock *to* Chicago on the weekends—unlike other urban areas, where families *escape from* the city. When the weather is warm, you'll find that suburbanites, Wisconsinites, Iowans, and families from other surrounding states head to our city to enjoy the cool lake breezes.

Chicago's a no-nonsense Midwestern city, and most establishments are laid-back and open-minded. You won't get the kind of urban snobbery you might experience in other big cities. For the most part, Chicagoans are "nice"—another Midwestern quality—meaning you are more likely to get a sympathetic smile than the evil eye when trying to calm a crying child.

1 SIGHTS BY NEIGHBORHOOD

THE LOOP & VICINITY

Adler Planetarium & Astronomy Museum ★, p. 157
Art Institute of Chicago ★★★, p. 178
Chicago Archicenter, p. 179
Chicago Cultural Center ★, p. 180
Chicago Fed Money Museum, p. 180
Chicago Public Library/Harold Washington Library Center, p. 181
The Field Museum of Natural History ★★★, p. 162
Glessner House, p. 196
John G. Shedd Aquarium ★★★, p. 165
The Loop Sculpture Tour ★★, p. 168
Millennium Park ★★★, p. 168
Museum Campus ★★★, p. 170
Museum of Contemporary Photography, p. 185
National Vietnam Veterans Art Museum, p. 186
Sears Tower Skydeck ★, p. 177
Spertus Museum, p. 190

THE NORTH SIDE
Near North/Magnificent Mile

Chicago Children's Museum ★★, p. 160
Chicago Water Tower—City Gallery, p. 181
The Hancock Observatory ★★, p. 175
McCormick Tribune Freedom Museum, p. 184

Museum of Contemporary Art ★,
  p. 184
Navy Pier ★, p. 174
Newberry Library, p. 186

The Gold Coast
International Museum of Surgical
  Science, p. 183
The Lakefront ★★★, p. 167

Lincoln Park
Chicago History Museum ★, p. 180
Lincoln Park Conservatory ★, p. 199
Lincoln Park Pritzker Children's Zoo
  & Farm-in-the-Zoo ★, p. 197
Lincoln Park Zoo ★★★, p. 197
North Avenue Beach, p. 216
Peggy Notebaert Nature
  Museum ★★, p. 200

Uptown & Andersonville
Swedish-American Museum Center ★,
  p. 190

THE WEST SIDE
Near West
Garfield Park Conservatory ★, p. 199
Intuit: The Center for Intuitive and
  Outsider Art, p. 183
Jane Addams Hull House Museum,
  p. 184
Polish Museum of America, p. 188

Pilsen
National Museum of Mexican Art ★,
  p. 185

Hyde Park
DuSable Museum of African-American
  History, p. 182
Museum of Science and
  Industry ★★★, p. 170
Oriental Institute Museum ★, p. 187
Robie House ★★, p. 194
The Smart Museum of Art ★, p. 189

The Suburbs
Brookfield Zoo ★★★, Brookfield,
  p. 196
Fox River Trolley Museum, South
  Elgin, p. 188
The Frank Lloyd Wright Home &
  Studio ★★★, Oak Park, p. 194
Hamill Family Play Zoo ★★★,
  Brookfield, p. 165
Illinois Railway Museum, Union,
  p. 188
Morton Arboretum, Lisle, p. 200
Six Flags Great America, Gurnee,
  p. 191
Unity Temple ★, Oak Park, p. 195

EXPLORING CHICAGO WITH YOUR KIDS

6

KIDS' TOP 10 ATTRACTIONS

2 KIDS' TOP 10 ATTRACTIONS

Adler Planetarium & Astronomy Museum★ All ages. The building may be historic, but some of the attractions here will captivate the most jaded video game addict in your family. The Western Hemisphere's first planetarium was founded by Sears, Roebuck & Co. executive Max Adler, who imported a Zeiss projector from Germany in 1930.

The good news for present-day visitors is that the planetarium has been updated since then. Your first stop should be the modern Sky Pavilion, where the don't-miss experience is the **StarRider Theater,** which propels passengers on an exhilarating voyage of discovery into the infinity of space. Settle down under the massive dome, and you'll take a half-hour interactive virtual-reality trip through the Milky Way and into deep space, featuring a computer-generated 3-D graphics projection system. You participate in the journey by operating controls on the armrests. Six high-resolution video projectors form a seamless image above your head—you'll feel like you're literally floating in space. If you're looking for more entertainment, the **Sky Theater** shows movies with an astronomical bent.

6

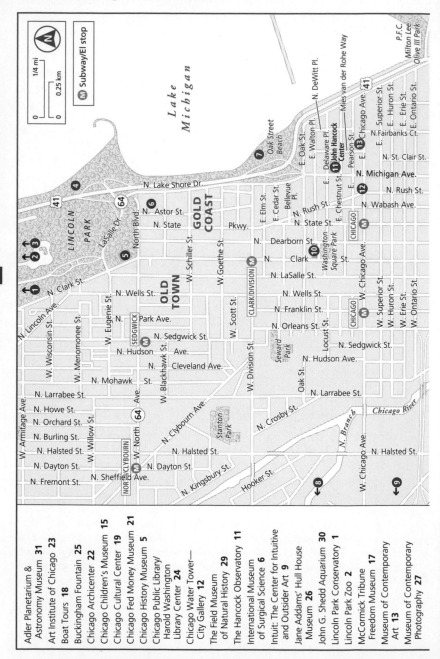

Adler Planetarium &
Astronomy Museum **31**
Art Institute of Chicago **23**
Boat Tours **18**
Buckingham Fountain **25**
Chicago Archicenter **22**
Chicago Children's Museum **15**
Chicago Cultural Center **19**
Chicago Fed Money Museum **21**
Chicago History Museum **5**
Chicago Public Library/
Harold Washington
Library Center **24**
Chicago Water Tower—
City Gallery **12**
The Field Museum
of Natural History **29**
The Hancock Observatory **11**
International Museum
of Surgical Science **6**
Intuit: The Center for Intuitive
and Outsider Art **9**
Jane Addams' Hull House
Museum **26**
John G. Shedd Aquarium **30**
Lincoln Park Conservatory **1**
Lincoln Park Zoo **2**
McCormick Tribune
Freedom Museum **17**
Museum of Contemporary
Art **13**
Museum of Contemporary
Photography **27**

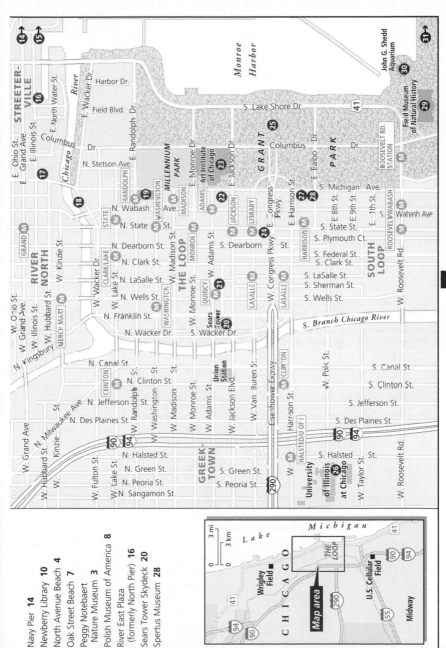

Navy Pier **14**

Newberry Library **10**

North Avenue Beach **4**

Oak Street Beach **7**

Peggy Notebaert
Nature Museum **3**

Polish Museum of America **8**

River East Plaza
(formerly North Pier) **16**

Sears Tower Skydeck **20**

Spertus Museum **28**

Recent shows have included *Secrets of Saturn* and *Mars Now!*, both of which are updated as new discoveries are made.

The planetarium's exhibition galleries feature a variety of displays and interactive activities. If you're going to see only one exhibit with your kids, check out **Shoot for the Moon,** an exhibit on lunar exploration that's full of interactive stations (it also showcases the personal collection of astronaut Jim Lovell, captain of the infamous Apollo 13 mission, who now lives in the Chicago suburbs). Other exhibits include **Bringing the Heavens to Earth,** which traces the ways different cultures have tried to make sense of astronomical phenomena. Also of special interest is the planetarium's signature exhibit, **From the Night Sky to the Big Bang,** which traces changing views of the cosmos over 1,000 years and features artifacts from the planetarium's extensive collection of historical astronomical instruments. (*Warning:* This one is best suited for older kids, unless your kid is a real astronomy fan.)

The museum's cafe provides views of the lakefront and skyline. On the first Friday evening of the month, visitors can view dramatic close-ups of the moon, planets, and distant galaxies through a closed-circuit monitor connected to the planetarium's Doane Observatory telescope.

To find out what to look for in this month's sky, call the Nightwatch 24-Hour Hot Line (✆ **312/922-STAR** [922-7827]), or check out the planetarium's website.

Families might want to make a point of visiting during **"Far Out Fridays,"** on the first Friday of each month from 4:30 to 10pm, which feature special activities suited to kids, including telescope viewings and sky shows. Admission is $20 for adults, $17 for kids, a real deal when you consider all of the activities it includes.

1300 S. Lake Shore Dr. ✆ **312/322-STAR** [322-7827]. www.adlerplanetarium.org. Admission $10 adults, $8 seniors, $6 children 4–17, free for children 3 and under; admission including 1 show and audio tour $19 adults, $17 seniors, $15 children. Free admission Mon–Tues Oct–Nov and Jan–Feb. Memorial Day to Labor Day daily 9:30am–4:30pm; Sat–Sun 9am–6pm; 1st Fri of every month until 10pm; until 6pm daily Memorial Day to Labor Day. StarRider Theater and Sky Shows run throughout the day; call main number for current times. Bus: 12 or 146.

Chicago Children's Museum ★★ **All ages.** Parents rave about the Chicago Children's Museum, now in existence for over 25 years. Since it moved to Navy Pier in 1996, the museum has become one of the most popular cultural attractions in the city. The three-story museum has areas especially for preschoolers as well as for children up to age 10. Several permanent exhibits allow kids a maximum of hands-on fun, and there are always creative temporary exhibitions on tap as well. **Dinosaur Expedition** re-creates an expedition to the Sahara, allowing kids to experience camp life, conduct scientific research, and dig for the bones of *Suchomimus,* a Saharan dinosaur recently discovered by Chicago paleontologist Paul Sereno (a full-scale model stands nearby). Another permanent exhibit, **Play It Safe,** addresses possible safety issues in an interactive house and backyard. **WaterWays** allows visitors to learn about the uses and benefits of water resources by constructing dams to direct the flow of water, constructing fountains, and teaming up with others to blast a stream of water 50 feet in the air. Art meets technology in Big Backyard, an urban garden filled with enormous insects, giggling flowers, giant toadstools and other fantasy creations. Through innovative technology, you can immerse yourself in the action and discover what it's like to be part of the city's landscape. There's also a three-level schooner that children can board for a little climbing, from the crow's nest to the gangplank; **Kids Town,** a kid-scaled cityscape with everything from a gas station to a city bus that children 4 and under can touch and explore; and an arts-and-crafts

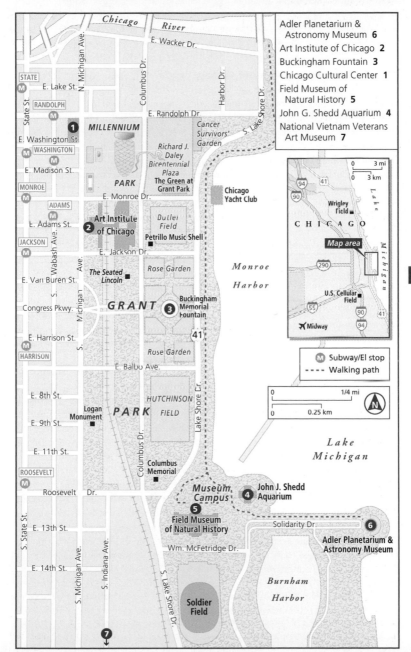

Adler Planetarium &
Astronomy Museum **6**
Art Institute of Chicago **2**
Buckingham Fountain **3**
Chicago Cultural Center **1**
Field Museum of
Natural History **5**
John G. Shedd Aquarium **4**
National Vietnam Veterans
Art Museum **7**

Chicago River
E. Wacker Dr.
N. Michigan Ave.
Columbus Dr.
Harbor Dr.
S. Lake Shore Dr.

STATE
E. Lake St.
State St.
RANDOLPH
E. Randolph Dr.
MILLENNIUM
E. Washington St.
WASHINGTON
E. Madison St.
MONROE
PARK
E. Monroe Dr.
ADAMS
E. Adams St.
Art Institute
of Chicago **2**
JACKSON
Wabash Ave.
E. Jackson Dr.
The Seated
Lincoln
Rose Garden
E. Van Buren St.
Michigan Ave.
Congress Pkwy.
GRANT
Buckingham
Memorial
Fountain **3**
E. Harrison St.
HARRISON
Rose Garden
E. Balbo Ave.
Lake Shore Cr.
E. 8th St.
HUTCHINSON
FIELD
Logan
Monument
E. 9th St.
PARK
E. 11th St.
ROOSEVELT
Columbus Dr.
Columbus
Memorial
Roosevelt Dr.
S. State St.
E. 13th St.
S. Michigan Ave.
S. Indiana Ave.
E. 14th St.
S. Lake Shore Dr.

Cancer
Survivors'
Garden
Richard J.
Daley
Bicentennial
Plaza
The Green at
Grant Park
Chicago
Yacht Club
Butler
Field
Petrillo Music Shell

Monroe
Harbor

Museum
Campus **5**
Field Museum
of Natural History
Wm. McFetridge Dr.

John J. Shedd
Aquarium **4**
Solidarity Dr. **6**
Adler Planetarium &
Astronomy Museum

Lake
Michigan

Burnham
Harbor

Soldier
Field

7

0   3 mi
0   3 km
94   41
90
Wrigley
Field
CHICAGO
Map area
290
U.S. Cellular
Field
55
Midway
90
41
94
Lake Michigan

Ⓜ Subway/El stop
---- Walking path

0   1/4 mi
0   0.25 km
N

EXPLORING CHICAGO WITH YOUR KIDS

6

KIDS' TOP 10 ATTRACTIONS

area where visitors can create original artwork to take home. The museum store is filled with educational and multicultural books, science toys, videos, music, and art supplies.

Navy Pier, 700 E. Grand Ave. (©) **312/527-1000.** www.chicagochildrensmuseum.org. Admission $9 adults and children, $8 seniors. Free admission the first Mon of every month for ages 15 and under; free admission for all Thurs 5–8pm. Sun–Wed and Fri 10am–5pm; Thurs and Sat 10am–8pm. Subway/El: Red Line to Grand/State; transfer to city bus or Navy Pier's free trolley bus. Bus: 29, 56, 65, or 66.

The Field Museum of Natural History ★★★ All ages. Kids love the Field Museum for its wide-open spaces—we're talking 9 acres of floor space—giant dinos, and hands-on exhibits. Little ones can indulge their inner Indiana Jones by exploring the shadowy tunnels of an Egyptian tomb or feeling the thrill of a passage across the Pacific Ocean in an outrigger canoe. Or explore the African continent by visiting a royal Cameroon palace, witnessing savanna wildlife, and traveling across the Sahara and back to Nigeria. Gleaming gems, giant stuffed elephants, mummies, and Native American artifacts will have your kids enthralled. Scores of permanent and temporary exhibitions—some interactive, but most requiring the old-fashioned skills of observation and imagination—can boggle the mind with their sheer quantity. Some of the diorama-type exhibits have gotten musty over time, but many others have been completely overhauled, with plenty of activities to keep kids interested.

Start out in the grand **Stanley Field Hall** (where you enter from either the north or the south end). Standing proudly at the north side is the largest, most complete *Tyrannosaurus rex* fossil ever unearthed. Named **"Sue" ★★** for the paleontologist who found the dinosaur in 1990 in South Dakota, the specimen was acquired by the museum for a cool $8.4 million following a high-stakes bidding war. The real skull is so heavy that a lighter copy had to be mounted on the skeleton; the actual one is on display nearby.

Families should head downstairs for two of the most popular kid-friendly exhibits. The pieces on display in **Inside Ancient Egypt ★** were brought to the museum in the early 1900s, after researchers in Saqqara, Egypt, excavated two of the original chambers from the tomb of Unis-ankh, son of the Fifth Dynasty ruler Pharaoh Unis. This *mastaba* (tomb) of Unis-ankh now forms the core of a spellbinding exhibit that realistically depicts scenes from Egyptian funeral, religious, and other social practices. Visitors can explore aspects of the day-to-day world of ancient Egypt, viewing 23 actual mummies and realistic burial scenes, a living marsh environment and canal works, the ancient royal barge, a religious shrine, and a reproduction of a typical marketplace of the period. Many of the exhibits allow hands-on interaction, and there are special activities for kids, such as making parchment from living papyrus plants.

Next to the Egypt exhibit you'll find **Underground Adventure,** a "total immersion environment" populated by giant robotic earwigs, centipedes, wolf spiders, and other subterranean critters. The Disneyesque exhibit is a big hit with kids, but—annoyingly—requires an extra admission charge ($7 on top of regular admission for adults, $3 for kids). While you're downstairs, plug a dollar bill into one of the old-fashioned wax-molding machines and watch as your very own red *T. rex* or green brontosaurus is shaped in front of your eyes. Kids get a thrill out of taking home their very own Field Museum dino.

The "peoples of the world" exhibits are not only mind-opening, but also great fun. **Traveling the Pacific** is hidden up on the second floor, but it's definitely worth a stop. Hundreds of artifacts from the museum's oceanic collection re-create scenes of island life in the South Pacific. (There's even a full-scale model of a Maori meetinghouse.) **Africa,** an assemblage of African artifacts and provocative, interactive multimedia presentations, takes viewers to Senegal, to a Cameroon palace, to the savanna and its wildlife, and on a

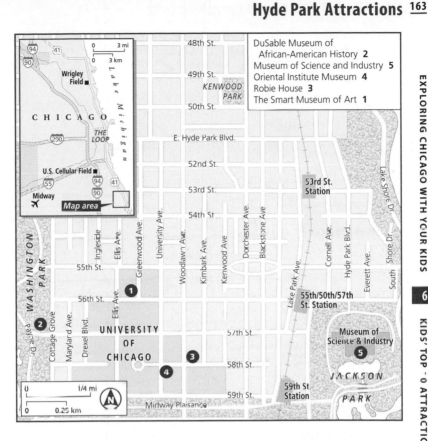

DuSable Museum of African-American History **2**
Museum of Science and Industry **5**
Oriental Institute Museum **4**
Robie House **3**
The Smart Museum of Art **1**

"virtual" journey aboard a slave ship to the Americas. Native Chicagoans will quickly name two more signature highlights: the taxidermied bodies of **Bushman** (a legendary lowland gorilla who made international headlines while at the city's Lincoln Park Zoo) and the **Man-Eating Lions of Tsavo.** (The pair of male lions munched nearly 140 British railway workers constructing a bridge in East Africa in 1898; their story is featured in the film *The Ghost and the Darkness.*)

The museum's newest permanent exhibit, the **Crown Family Playlab** (located directly inside the museum's East entrance) is aimed at kids and enhances the museum experience even for the littlest ones. Inside is a well-stocked art room complete with kiln, where museum employees are on hand to encourage budding artists. My suggestion is to visit the Playlab last: First, the kids will likely be itching to get hands-on by then, and second, you'll have a hard time tearing them away from the Playlab to visit any other exhibits. Plus, in the Playlab, the kids can act out (in a positive way!) what they've seen in the rest of the museum, by dressing up like woodland animals, digging for dinosaur bones, or picking ears of corn in a Pueblo.

The museum hosts special traveling exhibits, as well as numerous lectures, book signings, multiethnic musical and dance performances, storytelling events, and family activity days

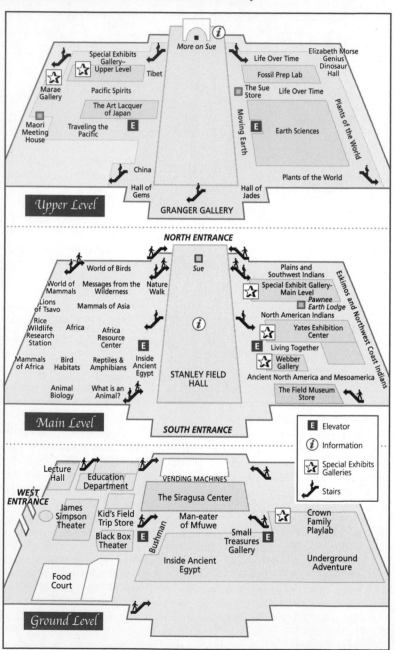

Upper Level

More on Sue

Special Exhibits Gallery– Upper Level

Tibet

Life Over Time

Elizabeth Morse Genius Dinosaur Hall

Fossil Prep Lab

Marae Gallery

Pacific Spirits

The Sue Store

Life Over Time

The Art Lacquer of Japan

E

Plants of the World

Maori Meeting House

Traveling the Pacific

Moving Earth

E

Earth Sciences

China

Plants of the World

Hall of Gems

GRANGER GALLERY

Hall of Jades

NORTH ENTRANCE

Main Level

World of Birds

Sue

Plains and Southwest Indians

World of Mammals

Messages from the Wilderness

Nature Walk

Special Exhibit Gallery– Main Level

Lions of Tsavo

Mammals of Asia

Pawnee Earth Lodge

Rice Wildlife Research Station

Africa

Africa Resource Center

North American Indians

Yates Exhibition Center

Mammals of Africa

Bird Habitats

Reptiles & Amphibians

Inside Ancient Egypt

E

Living Together

Webber Gallery

Animal Biology

What is an Animal?

STANLEY FIELD HALL

Ancient North America and Mesoamerica

The Field Museum Store

Eskimos and Northwest Coast Indians

SOUTH ENTRANCE

Ground Level

Lecture Hall

Education Department

VENDING MACHINES

E Elevator

WEST ENTRANCE

The Siragusa Center

(i) Information

James Simpson Theater

Kid's Field Trip Store

Man-eater of Mfuwe

Crown Family Playlab

Special Exhibits Galleries

Black Box Theater

Bushman

E

Small Treasures Gallery

E

Stairs

Inside Ancient Egypt

Underground Adventure

Food Court

throughout the year. The Corner Bakery cafe, located just off the main hall, serves fare
that's a cut above the usual museum victuals. (To skip the lunchtime lines, pick up one
of the premade salads or sandwiches and head for the cash register.) Families also flock
to the McDonald's on the lower level. Allow 3 hours.

Roosevelt Rd. and Lake Shore Dr. (C) **312/922-9410** or 312/341-9299 TDD (for hearing-impaired callers).
www.fieldmuseum.org. Admission $12 adults; $7 seniors and students with ID; $7 children 3–11; free for
teachers, armed-forces personnel in uniform, and children 2 and under. Free admission Mon–Tues mid-
Sept to Nov and Jan–Feb. Daily 9am–5pm. Closed Dec 25. Bus: 6, 10, 12, 130, or 146.

Hamill Family Play Zoo ★★★   All ages. Located within Chicago's largest zoo, the
Brookfield Zoo (located in west suburban Brookfield), the Hamill Family Play Zoo lets
kids talk to the animals in an up-close-and-personal way. In fact, the kids' zoo was
designed to help kids, from infants to age 10, develop feelings of kinship with the natural world. Children can touch domesticated animals, help care for animals, search for
insects under logs, watch zookeepers prepare animal food, pretend to be a veterinarian,
plant seeds, build feeders, and more. You'll find 300 individual animals from 58 species
here, and specially trained staff is on hand to help make the most of your visit.

Other Brookfield Zoo exhibits let kids encounter bathing hippos and laugh at the
antics of the orangutans. In total, the Brookfield Zoo is spread over 216 acres with 2,700
animals in residence. Kid favorites are Siberian tigers, snow leopards, giraffes, green sea
turtles, and baboons. All the animals live in naturalistic environments that allow them to
live side by side with other inhabitants of their regions (see the Brookfield Zoo review in
the "Zoos" section later in this chapter for more information).

First Ave. and 31st St., Brookfield. (C) **708/485-0263.** www.brookfieldzoo.org. Admission to Play Zoo
$3.50 adults, $2.50 seniors and children 3–11 (in addition to paying the general Brookfield Zoo admission
of $10 adults, $6 seniors and children 3–11, free for children 2 and under). Free admission Tues and Thurs
Oct–Feb. Memorial Day to Labor Day daily 9:30am–6pm (Sun until 7:30pm); fall–spring daily 10am–5pm.
Parking $8. To reach the zoo from downtown, take the Stevenson (I-55) and Eisenhower (I-290) expys 14
miles west of the Loop. Subway/El: 304 or 311.

John G. Shedd Aquarium ★★★   All ages. What do kids love best about the
Shedd? The dolphin show! But there's plenty more to see and do here. Thousands of
denizens of river, lake, and sea populate the standard aquarium tanks and elaborate new
habitats at this marble octagon building. Opened in 1930, the Shedd debuted in auspi-
cious fashion: It had the greatest variety of sea life ever exhibited at one institution and
was the first inland aquarium to maintain permanent exhibits of both saltwater and
freshwater animals. Today, it is one of the world's largest indoor aquariums. The only
downside to the Shedd is its steep admission price, which can really add up for a family
($23 for adults and $16 for children). You can keep your costs down by buying the
"Aquarium Only" admission, but you'll miss some of the most stunning exhibits (including the dolphin show). A CityPass can also save you money if you visit enough of the
other included attractions.

The first thing you'll see as you enter is the **Caribbean Coral Reef** exhibit. This
90,000-gallon circular tank occupies the Beaux Arts–style central rotunda, entertaining
spectators who press up against the glass to ogle divers feeding nurse sharks, barracudas,
stingrays, and a hawksbill sea turtle. A roving camera connected to video monitors on the
tank's periphery gives visitors close-ups of the animals inside. It's worth sticking around
to catch one of the daily feedings, when a diver swims around the tank and talks into a
microphone about the species inside and their eating habits.

Do-It-Yourself Sightseeing

There comes a time in every parent's life when you decide that trying to force your kids on a guided tour (and trying to enforce good behavior while on that tour) is simply not worth it. If that's the case, an inexpensive and low-pressure way to tour the city is by hopping aboard one of Chicago's El trains or buses. And what kid doesn't love a train or bus ride? Do-it-yourselfers can take their own tour for the cost of subway or bus fare—$2, plus 25¢ for a transfer (good for a return trip if you use it within 2 hr.). Here are some of the city's best sightseeing routes:

- **Brown line** (trip duration 20 min.; daily). Ride from the Loop to Belmont Station. You get a bird's-eye view of downtown, gentrified loft districts, and a number of historic neighborhoods. Start at the big El station at Clark and Lake streets and get on the northbound train.

- **No. 151 Sheridan bus** (trip duration 30 min.; daily). Pick up the 151 downtown on Michigan Avenue (the bus stops every 2 blocks on the ave.) and ride it north to Belmont. You cover Lake Shore Drive and Lincoln Park. If you take the bus south, you travel State Street and wind up at Union Station.

- **No. 146 Marine–Michigan bus** (trip duration 20 min.; daily). This express bus allows you to take in North Michigan Avenue, State Street, and the Museum Campus. Pick up the bus on Sheridan and Diversey going south. (You can also pick up the 146 along Michigan Ave., although it has fewer stops than the 151.) You see the Harold Washington Library, the Art Institute of Chicago, the Chicago Cultural Center, and the landmark Water Tower.

- **No. 10 Museum of Science and Industry bus** (trip duration 35 min.; weekends year-round, daily in summer and winter holiday season). From North Michigan Avenue at the Water Tower (the stop is in front of Borders on Michigan Ave. across from Water Tower Place), ride south to the Museum Campus. You see Grant Park, the Art Institute of Chicago, the University of Chicago, and Chinatown.

The exhibits surrounding the Caribbean coral reef re-create different marine habitats around the world. The best is **Amazon Rising: Seasons of the River,** a 10,000-square-foot exhibit with more than 250 species of animals—including piranhas, birds, sloths, insects, spiders, snakes, caiman lizards, and monkeys—on display in this re-creation of the Amazon basin.

You'll pay extra to see the other Shedd highlights; but they're quite impressive, so I'd suggest shelling out for at least one, assuming your kids won't run out of gas before then. The 3-million-gallon saltwater **Oceanarium** ★★ is an indoor marine mammal pavilion that re-creates a Pacific Northwest coastal environment and also happens to be the largest of its kind in the world. With its wall of windows revealing the lake outside, the Oceanarium creates a stunning optical illusion of one uninterrupted expanse of sea. As you follow a winding nature trail, you encounter beluga whales, white-sided dolphins, Alaskan sea otters, and harbor seals. A colony of penguins in a separate exhibit area inhabits

Tips **Website Extras**

Scanning the websites of museums and other attractions before you visit can enhance your trip when you get here. At the **Field Museum of Natural History** website (www.fieldmuseum.org), you can download an mp3 audio tour of the museum's permanent collection; you can also print out a Family Adventure Tour, which sends kids on a scavenger hunt throughout the museum. The **Millennium Park** mp3 audio tour (available at www.millenniumpark.org) includes interviews with the artists who created the park's eye-catching artwork. And if you're intimidated by the massive size of the **Museum of Science and Industry,** check out the website's Personal Planner, which will put together a customized itinerary based your family's interests (www.msichicago.org).

a naturalistic environment meant to resemble the Falkland Islands in the southern sea off Argentina. You can observe all these sea mammals at play through large underwater viewing windows. On a fixed performance schedule in a large pool flanked by an amphitheater, a crew of friendly trainers puts the dolphins through their paces of leaping dives, breaches, and tail walking. Check out the Oceanarium schedule as soon as you get to the Shedd; seating space fills up quickly for the shows, so you'll want to get there early. If you're visiting during a summer weekend, you may also want to buy your Oceanarium ticket in advance to make sure you can catch a show that day.

The newest signature exhibit is **Wild Reef—Sharks at Shedd ★★**, a series of 26 interconnected habitats that house a Philippine coral reef patrolled by sharks and other predators. The floor-to-ceiling windows bring the toothy swimmers up close and personal (they even swim over your head in certain spots). The Shedd mounts temporary exhibitions, so call ahead for the latest. A recent feature was Sea Star Quest, with a touch pool that made for the most interactive, kid friendly exhibit in the Shedd's 74-year history. Look for more of the same as the Shedd strives to give guests a better firsthand understanding of sea creatures.

If you want a quality sit-down meal in a restaurant with a spectacular view of Lake Michigan, check out Soundings, inside the aquarium. There's also a family-friendly cafeteria. Allow 3 hours.

1200 S. Lake Shore Dr. © **312/939-2438.** www.sheddaquarium.org. All-Access Pass (to all exhibits) $23 adults, $16 seniors and children 3–11, free for children 2 and under; admission to the aquarium and Wild Reef $18 adults, $14 seniors and children 3–11; aquarium only, $8 adults, $6 children and seniors. Free admission to aquarium only Mon–Tues Oct–Nov and Jan–Feb. Memorial Day to Labor Day daily 9am–6pm; early Sept to late May Mon–Fri 9am–5pm, Sat–Sun 9am–6pm. Bus: 6 or 146.

The Lakefront ★★★ All ages. Chicago was blessed with forefathers with foresight. Thanks to them, the lakefront was declared in 1836 to be public ground "to remain forever open, clear, and free" from construction—that's why you won't find warehouses, docks, and private businesses along our beautiful lakeshore, as you do in many other cities. Instead, join Chicagoans in reveling in 30 miles of sand beaches, green lawns, flower beds, and bicycle paths. More than half of the 2,800 acres of lakefront were created by filling in the lake and building a string of splendid lakeshore parks (from north to south, Lincoln, Grant, Burnham, Jackson, Rainbow, and Calumet). Chicagoans take full advantage of the lakefront to walk, rollerblade, bike, run, swim, picnic, and play

(Value) The Loop Tour Train

For a distinctive downtown view at an unbeatable price—free!—hop aboard the **Loop Tour Train,** a special elevated train that runs on Saturday from May to September. Docents from the Chicago Architecture Foundation point out notable buildings along the way and explain how the El shaped the city. Riders must pick up tickets at the Chicago Cultural Center, 77 E. Randolph St., beginning at 10am on the day of the tour; tours leave at 11, 11:40am, 12:20, and 1pm from the Randolph/Wabash El station. For more information, call (C) **312/744-2400,** or visit www.cityofchicago.org/exploringchicago.

volleyball. Most activity takes place around **Oak Street Beach** (just north of the Magnificent Mile) and **North Avenue Beach** (several blocks north of Oak St.). One Chicago mom told me that a favorite activity of her kids is to sit on a bench at the beach and count the dogs as they go by. It's just that simple—kids' entertainment doesn't always have to come at a price.

The Loop Sculpture Tour ★★ Ages 5 & up. In the spirit of emphasizing free, flexible, and outdoor activities for kids, I can't fail to note the self-guided tour that lets you navigate through Grant Park and much of the Loop to view some 100 examples of Chicago's monumental public art. With the help of a very comprehensive free booklet, *The Chicago Public Art Guide* (free at the Chicago Cultural Center, 78 E. Washington St.), you'll get info on how to find the best examples of monumental public art. You also can conduct a self-guided tour of the city's public sculpture by following our "Loop Sculpture Tour" map on p. 169.

One of the newer additions is the massive elliptical sculpture ***Cloud Gate*** (known as "the Bean," because it looks like a giant silver kidney bean) by British artist Anish Kapoor. The sculpture, in Millennium Park, was Kapoor's first public commission in the U.S. The single-most-famous sculpture is **Pablo Picasso's *Untitled,*** located in Daley Plaza and constructed out of Cor-Ten steel, the same gracefully rusting material used on the exterior of the Daley Center behind it. Perhaps because it was the buttoned-down Loop's first monumental modern sculpture, its installation in 1967 was met with hoots and heckles, but today "the Picasso" enjoys semiofficial status as the logo of modern Chicago. It is by far the city's most popular photo opportunity among visiting tourists. Kids can view the Picasso from various perspectives and try to decide: Does its mysterious shape look like a woman, a bird, or a dog? At noon on weekdays during warm-weather months, you'll likely find a dance troupe, musical group, or visual-arts exhibition there as part of the city's long-running "Under the Picasso" multicultural program. Call (C) 312/346-3278 for weekly updates of events.

Millennium Park ★★★ All ages. One of Chicago's grandest public-works projects ever produced is Millennium Park. It's not easy to create new icons for a city, but many of Millennium Park's installations have already come to symbolize Chicago. In fact, I dare you to stand with your toes in the water at the Crown Fountain, surveying the spectacular cityscape of South Michigan Avenue, and not feel an irrepressible urge to uproot your family and move into a condo in downtown Chicago. The park has been a strikingly beautiful success, and thank goodness Chicago's donors and government saw fit to overspend the budget by leaps and bounds and go far beyond the deadline for opening to

The Loop Sculpture T...

1 *Untitled ("The Picasso"),*
  Pablo Picasso (1967)

2 *Chicago,* Joan Miro (1981)

3 *Monument with Standing Beast,*
  Jean Dubuffet (1984)

4 *Freeform,* Richard Hunt (1993)

5 *Flight of Daedalus and Icarus,*
  Roger Brown (1990)

6 *Dawn Shadows,* Louise Nevelson (1983)

7 *Loomings* and *Knights and Squires,*
  Frank Stella

8 *Batcolumn,* Claes Oldenburg (1977)

9 *The Universe,* Alexander Calder (1974)

10 *Gem of the Lakes,* Raymond Kaskey (1990)

11 *San Marco II,* Ludovico de Luigi (1986)

12 *The Town-Ho's Story,* Frank Stella (1993)

13 *Ruins III,* Nita K. Sutherland (1978)

14 *Flamingo,* Alexander Calder (1974)

15 *Lines in Four Directions,* Sol Lewitt (1985)

16 *The Four Seasons,* Marc Chagall (1974)

17 *Untitled Sounding Sculpture,*
  Harry Bertoia (1975)

18 *Cloud Gate,* Anish Kapoor (2004)

19 *Large Interior Form,* Henry Moore (1983)

20 *Celebration of the 200th Anniversary
  of the Founding of the Republic,*
  Isamu Noguchi (1976)

21 *The Fountain of the Great Lakes,*
  Lorado Taft (1913)

ensure a place like this. It's really an example of what a modern park can be. Compare the Crown Fountain, Millennium Park's interactive fountain, with the grande dame of Chicago fountains, Buckingham Fountain (just to the south in Grant Park), which is lovely but untouchable, and you'll see how far we've come. Even the sculpture is interactive—"the bean" by Anish Kapoor is essentially a gigantic 3-D mirror. Kids and adults are equally attracted to its reflective surface and house-of-mirrors qualities. The Crown Fountain is another kid favorite, with its two 50-foot glass-brick towers facing each other across a black granite plaza, with water cascading down their sides. Faces of Chicagoans are projected through the glass blocks and change at regular intervals—and watch out, because water spews from their mouths when you least expect it. It's public art with a sense of humor. The Jay Pritzker Pavilion, with its Frank Gehry–designed band shell, is a sight to behold, and the BP Pedestrian Bridge, also designed by Gehry, curves and winds its way over Columbus Drive, providing changing views of the cityscape as you walk. Gardens of native plants are just beginning to flourish, and by the next edition of this book, you will surely feel that you are walking through a Midwestern prairie as you stroll the Lurie Garden, with 250 varieties of native perennial plants. All in all, this is a must-see, must-experience park. You can lunch at the **Park Grill** (✆ **312/521-7275;** www.parkgrillchicago.com; daily 11am–10:30pm), an eatery overlooking the McCormick Tribune Plaza ice-skating rink. Next door to the grill, Park Café offers takeout salads and sandwiches. Parking is easy, too, with plentiful underground lots at reasonable rates of around $14/day. Free walking tours of the park are offered daily Memorial Day through October at 11:30am and 1pm, starting at the Park's Welcome Center, 201 E. Randolph St. (✆ **312/742-1168**).

Michigan Ave., from Randolph Dr. on the north to Monroe Dr. on the south, and west to Columbus Dr. ✆ **312/742-1168.** www.millenniumpark.org. Daily 6am–11pm. El: Blue Line to Washington; Red Line to Lake; Brown, Green, Orange, or Purple Line to Randolph.

Museum Campus ★★★ **All ages.** The most beautiful collection of museums in any city in the United States lies southeast of Grant Park on Chicago's glistening lakefront. Okay, so I am cheating a little by making "Museum Campus" one single kids' favorite. But ever since the city connected its great trio of museums (The Field Museum of Natural History, John G. Shedd Aquarium, and the Adler Planetarium & Astronomy Museum) on a landscaped 57-acre campus—thus, "Museum Campus"—they've felt like one destination. With terraced gardens and broad walkways, it's easy for pedestrians to visit these three beloved institutions. A large indoor parking lot is accessible from Lake Shore Drive southbound; you can park there all day for $15. Be aware that there is no public parking during Chicago Bears games in the fall; Soldier Field is next to the Museum Campus, and football fans get first dibs on all the surrounding parking spaces.

To get to the Museum Campus from the Loop, head east across Grant Park from Balbo St. and S. Michigan Ave., trekking along the lakeshore route to the Field Museum, the aquarium, and the planetarium. Or you can make your approach on the path that begins at 11th St. and Michigan Ave. Follow 11th to the walkway that spans the Metra tracks. Cross Columbus Dr. and then pick up the path that will take you under Lake Shore Dr. and into the Museum Campus. The CTA bus 146 will take you from downtown to all 3 of these attractions. Call ✆ **836-7000** (from any city or suburban area code) for the stop locations and schedule.

Museum of Science and Industry ★★★ **All ages.** Generations of children recount fond memories of this world-famous museum, the granddaddy of interactive museums, with some 2,000 exhibits. Good news: The museum is still thrilling kids today. In fact, if you can visit only one museum in Chicago with your children, this should be the one—hands down. Ask anyone who grew up around Chicago and he or she will reminisce about school field trips to the museum, bringing cans of soda wrapped in tin foil, and seeing a favorite exhibit—the *U-505* ★★ and **Coal Mine** ★ inevitably top the list of favorites from the past. The *U-505* is a German submarine that was captured in 1944 and brought to the museum 10 years later. In 2004 the U-boat was closed and underwent a restoration process to bring it back to its former glory, housed indoors (for many decades, it was exposed to the elements) in a new 35,000-square-foot exhibit. Your kids will undoubtedly join the legions who have been fascinated by the claustrophobic reality of underwater naval life. The full-scale Coal Mine, which dates back to 1934, now incorporates modern mining techniques into the exhibit. A guided tour of the sub's interior costs $5 extra, and isn't recommended for young children, but the exhibit is worth visiting even if you don't go inside. Get to both of these exhibits quickly after the museum opens because they attract amusement-park-length lines during the day.

Kids who love planes, trains, and automobiles shouldn't miss **All Aboard the Silver Streak!,** the museum's Burlington Pioneer Zephyr, the world's first streamlined, diesel-electric, articulated train, which was moved indoors and installed in the museum's three-story underground parking garage. A simulated train station has been installed along the 197-foot-long Zephyr, and visitors can explore the train and its onboard interactive exhibits. **The Great Train Story,** which replaces the museum's 60-year-old model railroad exhibit, takes up 3,500 square feet and depicts the winding rail journey between Chicago and Seattle. Kids can drive a Metra Train (our commuter line to the suburbs), open a drawbridge over the Chicago River, harvest timber in the Cascade Range, and bore a tunnel through the Rocky Mountains. For airplane fans, **Take Flight,** an aviation exhibit, features a full-size 727 airplane that revs up its engines and replays the voice recordings from a San Francisco–to–Chicago flight.

Computer addicts should be entranced by **Networld,** which offers a flashy immersion into the Internet (with plenty of interactive screens). More low-tech—but still fascinating—is the giant walk-through **model of the human heart** ★.

One of my favorites (especially for city kids who don't get much exposure to rural life) is **The Farm** (where children can sit at the wheel of a giant combine) and the **chick hatchery** inside the exhibit **Genetics: Decoding Life,** where you can watch as tiny newborn chicks poke their way out of eggs. Educational exhibits include **Enterprise,** which lets visitors take on the role of CEO for a day as they immerse themselves in the goings-on of a virtual company. And, not to be sexist, but girls (myself included) love **Colleen Moore's Fairy Castle,** a lavishly decorated miniature palace filled with priceless treasures. (Yes, those are real diamonds and pearls in the chandeliers.) The castle is hidden away on the lower level. Younger children up to age 10 love to spend time at the **Idea Factory,** a "learning through play" environment that allows kids to explore scientific principles themselves.

A major addition to the museum is the **Henry Crown Space Center,** where the story of space exploration, still in its infancy, is documented in copious detail, highlighted by a simulated space-shuttle experience through sight and sound at the center's five-story **OMNIMAX Theater.** The theater offers double features on weekends; call for show times.

When you've worked up an appetite, you can visit the museum's large and above-average food court and the ice-cream parlor, and there is also an excellent gift shop. Allow a minimum of 3 hours for your visit; a comprehensive visit can take all day, especially if you catch an OMNIMAX movie.

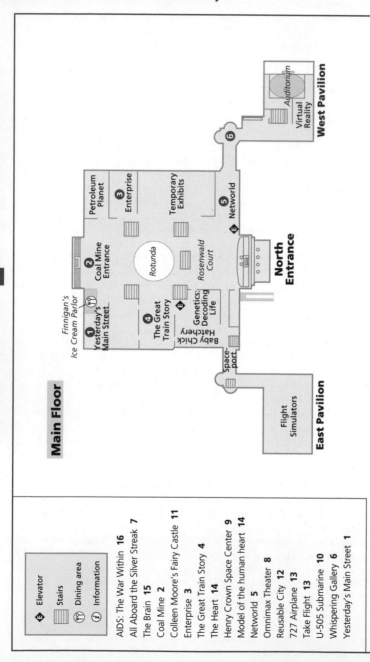

Main Floor

West Pavilion

Auditorium

Virtual Reality

6

Petroleum Planet

Enterprise 3

Temporary Exhibits

Networld 5

Coal Mine Entrance 2

Rotunda

Finnigan's Ice Cream Parlor

Yesterday's Main Street 1

The Great Train Story 4

Rosenwald Court

Genetics: Decoding Life

Baby Chick Hatchery

North Entrance

Space-port

Flight Simulators

East Pavilion

AIDS: The War Within **16**
All Aboard the Silver Streak **7**
The Brain **15**
Coal Mine **2**
Colleen Moore's Fairy Castle **11**
Enterprise **3**
The Great Train Story **4**
The Heart **14**
Henry Crown Space Center **9**
Model of the human heart **14**
Networld **5**
Omnimax Theater **8**
Reusable City **12**
727 Airplane **13**
Take Flight **13**
U-505 Submarine **10**
Whispering Gallery **6**
Yesterday's Main Street **1**

⊕ Elevator
▥ Stairs
🍴 Dining area
ⓘ Information

41 E. Superior St. (at Wabash Ave.). ℂ **312/266-0400.** Kids' menu, highchairs, boosters. Reservations accepted only for parties of 10 or more. Main courses $9–$15; kids' menu $4. AE, DC, DISC, MC, V. Mon–Wed 11:30am–midnight; Thurs–Sat 11:30am–2pm; Sun 11am–11pm. Subway/El: Red Line to Chicago/State.

INEXPENSIVE

Big Bowl ★ (Value) ASIAN   You know you're in a kid-friendly Asian restaurant when you sit down and crayons and a bowl of white rice are brought to the table. Big Bowl also has a great kids' menu—no cheeseburgers, just smaller portions of the same Asian food the adults eat. Okay, so the restaurant is yet another creation of Rich Melman's Lettuce Entertain You empire. But it's friendly, affordable, and the kind of place that's got dishes so addictive, I dare you to go only once during your visit. Start with a glass of the signature fresh ginger ale or a fresh-brewed fruit-flavored iced tea; either will wake up your taste buds. The menu covers a range of Asian specialties, including Chinese pot stickers, Thai curries, and Vietnamese spring rolls. The indecisive can go with one of several combinations, each offering a mix of soup, salad, appetizers, or noodles. The straightforward crunchy sesame chicken is a reliable standby, mixing crispy chicken pieces with fresh Asian vegetables in a light soy sauce. Other good bets are the teriyaki beef and spicy flat noodles with tofu and veggies. You can also put together your own mix of flavors at the large stir-fry bar. If you're looking for delivery, Big Bowl will rush pot stickers to your hotel, no problem. Big Bowl has another Chicago location, which re-creates the same upscale diner decor, at 60 E. Ohio St., just off the Magnificent Mile and near kid-frequented spots such as ESPN Zone (ℂ **312/951-1888**).

6 E. Cedar St. (at Rush St.). ℂ **312/640-8888.** www.bigbowl.com. Kids' menu, highchairs, boosters. Reservations not accepted. Main courses $9–$15; kids' menu $5–$8. AE, DC, DISC, MC, V. Sun–Thurs 11:30am–10pm; Fri–Sat 11:30am–11pm. Subway/El: Red Line to Clark/Division.

Billy Goat Tavern ★ (Value) BREAKFAST/BURGERS   "Cheezeborger, Cheezeborger—No Coke . . . Pepsi." Viewers of the original *Saturday Night Live* will certainly remember the classic John Belushi routine, a moment in the life of a crabby Greek short-order cook. The comic got his material from the Billy Goat Tavern, located under North Michigan Avenue near the bridge that crosses to the Loop (you'll find it by walking down the steps across the street from the Chicago Tribune building). BUTT IN ANYTIME says the sign on the red door with the picture of the billy goat on it. The tavern has traditionally been a hangout for the newspaper workers and writers who occupy the nearby Tribune Tower and Sun-Times Building, but its *Saturday Night Live* fame attracts droves of tourists, a la the *Cheers* bar in Boston. The tavern serves beer and greasy food (including, of course, "cheezeborgers" and "No Pepsi. Coke! No fries! Chips!"). Families will feel most at home during lunchtime, when tourists and office workers pop in for a quick burger.

For the same "cheezeborgers" in less grungy, and more kid-friendly, surroundings, head to the Billy Goat's outpost on Navy Pier (ℂ **312/670-8789**).

430 N. Michigan Ave. ℂ **312/222-1525.** No kids' menu. Reservations not accepted. Menu items $4–$8 No credit cards. Mon–Fri 7am–2am; Sat 10am–3am; Sun 11am–2am. Subway/El: Red Line to Chicago/State.

California Pizza Kitchen PIZZA   Way, way back in the early 1990s, "CPK" was plying its new concept of exotic toppings made on individual-size pies. The concept is a bit stale, but kids still get a kick out of creating and swapping pieces of their individual pizzas. Names like tandoori chicken, Hawaiian, BLT, Peking duck, and grilled burrito

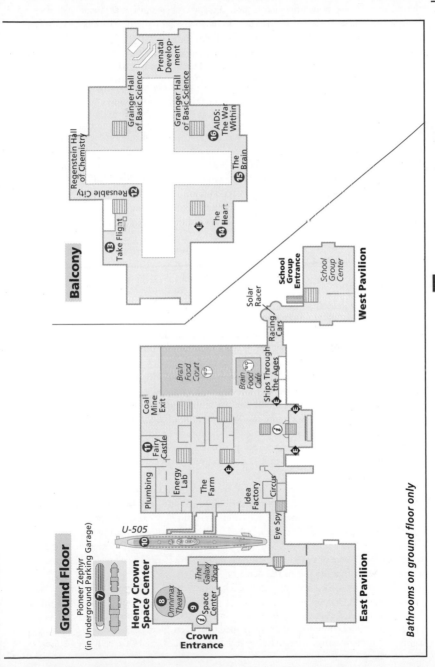

Balcony

Regenstein Hall of Chemistry

Grainger Hall of Basic Science

Prenatal Development

Grainger Hall of Basic Science

13 Take Flight

12 Reusable City

16 AIDS: The War Within

15 The Brain

14 The Heart

Ground Floor

Pioneer Zephyr (in Underground Parking Garage)

7

U-505

10

Plumbing

Energy Lab

The Farm

Idea Factory

Coal Mine Exit

11 Fairy Castle

Brain Food Court

17

Brain Food Café

Ships Through the Ages

Circus

Eye Spy

Solar Racer

Racing Cars

School Group Entrance

School Group Center

West Pavilion

Henry Crown Space Center

8 Omnimax Theater

The Galaxy Shop

9 Space Center

Crown Entrance

East Pavilion

Bathrooms on ground floor only

Although the museum is quite a distance from the rest of Chicago's tourist attractions, the museum is easy enough to reach without a car; your best options are the no. 6 Jeffrey Express bus and the Metra Electric train from downtown (the no. 10 bus runs from downtown to the museum's front entrance in the summer).

57th St. and Lake Shore Dr. (C) **800/468-6674** outside the Chicago area, 773/684-1414, or TTY 773/684-3323. www.msichicago.org. Admission to museum only, $11 adults, $9 seniors, $7 children 3–11, free for children 2 and under. Free admission Mon–Tues mid-Sept to Nov and Jan–Feb. Combination museum and OMNIMAX Theater $17 adults, $15 seniors, $12 children 3–11, free for children 2 and under on an adult's lap. Memorial Day to Labor Day Mon–Sat 9:30am–5:30pm; Sun 11am–5:30pm; early Sept to late May Mon–Sat 9:30am–4pm; Sun 11am–4pm. Closed Dec 25. Bus: 6 or Metra Electric to 57th St. and Lake Park Ave.

Navy Pier ★ **All ages.** After you've spent a couple of fun-filled hours at the Chicago Children's Museum, check out Navy Pier—Chicago's top tourist attraction. Built during World War I, this 3,000-foot-long pier has been a ballroom, a training center for Navy pilots during World War II, and a satellite campus of the University of Illinois. But any military aura is long gone, now that the place has been transformed into a bustling tourist mecca. A combination of carnival, food court, and boat dock, the pier makes a fun place to stroll (if you don't mind crowds). To get the best views of the city, walk all the way down to the end.

Midway down the pier are the Crystal Gardens, with 70 full-size palm trees, dancing fountains, and other flora in a glass-enclosed atrium; a carousel and kiddie carnival rides; and a 15-story Ferris wheel, a replica of the original that debuted at Chicago's 1893 World's Fair. The 50 acres of pier and lakefront property also are home to the aforementioned Chicago Children's Museum (p. 160), a 3-D **IMAX theater** ((C) **312/595-0090**), a small ice-skating rink, and the Chicago Shakespeare Theater (p. 259). Naturally, there are a handful of rather bland shops and pushcart vendors. Dining options include a food court, an outpost of Lincoln Park's popular Charlie's Ale House, and the white-tablecloth seafood restaurant Riva. You'll also find a beer garden with live music; Joe's Be-Bop Cafe & Jazz Emporium, a Southern-style barbecue restaurant with live music nightly; and Bubba Gump Shrimp Co. & Market, a casual family seafood joint. Summer is one long party at the pier, with fireworks on Wednesday and Saturday evenings.

The **Smith Museum of Stained Glass Windows** sounds dull, but is actually a remarkable installation of more than 150 stained-glass windows set in illuminated display cases. Occupying an 800-foot-long expanse on the ground floor of Navy Pier, the free museum features works by Frank Lloyd Wright, Louis Sullivan, John LaFarge, and Louis Comfort Tiffany.

Navy Pier schedules a variety of conventions and trade shows, including an international art exposition in May, pro-tennis exhibitions, and a flower and garden show. There's something for everyone, but the commercialism of the place might be too much for some. In that case, take the ¹/₂-mile stroll to the end of the pier, east of the ballroom, where you can find a little respite and enjoy the wind, the waves, and the city view, which is the real delight of a place like this. Or unwind in **Olive Park,** a small sylvan haven with a sliver of beach that lies just to the north of Navy Pier.

You'll find, moored along the south dock, more than half a dozen different sailing vessels, including a couple of dinner cruise ships, the pristine white-masted tall ship *Windy* (ask about the special "Pirate" sails), and the 70-foot speedboats *Seadog I, II,* and *III.* In the summer months, water taxis speed between Navy Pier and other Chicago sights. For more specifics on sightseeing and dinner cruises, see "Lake & River Cruises," p. 204. Allow 2 to 3 hours.

(Value) **Museum Free Days**

If you time your visit right, you can save yourself some admission fees—but not during prime tourist season. While some major museums offer free admission at specific times year-round, others schedule free days only during the slowest times of the year (usually late fall and the dead of winter); keep in mind that you will still have to pay for special exhibitions and films on free days. The good news? Some smaller museums never charge admission.

Monday: Adler Planetarium (Oct–Nov and Jan–Feb); Chicago History Museum; Museum of Science and Industry (mid-Sept through Nov and Jan–Feb); and Shedd Aquarium (Oct–Nov and Jan–Feb; Oceanarium admission extra).

Tuesday: Adler Planetarium (Oct–Nov and Jan–Feb); Museum of Contemporary Art; Museum of Science and Industry (mid-Sept through Nov and Jan–Feb); Shedd Aquarium (Oct–Nov and Jan–Feb; Oceanarium admission extra); and Spertus Museum (10am–noon).

Thursday: Art Institute of Chicago (5–8pm only, until 9pm Memorial Day to Labor Day); Chicago Children's Museum (5–8pm only); and Spertus Museum (3–7pm).

Sunday: DuSable Museum of African-American History.

Always Free: Chicago Cultural Center, Garfield Park Conservatory, David and Alfred Smart Museum of Art, Jane Addams Hull-House Museum, Lincoln Park Conservatory, Lincoln Park Zoo, National Museum of Mexican Art, Museum of Contemporary Photography, and Newberry Library.

---

600 E. Grand Ave. (at Lake Michigan). (C) **800/595-PIER** (800/595-7437, outside the 312 area code) or 312/595-PIER. www.navypier.com. Free admission. Summer Sun–Thurs 10am–10pm, Fri–Sat 10am–midnight; fall–spring Mon–Thurs 10am–8pm, Fri–Sat 10am–10pm, Sun 10am–7pm. Parking $19/day weekdays; $23/day weekends. Parking lots fill quickly. Bus: 29, 65, 66, 120, or 121. Free trolley buses make stops on Grand Ave. and Illinois St. from State St. Subway/El: Red Line to Grand/State; transfer to city bus or board a free pier trolley bus.

---

3 BEST VIEWS

Sweeping views of the city from north to south are one of the main attractions of the many **boat tours** that leave from Navy Pier. Hop aboard and get the lay of the land from a waterborne vantage point. It's the best way to see how the city sweeps from Museum Campus in the south, to the Loop, across the Chicago River, and up through the Magnificent Mile, then on to the condo buildings that populate the lakefront moving north to the suburbs. See "Kid-Friendly Tours," later in this chapter, for a full listing of boat-tour options.

The Hancock Observatory ★★ **All ages.** Kids can play "count the rooftop pools" from the 1,000-foot-high observation deck as they look down (way down) on the residential neighborhoods below. For my money, the Hancock Center offers the best views in town. Why? It offers an excellent panorama of the city and an intimate view of nearby

Walker's Warning

Chicago is a great city to explore on foot, but I must warn people against trying to cross Lake Shore Drive on foot. People have been seriously injured and even killed attempting to dodge the traffic on the drive. Look for the pedestrian underpasses at Chicago Avenue, Oak Street, and North Avenue, among other locations.

Lake Michigan and various shoreline residential areas. (Many people don't agree with me, however, because more than 1.5 million people go up the Sears Tower each year.)

Although it's not as famous as the Sears Tower, for many local residents, the Hancock remains the archetypal Chicago skyscraper, with its bold, tapered shape and exterior steel cross-bracing design. The building rises to a total height of 1,107 feet above Michigan Avenue—1,456 feet if you count its twin 349-foot antennas. The view from the top of Chicago's third-tallest building is enough to satisfy, and some high-tech additions to the experience include "talking telescopes" with sound effects and narration in four languages, history walls illustrating the growth of the city, and the Skywalk open-air viewing deck—a "screened porch" that allows visitors to feel the rush of the wind at 1,000 feet. It's a sky-high step outside. Kids can check out the building's infrastructure on computers and locate 80 Chicago attractions on virtual-reality television screens. On a clear day, you can see portions of the three states surrounding this corner of Illinois (Michigan, Indiana, and Wisconsin), for a radius of 40 to 50 miles. The view up the North Side is particularly dramatic. It stretches from the nearby Oat Street and North Avenue beaches, along the green strip of Lincoln Park, to the line of high-rises tracing the shoreline that suddenly halt just below the boundary of the northern suburbs. A high-speed elevator carries passengers to the observatory in 40 seconds, and the entrance and observatory are accessible for people with disabilities. Allow 1 hour.

"Big John," as it's referred to by some locals, also has a sleek restaurant, **The Signature Room at the 95th,** with an adjoining lounge. (For about the same cost as the observatory, you can take in the views with libation in hand.) During the day plenty of tourists make the place kid-friendly; at night it's more adult-oriented. In the afternoon it's not very crowded, so don't be afraid to bring the family for refreshments.

94th floor of the John Hancock Center, 875 N. Michigan Ave. (enter on Delaware St.). ✆ **888/875-VIEW** (875-8439) or 312/751-3681. www.hancock-observatory.com. Admission $11 adults, $8 seniors, $6.50 children 5–12, free for children 4 and under. Daily 9am–11pm. Bus: 145, 146, 147, or 151. Subway/El: Red Line to Chicago/State.

Navy Pier   All ages. Because Navy Pier juts 3,000 feet into Lake Michigan, the view from the end of the pier looking toward the city is fabulous—the next best thing to seeing the Chicago skyline by boat. And, if you like heights, hop aboard the Ferris wheel and get a 15-story-high vantage point. Go early in the morning to see the sun rise, the rays gleaming off the glass Mies van der Rohe buildings lining Lake Shore Drive. Surrounded by Lake Michigan, lush gardens, and sculpture, the view from the Navy Pier is one of the best in the city. See the review in the previous section for more details about the other attractions at Navy Pier.

600 E. Grand Ave. (at Lake Michigan). ✆ **800/595-PIER** (800/595-7437, outside the 312 area code), or 312/595-PIER. www.navypier.com.

North Avenue Beach   All ages. One of the most famous views of Chicago (and one that you'll find in many guidebooks as a featured photo) is taken on the lakefront bike path, looking south to the John Hancock Center. To get a photo of your family in this picture-perfect scene, walk north on Lake Shore Drive to the tunnel at North Avenue that leads under Lake Shore Drive to North Avenue Beach. Once on the lakefront path, turn south toward the city, and you will have your photo opportunity. (Just watch out for cyclists, skaters, runners, and dog walkers if it's a nice summer day!) See "Enjoying the 'Third Coast': Chicago's Beaches," in chapter 8, for more information.

Lake Shore Dr. at North Ave. ⓒ **312/742-PLAY** (742-7529) for Chicago Park District and beach information.

Sears Tower Skydeck ★ (Overrated   All ages. When you stand on a perch this high and view the trains, river traffic, and expressways streaming with cars, you can teach your kids the meaning of the term "transportation hub." Sears Tower is one of Chicago's most popular attractions. Since its debut in 1973, the Sears Tower's lock on the crown of "world's tallest building" has been a source of civic pride for the city. Sadly, the building's namesake, Sears, sold the building and moved to cheaper suburban offices in 1992. Another blow to morale came when Petronas Towers in Kuala Lumpur, Malaysia, went up and laid claim to the title of world's tallest buildings. (The Sears Tower has since put up a 22-ft. antenna in an attempt to win back the title—and for what it's worth, the building is still listed as the tallest building in the world under the category of "including antenna.") And now, Burj Dubai is developing as a new contender. Tallest-building posturing aside, this is still a great place to orient your family to the city, but I wouldn't put it on the top of must-see sights for any family with limited time or limited patience for crowds.

The view from the 103rd-floor Skydeck is everything you'd expect it to be—once you get there. Unfortunately, you're usually stuck in a very long, very noisy line, so by the time you make it to the top, your patience could be as thin as the atmosphere up there. *One suggestion:* I once went up the tower at night on a weeknight, a couple of hours before closing (in summertime, it stays open until 10pm). We had the observation deck practically to ourselves. If that's too late for your kids, try the late afternoon, when crowds have thinned. On a clear day, visibility extends up to 50 miles, and you can catch glimpses of the surrounding states. Despite the fact that it's called a "skydeck," you can't actually walk outside (though I can't understand why you'd want to—but that's just my fear of heights speaking!). The 70-second high-speed elevator trip will feel like a thrill ride for some, but it's a nightmare for anyone with even mild claustrophobia. Allow 1 hour, more if there's a line.

Ⓜ**oments   A Great View**

After visiting the Lincoln Park Zoo or the Peggy Notebaert Nature Museum, take a stroll on Fullerton Avenue to the bridge that runs over the lagoon (just before you get to Lake Shore Dr.). Standing on the south side of Fullerton Avenue, you'll have a great view of the Chicago skyline and Lincoln Park—and an excellent backdrop for family souvenir photos. This path can get very crowded on summer weekends, so I suggest trying this photo op during the week.

233 S. Wacker Dr. (enter on Jackson Blvd.). ☎ **312/875-9696.** www.the-skydeck.com. Admission $13 adults, $9.50 seniors and children 3–12, free for children 2 and under. Apr–Sept daily 10am–10pm; Oct–Apr daily 10am–8pm. Subway/El: Brown, Purple, or Orange Line to Quincy; Red or Blue Line to Jackson; then walk a few blocks west. Bus: 1, 7, 126, 146, 151, or 156.

4 MORE CHICAGO MUSEUMS

Chicago has plenty of museums that make every effort to turn a bored child into a stimulated one. Many of the city's museums are leaders in the "please touch me" school of interactive exhibitions, with buttons and lights and levers and sounds and bright colors, and activities for kids at special exhibitions.

Art Institute of Chicago ★★★ All ages. Chicago's pride and joy is a warm, welcoming museum—one that's never too stuffy to embrace kids. You know this is a museum with a winning sense of whimsy when at the holidays, the famous lion sculptures that guard its entrance sport Santa hats. As this book goes to press, the museum is undergoing a historic addition, the Modern Wing, which will open in May 2009. The map (p. 161) shows the new addition, and exciting changes are planned at the museum that will make it even more welcoming to families (first and foremost, children 11 and under get in to the museum for free). With the addition of the Modern Wing, the size of the family/education center will double. The new Ryan Education Center will be an impressive 20,000 square feet, and use the entire first floor of the East pavilion of the Modern Wing. The light-filled, beautiful space will include studio space, classrooms, library (with computers), teacher resources, and its own galleries, and—best of all—families can enter the space without paying admission to the museum (as they do now). The museum will also be increasing its kids programming.

In other parts of the museum, kids will be entranced by the **Thorne Miniature Rooms,** filled with tiny reproductions of furnished interiors from European and American history (heaven for a dollhouse fanatic). Another popular attraction is the original **Trading Room of the old Chicago Stock Exchange,** salvaged when the Adler and Sullivan Stock Exchange building was demolished in 1972. One parent says her boys love the great hall of **European arms and armor** dating from the 15th to the 19th centuries. Composed of more than 1,500 objects, including armor, horse equipment, swords, daggers, pole arms, and maces, it's one of the most important assemblages of its kind in the country. (If you do head down here, don't miss Marc Chagall's stunning stained-glass windows at the end of the gallery.)

If you have older kids, you'll find an array of works to satiate any interest: Japanese *ukiyo-e* prints, ancient Egyptian bronzes and Greek vases, 19th-century British photography, masterpieces by most of the greatest names in 20th-century sculpture, or modern

---

Ⓜ**Moments** **Photo Op**

For a great photo op, walk on Randolph Street toward the lake in the morning. That's when the sun, rising in the east over the lake, hits the string of high-rises that line South Michigan Avenue—giving you the perfect backdrop for an only-in-Chicago picture.

Tips **Touring the Art Institute**

Keeping track of your kids in the crowds that flood the Art Institute during its peak days might reduce your enjoyment of your favorite masterpieces.

Your best bet is to avoid the craziest times: Many people don't realize the museum is open on Monday, so the galleries are relatively subdued. Wednesday is a close second. Tuesday tends to draw the masses because the Art Institute is free and open late (until 8pm). Try to arrive when the doors open in the morning or else during the lunchtime lull. **Another tip:** If the Michigan Avenue entrance is crowded, head around to the entrance on the Columbus Drive side, which is usually less congested and is more convenient to the Grant Park underground parking garage. There's also a small gift shop near the Columbus Drive entrance that you might want to check out if the main shop is too bustling.

American textiles. No matter how many times you visit, there are always new works to be seen and special shows that draw in even more crowds.

For a good general overview of the museum's collection, take the free "Highlights of the Art Institute" tour, given at 2pm on Tuesday, Saturday, and Sunday. Those with limited time and kids with limited patience for tours should head straight to the museum's renowned collection of Impressionist art (including one of the world's largest collections of Monet paintings), one of the more highly trafficked areas of the museum. Among the treasures here you'll find Seurat's pointillist masterpiece *Sunday Afternoon on the Island of La Grande Jatte.* Your second must-see area is the galleries of European and American contemporary art, ranging from paintings, sculptures, and mixed-media works from Pablo Picasso, Henri Matisse, and Salvador Dalí through Willem de Kooning, Jackson Pollock, and Andy Warhol. Visitors are sometimes surprised when they discover many of the icons that hang here. (Grant Wood's *American Gothic* and Edward Hopper's *Nighthawks* are two that bring double takes from many visitors.)

If you want to steer clear of the crowds, you'll find more breathing room in the galleries of Indian, Himalayan, and Southeast Asian art. Other recommended exhibits are the collection of delicate mid-19th-century glass paperweights in the museum's famous Arthur Rubloff collection.

The museum also has a cafeteria and an elegant full-service restaurant, a picturesque courtyard cafe (June–Sept), and a large shop. There is a busy schedule of lectures, films, and other special presentations, as well as guided tours, to enhance your viewing of the art.

111 S. Michigan Ave. (at Adams St.). ℂ **312/443-3600.** www.artic.edu. Admission $12 adults, $7 seniors and students with ID, free for children 11 and under. Additional cost for special exhibitions. Free admission Thurs 5–8pm. Mon–Fri 10:30am–5pm (Thurs until 8pm, until 9pm Thurs–Fri Memorial Day to Labor Day); Sat–Sun 10am–5pm. Closed Jan 1, Thanksgiving, and Dec 25. Subway/El: Green, Brown, Purple, or Orange Line to Adams; Red Line to Monroe/State or Jackson/State. Bus: 3, 4, 60, 145, 147, or 151.

Chicago Archicenter **Ages 13 & up.** Chicago's architecture is one of the city's main claims to fame, and a quick swing through this center will help you understand why. Run by the well-regarded Chicago Architecture Foundation, it's conveniently located across the street from the Art Institute. Still trying to figure out the difference between Prairie School and postmodern? Stop in here for a lesson. Exhibits include a scale model of downtown Chicago, profiles of the people and buildings that shaped the city's look, and a searchable database with pictures and information on many of Chicago's best-known skyscrapers. "Architecture ambassadors" are on hand to provide information on tours run by the foundation (see "Chicago Architecture Foundation Tours," p. 202). Two galleries feature changing exhibits about ongoing Chicago design projects—so you can see first-hand how local architecture continues to evolve. There's also an excellent gift shop filled with architecture-focused books, decorative accessories, and gifts. Allow a half-hour, more if you want to browse in the store.

224 S. Michigan Ave. © 312/922-3432. www.architecture.org. Free admission. Exhibits Mon–Sat 9:30am–4pm. Shop and tour desk Mon–Sat 9am–6:30pm; Sun 9am–6pm. Subway/El: Brown, Green, Orange, or Purple Line to Adams; Red Line to Jackson. Bus: 3, 4, 145, 147, or 151.

Chicago Cultural Center ★ (Finds) **Ages 3 & up.** Free family programs are the main attraction of this landmark building, built in 1897 as the city's public library and transformed into a showplace for visual and performing arts in 1991. Its basic Beaux Arts exterior conceals a sumptuous interior of rare marble, fine hardwood, stained glass, polished brass, and mosaics of Favrile glass, colored stone, and mother-of-pearl inlaid in white marble. The crowning centerpiece is Preston Bradley Hall's majestic Tiffany dome, said to be the largest of its kind in the world.

The building also houses one of the Chicago Office of Tourism's visitor centers, which makes it a good place to kick-start your visit. If you stop in to pick up tourist information and take a quick look around, your visit won't take longer than 15 minutes, but the Cultural Center also hosts an array of art exhibitions, concerts, films, lectures, and other special events (many free), which might convince you to extend your time here. Programs might include African drumming, a recital by a mezzo-soprano from the Lyric Opera, or readings by Chicago playwrights. A long-standing tradition is the 12:15pm Dame Myra Hess Memorial classical concert every Wednesday in the Preston Bradley Hall.

Guided architectural tours of the Cultural Center are offered Wednesday, Friday, and Saturday at 1:15pm. For information, call © **312/744-8032.**

78 E. Washington St. © 312/744-6630, or 312/FINE-ART (346-3278) for weekly events. www.cityofchicago. org/exploringchicago. Free admission. Mon–Thurs 10am–7pm; Fri 10am–6pm; Sat 10am–5pm; Sun 11am–5pm. Closed major holidays. Subway/El: Brown, Green, Orange, or Purple Line to Randolph; Red Line to Washington/State. Bus: 3, 4, 20, 56, 60, 145, 146, 147, 151, or 157.

Chicago Fed Money Museum It's not worth a special trip (unless you're a huge monetary-policy geek), but the Visitors Center at the Federal Reserve Bank of Chicago can make for a surprisingly kid-friendly stop if you're touring the Loop's other attractions. Offering more than just the standard history-of-banking exhibits, the center has kid-friendly features such as a giant cube that holds a million dollars, and an exhibit that lets kids try to detect counterfeit bills. And, yes, there's even a section where visitors can learn how changes in interest rates affect the economy. Free guided tours are given weekdays at 1pm. Allow a half-hour.

230 S. LaSalle St. (at Quincy St.). © 312/322-2400. www.chicagofed.org. Free admission. Mon–Fri 9am–4pm. Closed Federal holidays. Subway/El: Brown Line to Quincy/Wells. Bus: 134, 135, or 156.

Chicago History Museum ★ **Ages 3 & up.** The Chicago History Museum, located at the southwestern tip of Lincoln Park, is one of the city's oldest cultural institutions (founded in 1856), but it's reinvented itself for the 21st century. The main, must-see exhibit is **Chicago: Crossroads of America,** which fills the museum's second floor. A survey of the city's history—from its founding as a frontier trading post to the riots at the 1968 Democratic Convention—it's filled with photos, artifacts, and newsreels that make the past come alive; surrounding galleries track the development of local sports teams, architecture, music, and art. Although the exhibit is geared toward families with older children (you can even download an mp3 audio tour for teenagers from the museum's website), little ones will love the re-creation of an 1890s El station, where they can run inside the city's first elevated train. Another museum highlight is the hall of dioramas that re-create scenes from Chicago's past. Although they've been around for decades (and are decidedly low-tech), they're a fun way to trace the city's progression from a few small cabins to the grand World's Columbian Exposition of 1893. Another must-see is the Costume and Textile Gallery, which showcases pieces from the museum's renowned collection of historical clothing, including Michael Jordan's basketball uniform, dresses made by 19th-century immigrants, and gowns by French designer Christian Dior. The Children's Gallery on the ground floor has interactive exhibits for kids, including a giant table where you can experience the "Smells of Chicago" (not all pleasant, either!). A dress-up area allows kids to deck themselves out as a real Chicago hot dog with all the fixings.

The History Museum presents a wide range of lectures, seminars, and tours, including walking tours of the surrounding neighborhood, check the museum's website for details, as the schedules change frequently. Allow 1 to 2 hours.

1601 N. Clark St. (at North Ave.). © **312/642-4600.** www.chicagohistory.org. Admission $12 adults, $10 seniors and students, free for children 12 and under. Free admission Mon. Mon–Sat 9:30am–4:30pm (until 8pm Thurs); Sun noon–5pm. Research center Tues–Sat 1–4pm; Fri 10am–4:30pm. Bus: 11, 22, 36, 72, 151, or 156.

Chicago Public Library/Harold Washington Library Center Ages 2 & up.
This massive red-brick neoclassical edifice—occupying an entire city block at State Street and Congress Parkway—is the largest public library in the world. The Harold Washington Library Center is named in memory of Chicago's first and only African-American mayor, who died of a heart attack in 1987 at the beginning of his second term in office. There's a stunning 52-foot glass-domed winter garden on the top floor. On the second floor is another treasure: the vast **Thomas Hughes Children's Library,** housing more than 100,000 volumes, which makes an excellent resting spot for families. The library presents an interesting array of events and art exhibitions worth checking out, and is an excellent resting spot for families touring the Loop. A 385-seat auditorium is the setting for a unique mix of dance and music performances, author talks, and children's programs, including readings by librarians, puppet shows, and visits from book characters. (For example, kids might meet "Angelina Ballerina" and make crowns with her.) The library also has a cafe adjacent to the ninth-floor winter garden, and a coffeehouse and used-book store on the ground floor. Want to check your e-mail? Stop by the third-floor Computer Commons, which has about 75 terminals available for public use. Allow a half-hour.

400 S. State St. © **312/747-4300.** www.chipublib.org. Free admission. Mon–Thurs 9am–7pm; Fri–Sat 9am–5pm; Sun 1–5pm. Closed major holidays. Subway/El: Red Line to Jackson/State; Brown Line to Van Buren/Library. Bus: 2, 6, 11, 29, 36, 62, 145, 146, 147, or 151.

Chicago Water Tower—City Gallery All ages.
Along with the pumping station across the street, the Chicago Water Tower is one of only a handful of buildings to survive the Great Chicago Fire of 1871. It has long been a revered symbol of the city's resilience and fortitude, although today—more than 130 years after it first rose to a once-mighty height of 154 feet—the Water Tower is dwarfed by the high-rise shopping centers and hotels of North Michigan Avenue. The Gothic-style limestone building now has been

reinvented as an art gallery. While this may be a welcome and inventive use of the structure, it's actually an idea that first cropped up in 1948 but was never acted upon. The spiffed-up interior is intimate and sunny, and it's a refreshing pit stop of culture on your way to the Water Tower shopping center or pumping-station tourist information center across the street. Exhibits have included works by Chicago-based photographer Victor Skrebneski. Allow a half-hour.

806 N. Michigan Ave. (btw. Chicago Ave. and Pearson St.). © **312/742-0808.** Free admission. Mon–Sat 10am–6:30pm; Sun 10am–5pm. Bus: 3, 145, 146, 147, or 151.

DuSable Museum of African-American History   *Ages 5 & up.* The DuSable Museum is a repository of the history, art, and artifacts pertaining to the African-American experience and culture. Named for Chicago's first permanent settler, Jean Baptiste Point du Sable, a French-Canadian of Haitian descent, it is admirable not so much for its collections and exhibits as for the inspiring story behind its existence. Founded in 1961 with a $10 charter and minimal capital, the museum began in the home of Dr. Margaret Burroughs, an art teacher at the city's DuSable High School. In 1973, as a result of a community-based campaign, the museum took up residence in its present building (a former parks administration facility and police lockup) on the eastern edge of Washington Park. With no major endowment to speak of, the DuSable Museum has managed to accumulate a respectable collection of more than 13,000 artifacts, books, photographs, art objects, and memorabilia. Its collection of paintings, drawings, and sculpture by African-American and African artists is excellent.

In 1993 the DuSable Museum added a 25,000-square-foot wing named in honor of the city's first and only African-American mayor, Harold Washington. The permanent exhibit on Washington contains memorabilia and personal effects, and surveys important episodes in his political career. The museum also has a gift shop, a research library, and an extensive program of community-related events, such as a jazz and blues music series, and other cultural events, all presented in a 466-seat auditorium. Youth programming and workshops are also scheduled year-round, including a film series.

740 E. 56th Place. © **773/947-0600.** www.dusablemuseum.org. Admission $3 adults, $2 students and seniors, $1 children 6–13, free for children 5 and under. Free admission Sun. Tues–Sat 10am–5pm; Sun noon–5pm. Closed major holidays. Subway/El: Metra Electric train to 57th St. and Lake Park Ave., then a short cab ride. Bus: 6.

Historic Pullman ★★   *Ages 10 & up.* Railway magnate George Pullman was a fabulously wealthy industrialist, and he fancied himself more enlightened than his 19th-century peers. So when it came time to build a new headquarters for his Pullman Palace Car Company, he dreamed of something more than the standard factory surrounded by tenements. Instead, he built a model community for his workers, a place where they could live in houses with indoor plumbing and abundant natural light—amenities almost unheard of for industrial workers in the 1880s. Pullman didn't do all this from the goodness of his heart; he hoped that the town named after him would attract the most skilled workers (who would, not coincidentally, be so happy here that they wouldn't go on strike). As one of the first "factory towns," Pullman caused an international sensation and was seen as a model for other companies. The happy workers that Pullman envisioned, however, did not entirely cooperate, going on strike in 1894, frustrated by the company's control over every aspect of their lives.

Today the Pullman district makes a fascinating stop for families with kids interested in history or architecture. Although many of the homes are private residences, a number of public buildings still stand (including the lavish Hotel Florence, the imposing Clock Tower, and the two-story colonnaded Market Hall). A fire damaged some buildings in the late 1990s, but Pullman has thankfully been recognized as a unique historic site, and much-needed repairs are underway. You can walk through on your own (stop by the visitor center for a map), or take a guided tour at 1:30pm on the first Sunday of the month, from May to October ($5 adults, $4 seniors, $3 students). Allow 1¹/₂ hours for the guided tour.

11141 S. Cottage Grove Ave. ⓒ **773/785-8901.** www.pullmanil.org. Visitor center Tues–Sun 11am–3pm. Free admission. Train: Metra Electric Line to Pullman (111th St.), turn right on Cottage Grove Ave. and walk 1 block to the visitor center.

International Museum of Surgical Science (Finds   Ages 12 & up. This museum

is not for the faint of stomach. (Although I lived three doors down from this museum for 7 years, I was afraid to set foot inside—maybe it was the real skeletons they put in the windows every Halloween that scared me off?) Run by the International College of Surgeons, the museum is housed in a historic 1917 Gold Coast mansion designed by the noted architect Howard Van Doren Shaw, who modeled it after Le Petit Trianon at Versailles. Displayed throughout its four floors are surgical instruments, paintings, and sculpture depicting the history of surgery and healing practices in Eastern and Western civilizations. The exhibits are old-fashioned (no interactive computer displays here!) but that's part of the museum's odd appeal.

You'll look at your doctor in a whole new way after viewing the trepanned skulls excavated from an ancient tomb in Peru. The accompanying tools were used to bore holes in patients' skulls, a horrific practice thought to release the evil spirits causing their illnesses. (Some skulls show signs of new bone growth, meaning that some lucky headache-sufferers actually survived this low-tech surgery.) There are also battlefield amputation kits, a working iron-lung machine in the polio exhibit, and oddities such as a stethoscope designed to be transported inside a top hat. Other attractions include an apothecary shop and dentist's office (ca. 1900), re-created in a historical street exhibit, and the hyperbolically christened "Hall of Immortals," a sculpture gallery depicting 12 historic figures in medicine, from Hippocrates to Madame Curie. Allow 1 hour.

1524 N. Lake Shore Dr. (btw. Burton Place and North Ave.). ⓒ **312/642-6502.** www.imss.org. Admission $8 adults, $4 seniors and students. Tues–Sat 10am–4pm; May–Sept Sun 10am–4pm. Bus: 151.

Intuit: The Center for Intuitive and Outsider Art   Ages 3 & up. Chicago is

home to an active community of collectors of so-called outsider art, a term attached to a group of unknown, unconventional artists who do their own artwork without any formal training or connection to the mainstream art world. Often called folk or self-taught artists, their work is highly personal and idiosyncratic, and they work in a range of media, from bottle caps to immense canvases. Intuit was founded in 1991 to bring attention to these artists through exhibitions and educational lectures. Housed in the warehouse district northwest of the Loop, with two galleries and a performance area, Intuit is slowly gaining a higher profile on the city's art scene. The museum offers a regular lecture series, and if you time your visit right, you might be here for one of the center's tours of a private local art collection. Intuit doesn't offer special programs for kids, but events like quilt sales featuring textiles in the African-American improvised tradition, or graffiti art, should satisfy them.

756 N. Milwaukee Ave. (at Chicago and Ogden aves.). ⓒ **312/243-9088.** www.art.org. Free admission. Tues–Sat 11am–5pm (Thurs until 7:30pm). Subway/El: Blue Line to Chicago. Bus: 56 or 66.

Jane Addams Hull-House Museum **Ages 8 & up.** Three years after the 1886 Haymarket Riot, a young woman named Jane Addams bought a mansion on Halsted Street that had been built in 1856 as a "country home" but was now surrounded by the shanties of the immigrant poor. Here Addams and her co-worker, Ellen Gates Starr, launched the American settlement-house movement with the establishment of Hull House, an institution that endured on this site in Chicago until 1963. (It continues today as a decentralized social-service agency known as Hull House Association.) Orphans found a home here, and immigrants received healthcare, job training, and English lessons. In 1963 all but two of the settlement's 13 buildings, along with the entire residential neighborhood in its immediate vicinity, were demolished to make room for the new University of Illinois at Chicago campus, which now owns the museum buildings. Of the original settlement, what remains today are the Hull-House Museum (the mansion itself) and the residents' dining hall, snuggled among the ultramodern, poured-concrete buildings of the university campus. Inside are the original furnishings, Jane Addams's office, and numerous settlement maps and photographs. Rotating exhibits re-create the history of the settlement and the work of its residents, showing how Addams was able to help transform the dismal streets around her into stable inner-city environments. Allow a half-hour.

University of Illinois at Chicago, 800 S. Halsted St. (at Polk St.). ✆ **312/413-5353.** www.uic.edu/jaddams/hull. Free admission. Tues–Fri 10am–4pm; Sun noon–4pm. Closed university holidays. Subway/El: Blue Line to Halsted/University of Illinois. Bus: 8.

McCormick Tribune Freedom Museum **Ages 12 & up.** As you might guess from the name, the *Chicago Tribune* newspaper is the guiding force behind this celebration of the First Amendment. Thankfully, though, this is no corporate-PR stunt, but rather a thought-provoking overview of how the freedom of speech impacts our daily life. Aimed predominantly at junior-high and high-school students, it includes the requisite high-tech bells and whistles aimed at jaded young attention spans (such as computer kiosks where you can listen to once-banned songs, or take sides in a free-speech debate), and during the week, you might be surrounded by loud school groups. But some of the exhibits—such as the stories of reporters who were jailed for telling the truth—are emotionally affecting, and it makes an easy stop during a walk along Michigan Avenue. Allow 1 hour.

445 N. Michigan Ave. (btw. Illinois St. and the Chicago River). ✆ **312/222-4860.** www.freedommuseum. us. Admission $6, free for children 5 and under. Wed–Mon 10am–6pm. Closed Thanksgiving, Christmas, and New Year's Day. Bus: 56 or 66. Subway/El: Red Line to Grand. Bus: 145, 146, 147, or 151.

Museum of Contemporary Art ★ **Ages 5 & up.** The MCA is the largest contemporary-art museum in the country, emphasizing experimentation in a variety of media—painting, sculpture, photography, video and film, dance, music, and performance. To be honest, some of the works are challenging enough for adults, much less kids, but kids might get into some of the touring shows, which have included Roy Lichtenstein, Cindy Sherman, and Chuck Close.

Sitting on a front-row piece of property between the lake and the historic Water Tower, the classically styled building, clad in aluminum panels, is a subdued, almost-somber presence, and the steep rise of stairs leading to the entrance is monumental yet a bit daunting. But don't let the gloomy exterior get you down; the interior spaces are more vibrant, with a sun-drenched two-story central corridor, elliptical staircases, and three floors of exhibition space.

You can see the MCA's highlights in about an hour, although art lovers will want more time to wander (especially if a high-profile exhibit is in town). Your first stop should be the handsome barrel-vaulted galleries on the top floor, dedicated to pieces from the

(Fun Facts **Rock Around the World**

The impressive Gothic **Tribune Tower,** just north of the Chicago River on the east side of Michigan Avenue, is home to one of the country's media giants, the *Chicago Tribune* newspaper. It's also notable for an array of architectural fragments jutting out from the exterior—kids love getting hands-on here by touching stones from all over the world. The newspaper's notoriously despotic publisher, Robert R. McCormick, started the collection shortly after the building's completion in 1925, gathering pieces during his world travels. *Tribune* correspondents then began supplying building fragments that they acquired on assignment. Each one now bears the name of the structure and country whence it came. There are 138 pieces in all, including chunks and shards from the Great Wall of China, the Taj Mahal, the White House, the Arc de Triomphe, the Berlin Wall, the Roman Colosseum, London's Houses of Parliament, the Great Pyramid of Cheops in Giza, Egypt, and the original tomb of Abraham Lincoln in Springfield, Illinois.

permanent collection. For visitors who'd like a little guidance for making sense of the rather challenging works found at a contemporary-art museum, there is an audio tour for rent, as well as a free daily tour (1 and 6pm Tues; 1pm Wed–Fri; 11am, noon, 1, and 2pm Sat–Sun). In addition to a range of special activities and educational programming, including films, performances, and a lecture series in a 300-seat theater, the museum features Puck's at the MCA, a cafe operated by Wolfgang Puck of Spago restaurant fame, with seating that overlooks a 1-acre terraced sculpture garden. The museum store has one-of-a-kind gift items that make it worth a stop even if you don't visit the museum. Allow 1 to 2 hours.

220 E. Chicago Ave. (1 block east of Michigan Ave.). **(** **312/280-2660.** www.mcachicago.org. Admission $10 adults, $6 seniors and students with ID, free for children 12 and under. Free admission Tues. Tues 10am–8pm; Wed–Sun 10am–5pm. Closed Jan 1, Thanksgiving, and Dec 25. Subway/El: Red Line to Chicago/State. Bus: 3, 10, 66, 145, 146, or 151.

Museum of Contemporary Photography **Ages 8 & up.** Columbia College's photography museum sometimes has shows that kids find appealing (one show featured fairy tale–based photography aimed at preteens; another featured photos of twins)—so call or check out the website for current shows. Ensconced in a ground-floor space at the college, a progressive arts- and media-oriented institution that has the country's largest undergraduate film department and a highly respected photojournalism-slanted photography department, the Museum of Contemporary Photography is the only museum in the Midwest of its ilk. As the name indicates, it exhibits, collects, and promotes modern photography, with a special focus on American works from 1959 to the present. Rotating exhibitions showcase images by both nationally recognized and "undiscovered" regional artists. Related lectures and special programs are scheduled during the year. Allow 1 hour.

600 S. Michigan Ave. **(** **312/344-7104.** www.mocp.org. Free admission. Mon–Wed and Fri 10am–5pm; Thurs 10am–8pm; Sat noon–5pm. Subway/El: Red Line to Harrison. Bus: 6, 146, or 151.

National Museum of Mexican Art ★ **All ages.** Chicago's vibrant Pilsen neighborhood, just southwest of the Loop, is home to one of the nation's largest Mexican-American communities. Ethnic pride emanates from every doorstep, *taqueria,* and bakery and the multitude of colorful murals splashed across building exteriors and alleyways. But this institution—the only Latino museum accredited by the American Association of Museums—may be the neighborhood's most prized possession. That's quite an accomplishment, given that the Mexican Fine Arts Center Museum was founded in 1987 by a passel of public schoolteachers who pooled $900 to get it started.

The museum is very family-oriented, offering a deluge of educational workshops for kids and parents: It's truly a living museum. There are wonderful exhibits to be sure, showcasing Mexican and Mexican-American visual and performing artists, and often drawing on the museum's permanent collection of more than 2,400 works. But it's the visiting artists, festival programming, and community participation where the museum really shines. Its Day of the Dead celebration, which runs for about 8 weeks beginning in September, is one of the most ambitious in the country. The Del Corazon Mexican Performing Arts Festival, held in the spring, features programs by local and international artists here and around town. And the Sor Juana Festival, presented in the fall, honors Mexican writer and pioneering feminist Sor Juana Ines de la Cruz with photography and painting exhibits, music and theater performances, and poetry readings by Latina women.

The museum also has a splendid gift shop, and it stages a holiday market, featuring gift items from Mexico, on the first weekend in December. Allow 1 hour.

1852 W. 19th St. (a few blocks west of Ashland Ave.). 🕐 **312/738-1503.** www.nationalmuseumofmexican art.org. Free admission. Tues–Sun 10am–5pm. Subway/El: Blue Line to 18th St. Bus: 9.

National Vietnam Veterans Art Museum Ⓕ**inds** **Ages 12 & up.** Junior high kids and older can emerge from this unique museum with a better understanding of the Vietnam War and the lives touched by this experience. This museum houses one of the most stirring art collections anywhere—and the only one of its kind in the world—telling the story of the men who fought in Vietnam. Since the war, many of the veterans made art as personal therapy, never expecting to show it to anyone, but in 1981 a small group of them began showing their works together in Chicago and in touring exhibitions. The collection has grown to more than 700 paintings, drawings, photographs, and sculptures from all over the country and other countries, including Vietnam. Titles such as *We Regret to Inform You, Blood Spots on a Rice Paddy,* and *The Wound* should give you an idea of the power of the images in this unique legacy to the war. Housed in a former warehouse in the Prairie Avenue district south of the Loop, the museum is modern and well organized. An installation that's suspended from the ceiling, **Above & Beyond ★**, comprises more than 58,000 dog tags with the names of the men and women who died in the war—the emotional effect is similar to that of the Wall in Washington, D.C. The complex also houses a small theater, a cafe open for breakfast and lunch, a gift shop, and an outdoor plaza with a flagpole that has deliberately been left leaning because that's how veterans saw them in combat. Allow 1 hour.

1801 S. Indiana Ave. (at 18th St.). 🕐 **312/326-0270.** www.nvvam.org. Admission $10 adults, $7 seniors and students with ID. Tues–Fri 11am–6pm; Sat 10am–5pm; Sun noon–5pm. Closed major holidays. Bus: 3 or 4.

Newberry Library **Ages 12 & up.** Got a bookworm in the family? The Newberry Library is a bibliophile's dream. Established in 1887 at the bequest of the Chicago merchant and financier Walter Loomis Newberry, the noncirculating research library today contains many rare books and manuscripts (such as Shakespeare's first folio and Jefferson's copy of *The Federalist Papers*). Although most of the library is off-limits to kids 15 and under, the library does hold children's story hours throughout the year. It also houses a vast depository of published resources for those who are seriously delving into American and European history and literature, as well as other aspects of the humanities from the late Middle Ages onward. The library is also a major destination for genealogists digging at their roots, and its holdings are now open for the use of the public for free (over the age of 16 with a photo ID). The collections, many items of which are displayed during an ongoing series of public exhibitions, include more than 1.5 million volumes and 75,000 maps, housed in a comely five-story granite building, designed in the Spanish-Romanesque style by Henry Ives Cobb and built in 1893. For an overview, take a free 1-hour tour Thursday at 3pm or Saturday at 10:30am. The library also operates a fine bookstore and sponsors a series of concerts (including those by its resident early-music ensemble, the Newberry Consort), lectures, and children's story hours throughout the year. One popular annual event that older kids might enjoy is the "Bughouse Square" debates. Held across the street in Washington Square Park, the debates re-create the fiery soapbox orations of the left-wing agitators in the 1930s and 1940s. Allow a half-hour.

60 W. Walton St. (at Dearborn Pkwy.). © **312/943-9090** or 312/255-3700 for programs. www.newberry. org. Reading room Tues–Thurs 10am–6pm; Fri–Sat 9am–5pm. Exhibit gallery Mon and Fri–Sat 8:15am–5:30pm; Tues–Thurs 8:15am–7:30pm. Subway/El: Red Line to Chicago/State. Bus: 22, 36, 125, 145, 146, 147, or 151.

Oriental Institute Museum ★ Ⓕⁱⁿᵈˢ **Ages 10 & up.** Don't skip this museum because of its intimidating name. Kids love the Egyptian artifacts here (including mummies and toys and clothes from ancient Egyptian children). Located near the midpoint of the University of Chicago campus, just north of the Memorial Chapel, the Oriental Institute houses one of the world's major collections of Near Eastern art. Although most of the galleries have been renovated within the past few years, this is still a very traditional museum: lots of glass cases, very few interactive exhibits (that's why I recommend it only for older kids—young children won't be interested). It won't take you long to see the highlights here—and a few impressive pieces make it worth a stop for history and art buffs.

Your first stop should be the **Egyptian Gallery** ★★, which showcases the finest objects among the 35,000 artifacts from the Nile Valley held by the museum. At the center of the gallery stands a monumental 17-foot solid-quartzite **statue of King Tutankhamen,** the boy king who ruled Egypt from about 1335 to 1324 B.C. The largest Egyptian sculpture in the Western Hemisphere (tipping the scales at 6 tons), the Oriental Institute excavated it in 1930. The surrounding exhibits, which document the life and beliefs of Egyptians from 5000 B.C. to the 8th century A.D., have a wonderfully accessible approach that emphasizes themes, not chronology. Among them are mummification (14 mummies are on display—five people and nine animals), kingship, society, writing (including a deed for the sale of a house, a copy of the *Book of the Dead,* and a schoolboy's homework), family, art, tools and technology, occupations, popular religion, medicine, the gods, food, games, clothing, and jewelry. Kids will be especially interested in two fragile objects used by Egyptian children: papyrus documents and a child's linen tunic from 1550 B.C.

The institute also houses important collections of artifacts from civilizations that once flourished in what are now Iran and Iraq. The highlight of the **Mesopotamian Gallery** ★ is a massive, 16-foot-tall sculpture of a winged bull with a human head, which once stood in the palace of Assyrian King Sargon II. The gallery also contains some of the earliest man-made tools ever excavated, along with many other pieces that have become one-of-a-kind since the looting of the National Museum in Baghdad in 2003. Other galleries are filled with artifacts from Sumer, ancient Palestine, Israel, Anatolia, and Nubia.

For Train Lovers

Chicago and trains go together like, well, kids and trains. From little red street-cars to thundering steam trains, two area museums are the places to ride the rails—and maybe even learn a bit about history.

At the **Fox River Trolley Museum** (© **847/697-4676;** www.foxtrolley.org) in west suburban South Elgin, hop a trolley and ride a real electric railway that first opened on July 4, 1896. The 3-mile ride takes you along the banks of the scenic Fox River. The Aurora, Elgin, and Fox River Electric Co. Interurban Line once connected communities along the Fox River, including Carpentersville, Elgin, Aurora, and Yorkville. The railway was abandoned to passenger traffic in 1935, and in 1972 the museum purchased part of the line. At the museum you can check out antique trolleys from 1891 to 1952. The museum's most popular annual event is the Pumpkin Trolley, run on 2 weekends in October. Ride the trolley to the museum's pumpkin patch, pick your own, and head back to the museum for a picnic lunch and a visit to the museum store.

The museum is at 361 S. LaFox St. (Illinois Rte. 31) in South Elgin, about 40 miles west of Chicago. Fares are $3.50 for adults, and $2 for seniors and children 3 to 11. Additional rides are 50¢. Open dates change yearly: In 2008, the museum was open on Sundays from May 11 to November 2 from 11am to 5pm, and on Saturdays from June 28 to August 1, and October 11, 18, and 25 from 11am to 5pm. Check the website for dates in 2009 and beyond. To get there, take I-90 or U.S. Rte. 20 west to Elgin, and exit on Illinois Rte. 31 southbound. To make it an all-train day, take the Metra commuter train to Elgin on the Milwaukee District West Line. Then take Pace bus no. 801 to State Street, South Elgin, and walk 3 blocks south to the museum (or take a taxi from the Elgin train station).

America's largest railway museum is the **Illinois Railway Museum** (www.irm.org) located in Union, about 60 miles northwest of Chicago. With 120 acres

The gift shop at the Oriental Institute, called the Suq, stocks many unique items, including reproductions of pieces in the museum's collection. Allow 1 hour.

1155 E. 58th St. (at University Ave.). © **773/702-9514.** http://oi.uchicago.edu. Free admission; suggested donation $5 adults, $2 children. Tues and Thurs–Sat 10am–6pm (Wed until 8:30pm); Sun noon–6pm. Bus: 6 or Metra Electric train to 57th St. and Lake Park Ave.

Polish Museum of America **Ages 6 & up.** One million people of Polish ancestry live in Chicago, giving the city the largest Polish population outside of Warsaw. So it's no surprise that Chicago is the site of the Polish Museum of America, located in the neighborhood where many of the first immigrants settled. This museum has one of the most important collections of Polish art and historical materials outside Poland. (It is also the largest museum in the United States devoted exclusively to an ethnic group.) The museum's programs include rotating exhibitions, films, lectures, and concerts, and a permanent exhibit about Pope John Paul II. There is also a library with a large Polish-language collection, and archives where visitors can research genealogical history (call in

and 400 engines and cars, sprawling rail lines crisscross the property. (Be sure to look both ways before crossing any tracks!) The museum has a 5-mile rail line, where you'll find steam, diesel, and heavy electric trains chugging along, and a mile-long streetcar loop. On the weekend you can jump on a steam or diesel train from the museum's East Union depot (built around a station dating from 1851) and take a 40-minute round-trip ride to Kishwaukee Grove, passing prairie and farmland. Whether you get on a steam locomotive with its hissing brakes and billowing steam, a diesel dating from the 1950s, or an Electroliner, which ran between Chicago and Milwaukee until 1963 and is powered by overhead wires, you're in for a thrill. Smaller trains depart from the 50th Avenue rapid transit station built in 1910 and removed from Cicero.

A streetcar line encircles the museum grounds so you can hop on and off at different "barns" that house everything from red cabooses to luxurious private passenger cars from the late 1800s. Call ⓒ **800/BIG-RAIL** (244-7245) or 815/ 923-4000 in advance to find out which trains are operating. Diesels operate most weekends and holidays, but steam trains run only about 12 times a season. Electric cars run daily.

The museum is open April through October. Grounds are open from 9am to 6pm on weekends, 10am to 5pm on weekdays. Trains run on weekends from 10:30am to 5pm, and weekdays from 10am to 4pm. Rides cost $8 to $12 (depending on the trains running) for adults, and $4 to $8 for children, with family maximums of $25 to $45. To get there, take I-90 to U.S. Rte. 20. Take the Marengo exit and drive northwest on Rte. 20 to Union Road. Go north on Union Road.

advance if you want to look through those records). Parents should request a "seek and find" booklet with questions for kids (and get a free Polish Museum pen, too).

984 N. Milwaukee Ave. (at Augusta Blvd.). ⓒ **773/384-3352.** www.polishmuseumofamerica.org. Suggested donation $5 adults, $4 students, $3 children 11 and under. Fri–Wed 11am–4pm. Subway/El: Blue Line to Division.

The Smart Museum of Art ★ Ages 5 & up. The University of Chicago's fine-arts museum looks rather modest, but it packs a lot of talent into a compact space. Its permanent collection of more than 7,000 paintings and sculptures spans Western and Eastern civilizations and ranges from classical antiquity to the present day. Bona fide treasures include ancient Greek vases, Chinese bronzes, and old-master paintings; Frank Lloyd Wright furniture; Tiffany glass; sculptures by Degas, Matisse, and Rodin; and 20th-century paintings and sculptures by Mark Rothko, Arthur Dove, Mexican muralist Diego Rivera, Henry Moore, and Chicago sculptor Richard Hunt. Built in 1974, the contemporary building doesn't really fit in with the Gothic style of other campus buildings, but its sculpture garden and outdoor seating are available for families, who are welcome to picnic on the lawn. The museum is reaching out to families through Smart-Kids programs, which offer hands-on art activities. The museum also has a gift shop and a cafe.

5550 S. Greenwood Ave. (at E. 55th St.). ✆ **773/702-0200.** http://smartmuseum.uchicago.edu. Free admission; donations welcome. Tues–Wed and Fri 10am–4pm (Thurs until 8pm); Sat–Sun 11am–5pm. Closed major holidays. Bus: 6.

Spertus Museum Ages 5 & up. The Spertus Museum, an extension of the Spertus Institute of Jewish Studies, showcases intricately crafted and historic Jewish ceremonial objects, textiles, coins, paintings, and sculpture, tracing 5,000 years of Jewish heritage. In 2007, the museum moved to a new, contemporary building, with an angled glass facade that marks a welcome change from the solemn, solid structures surrounding it. Highlights of the building include a 400-seat theater for lectures and films; an interactive exhibit space designed for kids; and a kosher cafe operated by Chef Wolfgang Puck's catering company. Researchers can register to visit the Asher Library or study the Chicago Jewish Archives collection. The museum shop carries a large selection of art, books, music, videos, and contemporary and traditional Jewish ceremonial gifts. Allow 1 hour.

610 S. Michigan Ave. ✆ **312/322-1747.** www.spertus.edu. Admission $7 adults; $5 seniors, students, and children. Free admission Tues 10am–noon and Thurs 3–7pm. Sun–Wed 10am–6pm; Thurs 10am–7pm; Fri 10am–3pm. Validated parking in nearby lots. Subway/El: Red Line to Harrison; Brown, Purple, Orange, or Green Line to Adams. Bus: 3, 4, 6, 145, 147, or 151.

Swedish-American Museum Center ★ Ages 2 & up. Chicago parents recommend a visit to this storefront museum, which chronicles the Swedish immigrant contribution to American life. The museum is a hub of activity, with cultural lectures, concerts, and classes and folk dancing geared to Swedish Americans, some of whom still live in the surrounding Andersonville neighborhood. The **Children's Museum of Immigration** is located on the third floor, where Swedish crafts demonstrations and classes, as well as language classes, are offered. Geared toward kindergartners through sixth graders, the museum lets kids experience the journey from the Old World. They can step inside an authentic Swedish farmhouse and do chores on the farm, board a steamship for America, and begin a new life in a log cabin.

The permanent exhibits on display draw on a small collection of art and artifacts dating to the mass immigration of Swedes to Chicago 2 centuries ago. Temporary exhibitions (usually Swedish folk art) are mounted four times a year. There's also a nice gift shop that sells Orrefors glassware; books on Swedish folk art, decorating, and cooking; children's toys; and holiday knickknacks. Strolling down this stretch of Clark Street, where Swedish bakeries and gourmet-food stores are interspersed with an attractive mix of restaurants, bars, cafes, and theater companies, is the best reason for stopping in here.

5211 N. Clark St. (near Foster Ave.). ✆ **773/728-8111.** www.samac.org. Admission $4 adults, $3 seniors and students, $10 family rate, free for children under 1. Free the 2nd Tues of the month. Tues–Fri 10am–4pm; Sat–Sun 11am–4pm. Subway/El: Red Line to Bryn Mawr, then walk several blocks west to Clark. Bus: 22.

5 BEST RIDES

The best ride in the city is the El, with boat tours of the river and lake a close second (see "Kid-Friendly Tours," later in this chapter). Other rides are tucked away in Chicago's top attractions: Don't miss the endangered-species merry-go-round at Lincoln Park Zoo and

seekers should head directly to an amusement park.

Six Flags Great America   All ages. One of the Midwest's biggest theme/amusement parks is located midway between Chicago and Milwaukee on I-94 in Gurnee, Illinois. The park has more than 100 rides and attractions and is a favorite of roller coaster devotees. There are a whopping 10 of them here, including the nausea-inducing Déjà vu, where riders fly forward and backward over a twisting, looping inverted steel track, and Superman, where you speed along hanging head first (with your legs dangling). Other don't-miss rides for the strong of stomach include the Iron Wolf, where you do corkscrew turns and 360-degree loops while standing up, and the American Eagle, a classic wooden coaster. Because this is a place that caters to families, you'll also find plenty to appeal to the young set. The Looney Tunes National Park is full of kiddie rides with a cartoon theme; other worthwhile stops include the double-decker carousel and bumper cars. Six Flags also has live shows, IMAX movies, and restaurants. If you take the trouble to get out here from the city, allow a full day.

I-94 at Rte. 132 E., Gurnee. ℂ **847/249-4636.** www.sixflags.com. Admission (including unlimited rides, shows, and attractions) $43 adults, $35 seniors and children over 54 in. tall, free for children 3 and under. Daily May 10am–7pm; June–Aug 10am–10pm; weekends only in Sept 10am–7pm. Parking $10. Take I-94 or I-294 W. to Rte. 132 (Grand Ave.). Approximate driving time from Chicago city limits is 45 min.

6 HISTORIC HOUSES

OAK PARK

Architecture and literary buffs alike make pilgrimages to Oak Park, a nearby suburb on the western border of the city that is easily accessible by car or train. Bookworms flock here to see the town where Ernest Hemingway was born and grew up, while others come to catch a glimpse of the Frank Lloyd Wright–designed homes that line the well maintained streets.

Getting There

BY CAR   Oak Park is 10 miles due west of downtown Chicago. By car, take the Eisenhower Expressway (I-290) west to Harlem Avenue (Ill. 43) and exit north. Continue on Harlem north to Lake Street. Take a right on Lake Street and continue to Forest Avenue. Turn left here, and immediately on your right you'll see the **Oak Park Visitor Center** (see below).

BY PUBLIC TRANSPORTATION   Take the Green Line west to the Harlem stop, roughly a 25-minute ride from downtown. Exit the station onto Harlem Avenue, and proceed north to Lake Street. Take a right on Lake Street, follow it to Forest Avenue, and then turn left to the **Oak Park Visitor Center** (see below).

BY TOUR   The **Chicago Architecture Foundation** regularly runs guided tours from downtown Chicago to Oak Park. For details, see "Chicago Architecture Foundation Tours," p. 202.

Visitor Information

The **Oak Park Visitor Center,** 158 Forest Ave. (ℂ **888/OAK-PARK** [625-7275]; www.visitoakpark.com), is open daily from 10am to 5pm April through October, and from 10am to 4pm November through March. Stop here for orientation, maps, and guidebooks.

The (Frank Lloyd) Wright Stuff

Oak Park has the highest concentration of houses or buildings anywhere designed and built by Wright, probably the most influential figure in American architectural history. People come here to marvel at the work of a man who saw his life as a twofold mission: to wage a single-handed battle against the ornamental excesses of architecture, Victorian in particular, and to create in its place a new form that would be at the same time functional, appropriate to its natural setting, and stimulating to the imagination.

Not everyone who comes to Oak Park shares Wright's architectural philosophy. But scholars and enthusiasts admire Wright for being consistently true to his own vision, out of which emerged a unique and genuinely American architectural statement. The reason for Wright's success could stem from the fact that he himself was a living exemplar of a quintessential American type. In a deep sense, he embodied the ideal of the self-made and self-sufficient individual who had survived, even thrived, in the frontier society—qualities that he expressed in his almost-puritanical insistence that each spatial or structural form in his buildings serves some useful purpose. But he was also an aesthete in Emersonian fashion, deriving his idea of beauty from natural environments, where apparent simplicity often belies a subtle complexity.

The three principal ingredients of a tour of Wright-designed structures in Oak Park are the **Frank Lloyd Wright Home & Studio tour,** the **Unity Temple tour,** and a **walking tour**—guided or self-guided—to view the exteriors of homes throughout the neighborhood that were built by the architect. Oak Park has, in all, 25 homes and buildings by Wright, constructed between the years 1892 and 1913, which constitute the core output of his Prairie School period. Visiting another 50 dwellings of architectural interest by Wright's contemporaries, scattered throughout this community and neighboring River Forest, is also worthwhile.

There's a city-operated parking lot next door. The heart of the historic district and the Frank Lloyd Wright Home and Studio are only a few blocks away.

An extensive tour of the neighborhood surrounding the Frank Lloyd Wright Home and Studio leaves from the **Ginkgo Tree Bookshop,** 951 Chicago Ave. (✆ **708/848-1606**), on weekends from 10:30am to 4pm (tour times are somewhat more limited Nov–Feb). This tour lasts 1 hour and costs $12 for adults and $10 for seniors and students ages 11 to 18, and $5 for children 4 to 10. If you can't make it to Oak Park on the weekend, you can follow a self-guided map and audiocassette tour of the historic district for the same price; the audio tour is available at the Ginkgo Tree Bookshop from 10am to 3:30pm. In addition to homes designed by Wright, you will see that of several of his disciples, as well as some very charming examples of the Victorian styling that he so disdained. A more detailed map ($3 at the bookshop), *Architectural Guide Map of Oak Park and River Forest,* includes text and photos of all 80 sites of interest in Oak Park and neighboring River Forest.

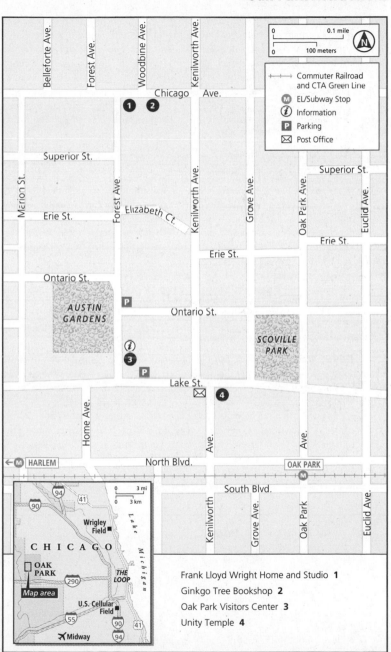

Frank Lloyd Wright Home and Studio **1**

Ginkgo Tree Bookshop **2**

Oak Park Visitors Center **3**

Unity Temple **4**

The Frank Lloyd Wright Home & Studio ★★★ **Ages 6 & up.** For the first 20 years of Wright's career, this remarkable complex served first and foremost as the sanctuary from which Wright was to design and execute more than 130 of an extraordinary output of 430 completed buildings. During this highly fertile period, the house was Wright's showcase and laboratory, but it also embraces many idiosyncratic features molded to his own needs rather than those of a client. The home began as a simple shingled cottage that Wright built for his bride in 1889 at the age of 22, but it became a work in progress, as Wright remodeled it constantly over the years. With its many add-ons—including a barrel-vaulted children's playroom and a studio with an octagonal balcony suspended by chains—the place has a certain whimsy that others might have found less livable. This, however, was not an architect's masterpiece, but the master's home, and every room in it can be savored for the view it reflects of the workings of a remarkable mind. The Home and Studio Foundation has restored the residence and studio to its 1909 vintage—the year Wright left the house.

The special guided Junior Architecture Tour presents the home through the eyes of the six Wright children who grew up here. (One of those children later invented Lincoln Logs.) Tours, which are for kids age 6 to 14, are led the fourth Saturday of the month from January to November and last 45 minutes. What's most special is that the tours are given by the Preservation Trust's Junior Interpreters, specially trained 5th- through 10th-grade students. Tour cost is $3.

951 Chicago Ave. ⓒ **708/848-1976.** www.wrightplus.org. Admission $12 adults, $10 seniors and students 11–18, $5 children 4–10. Combined admission for Home & Studio tour and guided or self-guided historic district tour (see below) $20 adults, $10 seniors and students 11–18, $5 children 4–10. Admission to home and studio is by guided tour only; tours depart from the Ginkgo Tree Bookshop Mon–Fri 11am, 1, and 3pm; Sat–Sun every 20 min. 11am–3:30pm. Closed Jan 1, last week in Jan, Thanksgiving, and Dec 25. Facilities for people with disabilities are limited; please call in advance.

Robie House ★★ **Ages 10 & up.** One of Frank Lloyd Wright's finest works, the Robie House is considered among the masterpieces of 20th-century American architecture. The open layout, linear geometry of form, and craftsmanship are typical of Wright's Prairie School design. Completed in 1910 for inventor Frederick Robie, a bicycle and motorcycle manufacturer, the home is also notable for its exquisite leaded- and stained-glass doors and windows. It's also among the last of his Prairie School–style homes: During its construction, Wright abandoned both his family and his Oak Park practice to follow other pursuits, most prominently the realization of his Taliesin home and studio in Spring Green, Wisconsin. Docents from the Frank Lloyd Wright Preservation Trust lead tours here, although until the end of October 2009, the tours will be limited to the

---

ⓘ Tips **The Wright Plus Tour**

Die-hard fans of the architect will want to plan to be in town the third Saturday in May for the annual Wright Plus Tour, during which the public can tour several Frank Lloyd Wright–designed homes and several other notable Oak Park buildings, in both the Prairie School and the Victorian styles, in addition to Wright's home and studio and the Unity Temple. The tour includes 10 buildings in all. Tickets go on sale March 1 and can sell out by mid-April. Call ⓒ **708/848-1976** (Frank Lloyd Wright Home & Studio; www.wrightplus.org) for details and ticket information.

(Finds) **More Frank Lloyd Wright Homes**

In addition to Robie House, several of Wright's earlier works, still privately owned, dot the streets of Hyde Park, such as the **Heller House,** 5132 S. Woodlawn Ave. (1897); the **Blossom House,** 1332 E. 49th St. (1882); and the **McArthur House,** 4852 S. Kenwood Ave. (1892). These homes are not open to the public but can be admired from the sidewalk.

hours of 11am to 3pm on Saturdays, as a massive, 10-year restoration project accelerates to be completed in time for the house's 100th anniversary in 2010. Advance ticket purchases are recommended. After October 2009, please call or check the website for new details. Allow 2 hours.

5757 S. Woodlawn Ave. (at 58th St.). (C) **773/834-1847.** www.gowright.org. Admission $12 adults, $10 seniors and children 7–18, free for children 6 and under. Mon–Fri tours at 11am, 1, and 3pm; Sat–Sun every half-hour 11am 3:30pm. Bookshop daily 10am–5pm. Bus: 6 or Metra Electric train to 57th St. and Lake Park Ave.

Unity Temple ★ Ages 10 & up. After fire destroyed its church around 1900, a Unitarian Universalist congregation asked one of its members, Frank Lloyd Wright, to design an affordable replacement. Using poured concrete with metal reinforcements—a necessity, owing to the small budget of $40,000 allocated for the project—Wright created a building that on the outside seems as forbidding as a mausoleum but that on the inside contains in its detailing the entire architectural alphabet of the Prairie School that has since made Wright's name immortal. Following the example of H. H. Richardson (of Glessner House fame; see below), Wright placed the building's main entrance on the side, behind an enclosure—a feature often employed in his houses as well—to create a sense of privacy and intimacy. Front entrances were too anonymous for these two architects. Wright complained, furthermore, that other architectural conventions of the church idiom, such as the nave in the Gothic-style cathedral across from the future site of Unity Temple, were overpowering. Of that particular church, he commented that he didn't feel a part of it.

Yet his vision in this regard was somewhat confused and contradictory. He wanted Unity Temple to be "democratic." But perhaps Wright was unable to subdue his own personal hubris and hauteur in the creative process, for the ultimate effect of his chapel, and much of the building's interior, is very grand and imperial. Unity Temple is no simple meetinghouse in the tradition of Calvinist iconoclasm. Instead, its principal chapel looks like the chamber of the Roman Senate. Even so, the interior, with its unpredictable geometric arrangements and its decor reminiscent of Native American art, is no less beautiful.

Wright used color sparingly within Unity Temple, but the pale, natural effects that he achieved are owed in part to his decision to add pigment to the plaster rather than use paint. Wright's use of wood for trim and other decorative touches is still exciting to behold; his sensitivity to grain and tone and placement was akin to that of an exceptionally gifted woodworker. Wright was a true hands-on, can-do person; he knew the materials he chose to use as intimately as the artisans who carried out his plans. And his stunning, almost-minimalist use of form is what still sets him apart as a relevant and brilliant artist. Other details to which the docent guide will call your attention, as you

The Pride of Prairie Avenue

Prairie Avenue, south of the Loop, was the city's first "Gold Coast," and its most famous address is **Glessner House,** a must-see for anyone interested in architectural history. The only surviving Chicago building designed by Boston architect Henry Hobson Richardson, it represented a dramatic shift from traditional Victorian architecture when it was built in 1886 (and inspired a young Frank Lloyd Wright).

The imposing granite exterior gives the home a forbidding air. (Railway magnate George Pullman, who lived nearby, complained, "I do not know what I have ever done to have that thing staring me in the face every time I go out my door.") But step inside and the home turns out to be a welcoming, cozy retreat, filled with Arts and Crafts furniture and decorative arts.

Visits to Glessner House are by guided tour only. Tours are given Wednesday to Sunday at 1, 2, and 3pm year-round (except major holidays). Tours are first-come, first-served, with no advance reservations except for groups of 10 or more. It's located at 1800 S. Prairie Ave. (© **312/326-1480;** www.glessner house.org). Admission is $10 for adults, $9 for students and seniors, and $5 for children 5 to 12. Bus: 1, 3, or 4 from Michigan Avenue at Jackson Boulevard (get off at 18th St.).

complete a circuit of the temple, are the great fireplace, the pulpit, the skylights, and the clerestory (gallery) windows. Suffice it to say, Unity Temple—only one of Wright's masterpieces—is counted among the 10 greatest American architectural achievements.

875 Lake St. © **708/383-8873.** http://unitytemple-utrf.org. Self-guided tours $8 adults; $6 seniors, children 6–12, and students with ID. Free guided tours weekends at 1, 2, and 3pm. Mon–Fri 10:30am–4:30pm; Sat–Sun 1–4pm. Church events can alter the schedule; call in advance.

7 ZOOS

Brookfield Zoo ★★★   All ages. Brookfield is the Chicago area's largest zoo. In contrast to the rather efficient Lincoln Park Zoo, Brookfield is spacious and spreads out over 216 acres with 2,700 animal residents—camels, dolphins, giraffes, baboons, wolves, tigers, green sea turtles, Siberian tigers, snow leopards, and more—living in naturalistic environments that put them side by side with other inhabitants of their regions. These creative indoor and outdoor settings—filled with activities to keep kids interested—are what set Brookfield apart.

Start out at *Habitat Africa!* ★★, a multiple-ecosystem exhibit that encompasses 30 acres—about the size of the entire Lincoln Park Zoo. Then wander through some of the buildings that allow you to see animals close up; my personal favorites are *Tropic World* ★, where you hang out at treetop level with monkeys, and *Australia House,* where fruit bats flit around your head. *The Living Coast* ★★ explores the west coast of Chile and Peru, and includes everything from a tank of plate-size moon jellies to a rocky shore where Humboldt penguins swim and nest as Inca terns and gray gulls fly freely overhead. *The*

Lincoln Park Zoo

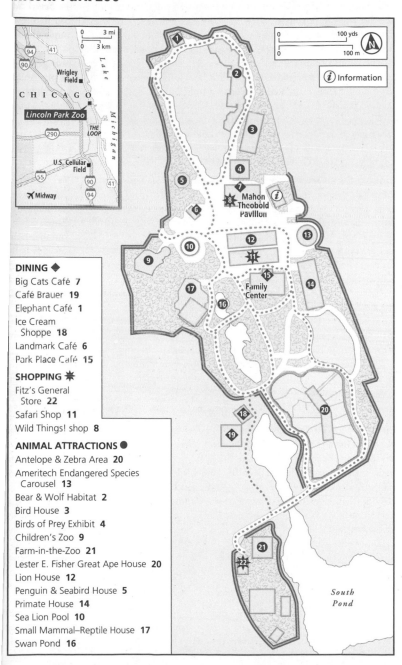

Mahon Theobold Pavilion

Family Center

South Pond

Information

DINING ◆

Big Cats Café **7**

Café Brauer **19**

Elephant Café **1**

Ice Cream Shoppe **18**

Landmark Café **6**

Park Place Café **15**

SHOPPING ✳

Fitz's General Store **22**

Safari Shop **11**

Wild Things! shop **8**

ANIMAL ATTRACTIONS ●

Antelope & Zebra Area **20**

Ameritech Endangered Species Carousel **13**

Bear & Wolf Habitat **2**

Bird House **3**

Birds of Prey Exhibit **4**

Children's Zoo **9**

Farm-in-the-Zoo **21**

Lester E. Fisher Great Ape House **20**

Lion House **12**

Penguin & Seabird House **5**

Primate House **14**

Sea Lion Pool **10**

Small Mammal–Reptile House **17**

Swan Pond **16**

Swamp re-creates the bioregions of a southern cypress swamp and an Illir
and discusses what people can do to protect wetlands. The dolphins at t
Panorama ★★ put on an amazing show that has been a Brookfield 2
years. If you go on a weekend, buy tickets to the dolphin show at least a c
before the one you plan to attend, because they tend to sell out quickly.

The **Hamill Family Play Zoo** is a wonderful stop for kids. They not
animals but also can build habitats, learn how to plant a garden, and eve
dress-up. The only catch: the separate admission fee ($3.50 adults, $2
Allow 3 hours.

First Ave. and 31st St., Brookfield. ℃ **708/485-0263.** www.brookfieldzoo.org. Admissic
seniors and children 3–11, free for children 2 and under. Free admission Tues and Thurs
rial Day to Labor Day daily 9:30am–6pm (Sun until 7:30pm); fall–spring daily 10am–5p
venson (I-55) and Eisenhower (I-290) expys 14 miles west of the Loop. Bus: 304 or 311.

Lincoln Park Pritzker Children's Zoo & Farm-in-the-Zoo ★ ⟨Val

After gazing upon the animals from afar in the rest of the Lincoln Park
come here for some hands-on experience. Unlike many other children's zoo
baby animals at the Pritzker Children's Zoo; instead, the outdoor habitats fi
of the North American woods, including wolves, beavers, and otters. The
tats are fun to explore, with interactive displays, but the highlight for mc
indoor Treetop Canopy Climbing Adventure, a 20-foot-high wood-ar
(encased in safety netting) that kids can scramble up and down (there are als
padded play areas for little ones). The best (meaning newest and cleanest)
the zoo are located in this building.

The Farm-in-the-Zoo is a working reproduction of a Midwestern farm, cc
a white-picket-fenced barnyard. You can see live demonstrations of butter c
weaving, and watch the cows being milked. Thanks to the chicken coops, an
with livestock, including cows, sheep, and pigs, even the aroma is authenti
Main Barn (filled with interactive exhibits), the main attraction is the huge
tractor that kids can climb up into and pretend to drive. Allow 1 hour.

2200 N. Cannon Dr. ℃ **312/742-2000.** www.lpzoo.com. Free admission. Daily 9am–5pm. Bi

Lincoln Park Zoo ★★★ ⟨Value⟩ **All ages.** One of Chicago's don't-mis

for kids, Lincoln Park Zoo occupies a scant 35 acres, and its landmark Georg
brick buildings and modern structures sit among gently rolling pathways, ve
and a kaleidoscopic profusion of flower gardens. It's so compact that a tour of
habitats takes all of 2 or 3 hours—a convenience factor even more enticing
consider that the nation's oldest zoo (it was founded in 1868) stays open 365
and is one of the last free zoos in the country. Lincoln Park Zoo has held a s
in the hearts of Chicagoans since the days of Bushman, the mighty lowland
captivated the world in the 1930s and 1940s and now suffers the ignominio
stuffed exhibit at the Field Museum of Natural History. The late Marlon Perki
ary host of the *Mutual of Omaha's Wild Kingdom* TV series, got his start here
director, and filmed a pioneering TV show called *Zoo Parade* (*Wild Kingdom*'
sor) in the basement of the old Reptile House.

The zoo has taken on an ambitious modernization, renovating and expandir
to reflect natural habitats. For years, the star attraction has been the lowland
the **Regenstein Center for African Apes** ★. The zoo has had remarkable
breeding both gorillas and chimpanzees, and watching these ape families is me:

Regenstein African Journey ★★, a series of linked indoor and outdoor habitats, is home to elephants, giraffes, rhinos, and other large mammals; large glass-enclosed tanks allow visitors to go face-to-face with swimming pygmy hippos and (not for the faint of heart) a rocky ledge filled with hissing cockroaches from Madagascar.

The **Small Mammal–Reptile House** is a state-of-the-art facility, housing 200 species and featuring a glass-enclosed walk-through ecosystem simulating river, savanna, and forest habitats. The popular **Sea Lion Pool,** home to harbor seals, gray seals, and California sea lions, features an underwater viewing area spanning 70 feet and an amphitheater.

The Park Place Café food court is in a historic building that originally housed Chicago's first aquarium. In fine weather, take your trays outside on the large patio area, and watch the nearby monkeys doing acrobatics. The Mahon Theobold Pavilion features a sprawling indoor gift shop and a unique rooftop eatery called Big Cats Café that opens at 8am (1 hr. before the exhibits do) and serves fresh-baked muffins and scones, focaccia sandwiches, salads, and flatbreads. *Tip:* For best animal viewing, go on a temperate weather day—in really hot weather, the animals tend to be lethargic (like human beings, I guess!). Allow 3 hours.

2200 N. Cannon Dr. (near Lake Shore Dr. at Fullerton Pkwy.). (ℂ **312/742-2000.** www.lpzoo.com. Free admission. Buildings daily 10am–5pm (until 6:30pm Sat–Sun Memorial Day to Labor Day); grounds 9am–6pm (until 7pm Memorial Day to Labor Day and until 5pm Nov 1–Mar 31). Parking $14 for up to 3 hr. in on-site lot. Bus: 151 or 156.

---

8 GARDENS & CONSERVATORIES

Garfield Park Conservatory ★   **All ages.** Designed by the great landscape architect Jens Jensen in 1907, Garfield Park Conservatory is one of the largest gardens under glass in the world at 2 acres in size. And it's open 365 days a year from 9am to 5pm, with free admission. Surprisingly, it took a blockbuster exhibit by glass artist Dave Chihuly a few years ago for many Chicagoans to "discover" the conservatory.

Chicago parents give the conservatory a thumbs-up for the special kids' area, which features a slide, climbing equipment, and a big pile of dirt (and digging tools), all within an environment that feels downright tropical. Educational displays such as plants, pods, and insects, and staff members who work with kids, ensure that some learning gets done along with digging. Unfortunately, the conservatory is surrounded by a rather blighted neighborhood with a high crime rate. I advise driving there and forgoing public transportation. Allow 1 hour.

300 N. Central Park Ave. (ℂ 312/746-5100. Free admission. Daily 9am–5pm. Free parking in an adjacent lot.

Lincoln Park Conservatory ★   **All ages.** Just beyond the zoo's northeast border is a lovely botanical garden housed in a soaring glass-domed structure. Inside are four great halls filled with thousands of plants that, unless you're an avid horticulturist, will take you perhaps a half-hour to explore. The Palm House features giant palms and rubber trees (including a 50-ft. fiddle leaf rubber tree dating from 1891), the Fernery nurtures plants that grow close to the forest floor, and the Tropical House is a shiny symphony of flowering trees, vines, and bamboo. The fourth environment is the Show House, where seasonal flower shows are held.

Even better than the plants inside, however, might be what lies outside the front doors. The expansive lawn with its French garden and lovely fountain on the conservatory's south side is one of the best places in town for an informal picnic (especially nice if you're visiting the zoo and want to avoid the congestion at its food concession venues). Allow a half-hour.

Fullerton Ave. (at Stockton Dr.). ⓒ **312/742-7736.** Free admission. Daily 9am–5pm. Bus: 73, 151, or 156.

9 NATURE CENTERS

Morton Arboretum   All ages. Should your visit to Chicago coincide with Arbor Day, here's the place to celebrate: More than 3,000 kinds of trees, shrubs, and vines grow on the 1,700-acre site in west suburban Lisle. The place has been spruced up lately (sorry for the pun), with improvements to many of the facilities' buildings. Special areas include the Illinois Tree Trails' woodlands, meadows, and marshes; an area with sugar maples (colorful in the fall); a crab apple orchard (splendid when the trees are in full bloom); and a prairie with tall grasses and flowers that blossom in summer and fall. The arboretum also features trees from other countries. Most of the 13 miles of trails are covered with wood chips, so they are not stroller-friendly. If your kids are young, it's best to see the landscape by car along 11 miles of one-way roads or take a bus tour. One-hour tram tours depart at noon and 1:15pm Wednesday, Saturday, and Sunday from May to October. Cost for the tram is $4 per seat, and $3 for children ages 3 to 12. Stop by the visitor center for additional information. Light meals are available in the Ginkgo Restaurant, sandwiches and soups are served in the coffee shop, and there's a picnic area near a small lake.

4100 Illinois Hwy. 53 (at I-88, the East-West Tollway), Lisle. ⓒ **630/719-2400.** www.mortonarb.org. Admission $9 adults, $8 seniors, $6 children 3–12, free for children 2 and under. Reduced admission fees Wed. Daily year-round, 7am–7pm or sunset, whichever is earlier. Visitor center daily Nov–Feb 8am–5pm, Mar–Oct 8am–6pm; Gingko Tree restaurant daily 11am–3pm; coffee shop daily 9am–5pm. Free parking. Subway/El: Metra train stops at Lisle, 1¹⁄₂ miles away; cabs available.

Peggy Notebaert Nature Museum ★★   All ages. Built on an ancient sand dune—once the shoreline of Lake Michigan—this museum bills itself as "an environmental museum for the 21st century." Most of the exhibits here are hands-on, and designed for kids.

Shaded by huge cottonwoods and maples, the sand-colored exterior with its horizontal lines composed of interlocking trapezoids itself resembles a sand dune. Rooftop-level walkways give strollers a view of birds and other urban wildlife below. Paths wind through gardens planted with native Midwestern wildflowers and grasses, and trace the shore of the North Pond. Inside, large windows throughout create a dialogue between the outdoor environment and the indoor exhibits designed to illuminate it. The 73,000-square-foot facility features plenty of exhibits on nature and the interaction between human activities and the environment.

Throughout, the focus is on interactivity, done with imagination and intelligence. Don't miss the **Butterfly Haven ★**, a greenhouse habitat where about 25 Midwestern species of butterflies and moths carry on their complex life cycles. Wander through as a riot of color flutters all around you. Another top exhibit is **Extreme Green House,** a full-size bungalow that's home to the offbeat Green Family. Join them on a tour of their house and learn how every nook and cranny is connected with nature. **Riverworks** is a water-play exhibit that gives children a chance to splash around while building dams and maneuvering boats along a miniriver. I'd also recommend the **Hands-On Habitat ★**,

designed for children 3 to 7; kids can climb a two-story treehouse, coast down a wiggly
"worm" slide, and peer through "bug" binoculars that re-create how insects see the world.

The sunny Butterfly Cafe offers fresh, healthful meals cafeteria-style. In summer get there early to enjoy coffee and a muffin—and the lovely surroundings—with joggers and other locals. Allow 1 hour.

Fullerton Ave. and Cannon Dr. ℂ **773/755-5100.** www.chias.org. Admission $7 adults, $5 seniors and students, $4 children ages 3–12, free for children 2 and under. Free admission Thurs. Mon–Fri 9am–4:30pm; Sat–Sun 10am–5pm. Closed Thanksgiving, Dec 25, and Jan 1. Bus: 151 or 156. Free trolley service from area CTA stations and parking garages Sat–Sun and holidays. Visit museum website for route information and schedule.

---

10 WATER PARKS

Coco Key Water Resort   Ages 2 to 12. The Chicago area's first major indoor water resort opened at the end of 2006 in northwest suburban Arlington Heights and offers the usual water park fare of four water slides, indoor adventure river for tubing, and plenty of opportunities to get sprayed and splashed. It's all done in a decor that replicates the tropical appeal of Key West. One unique feature: You can rent a private cabana for the day, a good option for chilling out and getting away from the noise and commotion, plus a television, a refrigerator, and a safe for your valuables. For the adults, the Wet Rooster Bar is a nice feature, as it sits slightly above the water activities, allowing you to relax with a tropical-themed drink while keeping an eye on your kids. (If you're hungry, the usual fast-food fare is available from A&W or Pizza Hut.) A zero-depth splash pool with burbling fountains and a wading pool with water basketball should keep the littlest ones happy. For the older kids, there are four body- and raft-water slides that seemingly start at the ceiling and wind their thrilling ways down.

It's for all ages, but during my visit, it seemed the youngest that could really take advantage of the activities would be about age 2; kids older than 12 might lose interest in this sort of thing! There's an extensive arcade adjacent to the water park. The resort itself is attached to the Sheraton Chicago Northwest, which underwent a major renovation while the water park was being built. The water park makes for a great getaway within an hour of the city, particularly nice on a wintry weekend. Allow a full day.

3400 W. Euclid Ave., Arlington Heights. ℂ **847/394-2000.** www.cocokeywaterresort.com. Admission (day pass) Mon–Thurs $25 adults and children; Fri–Sun and holidays $39; free for children 2 and under. Sun–Thurs 10am–9pm; Fri–Sat and holidays 10am–10pm. Take I-90, I-94, or I-290 north to Arlington Heights. Approx. driving time from Chicago Loop 45 min.

---

11 KID-FRIENDLY TOURS

If you're in town for a limited time, an organized tour may be the best way to get a quick overview of the city's highlights. Some tours—such as the boat cruises on Lake Michigan and the Chicago River—can give you a whole new perspective on the city's landscape. Because Chicago caters to sophisticated travelers from all over the world, many tours go beyond sightseeing to explore important historical and architectural landmarks in depth. These specialized tours can help you appreciate buildings or neighborhoods that you might otherwise have passed by without a second glance.

CARRIAGE RIDES

6

Noble Horse (✆ **312/266-7878**) maintains the largest fleet of antique horse carriages in Chicago, stationed around the old Water Tower Square at the northwest corner of Chicago and Michigan avenues. Each of the drivers, outfitted in a black tie and top hat, has his or her own variation on the basic Magnificent Mile itinerary (you can also do tours of the lakefront, river, Lincoln Park, and Buckingham Fountain). The charge is $35 for each half-hour for up to four people. The coaches run year-round, with convertible coaches in the warm months and enclosed carriages furnished with wool blankets on bone-chilling nights. There are several other carriage operators, all of whom pick up riders in the vicinity.

ORIENTATION TOURS

Chicago Trolley Company   All ages. Chicago Trolley Company offers guided tours on a fleet of rubber-wheeled "San Francisco–style" trolleys that stop at a number of popular spots around the city, including Navy Pier, the Grant Park museums, the Museum of Science and Industry, Lincoln Park Zoo, and the cluster of theme restaurants in River North. If you can bear the touristy-ness of it all, you'll find that the tours are fun and informative, especially if you get a good driver. You can stay on for the full $1^{1}/_{2}$-hour ride or get on and off at each stop. The trolleys operate year-round, but in the winter you won't need to bundle the kids in snowsuits: The vehicles are enclosed and heated in the chilliest months. The same company also operates the Chicago Double Decker Company, which has a fleet of London-style, red, two-story buses. The buses follow the same route as the trolleys; if you buy an all-day pass, you can hop from bus to trolley at any point. You can buy tickets online or at any of the stops.

✆ **773/648-5000.** www.chicagotrolley.com. All-day hop-on, hop-off pass $25 adults, $20 seniors, $10 children 3–11. Family package (2 adults, 2 children) $64. Daily 9am–5pm (until 6:30pm Apr–Oct).

Gray Line   Ages 8 & up. Part of a company that offers bus tours worldwide, Gray Line Chicago gives professional tours in well-appointed buses. Most tours run 3 to 4 hours, so this is recommended only for kids who will sit for that long. Tours include lunch and feature highlights of downtown or various neighborhoods; some tours also include a cruise on Lake Michigan or a visit to the Sears Tower Skydeck.

27 E. Monroe St., Ste. 515. ✆ **800/621-4153** or 312/251-3107. www.grayline.com. Tours $20–$50.

CHICAGO ARCHITECTURE FOUNDATION TOURS

Chicago Architecture Foundation ★★★   Chicago's architecture is world famous. Luckily, the Chicago Architecture Foundation offers first-rate guided tours to help visitors understand what makes this city's skyline so special. The foundation offers walking, bike, boat, and bus tours to more than 60 architectural sites and environments in and around Chicago, led by nearly 400 trained and enthusiastic docents (all volunteers). I highly recommend taking at least one CAF tour while you're in town—they help you look at (and appreciate) the city in a new way. Tours are available year-round but are scheduled less frequently in winter.

One of the CAF's most popular tours is the $1^{1}/_{2}$-hour **Architecture River Cruise,** which glides along both the north and the south branches of the Chicago River. Although you can see the same 50 or so buildings by foot, traveling by water lets you enjoy the buildings from a unique perspective. The excellent docents also provide interesting historical details, as well as some fun facts (David Letterman once called the busts of the nation's retailing legends that face the Merchandise Mart the "Pez Hall of Fame").

(Finds) The Wright Stuff in the Gold Coast

Architecture junkies also might want to inquire about house tours of the **Charnley-Persky House** (© **312/915-0105** or 312/573-1365), designed by Frank Lloyd Wright and Louis Sullivan in 1891. The house is located in the Gold Coast at 1365 N. Astor St. and would make a nice highlight to an informal walking tour of the area. One-hour tours are given on Wednesday at noon (free) and Saturday from April to November at 10am and 1pm ($5); reservations are not accepted.

The docents generally do a good job of making the cruise enjoyable for visitors with all levels of architectural knowledge. In addition to pointing out buildings—Marina City, the Civic Opera House, the Sears Tower—they approach the sites thematically, explaining, for example, how Chicagoans' use of and attitudes toward the river have changed over time.

Tours are $28 per person weekdays, $30 on weekends and holidays, and begin hourly every day June through October from 11am to 3pm (with more limited schedules in May and Nov). The trips are extremely popular, so purchase tickets in advance through **Ticketmaster** (© **312/902-1500;** www.ticketmaster.com), or avoid the service charge and buy tickets at one of the foundation's tour centers or from the boat launch on the southeast corner of Michigan Avenue and Wacker Drive.

If you want to squeeze a lot of sightseeing into a limited time, try **Highlights by Bus,** a 3¹/₂-hour overview tour that covers the Loop, Hyde Park—including a visit to the interior of Frank Lloyd Wright's Robie House—and the Gold Coast, plus several other historic districts. Tours start at 9:30am on Wednesday and Saturday from December to March, from April to November on Wednesday, Friday, Saturday, and Sunday. Tickets are $40 for adults and $35 for students and seniors.

A 4-hour **Frank Lloyd Wright by Bus** tour, which visits Frank Lloyd Wright sights in Oak Park ($52 adults; $48 seniors and students), is available on Tuesdays from May to October. Also available is the **Frank Lloyd Wright Neighborhoods by Bus** tour ($40 adults; $35 seniors and students), which goes through three neighborhoods and provides commentary on more than 25 houses—but does not take visitors inside Wright's home and studio. Some of the tours are pretty long and involved for younger kids (such as the 4-hr. bus tour of Frank Lloyd Wright sites in Oak Park), but check the website or call for the latest and greatest offerings. For example, a one-time summer tour called "A View from the Road" offered a tour of Chicago's roadside attractions. The tour included a lunch stop at the famed Superdawg drive-in with commentary by its owner and designer, and visits to the original Ray Kroc McDonald's in Des Plaines and the Leaning Tower YMCA in Niles (yes, it's a replica of the Leaning Tower of Pisa!). Other special theme bus tours have included Chicago movie palaces and historic churches. Like I said, you never know, so give them a call.

If you prefer exploring on your own, the CAF offers a variety of guided walking tours. For first-time visitors, I highly recommend two tours for an excellent introduction to the dramatic architecture of the Loop. **Historic Skyscrapers** (10am–3pm Wed–Tues) covers buildings built between 1880 and 1940, including the Rookery and the Chicago Board of Trade; **Modern Skyscrapers** (1pm daily; additional tour at 5:30pm on Fri) includes modern masterpieces by Mies van der Rohe and postmodern works by contemporary architects. The 2-hour tours cost $15 each for adults and $12 each for seniors and students.

The CAF also offers more than 50 **neighborhood tours,** visiting the Gold Coast, River North, Grant Park, Old Town, the Jackson Boulevard Historic District, and even Lincoln Park Zoo. Most cost $10 and last a couple of hours.

Departing from the Chicago ArchiCenter, 224 S. Michigan Ave.; a few tours leave from the John Hancock Center, 875 N. Michigan Ave. ℂ **312/922-3432,** or 312/922-TOUR (922-8687) for recorded information. www.architecture.org. Tickets for most walking tours $10–$15. Subway/El: Brown, Green, Purple, or Orange Line to Adams, or Red Line to Jackson.

LAKE & RIVER CRUISES

Getting out on the lake is a great way to take in Chicago's incredible skyline from a new vantage point. Don't forget that you're always going to be at the mercy of the weather if you book in advance: I've taken sightseeing cruises in the rain—luckily, most boats have plenty of covered areas for this reason. But when the weather cooperates, the sight of sunlight glinting off the city's skyscrapers never fails to thrill.

Chicago from the Lake　All ages. This company runs 90-minute architectural river cruises and lake and river historical cruises that explore the development of the city. Complimentary coffee, lemonade, cookies, and muffins are served. For tickets, call or stop by the company's ticket office, located on the lower level on the east end of River East Plaza. Reservations are recommended.

Departing from Ogden Slip adjacent to River East Plaza (formerly North Pier) at the end of E. Illinois St. ℂ **312/527-2002.** www.chicagoline.com. Tickets $32 adults, $30 seniors, $18 children 7–18, free for children 6 and under. Daily May–Oct.

Mystic Blue Cruises　All ages. A more casual alternative to fancy dinner cruises, this is promoted as a "fun" ship (that means DJs at night, although you'll also be treated to some live entertainment no matter when you sail). Daily lunch and dinner excursions are available, as well as midnight voyages on weekends.

Departing from Navy Pier. ℂ **877/299-7783.** www.mysticbluecruises.com. Lunch cruises $32–$37, dinner $60–$80, midday cruise $25, moonlight cruise $30. Cruises run year-round.

Shoreline Sightseeing　All ages. Shoreline schedules 30-minute lake cruises called Skyline Boat Tours, every half-hour, from its three dock locations: the Shedd Aquarium, Navy Pier, and Buckingham Fountain in Grant Park. It's a great way to get a quick primer about famous landmarks and a panoramic view of the city skyline in a short time. Shoreline has also gotten in on the popularity of architecture tours by offering its own version, narrated by an architectural guide (with higher prices than their regular tours). A **water taxi** also runs every half-hour from Navy Pier to both the Sears Tower and the Shedd Aquarium. One-way tickets for the water taxi cost $3 to $13, depending on how far you travel.

Departing from Navy Pier, Shedd Aquarium, and Buckingham Fountain in Grant Park. ℂ **312/222-9328.** www.shorelinesightseeing.com. Tickets weekdays $14 adults, $13 seniors, $6 children 11 and under ($1 more per ticket on weekends). May–Sept daily. Tours depart hourly 10am–5:00pm Memorial Day to Labor Day; every 30 min. 10am–4pm May and Sept.

The Spirit of Chicago　Ages 12 & up. This luxury yacht offers a variety of wining and dining harbor cruises, from a lunch buffet to the Moonlight Dance Party. Children are allowed, with some restrictions; otherwise, book a sitter and hit one of the cruises. This can be a fairly pricey night out if you go for the whole dinner package.

Departing from Navy Pier. ℭ **866/211-3804.** www.spiritcruises.com. Lunch cruises $40–$50, dinner (seated) $80–$110, sunset and midnight cruises $32. Ask about children's rates. Daily year-round.

Wendella Sightseeing Boats   All ages. Wendella is the granddaddy of all sightseeing operators in Chicago. Started in 1935, it's run by the original owner's son, Bob Borgstrom, whose own two sons serve as captains. You won't find a more authoritative source on the Chicago River than Borgstrom.

Wendella operates a 1-hour water tour along the Chicago River, and a 1¹/₂-hour tour along the river and out onto Lake Michigan (one of the highlights for kids is passing through the locks that separate the river from the lake). Boats run from late April to early October. The 2-hour sunset tour runs Memorial Day to Labor Day starting at 7:45pm. Scheduling for cruises depends on the season and the weather, but cruises usually leave every hour during the summer.

Departing from Michigan Ave. and Wacker Dr. (north side of the river, at the Wrigley Bldg.). ℭ **312/337-1446.** www.wendellaboats.com. Tickets $22 adults, $20 seniors, $11 children 3–11, free for children 2 and under. Daily late Apr–early Oct.

Windy   **Ages 8 & up.** One of the more breathtaking scenes on the lake is watching this tall ship approach the docks at Navy Pier. The 148-foot-long, four-masted schooner (and its new sister ship, the *Windy II*) sets sail for 90-minute cruises two to five times a day, both day and evening. Of course, the boats are at the whims of the wind, so every cruise charts a different course. Passengers are welcome to help raise and trim the sails and occasionally take turns at the ship's helm (with the captain standing close by). Ask about "Pirate" cruises for the kids. The boats are not accessible for people with disabilities.

Departing from Navy Pier. ℭ **312/595-5555.** Tickets $27 adults, $20 seniors and children 11 and under. Tickets go on sale 1 hr. before the 1st sail of the day at the boat's ticket office, on the dock at Navy Pier. Reservations (except for groups) are not accepted. Call for sailing times.

SPECIAL-INTEREST TOURS

NEIGHBORHOOD TOURS   It's a bit of a cliché to say that Chicago is a city of neighborhoods, but if you want to see what really makes Chicago special, that's where you have to go. And if you're a bit intimidated by public transportation and getting around a less tourist-friendly area of the city, an escorted tour is the perfect way to see places you'd otherwise miss. Sponsored by the Department of Cultural Affairs, **Chicago Neighborhood Tours** (ℭ 312/742-1190; www.chgocitytours.com) are 4- to 5-hour narrated bus excursions to about a dozen diverse communities throughout the city. Embarking from the Chicago Cultural Center, 77 E. Randolph St., every Saturday (not on major holidays and not during Jan, generally, so call first), the tours visit different neighborhoods, from Chinatown and historic Bronzeville on the South Side to the ethnic enclaves of Devon Avenue and Uptown on the North Side. Neighborhood representatives serve as guides and greeters along the way as tour participants visit area landmarks, murals, museums, and shopping districts. Tickets (including a light snack) are $25 for adults and $20 for seniors, students, and children 8 to 18. Several specialty tours have recently been added to the mix, including Literary Chicago; the Great Chicago Fire; Roots of Blues, Gospel & Jazz; Threads of Ireland; Jewish Legacy; and an Ethnic Cemetery tour. These tours, which generally run 4 to 6 hours and include lunch, are more expensive ($40).

The Chicago History Museum offers a handful of walking tours every summer of the **Gold Coast, Old Town,** and **Lincoln Park** neighborhoods. Led by museum docents, they average about four per month from June to August. Day and evening tours are available, and a few specialty walking tours usually are given as well. Tours are $10 per person, and registration is recommended but not required. Touts depart from the CHS museum at Clark Street and North Avenue, and light refreshments are served afterward. In the summer and fall, the museum also offers a few half-day and daylong bus tours called **"Exploring Chicago,"** which cover unique themes or aspects of the metropolitan area's history. Led by historians and scholars, they take place in the city and surrounding areas ($40). Tours depart from the Chicago History Museum at Clark Street and North Avenue. Call © **312/642-4600,** or visit the museum's website (www.chicagohistory.org) for schedules.

Groups can arrange tours of Chicago's **"Black Metropolis,"** the name given to a South Side area of Bronzeville, where African Americans created a flourishing business-and-artistic community after World War II. Contact **Tour Black Chicago** (© **773/684-9034;** www.tourblackchicago.com) for more information.

GANGSTER TOURS   **Untouchable Tours,** or so-called "gangster tours" (© **773/881-1195;** www.gangstertour.com), is the only bus tour that takes you to all of the city's old hoodlum hangouts from the Prohibition era. The focus is definitely more on entertainment (guides with names like "Al Dente" and "Ice Pick" appear in costume and role-play their way through the tour) than a seriously historical take on the era. But the bus trip gives you a pretty thorough overview of the city, in addition to the gangster hot spots. You'll see the site of O'Bannion's flower shop, the site of the St. Valentine's Day massacre, and much more. The tour is pretty tame, but if you have impressionable young ones, use your discretion; kids over age 8 should be fine. The cost is $25 for adults, $19 for children. Tours, which depart from the southeast corner of Clark and Ohio streets, run Monday to Wednesday at 10am; Thursday at 10am and 1pm; Friday at 10am, 1, and 7:30pm; Saturday at 10am, 1, and 5pm; and Sunday at 10am and 1pm.

GHOST TOURS   Another offbeat way to experience the real "spirit" of Chicago is to take a narrated **supernatural bus tour** of cemeteries, murder sites, Indian burial grounds, haunted pubs, and other spooky places. Richard Crowe, who bills himself as a "professional ghost hunter," spins out ghost stories, legends, and lore on the 4-hour trip, held both day and night (afraid of the dark?). I'd take only teens on these tours due to touchy subject matter and the rather expensive price; use your discretion. Tickets are $39 per person and tours depart from the Clybourn Place shopping mall, 1800 N. Clybourn. Two-hour **supernatural boat excursions** are available for $25 per person in July and August through Labor Day weekend, and board at 9:30pm from the Mercury boat dock, at Michigan Avenue and Wacker Drive. Reservations are required for each tour; call © **708/499-0300** or visit www.ghosttours.com. Tours are offered once or twice a month Friday and Saturday nights; call for exact schedule. As you might imagine, Crowe's tours get especially popular around Halloween, so you'll definitely want to reserve well ahead of time if that's when you want to go.

CEMETERY TOURS   Don't be scared away by the creepy connotations. Some of Chicago's cemeteries are as pretty as parks, and they offer a variety of intriguing monuments that offer insight into the city's history.

One of the best area cemeteries is **Graceland,** which stretches along Clark Street in the Swedish neighborhood of Andersonville. The land between Irving Park Road and Montrose Avenue, running for about a mile along Clark Street, is occupied exclusively by cemeteries—primarily Graceland. Here you can view the tombs and monuments of many Chicago notables. When Graceland was laid out in 1860, public parks as such did not exist. The elaborate burial grounds that were constructed in many large American cities around this same time had the dual purpose of relieving the congestion of the municipal cemeteries closer to town and providing pastoral recreational settings for the Sunday outings of the living. Indeed, cemeteries like Graceland were the precursors of such great municipal green spaces as Lincoln Park. Much of Lincoln Park, in fact, had been a public cemetery since Chicago's earliest times. Many who once rested there were reinterred in Graceland when the plans for building Lincoln Park went forward.

The Chicago Architecture Foundation (✆ 312/922-3432; www.architecture.org) offers walking tours of Graceland on selected Sundays during August, September, and October. The tour costs $10 per person and lasts about 2 hours. Among the points of interest you will discover as you meander the paths of these 121 beautifully landscaped acres are the Ryerson and Getty tombs, famous architectural monuments designed by Louis Sullivan. Sullivan himself rests here in the company of several of his most distinguished colleagues: Daniel Burnham, Ludwig Mies van der Rohe, and Howard Van Doren Shaw, an establishment architect whose summer home in Lake Forest, called Ragdale, now operates as a writers' and artists' colony. Some of Chicago's giants of industry and commerce are also buried at Graceland, including Potter Palmer, Marshall Field, and George Pullman. The Chicago Architecture Foundation offers tours of some other cemeteries, as well, including the Oak Woods Cemetery, Rosehill Cemetery, and the suburban Lake Forest Cemetery. Call for details. **Oak Woods,** located just south of Hyde Park on the city's south side, is the final resting place for many of Chicago's most famous African-American figures, including Jesse Owens, Ida B. Wells, and Mayor Harold Washington.

7

Neighborhood Strolls

The best way to get a feel for Chicago is to stroll its streets. Every block brings interesting window-shopping, people-watching, or snippets of conversation that are sure to keep you and the wee ones entertained. The orderly configuration of Chicago's streets and the excellent public transportation system make walking a breeze—when you get tired, you can hop on a bus or the El without having to veer too far off your course.

This chapter provides brief walks that will give you a snapshot of the city's most frequented neighborhoods.

1 NEAR NORTH/MAGNIFICENT MILE

North Michigan Avenue is known as the Magnificent Mile, from the bridge spanning the Chicago River on the south end to Oak Street on the northern tip. Many of the city's best hotels, shops, and restaurants are to be found on and around elegant Michigan Avenue. But never fear: Michigan Avenue offers excellent family shopping, too. Scattered among the shops owned by Gucci, Salvatore Ferragamo, and Cartier are more kid-friendly stops such as American Girl Place and Niketown. You and your kids will feel right at home making your way up this storied avenue. Strolling the entire mile will take you half a day, since you'll want to stop frequently. Of course, if you're determined to avoid the shops, you can do it in less than an hour—but who'd want to?

Start at the **Riverwalk** that goes along the north side of the Chicago River. Walk down the steps on the east side of Michigan Avenue that lead off the Michigan Avenue Bridge. You can walk east for a short distance and see the plaza of the NBC Tower, as well as some of the newest condominium and town house developments along the river. Backtrack and continue north on Michigan Avenue. You'll run right into the **Chicago Tribune Tower.** The tower is notable for its signature array of stones jutting out from the exterior. The collection was started shortly after the building's completion in 1925 by the newspaper's notoriously despotic publisher, Robert R. McCormick, who gathered them during his world travels. *Tribune* correspondents then began supplying stone souvenirs encountered on assignment. Each one now bears the name of the structure and country whence it came. There are 138 stones in all, including chunks and shards from the Great Wall of China, the Taj Mahal, the White House, the Arc de Triomphe, the Berlin Wall, the Roman Colosseum, London's Houses of Parliament, the Great Pyramid of Cheops in Giza, Egypt, and the original tomb of Abraham Lincoln in Springfield. Send your kids on a scavenger hunt to see how many they can find. **Hint:** Inside the *Tribune*'s lobby, there's a brochure telling you where they are.

Chicago Neighborhoods

Turn to chapter 2 for more descriptions of Chicago neighborhoods. Also see p. 53 for a map of the neighborhoods.

Walk This Way: Chicago's Underground Pedway

Rainy day? Snowy? So windy you're afraid your kids will blow away? Take a break and cruise around Chicago's Loop through the not-so-secret underground **Pedway.** The city started building tunnels to connect subway stations in the early 1950s, and today the underground system of tunnels covers 23 blocks that are fun for kids to explore. You'll find stores, restaurants, and other businesses. Don't worry—if you ever get lost, just look for an exit and go up to street level to get your bearings (and you can pick up a map at the Chicago Cultural Center).

A good spot to enter the Pedway is the State Street subway station, between Randolph and Washington streets. On the stretch west of State Street, you'll find a newsstand selling snacks and fresh fruits, a barbershop, a Starbucks, a big gift store, and a food court. Beneath the Chicago Cultural Center, your children can look through the window at a radio station that broadcasts books for the blind. Farther along, at the Athletic Club, kids can see a seven-story climbing wall and watch office workers working out at lunchtime. The eastern section is the most elegant—it travels under several hotels and has a shopping concourse.

Continue north along Michigan Avenue. When you reach Chicago Avenue, just ahead of you is the **Chicago Water Tower** (not to be confused with a mall of the same name, located cater-cornered from the real tower). Michigan Avenue's best-known landmark is dwarfed by high-rises today but still gleams like a fairy tale castle. Surrounded by lawns and park benches, the tower is illuminated at night, and street musicians often play here. Chicagoans are proud of their talisman, one of the few buildings to survive the Great Fire of 1871. (And it serves a real purpose by covering an ugly, 138-ft.-high standpipe used in connection with pumping water from Lake Michigan.) The Gothic-style limestone building now houses an art gallery and is a refreshing cultural pit stop. Across the street the pumping station has been transformed into a tourist information center.

To conclude your walk up Michigan Avenue, step across the street to **Ghirardelli's** (located on DeWitt, half a block west of Michigan Ave.) and grab an ice-cream cone, or, in chilly weather, a foamy mug of hot chocolate. If you walk 1 block north, you can enjoy your ice cream in the shaded, ivy-covered courtyard of **Fourth Presbyterian Church,** at Chestnut Street and Michigan Avenue—a tranquil spot just steps from the bustle of Michigan Avenue.

2 THE LOOP

South Michigan Avenue is less congested than its northerly branch, the Magnificent Mile. Down here you can amble along and take in a couple of Chicago's famous museums and two parks, including Millennium Park, which was completed in 2004, and has become Chicago's second-largest tourist draw after Navy Pier. South Michigan Avenue can be strolled in an hour or two, but if you stop to check out building lobbies and have

Tips **Sorting Out the Post Office**

While you're near the Loop, treat your kids to a look at the inner workings of the **Chicago Main Post Office,** 433 W. Harrison (© **312/983-7550**), and see for yourselves what happens to the letters you send. The 90-minute tour includes the sorting process, a look at the latest automated equipment, and an enormous stamp collection. The tour is suggested for ages 10 and older and reservations are required; call the number above to arrange a time. Admission is free.

lunch, it can be a half-day event. Because this walk focuses on architecture, it's best for older children and teens.

Cross the Chicago River on the Michigan Avenue Bridge and walk south, into the Loop business district. On this easterly fringe of the Loop lie some of Chicago's top cultural institutions and parks. Continue south, past Lake and Randolph streets. On your left, you will see a clearing: This is **Millennium Park,** on the north end of Grant Park along Michigan Avenue. Admire the dramatic music pavilion designed by Frank Gehry, and check out the large public art displays. At the corner of Michigan and Randolph is a huge Beaux Arts–style building, called the **Chicago Cultural Center.** Built in 1897 as the city's public library, the Cultural Center is now your home base for tourist information. Go in, pick up all the information you need, and, while you're at it, check out the building's stunning interior. Free tours guide visitors up a sweeping staircase of white Italian marble to admire what is, for my money, the most stunning interior in Chicago. At the top of the staircase is a majestic Tiffany dome, believed to be the world's largest. You'll also discover mosaics of Favrile glass, colored stone, and mother-of-pearl inlaid in white marble.

As you stroll south from the Cultural Center, you're seeing "Michigan Avenue Cliff," a particularly impressive great wall of buildings that stretches south to Congress Parkway (location of the Auditorium Bldg.). It's a visual treat for architecture lovers and novices alike.

Abutting the park on the south, facing Adams Avenue, is the **Art Institute.** Save the tour for another time—for now, climb the steps and visit the stone lions. Watch the other people who are sitting on the steps people-watching. If you need a break, stop in the outdoor cafe. Parents can get a glass of wine while the kids can enjoy a lemonade.

Farther south on the avenue is the **Fine Arts Building,** constructed in 1885 as a showroom for Studebaker carriages, and converted into an arts center in 1917. The building houses two theaters, offices, shops, and studios for musicians, artists, and writers. Frank Lloyd Wright, sculptor Lorado Taft, and L. Frank Baum, author of *The Wonderful Wizard of Oz,* had offices here. Located throughout the building are a number of interesting studios and musical instrument shops. Take a quick walk through the marble-and-wood lobby, which suggests something monastic and cloister-like, or visit the top floor to see the spectacular murals (and to get there, you'll be fortunate to ride in an old-fashioned elevator manned by a real, live operator!).

Last stop on our south Michigan Avenue tour is the **Auditorium Building.** This wonder of architecture was designed and built in 1889 by Louis Sullivan and Dankmar Adler. At the time, it was the heaviest (110,000 tons) and most massive modern building on earth, the most fireproof building ever constructed, and the tallest building in Chicago. It was also the first large-scale building to be electrically lighted, and its theater was the first in the country to install air-conditioning. The lobby fronting Michigan Avenue has faux ornamental marble columns, molded ceilings, mosaic floors, and Mexican onyx walls. If this inspires you and your kids, take the elevator to the 10th-floor library reading room and have a look at what was once the city's first top-floor dining room. Soak in the decorative details and show your kids that they just don't make them like this anymore—the barrel-vaulted, muraled ceiling, and marvelous views of Grand Park and the lake will make architecture fans out of novices.

3 THE GOLD COAST

Walking north on **Lake Shore Drive** from North Michigan Avenue, you will enter a neighborhood known as the Gold Coast. The neighborhood runs from about Oak Street on the south to North Avenue on the north and includes some of Chicago's most desirable real estate and historic architecture. This is the classic "old money" neighborhood of Chicago, where many of the city's wealthiest citizens built homes after the 1871 fire. Sadly, starting in the late 1950s, most of the mansions that once lined Lake Shore Drive were slowly torn down and high-rises built in their stead, but you can see the remnants of Chicago's storied past in the three mansions still standing near Lake Shore Drive's intersection with Goethe Street. This hour-long stroll is suitable for the whole family and can be combined with a foray into Lincoln Park to make a day's worth of activities.

To get a feel for the neighborhood, walk up Lake Shore Drive to **Schiller Street.** Turn left and walk 1 block to **Astor Place.** Turn right onto Astor and enjoy the amble past stately mansions and beautiful brownstones. (Just a block or two farther west, State and Dearborn sts. also feature homes fit for magazine covers.) Once you reach **North Avenue,** you'll see a red-brick mansion on your left. This is the home of Cardinal Francis George, Catholic archbishop of Chicago, and is owned by the Catholic archdiocese of Chicago. Ask your kids to count the chimneys—I bet they'll lose track once they pass 10! (There are a total of 17.)

You can continue on into **Lincoln Park,** or turn back south. If you go south, walk 1 block west to State Street and follow that to Division Street. From there going south, you will find a thriving zone of restaurants, bars, and nightclubs, many featuring sidewalk seating—all the better to view the beautiful people who frequent the area.

4 OLD TOWN

This residential neighborhood is best known as the home of the Second City comedy troupe for the past 30-plus years. A hippie haven of the 1960s and 1970s, Old Town now includes a newly gentrified Cabrini Green (located on the far southern border of Old Town), America's most notorious housing project, which began falling to the wrecking ball in the late 1990s. The northern part of Old Town, particularly the area north of North Avenue and west of Wells Street, has a lovely residential neighborhood, and on any given day, you will see plenty of strollers and parents with kids in tow. I'd allow a couple of hours to stroll through the neighborhood, including time to linger in the shops.

To get the flavor of Old Town, start at the intersection of Wells Street and North Avenue. On the northwest corner is **Pipers Alley,** a shopping complex containing a large

Chicago & the Great Black Migration

From 1915 to 1960, hundreds of thousands of black Southerners poured into Chicago, trying to escape segregation and seeking economic freedom and opportunity. The so-called "Great Black Migration" radically transformed Chicago, both politically and culturally, from an Irish-run city of recent European immigrants into one in which no group had a majority and in which no politician—white or black—could ever take the black vote for granted. Unfortunately, the sudden change gave rise to many of the social and economic disparities that still plague the city, but it also promoted an environment in which many black men and women could rise from poverty to prominence.

Between 1910 and 1920, Chicago's black population almost tripled, going from 44,000 to 109,000; between 1920 and 1930, it more than doubled, to 234,000. The Great Depression slowed the migration to a crawl, with 278,000 blacks residing here in 1940. But the boom resumed when World War II revived the economy, causing the black population to skyrocket to 492,000 between 1940 and 1950. The postwar expansion and the decline of Southern sharecropping caused the black population to nearly double again, to 813,000, by 1960.

Although jobs in the factories, steel mills, and stockyards paid much better than those in the cotton fields, Chicago was not the paradise that many blacks envisioned. Segregation was almost as bad here as it was down South, and most blacks were confined to a narrow "Black Belt" of overcrowded apartment buildings on the South Side. But the new migrants made the best of their situation, and for a time in the 1930s and 1940s, the Black Belt—dubbed "Bronzeville" or the "Black Metropolis" by the community's boosters—thrived as a cultural, musical, religious, and educational mecca, much as New York's Harlem did in the 1920s. As journalist and Great Migration historian Nicholas Lemann writes in The Promised Land: The Great Black Migration and How It Changed America, "Chicago was a city where a black person could be somebody."

Some of the Southern migrants who made names for themselves in Chicago included black separatist and Nation of Islam founder Elijah Muhammed; Robert S. Abbott, publisher of the powerful Chicago Defender newspaper, who launched a "Great Northern Drive" to bring blacks to the city in 1917; Ida B. Wells, the crusading journalist who headed an antilynching campaign; William Dawson, for many years the only black congressman; New Orleans–born jazz pioneers Jelly Roll Morton, King Oliver, and Louis Armstrong; Native Son author Richard Wright; John H. Johnson, publisher of Ebony and Jet magazines and

cinema, Starbucks, restaurants, and shops. Directly to the north is **Second City.** Walk north up Wells Street. Small retail shops, florists, cafes, bread stores, and more line the street. When you reach the intersection with Lincoln Avenue, turn back and head south down the opposite side of the street. Cross North Avenue going south. Kids will be magnetically attracted to the colorful fish swimming around the front windows of **Old**

one of Chicago's wealthiest residents; blues musicians Willie Dixon, Muddy Waters, and Howlin' Wolf; Thomas A. Dorsey, the "father" of gospel music, and his greatest disciple, singer Mahalia Jackson; Robert Taylor, head of the Chicago Housing Authority, after whom the CHA's most notorious buildings are named; and Ralph Metcalfe, the Olympic-gold-medalist sprinter who turned to politics once he got to Chicago, eventually succeeding Dawson in Congress.

When open housing legislation enabled blacks to live in any neighborhood, the flight of many Bronzeville residents to less crowded areas took its toll on the remaining community. Through the 1950s almost a third of the housing became vacant, and by the 1960s the great social experiment of urban renewal through wholesale land clearance and the creation of large tracts of public housing gutted this once-thriving neighborhood.

In recent years, however, community and civic leaders appear committed to restoring the neighborhood to a semblance of its former glory. Landmark status has been secured for several historic buildings in Bronzeville, including the **Liberty Life/Supreme Insurance Company,** 3501 S. King Dr., the first African-American–owned insurance company in the northern United States, and the **Eighth Regiment Armory,** which, when completed in 1915, was the only armory in the United States controlled by an African-American regiment. The former home of the legendary **Chess Records** at 2120 S. Michigan Ave.—where Howlin' Wolf, Chuck Berry, and Bo Diddley gave birth to the blues and helped define rock 'n' roll—now houses a museum and music education center, **Blues Heaven Foundation** (✆ 312/808-1286), set up by Willie Dixon's widow, Marie Dixon, with financial assistance from rock musician John Mellencamp. Entertainer Lou Rawls, who grew up at 45th Street and King Drive (formerly South Pkwy.), is building the Lou Rawls Theater and Cultural Center at the famous crossroads of 47th Street and King Drive, where Chicago's fabled Regal Theater once stood and hosted performances by such legends as Count Basie, Duke Ellington, and Ella Fitzgerald. Along Dr. Martin Luther King, Jr., Drive, between 24th and 35th streets, several **public art installations** now celebrate Bronzeville's heritage as well. The most poignant of them is sculptor Alison Saar's *Great Northern Migration* **bronze monument,** at King and 26th, depicting a suitcase-toting African-American traveler standing atop a mound of worn shoe soles.

For tours of Bronzeville, contact the Chicago Office of Tourism's **Chicago Neighborhood Tours** (✆ 312/742-1190).

Town Aquarium, a shop located on the west side of the street at 1538 N. Wells St. Don't miss stopping at **Twisted Sister Bakery,** 1543 N. Wells St., where you'll find a homey atmosphere to sit and rest your weary feet, plus surprisingly sophisticated takes on the usual cakes, cookies, eclairs, and cupcakes.

5 LINCOLN PARK

Chicago's most popular residential neighborhood is fashionable Lincoln Park. Stretching from North Avenue to Diversey Parkway, it's bordered on the east by the huge park of the same name, which is home to two major museums and one of the nation's oldest zoos (established in 1868). You'll find it easy to spend a whole day and evening in Lincoln Park and the surrounding neighborhood. Thanks to the museums, zoo, and beach, plus shopping and restaurants in the surrounding neighborhood, there's something for all ages.

To explore the park, start at the **Chicago History Museum,** at Clark Street and North Avenue. You can pick up a walking path behind the building and pass through a pedestrian tunnel that takes you underneath a busy street and into the heart of the park. You'll have company on the wide gravel path—joggers, bikers, and dog walkers make good use of this route. Veer right coming out of the tunnel and walk past the baseball fields to the pedestrian bridge. If you cross the bridge going over Lake Shore Drive, you'll wind up on **North Avenue Beach,** Chicago's busiest beach. In the summer this is beach-volleyball central. Take your shoes off, dig your toes in the sand, and check out Lake Michigan's water temperature. (***Warning:*** It will be cold, even in Aug!) Your kids might want to explore the beach house, designed like a real boat, and you can pick up some ice cream and cool drinks inside.

Now that you've seen the park, it's time to check out the neighborhood of the same name. The trapezoid formed by **Clark Street, Armitage Avenue, Halsted Street,** and **Diversey Parkway** contains many of Chicago's most happening bars, restaurants, retail stores, music clubs, and off-Loop theaters. One manageable area to explore on foot is the Armitage Avenue area, which starts at the intersection of Halsted Street and Armitage Avenue. Strolling west on Armitage Avenue, you'll find a string of charming boutiques, featuring shoes and clothing for kids and adults, outdoor outfitters, home decor, and more. Should you choose to go north on Halsted from Armitage Avenue, you'll find more shops, including GapKids and other chain stores. Going south from Halsted on Armitage, you will find restaurants and the nationally acclaimed theater, **Steppenwolf Theatre Company.**

6 ANDERSONVILLE

This formerly Scandinavian neighborhood stretches several blocks along North Clark Street immediately north of Foster Avenue. Today, a burgeoning community of gays and lesbians makes Andersonville their home, and immigrant groups have moved in. You might want to have lunch at **Ann Sather** at 5207 N. Clark St. (p. 149) and walk the meal off by strolling up and down Clark Street for an hour or two.

Clark Street going north from Foster is a very walkable small stretch that includes the **Swedish-American Museum Center** (p. 190), a Scandinavian deli, a Swedish bakery, and two good Swedish restaurants. Since the wave of Scandinavian immigrants ended over 100 years ago, new immigrants have moved in. You'll find excellent Middle Eastern restaurants, including a northern branch of **Reza's** (p. 134), and delis with barrels of olives, figs, and other Middle Eastern delicacies. Make sure to stop at **Women & Children First** (p. 242), a wonderful bookstore for kids (and women). Stop for a bite at stroller-friendly **Kopi—A Traveler's Café,** where you can get a mean mango smoothie, or at Ann Sather, where you can get gooey fresh-baked cinnamon rolls (plus free advice for moms from the very motherly owner).

7 BUCKTOWN/WICKER PARK

Home to the third-largest concentration of artists in the country, this neighborhood is rapidly gentrifying. Over the past century the area has hosted waves of German, Polish, and, most recently, Spanish-speaking immigrants (not to mention writer Nelson Algren). Heading north on Damen Avenue, you'll pass hot new restaurants, stores featuring the latest in alternative culture, and loft-dwelling yuppies surfing the gentrification wave that's washing over this still-somewhat-gritty neighborhood.

The go-go gentrification of the Bucktown/Wicker Park area has been followed by not only a rash of restaurants and bars, but also retailers with an artsy bent reflecting the neighborhood's bohemian spirit. Mixed in with old neighborhood businesses, such as discount furniture stores and religious-icon purveyors, is a proliferation of antiques-furniture shops, too-cool-for-school clothing boutiques, and eclectic galleries and gift emporiums. Teenagers will love this walk—in 2001 the neighborhood was the location for MTV's *The Real World: Chicago,* so if your kids have watched the show, either originally or in its plentiful reruns, they might recognize many of the area's restaurants and bars.

To get a feel for the neighborhood's artsy vibe, stroll up and down Damen Avenue, starting from the intersection with North Avenue. Head north for the best concentration of restaurants and shops. One notable kids' store along your path is the children's clothing store **The Red Balloon Company,** 2060 N. Damen (p. 248). When you're ready for a break, stop at **Silver Cloud Bar & Grill,** 1700 N. Damen, for grilled cheese and tomato soup (p. 153), or pop across the street to **Northside Café,** 1635 N. Damen, for a burger or a beverage on the huge outdoor patio (p. 153).

8

For the Active Family

With its wide blue lake and emerald string of parks, Chicago is one big playground for kids. The city's ample green space means it's easy to get out and be active. Whether your kids like water-based sports or activities on solid ground, you'll probably be able to find it here.

A handy resource for those interested in the sporting life is *Windy City Sports* (© 312/421-1551; www.windycitysports. com), a free monthly publication that you'll find at many retail shops, grocery stores, and bars and cafes.

1 ENJOYING CHICAGO'S BEACHES

Public beaches line Lake Michigan all the way up north into the suburbs and Wisconsin, and southeast through Indiana and into Michigan. The most well known is **Oak Street Beach ★**; its location at the northern tip of the Magnificent Mile creates some interesting sights as sun worshipers sporting swimsuits and carting coolers make their way down Michigan Avenue. The most popular is **North Avenue Beach,** about 6 blocks farther north, which has developed into a volleyball hot spot. With its landmark steamship-shaped beach house and Venice Beach–style gym, this is where the Lincoln Park singles come to play, check each other out, and fly by on bikes and in-line skates. Even though families might be outnumbered by singles, the atmosphere is open and easy, and you won't feel out of place in the least. The beach has a **Bike & Roll** shop (© 312/729-1000) for renting bicycles (May 1–Sept 31), a chess pavilion, and **Castaways Bar & Grill** (© 773/281-1200; www.stefanirestaurants.com), which is open seasonally for sandwiches. It's also the place to be during the annual Air and Water Show, which takes place along the waterfront in August.

For more seclusion, try **Ohio Street Beach,** an intimate sliver of sand in tiny Olive Park, just north of Navy Pier, which, incredibly enough, remains largely ignored despite its central location. If you have a car, head up to **Montrose Beach,** a beautiful unsung treasure about midway between North Avenue Beach and Hollywood-Ardmore Beach (with plenty of free parking). Long popular with the city's Hispanic community, it has an expanse of beach mostly uninterrupted by piers or jetties, and a huge adjacent park with soccer fields and one big hill great for kite flying. Anglers can visit a small bait shop before heading for a nearby long pier designated for fishing, and teens can find a pickup game of volleyball here during the warmer months. **Hollywood-Ardmore Beach** (officially Kathy Osterman Beach), at the northern end of Lake Shore Drive, is a lovely crescent that's less congested and has steadily become more popular with gays who've moved up the lakefront from the Belmont Rocks, a longtime hangout.

If you've brought the family pooch along, you might want to take him for a dip at the **doggie beach** south of Addison Street, at about Hawthorne and Lake Shore Drive—although this minute spot aggravates some dog owners because it's situated in a harbor where the water is somewhat fouled by gas and oil from nearby boats. *Tip:* Try the south

(Also consider that, in off season, all beaches are fair game for dogs.)

Beaches officially open with a full retinue of lifeguards on duty beginning about June 20, but swimmers can wade into the chilly water from Memorial Day to Labor Day. Only the bravest souls venture into the water before July, when the temperature creeps up enough to make swimming an attractive proposition. Please take note that not the entire lakefront is beach, and don't do anything stupid such as diving off the rocks. Be extremely careful with your kids. The lake has drop-offs at points along the shore, and kids can easily and quickly get into deeper water. Lake Michigan can develop large waves, too, so exercise the same caution you would at the ocean.

Oak Street, North Avenue, Loyola, Osterman, Montrose, South Shore, and Rainbow beaches are wheelchair- and stroller-friendly—they offer specially designed mats that create a path over the sand to the water. For questions about the 29 miles of beaches and parks along Lake Michigan, call the park district's lakefront region office at © **312/742-5239.**

2 GREEN CHICAGO: CITY PARKS

Thanks to architect Daniel Burnham and his coterie of visionary civic planners—who drafted the revolutionary 1909 Plan of Chicago in the aftermath of the Great Chicago Fire of 1871—the city's wide-open lakefront park system is unrivaled by most major metropolises. Downtown Chicago has two extensive downtown parks: Grant Park on the southern end of Michigan Avenue, and Lincoln Park, starting at North Avenue.

GRANT PARK ★★★

Modeled after the gardens at Versailles, Grant Park is Chicago's front yard, composed of giant lawns segmented by *allées* of trees, plantings, and paths, and pieced together by major roadways and a network of railroad tracks. Covering the greens is a variety of public recreational and cultural facilities (although these are few in number and nicely spread out, a legacy of mail-order magnate Aaron Montgomery Ward's *fin de siècle* campaign to limit municipal buildings in the park). Incredibly, the entire expanse was created from sandbars, landfill, and Chicago Fire debris; the original shoreline extended all the way to Michigan Avenue. Grant Park is the major venue for festivals in the city, but although it's beautiful, it has fewer attractions for families than Lincoln Park (see review below).

The immense **Buckingham Fountain,** accessible along Congress Parkway, is the baroque centerpiece of the park, composed of pink Georgia marble and patterned after—but twice the size of—the Latona Fountain at Versailles, with adjoining esplanades beautified by rose gardens in season. Throughout the late spring and summer, the fountain spurts columns of water up to 165 feet in the air, illuminated after dark by a whirl

---

(Fun Facts) **Did You Know?**

Buckingham Fountain's jets and electric light displays are actually controlled by a computer 700 miles away in Atlanta.

of colored lights, and building toward a grand finale before it shuts down for the night at 11pm. You'll find concession areas and restrooms here, as well.

Favorite annual events are the free outdoor blues festival (in June) and the jazz festival (Labor Day). **Taste of Chicago** (✆ 312/744-3315), purportedly the largest food festival in the world (the city estimates its annual attendance at over 3.5 million), takes place every summer for 10 days around the July 4th holiday. Local restaurants serve up more ribs, pizza, hot dogs, and beer than you'd ever want to see, let alone eat. (See chapter 2 for a comprehensive listing of summer events in Grant Park.)

Scattered about the park are a number of sculptures and monuments, including a heroic sculpture of two Native Americans on horseback titled *The Spearman and the Bowman* (at Congress Pkwy. and Michigan Ave.), which has become the park's trademark since it was installed in 1928, as well as likenesses of Copernicus, Columbus, and Lincoln *(The Seated Lincoln),* the latter by the great American sculptor Augustus Saint-Gaudens, located on Congress Parkway between Michigan Avenue and Columbus Drive. On the western edge of the park, at Adams Street, is the **Art Institute** (p. 178), and at the southern tip of the Museum Campus are **The Field Museum of Natural History** (p. 162), the **Adler Planetarium** (p. 157), and the **John G. Shedd Aquarium** (p. 165). At the north end of the park, adjacent to the nascent Millennium Park, is Daley Bicentennial Park, featuring an outdoor sports plaza with a dozen lighted tennis courts, a rink for ice-skating in the winter and 'blading or roller-skating in the summer, and a field house.

331 E. Randolph St. ✆ **312/742-7648.** Subway/El: Brown Line to the Loop. Bus: 3, 4, 6, 60, 146, or 151.

LAKE SHORE PARK

Located just behind the Museum of Contemporary Art, this park has a view of the lake, and packs some good facilities into a small space. (If you enjoy a meal in the dining room at American Girl Place on the second floor of the adjacent Water Tower Place mall, you might have the pleasure of overlooking this lovely park.) You'll find baseball diamonds, a fitness center, a gym for basketball, an outdoor running track, and tennis courts. Again, although it's tiny, this green space is a big find for families staying in the heart of the city.

808 N. Lake Shore Dr. (at Chicago Ave., 3 blocks east of Michigan Ave.). ✆ **312/742-PLAY** (742-7529). Bus: 151.

LINCOLN PARK ★★★

Straight and narrow Lincoln Park begins at North Avenue and follows the shoreline of Lake Michigan northward 6 miles to Ardmore Avenue (not far from the East Asian enclave radiating from Argyle Ave. and quaint Andersonville), making it the city's largest park. Within its elongated 1,200 acres are a world-class zoo, a half-dozen bathing beaches, a botanical conservatory, two excellent museums, a golf course, and the usual meadows, formal gardens, sporting fields, and tennis courts typical of urban parks. Attractions in the park include the **Chicago History Museum** (p. 180), **Lincoln Park Zoo** (p. 197), **Lincoln Park Conservatory** (p. 199), and **Peggy Notebaert Nature Museum** (p. 200).

The park's lakes, trails, and pathways make it ideal for biking, hiking, picnicking, and enjoying nature. Baseball, softball, and soccer fields, and basketball and tennis courts are concentrated mainly around the South Field, Waveland, and Montrose sections. You'll find archery and a 9-hole golf course in the Waveland area; minigolf and a driving range are located near Diversey Harbor. Families can rent paddle boats and explore the South

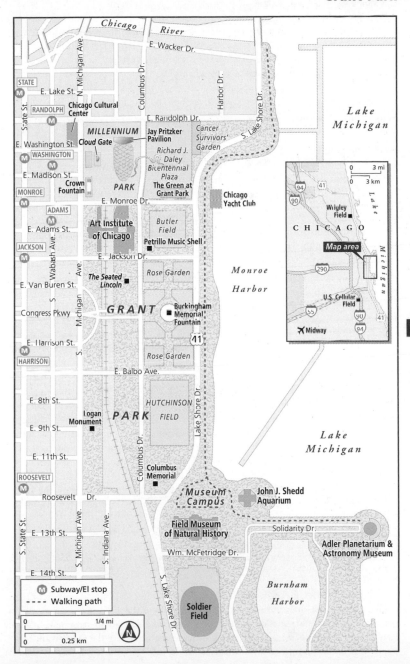

Moments **A Great View**

After a visit to the Lincoln Park Zoo or the Peggy Notebaert Nature Museum, take a quick stroll on Fullerton Avenue to the bridge that runs over the lagoon (just before you get to Lake Shore Dr.). Standing on the south side of Fullerton Avenue, you'll have a great view of the Chicago skyline and Lincoln Park—an excellent backdrop for family souvenir photos. This path can get very crowded on summer weekends, so I suggest trying this photo op during the week.

Pond from a little dock in front of Café Brauer, on the northwest side of lovely South Pond ($12 per half-hour for four-person paddle boats; $16 per half-hour for swan boats, which seat two and are shaped like—you guessed it—a giant white swan). You can also rent boats from the boathouse on North Pond. Boat rentals are available May through September.

Families with small children won't want to miss the **Farm-in-the-Zoo** (p. 197), on the southern end of South Pond. Five barns house cows, chickens, horses, goats, and other livestock. Kids can get a farmhand's-eye view of butter churning, milking, and other farm activities throughout the day.

The **statue of the standing Abraham Lincoln** (just north of the North Ave. and State St. intersection) in the park that bears his name is one of two in Chicago by Augustus Saint-Gaudens (*The Seated Lincoln* is in Grant Park). Saint-Gaudens also did the Bates Fountain near the conservatory. The statue marks the southern boundary of the park.

A one-time Chicago dining institution near the zoo, **Café Brauer** (www.cafebrauer. com; p. 143) is a stunning facility. Operating a cafe and ice-cream parlor on the ground floor, and a ballroom called the Great Hall on the second floor that's flanked by two curving loggias, the Brauer restores some of the elegant atmosphere that characterized the park around 1900, when this landmark building was erected. (If you visit on a weekend, chances are good that caterers will be setting up for a wedding in the Great Hall, but they'll usually let you in to sneak a peek.) Architect Dwight Perkins, who created this gem of a building, was one of the leaders of Chicago's Prairie School architecture movement, and Brauer is undeniably his masterwork. Best of all, though, is the picture-postcard view from the adjacent bridge spanning the pond of the John Hancock Center and neighboring skyscrapers beyond Lincoln Park's treetops.

If you're looking for an evening's entertainment, check out the **Theater on the Lake,** Fullerton Avenue, for open-air theater with a relaxed setting. For information, call ① **312/ 742-7994.**

Bounded by Lake Shore Dr. from North Ave. to Bryn Mawr Ave. ① **312/742-7726.** The park's visitor center is in the Lincoln Park Cultural Center, 2045 N. Lincoln Park W. Park daily dawn–dusk. Visitor center year-round Mon–Thurs 9am–9pm; Fri 11am–7pm; Sat 8am–4pm; Sun 11am–5pm. Bus: 22, 145, 146, 147, 151, or 156.

MILLENNIUM PARK ★★★

At the north end of Grant Park along Michigan Avenue is the city's newest urban show-piece. The architectural highlight of the park is the Frank Gehry–designed Pritzker Music Pavilion, home of the free summer music concerts performed by the Grant Park Symphony Orchestra. Another popular attraction is the huge elliptical sculpture by British

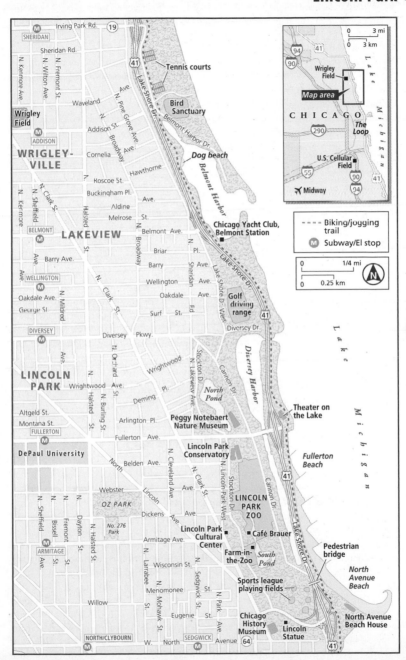

artist Anish Kapoor, his first public work in the U.S. Once you see the sculpture, officially titled *Cloudgate,* you'll see why most Chicagoans affectionately call it "the Bean." For much more on the park, see p. 168 in chapter 6.

PING TOM MEMORIAL PARK

Families touring Chinatown should make a point of stopping at this wonderfully themed playground and park. Brightly colored swing sets, rubberized surfacing, and signs in Mandarin and English are surrounded by grounds landscaped with plants indigenous to China, such as bamboo. The park shelter is of Chinese design. It's all part of the Chicago Park District's new efforts to make parks attractive to both kids and adults, and appropriate to their neighborhood. You'll find the park at 300 W. 19th St.

300 W. 19th St. ℂ **312/742-PLAY** (742-7529). Subway/El: Orange Line to Cermak.

WASHINGTON SQUARE PARK

This little park, built on 3 acres, may have been named after New York's Washington Square Park, which is in a similarly elegant neighborhood. Although small in size, its location is wonderful, just west of the Magnificent Mile. If you need a place for your kids to run free after a day of shopping or touring, this park will give them some open space and immerse you in a "neighborhood" area, not far from busy Michigan Avenue.

The park has had its ups and downs, following the fortunes of the neighborhood. Surrounded by fine residences and churches in the late 1800s, the neighborhood fell upon harder times in the 1910s, when many mansions were converted into flophouses. The park earned the nickname "Bughouse Square." Like Speakers' Corner in London's Hyde Park, Washington Square became a popular spot for soapbox orators. Artists, writers, political radicals, and hobos pontificated, read poetry, and ranted and raved.

In the late 1990s, the park district, city, and neighborhood organizations restored the park by reconstructing a historic Victorian fountain and installing period lighting, fencing, and new plantings. Today the park is surrounded by historic mansions, new condo buildings, and **Newberry Library** (p. 186).

901 N. Clark St. (at Delaware St.). ℂ **312/742-PLAY** (742-7529). Bus: 11.

3 PLAYGROUNDS IN THE CITY CENTER

Chicago has a network of 552 city parks—most of which have playgrounds. To find information on a neighborhood park, go to **www.chicagoparkdistrict.com** or call ℂ **312/742-PLAY** (742-7529) for a list of parks and their facilities.

One of the most centrally located children's playgrounds is at **Daley Bicentennial Plaza in Millennium Park,** at 337 E. Randolph St. The playground is set in the shadow of downtown skyscrapers at Randolph Street and Lake Shore Drive, which has fine views of the skyline and the lake. Kids will find all-new equipment for climbing, playing, and interacting, including swing sets and more, on a safe, rubberized surface. In addition to the play area, the plaza also has a fitness center, locker rooms, and tennis courts, plus ice-skating in the winter. (For more on the skating rink, see "Sports & Games," below.)

Another heavily used playground is **Seneca Playlot Park,** 228 E. Chicago Ave., just west of Chicago's venerable pumping station on Michigan Avenue. Seneca Park features both a lawn with shaded walkways and a play lot with a standard swing set, slide, and more. Though it's small and could use a little updating, Seneca provides a quiet oasis near

the bustling Magnificent Mile. On the lawn sit two recent sculptures by nationally recognized artists: *Ben,* a bronze horse by sculptor Debra Butterfield, and *Farmer's Dream,*
an abstract piece by sculptor Richard Hunt. The play lot is named for Eli Schulman
(1910–88), a well-known restaurateur who founded Eli's, the Place for Steak, and who
was active in promoting recreational activities for children. The park itself takes its name
from adjacent Seneca Street, named for the Iroquois tribe of upstate New York.

4 SPORTS & GAMES

BASEBALL

Chicago's Park District offers baseball in many of its 552 parks; one diamond that's easily
accessible and in a central location is **Lincoln Park.** The baseball fields are on the southern tip, just north of the Chicago Historical Society. Even if a game is underway, you'll
find some room to throw a ball back and forth with your child. For more information
on baseball in city parks, visit www.chicagoparkdistrict.com.

Chicago parents who want to get kids involved in baseball should contact **Little
League.** Kids ages 5 to 12 can participate. Teams change every year, so the best way to
find one near you is to visit www.littleleague.org. Click on the "Finding a Local League"
link to start your search for a team for your child.

Still basking in their stunning World Series win in 2005, the **Chicago White Sox**
attract the same kind of loyalty as the Chicago Cubs. At their home, **U.S. Cellular Field,**
333 W. 35th St. (© 312/674-1000; www.whitesox.mlb.com), the White Sox do a great
job getting kids excited about baseball. Before every home game, White Sox Training
Center coaches conduct a baseball clinic. Kids can practice in the batting cages, at the
base-running drill, and in the practice pitching areas. It's all free of charge. Enter U.S.
Cellular Field at Gate 3 or ask a Guest Services Representative how to get there. FUN-
damentals, as the program is called, opens the gates about 1½ hours before game time
and stays open for 1½ hours after the game starts. (If you're hungry after your pregame
workout, stop by the Pepsi Kids Corner near Section 100 for kids' concessions like peanut-butter-and-jelly sandwiches, plus other kid favorites. Near Section 101, you'll find a
kids' gift shop, featuring kids' souvenirs and apparel.)

If it's a little batting practice you're seeking, head for the batting cages **Sluggers Sports
Bar,** near Wrigley Field at 3540 N. Clark St. (© 773/248-0055). This neighborhood
sports bar is super–kid-friendly. Dozens of TV screens bring in games via satellite, providing a fitting backdrop for you and your kids to test your skill in the batting cages. The
upstairs batting cages approximate both softball and baseball pitches; there's also Pop-a-
Shot and high-ball (a basketball-type game played on a trampoline) and an arcade. In the
northern suburbs, try **Skokie Sports Park,** 3459 Oakton (© 847/674-1500). The cages
are open April through October, Sunday to Thursday from 8am to 10pm, and Friday and
Saturday from 8am to 11pm.

BASKETBALL

One of Chicago's better public parks to catch (or watch) a game of hoops is **Blackhawk
Park,** at 2318 N. Lavergne Ave. in the Irving Park neighborhood (© 773/746-5014). A
basketball court and baseball and softball fields dot the grounds of this family-friendly
park. Basketball programs are offered for ages 5 and up. You'll also find an outdoor

playground and spray pool and an indoor swimming pool. Park hours are Monday through Friday from 8am to 9pm and Saturday and Sunday from 9am to 5pm. Also recommended for their excellent kids' basketball programs are **Oz Park,** at 2021 N. Burling in the Lincoln Park neighborhood; **Portage Park,** 4100 N. Long Ave. on the northwest side; and **Independence Park,** at 3945 Springfield Ave. in the Irving Park neighborhood.

You can walk in to any **YMCA of Metropolitan Chicago** and use the gym to play basketball for a small fee. The most centrally located YMCA in the downtown area is New City YMCA, located at 1515 N. Halsted, at Clybourn (© **312/440-7272**). For more information, see www.ymcachgo.org.

BIKING

Biking is a great way to see the city, particularly the lakefront, along which a bike path extends for more than 18 miles. The stretch between Navy Pier and North Avenue Beach gets extremely crowded in the summer (you're jostling for space with in-line skaters, joggers, and dawdling pedestrians). If you're looking for more wide-open spaces, I recommend biking south from Navy Pier—once you're past the Museum Campus, traffic on the trail is light, and you can cruise all the way to Hyde Park. If you want a more leisurely tour with good people-watching potential, head north (through the crowds) and be patient—once you pass Belmont Harbor, the traffic lets up somewhat. It's possible to ride all the way to Hollywood Beach, where the lakefront trail ends—a great workout.

To rent bikes, try **Bike Chicago,** which has locations at Navy Pier (© **312/595-9600**), North Avenue Beach (© **773/327-7206**), Millennium Park (© **888/BIKE-WAY** [245-3929]), the Riverwalk (Wacker Drive and Columbus Street—take the stairs down to the river; © **312/595-9600**), and at the north end of the lakefront bike path at Foster Beach (© **773/275-2600**). Open from 8am to 8pm May through October (weather permitting), Bike Chicago stocks mountain and touring bikes, kids' bikes, kids' seats and trailers for any kids too young for a bike, strollers, and—most fun of all—quadcycles, which are four-wheeled contraptions equipped with a steering wheel and canopy that can accommodate four or five people. Rates for bikes start at $8 an hour ($6 for kids' bikes) and range up to about $34 a day (higher for high-end road bikes), with helmets, pads, and locks included. You can also rent bike seats for kids and wagons (the covered version that you pull behind your bike). If you'd like to cycle your way past some Chicago landmarks, guided tours are also available.

Both the park district (© **312/742-PLAY** [742-7529]) and the **Chicagoland Bicycle Federation** (© **312/427-3325;** www.biketraffic.org) offer free maps that detail popular biking routes. The latter, which is the preeminent organization for cyclists in Chicago, also sells a much larger, more extensive map for $6.95 that shows routes within a seven-county area. They sponsor a number of bike rides throughout the year, including the highly enjoyable **Boulevard Lakefront Tour,** held in mid-September, which follows the historic circle of boulevards that had their genesis in the Chicago Plan of 1909. It starts in Hyde Park at the University of Chicago campus.

A word of caution: Locking your bike anywhere you go is a no-brainer. More important, though, is never heading anywhere on the city's streets without first strapping on a helmet. Chicago Mayor Richard M. Daley is an avid cyclist himself and has tirelessly promoted the addition of designated bike lanes along many main thoroughfares. But, that said, most cabbies and drivers tend to ignore them. Bike with extreme caution on city streets (you can get a ticket for biking on the sidewalks), and stick to the lakefront path if you're not an expert rider.

BOWLING

What better way to bond as a family than an evening of gutter-dusting? Two popular hangouts mix teens, serious league bowlers, and families in an irresistible recipe for fun. At **Diversey River Bowl,** 2211 W. Diversey Ave. (✆ **773/227-5800;** www.drbowl.com), tunes spun by a DJ (from an eclectic 300-CD collection) will get your feet tapping as you lace your bowling shoes. You'll find plenty of 20-somethings here on weekends, many of whom play in leagues. Prepare for a wait: It can be an hour. The festive atmosphere is complemented by a collection of bowling pins signed by "bowling greats" such as Dolly Parton and Eddie Vedder. Lanes are open Monday through Friday from noon to 2am; on Saturday and Sunday, leagues are usually scheduled, but there are always open lanes reserved for nonleague bowlers. Cost is $19 per hour per lane Monday through Thursday, and $32 per hour per lane on Friday and Saturday. Shoe rental is $3.

Adjacent to Hotel Sax and House of Blues is **10pin,** a 24-lane alley located at 330 N. State St. (✆ **312/644-0300**). With eight large-screen televisions and a mahogany and marble bar, this place offers a more upscale take on bowling. A grill serves up thin-crust pizzas, salads, sandwiches, and fried chicken; eat in the restaurant or at your lane. Cost is $4.95 per player per game until 5pm; $6.95 per person per game after 5pm.

Another option is **Waveland Bowl,** 3700 N. Western Ave. (✆ **773/472-5900**). Open 24/7, Waveland has 40 lanes and gets pretty loud when busy. Even though the place is huge, expect to wait your turn.

When in the suburbs, **Brunswick Zone** is your best bet and birthday-party central. One plus for families is the video games. The company has lanes in suburban Algonquin, Carol Stream, Deerfield, Deer Park, Glendale Heights, Kankakee, Mount Prospect Naperville, Niles, Oak Lawn, Palatine, Roselle, Waukegan/Lakehurst, and Woodridge. For phone numbers or to make online reservations, visit **www.brunswickbowling.com**.

CLIMBING

Sorry to point out the obvious, but Chicago has no hills, much less mountains. (When I was in a training group for the Chicago Marathon, we did our hill training by running up the corkscrew ramp in the John Hancock Center parking garage—that's how serious Chicago's hill shortage is!) Your best option for climbing in the city is "Mount Chicago," at the **Lakeshore Athletic Club–Illinois Center** (✆ **312/616-9000;** www.lsac.com). One of the most impressive climbing facilities built anywhere in the world, the man-made wall rises 110 feet (that's seven-and-a-half stories!). Kids ages 5 and up can climb on Saturday 10am to 5pm and Sunday 10am to 1pm. You don't have to be a member to use the wall. Cost for kids is $15 for an orientation class. Kids' classes and private lessons are available; classes take place for 6 consecutive weekends and require preregistration. Even if you don't have previous experience, adults, too, can venture onto the wall through an orientation and safety class (all while wearing a protective harness, of course). The club is located at 211 N. Stetson, 1 block east of North Michigan Avenue at Lake Street. To get there, take any bus that serves Michigan Avenue.

Chicago residents who want to enroll their kids in classes might investigate the indoor rock climbing at **Lakeshore Academy,** at 937 W. Chestnut, near the intersection of Halsted and Chicago (✆ **312/563-9400;** www.lakeshoreacademy.com). Membership is $100 per year for a family and lasts until the same term 1 year later, and classes are organized by age group for kids from age 5 to 16. "Hidden Peak," as the climbing area is called, is a great way to discover the challenge of indoor rock climbing. Staffed with experienced and friendly people, Hidden Peak offers tons of user-friendly programs for kids (and adults). *Tip:* A fun option for a birthday party is climbing parties, held for kids ages 6 and up, Lakeshore Academy gives these parties over a 2-hour period on Saturday and Sunday evenings, or Sunday mornings. Check out the website for more information.

FISHING

The Chicago Park District runs fishing programs for kids; for the latest details, check out **www.chicagoparkdistrict.com**. One program, "Fish 'n Kids," provides rods, reels, bait, and instruction for four daily 45-minute sessions at all Chicago Park District lagoons and at four lakefront locations. The Sam Romano Youth Fishing Derby (named for a charter boat captain who loved fishing and kids), which runs all summer, is open to kids ages 8 to 15. Kids enter their catches in a category: rock bass, panfish, catfish, and carp. Twenty kids in each category win prizes of new fishing equipment.

Want to do battle with the scrappy coho salmon, or tie into a tackle-testing, arm-aching 20-pound chinook? Salmon fishing has been popular on Lake Michigan since Pacific species were introduced in the 1970s. Gather a group of six (to split the cost of about $400 for 5 hr. of fishing) and be prepared to start at dawn. You can find a charter boat through the **Chicago Sportfishing Association** (© **312/922-1100;** www.great-lakes.org), with boats available in both Burnham and Millennium (on the south side) and Diversey and Montrose (on the north side) harbors.

Lake perch are another popular Lake Michigan fish—they won't give you the fight that salmon do, but they are fun to catch and good to eat. (Pan-fried is the way to go.) They are plentiful from May to August. Jumbo perch weigh in at 1 pound and are caught with ultralight spinning tackle or hand lines rigged with multiple hooks. Check sporting-goods stores for equipment and bait. The local anglers' favorite spot is Montrose Harbor Pier, east of Lake Shore Drive at Wilson Avenue. Harbor fishing is allowed in designated areas of Belmont, Montrose, Diversey, DuSable, Monroe, Burnham, 59th Street, and Jackson Inner and Jackson Outer harbors. To find out more, call **Chicago Park District** harbor information at © **312/747-7527.**

GOLF

Chicago has an impressive number of golf options within the city limits. The Chicago Park District offers six courses, three driving ranges, and three learning centers. Don't let a little cold weather stop you: As further evidence of the hardiness of Chicagoans, the golf courses are open year-round, even on Christmas Day! For tee times and information, call © **312/245-0909.** Most recommended for kids is the **Diversey Driving Range,** 141 W. Diversey Pkwy. (© **312/742-7929**), in Lincoln Park just north of Diversey Harbor; it's a fun way to get outside after dinner on a summer evening. This two-level range attracts all players, from show-off scratch golfers to shanking beginners. The price is right ($9 for a bucket of balls), and the setting is pretty much perfect.

One of the most popular golf courses operated by the Chicago Park District is the 9-hole **Sydney Marovitz Course,** 3600 N. Lake Shore Dr., at Waveland Avenue. Many Chicagoans refer to it simply as "Waveland." Thanks to its picturesque lakefront location, it's always busy on weekends; so make a reservation well in advance, and don't expect a quick round—this is where beginners come to practice. Another good bet, and one that's usually less crowded, is the 18-hole course in **Jackson Park** at 63rd Street and Stoney Island Avenue. These city-run courses are open mid-April through November. For information on greens fees, locations, and hours, call the **Chicago Park District** golf office (© **312/245-0909**), or go to www.cpdgolf.com.

No Horsing Around

Let me be frank: Horseback riding in downtown Chicago is impossible. About the closest you can get is a horse-and-buggy ride. Carriages depart from the southwest corner of Michigan Avenue and Pearson Street (next to the Water Tower). For $35 for a half-hour ride (for up to four people), it's a picturesque way to take in the city's sights. The rides are operated by the Noble Horse Theater, which owns Chicago's historic riding hall, which dates back to 1871 and is located at 1410 N. Orleans Ave. To see a Noble Horse performance, call the **Noble Horse** at ✆ **312/266-7878;** www.noblehorsechicago.com.

If you're planning on visiting the suburbs and want to play a round on one of the many plush and pricey suburban courses, visit the website of the Chicago District Golf Association at www.cdga.org.

In the northern suburbs, **Skokie Sports Park,** 3459 Oakton (✆ **847/674-1500;** www.skokieparkdistrict.com), has an 18-hole around-the-world–themed miniature golf course, a 9-hole miniature golf course for the smallest tots, a two-tiered driving range, and junior golf lessons. The Traveler's Quest miniature golf course, geared toward older kids and adults, lets you putt around the Eiffel Tower and over the waterfall near Easter Island. Check out the African water hole (in which you putt into the hippo's mouth), the Japanese garden with lanterns with its sizable hazards, and the Great Wall of China. The park is open April through October Sunday through Thursday from 8am to 10pm, Friday and Saturday until 11pm.

In nearby Lincolnwood, **Novelty Golf and Games,** 3550 W. Devon Ave. (✆ **847/679-9434;** www.noveltygolf.com), has miniature golf, batting cages, a video arcade, and an ice-cream parlor. It's a 50-year-old operation that's open Saturday and Sunday from 11am to dusk from early March to late October, weather permitting.

ICE-SKATING

Whether you and your kids are executing graceful toe loops or merely stumbling across the rink, you can hit the ice in the heart of Chicago's Loop. The city's premier skating destination is the **McCormick Tribune Ice Rink** at Millennium Park, 55 N. Michigan Ave., at the intersection of Michigan Avenue and Monroe Street (✆ **312/742-5222;** www.millenniumpark.org). The location is unbeatable. You'll skate in the shadows of grand skyscrapers and within view of the lake. The rink is open daily from 9am to 9pm, November to March. Admission is free, and skate rentals are $10. Try going on a weeknight when the city lights sparkle over you, and grab a hot chocolate from a vending machine to warm up before hitting the ice.

Year-round skating and ice-skating lessons are available at the only city-run indoor ice arena at **McFetridge Sports Complex** (known to many Chicago residents as California Park) located in the Lakeview neighborhood at 3845 N. California Ave., at Irving Park Road (✆ **773/478-2609**). Open skating sessions in the indoor rink are held Wednesday and Friday afternoons from 3:30 to 5pm, and Saturday and Sunday from 4:30 to 6pm. Skates can be rented for $3 a pair; the rink fee is $5 for ages 13 and up, $4 for ages 12 and under. The rink is huge and can be very crowded on weekends. You might want to take advantage of the free skating lessons, available on Monday from 5:15 to 5:55pm.

There's also a relatively small rink at **Navy Pier,** 600 E. Grand Ave. (© **312/595-PIER** [595-7437]).

IN-LINE SKATING

In-line skaters have been taking over Chicago's sidewalks, streets, and bike paths since the early 1990s. Numerous rental places have popped up, and several sporting-goods shops that sell in-line skates also rent them. The rentals generally include helmets and pads. **Bike Chicago,** with locations at Navy Pier (© **312/595-9600**), North Avenue Beach (© **773/327-7206**), Millennium Park (© **888/BIKE-WAY** [245-3929]), and more, charges $8 an hour or $30 a day (you can have the skates 8am–8pm).

The best route to skate, of course, is the lakefront trail that leads from Lincoln Park down to Oak Street Beach. Beware, though, that those same miles of trail are claimed by avid cyclists—and I've seen plenty of collisions between 'bladers and bikers. Approach Chicago lakefront traffic as carefully as you would a major expressway!

SAILING

It seems a shame to just sit on the beach and watch all those beautiful sailboats gliding across the lake. Go on, get out there. The **Chicago Sailing Club,** in Belmont Harbor (© **773/871-SAIL** [871-7245]; www.chicagosailingclub.com), rents J-22 and J-30 boats from 9am to sunset, weather permitting, May through October. A J-22 holds four or five people. Rates for a J-22 range from $45 to $65 an hour (with an extra cost per hr. for a skipper). A J-30 accommodates up to 10 people and can sail at night. Rates are $80 to $100 per hour, plus the extra hourly fee if you want a skipper. If you want to take the boat out without a skipper, you need to demonstrate your skills first (and pay an additional checkout fee). Those who'd rather sit back and relax while a pro does the sailing can charter a boat here as well. Reservations are recommended.

SWIMMING

The Chicago Park District maintains about 30 indoor pools for lap swimming and general splashing around, but none is particularly convenient to downtown. If you are a resident, you should check out your local park (to find out where parks are located, see www.chicagoparkdistrict.com). Some neighborhoods have incredible facilities that are safe and clean. For example, **Portage Park,** on Chicago's northwest side at 4100 Long Ave. (© **773/685-7235**), has a stunning outdoor Olympic-size pool, a diving board with three levels and its own dive pool, and a kids' pool with a water playhouse, waterfalls, and more. It's absolutely wonderful, and it's free. The neighborhood is populated by Hispanic and eastern European immigrants, and tons of kids jam the pool every summer weekend. Another great park for swimming is **Blackhawk Park,** at 2318 N. Lavergne Ave. in the Irving Park neighborhood (© **312/746-5014**). You'll find an outdoor spray pool and an indoor swimming pool. Pool hours vary according to age: Youth swim is at 3pm, teen swim at 5pm, and family swim at 7pm.

Still, my advice to visitors would be to skip the park district pools, because many are in off-the-beaten-track neighborhoods. As a visitor, your best bet for summer swimming is **Lake Michigan,** where beaches are open for swimmers Memorial Day through Labor Day from 9am to 9:30pm in areas watched over by lifeguards (no swimming off the rocks, please). It's a safe place to swim and a uniquely "Chicago" experience. How often do you and your kids get the chance to take a dip in a Great Lake? Watch the news for beach closings, which happen occasionally, as the water is tested daily for bacteria. If you're a serious lap swimmer, you'll find company along the wall beginning at Ohio Street Beach, located slightly northwest of Navy Pier. The Chicago Triathlon Club marks a course here each summer with a buoy at both the $^1/_4$- and $^1/_2$-mile marks. This popular swimming route follows the shoreline in a straight line. The water is fairly shallow. For more information, call the park district's beach and pool office (© **312/742-PLAY** [742-7529]).

The Chicago Park District manages 31 beaches along 24 miles of lakefront. Amenities vary, but most have a comfort station or a beach house and food vendors selling hot dogs, burgers, and soda. The two beaches I can recommend without hesitation are **Oak Street Beach** and **North Avenue Beach.** Both also feature a broader menu for dining: The Oak Street Beachstro (p. 216) serves gourmet salads, beef tenderloin, grilled salmon, and Key lime pie; the restaurant in the beach house at North Avenue Beach serves Jamaican jerk chicken and specialty ice cream.

For more information, call the park district's beach and pool office at © **312/747-0832.**

TENNIS

The best—and cheapest—tennis in the city is found at **Waveland Courts,** located on Lake Shore Drive at Addison. For about $5 per hour, you can play on these public courts. It's first-come, first-served, so get there early—the park is open from 6am to 11pm. Pay before you play at the trailer close to the Addison entrance. Tennis buffs report that the availability of courts is pretty good in the morning. League play takes place in the evenings, and it's difficult to get a court. Any nontennis players in your family can play golf, which is also available here.

If it's lessons you're seeking, head for **McFetridge Sports Complex,** 3845 N. California Ave. (© **773/478-2609**). Students here report that the tennis pros are great, lessons are good, and the price is right. Court fees are $17 per hour during the day, and $26 per hour in the evening. You'll have no problem booking an indoor court in the summer, but in the winter make sure to book ahead.

5 INDOOR PLAYGROUNDS

The only city-run indoor playground is free, highly recommended, and located in **Garfield Park Conservatory;** see p. 199 for a full description.

The national chain **Gymboree** offers a series of classes for kids from newborn to age 4 in a playscape with slides, inflatable logs, colorful mats, and all kinds of things to jump on and crawl inside. A Gymboree teacher leads the way with activities and songs. Visitors can call ahead to request space in one of the classes; most local parents sign up for a full series. In Chicago, one location is at 3158 N. Lincoln Ave. (© **773/296-4550;** www.gymboree.com). You'll also find branches in suburban Wilmette, Skokie, Northbrook, and Wheaton.

Odyssey Fun World (www.odysseyfunworld.com), in west suburban Naperville and Tinley Park, features 250 video games and rides, plus a Little Tykes playground, a four-level soft playland (for kids 12 and under), a roller coaster simulator, a cafe, a rock-climbing-wall thrill ride, paintball, and some outdoor attractions, including 36 holes of adventure golf, go-cart tracks, and batting cages. Each activity has a fee, and games require tokens (usually 25¢ each, less if bought in quantity); admission to the soft playground is free, but costs for rides are charged individually and range from $3 to $10 per ride. Locations are at 19111 S. Oak Park Ave., Tinley Park (📞 **708/429-3800**), and 3440 Odyssey Court, Naperville (📞 **630/416-2222**).

6 CLASSES & WORKSHOPS

Chicago Children's Museum   Many wonderful classes are available at the museum. The array might include wintertime decorating of fleece scarves that kids can wear, making glitzy bookmarks, designing quilt squares of kids' favorite books, or dancing out storybook classics such as *The Gingerbread Man*. Classes are available for all ages. They change often, so see the "Activities" section of the website.

At Navy Pier, 700 E. Grand Ave. 📞 **312/527-1000.** www.chicagochildrensmuseum.org. Class fee included in museum admission fee ($9 adults and children, $8 seniors). Subway/El: Red Line to Grand/State; transfer to city bus or Navy Pier's free trolley bus. Bus: 29, 56, 65, or 66.

The Field Museum of Natural History   From fossil-hunting field trips to hands-on seminars on the mythology and crafts of the Incas, to an immersive workshop in video storytelling, the Field Museum offers workshops year-round for families. For more information, see the "Education" section of www.fmnh.org or call 📞 **312/665-7400.**

Roosevelt Rd. and Lake Shore Dr. 📞 **312/922-9410** or 312/341-9299 TDD (for hearing-impaired callers). www.fieldmuseum.org. Bus: 6, 10, 12, 130, or 146.

Lill Street Art Center   This center for working artists offers a huge array of classes for kids from 2 years old and up, involving pottery, watercolors, singing, and more. If you want to drop in, you can browse the studios, where the kids can see the artists at work.

1021 W. Lill, 3 blocks north of Fullerton St. in the DePaul University area. 📞 **773/477-6185.** www.lillstreet.com. 10-week-long kids' courses start at $140 (single lessons not available). Gallery hours Tues–Sat 11am–6pm; Sun noon–5pm. Subway/El: Red Line to Fullerton.

Museum of Science and Industry   Who knows how many current chemists, biologists, and real-life rocket scientists were once inspired by this museum? Get your young Einstein involved in the wonders of science with "Saturday Science Clubs," where kids can engage in hands-on science and technology activities. Participants are encouraged to work together to investigate scientific issues and develop problem-solving skills. Club activities cover subjects such as chemistry, physics, flight, electric circuitry, and forensics. Morning science clubs run from 9:30am to noon. Afternoon clubs run from 1 to 3:30pm. Workshops are for kids in grades six to nine. For current offerings, see the "Education" section of the website www.msichicago.org, or call 📞 **773/684-7844,** ext. 2687.

57th St. and Lake Shore Dr. 📞 **800/468-6674** outside the Chicago area, 773/684-1414, or TTY 773/684-3323. www.msichicago.org. Bus: 6, 10, 55, 151, or 156.

Old Town School of Folk Music   Chicago's premier music education center offers kids' classes in music, dance, art, and theater as well as private lessons. Children's courses last 8 or 16 weeks, and are 45 minutes to 1 hour in length. Visitors, however, can get a taste of the fun by trying out a class. You can show up the day of the class and pay in the range of $15 to attend that day. (Art classes are excluded.) Drop-in opportunities include the Wiggle Worms class, a music-and-movement class that Chicago parents say is the absolute most fun class in the city for small children (about 6 months–3 years).

Teen classes are just for students ages 11 to 18, and are offered during after-school and weekend hours. All classes meet once a week, and most are 80 minutes in length, in a relaxed group atmosphere of 8 to 12 students. Most teen music classes cost about $90 for 8 weeks of classes; theater classes run 16 weeks. Starlight: Teen Open Mic at the Old Town School takes the stage from 7 to 10pm on the second Friday of every month. Call for information or to be added to the Teen Open Mic mailing list. This new monthly event is a showcase for musicians, actors, and audience members at the 909 W. Armitage Ave. location.

4544 N. Lincoln Ave. ✆ **773/728-6000.** www.oldtownschool.org. Subway/El: Brown Line to Western.

Shopping with Your Kids

When I talked to other Chicago parents about shopping with their kids, they often joked, "The best shopping experience is *no* shopping experience!" True, shopping with kids can be a strain, and maybe this chapter is better titled "Shopping *for* Your Kids." To keep kids interested during your shopping expeditions, I've included some stores that wouldn't necessarily be considered children's stores but which kids find fascinating—stores that sell thousands of different buttons, for example.

For more on shopping for adults in Chicago, pick up a copy of *Frommer's Chicago*. This chapter concentrates on the Magnificent Mile, State Street, and several trendy neighborhoods, where you'll find one-of-a-kind shops and boutiques that make shopping such an adventure. It also includes a sampling of retailers organized by merchandise category.

1 THE SHOPPING SCENE

SHOPPING HOURS & SALES TAXES

As a general rule, stores are open Monday through Saturday from 10am to 6 or 7pm, and Sunday from noon to 6pm. Neighborhood stores tend to keep later hours, with some remaining open until 8pm Monday through Saturday and until 6pm on Sunday. Many stores are open later on Thursday, and almost all have extended hours during the holiday season. Nearly all the stores in the Loop are open for daytime shopping only, generally Monday through Saturday from 9 or 10am to no later than 6pm. (The few remaining big downtown department stores have some evening hours; see below.) Many Loop stores not on State Street are closed Saturday; on Sunday the Loop—except for a few restaurants, theaters, and cultural attractions—shuts down.

You might do a double take after checking the total on your purchase: At 10.25%, the state and local sales taxes on nonfood items is the steepest in the country.

SHOPPING DISTRICTS

The Magnificent Mile

The nickname "Magnificent Mile" refers to the roughly mile-long stretch of North Michigan Avenue between Oak Street and the Chicago River. As Chicago's top shopping destination, the Magnificent Mile is magnificent not because of the sightseeing or the architecture: The stores are the thing. The density of first-rate shopping is, quite simply, unmatched anywhere. Even jaded shoppers from other worldly capitals are delighted at the ease and convenience of the stores concentrated here. Taking into account that tony Oak Street is just around a corner (again, if you want to hit Hermès and Prada, I must

American Girl Place **9**
Barbara's Bookstore **13**
Bloomingdale's **4**
Blue Chicago Store **15**
Borders **7**
Chicago Place **12**
GapKids and babyGap **16**
Ghiradelli Chocolate Shop **6**
Jazz Record Mart **17**
Madison and Friends **1**

Neiman-Marcus **10**
Niketown **14**
900 North Michigan
  Avenue **5**
Nordstrom **19**
Saks Fifth Avenue **11**
Urban Outfitters **3**
Water Tower Place **8**
The Shops at
  North Bridge **18**

refer you to *Frommer's Chicago*), the overall area is a little like New York's Fifth Avenue and Beverly Hills's Rodeo Drive rolled into one. Whether your passion is Bulgari jewelry, Prada suits, or Salvatore Ferragamo footwear, you'll find it on this stretch of concrete. This is the city's liveliest corridor: The sidewalks are packed in the summer and on weekends with hordes of shoppers strolling up and down the avenue and pausing to enjoy the many street performers who enliven this strip. Holidays on Michigan Avenue are a magical time, as the city knocks itself out with lights and music and a spectacular Christmas tree in the John Hancock Center plaza.

And don't think you're seeing everything by walking down the street: Michigan Avenue is home to several indoor, high-rise malls, where plenty more boutiques and restaurants are tucked away. The face of Michigan Avenue has been dramatically transformed since the first mall—Water Tower Place—went up on the north end of the street. Several more malls and large-scale, hotel-retail projects have followed. As the rush for square footage escalated (beginning in the late 1980s), many city residents lamented the metamorphosis of the street from a rather intimate and graceful promenade of 1920s buildings to a glitzy canyon of retail theater. Eager to get in on the action, national and international retailers—from middle-brow discounters to highbrow couture purveyors—have continued to look for front-row locations to squeeze into.

For the ultimate Mag Mile shopping adventure, start at one end of North Michigan Avenue and work your way to the other. This section lists some of the best-known kid-related shops on the avenue and on nearby side streets.

North Michigan Avenue & the Magnificent Malls

North Michigan Avenue is lined with shops and includes four of the aforementioned vertical malls—each a major shopping destination in its own right. These indoor malls offer shopping on multiple levels.

WATER TOWER PLACE Chicago's first—and still busiest—vertical mall is Water Tower Place, a block-size, marble-sheathed building at 835 N. Michigan Ave. (© **312/ 440-3165;** www.shopWaterTower.com), between East Pearson and East Chestnut streets. The mall's seven floors contain about 100 stores and house a dozen different cafes and restaurants. Notably for families, the mall is now home to **American Girl Place,** which occupies two floors of Water Tower Place, and has a ground floor entrance (you can enter through the mall's main lobby, but to get the full effect, use the doors of the store's main entrance on Chestnut St.).

Water Tower was the first big indoor mall to open downtown (in 1975), and its glass elevators and shiny gold trim gave the place a glamorous air. These days, after some recent renovations, the spiffed-up mall remains popular. Water Tower is a magnet for suburban teenagers (just like your mall back home!) and can get quite crowded during the summer tourist season. Most of its stores are part of national chains (Gap, Victoria's Secret, and the like); however, a few notable shops make it worth a stop, including hip young designs from the British store **French Connection** (fifth floor; © **312/932-9460**) and wearable women's clothing at **Eileen Fisher** (second floor; © **312/943-9190**). The department store anchoring the mall is **Macy's** (floors one to eight; © **312/335-7700;** p. 243). The second anchor is **American Girl Place** (floors one and two; © **877/247-5223;** p. 251). One of the mall's best features is the innovative **foodlife** food court, which contains more than a dozen stations, from burgers and pizza to Mexican and Moroccan, plus the **Mity Nice Grill** (© **312/335-4745**), a faux-1940s diner. Two movie complexes contain eight screens. Of note to kids are **Accent Chicago** (© **312/944-1354**),

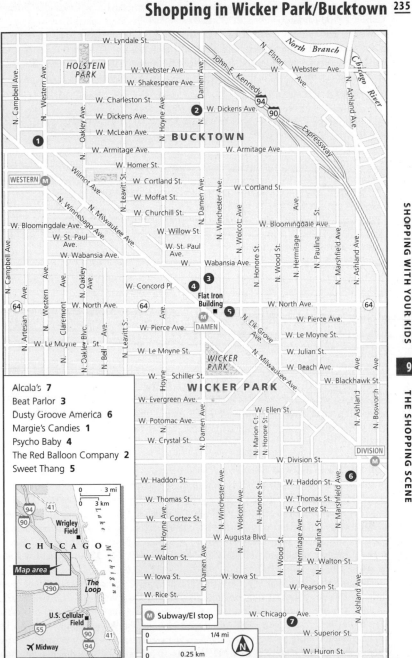

Alcala's **7**
Beat Parlor **3**
Dusty Groove America **6**
Margie's Candies **1**
Psycho Baby **4**
The Red Balloon Company **2**
Sweet Thang **5**

Ⓜ Subway/El stop

for T-shirts, pizza pans, logo sports gear, and other souvenirs that say "Chicago"; **Chicago Cubs Clubhouse Shop** (C 312/335-0807), for all the Cubs paraphernalia you can dream of; and **Gamers Paradise** (C 312/587-0077), with its large collection of board games, card games, video games, and more. The mall is home to **Abercrombie & Fitch** (p. 244), **Abercrombie, Limited Too, Claire's Boutique, MNG by Mango, Wet Seal,** and **Campus Colors,** with Chicago's largest selection of collegiate wear.

900 NORTH MICHIGAN AVE.   The most upscale of the Magnificent Mile's three vertical malls, 900 North Michigan (C 312/915-3916; www.shop900.com) is often called the "Bloomingdale's building" for its most prominent tenant. The mall avoids the tumult of Water Tower Place by appealing to a more upscale shopper, while still generating the vitality essential to a satisfying shopping spree. In addition to about 70 stores, there are a few good restaurants and a nice salon on the lower level.

Chic young teens will make a beeline for the second-level outpost of **Club Monaco** (C 312/787-8757), with minimalist casual-chic clothes at affordable prices. On the second floor, **J. Crew** (C 312/751-2739) sells sweaters, slacks, hats, belts, and other clothing featuring the scrubbed-clean look, popular with young teens to adults. You'll also want to check out the fifth floor, home to **Galt Toys** (p. 252), and **Mini Me** (p. 245), which features great kids' clothing. **Glove Me Tender** (C 312/664-4022) carries mitts for little hands if Chicago's weather turns chilly.

The mall's bathrooms are large, clean, and well equipped with infant changing areas; you'll find them on the second and fifth levels. *An added treat:* Shoppers are serenaded by live piano music on weekends from noon to 5pm on the second level. You'll also find kid-friendly restaurants, including **Frankie's Scallopine,** a casual Italian restaurant; **Potbelly Sandwich Works;** and **Oak Tree,** a bustling place on the sixth floor that welcomes families.

CHICAGO PLACE   The mall's main claim to fame is as the home of upscale retailer **Saks Fifth Avenue** (C 312/944-6500; p. 244). Inaugurated in 1991 at 700 N. Michigan Ave., Chicago Place (C 312/642-4811; www.chicago-place.com) features a food court on the eighth floor that has cheap eats and a bright and airy atmosphere, with a view that you'd usually pay dearly for at nearby luxury hotels. You'll find the usual mall favorites (McDonald's, Subway, Taco Bell). Grab one of the tables near the gigantic windows for a great Michigan Avenue view.

THE SHOPS AT NORTH BRIDGE   A solid concentration of kids' stores on the Mag Mile is found in this mall, at 520 N. Michigan Ave. (C 312/327-2300; www.theshops atnorthbridge.com). The newest of the Michigan Avenue malls, it opened in 2000. The third floor has several children's shops, the best of which is **The Lego Store** (C 312/494-0760). Look for the replicas of Chicago landmarks built out of those distinctive colored-plastic blocks, and be prepared to stay awhile: Kids can easily spend an hour here. Other stores of interest to kids are **Go! The Game Store** (C 312/840-9540) and **Oilily Kids** (p. 245).

The anchor of the mall is a four-story **Nordstrom** (C 312/379-4300). The mall includes the first Chicago location for **A/X Armani Exchange** (C 312/467-5702), Giorgio Armani's younger and more affordable line that's a big hit with teens. There's a large food court on the fourth level with local standouts like **Potbelly Sandwich Works** (p. 120) and a Chicago-style hot dog stand. Other eating options near the North Bridge mall include **Big Bowl** (p. 128), **ESPN Zone** (p. 127), **California Pizza Kitchen** (p. 128), and a host of fast-food outlets on the fourth floor.

Shopping in the Loop is mostly concentrated along State Street, from Randolph Street south to Congress Parkway (although there are stores sprinkled elsewhere, they're mostly in places that cater to office workers: drugstores, sandwich shops, and chain clothing stores). State Street was Chicago's first great shopping district. Between the time the first stores were established in 1852 and World War I, seven of the largest and most lavish department stores in the world were competing for shoppers' loyalties along a half-mile stretch between Randolph Street and Congress Parkway. The area has now been eclipsed by Michigan Avenue, and State Street is lined with discount stores and fast-food outlets. However, one grand old department store makes it worth a visit: **Macy's at State Street** (formerly Marshall Field's), 111 N. State St., at Randolph Street (© **312/781-1000;** p. 243). A city landmark and one of the largest department stores in the world, it occupies an entire city block and features the largest Tiffany glass mosaic dome in the U.S. If you're in Chicago between Thanksgiving and New Year's, Macy's has maintained a longtime Marshall Field's tradition: lavishly decorated holiday windows and breakfast or lunch served under the Great Tree in the store's restaurant, the Walnut Room.

Tips   Point Zero

If the quick change from north to south in the Loop confuses you, keep in mind that in Chicago, point zero for the purpose of address numbering is the intersection of State and Madison streets.

Although the other stores along State Street are not particularly distinctive—the place still has a no-frills aura compared to Michigan Avenue—it stays busy thanks to the thousands of office workers who stroll around during their lunch hour or after work. On weekends, the street is much more subdued. Stores that might be of interest to families are **Sears** (© **312/373-6000**), at the corner of State and Madison streets, and a large **Old Navy** store (p. 245), at Washington and State streets (© **312/551-0522**), which sells hip and cheap kids' wares.

Just off State Street, heading east on Randolph Street, is the **Gallery 37 Store,** 66 E. Randolph St. (© **312/251-0371**). The store sells goods made by Chicago youth ages 14 to 21 who are participants in the Gallery 37 arts training program. The not-for-profit pairs young artists with experienced artists. Proceeds from the sales of the paintings, jewelry, ceramics, decorated furniture, textiles, and sculptures benefit the program.

River North

Since the 1960s, when the Chicago Imagists (painters Ed Paschke, Jim Nutt, and Roger Brown among them) attracted international attention with their shows at the Hyde Park Art Center, the city has been a fertile breeding ground for emerging artists and innovative art dealers. Today, the primary gallery district is concentrated in the River North neighborhood, where century-old, red-brick warehouses have been converted into lofty exhibition spaces. More recently, a new generation of gallery owners has set up shop in the rapidly gentrifying West Loop neighborhood, where you'll find more cutting-edge work. The River North gallery district is an easy walk from many hotels; the West Loop may seem a little farther afield, but it's only a short cab ride from downtown. If you have young children, most of the galleries and home stores that line River North's streets are not recommended—protecting expensive artwork from toddlers is much too nerve-wracking! Older kids and

Fun Facts   Jewelers' Row

It's not quite as impressive as the Big Apple's diamond district, but Chicago's own "Jewelers' Row" is certainly worth a detour for rock hunters. Half a dozen high-rises along the Wabash Avenue El tracks in the heart of the Loop service the wholesale trade, but the one at 5 S. Wabash Ave. opens its doors to customers off the street. There's a mall-like retail space on the ground floor crammed with tiny booths manned by smooth-talking reps hawking their wares. You can grab a map here for a self-guided tour of the rest of the building's tenants. It's quite an experience because many of the booths are closet-size cubbyholes with hunched-over geezers who look as if they've been eyeballing solitaire and marquise cuts since the Roosevelt administration—Teddy, that is.

teens, however, might well enjoy browsing here and taking in the neighborhood's artsy vibe.

The River North gallery season officially gets underway on the first Friday after Labor Day in September. Besides fall, another great time to visit the district is from mid-July to August, when the Chicago Art Dealers Association presents **Vision,** an annual lineup of programs tailored to the public. Early September also offers the annual **Around the Coyote** festival in Wicker Park/Bucktown (© 773/342-6777 for information), when scores of artists open their studios to the public (the name refers to the now-departed Coyote Gallery, which used to stand at the corner of Damen and North aves.).

The *Chicago Reader,* a free weekly newspaper available at many stores, taverns, and cafes on the North Side, publishes a comprehensive listing of current gallery exhibitions, as does the quarterly *Chicago Gallery News* (www.chicagogallerynews.com), which is available free at the city's three visitor information centers. Another good resource is the **Chicago Art Dealers Association** (© 312/649-0065; www.chicagoartdealers.org); the group's website has descriptions of all member galleries. For descriptions of the city's top galleries, see "Art Galleries" under "Shopping A to Z," below.

Along with its status as Chicago's primary art-gallery district, River North—the area west of the Magnificent Mile and north of the Chicago River—has attracted many interesting home-design shops concentrated on Wells Street from Kinzie Street to Chicago Avenue. My favorites include **Manifesto,** 755 N. Wells St., at Chicago Avenue (© 312/664-0733), which offers custom-designed furniture, as well as imports from Italy and elsewhere in Europe; **Mig & Tig,** 540 N. Wells St., at Ohio Street (© 312/644-8277), a charming furniture and decorative-accessories shop; and **Lightology,** 215 W. Chicago Ave., at Wells Street (© 312/944-1000), a massive lighting store that carries a mind-boggling array of funky lamps, chandeliers, and glowing orbs from more than 400 manufacturers (even if you have no intention of flying home with a stack of lamps in your luggage, it's fun to browse).

Looming above the Chicago River at the southern end of River North is the **Merchandise Mart,** the world's largest commercial building. The massive complex was built in 1930 by Marshall Field & Company and was bought in 1945 by Joseph P. Kennedy (JFK's dad); the Kennedy family ran the Mart until the late 1990s. Now the building houses mostly interior design showrooms, which are open only to professional designers. One exception is **Luxe Home,** a collection of kitchen and bath showrooms on the first floor, all of which are open to the public (and worth a look for interior design junkies). Public tours of the whole complex are offered once a week, usually on Fridays ($12 adults; ℂ **312/527-7762** for dates and reservations).

Lincoln Park

I highly recommend shopping with kids in leafy Lincoln Park. Sidewalks are filled with parents and strollers on a weekend afternoon, giving this North Side neighborhood a warm, family vibe. Here you'll find a variety of specialty shops, most of which are found on the neighborhood's main commercial arteries: Armitage Avenue, Webster Avenue, Halsted Street, Clark Street, and Lincoln Avenue.

For kids, the highest concentration of stores is found on **Armitage Avenue** and **Halsted Street,** which form one of the finest 19th-century neighborhood commercial streetscapes remaining in Chicago. The district contains an excellent cross section of residential and commercial building types significant in the development of such streets, including small residential buildings and larger, multistory mixed-use buildings, and is especially noteworthy for the profusion of pressed-metal decoration, including bays, cornices, and corner turrets on many of the buildings.

Armitage Avenue has emerged as a shopping destination in its own right, thanks to an influx of wealthy young professionals who have settled into historic town homes on the neighboring tree-lined streets. The main shopping district is concentrated between Halsted Street and Racine Avenue; I'd suggest starting at the Armitage El stop (Brown Line) and working your way east to Halsted Street, and then wandering a few blocks north to Webster Street. The shops and boutiques here, which sell everything from artisan-made apparel to interesting, offbeat gifts, are geared toward a sophisticated, well-heeled shopper, and make for great browsing. As you stroll the area, you'll get some sense of its strong community spirit, with neighbors greeting each other and catching up on street corners. To give you a sampling of the number of children's boutiques in this area, clothing stores include **The Second Child, GapKids,** and **LMNOP.** All are covered in detail under "Fashion," later in this chapter.

Lakeview

A few major north-south thoroughfares— Lincoln Avenue, Clark Street, and Broadway— are the main shopping streets in both Lincoln Park (south of Diversey Pkwy.) and Lakeview (north of Diversey). Most of the shops cater to young singles who live in the

---

ⓕinds Pamper Yourself

Mom, you need a little treat for yourself, too—take a break at one of the beauty stores concentrated within a few blocks of each other on Halsted Street. The mood is flashy and hip at **Fresh,** 2040 N. Halsted St. (ℂ **773/404-9776**), where the sleek shelves are filled with skin treatments, at-home spa supplies, and their own line of cosmetics. To get really creative, visit cozy **Aroma Workshop,** 2050 N. Halsted St. (ℂ **773/871-1985**), where you can mix up your own custom-scented body lotions and perfumes. A few blocks south, you can browse the all-natural soaps, creams, and bubble baths at **Lush,** 859 W. Armitage Ave. (ℂ **773/281-LUSH** [281-5874]).

surrounding apartment buildings; you'll find plenty of minimart groceries, some clothing and shoe boutiques, and the occasional used-book store, but not much that's worth a special trip.

SOUTHPORT AVENUE   Shoppers will find elements of both prosperous Lincoln Park and alternative-ish Wicker Park when they're wandering along Lakeview's principal commercial avenue. With the **Music Box Theater** (✆ 773/871-6604) at 3733 N. Southport Ave., north of Addison Street, as its anchor, this gentrifying retail row, popular with the stroller set, has an interesting mix of quirky and artsy merchants and restaurateurs. Start at Roscoe Street and walk north to find a string of hip kids' clothing and toy boutiques. Nearby, on Ashland Avenue, you'll find **Bebe Elegante,** 3338 N. Ashland (btw. Belmont and Addison; ✆ 773/477-2323), and on Lincoln Avenue, **Building Blocks Toy Store,** 3306 N. Lincoln (just north of Belmont; ✆ 773/525-6200).

BELMONT AVENUE & CLARK STREET   Radiating from the intersection of Belmont Avenue and Clark Street is a string of shops catering to rebellious kids on tour from their homes in the 'burbs. (The Dunkin' Donuts on the corner is often referred to as "Punkin' Donuts" in their honor.) If you have preteens or young teens, they will be fascinated by the youth culture, the street life—and the shops.

Alley, 3228 N. Clark St., at Belmont Avenue (✆ 773/883-1800), is an "alternative shopping complex" selling everything from plaster gargoyles to racks of leather jackets. *Warning:* The store has separate shops specializing in condoms, cigars, and bondage wear—you will want to monitor your teens carefully here.

Tragically Hip, a storefront women's boutique at 931 W. Belmont Ave. (✆ 773/549-1500), next to the Belmont El train stop, has outlasted many other similar purveyors of cutting-edge women's apparel.

You can get plugged in to what the kids are reading at **Chicago Comics,** 3244 N. Clark St. (✆ 773/528-1983), considered one of the best comics shops in the country. Besides the usual superhero titles, you'll find lots of European and Japanese comics, along with underground books and 'zines.

Wicker Park/Bucktown

The go-go gentrification of the Wicker Park/Bucktown area has been followed by not only a rash of restaurants and bars, but also retailers with an artsy bent reflecting the neighborhood's bohemian spirit. Mixed in with old neighborhood businesses, such as discount furniture stores and religious-icon purveyors, is a proliferation of antiques-furniture shops, too-cool-for-school clothing boutiques, and eclectic galleries and gift emporiums. Although the neighborhood focus is art, collectibles, and hip adult clothing, you'll find a few kids' stores, including **The Red Balloon Company,** 2060 N. Damen (✆ 773/489-9800; p. 248). For a new twist on custom clothing, stop by **The T-Shirt Deli,** 1739 N. Damen Ave. (✆ 773/276-6266; www.tshirtdeli.com), where you and your kids can order up your own personalized T-shirt creation. Choose from hundreds of vintage logos, add your own lettering, and your shirt will be printed while you wait (and to thrill your kids, the shirt is packaged up in a paper bag with a side of potato chips).

West Division Street

Once home to just a few pioneering restaurants, Division Street is quickly being transformed from a desolate urban landscape to a hot shopping destination. It's a work in progress (you'll still find some boarded-up buildings among the cool boutiques), but for

Teens will get a thrill when you settle down at a local coffeehouse and soak in Wicker Park's artsy vibe. **Earwax Café,** 1564 N. Milwaukee Ave. (© **773/772-4019**), attracts the jaded and pierced set with a no-frills, slightly edgy atmosphere. **Filter,** across the street at 1585 N. Milwaukee Ave. (© **773/227-4850**), is a little more welcoming; comfy couches fill the main dining room, which is adorned with paintings by local artists. Both cafes are near the bustling intersection of North, Milwaukee, and Damen avenues—the heart of Wicker Park—and draw a steady stream of locals. It's here you'll realize that Wicker Park is really just a small town—with cooler hair and funkier shoes.

now this is what Wicker Park used to be: a place where rents are still cheap enough for eager young entrepreneurs.

Start at the Division El stop on the Blue Line, and head west along Division; most stores are concentrated between Milwaukee and Damen avenues (a round-trip walk will take about a half-hour). Along the way, you'll stroll past eclectic clothing and shoe boutiques, bath-and-beauty shops, and home-decor stores such as **Porte Rouge,** 1911 W. Division St. (© **773/269-2800**), which is filled with French antiques and housewares (they'll even offer you a complimentary cup of tea). The mix of people living here—from working-class Latino families to self-consciously edgy young singles—makes the local cafes great for people-watching.

While singles make up most of the population, West Division Street is full of options for kids too, including a **Building Blocks Toy Store** at 2130 W. Division St. (© **773/235-1888**) and **Bullfrogs and Butterflies** (again, toys) at 2124 W. Division St. (© **773/661-1632**).

2 SHOPPING A TO Z

As you might expect, Chicago has shops selling just about anything your kids could want or need, be it functional or ornamental, whimsical or exotic. The following list only scratches the surface, but it will give you an idea of the range of merchandise available.

ARTS & CRAFTS

1154 Lill Studio ★ (Finds) Purse-aholics and wannabe designers will find fashion heaven at this custom-handbag shop. Pick a style (which includes everything from evening purses to diaper bags), and then browse the huge selection of fabrics to create your own custom interior and exterior. Your finished creation can be picked up in a few weeks or shipped to your home. Not feeling particularly creative? There's also a selection of premade bags. Personal handbag parties can be arranged for groups of five or more. 904 W. Armitage Ave. (at Fremont St.). © 773/477-LILL (477-5455). Subway/El: Brown Line to Armitage.

Pearl Art and Craft Supplies Graphic designers, artists, and arts and crafts aficionados flock to Pearl for every art supply known on earth. If you need to pick up supplies for a rainy-day project, you'll love Pearl. 255 W. Chicago Ave. (at Franklin St.). © 312/915-0200. www.pearlpaint.com. Subway/El: Brown Line to Chicago.

Barbara's Bookstore   This haven for small, independent press titles also has extensive selections of everything current. In addition, it has a well-stocked children's section, with sitting areas for the tots to peruse the books. If you enjoy author readings, call the store to see if your visit coincides with that of one of your favorite writers. There are a total of five Chicago-area branches, including one on the lower level at Macy's. 111 N. State St., lower level (℃ 312/781-3033; www.barbarasbookstore.com), and in the Sears Tower, 233 S. Wacker Dr., Lower Level 1 (℃ 312/466-0223).

Barnes & Noble   This two-level store is cozily situated on a lovely curving shopping street, and has a street-level cafe, in case you get the munchies while perusing the miles of books. Check out postings for readings, book groups, and other special events. The children's section offers easy access to picture books, first readers, and young-adult books, plus cozy reading nooks. There's another store in the Merchandise Mart, Suite 204 (℃ 312/329-1881), in Lincoln Park, at 659 W. Diversey Ave., 1 block west of Clark Street (℃ 773/871-9004), and one at 1441 W. Webster Ave., at Clybourn Avenue (℃ 773/871-3610). 1130 N. State St. (at Elm St.). ℃ 312/280-8155. Subway/El: Red Line to Clark/Division.

Borders   You couldn't ask for a better location, right across from Water Tower Place. Head to the lower level for the kids' section, which features a particularly impressive collection of picture books. There are carpeted platforms for sitting and perusing. This place is like a mini–department store, with books, magazines, CDs, and computer software spread over four floors, and a cafe with a view overlooking the Mag Mile. There are also author readings, book signings, and other special events. There's also a Borders in the Loop at 150 N. State St., at Randolph Street (℃ 312/606-0750); one at North and Halsted, at 755 W. North Ave. (℃ 312/266-8060); one in Lincoln Park at 2817 N. Clark St., at Diversey Avenue (℃ 773/935-3909); and one in Uptown, 4718 N. Broadway (℃ 773/334-7338). 830 N. Michigan Ave. (at Pearson St.). ℃ 312/573-0564. Subway/El: Red Line to Chicago.

Unabridged Books   This quintessential neighborhood bookseller in the area known as Boys Town carries strong sections in gay and lesbian literature, travel, film, and sci-fi. Perhaps surprisingly, it's also known for its extensive collection of children's books. 3251 N. Broadway (btw. Belmont Ave. and Addison St.). ℃ 773/883-9119. Subway/El: Red Line to Addison.

Women & Children First   This feminist and children's bookstore holds the best selection in the city of titles for, by, and about women. Co-owner Linda Bubon holds a children's storybook hour every Wednesday at 10:30am; several book groups meet regularly as well, including one for mothers and daughters. The store also hosts frequent readings by the likes of Gloria Steinem, Amy Tan, Alice Walker, and Naomi Wolf. 5233 N. Clark St. (btw. Foster and Bryn Mawr aves.). ℃ 773/769-9299. Subway/El: Red Line to Berwyn.

DEPARTMENT STORES

Barneys New York   The first Midwest outpost of Barneys has the same look and feel of the New York original: minimalist-chic decor, high-priced fashions, and a fair amount of attitude from the sales staff. That said, the store has a stellar—if high-priced—shoe selection, along with always-interesting home accessories and a fun-to-browse cosmetics area full of specialty beauty products. In Lincoln Park, not far from the Armitage Avenue shopping district, you'll find **Barneys Co-Op,** 2209–11 N. Halsted St., at Webster Street

(📞 **773/248-0426**), which features collections from younger, up-and-coming designers—and lots of denim. 25 E. Oak St. (at Rush St.). 📞 **312/587-1700**. www.barneys.com. Sub-
way/El: Red Line to Chicago.

Bloomingdale's   The first Midwestern branch of the famed New York department
store, Bloomingdale's is on par in terms of size and selection with Macy's Water Tower
store. The sixth floor features kids' clothing. 900 N. Michigan Ave. (at Walton St.). 📞 **312/440-
4460**. Subway/El: Red Line to Chicago.

Macy's ★★★   When Macy's took over Marshall Field's—Chicago's best-known
"hometown" department store—in 2006, there was much local hand-wringing about
what the buyout meant for Field's grand State Street headquarters. Although Field's
iconic green awnings and shopping bags have been replaced by Macy's more dreary black,
the good news is that the store itself remains impressive, a testament to the days when
shopping downtown was an eagerly anticipated event rather than a chore. Now redubbed
Macy's on State Street, this block-long store is second in size only to Macy's New York
City flagship, and its impressive breadth of merchandise and historically significant interior make it a must-see for serious shoppers. A number of exclusive "miniboutiques" are
scattered throughout the overwhelming space, including the 28 Shop, which stocks the
latest from hot young designers; beauty stations where you can get a manicure and pick
up exclusive products; and a gourmet food department developed by celebrity chef Charlie Trotter. The enormous shoe department is another highlight, selling everything from
killer high heels (at killer prices) and boots to sneakers and casual sandals.

The Water Tower store, 835 N. Michigan Ave. (📞 **312/335-7700**), is a scaled-down but
respectable version of the State Street store. Its eight floors are actually much more manageable than the enormous flagship, and its merchandise selection is still vast (although this
branch tends to focus on the more expensive brands). 111 N. State St. (at Randolph St.).
📞 **312/781-1000**. www.macys.com. Subway/El: Red Line to Washington.

Neiman Marcus   Yes, you'll pay top dollar for designer names here—after all, the
store must live up to its "Needless Mark-ups" moniker—but Neiman's has a broader
price range than many of its critics care to admit. It also has some mighty good sales. The
four-story store, a beautiful environment in its own right, also sells cosmetics, shoes, furs,
fine and fashion jewelry, and menswear and children's wear. On the top floor is the children's department, plus a fun gourmet-food department and a pretty home-accessories
area. Neiman's has two restaurants: one relaxed, the other a little more formal. 737 N.
Michigan Ave. (btw. Superior St. and Chicago Ave.). 📞 **312/642-5900**. Subway/El: Red Line to
Chicago Ave.

Nordstrom   Nordstrom's spacious, airy design and trendy touches (wheat grass growing by the escalators, funky music playing on the stereo system) give it the feel of an
upscale boutique rather than an overcrowded department store. Kids' clothing is found
on the third floor, with a nice selection of clothing and gifts for infants through teens.
The selection of children's shoes is extensive. In the cosmetics department, you'll find a
wide array of smaller labels and an "open sell" environment (meaning you're encouraged
to try on makeup without a salesperson hovering over you). In keeping with the store's
famed focus on service, a concierge can check your coat, call a cab, or make restaurant
reservations. If you need a lift, Cafe Nordstrom offers a shopping break, with salads and
sandwiches. Set up cafeteria-style, the restaurant also features a Kid's Cafe. The bathrooms, one on each level, have infant-changing areas and women's lounges equipped with
upholstered chairs where you can comfortably and semiprivately nurse an infant. The

Shops at North Bridge, 55 E. Grand Ave. (at Rush St.). © **312/379-4300.** www.nordstrom.com. Subway/El: Red Line to Grand.

Saks Fifth Avenue Saks Fifth Avenue might be best known for its designer collections—Valentino, Chloe, and Giorgio Armani, to name a few—but the store also does a decent job of buying more casual and less-expensive merchandise. Check out, for example, Saks's own Real Clothes or The Works women's lines. Plus, the store has very good large-size and petite women's apparel departments. The children's department has a variety of casual and dress clothes, as well as a few stuffed animals. The men's department is in a separate building across Michigan Avenue. Don't forget to visit the cosmetics department, where Saks is known, in particular, for its varied fragrance selection. Chicago Place, 700 N. Michigan Ave. (at Superior St.). © **312/944-6500.** www.saksfifthavenue. com. Subway/El: Red Line to Chicago/State.

DOLLS & DOLLHOUSES

Think Small If your child dreams of building (in other words, dreams of having mom and dad build) a dollhouse, you'll find everything you need here. Sometimes the path of least resistance is best: In that case, check out the ready-made dollhouses that are available for purchase. You can also buy the dolls and furniture that will reside in the house. For those ambitious enough to build their child's dream house themselves, the store offers workshops on Wednesday, Thursday, Saturday, and Sunday. You can drop in, but it might be a good idea to call ahead before you go. The fee is about $80, and includes the use of tools and paintbrushes, paper goods, wood glue, and cleaning materials. 3209 N. Clark St. (at W. Belmont St.). © **773/477-1920.** Subway/El: Red Line to Belmont.

FASHION

Abercrombie & Fitch The cool "uniform" of preference for middle school kids is anything Abercrombie. Clothes here are pricey but well made, and if you break down and buy just a T-shirt, it shouldn't break your budget. Water Tower Place, 849 Michigan Ave. © **312/274-9859.** www.abercrombie.com. Subway/El: Red Line to Chicago/State.

Alcala's Do your kids dream of the open range? Here's just the spot to help them look the part. Cowboy hats, boots, shirts, jeans, and chaps for miniature cowpokes are the focus at Alcala's. And to prove that you're never too young to start appreciating the Wild West, soft leather booties get even the littlest cowpokes off to the right start. 1733 W. Chicago Ave. (at Wood St.). © **312/226-0152.** www.alcalas.com.

Anthropologie Eclectic and funky clothes that appeal to the young teen set and up (sorry, females only) and a mix of new and vintage home furnishings and accessories make this store a delight to browse. 1120 N. State St. © **312/255-1848.** www.anthropologie. com. Subway/El: Red Line to Clark/Division.

GapKids and babyGap Classic and fun, although definitely not avant-garde, Gap produces reliable clothes and accessories for kids. Inventory turns quickly here, so it's easy to pick up a few things on sale. The store has four locations in Chicago. The largest store is at 555 N. Michigan Ave., where you'll find a large kids and baby section on the lower level. (1) 555 N. Michigan Ave. (at E. Ohio St.). © **312/335-1896.** Subway/El: Red Line to Grand/ State. (2) 1740 N. Sheffield (at W. Webster St.). © **312/944-6742.** Subway/El: Red Line to Sheffield. (3) 3216 N. Broadway Ave. (at W. Wellington St.). © **773/929-4085.** Subway/El: Brown Line to Diversey. (4) 3155 N. Lincoln Ave. (at W. Barry St.). © **773/883-9050.** Subway/El: Brown Line to Wellington.

Grow For a look at the future of baby style, trek out to this trendy boutique in the up-and-coming West Division Street neighborhood. The bright, open space showcases streamlined, ultramodern kids' furniture (such as bubble-shaped high chairs that would look right at home on *The Jetsons*), as well as clothing made of organic fabrics. Sure, many of the environmentally friendly products on display are out of most parents' price range, but families that have had their fill of plastic kiddy gear will have fun browsing here. 1943 W. Division St. (at Damen Ave.). ☏ 773/489-0009. Subway/El: Blue Line to Division.

Gymboree Bright colors and strong patterns are the trademark of Gymboree clothing. You'll find items here for infants up to age 7. The chain also runs play centers (see "Indoor Playgrounds," in chapter 8). Clybourn Galleria, 1845 N. Clybourn ☏ 773/525-2080. www.gymboree.com. Subway/El: Red Line to Clybourn.

LMNOP Nothing ordinary about the children's clothing you'll find here, for ages newborn to 6 years. 2570 N. Lincoln Ave. (at Sheffield Ave.). ☏ 773/975-4055. Subway/El: Red or Brown Line to Fullerton.

Madison and Friends When Chicago parents with a money's-no-object attitude go shopping for special-occasion clothing for kids, they make a beeline for Madison and Friends. The selection is top-of-the-line, the inventory large and unique. You'll find baby-size leather jackets and yoga pants for toddlers. A separate back room caters to older kids and 'tweens—with a staggering array of jeans. You can find clothing here for kids from newborn to size 16. 940 N. Rush St. (at Oak St.). ☏ 312/642-6403. www.madisonandfriends. com. Subway/El: Red Line to Chicago.

Mini Me This store specializes in European-style clothing for girls from infant to age 10 and boys up to size 4. In the mall at 900 N. Michigan Ave. ☏ 312/988-4011. Subway/El: Red Line to Chicago/State.

Oilily Kids Even if you don't mix plaids and florals on a daily basis (a trademark of this designer), just one of Oilily's distinctive and colorful items can perk up a wardrobe from infant to size 12. Clothes are the focus, but some accessories like quilts and backpacks are also offered. To keep kids happy while you shop, rolling wooden chairs and blocks are on hand. The Shops at North Bridge, 520 N. Michigan Ave. ☏ 312/527-5747. Subway/ El: Red Line to State/Grand.

Old Navy ⟨**Value**⟩ The lower-priced relative of Gap carries an extensive collection of kids' clothes, from infants and up. Sales here are fantastic—and frequent. Clothes are trendy and stylish. The collection for boys is great, a refreshing change for moms who are frustrated with the ho-hum choices available at most stores. The store has three Chicago locations. The biggest and best is the State Street location. (1) 35 N. State St. (at E. Washington St.). ☏ 312/551-0523. Subway: Brown, Purple, Green, or Orange Line to Randolph/Wabash and walk 1 block south and 1 block west; or Red Line to Washington/State. (2) 1596 W. Kingsbury (at North Ave.). ☏ 312/397-0624. Subway/El: Red Line to Clybourn. (3) 1730 W. Fullerton Ave. (at N. Clybourn Ave.). ☏ 773/871-0613. Subway/El: Red Line to Fullerton.

Psycho Baby The opening of this everything-for-baby shop is a definitive sign that Bucktown has gentrified. The prices may sometimes cause a double take ($60 for shoes that your kid will outgrow in 3 months), but the creative selection and happy vibe make it fun for browsing. 1630 N. Damen Ave. (1 block north of North Ave.). ☏ 773/772-2815. www. psychobabyonline.com. Subway/El: Blue Line to Damen.

The Second Child ⟨**Value**⟩ This consignment store sells children's clothing for infants through size 14, plus toys, furniture, and equipment for kids (and maternity clothes if

Tips From Chicago with Love

Need to bring some Chicago gifts home for friends and family? With more national chain stores hitting town, it's getting harder to find distinctive, only-in-Chicago souvenirs. Here are some unique ideas:

- The **Archicenter Shop,** at 224 S. Michigan Ave. ((C) **312/922-3432;** www. architecture.org), sells some of the coolest gifts in town. This bright, sleek shop is part of the Chicago Architecture Foundation, so everything in stock—including toys, photography books, tour guides, and stationery—has a definite sense of style. Whether you're in the market for a $900 reproduction of a vase from Frank Lloyd Wright's Robie House or a more affordable black-and-white photo of the city skyline, it's well worth stopping in.

- The *Chicago Tribune* store, at 435 N. Michigan Ave. ((C) **312/222-3080**), has your standard tourist selection (CHICAGO emblazoned on everything from shirts to shot glasses). But this is also a good place to pick up Cubs memorabilia (the Tribune Company owns the team), along with books from some of the city's top journalists. You can also order reproductions of the *Tribune*'s front page or color prints of photos from the newspaper's archives.

- **Sports Authority,** at 620 N. LaSalle St. ((C) **312/337-6151**), is the largest sporting-goods store in the city, and the best place to find jerseys and hats from Chicago's other pro sports teams. The victorious Jordan years might be behind us, but his shirts still sell well here.

- **City of Chicago Store,** in the Water Works Visitor Center, right off of Michigan Avenue at 163 E. Pearson St. ((C) **312/742-8811**), is a convenient stop for Chicago-related souvenirs and gifts, including truly one-of-a-kind pieces of retired municipal equipment (although the parking meters I've seen for sale here might be a little difficult to stuff into your suitcase).

- **The Savvy Traveller,** at 310 S. Michigan Ave., at Van Buren Street ((C) **312/913-9800;** www.thesavvytraveller.com), is where smart travelers buy their gear. This Loop specialty store carries just about everything a traveler might need, from maps to rain gear to games that keep the kids occupied on long car trips.

you've got another on the way). Yes, the merchandise is secondhand, but thanks to the store's location in the tony Lincoln Park neighborhood, it's *upscale* secondhand. You'll find name brands and excellent quality. The store ensures that its collection of furniture and equipment meets current safety standards. Lock your stroller just outside the building and take the stairs up. 954 W. Armitage (just east of N. Sheffield Ave.). (C) **773/883-0880.** www.2ndchild.com. Subway/El: Red Line to Sheffield.

Urban Outfitters Fun, funky, and offbeat clothing and accessories, from beanbag chairs to trendy clothing and glittery nail polish, sure to please young teens. There's a second location in Lincoln Park, at 2352 N. Clark St. ((C) **773/549-1711**). 935 N. Rush St. (at Walton St.). (C) **312/640-1919.** www.urbanoutfitters.com. Subway/El: Red Line to Chicago/State.

Ash's Magic Shop Mr. Ash, a real-life magician with a love of his craft, stocks his shop with tricks, jokes, books, and videos that will make you believe in magic, too. 4955 N. Western Ave. (at W. Argyle). www.ashs-magic.com. © 773/271-4030. Subway/El: Brown Line to Western.

Fantasy Costumes (Finds) Not exactly a toy store, this sprawling costume shop (covering an entire city block) is nonetheless devoted to make-believe and is just as fun. The store stocks more than a million items, including 800 styles of masks (priced $1–$200) and all the accessories and makeup needed to complete any costume. There's also a full-service wig salon here. 4065 N. Milwaukee Ave. (west of Cicero Ave.). © 773/777-0222. www.fantasycostumes.com. Subway/El: Blue Line to Irving Park.

Uncle Fun (Finds) Uncle Fun and his staff travel the world to bring home bobbing-head figurines, accordions, and stink bombs from all corners of the earth—for the sole purpose of tickling your fancy. Bins and cubbyholes are stuffed full of the standard joke toys (rubber-chicken key chains and chattering windup teeth), but you'll also find every conceivable modern pop-culture artifact, from Jackson Five buttons to demon-on-wheels *Speed Racer*'s Mach-Five model car. 1338 W. Belmont Ave. (near Southport Ave.). © 773/477-8223. www.unclefunchicago.com. Subway/El: Red or Brown Line to Belmont.

MUSIC

Beat Parlor If the idea of hanging out with local DJs appeals to your kids, then Beat Parlor is your place. In the city where house music was born, Howard Bailey's Bucktown shop sells lots of it, plus plenty of hip-hop and local DJs' mix tapes, on CD and vinyl. The store's two turntables are always in use by cutters checking out new merchandise. 1653 N. Damen Ave. (btw. North and Wabansia aves.). © 773/395-CUTS (395-2887). Subway/El: Blue Line to Damen.

Blue Chicago Store (Finds) Here's one that's near and dear to my blues-loving heart—a store that's dedicated to teaching kids about the blues. America's original contribution to the world of music, and the basis for jazz and rock 'n' roll, is alive and thriving in Chicago. Treat your kids to a stop here, pick up some books, and maybe even plan to attend the Saturday-night dance-athons that are open to all ages. 534 N. Clark (at W. Grand Ave.). © 312/661-1003. www.bluechicago.com. Subway/El: Red Line to State/Grand.

Dusty Groove America In 1996, using a rickety old PC, Rick Wojcik and John Schauer founded an online record store, www.dustygroove.com. Since then, the operation has expanded in both cyberspace and the real world. Dusty Groove covers a lot of ground, selling soul, funk, jazz, Brazilian, lounge, Latin, and hip-hop music on new and used vinyl and all new CDs. For the most part, selections are either rare or imported, or both. 1120 N. Ashland Ave. (1 block south of Division St.). © 773/342-5800. Subway/El: Blue Line to Division.

Guitar Center When your kids are, oh, somewhere around age 12 and decide it's time to start their own garage band, you'll need to find the one store that can satisfy their needs. Guitar Center is it: Your kids can check out the keyboards, music software, recording equipment, dance-music gear, drums, amplifiers, basses, acoustic guitars, accessories, and vintage instruments. 2633 N. Halsted (at Diversey). © 773/248-2808. www.guitarcenter.com. Subway/El: Brown Line to Wellington.

Jazz Record Mart (Finds) This is possibly the best jazz record store in the country. It's so cool, even your disenchanted teenager will love it, despite herself. The first of four rooms houses the "Killers Rack," a display of albums that the store's owners consider essential to any jazz collection. In addition to jazz, there are bins filled with blues, Latin, and "New Music"; the albums in the record rooms are filed alphabetically and by category (vocals, big band, and so on), and there are a couple of turntables to help you spend wisely. Jazz Record Mart also features a stage, with seating for 50, where local and national artists coming through town entertain with in-store performances. 27 E. Illinois St. (btw. Wabash Ave. and State St.). ✆ **312/222-1467.** Subway/El: Red Line to Grand.

Little Strummer   Located in the Old Town School of Folk Music, which offers music classes for children, this compact store stocks every kind of mini-instrument imaginable, from accordions and guitars to wind chimes and music boxes. There's also a good selection of music-related games and kids' CDs. 909 W. Armitage Ave. (at Halsted St.). ✆ **773/751-3410.** Subway/El: Brown Line to Armitage.

New Sound Gospel   Chicago is the birthplace of gospel music, and now, thanks to artists such as Kirk Franklin, it has also become big business. All the major labels have gospel music divisions, and this store on the city's far South Side is the best place in town to browse the full range of what's available. Not sure where to start? Ask the store's expert staff for advice—here's where you'll find everything from gospel's greatest to groups with names such as Gospel Gangstaz. 10723 S. Halsted St. (✆ **773/785-8001**). Subway/El: Red Line to 95th/Dan Ryan, then 108 Halsted bus to 107th St.

Reckless Records   The best all-around record store for music that the cool kids listen to, Reckless Records wins Brownie points for its friendly and helpful staff. You'll find new and used CDs and albums in a variety of genres (psychedelic and progressive rock, punk, soul, and jazz) here, along with 'zines and a small collection of DVDs. There are also locations in Wicker Park, at 1532 N. Milwaukee Ave. (✆ **773/235-3727**), and the Loop, 26 E. Madison St. (✆ **312/795-0878**). 3157 N. Broadway (at Belmont Ave.). ✆ **773/404-5080.** Subway/El: Red or Brown Line to Belmont.

SHOES

Piggy Toes   European makers are featured in this boutique's selection of shoes, sandals, and boots, plus hats, socks, tights, and other accessories. Shoe sizes for infants through children's size 6. 2205 N. Halsted (at W. Belden Ave.). ✆ **773/281-5583.** www.ptoes.com. Subway: Brown Line to Armitage.

Steve Madden ⟨Value⟩   Funky and inexpensive, Steve Madden specializes in the platform, chunky-heel style of shoe. Your teenage daughter probably covets Steve Maddens already. Boys' styles are appearing in the store as well, although it's still female-dominated territory. Most styles start at size 5. When a sale is on, you can sometimes pick up a pair for as little as $15. Water Tower Place, 845 N. Michigan Ave. ✆ **312/440-1590.** www.stevemadden.com. Subway/El: Red Line to Chicago/State.

SHOWER & BABY GIFTS

The Red Balloon Company ⟨Finds⟩   This creative little shop in the trendy Wicker Park neighborhood sells casual clothes for infants through age 8, hand-painted furniture, linens, and books. It's a great place to find a special gift. Children's classic books such as *The Red Balloon, The Lonely Doll,* and *Mike Mulligan and His Steam Shovel* are displayed atop decoupaged bedroom furnishings. There are lots of vintage-inspired items, too, including Pinecone Hill reversible blankets, caps, and burp cloths. The store features antiques and one-of-a-kind pieces. If there's a furniture item you want made, just ask the staff—some items can be custom-made. A second location is found in Andersonville, at 5407 N. Clark (at Balmoral; ✆ 773/989-8500). 2060 N. Damen Ave. (at W. Armitage Ave.). ✆ 773/489-9800. www.theredballoon.com. Subway/El: Blue Line to Damen.

SPORTS STUFF

Fleet Feet Sports (Finds)   This store, owned by a former banker who decided to follow his love of running to create a new business, is a wonderful place to buy shoes for little athletes. Although running is the forte here, you can buy all types of athletic shoes. The staff is made up of athletes who can relate when you complain about your sore Achilles—and better yet, they can find a pair of shoes that will help. You'll even get a chance to hop on a treadmill to get your running gait videotaped. The staff will assess your style and bring you a variety of shoes to try. (**Note:** Don't ask to try on a pair of shoes simply because you like the color. That request is sure to get you a disapproving look!) There's a second location in the Lincoln Square neighborhood, at 4555 N. Lincoln (✆ 773/271-3338). 1620 N. Wells St. (at North Ave., in the Pipers Alley complex). ✆ 312/587-3338. www.fleetfeetchicago.com. Subway/El: Brown Line to Sedgwick.

Kozy's Cyclery   A Chicago favorite, this third-generation family-owned business has been selling and servicing bikes for 56 years. You'll find name brands, a vast collection of accessories, and store personnel with opinions you can trust. If you're a Chicago resident, you can count on complete servicing for your bikes, and the staff will connect you with all kinds of cycling resources. Check out Kozy's online catalog (www.kozy.com), complete with photos, to get an idea of what the shop carries. (For out-of-towners, shipping is available.) The store has four locations. (1) 601 S. LaSalle (at W. Harrison St.). ✆ 312/360-0020. Subway/El: Blue Line to LaSalle. (2) 1451 W. Webster (at N. Clybourn Ave.). ✆ 773/528-2700. Subway/El: Brown Line to Armitage. (3) 3712 N. Halsted (at W. Waveland Ave.). ✆ 773/281-2263. (4) 219 W. Erie. ✆ 312/266-1700. Subway/El: Red Line to Addison.

Momentum   This store takes running seriously, but you don't have to be a marathoner to shop here. The knowledgeable sales staff takes the time to find the shoe that's right for you, no matter what your fitness level. The store also stocks running apparel and accessories as well as swimwear. 2001 N. Clybourn Ave. (btw. North and Fullerton aves.). ✆ 773/525-7866. Subway/El: Brown Line to Armitage.

 Pop On In

Across the street from Niketown, you'll probably see a line of people trailing out from the **Garrett Popcorn Shop,** 670 N. Michigan Ave. (✆ 312/944-2630), a 50-year-old landmark. Join the locals in line and pick up some caramel corn for a quick sugar rush.

Niketown   When Niketown opened some 10 years ago, it was truly something new: a store that felt more like a funky sports museum than a place hawking running shoes. In the days when Michael Jordan was the city's reigning deity, Niketown was the place to bask in his glory. These days Niketown is no longer unique to Chicago (it has sprung up in cities from Atlanta to Honolulu), and the store's celebration of athletes can't cover up the fact that the ultimate goal is to sell expensive shoes. But the crowds keep streaming in—and snatching up products pitched by Niketown's patron saints, Michael Jordan and Tiger Woods. 669 N. Michigan Ave. ✆ 312/642-6363. Subway/El: Red Line to Grand.

SHOPPING WITH YOUR KIDS

9

SHOPPING A TO Z

Sports Authority   The largest sporting-goods store in the city, the flagship store of this chain offers seven floors of merchandise, from running apparel to camping gear. Sports fans will be in heaven in the first- and fifth-floor team merchandise departments, where Cubs, Bulls, and Sox jerseys abound. Cement handprints of local sports celebs dot the outside of the building; step inside to check out the prints from Michael Jordan and former White Sox slugger Frank Thomas. 620 N. LaSalle St. (at Ontario St.). © 312/337-6151. Subway/El: Red Line to Grand.

STROLLERS, CRIBS & FURNITURE

Bellini   Outfitting your dream nursery? Head to this high-end boutique for furniture with Italian design and a distinctly contemporary flair. (And even if some prices are a bit out of your budget stratosphere, you'll at least find inspiration.) Cribs, changing tables, armoires, and rocking chairs are on offer, plus items to achieve just the right decor. Clothing and accessories for baby top off the selection here. 1800 N. Clybourn. © 312/981-6301. www.bellini.com. Subway/El: Brown Line to Fullerton.

The Right Start   Gadgets for babies and toddlers and sanity-saving devices such as bouncers, swings, and ExerSaucers are the focus here. If Junior is suddenly up and walking and you need to baby-proof your home, this store is your source for gates, electrical-outlet covers, and cabinet locks. It's a chain, but you can't beat the convenience of being able to buy so many gadgets in one location. 2121 N. Clybourn Ave. (at N. Wayne St. in the Market Square Shopping Center). © 773/296-4420. www.therightstart.com. Subway/El: Brown Line to Armitage.

SWEETS FOR THE SWEET

Bittersweet   Run by Judy Contino, one of the city's top pastry chefs and bakers of all things sweet and sinful, this Lakeview cafe and shop is sought out by brides-to-be and trained palates who have a yen for gourmet cakes, cookies, tarts, and ladyfingers. The rich chocolate mousse cake, a specialty of the house, is out of this world. 1114 W. Belmont Ave. © 773/929-1100. Subway/El: Red Line to Belmont.

Ethel's Chocolate Lounge   A celebration of all things chocolate, this bright, candy-colored cafe has a distinctly feminine vibe; I have yet to see a group of guys huddling on one of the hot-pink couches (although I have taken my young sons and they don't seem to mind, as long as there's hot chocolate involved!). But what better way to catch up with a girlfriend than over a selection of gourmet truffles or a pot of hot chocolate? The chocolates are a tad pricey—more than a dollar per piece—but they run the range from espresso-flavored truffles to the "Etheltini" (a dark-chocolate square spiked with vodka and dry vermouth). Ethel's also has locations inside the 900 North Michigan Avenue mall (© 312/440-9747) and along the Armitage Avenue shopping strip, 819 W. Armitage Ave. (© 773/281-0029). 520 N. Michigan Ave. (inside the Westfield North Bridge mall). © 312/464-9330. www.ethelschocolate.com. Subway/El: Red Line to Grand.

Ghirardelli Chocolate Shop & Soda Fountain   This Midwest outpost of the famed San Francisco chocolatier, just half a block off the Mag Mile, gets swamped in the summer, but they've got their soda-fountain assembly line down to a science. In addition to the incredible hot-fudge sundaes, there's a veritable mudslide of chocolate bars, hot-cocoa drink mixes, and chocolate-covered espresso beans to tempt your sweet tooth. 830 N. Michigan Ave. © 312/337-9330. Subway/El: Red Line to Chicago.

Margie's Candies (Value   This family-run candy and ice-cream shop hasn't changed much since it opened in 1921. It still creates some of the city's finest handmade fudge, whether it comes in a box or melted over a banana split served in a clamshell dish. The store is known for its turtles—chocolate-covered pecan and caramel clusters—and may be the only place in the city still selling rock candy on wooden sticks. 1960 N. Western Ave. (just north of Armitage Ave.). © 773/384-1035. Subway/El: Blue Line to Western.

Sweet Thang When bopping around Wicker Park's boutiques and quirky shops, don't miss Bernard Runo's Euro-style cafe for a tasty treat to tide you over. Runo, a classically trained pastry chef who has worked in the kitchens of the city's best hotels and learned his trade in France, imports most of the ingredients for his croissants, cookies, tarts, and other pastries from across the pond. The cafe has a laid-back atmosphere, with red distressed walls covered with abstract art and Parisian-style tables and chairs that are set outside in warm weather. 1921 W. North Ave. © 773/772-4166. Subway/El: Blue Line to Damen.

Vosges Haut-Chocolat (Finds) Some of the works of chocolatier Katrina Markoff might be a reach for kids (such as wasabi-flavored truffles), but chocolate bars and the best toffee I've ever tasted are a hit no matter what the age range. Markoff studied at Le Cordon Bleu in Paris and honed her skills throughout Europe and Asia. Her exotic gourmet truffles—with fabulous names such as absinthe, mint julep, wink of the rabbit, woolloomooloo, and ambrosia—are made from premium Belgian chocolate and infused with rare spices, seasonings, and flowers from around the world. The store—which looks more like a modern art gallery than a chocolatier—includes a gourmet-hot-chocolate bar, where you're welcome to sit and sip. Vosges also has a small store on trendy Armitage Avenue (951 W. Armitage Ave.; © 773/296-9866). 520 N. Michigan Ave. (in Shops at North Bridge). © 312/644-9450. Subway/El: Red Line to Grand.

THEME STORES

American Girl Place One of Chicago's hottest family destinations, this two-story doll emporium attracts hordes of young girls (and parents with credit cards at the ready) hooked on the popular mail-order doll company's line of historical character dolls. In its new digs in Water Tower Place (it now occupies two levels of the former Lord & Taylor department store), the new store's cafe is a nice spot for a special mother-daughter lunch or afternoon tea. The view to the north, overlooking a park and the Museum of Contemporary Art, is lovely. Breakfast, lunch, tea, and dinner seatings are available 7 days a week. Reservations are needed for the cafe (call well in advance—2 months is not excessive—to avoid disappointing the American Girl in your life). Brunch is $19, lunch is $21, afternoon tea is $17, and dinner is $22 (all per person). Most notably, the theater has been eliminated from the new store. However, a couple of new features should enchant girls. Don't miss your chance to have your daughter (and her doll) featured on a huge overhead screen near the Chestnut Street entrance. Simply visit the photo studio and, if you choose, you'll instantly be projected onto the screen for all to see. (You can also take home a souvenir issue of *American Girl* magazine with your daughter's photo on the cover.) There's a large book store near the Michigan Avenue entrance. As you progress farther into the store, you'll walk along a storefront area called Avenue AG, with kiosks offering design-it-yourself T-shirts and other products, plus services for your doll (the Doll Hair Salon now offers doll ear piercing in addition to hair styling!). All of the American Girl dolls from different eras of U.S. history, plus their many accessories, are for sale here. Dioramas for each doll change with the seasons. Check the website for a full lineup of special events, from lessons on how to cook like a pro to visits with American Girl book authors. You'll need at least 2 hours to explore the store. If you include a meal in the cafe, this can practically be a full-day activity (for a review of the American Girl Place Cafe, see p. 123). 835 N. Michigan Ave. (C) **877/AG-PLACE** (247-5223). www.americangirlplace.com. Subway/El: Red Line to Chicago/State.

TOYS

Chicago Harbor On breezy days when the wind is just right off of Lake Michigan, stop in to Kite Harbor to pick up a colorful kite. (There are the standard kid-size kites, all the way up to spectacular jumbo kites for the ambitious—or experienced.) The shop stocks all sorts of flying objects, from boomerangs to whirligigs, and even juggling sets. 5445 N. Harlem Ave. (Higgins Rd.). (C) **773/467-1428.** Subway/El: Blue Line to Harlem.

Dorby Magoo & Co. (Finds) What's not to love about a toy store that's laid out like your own home? Kids feel an immediate welcome as they look for toys in the bedroom or books in the library. There's even a living room, den, kitchen, and bathroom. Birthday parties can be scheduled for the dining room and backyard area (complete with AstroTurf "grass" and a ceiling painted to look like the sky). Each section is labeled with an age range, from infants on up, to make gift shopping easy, and there's a stellar collection of arts-and-crafts projects. You'll also find bins of cheap classics like superballs and plastic rings. Gag gifts, like fake prechewed gum and whoopee cushions, are also in abundance. 2744 N. Lincoln Ave. (at W. Diversey Pkwy.). (C) **773/935-2663.** Subway/El: Brown Line to Diversey.

Galt Toys This shop sells its own brand of toys, which are known for their craftsmanship, quality, and design. The staff is especially helpful when you're desperately seeking, say, a few toys to keep a toddler entertained on your flight home. There's a full selection of Baby Einstein DVDs, books, and other products, as well as Chicco brand plastic toys and much, much more. In the mall at 900 N. Michigan Ave. (C) **312/440-9550.** Subway/El: Red Line to Chicago/State.

LEGO Store You'll marvel at replicas of Chicago landmarks, made entirely of LEGOs. Special-edition sets for young builders who want to create huge animals and people are often featured, too. A LEGO Construction Zone just outside of the store lets kids design and build in their own play area with a life-size race car built from LEGO bricks; LEGO walls; and tables. The play zone is open daily from 11am to 5:30pm. The Shops at North Bridge, 520 N. Michigan Ave. (C) **312/494-0760.** www.lego.com. Subway: Red Line to Grand/State.

Timeless Toys From the hardwood floor to its beautifully restored tin ceiling, Timeless Toys Ltd. is packed with items of all kinds. Musical instruments, art supplies, and costumes get kids interested in the arts. The store carries baby toys from brands like Lamaze and Sassy, all the way up to more involved toys for older kids, such as Brio train sets and Plan Toys wooden dollhouses. 4749 N. Lincoln Ave. (at Lawrence). (C) **773/334-4445.** www.timelesstoyschicago.com. Subway: Brown Line to Western.

Toys Et Cetera Tired of mass-market toys? Make a trek to visit this special toy store. Although it's known for its excellent website, you'll have more fun at the real store. The space is small but packed with educational puzzles and games, and toys, toys, toys. (Check out the wide assortment of dolls.) Dress-up clothes and an arts-and-crafts area round out the store. There are also three other Chicago-area locations, at 1502 E. 55th St. in Hyde Park ((C) **773/324-6039**); 2037 N. Clybourn Ave. ((C) **773/348-1772**); and 711 Main St. in north suburban Evanston ((C) **847/475-7172**). 5311 N. Clark St. (at Berwyn Ave.). (C) **773/769-5311.** www.toysetcetera.com. Subway/El: Red Line to Berwyn.

Entertainment for the Whole Family

For most families, showbiz central in Chicago is the North Loop theater district. Particularly along State and Randolph streets, the district is bustling with energy (even after dark). These glorious old theaters host the traveling Broadway productions that attract families. Thanks to extensive renovation efforts, performers have some impressive venues where they can strut their stuff.

Chicago is a regular stop on the big-name entertainment circuit, whether it's the national tour of Broadway shows such as *Rent* and *Cabaret* or pop music acts such as U2, the Dave Matthews Band, or Bruce Springsteen (all of whom sell out multiple nights at stadiums when they come to town). High-profile shows such as Monty Python's *Spamalot* and Mel Brooks's stage version of *The Producers* had their first runs here before moving on to New York.

While Chicago's off-Loop theaters, such as Steppenwolf Theatre, have built their reputations on a gritty style of acting (and a repertoire geared to adults), Chicago has plenty of theater companies that are less avant-garde and more attuned to the younger set. Even the city's blues community sees the wisdom of bringing the next generation into the fold, with special nights that are smoke and alcohol free. In the classical realm, the Chicago Symphony supports a youth symphony. Even Chicago's opera companies make an effort to reach out to kids—so don't count anything out!

FINDING OUT WHAT'S ON Check out *Chicago Parent Magazine* (© 708/386-5555; www.chicagoparent.com) for calendars of upcoming cultural events targeted to kids. You can usually pick up free copies of the magazine at public libraries, bookstores, toy stores, and kids' clothing stores. The City of Chicago has cultural listings on its website at **www.cityof chicago.org/tourism**. For theater, you can't beat **www.chicagoplays.com**, the website for the League of Chicago Theatres. The site links you to more than 130 Chicago-area theaters, and provides an online database of all current and upcoming productions, updated weekly. (They are also categorized so you can look up "children's theater.") The league's Hot Tix website (**www.hottix.org**) has twice-daily posts offering half-price tickets at the seven Chicago-area Hot Tix locations.

Chicago Dance and Music Alliance's website, **www.chicagoperformances.org**, provides listings on performances in these categories: Cultural Center, Ravinia, Grant Park, Dame Myra Hess Memorial Concerts, Jazz, Children's, and Dance. The website also provides a calendar where you can search for events by date.

For up-to-date entertainment listings, check the local newspapers and magazines, particularly on Fridays, when the *Chicago Tribune* and the *Chicago Sun-Times* produce special entertainment sections. The *Chicago Reader* and *New City* are two free weekly tabloids with extensive listings, and the monthly *Chicago* magazine offers entertainment coverage. The *Tribune*'s entertainment-oriented website, **www.metromix. com**, is an excellent source for reviews of cultural events, and the *Reader*'s website, **www.chireader.com**, is known for having

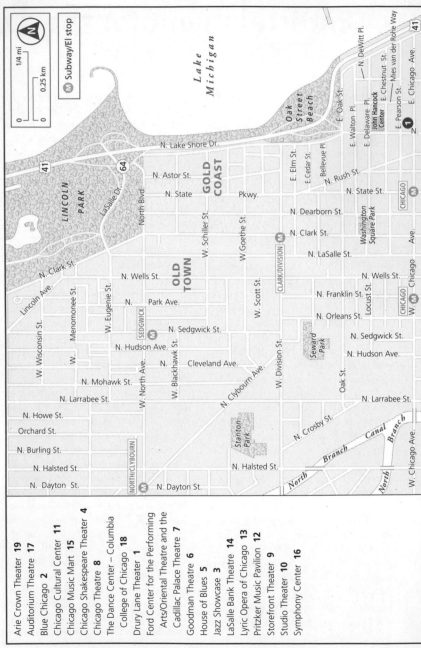

Arie Crown Theater **19**
Auditorium Theatre **17**
Blue Chicago **2**
Chicago Cultural Center **11**
Chicago Music Mart **15**
Chicago Shakespeare Theater **4**
Chicago Theatre **8**
The Dance Center – Columbia
  College of Chicago **18**
Drury Lane Theater **1**
Ford Center for the Performing
  Arts/Oriental Theatre and the
  Cadillac Palace Theatre **7**
Goodman Theatre **6**
House of Blues **5**
Jazz Showcase **3**
LaSalle Bank Theatre **14**
Lyric Opera of Chicago **13**
Pritzker Music Pavilion **12**
Storefront Theater **9**
Studio Theater **10**
Symphony Center **16**

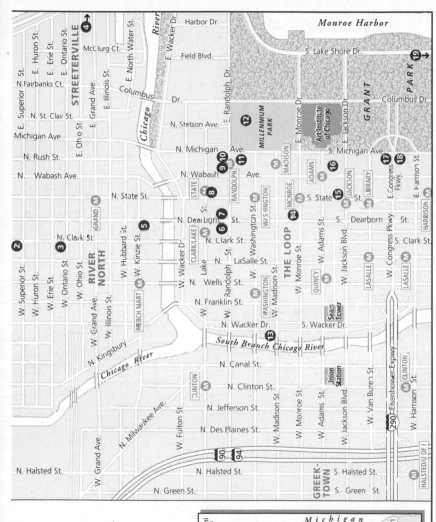

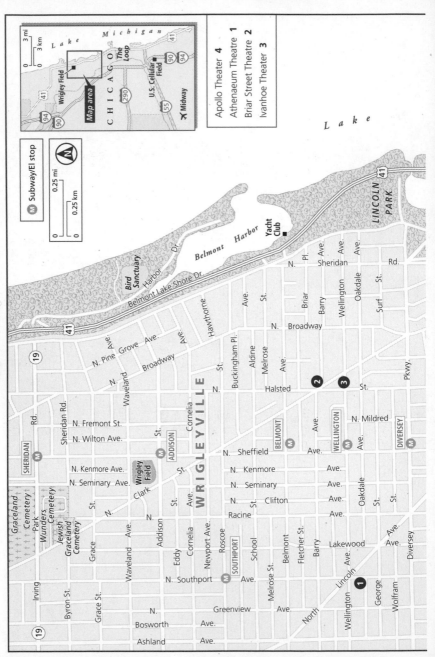

Apollo Theater **4**
Athenaeum Theatre **1**
Briar Street Theatre **2**
Ivanhoe Theater **3**

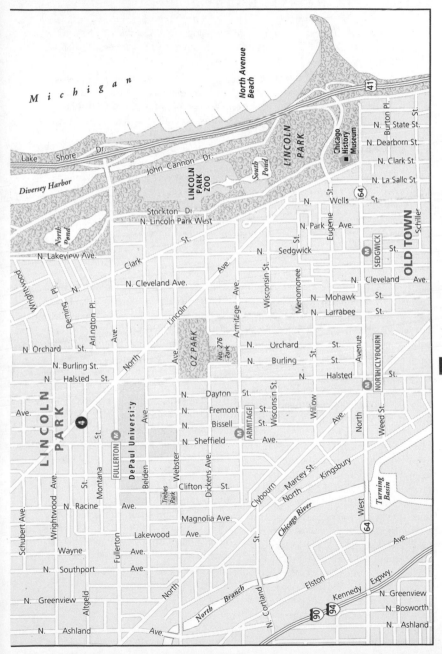

Tips   ## Scoring the Elusive Ticket

Will Junior be crushed if you miss the traveling Broadway show he's been dreaming about seeing? Here are some tips for coming out a hero in your kids' eyes by getting tickets when demand is high:

- Hard-core Chicago theatergoers say the best way to score tickets is to **head right for the box office,** even for a hot show. (This is how I got tickets to *The Producers*—on the day of the show—when it was previewed in Chicago!) Don't phone. This way, you avoid those additional fees—and you will probably get better seats than you would by phone.

- **Use Hot Tix.** In New York plentiful half-price tickets usually means the show is a loser. In Chicago the League of Chicago Theatres expects all its members to offer tickets to its Hot Tix program, whether the show is a hit or a flop.

- **Catch shows while they're still in previews.** Tickets are less expensive and more plentiful. If you want to see the cast in ideal form, get tickets for the final preview, which might coincide with the press opening.

one of the most complete weekly listings of cultural happenings. The local Citysearch website, **http://chicago.citysearch.com**, is also an excellent source of information, with lots of opinionated reviews.

GETTING TICKETS   Why pay full price? **Hot Tix** (www.hottix.org) offers half-price tickets on the day of the show to more than 125 theaters throughout the Chicago area (on Fri, you can also purchase tickets for weekend performances). Tickets are sold Sunday through Thursday for the day of performance. You must buy the tickets in person at a Hot Tix outlet; the main Hot Tix box office is at 72 E. Randolph St., between Wabash and Michigan avenues. If the show you've got your heart set on doesn't have half-price tickets available, never fear: Hot Tix is also a Ticketmaster outlet selling full-price tickets to all Ticketmaster events. A second, smaller Hot Tix outlet is located in the heart of the city's shopping district, in the old pumping station at Michigan and Chicago avenues,

which is now the **Chicago Water Works Visitor Center.** Its entrance is at 163 E. Pearson St., across from the Water Tower Place mall. Hot Tix locations are open 10am to 6pm Tuesday through Saturday, and 11am to 4pm on Sunday. The Hot Tix website (www.hottix.org) lists what's on sale for that day, with frequent updates (the time of the updates is posted at the top of the website).

In addition, a few theaters offer last-minute discounts on their leftover seats. Steppenwolf Theatre Company often has $20 seats available beginning at 11am on the day of a performance; call or stop by the Audience Services at the theater. The "Tix at Six" program at the Goodman Theatre offers half-price, day-of-show tickets; many of them are excellent seats that have been returned by subscribers. Tickets go on sale at the box office at 6pm for evening performances and at noon for matinees.

1 THE BIG VENUES

Arie Crown Theater Musicals and pop acts are the focus here; a renovation has improved what were terrible acoustics (Elton John once interrupted a performance to complain about the sound), but this is still a massive, somewhat impersonal hall, and cheaper seats might well be in nosebleed territory. 2301 S. Lake Shore Dr., in the McCormick Place convention center at 23rd St. and Lake Shore Dr. © 312/791-6190. Bus: 3 or 4.

Auditorium Theatre This beautiful theater is a certified national landmark. Built in 1889 by Louis Sullivan and Dankmar Adler, the grand hall hosts mostly musicals and dance performances. Even if you don't catch a show here, stop by for a tour. The occasional show will appeal to kids, from the Joffrey Ballet of Chicago's *The Nutcracker* to a performance by indie rockers Smashing Pumpkins. 50 E. Congress Pkwy., btw. Michigan and Wabash aves. © 312/922-2110. www.auditoriumtheatre.org. Subway/El: Brown, Green, Orange, or Purple Line to Library/Van Buren, or Red Line to Jackson. Bus: 145, 147, or 151.

Briar Street Theatre Since 1997, the New York City performance phenomenon known as **Blue Man Group** has transformed this 625-seat theater, beginning with the lobby, which is now a jumble of tubes and wires and things approximating computer innards. The show—which mixes percussion, performance art, mime, and rock 'n' roll—has become an immensely popular permanent fixture on the Chicago theater scene. The three strangely endearing performers, whose faces and heads are covered in latex and blue paint, know how to get the audience involved. Your first decision: Do you want the "splatter" or the "nonsplatter" seats? (The former necessitates the donning of a plastic sheet.) I dare you to find a kid who doesn't get a kick out of seeing the Blue Men stuff their faces (literally) with marshmallows. Of all the long-running hits in Chicago, this is the one to beat—and the best kid-pleaser in town. And although the show is a great pick for older children, it's not recommended for kids 4 and under. This show is often a sell-out, so call for tickets in advance. 3133 N. Halsted St. (at Briar St.). © 773/348-4000. Tickets $46–$56. Subway/El: Red or Brown Line to Belmont.

Chicago Cultural Center (Value) Built in 1897, the Cultural Center's mandate has always been to provide the people of Chicago with access to the arts. Fortunately for families, children's shows are a major thrust of their programming, especially on Saturday and sometimes Sunday. The center puts on workshops and performances for children several times a month and major festivals four times a year. Concerts featuring Thai music or dance programs depicting the history and architecture of Chicago are just a few of the types of programs you might find. Your children can become familiar with many performing arts genres and with the artists themselves. Best of all, it's free. 78 E. Washington St. © 312/346-3278. Free tickets. Subway: Red or Brown Line to Randolph and State.

Chicago Shakespeare Theater Normally I wouldn't recommend that parents take kids to a performance of Shakespeare, especially with audiences as dedicated as those who attend this theater. However, this company does a great job of making Shakespeare accessible to kids. Shows like *Leaping Leopold! The Mozart Show* welcome kids age 4 and up (the eighth collaboration btw. Chicago Chamber Musicians and Chicago Shakespeare Theater), and other offerings that bring abbreviated versions of the Bard's work to life (the 2004 selection was a 75-min. abridgement of *Comedy of Errors*). This group's home on Navy Pier is a visually stunning, state-of-the-art jewel. The centerpiece of the glass-box complex, which rises seven stories, is a 525-seat courtyard-style theater patterned loosely after the Swan Theater in Stratford-upon-Avon. The complex also houses a 180-seat

(Tips) Going to the Show by El or Bus

You have several public transportation options when stepping out on a budget. Bus and El (train/subway) rides cost $2 plus 25¢ for transfers. For more information on Chicago's public transportation system, see chapter 2.

- **Chicago Theatre:** Green, Purple, Orange, or Brown Line El to State and Lake, or State Street bus (no. 2, 6, 10, 11, 29, 36, 44, 62, or 146) to corner of State and Lake.

- **Ford Center for the Performing Arts:** Green, Purple, Orange, or Brown Line El to Randolph, or State Street bus (no. 2, 6, 10, 11, 29, 36, 44, 62, or 146) to corner of Randolph and State.

- **Goodman Theatre:** Green, Purple, Orange, or Brown Line El to Randolph, or State Street bus (no. 2, 6, 11, 29, 36, 44, 62, or 146) to corner of State and Randolph, and walk 1 block west to Dearborn.

- **LaSalle Bank Theatre (formerly the Shubert Theatre):** Red Line El to Monroe, or State Street bus (no. 2, 6, 10, 11, 29, 36, 44, 62, or 146) to corner of Monroe and State.

- **Lyric Opera of Chicago:** Metra train to Northwestern station, or take the Green, Purple, Brown, or Orange Line El to Washington. Take the Madison Street bus (no. 14, 20, 56, 131, or 157) to the corner of Madison and Wacker.

- **Petrillo Music Shell:** Green, Purple, Brown, or Orange Line El to Adams, or the Michigan Avenue bus (no. 3, 4, 60, 145, 147, or 151) to the corner of Michigan and Jackson.

- **Steppenwolf Theatre Company:** Red Line El to North and Clybourne, or bus no. 33 or 41 to corner of North and Halsted.

- **Symphony Center:** Green, Purple, Brown, or Orange Line El to Adams, or the Michigan Avenue bus (no. 3, 4, 60, 145, 147, or 151) to the corner of Michigan and Jackson.

studio theater, an English-style pub, and lobbies with commanding views of Lake Michigan and the Chicago skyline. The Jentes Family Auditorium is the venue for the kid-friendly shows, while the main theater presents three plays a year—almost always by the Bard—with founder and artistic director Barbara Gaines usually directing one of the shows. 800 E. Grand Ave. (© **312/642-2273.** www.chicagoshakes.com. Tickets $40–$67. Discounted parking in attached garage. Subway/El: Red Line to Grand, then bus 29 to Navy Pier.

Chicago Theatre   This 1920s music palace has been reborn as an all-purpose entertainment venue, hosting everything from pop acts and magicians to stand-up comedy. 175 N. State St. (at Lake St.). (© **312/443-1130.** Subway/El: Red Line to Lake/State; Brown or Orange Line to Clark/Lake.

Ford Center for the Performing Arts/Oriental Theater and the Cadillac Palace Theater   Late 1990s renovations of these opulent theaters inevitably required corporate sponsorship—in this case, from car companies—transforming them into the

Cadillac Palace and the awkwardly named Ford Center for the Performing Arts/Oriental Theater. Both book major touring shows and are well worth a visit for arts buffs. The Oriental's fantastical Asian look includes elaborate carvings almost everywhere you look; dragons, elephants, and griffins peer down at the audience from the gilded ceiling. The Palace features a profusion of Italian marble surfaces and columns, gold-leaf accents a la Versailles, huge decorative mirrors, and crystal chandeliers. If you'd like to get a look at these historic theaters for a fraction of the ticket price, guided tours of the Oriental and the Cadillac Palace Theaters start at 11am Saturday and cost $10 per person; meet in the Oriental lobby. For show schedules at the Ford, Cadillac, and LaSalle Bank theaters, call © **312/977-1700,** or visit www.broadwayinchicago.com. Oriental Theater: 24 W. Randolph St. © **312/977-1700.** Cadillac Palace Theater: 151 W. Randolph St. © **312/384-1510.** Subway/El: Brown Line to Randolph.

Goodman Theatre Chicago kids (and their parents) come back year after year for the Goodman's annual production of *A Christmas Carol,* a Chicago holiday tradition. The show runs from mid-November to the end of December. Book well in advance; the run always sells out. It's a great way for families to experience the Goodman's state-of-the-art theater complex in the heart of Chicago's revitalized downtown theater district. The project was a total gut rehab of the historic Harris and Selwyn theaters, a pair of former rococo movie houses. None of the historic bric-a-brac was retained; the new building has a very modern, minimalist feel (the side of the building glows with different colors in the evenings). The centerpiece—the 830-seat Albert Ivar Goodman Theatre—is a brand-new limestone-and-glass structure. Connected to the main theater is another addition, a cylindrical, glass-walled building housing shops, the 400-seat Owen Theatre, and Italian restaurant Petterino's. The Goodman is the dean of legitimate theaters in Chicago, producing both original productions and familiar standards, including everything from Shakespeare to musicals. Productions at the Goodman are always solid; you may not see anything revolutionary, but you'll get some of the best actors in the city. 170 N. Dearborn St. © **312/443-3800.** www.goodman-theatre.org. Tickets $30–$50 main stage, $10–$30 studio. Subway/El: Red Line to Washington/State or Lake/State; Brown or Orange Line to Clark/Lake.

LaSalle Bank Theatre Built in 1906 as a home for vaudeville, the LaSalle Bank Theatre (formerly the Shubert) books mostly big-name musicals and sometimes comedy performers. A lot of the musicals are great family fare, so you may well find yourself here. If you get balcony seats, be aware that you are going to be way, way up. The view is still good, but if you have any fear of heights (or want to see expressions on the performers' faces), you might want to try for tickets on the main floor. 22 W. Monroe St. © **312/977-1700.** Subway/El: Red Line to Washington.

ⓘ**ps** **Finding a Better Seat**

Most of Chicago's grand old theaters have balconies that go way, way up toward the ceiling—and if you're stuck in the cheap seats, you'll be straining to see what's happening onstage. Although theaters are very strict about checking tickets when you arrive, the ushers relax during intermission. So scope out empty seats during the first act, and then move down to better (and much pricier) spots for the rest of the show.

ENTERTAINMENT FOR THE WHOLE FAMILY

10

THE BIG VENUES

If You Have a Sitter: The Music Scene

Chicago is home to the world's most popular and widely heard style of blues and is an important venue for jazz. So book a sitter, grab some dinner, and then head for one of these standout clubs. Just remember, it's going to be a late night: Many music venues don't get hopping until after 11pm. Plan to arrive between 9 and 10pm to allow time to get seats in the club, have a drink, and relax before the show. Most clubs continue to pulse until the wee hours, depending on what's happening onstage.

FIRST, HOW TO CATCH THE BLUES:
Celebrate the women of blues at **Blue Chicago,** 736 and 536 N. Clark St., River North (✆ **312/642-6261;** www.bluechicago.com), which showcases top female talent. The cover charge is $6 to $8.

B.L.U.E.S., 2519 N. Halsted St. between Wrightwood and Fullerton avenues, Lincoln Park (✆ **773/528-1012;** www.chicagobluesbar.com), satisfies the most ardent fans with live music 365 days a year, since 1979. The dark, narrow club places patrons up close to performers. As at Kingston Mines (described later in this box), expect to spend the evening standing. The cover is $5 to $10.

If Chicago is the body and soul of blues music, then **Buddy Guy's Legends,** 754 S. Wabash Ave. between Balbo and 8th streets, South Loop (✆ **312/427-0333;** www.buddyguys.com), is its heart. Everyone from Eric Clapton to Muddy Waters has stopped in to jam and listen to the best in blues at this club owned and operated by blues legend Buddy Guy. Every January, Guy plays a series of shows that sell out early. The cover charge is $10 to $15.

A great place to see a show, the **House of Blues,** 329 N. Dearborn St. at Kinzie Street, River North (✆ **312/923-2000;** www.hob.com), could more appropriately be called the House of Pop. Although it's decorated with Mississippi Delta folk art, the bands that play here tend to be rock groups, '80s novelty acts, and the occasional hip-hop or reggae. Concerts are in a theater that re-creates a gilded European opera house (minus the seats), and stage views are pretty good no matter where you stand. A restaurant also serves lunch and dinner with hometown blues accompaniment. The popular Sunday gospel brunch, offering a Southern-style buffet, brings a different Chicago gospel choir to the stage each week; the three weekly "services" often sell out, so get tickets in advance. The cover varies from about $15 to $45 for a big name.

Kingston Mines, 2548 N. Halsted St. between Wrightwood and Fullerton avenues, Lincoln Park (✆ **773/477-4646;** www.kingstonmines.com), has two stages' worth of blues greats. It may not be up to par with Buddy Guy's, but

Lookingglass Theatre Company ★ A rising star on the Chicago theatrical scene, Lookingglass produces original shows and unusual literary adaptations in a highly physical and visually imaginative style. (Its location in the Water Tower Pumping Station—just off Michigan Ave. and within walking distance of many downtown hotels—makes it

it's certain to satisfy your craving for down-home blues. Performances last until 4am on Saturdays. The cover charge is $10 to $15.

IF YOU PREFER TO JAZZ UP THE NIGHT:

Live jazz is performed virtually round-the-clock, mostly by nationally known musicians, at **Andy's Jazz Club,** 11 E. Hubbard St. between State Street and Wabash Avenue, River North (© **312/642-6805;** www.andysjazzclub.com). This loud, grungy hangout for serious jazz fans offers 3-hour sets at lunch on weekdays and music throughout the evening all week. The kitchen stays open late; pizza and burgers are decent. Depending on the day of the week and the time you arrive, the cover charge is $5 to $10.

Green Dolphin Street, 2200 N. Ashland Ave. at Webster Avenue, Lincoln Park (© **773/395-0066;** www.jazzitup.com), is a retro supper club that's slick— and pricey. Stylish patrons in their 30s to 50s enjoy seafood and contemporary American cuisine from a celebrated kitchen and then head to an adjacent room that accommodates 200 people for live jazz. The music ranges from headliners, such as Wynton Marsalis, to experimental artists, plus Latin jazz and big-band music. Cover is $5 to $20.

Known for great jazz in a historical setting, **Green Mill,** 4802 N. Broadway at Lawrence Avenue, near Andersonville (© **773/878-5552;** www.greenmilljazz. com), was established in 1907 and frequented by infamous mobster Al Capone. You hear Latin jazz, big-band jazz, jazz piano, and more. On Tuesday and Thursday nights, jitterbugging hipsters swarm to the club for Prohibition-era swing and big-band music. On Sunday, the club hosts Chicago's best-known poetry slam. The cover ranges from $6 to $15.

Joe Segal, founder of **Jazz Showcase,** 806 S. Plymouth Court, in the historic Dearborn Station building (© **312/360-0234;** www.jazzshowcase.com), books some of the hottest names in the business. With two performances each night (open to audiences of all ages) and a 4pm Sunday matinee, this club is ushering in the next generation of fans. The cover charge is $20 to $25.

If you're in the mood for bubbly, **Pops for Champagne,** 601 N. State St. at Ohio Street (© **312/266-7677;** www.popsforchampagne.com), offers more than 100 labels, and Pops Jazz Club offers live music 5 nights a week (Tues–Sat), beginning at 9pm. Cover charge is $15 Friday and Saturday; no cover is charged Tuesday through Thursday. Located in historic Tree Studios (a former artists' colony in the heart of River North), this is one of Chicago's hot spots for couples seeking a romantic night out.

especially visitor-friendly, and perfect for a parents' night out—get a sitter and treat yourselves!) The company, founded more than a decade ago by graduates of Northwestern University (including *Friends'* David Schwimmer), stages several shows each year. Recent offerings included *Metamorphoses,* a sublime and humorous modern recasting of

Ovid's myths that became a hit in New York, and *Lookingglass Alice,* an acrobatic retelling of *Alice in Wonderland.* Ensemble member Mary Zimmerman—who directed *Metamorphoses*—has built a national reputation for her creative interpretations of literature, so if she's directing a show while you're in town, don't miss it. Schwimmer also appears here occasionally, as either an actor or a director. Lookingglass shows emphasize visual effects as much as they do acting, whether it's having performers wade through a giant shallow pool or take to the sky on a trapeze. 821 N. Michigan Ave. (at Chicago Ave.). © **312/337-0665.** www.lookingglasstheatre.org. Tickets $25–$55. Subway/El: Red Line to Chicago.

North Shore Center for the Performing Arts in Skokie　This north suburban theater is home to the well-respected Northlight Theater, the Skokie Valley Symphony Orchestra, and a series of touring acts, including comics, dance troupes, and children's programs. 9501 Skokie Blvd., Skokie. © **847/673-6300.** To reach the theater, take the Edens Expwy. and exit at Old Orchard Rd.; go right onto Old Orchard; make a right onto Skokie Blvd. The theater is at the intersection of Skokie Blvd. and Golf Rd.

Rosemont Theatre　A major venue for traveling shows, this is a top suburban stop for musicals and concerts. *Radio City Christmas Spectacular Starring the Rockettes* and *Bear and the Big Blue House* are recent shows that have appealed to kids of a wide age range. 5400 River Rd. in Rosemont, near O'Hare Airport. © **847/671-5100.**

Storefront Theater　Every kind of lively art, from theater, dance, performance art, chamber opera, puppetry, and cabaret to staged readings, finds a home here. Located in the Gallery 37 Center for the Arts, in the heart of the Loop's revitalized theater district, this state-of-the-art black box theater provides a forum for Chicago's best artists to show off their accomplishments. 66 E. Randolph St. © **312/742-8497.** Subway/El: Brown Line to Randolph.

Studio Theater (Value)　When you pop in to the Chicago Cultural Center, you might find yourself seeing a show here, at an intimate stage. The theater is used as an incubator space, giving Chicago's best off-Loop theater companies the opportunity to share their work with downtown audiences. The Department of Cultural Affairs provides the space for free to encourage the growth of new creative talent. Ticket prices are kept low or admission is free for select events to allow everyone the chance to enjoy some of Chicago's best theater. 77 E. Randolph St. © **312/744-6630.** Subway/El: Brown, Green, Orange, or Purple Line to Randolph, or Red Line to Washington/State. Bus: 3, 4, 20, 56, 60, 127, 131, 145, 146, 147, 151, or 157.

Symphony Center　Symphony Center is the building that encompasses Orchestra Hall, home of the Chicago Symphony Orchestra. Expanded and renovated a few years back, the building now includes a six-story sky-lit arcade, recital spaces, and the fine-dining restaurant Rhapsody. While the CSO is the main attraction (and it's off-limits to kids 11 and under), the Symphony Center hosts a family matinee series, plus a series of piano recitals, classical and chamber music concerts, and the occasional jazz or pop artist. 220 S. Michigan Ave., btw. Adams St. and Jackson Blvd. © **312/294-3000.** Subway/El: Red Line to Washington/State. Bus: 3, 4, 20, 56, 60, 127, 145, 146, 147, 151, or 157.

Victory Gardens Theater (Finds)　Victory Gardens is one of the few pioneers of off-Loop theater that has survived from the 1970s. Highly recommended for a parents' night out, the company was rewarded for its unswerving commitment to developing playwrights with a Tony Award for regional theater in 2001—a real coup for a relatively small theater. The five or six productions presented each season are new works, many developed through a series of workshops. The plays tend to be accessible stories about real

feature nationally known actors, the casts are always first-rate, and the plays usually leave you with something to think about (or passionately discuss) on the way home.

Victory Gardens stages shows at its main stage inside the former Biograph movie theater (known in Chicago lore as the place where the FBI gunned down bank robber John Dillinger in 1934). Smaller independent companies play on four smaller stages at the Victory Gardens Greenhouse Theater, 2257 N. Lincoln Ave., a few blocks south. 2433 N. Lincoln Ave. (1 block north of Fullerton Ave.). ⓒ 773/871-3000. www.victory gardens.org. Tickets $30–$45. Subway/El: Red or Brown Line to Fullerton.

---

2 SEASONAL EVENTS

Chicago Human Rhythm Project (Finds   **Ages 6 & up.** This group performs an annual tap dance festival that was created in 1990 and brings together tap and percussive dancers from all over the world. It's an impressive sight (and sound). Dancers spend a month in Chicago, taking a series of workshops and outreach programs. It all culminates in a stirring week of performances in July and August at locations throughout the city and suburbs. ⓒ 773/281-1825. www.chicagotap.com. Tickets about $20.

A Christmas Carol   Ages 6 & up. This beloved Chicago holiday tradition is a darker and more operatic take on the classic story—along the lines of a Tim Burton movie. Kids love it, parents love it, and theater buffs love the fact that the Goodman didn't turn the show, admittedly one of the darker Christmas stories ever penned, into a sugarcoated Broadway event. In fact, the show is even better for being more of a serious play and ghost story—it makes the ending even more uplifting. The show runs every year from the third weekend in November until just before Christmas. 170 N. Dearborn St. ⓒ 312/ 443-3800. www.goodman-theatre.org. Tickets $30–$50. Subway/El: Red Line to Washington/ State or Lake/State; Brown or Orange Line to Clark/Lake.

Dance Chicago (Value   **Ages 5 & up.** In addition to Chicago Human Rhythm Project (reviewed above), the Athenaeum also hosts the annual Dance Chicago, a highly engaging month-long festival showcasing the talents of up-and-coming contemporary-dance companies and choreographers. It usually takes place in November. In recent years the programs have included jazz, hip-hop, tap, ballroom, tango, salsa, swing, and more. A kids' show called *Dance for Kids, Too!* generally runs every Saturday afternoon at a cost of $12 for adults and $5 for kids ages 4 and up. (To attend the evening programs, kids need to be age 5 or older.) The kids' program features numerous dance companies, both youth and professional, whose work is geared to families. At the Athenaeum Theatre, 2936 N. Southport Ave. (at Lincoln Ave.). ⓒ 773/989-0698. www.dancechicago.com. Tickets $5–$25. Subway/El: Brown Line to Wellington.

Grant Park Music Festival   All ages. A great Chicago event takes place from late June to August: the series of free outdoor classical music concerts given by the Grant Park Symphony and Chorus, as well as a number of visiting artists. They perform in the Frank Gehry–designed Pritzker Music Pavilion in Millennium Park (with the surrounding Loop skyscrapers creating an impressive backdrop). Featuring Gehry's signature sinuous lines, the pavilion is surrounded by dramatic ribbons of curved steel. The Grant Park Symphony not only looks better than ever, but sounds great, too, thanks to a state-of-the-art sound system. The Grant Park Music Festival has been a Chicago tradition since

A Do-It-Yourself Messiah

Fancy yourself an ecclesiastical crooner? Should you be in town over the Christmas holidays, don't skip the **Do-It-Yourself** *Messiah,* an extraordinarily popular and rousing rendition of the Handel classic. Staged at the opulent Civic Opera House, the program enlists audience members as part of a 3,500-voice chorus, who are accompanied by a volunteer orchestra and four professional soloists. Even if you and your kids don't join in the singing, just sitting in the audience and absorbing the roof-raising aural power that fills the theater guarantees goose bumps. This is a hot, hot, hot ticket, and they are available starting in mid-November (tickets are free, but limited to four per household) by calling the Civic Opera House box office at ☎ **312/332-2244.**

1931, when Mayor A. J. Cermak suggested free concerts to lift Chicagoans' spirits. Concerts are held Wednesday through Sunday, with most performances beginning at 7:30pm. Bring a blanket if you plan to sit on the lawn; seats in the band shell are reserved for subscribers, but unclaimed seats are offered to the public about 15 minutes before the concert begins. It's a great way for families to enjoy music together. If you sit in the back, your kids will find plenty of company—it looks like a veritable playground of kids back there. Selections might include Broadway favorites, Bernstein, Mozart, Brahms, Cole Porter, and Gershwin. Pritzker Music Pavilion, at the cover of Michigan Ave. and Randolph St. ☎ **312/742-4763.** www.grantparkmusicfestival.com. Subway/El: Red Line to Washington/State or Brown, Orange or Green Lines to Randolph/Wabash.

The Nutcracker **Ages 8 & up.** When the Joffrey Ballet of Chicago moved here several years ago, it brought along a new holiday tradition: its annual production of *The Nutcracker.* The ballet is performed at the beautiful Auditorium Theatre for 3 weeks in December. It's simply the best version in town, with a live orchestra helping to bring Tchaikovsky's holiday tale to life. Office: 70 E. Lake St. ☎ **312/739-0120.** www.joffrey.com. Tickets $25–$100. Auditorium Theatre, 50 E. Congress Pkwy. Bus: 145, 147, or 151. Subway/El: Brown, Green, Orange, or Purple Line to Library/Van Buren, or Red Line to Jackson.

Ravinia Festival (Finds **All ages.** Ravinia, summer home of the Chicago Symphony Orchestra in suburban Highland Park, is a Chicago summer tradition. The festival strives to be family-friendly by maintaining low ticket prices and inviting patrons to pack their own picnics and sit on the lawn. There's even a series of **Kraft Kids Concerts** that reach out to the next generation of music lovers on various Saturdays and Sundays. In the past the series has featured the Ravinia Festival Jazz Mentors with the Muntu Dance Theatre of Chicago, Ravinia Festival Orchestra, Chicago Human Rhythm Project, the Apollo Chorus, River North Dance Chicago, the Joffrey Ballet, and more. Held about eight times each summer, the kids' concerts usually begin at 11am on Saturday, or 2pm on Sunday, and have a discounted price of about $15 for reserved seats (in the Pavilion) and $5 for lawn tickets. My advice? Bring a picnic lunch and stake out a spot on the lawn (with the added bonus that your kids can run and burn off excess energy).

If your kids are a bit older, they'll enjoy joining Chicago natives by chilling on the lawn while catching a pop act, dance performance, operatic aria, or blues concert. Tickets are available for the lawn and the covered pavilion, where you get a reserved seat and a view of the stage. The lawn is the real joy of Ravinia: sitting under the stars and a canopy of leafy branches while listening to music and indulging in an elaborate picnic (it's a local tradition to try to outdo everyone else by bringing candelabras and fine china). I've been here for everything from Beethoven symphonies to folksy singer-songwriters, and the setting has been magical every time. The lawn to the left of the stage is a popular place for families to spread out, but I'm partial to the tree-filled area on the right (the lights projected into the branches create a dramatic effect after the sun sets).

Don't let the distance from downtown discourage you from visiting, because an extremely convenient public-transportation system serves Ravinia. On concert nights, a special Ravinia Metra commuter train leaves at 5:50pm from the North Western train station at Madison and Canal streets (just west of the Loop). The train stops at the festival at 6:30pm, allowing plenty of time to enjoy a picnic before an 8 o'clock show. After the concert, trains wait right outside the gates to take commuters back to the city. The round-trip train fare is $5, a real bargain considering that traffic around the park can be brutal.

At the park, dining options range from the fine-dining restaurant **Mirabelle** (✆ 847/ 432-7550 for reservations) to prepacked picnic spreads from the **Gatehouse,** featuring gourmet items to go. For $10, you can rent a pair of lawn chairs and a table from booths set up near the park entrance. In case you're wondering about the weather conditions at concert time, dial Ravinia's Weather Line (✆ 847/433-5010). Green Bay and Lake-Cook rds., Highland Park. ✆ 847/266-5100 or 312/RAVINIA (728-4642). www.ravinia. org. Tickets: Pavilion $20–$75; lawn $10–$20. Most concerts are in the evening.

Ringling Bros. and Barnum & Bailey Circus   Ages 6 & up. Come one, come all to this massive circus, which stops in Chicago every fall for several weeks beginning in November. Three rings of glitzy, over-the-top entertainment are in store, from trapeze artists to the horses, tigers, elephants, and crocodiles that make up some of the 200 human and animal performers. There's nothing subtle about this show—in fact, smaller kids might be overwhelmed by the sheer size of the United Center, plus the flashing lights and eardrum-blasting music (the circus also visits suburban Rosemont at the smaller Allstate Arena, which might be a better choice for little ones). Still, at least once in your life, it's worth it to see this darn impressive "greatest show on earth." United Center, 1901 W. Madison St. ✆ 312/559-1212. www.ringling.com. Tickets $13–$85. Bus: 9 or 20.

SummerDance   Ages 5 & up. Now entering its tenth year, the annual Chicago SummerDance Festival usually runs from late June to August in the Spirit of Music Garden in Grant Park. Presented by the Chicago Department of Cultural Affairs, the festival features 1-hour dance lessons to taped music (you can learn everything from ballroom dancing to country line dancing), followed by dancing to live orchestras, every Thursday, Friday, and Saturday evening from 6 to 10pm, and Sunday afternoons beginning at 4pm, weather permitting. The festival also presents folk dance from Scandinavia, Israel, Ireland, Scotland, Wales, and others at various venues throughout the city. Grant Park, 601 S. Michigan (btw. Harrison and Balbo, across from Columbia College). For complete information on what's scheduled, call the Chicago Dept. of Cultural Affairs at ✆ 312/744-6630. Free admission. Subway/El: Red Line to Jackson.

3 THEATER

Chicago Playworks for Families and Young Audiences (Value)   **Ages 3 & up.** How can the 35,000 kids and adults who flock to see this company's performances each

Calling a Cab

Taxis are easy to hail in the Loop, on the Magnificent Mile and the Gold Coast, in River North, and in Lincoln Park, but if you go much beyond these key areas, you might need to call a cab. Try one of these cab companies:

* **Flash Cab** (📞 **773/561-1444**)
* **Yellow Cab** (📞 **312/TAXI-CAB** [312/829-4222])
* **Checker Cab** (📞 **312/CHECKER** [312/243-2537])

year be wrong? Founded in 1925 as Goodman Children's Theatre, Chicago Playworks later became part of DePaul University and is one of the first important children's theaters in the United States. The company presents three shows per season, which runs October through April. The performances are held in the historic Merle Reskin Theatre, where kids can cozy up in plush red seats and marvel at the sparkling chandeliers and grand scale of the surroundings. If you're a Chicago resident, you might want to try the season tickets, which entitle you to two free admission tickets to the Chicago Children's Museum at Navy Pier. Ask about the Ice Cream Social package, offered three times a year, which gets you into an after-show ice-cream bar and features discussion and an autograph session with the cast at the nearby Hilton Chicago, for the very reasonable ticket price of $5. Shows run from October to May, usually Tuesday and Thursday at 10am and Saturday at 2pm. Merle Reskin Theatre, 60 E. Balbo Dr. 📞 **312/922-1999.** http://theatreschool. depaul.edu. Tickets $8 and up. Subway/El: Red Line to Jackson.

The Children's Theater Fantasy Orchard   **Ages 3 & up.** Performing in the Ivanhoe Theater, Children's Theater Fantasy Orchard presents fairy and folk tales from around the world. Founded in 1990, the company now performs for 30,000 kids annually. Some 30 actors and technicians come up with new productions each year. In doing so, the company tries to depict universal struggles and truths as they stoke kids' imaginations. At Ivanhoe Theater, 750 W. Wellington Ave. 📞 **773/539-4211.** Tickets $7 for adults, $5 for kids. Subway/El: Brown, Purple, or Red Line to Wellington.

Drury Lane Theater   Drury Lane, located in Water Tower Place, presents revivals of Broadway productions in a 549-seat theater with stadium-type seating, which means your kids get a better view of the stage than in your average theater. With five productions each year, you might catch one the kids will enjoy. Recent shows have included "Meet Me in St. Louis," "The Full Monty," and "Grand Hotel." Dinner packages in conjunction with area restaurants and discounted Water Tower Place parking of $7 are offered. 175 E. Chestnut St. (just east of Michigan Ave.) 📞 **312/642-2000.** www.drurylanewater tower.com. Subway/El: Red Line to Chicago/State or 151 Bus to Chestnut.

Emerald City Theatre Company   **Ages 2 & up.** From Tarzan and Jane to Dr. Seuss classics, this relative newcomer to the kids' theater scene produces shows for kids ages 2 and up. The company is currently performing at the Apollo Theater, a modern theater with 400 seats—although that has changed from time to time throughout the years. Emerald City Theatre Company was founded in 1996, and recent shows have included *Dr. Dolittle, Cinderella, If You Take a Mouse to School, Aladdin, The Wizard of Oz, Narnia, Snow White,* and *Where the Wild Things Are.* Each season, Emerald City produces four shows, some of which are original works written for the company. Many Chicago kids had their first theater experience with Emerald City (named in honor of *The Wonderful*

A Brief Primer on Theater Etiquette for Kids

A night at the theater used to mean dressing formally and sitting stiffly. Although casual dress and equally casual manners have replaced much of the formality of a night at the theater, some rules of etiquette still prevail. Before heading to a show with your kids, you might want to talk through the following basic guidelines:

- Don't use cameras or video cameras in the theater. Taping is prohibited by law.

- Don't talk during a performance; it's distracting for other patrons who have paid a pretty penny for their seats (most touring Broadway shows cost well over $50 a ticket these days).

- Turn off beepers and cellphones. Most theaters will remind patrons of this rule before the curtain rises, as it seems inevitable that someone will forget, and that one ring will ruin everyone's enjoyment (and possibly the actors' concentration!).

- Rustling candy wrappers can be as much of a nuisance as a ringing cellphone. If you or your kids must eat candy, unwrap it before the show starts.

- Dress comfortably, but within bounds. You can anticipate seeing theatergoers dressed up for a blockbuster musical and dressed down for a storefront repertory, so dress accordingly. While Chicago is a relaxed Midwestern city, sweatshirts and jeans are too casual for the theater. For men, a nice sweater or collared shirt with slacks or jeans will work almost everywhere, and similar attire for women (sweaters, dress pants, or a skirt) is always appropriate.

- Make sure kids are fed before the show—squirming kids with growling stomachs do not make for a pleasant theater-watching experience for anyone, the kids especially.

- No need to tip the ushers. Acknowledging their help with a thank you or a pleasant nod or smile is all that's required. However, if you manage to battle your way to the bar during intermission, the beleaguered bartender will appreciate your tip.

- Take special care to be on time. Chicago theaters tend to be punctual, and tardy patrons usually must wait to be seated until the conclusion of the scene or musical number in progress. Arriving late for the opera can be especially troublesome. With acts lasting for over an hour, you'll be sitting outside watching the performance on a television—not a good use of your entertainment dollar.

ENTERTAINMENT FOR THE WHOLE FAMILY

10

THEATER

Wizard of Oz, written by Frank L. Baum while he lived in Chicago). At the Apollo Theater, 2540 N. Lincoln. Office: 2936 N. Southport. © **773/935-6100.** www.emeraldcitytheatre.com. Tickets $12 for children 2–12, $15 for ages 13 and up. Subway/El: Red or Brown Line to Fullerton.

Lifeline Theatre KidSeries **Ages 2 & up.** Lifeline Theatre—the grown-up version—has a faithful following who anticipate its creative stage adaptations of literary classics such as *Jane Eyre.* Its KidSeries plays are original adaptations of favorite children's books, and often include music written especially for them. These shows, which are presented on Saturday and Sunday afternoons, are great for even the youngest kids. Recent performances have included *Stuart Little; Giggle Giggle Quack,* about a farmer who goes on vacation and the duck who takes charge of the barnyard; and *Sophie's Masterpiece,* a tale about a spider with hidden artistic talents. After each performance, actors come out to the lobby to meet kids, give autographs, and answer questions. The theater is small—100 seats—and is in the Rogers Park neighborhood. Look for metered parking on Morse Avenue or free parking 3 blocks north of the theater at the corner of Glenwood and Estes avenues in the Trilogy, Inc. lot. 6912 N. Glenwood Ave. © **773/761-4477.** www. lifelinetheatre.com. Tickets $8–$10. Subway/El: Bus 147 to Sheridan and Arthur; transfer to bus 155 to Glenwood.

Medieval Times **Ages 6 & up.** Does jousting count as "theater"? This dinner-and-tournament show features knights competing in games, swordplay, jousting, and pyrotechnics. Sound familiar? You may have caught the act in the Jim Carrey film *The Cable Guy.* (Naturally, Jim Carrey got a bit too involved in the show, but in real life, kids shouldn't expect to find themselves wearing armor and riding horses.) It's pure kitsch, but if you can get off your high horse (so to speak), you might find yourself sucked in to the "drama." Besides, kids dig it. Guests dine on a four-course "medieval" banquet served by staff posing as "serving wenches." (Your kids might love the fact that you dig in with your hands—literally—because there's no silverware!) Performances take place on weekends, and during the holidays, Thursday nights are sometimes added. 2001 Roselle Rd. at I-90, Schaumburg. © **847/843-3900.** Tickets $63 for adults, $44 for children 12 and under. Matinee rates might be available, so call for showtimes and ticket prices.

4 CONCERTS

Blue Chicago (Finds) **Ages 8 & up.** A blues club for families? Yes, it's true—from 8pm to midnight on Saturday, the basement of the Blue Chicago store becomes a venue geared to families, featuring the music of the Gloria Shannon Blues Band. In fact, "Down in the Basement" is the only venue in Chicago that offers a regular live blues show for all ages. No alcohol is served and no smoking is allowed.

Blue Chicago pays homage to female blues belters with a strong lineup of the best women vocalists around. The 1940s-style brick-walled room, decorated with original artwork of Chicago blues vignettes, is open Monday through Saturday, with music beginning at 9pm. Admission allows you to club-hop between this venue and a second location, open Tuesday through Sunday, down the street at 536 N. Clark St. Next door, at 534 N. Clark, is the Blue Chicago Store, which sells blues-related clothing, merchandise, and artwork. 534 N. Clark St. (at the Blue Chicago store). © **312/642-6261.** www.bluechicago. com. Tickets $5 for adults, free for children 12 and under. Subway/El: Red or Brown Line to Chicago.

Chicago Children's Choir **Ages 6 & up.** Two self-produced concerts are performed each year, in May and December, by this multiracial, multicultural choral music-education program. Venues change, so call for information. This is not just any kids' choir: In the past, the choir performed with Bobby McFerrin at the Chicago Theatre. Founded in

1956, the choir trains nearly 3,000 young singers a year. The choir runs 61 in-school choruses in 40 Chicago elementary schools and five after-school Neighborhood Choirs. The showpiece is the 125-voice Concert Choir, which includes Treble and Chamber ensembles, Madrigals, and a Show Choir. Office: Chicago Cultural Center, 78 E. Washington, 5th floor. © 312/849-8300. www.ccchoir.org. Tickets $27–$47.

Chicago Opera Theater   Ages 8 & up. As the "other" opera company in town, Chicago Opera Theater doesn't get all the big names, but it does make opera accessible to a wider audience with an emphasis on American composers and performers who sing in English. It also helps that tickets are less expensive and more plentiful than those for the Lyric Opera. The opera has a wonderful educational outreach program that features one opera per season (a short one, usually!) that is performed by and for children. Call well in advance for tickets to the next performance, as they always sell out. No matter what the bill, the talent and production values are top-notch. Harris Theater for Music and Dance, 205 E. Randolph Dr. © 312/704-8414. www.chicagooperatheater.org. Tickets $30–$105 adults, children half-price. Subway/El: Red Line to Washington/State.

Chicago Symphony Orchestra   Ages 6 & up. The CSO does a nice job of outreach to young ones with the Kraft Family Matinee series, which exposes kids to the storytelling of music through classics. In the past, performances have included "special guests" such as Woofgang and Meowzart, who appear at performances of Stomp Your Foot!, and Underground Railway Theater puppeteers at performances of The Firebird. The series runs on select Saturdays at 11am and 12:45pm. Concerts are performed by members of the Chicago Symphony Orchestra and guest artists. Another kid favorite is the annual Halloween concert for ages 5 to 17. Kids are invited to wear costumes to the concert. Highlights include seeing Grainger Hall transformed into a haunted house, and participating in face painting and storytelling—and orchestra members dress in costumes, too.

Another option for kids is the Chicago Youth Symphony Orchestra, which performs at Orchestra Hall (© 312/939-2207; www.cyso.org). Founded in 1946, the orchestra is composed of a senior-level group of 105 top high-school musicians in the Chicagoland area. Recognized as one of the nation's best youth orchestras, the CYSO performs in November and May.

If your children are over age 12, they are welcome to attend a regular performance of the CSO, among the best in the world—a legacy of the late maestro Sir Georg Solti, who captured a record-breaking 31 Grammy awards for his CSO recordings and showcased the orchestra at other major musical capitals during frequent international tours. In addition to classical music, the "Symphony Center Presents" series has included some of the top jazz, world beat, Latin, and cabaret artists in the world in recent years. Although they're in high demand, good seats often become available on concert day. Call Symphony Center or stop by the box office to check availability.

Summertime visitors have an opportunity to hear a CSO performance at the delightful **Ravinia Festival** (p. 21) in suburban Highland Park, led by music director Christoph Eschenbach.

The **Civic Orchestra of Chicago,** the training orchestra of the Chicago Symphony since 1919, is also highly regarded and presents free programs at Orchestra Hall. The **Chicago Symphony Chorus** also performs there. Orchestra Hall, in Symphony Center, 220 S. Michigan Ave. © 312/294-3000. www.cso.org. Tickets $25–$110; box seats $185. Subway/El: Red Line to Jackson.

ENTERTAINMENT FOR THE WHOLE FAMILY

10

CONCERTS

Tips   **Chuckling the Night Away at a Comedy Club**

Chicago has always nurtured young comics, and while you're here, you might want to explore Chicago's comic side. From the storied Second City company to scrappier, up-and-coming troupes, Chicago is a training ground for the nation's best comedians. ComedySportz caters to families; if you are going to bring your teenagers to other clubs, it's advisable to call ahead to check out the show's content. The box office personnel should be able to warn you if the show will be too racy for your kids.

ComedySportz   Most improv-comedy shows aren't exactly family-friendly, but ComedySportz does away with the barlike atmosphere and R-rated topics to deliver shows that are funny for the whole family. Chicago's only all-ages professional improv troupe sets two groups of five comedians against each other to compete for audience applause. "It isn't *about* sports—it *is* a sport" is the tag line here. Catch the ComedySportz4Kids show on Saturdays at 2pm (kids 10 and under welcome; tickets $8). Kids can participate in the show, or just watch—either way, it's a blast. All ages (but I'd recommend it especially for kids 10 and up) are welcome at the troupe's shows at 8pm on Thursday, at 8 and 10pm on Friday, and at 6, 8, and 10pm on Saturday. 929 W. Belmont Ave. ℭ **773/549-8080.** www.comedysportzchicago.com. Tickets $21.

Second City   For more than 40 years, Second City has been the top comedy club in Chicago and the most famous of its kind in the country. Photos of famous graduates line the lobby walls, including Elaine May, John Belushi, and current *Saturday Night Live* cast members Tina Fey, Horatio Sanz, and Rachel Dratch. Today's Second City is a veritable factory of improv, with shows

House of Blues   **Ages 8 & up.** Gospel as well as blues originated in Chicago, and the House of Blues's popular Sunday gospel brunch, offering a Southern-style buffet, brings a different Chicago gospel choir to the stage each week; the three weekly "services" often sell out, so get tickets in advance. Kids will delight in the funky decor at the club, part of a nightclub, restaurant, and hotel complex that has breathed new life into Marina City. The largest outpost in the growing House of Blues chain, this 55,000-square-foot complex, extravagantly decorated with 600 pieces from owner Isaac Tigrett's collection of Mississippi Delta folk art, isn't really a blues club as much as a showcase for rock, R & B, zydeco, reggae, and everything else. 329 N. Dearborn St. (at Kinzie St.). ℭ **312/923-2000** for general information, 312/923-2020 for concert information. www.hob.com. Ticket prices vary depending on the act. Subway/El: Red Line to Grand.

Jazz Showcase   **Ages 8 & up.** The Segals make an effort to cultivate new generations of jazz lovers: Each Sunday, the club offers a 4pm matinee show that admits kids 11 and under for free and has a nonsmoking policy. Spanning more than 50 years and several locations, founder Joe Segal has become synonymous with jazz in Chicago. There are two shows a night (three on Sun), and reservations are recommended when a big-name headliner is featured. Such well-regarded musicians as McCoy Tyner, Clark Terry, Maynard Ferguson, and Ahmad Jamal have made appearances in recent years.

on two stages (the storied main stage and the smaller Second City ETC) and a hugely popular training school. The main-stage ensembles change frequently, and the shows can swing wildly back and forth on the hilarity meter. (I'd recommend making this a parents' night out—the subject matter is usually best appreciated by adults!) In recent years, the club has adopted the long-form improvisational program pioneered by ImprovOlympic (see below listing), which has brought much better reviews. Check the theater reviews in the *Reader*, a free local weekly, for an opinion on the current show. To sample the Second City experience, catch the free postshow improv session (it gets going around 10:30pm); no ticket is necessary if you skip the main show (except Fri). 1616 N Wells St. (in the Pipers Alley complex at North Ave.). ℂ **877/778-4707** or 312/337-3992. www.secondcity.com, Tickets about $20. Subway/El: Brown Line to Sedgwick.

ImprovOlympic (Finds) ImprovOlympic engages the audience as the talented cast solicits suggestions and creates original performances. Once a theme is decided, a series of skits, monologues, and songs are built around it. Unscripted nightly performances have included a variety of themes, from free-form pieces to shows loosely based on concepts such as *Star Trek* or dating. Like all improv, it's a gamble: It could be a big laugh, or the amateur performers could go down in flames. Successful alums include Mike Myers, the late Chris Farley, Tim Meadows, Andy Dick, and Conan O'Brien's former *Late Night* sidekick, Andy Richter. 3541 N. Clark St. (at Addison St.). ℂ **773/880-0199.** www.iochicago.net. Tickets $5–$18. Subway/El: Red Line to Addison.

The Segals' latest outpost is the new **Joe's Be-bop Cafe and Jazz Emporium** at Navy Pier, 600 E. Grand Ave. (ℂ **312/595-5299**), a Southern-style barbecue restaurant with live music nightly. 806 S. Plymouth Court (in the historic Dearborn Station bldg.). ℂ **312/360-0234.** www.jazzshowcase.com. Tickets $20–$25. Subway/El: Red Line to Grand.

Lyric Opera of Chicago **Ages 12 & up.** A major American opera company, the Lyric attracts top-notch singers from all over the world. Naturally, this is not the place for toddlers, but if you have kids in 7th through 12th grades, you might want to expose them to opera through the company's student matinees. Kids should be prepared for performances to run approximately 90 minutes. Their Lyric NExT program offers steeply discounted student tickets to the Opera's regular productions—as low as $20, when regular-priced seats are going for almost $200. Just soaking in the ambience at the glamorous and opulent opera house is quite an experience (even if you leave at intermission!). The handsome, 3,563-seat Art Deco Civic Opera House is the second-largest opera house in the country, built in 1929. Add to that the magnificence of the Lyric Opera Orchestra and chorus, the amazing sets and costumes, and the beautiful voices, and it's an experience your kids won't soon forget. Kids are encouraged to dress up for the occasion, and proper etiquette is expected. Ticket prices are $5 for the upper balcony,

$10 for the first balcony, $13 for the second section of the main floor, and $16 for box seats and the front section of the main floor.

If you can't snag tickets or if you visit during the opera's off season in February and March, you can still check out the theater by taking a tour (© 312/827-5685). Civic Opera House, at Madison St. and Wacker Dr. © 312/332-2244. www.lyricopera.org. Tickets $45–$165. Subway/El: Brown Line to Washington.

Old Town School of Folk Music (Finds) **All ages.** Country, folk, bluegrass, Latin, Celtic—the Old Town School of Folk Music covers a spectrum of indigenous musical forms. A full schedule of classes, concerts, and special events is geared to children ages 6 months to teen years. (For more on dropping in for a class, see chapter 8.) The school is best known as a training center offering a slate of music classes, but it also hosts everyone from the legendary Pete Seeger to bluegrass phenom Alison Krauss. The school's home, in a former 1930s library, is the world's largest facility dedicated to the preservation and presentation of traditional and contemporary folk music. The Old Town School also houses an art gallery showcasing exhibitions of works by local, national, and international artists; a music store selling an exquisite selection of instruments, sheet music, and hard-to-find recordings; and a cafe. The school hosts an annual Chicago Folk and Roots Festival in July in Wells Park at Lincoln and Montrose, with stage performances and an activity-and-crafts tent for kids. Headliners are name-brand performers such as Patti Smith. The school maintains another retail store and a schedule of children's classes at its first location, 909 W. Armitage Ave. 4544 N. Lincoln Ave. (btw. Wilson and Montrose aves.). © 773/728-6000. www.oldtownschool.org. Tickets $10–$25. Subway/El: Blue Line to Western.

5 MOVIES

Chicago has its share of multiplex theaters that feature kid fare. The **AMC River East,** at 322 E. Illinois, east of Columbus Drive (© **312/596-0333**), is Chicago's largest movie complex and features stadium seating and digital sound in all auditoriums. Other major downtown cinemas include **AMC Loews 600 N. Michigan Theaters,** at that address (© **312/255-9340**), and **AMC Lowes Pipers Alley 4,** 1608 N. Wells (© **312/642-6890**).

One IMAX and one OMNIMAX theater surround you with sights and sounds. **Navy Pier IMAX Theater** (www.imax.com; © **312/595-5629**) shows not only traditional

---

(Tips) **Facets' Film Festival**

Facets Multi-Media, 1517 W. Fullerton Ave. (© **773/281-4114;** www.facets.org; Subway/El: Red or Brown Line to Fullerton), a nonprofit group that screens independent film and video from around the world, is for the die-hard cinematic thrill-seeker. The group also hosts the **Chicago International Children's Film Festival** (Oct), the largest in the U.S. The festival screens more than 200 children's films from 40 countries—many of which you'll never see in mainstream theaters. Some 23,000 kids, adults, educators, and celebrities attend and run filmmaking workshops for kids. For more information about the film festival or to check out Facets' kids' programs, including Young Chicago Critics and Take One! Workshops, log on to **www.cicff.org**.

Chicago as Backdrop

Get warmed up for your trip to Chicago by renting one of these Chicago-based flicks:

- *Adventures in Babysitting* (1987)
- *Barbershop* (2002) and *Barbershop 2: Back in Business* (2004)
- *Batman Begins* (2005)
- *Blues Brothers 2000* (1998; note the original *Blues Brothers* movie is rated R)
- *The Break Up* (2006)
- *The Dark Knight* (2008)
- *Girls Just Want to Have Fun* (1985)
- *Ferris Bueller's Day Off* (1986)
- *High Fidelity* (2000)
- *My Big Fat Greek Wedding* (2002)
- *My Best Friend's Wedding* (1997)
- *Prelude to a Kiss* (1992)
- *The Fugitive* (1993)
- *While You Were Sleeping* (1995)
- *Save the Last Dance* (2001)

IMAX films on its six-story, 80-foot-wide screen, but also 3-D movies. The **OMNIMAX Theater** at the Museum of Science and Industry, 57th Street and Lake Shore Drive (© 773/684-1414; www.msichicago.org), usually presents movies in conjunction with exhibits. The theater also has an Omnilaser Fantasy light show featuring rock music and costs the same as a movie. To ensure tickets, reserve in advance—even if you have a ticket, get there early, because the line for seats begins forming about 20 minutes in advance.

6 DANCE

Ballet Chicago   **Ages 10 & up.** Under artistic director Daniel Duell, a former New York City Ballet dancer, the group is notable for its specialty: the ballets of Balanchine. The ballet performs one full-length story ballet a year, usually in April or May. © 312/251-8838. www.balletchicago.org. Tickets $12–$25.

The Dance Center—Columbia College Chicago   **Ages 10 & up.** Columbia College, a liberal arts institution specializing in the arts and media, has been growing by leaps and bounds in recent years. Its Dance Center—the hub of Chicago's modern dance milieu—features an intimate "black box" 275-seat performance space with stadium seating and marvelous sightlines. The Dance Center hosts at least a dozen performances a year by both international and national touring groups and homegrown choreographers. 1306 S. Michigan Ave. © 312/344-8300. www.colum.edu/dance_center. Tickets $15–$25. Subway/El: Red Line to Roosevelt. Bus: 151.

Hubbard Street Dance Chicago   **Ages 12 & up.** Dance lovers recommend that if you're going to see just one dance performance while you're in town, make it Hubbard Street, Chicago's best-known dance troupe whose mix of jazz, modern, ballet, and theater dance has won many devoted local fans. Sometimes whimsical, sometimes romantic, the crowd-pleasing 22-member ensemble incorporates a range of dance traditions, from Kevin O'Day to Twyla Tharp, who has choreographed pieces exclusively for Hubbard Street. Although the troupe spends most of the year touring, it has regular 2- to 3-week Chicago engagements in the fall and spring. In the summer the dancers often perform at Ravinia Festival (p. 21). Office: 1147 W. Jackson Blvd. © **312/850-9744.** www.hubbardstreet dance.com. Tickets $20–$75.

Joffrey Ballet of Chicago   **Ages 10 & up.** Now based in its own, brand-new home at 10 E. Randolph St. (at State St.), the Joffrey is committed to the classic works of the 20th century (all performances take place at the Auditorium Theatre; the Joffrey Tower is the location for rehearsals and training, although a box office is also found on-site). Its repertoire extends from the ballets of Arpino, Robert Joffrey, Balanchine, and Jerome Robbins to the cutting-edge works of Alonzo King and Chicago choreographer Randy Duncan. The Joffrey continues to draw crowds to its popular rock ballet, *Billboards,* which is set to the music of Prince, and tours internationally. The company is usually in town in the spring (Mar or Apr), fall (Sept or Oct), and December, when it stages its popular rendition of the holiday favorite *The Nutcracker.* 10 E. Randolph St. © **312/739-0120.** www.joffrey.com. Tickets $25–$135.

Muntu Dance Theatre of Chicago   **Ages 8 & up.** The tribal costumes, drumming, and energetic moves of this widely touring group, which focuses on both traditional and contemporary African and African-American dance, are always a hit with audiences. The company performs in town several times a year, at the Harris Theater for Music and Dance in December and in spring (Apr or May). Office: 6800 S. Wentworth Ave. © **773/602-1135.** www.muntu.com. Tickets $25–$50.

River North Dance Company   **Ages 10 & up.** Chicago can be a brutal testing ground for start-up dance companies, which have to struggle to find performance space and grab publicity. But the odds didn't buckle the well-oiled knees of the River North Dance Company. This terrifically talented jazz dance ensemble performs programs of short, Broadway-style numbers by established and emerging choreographers. You never know where they'll pop up next, so call for information on upcoming shows. Office: 1016 N. Dearborn St. © **312/944-2888.** www.rivernorthchicago.com. Tickets $25–$30.

7 PUPPET SHOWS

Redmoon Theater (Finds   **Ages 10 & up.** Redmoon Theater might well be the most intriguing and visionary theater company in Chicago. Founded in 1990, the company produces "spectacle theater," comprising masks, objects, and an international range of puppetry styles in indoor and outdoor venues around town—including, at least once a year lately, in Steppenwolf Theatre's studio space. Utterly hypnotic, highly acrobatic and visceral, and using minimal narration, their adaptations of Melville's *Moby Dick,* Mary Shelley's *Frankenstein,* Victor Hugo's *The Hunchback of Notre Dame,* and *Rachel's Love,* an original work based on Jewish folk tales, were revelations that have earned the company an ardent and burgeoning following. Every September, Redmoon presents a "spectacle," transforming a public park into a site for performance art, larger-than-life puppet shows, and dramatic visual effects. Office at 1438 W. Kinzie St. © **312/850-8440.** www.redmoon.org. Tickets $18–$22.

8 SPECTATOR SPORTS

Chicago is one of the country's great sports towns, and its fans are nothing if not loyal. For that reason, win or lose, attending a home game in any sport is an uplifting experience. And look on the bright side: When our teams aren't doing so well, it's a lot easier to get tickets to the games (unless you're talking about the perennially sold-out Cubs).

Chicago Bears   Ages 8 & up. The Bears play at a renovated Soldier Field, although the project was controversial and continues to be booed by architecture fans. But the original stadium, built to commemorate the soldiers of World War I, was undeniably shabby and low on amenities. The stadium's most distinctive feature, its classically inspired colonnade, was retained, but a giant addition that resembles a spaceship was crammed awkwardly on top (thus, the complaints that the place is an architectural disaster). But from a comfort perspective, the place is much improved. Regale your kids with stories of the notorious "Monsters of the Midway" who battered opponents into submission under the aegis of NFL founding father and legendary coach George "Papa Bear" Halas. There is still something quintessentially Chicago about bravely freezing off your derrière at Soldier Field, or, for that matter, grilling up ribs and brats in the parking lot before the Bears go to battle against our arch enemy, the Green Bay Packers. True story: I once sat through a Bears-Packers game late in the season in which it rained, then sleeted, then snowed (and still, it seemed that not one spectator left!). Just make sure you bring a thermos of hot chocolate for the kids and a flask of something warming for the adults before you experience "Bear Weather" for the first time. At Soldier Field, Lake Shore Dr. and 16th St. ✆ **847/295-6600.** www.chicagobears.com. Tickets $45–$300. Bus: 12, 127, 130, or 146.

Chicago Blackhawks   Ages 8 & up. The 'Hawks have a devoted, impassioned following of fans who work themselves into a frenzy with the first note of the "Star Spangled Banner." But don't expect any heroics on ice along the lines of past 'Hawks legends such as Bobby Hull and Tony Esposito. Any player who turns into a star and, hence, earns the right to restructure his contract for a higher salary is immediately traded by penny-pinching owner Bill Wirtz—derided by fans and local sportswriters as "Dollar Bill." Blackhawks's practices at "the Edge," the ice facility in west suburban Bensonville (near O'Hare Airport), are open to the public; for information, call ✆ **312/455-7000.** (Practices at the United Center are not open to the public.) For a more family-friendly and affordable hockey experience, catch the semipro **Chicago Wolves** at the Allstate Arena (✆ **847/724-GOAL** [724-4625]; www.chicagowolves.com). The team has been consistently excellent over the past few years and the games are geared toward all ages, with fireworks before the game and plenty of on- and off-ice entertainment (tickets $13–$30). Blackhawks at the United Center, 1901 W. Madison St. ✆ **312/455-4500.** www.chicago blackhawks.com. Tickets $15–$100. Bus: 9 or 20.

Chicago Bulls   Ages 8 & up. When it comes to basketball, Chicagoans prefer to live in the past, associating the Chicago Bulls with the days of Michael Jordan and the never-ending championships of the 1990s. Back in the glory days, the planet's most celebrated athlete, Michael Jordan, pulled off the impossible: replacing the world's perception of Chicago as gangster Al Capone's playground with an image of his royal Airness executing a signature tomahawk dunk. We started to take for granted the frenzied celebrations in the street that inevitably occurred each June in the wake of the latest championship crown. It was a wonderful boost for a perennially pessimistic sports-loving metropolis, and a rare, indelible moment when the city's white and black populations seemed to embrace in simple camaraderie and festivity. Although the team has rebounded somewhat from the dismal seasons that followed the departure of Michael Jordan and others, the current players don't inspire the same city-wide excitement. The upside for visitors? The Bulls don't consistently sell out, which might mean you can catch a game at the United Center—if your kids are basketball fans, it's well worth the price of admission to spend an evening here. At the United Center, 1901 W. Madison St. © 312/455-4000. www.nba. com/bulls. Tickets $20–$100; purchase through Ticketmaster at © 312/559-1212. Bus: 9 or 20.

Chicago Cubs **Ages 4 & up.** The Cubbies haven't made a World Series appearance since 1945 and haven't been World Champs since 1908, but don't let the team's less-than-stellar track record stop you. You must, absolutely must, take your kids to a game at Wrigley Field. Attend a day game. Buy a hot dog and box of Cracker Jacks, and join in the chorus of "Take Me Out to the Ball Game" during the seventh-inning stretch. (Since the death of longtime announcer Harry Caray, the crowd is led by a guest singer, often a visiting celebrity.) Because Wrigley Field is small, just about every seat is decent. Families might want to avoid the bleacher seats, because fans there can get a little overzealous in their rooting for the home team (and drinking). The ivy-covered outfield walls, hand-operated scoreboard, view of the shimmering lake from the upper deck, and w or l flag announcing the outcome of the game to the unfortunates who couldn't attend make Wrigley a pure slice of Americana. About a dozen tours of the ballpark are led each season on various Saturdays in the summer. Stops include the visitors' and home-team locker rooms, press box, security headquarters, and—thrill of thrills—a walk around the field itself. Tickets are $14 and are sold through the Wrigley Field ticket office (© 800/THE-CUBS [843-2827]), or stop by the box office at 1060 W. Addison St. The entire area around the stadium, known as Wrigleyville, is surrounded by souvenir shops, sports bars, and restaurants. One sandwich shop, the **Friendly Confines,** is actually located within the stadium itself, just off the sidewalk. **Sluggers,** a sports bar with real batting cages, is right around the corner from Wrigley at 3540 N. Clark St. (© 773/248-0055). At Wrigley Field, 1060 W. Addison St. © 773/404-CUBS (404-2827). www.cubs.mlb.com. Tickets $15–$50. Games do sell out (especially against longtime rivals such as the Mets), and most weekend and night games are sold out by Memorial Day; so it pays to call ahead. To order tickets in person, stop by the ticket windows at Wrigley Field Mon–Fri 9am–6pm, Sat 9am–4pm, and on game days. You can also order tickets online on the team website or call tickets.com at © 866/652-2827. Subway/El: Red Line to Addison. Bus: 22.

Chicago Fire **Ages 4 & up.** The city's Major League Soccer team launched in 1998 and quickly became a hit with families. The team plays at its own 20,000-seat stadium in suburban Bridgeview (about 12 miles southwest of downtown) from late May to October. Bringing your kids to a game is highly recommended—tickets are cheaper than for other professional sporting events, you can walk right up to the box office before a game and buy them, and kids understand soccer because many of them play it. During the summer, games usually take place in late afternoon or early evening. Regular fans of the Fire make the games fun, with organized stadium cheers and a band. The team reaches out to kids 12 and under with Sparky's Kids Club (Sparky the Dalmatian is the team's mascot), and to moms with the occasional Soccer Mom Saturday, with half-time games and prizes for moms. The occasional Kids' Fest features music, games, and clowns, so check the website for upcoming events. © 888/MLS-FIRE (657-3473). http://chicago.fire. mlsnet.com. Tickets $15–$40.

Chicago White Sox   Ages 4 & up. Despite their thrilling 2005 World Series win, the
White Sox struggle to attract the kind of crowds that the Cubs do. Located in the South
Side neighborhood of Bridgeport, the former Comiskey Park (now known as **U.S. Cellular Field**) has made a real effort to be family-friendly, although the sterile stadium and
the blighted neighborhood that surrounds it remain deterrents. When the owners
replaced the admittedly dilapidated former stadium with a concrete behemoth that lacks
the yesteryear charm of its predecessor, they did improve sightlines (if your kids are afraid
of heights, I'd recommend avoiding the vertigo-inducing upper-deck seats) and added
every conceivable amenity—from above-average ballpark food concessions to shops to
plentiful restrooms. The endearing quality about the White Sox is their blue-collar,
working-class aura with which so many Cubs-loathing southsiders identify. Games are
rarely sold out, but that makes this a bargain for bona fide baseball fans. U.S. Cellular
Field has the added bonus of pregame batting practice for kids (see "Sports & Games,"
in chapter 8). At U.S. Cellular Field, 333 W. 35th St. in the south side neighborhood of Bridgeport. ✆ **312/674-1000.** www.whitesox.mlb.com. Tickets $12–$45, half-price on Mon (kids get in
for $1 for certain Sun games). To get Sox tickets, call Ticketmaster at ✆ **866/SOX-GAME** (769-4263)
or visit the ticket office, Mon–Fri 10am–6pm, Sat–Sun 10am–4pm, with extended hours on
game days. Subway/El: Red Line to Sox/35th St.

DePaul Blue Demons   Ages 8 & up. The local college basketball team, the Blue
Demons, has a loyal following and is a good bet for an entertaining game at a reasonable
price. The season begins at the end of November. At the Allstate Arena, 6920 N. Mannheim
Rd., Rosemont. Tickets $9–$40; call ✆ **773/325-7526.** (Some of their games are at the United
Center.)

Northwestern Wildcats   Ages 8 & up. The smallest of the Big Ten colleges plays
football here. Although the team has occasionally surprised everyone by winning that
coveted spot in the Rose Bowl, more often, Northwestern crowds like to remind themselves why they attend Northwestern and not Michigan or Wisconsin or Ohio, with
cheers of "Someday, we'll be your boss" to opposing teams. At Ryan Field, 1501 Central St.,
in north suburban Evanston. ✆ **847/491-CATS** (491-2287). www.nusports.com. Tickets $25. Sub-
way/El: Purple Line to Central St., Evanston.

Thoroughbred Racing   Ages 6 & up. Arlington International Racecourse, with its
gleaming-white, palatial, six-story grandstand and lush gardens, is one of the most beautiful showcases for thoroughbred horse racing in the world. Arlington likes to say that it
caters to families, and it must be said that the ambience here is more Disney than den-
of-iniquity. It has a storied history stretching back to 1927, and its track has been graced
by such equine stars as Citation, Secretariat, and Cigar. The track's annual Arlington
Million (the sport's first million-dollar race) has attracted the top jockeys, trainers, and
horses in past years and recently became part of the new World Series Racing Championship, which includes the Breeders Cup races. Arlington's race days are thrilling to behold,
with all of racing's time-honored pageantry on display—from the bugler in traditional
dress to the parade of jockeys. Sunday is Family Day, with special activities for kids 12
and under. In the past, kids have been able to see a blacksmith shoe a horse, learn about
horse care from a groomer and the track veterinarian, and get goggles signed by jockeys.
Chicago parents should ask about the Junior Jockey Club, which keeps kids informed of
these activities. You can sign up through the website. At Arlington International Racecourse,
2200 W. Euclid Ave., Arlington Heights. ✆ **847/385-7500.** www.arlingtonpark.com. Seating
$3–$6. Gates Wed–Sun at 11am; post times are 1:05 and 3:05pm. Season runs June 13–Oct 28.

Take the Kennedy (I-94W) Expwy. to the I-90 Tollway and exit north on Rte. 53. Follow 53 north until you reach the Euclid exit. Or take the Metra train line to its Arlington Heights stop, which is within walking distance of the racecourse. General parking $4, valet parking $8.

9 STORY HOURS

Feel like you've read *The Cat in the Hat* about 10,000 times? Take your kids to one of these story hours and they can get their story fix while you get a rest—and you'll be inspiring a love of reading in your children.

Borders All ages. Kids can hear stories, with special visits from costumed characters, at this story hour, held at 11am on Tuesday on the lower level. 830 N. Michigan Ave. © **312/573-0564.** Free admission. Subway/El: Red Line to Chicago/State.

The Field Museum of Natural History   Ages 2 to 4. Designed for preschoolers, "Story Time" is a weekend afternoon event held at 1:30pm in the Living Together exhibit area that focuses on stories and projects that tie in with current exhibits. Roosevelt Rd. at Lake Shore Dr. © **312/665-7400.** Free with museum admission of $22 for adults, $12 for children. Bus: 146.

Thomas Hughes Children's Library at Harold Washington Library Center Ages 2 & up. Twice a month puppets act out stories, and Saturdays are packed with programs, including puppet shows, videos, crafts, author readings, and book signings. Toddler story times are offered at 10:30am on Mondays for kids 2 years and up and include storytelling, puppetry, music, movement, and a craft; you must sign up in advance, or if there's an opening, walk-ins are allowed. Baby "lapsit" story hours start at 10:30am on Mondays. Story times for preschoolers are available on a walk-in basis year-round at 10am Mondays. 400 S. State St. © **312/747-4200.** www.chicagopubliclibrary.org. Subway/El: Red Line to Jackson/State, Brown Line to Van Buren/Library.

Women and Children First   Ages 2 to 5. Books and poems are featured at this story hour for preschoolers, held Wednesday mornings from 10:30 to 11am. Store co-owner Linda Bubon performs five or more stories, including singing, dancing, and general silliness! Doors open at 10:15am. 5233 N. Clark St. © **773/769-9299.** Free admission. Subway/El: Red Line to Bryn Mawr, then walk several blocks west to Clark. Bus: 22.

10 ARCADES

ESPN Zone   Ages 7 & up. This 35,000-square-foot sports shrine provides arcade fans with sports-inspired video games plus the Sports Arena, where everyone can try out his or her skills. Future quarterbacks can try to throw the ball through moving cutouts. A simulated rock-climbing wall moves up and down like a vertical treadmill so you can never reach the top. You and your kids can dribble and shoot baskets on a half court, scoring points based on the difficulty of the shots you make. The basket can even be lowered so younger kids get a fair shot. And you can check your scores against those of the NBA players who showed off their stuff here. If hockey's your sport, you and your kids can pretend to be NHL players, with one of you taking shots on simulated ice while the other plays goalie. The Screening Room is a fan's nirvana, with a 16-foot screen surrounded by skybox viewing suites, along with another 37 monitors to cover everything

from the Super Bowl to the Madagascar Knee Volleyball Championships. 43 E. Ohio St.
© **312/644-ESPN** (644-3776). www.espnzone.com. Free admission; cost is $5 for a 15-point card, $15 for a 60-point card, and on up to $100 for a 700-point card. Games "cost" 2–10 points each. Bigger attractions, such as NHL Tonight and ESPN Bowling, are 10–24 points). Sun–Thurs 11am–11pm; Fri 11am–midnight; Sat 10am–midnight. Subway/El: Red Line to State/Grand.

LEGOLAND Discovery Centre   You'll need to make the trek out to the northwest suburbs to explore the first indoor LEGO world to open in the U.S., but for families with LEGO fans in their ranks, it's definitely worth a special trip. Located in The Streets of Woodfield (next to the gigantic Woodfield Mall), this stop is designed for kids ages 2 through 12. Featuring hands-on LEGO activities and life-sized LEGO adventures, you'll be able to fill a day here. The 30,000-square-foot facility combines LEGO model building and unusual construction challenges with theme park-like attractions such as a dragon ride, adventure trail, and 4D cinema incorporating fantastical LEGO creatures and LEGO-based special effects. If you've got young kids, there's a DUPLO play area, and you can take a break at the LEGO café (and of course, purchase a memento of your visit at the LEGO store). Don't miss visiting the special room with rotating exhibitions of work by master LEGO builders. Allow 3 hours. 601 N. Martingale Road (at the intersection of Martingale Road and Higgins Road), Schaumberg. © **866/929-8111.** www.legoland discoverycentre.com. Adults $19, seniors $17, children age 3 and up $15, children age 2 and under are free. Daily 10am–7pm (last tickets are sold at 5pm). Call for holiday hours. Subway/El: Blue Line to Rosemont Station. Transfer to the Route 606 Pace Bus to Woodfield Mall. Take the free Schaumburg Woodfield Trolley to the Streets of Woodfield stop. By car: take I-294 North to I-290 West to Illinois 72/Higgins Road Exit. Turn left onto Higgins Road, then turn right onto N. Martingale Road.

Side Trips from Chicago

Even with all that the city proper has to offer, if you're in town for more than a few days (or if you're staying with friends or relatives in the suburbs), you might want to venture beyond the city limits and check out some of the sights in the surrounding areas.

---

1 INDIANA DUNES STATE PARK

53 miles SE of Chicago (in Indiana)

This all-ages destination is my favorite for escaping to the great outdoors. The scenery, with dunes and grasses fronting the lake, is reminiscent of Cape Cod. Sending your kids running up, down, and around the dunes is a great way to burn off some energy, and tiring out your kids usually makes for a nice, quiet car ride back to the city!

ESSENTIALS

To get to the dunes, you'll need to drive. Take I-94 East to Ind. 49 North (east of Porter). Follow Ind. 49 north to Rte. 12. Travel east on Rte. 12 for 3 miles to the Dorothy Buell Memorial Visitor Center, which has restrooms and a gift shop with postcards, posters, and slides.

SEEING THE DUNES

You probably don't associate the words "sand dunes" with the Midwest, but a trip to Indiana Dunes State Park might change that. At the base of Lake Michigan, near Chesterton, Indiana, you'll find 15 miles of dunes so big you can't see over them; 3 miles of the dunes line sandy beaches. You can visit maple and oak forests, miles of sand piles covered with vegetation, marshes, and bogs, all in one state park. Plenty of well-marked trails help you explore.

Stop at the visitor center for a free map and a 10-minute slide show that will orient you. You might check out Cowles Bog, filled with ponds, wetlands, and marshes, plus delicate vegetation such as orchids, and not-so-delicate vegetation such as Venus' flytraps. West Beach offers a 3-mile trail that passes through a prairie zone, a conifer zone, and an oak forest–deciduous zone, and ends at a beach. If it's beachgoing that you're focused on, check out Kemil Beach, a long stretch of beautiful white sand. Finally, Mount Baldy is the largest "living" sand dune in the park, so named for the mounds of sand that are active in the wind.

1600 N. 25E, Chesterton, Indiana. © **219/926-1952.** www.in.gov. Free admission. Nature center summer daily 10am–5pm; beaches summer daily 11am–11pm. To park, you'll find some free lots, but some summer lots require payment.

WHERE TO EAT

There are no restaurants here, so bring a picnic. You'll find plenty of picnic areas in the park, some with barbecue pits. If you're staying in downtown Chicago, good places to

pick up sandwiches and drinks are Corner Bakery (p. 129) and Potbelly Sandwich Works **283** (p. 120).

2 KOHL CHILDREN'S MUSEUM

About 20 miles NW of Chicago

Children as young as 1 year old can enjoy this top-notch museum. (There are several infant play areas, which come in handy for younger siblings, but your kids will get more out of the museum once they're at least a year old.) In fact, many Chicago parents prefer Kohl to the Chicago Children's Museum on Navy Pier for its ease of access—you'll find much less of a crowd here than at Navy Pier. The museum has a brand-new facility that makes it worth a suburban stop.

ESSENTIALS

Glenview is on the North Shore, a swath of suburbia between Chicago and the state border of Wisconsin that is one of the nation's most affluent residential areas.

BY CAR From 94 northbound: Take Lake Avenue West exit heading west for 3 miles, then turn right onto Patriot Boulevard.

BY TRAIN Catch the **Metra** train (© **312/322-6777;** www.metrarail.com) from the Ogilvie Transportation Center at Madison and Canal streets in Chicago to the North Glenview station. Walk ¹/₂ mile west on West Lake Avenue to reach the museum on Patriot Boulevard.

SEEING THE MUSEUM

The Kohl Children's Museum packs a lot into its small square footage: The 200,000 visitors it hosts annually make it the most heavily visited museum per square foot in metropolitan Chicago. Opened in 1985, this museum is a hands-on, dress-up-and-pretend, blow-bubbles sort of place where your kids will amuse themselves for hours. They can shop at a simulated supermarket, take a voyage on a Phoenician sailing ship, and join in puppet shows and singalongs.

Permanent exhibits include **Car Care,** which provides a car wash with real blowers and rolling mops for kids to run through and operate, a car for kids to drive and repair, and an elaborate racetrack with cars that kids assemble on their own.

Dominick's, a grocery-store exhibit, gives children a chance to run the shop. Kids can role-play by pretending to be shoppers or the cashier. They're responsible for the workings of the store, from shopping to restocking to checking out. Other permanent exhibits include the **Hands-on House,** where you can be a home builder; **Water Works,** where kids can explore the wonders of water play; **Pet Vet,** a mocked-up veterinary clinic; and **Potbelly Sandwich Works,** where kids can run their own restaurant.

2100 Patriot Blvd., Glenview. © **847/832-6600.** www.kohlchildrensmuseum.org. Admission $6.50 adults and children, $5.50 seniors, free for children under 1. Mon 9:30am–noon (to 5pm June–Aug); Tues–Sat 9:30am–5pm; Sun noon–5pm.

MAKE A WEEKEND OF IT

The North Shore offers plenty of activities for families. Besides the Kohl Children's Museum, the **Chicago Botanic Garden,** with its kid-pleasing train garden (see below),

> (Moments) **A Suburban Respite**
>
> If you've made it up to the Baha'i Temple, take a stroll across Sheridan Road to **Gilson Park** for a taste of northern suburban life. Check out the sailors prepping their boats for a lake tour, families picnicking and playing Frisbee, and kids frolicking on the sandy beach. Access to the beach is restricted in the summer (the locals like to keep the Chicago riffraff out), but in the fall and spring, you're welcome to wander (just don't expect to take a dip in the frigid water).

is just a short drive away, as is one of the country's oldest malls, **Westfield Old Orchard Shopping Center** (www.westfield.com/oldorchard). This upscale, open-air mall features a fun hill-running outdoor play area, and is anchored by top-notch department stores including Nordstrom, Bloomingdale's, and Macy's. If you decide to stay, one hotel that caters to families is **Hampton Inn & Suites** (© 847/583-1111; www.hamptonsuites skokie.com). Not only do they have king and double suites with full-size kitchens (the bedrooms have their own televisions), but they also have a good-size pool with kid toys supplied, and free breakfast that's a cut above the average free hotel buffet.

While you're in the area, do some North Shore sightseeing with a drive over to Sheridan Road in Wilmette and the most visited of all the sights in the northern suburbs, the **Baha'i House of Worship,** an edifice that seems not of this earth. The gleaming white stone temple, designed by the French Canadian Louis Bourgeois and completed in 1953, is essentially a soaring nine-sided 135-foot dome, draped in a delicate lacelike facade, which strongly reveals the Eastern influence of the Baha'i faith's native Iran. Surrounded by formal gardens, it is one of seven Baha'i temples in the world, and the only one in the Western Hemisphere. The dome's latticework is even more beautiful as you gaze upward from the floor of the sanctuary, which, during the day, is flooded with light. Temple members give informal tours of the building to anyone who inquires; older children and adults with an interest in architecture will get the most out of a tour of the interior. Not only is the temple itself really a sight, but the drive on Sheridan Road is also one of the most beautiful in the Chicago area.

A word of caution if you're driving: The temple seems to appear out of nowhere as you round a particularly tight curve on Sheridan Road, and it can distract even the most focused of drivers. Take it slow and wait until you're safely parked before gazing skyward.

100 Linden Ave. (at Sheridan Rd.), Wilmette. © **847/853-2300.** www.us.bahai.org/how. Free admission. Visitor center daily May–Sept 10am–8pm; Oct–Apr 10am–5pm. Temple daily from 7am. Devotional services are held Mon–Sat at 12:15pm and Sun at 1:15pm (with choral accompaniment). To get there from Chicago, take the Red Line of the El north to Howard St. Change trains for the Evanston train and go to the end of the line, Linden Ave. (Or take the Purple/Evanston Express and stay on the same train all the way.) Turn right on Linden and walk 2 blocks east. If you're driving, take the Outer Dr. (Lake Shore Dr.) north, which feeds into Sheridan Rd.

WHERE TO EAT

After you see the Baha'i Temple, backtrack south on Green Bay road to **Walker Bros. Original Pancake House,** at 153 Green Bay Rd. (© 847/251-6000; www.walkerbros oph.com). The place is decorated with colorful Tiffany-style lamps, warm woodwork, deep booths, and extraordinary stained-glass art windows. Expect a wait on weekends. Top choices are apple pancakes, which arrive bubbling hot and glazed with cinnamon,

and German pancakes, fluffy pancakes dusted with powdered sugar and served with fruit.
Kids often go for the silver-dollar pancakes in chocolate chip, blueberry, or plain varieties.
Oven-baked omelets are another favorite. The restaurant also serves lunch and dinner,
and offers chicken teriyaki, roast beef, chicken Dijon, Reuben sandwiches, and salads. All
menu items are served throughout the day; it's open daily from 6:30am to 10pm.

---

3 CHICAGO BOTANIC GARDEN

About 25 miles N of Chicago

The Botanic Garden is a favorite of Chicago families because it's only a short drive from
the city but it offers a welcome change of scenery. Even young children will enjoy the
room to run (or ride in a stroller) along scenic trails, interspersed with waterfalls and
fountains. Older kids can explore the fruit-and-vegetable garden (so this is where bananas
come from!) and gardens of animal-shaped topiaries.

ESSENTIALS

BY CAR   Take I-90 (Kennedy Expwy.) to the Edens Expressway (I-94). Go north 20
miles and continue north on Rte. 41 and exit on Lake Cook Road. Turn right and go
$^1/_2$ mile to the garden.

BY TRAIN   You can take the **Metra** North Line (𝐶 **312/322-6777;** www.metrarail.
com) from Ogilvie Transportation Center at Madison and Canal streets in Chicago to
Glencoe. Connect to the 213 Pace Bus to reach the Botanic Garden.

TOURING THE GARDEN

Owned by the Forest Preserve District of Cook County and managed by the 110-year-
old Chicago Horticultural Society, this living preserve includes eight large lagoons and a
variety of distinct botanical environments—from the Illinois prairie to an English walled
garden to a three-island Japanese garden. To keep the visit manageable for kids, call ahead
to find out what's blooming and grab a map from the information desk when you arrive
to pick the gardens your family most wants to see. A tram tour lets kids cover more
ground without getting tired, which is a real possibility in this 385-acre garden.

Also on the grounds are a large fruit-and-vegetable garden, an Enabling Garden
(which shows how gardening can be adapted for people with disabilities), and a 100-acre
old-growth oak woodland. The living collections are composed of more than 1.2 million
plants, representing 7,000 plant types. If you're here in the summer, don't miss the extensive rose gardens (just follow the bridal parties who flock here to get their pictures taken).
The Botanic Garden also is home to an exhibit hall, an auditorium, a museum, a library,
education greenhouses, an outdoor pavilion, a carillon, a cafe, a designated bike path,
and a garden shop. Carillon concerts are given on Monday evenings at 7pm from June
21 to August 23, with a preliminary hour-long tour.

For kids, the highlight of the garden is the **Model Railroad Garden: Landmarks of
America,** which runs May through October (an additional $5 admission for adults; $3
for children ages 3–12). A family favorite, this enchanting outdoor exhibit takes visitors
from coast to coast with model trains, miniature representations of America's best-loved
landmarks, and colorful small-scale gardens. At the holidays, the garden creates an indoor
winter train garden called the Wonderland Express, which is truly magical. Check the
website or call to learn about upcoming events.

1000 Lake Cook Rd. (just east of Edens Expwy./I-94), Glencoe. ℂ **847/835-5440.** www.chicago-botanic. org. Free admission. Apr–Oct tram tours $5 adults, $4 seniors, $3 children 3–15. Daily 8am–sunset. Closed Dec 25. Parking $10.

WHERE TO EAT

The **Garden Café,** located within the Chicago Botanic Garden, serves soup, sandwiches, and salads as well as kids' favorites, in a cafeteria-style setting. In the summer you can sit on a patio overlooking water or at tables adjacent to the Rose Garden. It's open daily from 8am to 5pm.

4 DUPAGE CHILDREN'S MUSEUM

About 30 miles W of Chicago

Chicago's western suburbs are rapidly expanding. Naperville, a farming area not too many decades ago, is now one of Illinois's largest cities. Home to the DuPage Children's Museum, Naperville also has a historic downtown. The two make for a perfect day's outing. The museum is geared to all ages, but toddlers to age 8 will enjoy it most.

ESSENTIALS

BY CAR   Take the Eisenhower Expressway West (I-290) from Chicago. Take the I-294/I-88 West exit toward Indiana/Aurora. Merge onto I-88W, the East-West Tollway. Take the Naperville Road exit and turn right on Naperville Road. Turn right on East Ogden Avenue/U.S. 34. Turn left onto North Washington Street.

BY TRAIN   Catch the **Metra** Burlington Northern Santa Fe Line (ℂ **312/322-6777;** www.metrarail.com) from Union Station on Canal Street (btw. Adams and Jackson Blvd.) in Chicago to Naperville.

EXPLORING THE MUSEUM

DuPage Children's Museum is in Naperville, a historic, formerly rural community with a Main Street U.S.A. downtown district worthy of Norman Rockwell. (Naperville maintains a collection of 19th-century buildings in an outdoor museum setting known as Naper Settlement, with a lovely river walk.) At the museum, visit six "neighborhoods," where kids can learn about everything from construction to art. It's a great layout that eliminates walls, so you can keep an eye on your kids even if they are in different exhibits. **Creativity Connections** brings art, math, and science together; wee ones can enjoy black, white, and red patterns to stimulate their brains, look at themselves in mirrors, and change the color of a light's filter to see themselves in a new perspective, while older kids can play with shadows and light. **Build It** puts kid-size saws, hammers, and other real tools in kids' hands and lets them build a chair for a Beanie Baby, or saw wood. (Never fear, staff members are on hand to make sure everyone stays safe.) The littlest ones get to participate by hammering golf tees into Styrofoam and building with soft blocks. **Make It Move** turns kids into scientists experimenting with gravity. **AirWorks** lets kids walk through a wind tunnel and, with the wave of a special wand, fill up an air sock. **Water-Ways** shows kids how the power of water can be harnessed, and how to use sandbags to stop the rush of a waterfall. (Waterproof aprons are on hand to keep clothes dry.) Families with very young children should plan to spend about an hour here (or longer, if attention spans allow). Older children will be happy here for 2 to 3 hours.

301 N. Washington, Naperville. $\textcircled{C}$ **630/637-8000.** www.dupagechildrensmuseum.org. Admission $8.50
adults and children age 1 and over, $7.50 seniors, free for infants under age 1. Mon 9am–1pm; Tues–Wed
and Fri–Sat 9am–5pm; Thurs 9am–8pm; Sun noon–5pm.

WHERE TO EAT

The museum has a dining area with vending machines and a microwave, and nearby
you'll find plenty of fast-food restaurants. For a change of pace, try pizza at **Lou Malnati's,** 131 W. Jefferson St. ($\textcircled{C}$ **630/717-0700**).

5 WONDER WORKS

10 miles W of downtown Chicago

Wonder Works is the Chicago area's newest children's museum, located in Oak Park, a
historic and scenic suburb, with a wonderful downtown full of shops and restaurants.
Especially if your kids are over age 8, I'd recommend spending a day in Oak Park, visiting
the museum, and taking a tour of the Frank Lloyd Wright Home & Studio.

ESSENTIALS

BY CAR   Oak Park is about 30 minutes due west of downtown Chicago. Take North
Avenue west. You will travel about 9 miles straight on North Avenue to the museum,
which is at Elmwood and North avenues, just west of Ridgeland.

BY BUS   Take the no. 72 (North Ave.) bus from the corner of Clark Street and North
Avenue. It's about a 45-minute bus ride straight to the museum.

EXPLORING THE MUSEUM

This 6,500-square-foot museum is designed for kids up to age 10. It opened in 2003 and
as such is one of Chicago's newer children's museums.

One permanent exhibit is **Lights, Camera, Action!,** a performance area that allows
kids to be stars with a low-rise stage, costumes, and backdrops. Kids can sing a song,
entertain the audience, and record it all on videotape. Professional puppeteers and story-
tellers use the stage during special events throughout the year.

The **Great Outdoors** exhibit lets kids experience the wonders of the natural nighttime
world. Sounds and lighting set the mood and a canopy creates a beautiful night sky; tents
are set up near a glowing "campfire." Kids can also climb a ladder into a treehouse. A nature
trail lets kids wander through the "outdoors," with surprises around every corner.

The **Build It!** exhibit allows children to become construction workers, architects, and
engineers. Filled with a variety of small- and large-scale construction materials, this
exhibit lets children plan, design, and create anything they desire, while developing their
fine and gross motor skills.

6445 W. North Ave., Oak Park. $\textcircled{C}$ **708/383-4815.** www.wonder-works.org. Admission $5 ages 1 and over.
Wed–Sat 10am–5pm; Sun noon–5pm. Closed holidays.

WHERE TO EAT

An Oak Park tradition, **Petersen's,** at 1100 W. Chicago Ave. ($\textcircled{C}$ **708/386-6131;** www.
petersenicecream.com), is an ice-cream shop that's been serving up good ol' American
favorites since 1919. In addition to wonderfully rich ice cream (try the seasonal specials
that include peach in summertime and eggnog in winter), Petersen's also offers soup and
sandwiches for adults, and kiddie treats such as dinosaur-shaped chicken nuggets. But

the focus here is on dessert, so have your kids save plenty of room: The specialty is the Merry-Go-Round, a chocolate sundae topped with animal cookies and a parasol.

6 CUNEO MUSEUM & GARDENS

About 30 miles from downtown Chicago

Best for kids over 8, this historic mansion and grounds provide a glimpse into how people lived 100 years ago.

ESSENTIALS

The museum is not easily accessible by public transportation. To reach the museum **by car,** take the Kennedy (I-94W) expressway north to Rte. 60. Go west on Rte. 60 and then, at the Hawthorn Mall, turn north on Milwaukee Avenue (Rte. 21).

VISITING THE MUSEUM

This is a wonderful place for older kids to see how people lived in the early 20th century. The Cuneo Museum & Gardens was designed in 1914 by architect Benjamin Marshall for Samuel Insull, founder of the powerful Commonwealth Edison electric company and a partner of Thomas Edison. Its present-day name, however, comes from John F. Cuneo, a Chicago printing magnate, philanthropist, and gentleman farmer whose family lived at this vast, luxuriant estate from 1937 to 1990.

If you want to see how the other half lives, here's your chance. The palatial mansion is designed in an opulent Italianate style, with accents such as bold ironwork decor that are reminiscent of a Venetian palazzo. Eighteen of its 32 rooms are on exhibit to the public. The centerpiece is the **Great Hall,** featuring a 30-foot ceiling with skylights over a central courtyard surrounded by marble columns and arcaded balconies. You'll also "ooh" and "ahh" over the fanciful ceiling frescoes in the unusual double dining rooms and exquisite private chapel.

Cuneo was a connoisseur of art treasures, and the core of his collection is on display here, from old-master paintings and 17th-century tapestries to a custom-made gilt-wood piano and fine Capo di Monte porcelain. The estate's grounds, which at one time spanned 3,000 acres, are now a relatively modest 75 acres. They're quite lovely, with lakes, fountains, formal gardens, antique classical statuary, and even a few peacocks and swans. There's also a conservatory housing exotic plants, and Deer Park, a wooded enclosure that's about the only vestigial reminder of Hawthorn-Mellody Farms, a former farm and dairy operation that for years attracted families with its "Wild West Town," country store, and petting zoo.

1350 N. Milwaukee Ave., Vernon Hills. ✆ **847/362-3042.** www.cuneomuseum.org. Tour tickets $12 adults, $11 seniors, $7 children. Tues–Sun 10am–5pm. Guided tours Tues–Sat at 11am, 1, and 3pm. Grounds fee only (for touring the gardens in the summer without going into the house, for example) is $7. Free parking.

WHERE TO EAT

Hawthorne Center Mall, adjacent to the museum, features the usual array of fast-food and chain restaurants. For a more true-to-Chicago experience, head into Vernon Hills to the **Pizzeria Uno** at 545 Lakeview Pkwy. (✆ **847/918-8667**). Also nearby is the historic village of Long Grove, with the famed Long Grove Confectionary (✆ **847/634-0080;** www.longgrove.com).

Appendix: Fast Facts, Toll-Free Numbers & Websites

1 FAST FACTS: CHICAGO

AMERICAN EXPRESS Travel-service offices are located in the Loop at 55 W. Monroe St. (© **312/541-5440**) and just north of the Tribune Tower at 605 N. Michigan Ave.

AREA CODES The **312** area code applies to the Loop and the neighborhoods closest to it, including River North, North Michigan Avenue, and the Gold Coast. The rest of the city is under the **773** area code. Suburban area codes are **847** (north), **708** (west and southwest), and **630** (far west). You must dial "1" plus the area code for all telephone numbers, even if you are making a call within the same area code.

ATM NETWORKS/CASHPOINTS See "Money & Costs," p. 39.

AUTOMOBILE ORGANIZATIONS Motor clubs will supply maps, suggested routes, guidebooks, accident and bail-bond insurance, and emergency road service. The **American Automobile Association (AAA)** is the major auto club in the United States. If you belong to a motor club in your home country, inquire about AAA reciprocity before you leave. You may be able to join AAA even if you're not a member of a reciprocal club; to inquire, call AAA (© **800/ 222-4357;** www.aaa.com). AAA is actually an organization of regional motor clubs, so look under "AAA Automobile Club" in the White Pages of the telephone directory.

AAA has a nationwide emergency road service telephone number (© 800/AAA-HELP [222-4357]).

BABYSITTERS Check with the concierge or desk staff at your hotel, who are likely to maintain a list of reliable sitters with whom they have worked in the past. Many of the hotels work with the **American ChildCare Service** (© **312/644-7300;** www.americanchildcare.com), a state-licensed babysitting service that can match you with a sitter. The sitters are required to pass background checks, provide multiple child-care references, and be trained in infant and child CPR. It's best to make a reservation 24 hours in advance; the office is open from 9am to 5pm. Rates are about $19 per hour, with a 4-hour minimum and a $20 agency fee (you're also expected to give the sitter a cash tip).

BUSINESS HOURS Shops generally keep normal business hours, Monday through Saturday from 10am to 6pm. Most stores generally stay open late at least 1 evening a week. And certain businesses, such as bookstores, are almost always open during the evening hours all week. Most shops (other than those in the Loop) are now open on Sunday as well, usually from noon to 5pm. Malls are generally open until 7pm and on Sunday as well. Banking hours in Chicago are normally from 9am (8am in some cases) to 5pm Monday

through Friday, with select banks remaining open later on specified afternoons and evenings.

CAR RENTALS See "Toll-Free Numbers & Websites," p. 295.

DENTISTS The referral service of the **Chicago Dental Society** (© 312/836-7300; www.cds.org) can refer you to an area dentist; you can also get a referral online through the website. You also might try your hotel concierge or desk staff, who might keep a list of dentists.

DOCTORS In the event of a medical emergency, your best bet—unless you have friends who can recommend a doctor—is to rely on your hotel physician or go to the nearest hospital emergency room. **Northwestern Memorial Hospital** has a **Physician Referral Service** (© 877/926-4664). See also "Hospitals," below.

DRINKING LAWS The legal age for the purchase and consumption of alcoholic beverages is 21; proof of age is required and often requested at bars, nightclubs, and restaurants, so it's always a good idea to bring ID when you go out.

In Chicago, beer, wine, and other alcoholic beverages are sold at liquor stores and supermarkets. Bars may sell alcohol until 2am, although some nightclubs have special licenses that allow alcohol sales until 4am. Do not carry open containers of alcohol in your car or any public area that isn't zoned for alcohol consumption. The police can fine you on the spot. And nothing will ruin your trip faster than getting a citation for DUI (driving under the influence), so don't even think about driving while intoxicated.

DRIVING RULES See "Getting Around," p. 58.

ELECTRICITY Like Canada, the United States uses 110–120 volts AC (60 cycles), compared to 220–240 volts AC (50 cycles) in most of Europe, Australia, and New Zealand. Downward converters that change 220–240 volts to 110–120 volts

are difficult to find in the United States, so bring one with you.

EMBASSIES & CONSULATES All embassies are in the nation's capital, Washington, D.C. Some consulates are located in major U.S. cities, and most nations have a mission to the United Nations in New York City. If your country isn't listed below, call for directory information in Washington, D.C. (© 202/555-1212), or log on to **www.embassy.org/embassies**.

The embassy of **Australia** is at 1601 Massachusetts Ave. NW, Washington, DC 20036 (© 202/797-3000; www.austemb. org). There are consulates in New York, Honolulu, Houston, Los Angeles, and San Francisco.

The embassy of **Canada** is at 501 Pennsylvania Ave. NW, Washington, DC 20001 (© 202/682-1740; http://geo.international. gc.ca/can-am/washington). Other Canadian consulates are in Buffalo (New York), Detroit, Los Angeles, New York, and Seattle.

The embassy of **Ireland** is at 2234 Massachusetts Ave. NW, Washington, DC 20008 (© 202/462-3939; www.ireland emb.org). Irish consulates are in Boston, Chicago, New York, San Francisco, and other cities. See website for complete listing.

The embassy of **New Zealand** is at 37 Observatory Circle NW, Washington, DC 20008 (© 202/328-4800; www.nz embassy.com). New Zealand consulates are in Los Angeles, Salt Lake City, San Francisco, and Seattle.

The embassy of the **United Kingdom** is at 3100 Massachusetts Ave. NW, Washington, DC 20008 (© 202/588-7800; www.britainusa.com). Other British consulates are in Atlanta, Boston, Chicago, Cleveland, Houston, Los Angeles, New York, San Francisco, and Seattle.

EMERGENCIES For fire or police emergencies, call © 911. The nonemergency phone number for the Chicago Police Department is © 311. The city of Chicago

proclaims the following policy: "In emergency, dial 911 and a city ambulance will respond free of charge to the patient. The ambulance will take the patient to the nearest emergency room according to geographic location." If you desire a specific, nonpublic ambulance, call **Vandenberg Ambulance** (© **773/521-7777**).

GASOLINE (PETROL) At press time, the cost of gasoline (also known as gas, but never petrol) is fluctuating at just around $1.75 a gallon in Chicago. Taxes are included in the printed price. One U.S. gallon equals 3.8 liters or .85 imperial gallons. Fill-up locations are known as gas or service stations.

HOLIDAYS Banks, government offices, post offices, and many stores, restaurants, and museums are closed on the following legal national holidays: January 1 (New Year's Day), the third Monday in January (Martin Luther King, Jr., Day), the third Monday in February (Presidents' Day), the last Monday in May (Memorial Day), July 4 (Independence Day), the first Monday in September (Labor Day), the second Monday in October (Columbus Day), November 11 (Veterans Day/Armistice Day), the fourth Thursday in November (Thanksgiving Day), and December 25 (Christmas). The Tuesday after the first Monday in November is Election Day, a federal government holiday in presidential-election years (held every 4 years, and next in 2012).

For more information on holidays, see "Kids' Favorite Chicago Events," in chapter 2.

HOSPITALS The best hospital emergency room in Chicago is, by consensus, at **Northwestern Memorial Hospital,** 251 E. Huron St. (© **312/926-2000;** www. nmh.org), a state-of-the-art medical center right off North Michigan Avenue. The emergency department (© **312/926-5188** or 312/944-2358 for TDD access) is at 251 E. Erie St., near Fairbanks Court. For

an ambulance, dial © **911,** which is a free call.

INTERNET ACCESS Many Chicago hotels have business centers with computers available for guests' use. Computers with Internet access are also available to the public at the **Harold Washington Library Center,** 400 S. State St. (© **312/ 747-4300**), and at the Internet cafe inside the **Apple** computer store, 679 N. Michigan Ave. (© **312/981-4104**). Most Starbucks coffee shops and McDonald's restaurants in downtown Chicago have wireless Internet access available.

LEGAL AID If you are "pulled over" for a minor infraction (such as speeding), never attempt to pay the fine directly to a police officer; this could be construed as attempted bribery, a much more serious crime. Pay fines by mail, or directly into the hands of the clerk of the court. If accused of a more serious offense, say and do nothing before consulting a lawyer. Here the burden is on the state to prove a person's guilt beyond a reasonable doubt, and everyone has the right to remain silent, whether he or she is suspected of a crime or actually arrested. Once arrested, a person can make one telephone call to a party of his or her choice. International visitors should call their embassy or consulate.

LIQUOR LAWS Most bars and taverns have a 2am license, allowing them to stay open until 3am Sunday (Sat night); some have a 4am license and may remain open until 5am on Sunday.

LOST & FOUND Be sure to tell all of your credit card companies the minute you discover your wallet has been lost or stolen, and file a report at the nearest police precinct. Your credit card company or insurer may require a police report number or record of the loss. Most credit card companies have an emergency toll-free number to call if your card is lost or stolen; they may be able to wire you a cash

advance immediately or deliver an emergency credit card in a day or two. Visa's U.S. emergency number is © 800/847-2911 or 410/581-9994. American Express cardholders and traveler's check holders should call © 800/221-7282. MasterCard holders should call © 800/307-7309 or 636/722-7111. For other credit cards, call the toll-free number directory at © 800/555-1212.

If you need emergency cash over the weekend when all banks and American Express offices are closed, you can have money wired to you via **Western Union** (© 800/325-6000; www.westernunion. com).

MAIL At press time, domestic postage rates were 27¢ for a postcard and 42¢ for a letter. For international mail, a first-class letter of up to 1 ounce costs 94¢ (72¢ to Canada and Mexico); a first-class postcard costs the same as a postcard. For more information go to **www.usps.com** and click on "Calculate Postage."

If you aren't sure what your address will be in the United States, mail can be sent to you, in your name, c/o General Delivery at the main post office of the city or region where you expect to be. (Call © 800/275-8777 for information on the nearest post office.) The addressee must pick up mail in person and must produce proof of identity (driver's license, passport, and so on). Most post offices will hold your mail for up to 1 month, and are open Monday to Friday from 8am to 6pm, and Saturday from 9am to 3pm.

Always include zip codes when mailing items in the U.S. If you don't know your zip code, visit www.usps.com/zip4.

MAPS See "Getting to Know Chicago" in chapter 2.

NEWSPAPERS & MAGAZINES The *Chicago Tribune* (© 312/222-3232; www. chicagotribune.com) and the *Chicago Sun-Times* (© 312/321-3000; www.suntimes. com) are the two major dailies. *Time Out*

Chicago (© 312/924-9555; www.timeout chicago.com) is a weekly magazine that includes comprehensive roundups of the week's special events and performances. The *Chicago Reader* (© 312/828-0350; www.chicagoreader.com) is a free weekly that appears each Thursday, with all the current entertainment and cultural listings. *Chicago Magazine* (www.chicagomag. com) is a monthly that is widely read for its restaurant reviews. *CS* is a free lifestyle monthly that covers nightlife, dining, fashion, shopping, and other cultural pursuits. The *Chicago Defender* covers local and national news of interest to the African-American community. The Spanish-language *La Raza* (www.laraza.com) reports on stories from a Latino point of view. The *Chicago Free Press* (www.chicagofreepress. com) and *Windy City Times* (www.windy citytimes.com) publish both news and feature articles about gay and lesbian issues.

PASSPORTS The websites listed provide downloadable passport applications as well as the current fees for processing applications. For an up-to-date, country-by-country listing of passport requirements around the world, go to the "International Travel" tab of the U.S. State Department at **http://travel.state.gov**. International visitors to the U.S. can obtain a visa application at the same website. *Note:* Children are required to present a passport when entering the United States at airports. More information on obtaining a passport for a minor can be found at http://travel.state.gov. Allow plenty of time before your trip to apply for a passport; processing normally takes 4 to 6 weeks (3 weeks for expedited service) but can take longer during busy periods (especially spring). And keep in mind that if you need a passport in a hurry, you'll pay a higher processing fee.

For Residents of Australia You can pick up an application from your local post office or any branch of Passports Australia, but you must schedule an interview at the

passport office to present your application materials. Call the **Australian Passport Information Service** at ℂ **131-232,** or visit the government website at www.passports.gov.au.

For Residents of Canada Passport applications are available at travel agencies throughout Canada or from the central **Passport Office,** Dept. of Foreign Affairs and International Trade, Ottawa, ON K1A 0G3 (ℂ **800/567-6868;** www.ppt.gc.ca). *Note:* Canadian children who travel must have their own passport. However, if you hold a valid Canadian passport issued before December 11, 2001, that bears the name of your child, the passport remains valid for you and your child until it expires.

For Residents of Ireland You can apply for a 10-year passport at the **Passport Office,** Setanta Centre, Molesworth Street, Dublin 2 (ℂ **01/671-1633;** www.irlgov.ie/iveagh). Those under age 18 and over 65 must apply for a 3-year passport. You can also apply at 1A South Mall, Cork (ℂ **21/494-4700**), or at most main post offices.

For Residents of New Zealand You can pick up a passport application at any New Zealand Passports Office or download it from the website. Contact the **Passports Office** at ℂ **0800/225-050** in New Zealand or 04/474-8100, or log on to www.passports.govt.nz.

For Residents of the United Kingdom To pick up an application for a standard 10-year passport (5-yr. passport for children 15 and under), visit your nearest passport office, major post office, or travel agency, or contact the **United Kingdom Passport Service** at ℂ **0870/521-0410** or search its website at www.ukpa.gov.uk.

For Residents of the United States Whether you're applying in person or by mail, you can download passport applications from the U.S. State Department website at **http://travel.state.gov**. To find your regional passport office, either check the U.S. State Department website or call the **National Passport Information Center**'s toll-free number (ℂ **877/487-2778**) for automated information.

PHARMACIES Walgreens, 757 N. Michigan Ave., at East Chicago Street (ℂ **312/664-4000**), is open 24 hours. Both Walgreens and **CVS,** another major chain, have a number of downtown locations.

POLICE For emergencies, call ℂ **911.** This is a free call (no coins required). For nonemergencies, call ℂ **311.**

POST OFFICE The main post office is at 433 W. Harrison St. (ℂ **312/983-8182**); free parking is available. You can also find convenient branches in the Sears Tower, the Federal Center Plaza at 211 S. Clark St., the James R. Thompson Center at 100 W. Randolph St., and a couple of blocks off the Magnificent Mile at 227 E. Ontario St.

RADIO WBEZ (91.5 FM) is the local National Public Radio station, which plays jazz in the evenings. **WFMT** (98.7 FM) specializes in fine arts and classical music. **WXRT** (93.1 FM) is a progressive rock station whose DJs don't stick to corporate-sanctioned playlists but mix things up with shots of blues, jazz, and local music. If it's Top 40 you want to hear, tune in to 101.9 FM, and country music fans should dial in 99.5 FM. On the AM side of the dial, you'll find talk radio on **WGN** (720) and **WLS** (890)—two longtime stations that got their names from their immodest owners (respectively, that would be the *Chicago Tribune,* the "World's Greatest Newspaper," and Sears, the "World's Largest Store"). News junkies should tune to **WBBM** (780) for nonstop news, traffic, and weather reports, and sports fans will find company on the talk station **WSCR** (1160).

TAXES The United States has no value-added tax (VAT) or other indirect tax at the national level. Every state, county, and city may levy its own local tax on all purchases, including hotel and restaurant checks and airline tickets. These taxes will not appear on price tags.

In Chicago, the local sales tax is 10.25%. Restaurants in the central part of the city, roughly the 312 area code, are taxed an additional 1%, for a total of 11.25%. The hotel room tax is a steep 14.9%.

TELEGRAPH, TELEX & FAX Telegraph and telex services are provided primarily by Western Union. You can telegraph money, or have it telegraphed to you, very quickly over the Western Union system, but this service can cost as much as 15% to 20% of the amount sent.

Most hotels have **fax machines** available for guest use (be sure to ask about the charge to use it). Many hotel rooms are even wired for guests' fax machines. A less expensive way to send and receive faxes may be at stores such as The UPS Store (formerly Mail Boxes Etc.).

TIME The continental United States is divided into **four time zones:** eastern standard time (EST), central standard time (CST), mountain standard time (MST), and Pacific standard time (PST); Chicago is in the central time zone. Alaska and Hawaii have their own zones. For example, when it's 9am in Los Angeles (PST), it's 7am in Honolulu (HST), 10am in Denver (MST), 11am in Chicago (CST), noon in New York City (EST), 5pm in London (GMT), and 2am the next day in Sydney.

Daylight saving time is in effect from 1am on the second Sunday in March to 1am on the first Sunday in November, except in Arizona, Hawaii, the U.S. Virgin Islands, and Puerto Rico. Daylight saving time moves the clock 1 hour ahead of standard time.

TIPPING Tips are a very important part of certain workers' income, and gratuities are the standard way of showing appreciation for services provided. (Tipping is certainly not compulsory if the service is poor!) In hotels, tip **bellhops** at least $1 per bag ($2–$3 if you have a lot of luggage) and tip the **chamber staff** $1 to $2 per day (more if you've left a disaster area for him or her to clean up). Tip the **doorman** or **concierge** only if he or she has provided you with some specific service (for example, calling a cab for you or obtaining difficult-to-get theater tickets). Tip the **valet-parking attendant** $1 every time you get your car.

In restaurants, bars, and nightclubs, tip **service staff** 15% to 20% of the check, tip **bartenders** 10% to 15%, tip **checkroom attendants** $1 per garment, and tip **valet-parking attendants** $1 per vehicle.

As for other service personnel, tip **cab drivers** 15% of the fare; tip **skycaps** at airports at least $1 per bag ($2–$3 if you have a lot of luggage); and tip **hairdressers** and **barbers** 15% to 20%.

TOILETS You won't find public toilets or "restrooms" on the streets in most U.S. cities, but they can be found in hotel lobbies, bars, restaurants, museums, department stores, railway and bus stations, and service stations. Large hotels and fast-food restaurants are often the best bet for clean facilities. If possible, avoid the toilets at parks and beaches, which tend to be dirty; some may be unsafe. Restaurants and bars in resorts or heavily visited areas may reserve their restrooms for patrons.

TRANSIT INFO The **CTA** has a useful number to find out which bus or El train will get you to your destination: ✆ **836-7000** (from any area code in the city or suburbs) or TTY 836-4949.

VISAS For information about U.S. Visas go to **http://travel.state.gov** and click on "Visas." Or go to one of the following websites:

Australian citizens can obtain up-to-date visa information from the **U.S. Embassy Canberra,** Moonah Place, Yarralumla, ACT

from the Super Bowl to the Madagascar Knee Volleyball Championships. 43 E. Ohio St. **281**
© **312/644-ESPN** (644-3776). www.espnzone.com. Free admission; cost is $5 for a 15-point card,
$15 for a 60-point card, and on up to $100 for a 700-point card. Games "cost" 2–10 points each.
Bigger attractions, such as NHL Tonight and ESPN Bowling, are 10–24 points). Sun–Thurs
11am–11pm; Fri 11am–midnight; Sat 10am–midnight. Subway/El: Red Line to State/Grand.

LEGOLAND Discovery Centre   You'll need to make the trek out to the northwest
suburbs to explore the first indoor LEGO world to open in the U.S., but for families with
LEGO fans in their ranks, it's definitely worth a special trip. Located in The Streets of
Woodfield (next to the gigantic Woodfield Mall), this stop is designed for kids ages 2
through 12. Featuring hands-on LEGO activities and life-sized LEGO adventures, you'll
be able to fill a day here. The 30,000-square-foot facility combines LEGO model building and unusual construction challenges with theme park-like attractions such as a
dragon ride, adventure trail, and 4D cinema incorporating fantastical LEGO creatures
and LEGO-based special effects. If you've got young kids, there's a DUPLO play area,
and you can take a break at the LEGO café (and of course, purchase a memento of your
visit at the LEGO store). Don't miss visiting the special room with rotating exhibitions
of work by master LEGO builders. Allow 3 hours. 601 N. Martingale Road (at the intersection of Martingale Road and Higgins Road), Schaumberg. © **866/929-8111.** www.legoland
discoverycentre.com. Adults $19, seniors $17, children age 3 and up $15, children age 2 and
under are free. Daily 10am–7pm (last tickets are sold at 5pm). Call for holiday hours. Subway/
El: Blue Line to Rosemont Station. Transfer to the Route 600 Pace Bus to Woodfield Mall. Take
the free Schaumburg Woodfield Trolley to the Streets of Woodfield stop. By car: take I-294
North to I-290 West to Illinois 72/Higgins Road Exit. Turn left onto Higgins Road, then turn right
onto N. Martingale Road.

2600 (© 02/6214-5600), or by checking the U.S. Diplomatic Mission's website at http://usembassy-australia.state.gov/consular.

British subjects can obtain up-to-date visa information by calling the U.S. Embassy Visa Information Line (© 0891/200-290), or by visiting the "Visas to the U.S." section of the American Embassy London's website at www.usembassy.org.uk.

Irish citizens can obtain up-to-date visa information through the Embassy of the USA Dublin, 42 Elgin Rd., Dublin 4,

Ireland (© 353/1-668-8777), or by checking the "Consular Services" section of the website at http://dublin.usembassy.gov.

Citizens of New Zealand can obtain up-to-date visa information by contacting the U.S. Embassy New Zealand, 29 Fitzherbert Terrace, Thorndon, Wellington (© 644/472-2068), or get the information directly from the "For New Zealanders" section of the website at http://usembassy.org.nz.

WEATHER Check the weather on the Internet at www.chicagotribune.com or www.weather.com.

2 TOLL-FREE NUMBERS & WEBSITES

MAJOR U.S. AIRLINES
(*flies internationally as well)

Alaska Airlines
© 800/252-7522 (in U.S. and Canada)
www.alaskaair.com

American Airlines*
© 800/433-7300 (in U.S. and Canada)
© 020/7365-0777 (in U.K.)
www.aa.com

Continental Airlines*
© 800/523-3273 (in U.S. and Canada)
© 084/5607-6760 (in U.K.)
www.continental.com

Delta Air Lines*
© 800/221-1212 (in U.S. and Canada)
© 084/5600-0950 (in U.K.)
www.delta.com

go!
© 888/435-9462
www.iflygo.com
(interisland Hawaii only)

Hawaiian Airlines*
© 800/367-5320 (in U.S. and Canada)
www.hawaiianair.com

Northwest Airlines*
© 800/225-2525 (in U.S.)
© 870/0507-4074 (in U.K.)
www.flynaa.com

United Airlines*
© 800/864-8331 (in U.S. and Canada)
© 084/5844-4777 in U.K.
www.united.com

US Airways*
© 800/428-4322 (in U.S. and Canada)
© 084/5600-3300 (in U.K.)
www.usairways.com

MAJOR INTERNATIONAL AIRLINES

Air France
© 800/237-2747 (in U.S.)
© 800/375-8723 (U.S. and Canada)
© 087/0142-4343 (in U.K.)
www.airfrance.com

Air New Zealand
© 800/262-1234 (in U.S.)
© 800/663-5494 (in Canada)
© 0800/028-4149 (in U.K.)
www.airnewzealand.com

Air Tahiti Nui
- ✆ 877/824-4846 (in U.S. and Canada)
- www.airtahitinui-usa.com

Alitalia
- ✆ 800/223-5730 (in U.S.)
- ✆ 800/361-8336 (in Canada)
- ✆ 087/0608-6003 (in U.K.)
- www.alitalia.com

British Airways
- ✆ 800/247-9297 (in U.S. and Canada)
- ✆ 087/0850-9850 (in U.K.)
- www.british-airways.com

China Airlines
- ✆ 800/227-5118 (in U.S.)
- ✆ 022/715-1212 (in Taiwan)
- www.china-airlines.com

Delta Air Lines
- ✆ 800/221-1212 (in U.S. and Canada)
- ✆ 084/5600-0950 (in U.K.)
- www.delta.com

Hawaiian Airlines
- ✆ 800/367-5320 (in U.S. and Canada)
- www.hawaiianair.com

Japan Airlines
- ✆ 012/025-5931 (international)
- www.jal.com

Korean Air
- ✆ 800/438-5000 (in U.S. and Canada)
- ✆ 0800/413-000 (in U.K.)
- www.koreanair.com

Quantas Airways
- ✆ 800/227-4500 (in U.S. and Canada)
- ✆ 084/5774-7767 (in U.K.)
- ✆ 13 13 13 (in Australia)
- www.quantas.com

Philippine Airlines
- ✆ 800/I-Fly-Pal (435-9725) (in U.S. and Canada)
- ✆ 632/855-8888 (in Philippines)
- www.philippineairlines.com

Virgin Atlantic Airways
- ✆ 800/821-5438 (in U.S. and Canada)
- ✆ 087/0574-7747 (in U.K.)
- www.virgin-atlantic.com
- www.westjet.com

CAR-RENTAL AGENCIES

Alamo
- ✆ 800/GO-ALAMO (462-5266) (in U.S. and Canada)
- www.alamo.com

Avis
- ✆ 800/331-1212 (in U.S. and Canada)
- ✆ 084/4581-8181 (in U.K.)
- www.avis.com

Budget
- ✆ 800/527-0700 (in U.S.)
- ✆ 087/0156-5656 (in U.K.)
- ✆ 800/268-8900 (in Canada)
- www.budget.com

Dollar
- ✆ 800/800-4000 (in U.S.)
- ✆ 800/848-8268 (in Canada)
- ✆ 080/8234-7524 (in U.K.)
- www.dollar.com

Enterprise
- ✆ 800/261-7331 (in U.S.)
- ✆ 514/355-4028 (in Canada)
- ✆ 012/9360-9090 (in U.K.)
- www.enterprise.com

Hertz
- ✆ 800/645-3131
- ✆ 800/654-3001 (for international reservations)
- www.hertz.com

National
- ✆ 800/CAR-RENT (227-7368) (in U.S. and Canada)
- www.nationalcar.com

Rent-A-Wreck
☎ 800/535-1391
www.rentawreck.com

Thrifty
☎ 800/367-2277
☎ 918/669-2168 (international)
www.thrifty.com

MAJOR HOTEL & MOTEL CHAINS

Best Western International
☎ 800/780-7234 (in U.S. and Canada)
☎ 0800/393-130 (in U.K.)
www.bestwestern.com

Doubletree Hotels
☎ 800/222-TREE (222-8733)
 (in U.S. and Canada)
☎ 087/0590-9090 (in U.K.)
www.doubletree.com

Embassy Suites
☎ 800/EMBASSY (362-2779)
http://embassysuites1.hilton.com

Four Seasons
☎ 800/819-5053 (in U.S. and Canada)
☎ 0800/6488-6488 (in U.K.)
www.fourseasons.com

Hilton Hotels
☎ 800/HILTONS (445-8667)
 (in U.S. and Canada)
☎ 087/0590-9090 (in U.K.)
www.hilton.com

Holiday Inn
☎ 800/315-2621 (in U.S. and Canada)
☎ 0800/405-060 (in U.K.)
www.holidayinn.com

Hyatt
☎ 888/591-1234 (in U.S. and Canada)
☎ 084/5888-1234 (in U.K.)
www.hyatt.com

Marriott
☎ 877/236-2427 (in U.S. and Canada)
☎ 0800/221-222 (in U.K.)
www.marriott.com

Radisson Hotels & Resorts
☎ 888/201-1718 (in U.S. and Canada)
☎ 0800/374-411 (in U.K.)
www.radisson.com

Sheraton Hotels & Resorts
☎ 800/325-3535 (in U.S.)
☎ 800/543-4300 (in Canada)
☎ 0800/3253-5353 (in U.K.)
www.starwoodhotels.com/sheraton

Westin Hotels & Resorts
☎ 800/937-8461 (in U.S. and Canada)
☎ 0800/3259-5959 (in U.K.)
www.starwoodhotels.com/westin

Wyndham Hotels & Resorts
☎ 877/999-3223 (in U.S. and Canada)
☎ 050/6638-4899 (in U.K.)
www.wyndham.com

INDEX

GENERAL INDEX

AAA (American Automobile Association), 289
Abercrombie & Fitch, 244
Accent Chicago, 234
Accommodations, 73–106.
See also **Accommodations Index**
best, 6–8
concierges, 87
convention dates and, 75
The Gold Coast, 100–101
green-friendly, 45
landing the best room, 74
Lincoln Park and The North Side, 101–106
The Loop, 75–82
Near North and The Magnificent Mile, 84–97
price categories, 74
reservations, 73–74
River North, 97–100
tipping, 294
Active pursuits, 216–231. *See also specific activities*
beaches, 216–217
classes and workshops, 230–231
parks, 217–222
playgrounds, 222–223
sports and games, 223–229
Adler Planetarium & Astronomy Museum, 157, 160
Adventuring with Children, 34
African Americans
Chicago Public Library/ Harold Washington Library Center, 181
DuSable Museum of African-American History, 182
"Great Black Migration," 212–213
Oak Woods Cemetery, 207
tours, 206
Airfares, 27–29
Airlines, 26
food, 36–38
Airports, 29–31
security procedures, 17
transfers, 30–31
Air Tickets Direct, 28–29
AirTran Airways, 26
Air travel, 26–38
arriving at the airport, 26
children traveling solo, 32–34
documents needed by minors, 32
fun for kids, 36
green-friendly, 44
jet lag, 28
long-haul flights, 26–27
packing tips, 15
safe seats for kids, 31–32
safety instructions, 35
security measures, 30
Alaska Airlines, 31, 37
Alcala's, 244
Alley, 240
Ambulances, 291
AMC Loews 600 N. Michigan Theaters, 274
AMC Lowes Pipers Alley, 274
AMC River East, 274
American Airlines, 26
economy-class meal policy, 37
American Automobile Association (AAA), 289
American ChildCare Service, 289
American Express, 289
emergency number, 41
traveler's checks, 40
American Express Travelers Cheque Card, 40–41
American Girl Place, 234, 251–252
America West, 26
economy-class meal policy, 37
Amtrak, 39
Andersonville
brief description of, 56
walking tour, 214–215
Andersonville Midsommarfest, 22
Andy's Jazz Club, 263
Anthropologie, 244
Aquarium, John G. Shedd, 165–167
Arcades, 280–281
The Archicenter Shop, 246
Architecture
Chicago Archicenter, 179–180
Chicago Architecture Foundation tours, 202–204
Oak Park, 191–196
guided tours, 192, 194
Architecture River Cruise, 202–203
Area codes, 289
Arie Crown Theater, 259
Arlington International Racecourse, 279–280
Armitage Avenue, 239
Aroma Workshop, 239
Around the Coyote, 238
Art Institute of Chicago, 178–179, 210
Art museums and exhibits
Art Institute of Chicago, 178–179
Chicago Water Tower—City Gallery, 181–182
free days, 175
Intuit: The Center for Intuitive and Outsider Art, 183
The Loop Sculpture Tour, 168
Museum of Contemporary Art, 184–185

Museum of Contemporary
Photography, 185
National Museum of Mexi-
can Art, 185–186
National Vietnam Veterans
Art Museum, 186
Oriental Institute Museum,
187–188
The Smart Museum of Art,
189–190
Spertus Museum, 190
Arts and crafts, 241
Ash's Magic Shop, 247
Astor Place, 211
At Home Inn Chicago, 74
ATMs (automated-teller
machines), 39
Attractions, 156–207
best rides, 190–191
best views, 175–178
do-it-yourself sightseeing,
166
gardens and
conservatories, 199
historic houses, 191–196
nature centers, 200–201
by neighborhood, 156–157
top 10 attractions, 157–175
tours, 201–207
zoos, 196–199
Auditorium Building,
210–211
Auditorium Theatre, 259
Australia
customs regulations, 18
embassy and consulates,
290
passports, 292–293
visas, 294–295
Automobile rentals, 64
green-friendly, 45
Automobile travel, 63–64
green-friendly, 44
packing tips, 15
Auto Show, Chicago, 20
A/X Armani Exchange, 236

Babysitters, 289
Baha'i House of Worship
(Wilmette), 284
Ballet, 275, 276
Ballet Chicago, 275
Barbara's Bookstore, 242
Barnes & Noble, 242
Barneys Co-Op, 242–243
Barneys New York, 242–243
Baseball, 223
Basketball, 223–224

Beaches, 216–217
Beat Parlor, 247
Beauty stores, 239
Bebe Elegante, 240
Bed & breakfasts (B&Bs),
reservations, 74
Bellini, 250
Belmont Avenue, shopping,
240
The Big Top, 25
Bike & Roll, 216
Bike Chicago, 64, 224, 228
Biking, 64–65, 224
Boulevard Lakefront Bike
Tour, 24
Bittersweet, 250
Blackhawk Park, 223–224,
228
Bloomingdale's, 243
Blossom House, 195
Blue Chicago, 262, 270
Blue Chicago Store, 247
Blue Man Group, 259
Blues. See Jazz and blues
B.L.U.E.S., 262
Boat, RV & Outdoor Show, 20
Boat travel and cruises,
64, 204–206
Books
about Chicago, 65
game, for air travel, 36
on travel with kids, 34, 45
Bookstores, 242
Borders, 242
story hours, 280
Boulevard Lakefront Bike
Tour, 24
Boulevard Lakefront Tour,
224
Bowling, 225
Brain Quest for the Car, 36
Breakfast and brunch
restaurants, 132
Briar Street Theatre, 259
Bridgeport, 57
Brookfield Zoo, 196–197
Brunswick Zone, 225
Bucket shops, 28
Buckingham Fountain,
217–218
Buckingham Fountain Color
Light Show, 20
Bucktown/Wicker Park
brief description of, 57
restaurants, 133, 145,
150–154
shopping, 240
walking tour, 215
Buddy Guy's Legends, 262

Building Blocks Toy Store,
240, 241
Bulkhead row, 34
Bullfrogs and Butterflies, 241
Business hours, 289–290

Cabs, 62–63
tipping, 294
Cadillac Palace Theatre,
260–261
Calendar of events, 19–25
Cameras, digital, 38
Canada
customs regulations, 18
embassy and consulates,
290
passports, 293
Canaryville, 57–58
Carbon offsetting, 44
Carey Limousine of
Chicago, 30
Carousel (Navy Pier), 20–21
Car rentals, 64
green-friendly, 45
Carriage rides, 202
Carry-on luggage, 34–35
Car travel, 63–64
green-friendly, 44
packing tips, 15
Cellphones, 47–48
Celtic Fest Chicago, 24
Cemetery tours, 206–207
Charnley-Persky House, 203
Checker Cab, 63
Chicago Air & Water Show, 24
Chicago Archicenter,
179–180
Chicago Architecture Foun-
dation, tours, 202–204
Chicago Art Dealers
Association, 238
Chicago Auto Show, 20
Chicago Bears, 277
Chicago Bed and Breakfast
Association, 74
Chicago Blackhawks, 277
Chicago Blues Festival, 21
Chicago Boat, RV & Outdoor
Show, 20
Chicago Botanic Garden
(Glencoe), 283–284,
285–286
Chicago Bulls, 277–278
Chicago Children's Choir,
270–271
Chicago Children's Museum,
160, 162
classes, 230
Chicago Comics, 240

300 Chicago Convention & Tourism Bureau, 49, 73
Chicago Country Music Festival, 22
Chicago Cubs, 20, 278
Chicago Cubs Clubhouse Shop, 236
Chicago Cubs Convention, 19
Chicago Cultural Center, 49, 180, 210, 259
Chicago Dance and Music Alliance, 253
Chicago Dental Society, 290
Chicago Fed Money Museum, 180
Chicago Fire, 278
Chicago Gallery News, 238
Chicago Gospel Festival, 21
Chicago Greeter program, 50
Chicago Harbor, 252
Chicago History Museum, 180–181, 214
Chicago Human Rhythm Project, 265
Chicago International Children's Film Festival, 274
Chicago Jazz Festival, 24
Chicagoland Bicycle Federation, 64–65, 224
Chicago Limousine Services, 30
Chicago magazine, 50
Chicago Main Post Office, 210
Chicago Marathon, 25
Chicago Neighborhood Tours, 205
Chicago Office of Tourism, 12
Chicago Opera Theater, 271
Chicago Parent, 12, 49, 253
Chicago Place, 236
Chicago Playworks for Families and Young Audiences, 267–268
Chicago Public Library/Harold Washington Library Center, 181
Chicago Reader, 50, 238
Chicago River, 51. *See also* Boat travel and cruises
outdoor cafes, 119
Chicago Sailing Club, 228
Chicago Shakespeare Theater, 259–260
Chicago Sportfishing Association, 226
Chicago SummerDance, 23
Chicago Symphony Chorus, 271

Chicago Symphony Orchestra, 271
Chicago Theatre, 260
Chicago Transit Authority (CTA), 58–59
The Chicago Tribune store, 246
Chicago Tribune Tower, 185, 208
Chicago Trolley Company, 202
Chicago Visitor's Guide, 19
Chicago Water Tower, 209
Chicago Water Tower—City Gallery, 181–182
Chicago Water Works Visitor Center, 49
Hot Tix outlet, 258
Chicago White Sox, 20, 223, 279
Chicago Wolves, 277
Chicago Yacht Club's Race to Mackinac Island, 23
Children's Museum of Immigration, 190
Children's museums
Chicago Children's Museum, 160, 162
Children's Museum of Immigration, 190
Dupage Children's Museum (Naperville), 286–287
Kohl Children's Museum (Glenview), 283
Smith Museum of Stained Glass Windows, 174
Wonder Works (Oak Park), 287–288
The Children's Theater Fantasy Orchard, 268
Chinatown restaurants, 114
Chinese New Year Parade, 20
A Christmas Carol, 25, 265
Christmas Tree Lighting, 25
Cinemas, 274–275
Citicorp Visa, emergency number, 41
City of Chicago Store, 246
Civic Orchestra of Chicago, 271
Clark Street, shopping, 240
Classes and workshops, 230
Classical music, 270–271
Clear Pass, 17
Climate, 18–19
Climbing, 225
Clothing. *See also* Fashions
packing tips, 14–15

Cloud Gate, 168
Club Monaco, 236
Coco Key Water Resort (Arlington Heights), 201
Colds, kids with, 26
Comedy clubs, 272–273
ComedySportz, 272
Concerts, 270–274
Concierges, 87
Consolidators, 28
Continental Airlines, 26
economy-class meal policy, 38
Continental Airport Express, 30
Convention dates, 75
Credit cards, 40
Crime, 42–43
CS magazine, 50
CTA Paratransit, 31
Cuneo Museum & Gardens (Vernon Hills), 288
Customs regulations, 17–18

Daley Bicentennial Plaza in Millennium Park, 222
The Dance Center—Columbia College Chicago, 275
Dance Chicago, 265
Dance performances, 275–276
Daylight saving time, 294
Debit cards, 40
Deep vein thrombosis, 42
Delta Airlines, 26
economy-class meal policy, 38
Dentists, 290
Department stores, 242–244
DePaul Blue Demons, 279
Digital cameras, 38
Dining, 107–155. *See also* Restaurants Index
alfresco, 144–145
best, 8–11
breakfast and brunch, 132–133
Chinatown, 114
by cuisine, 108–111
Greektown, 115
green-friendly, 45
hot dogs, 154–155
Lincoln Park, 132, 139–148
alfresco, 145
Little Italy, 114
The Loop, 111–122
The Magnificent Mile and The Gold Coast, 123–130

The North Side, 132–133, 148–150
Pilsen, 115
pizza, 154
Polish, 123
price categories, 107
River North, 130–139, 145
suburban, 121
tipping, 294
tips for dining out in (relative) peace, 124–125
Wicker Park/Bucktown, 133, 145, 150–154
Wrigleyville, 148–150
  alfresco, 145
Disabilities, travelers with, 31
  accommodations, 73
Diversey River Bowl, 225
Doctors, 290
Doggie beach, 216–217
Do-It-Yourself *Messiah*, **266**
Dolls and dollhouses, 244
Dorby Magoo & Co., 252
Downtown, brief description of, 52
Drinking laws, 290
Driving rules, 63
Drury Lane Theater, 268
Dupage Children's Museum (Naperville), 286–287
DuSable Museum of African-American History, 182
Dusty Groove America, 247

East Monroe Garage, 64
Eating, 107–155. *See also*
  Restaurants Index
  aboard planes, 36–38
  alfresco, 144–145
  best, 8–11
  breakfast and brunch, 132–133
  Chinatown, 114
  by cuisine, 108–111
  Greektown, 115
  green-friendly, 45
  hot dogs, 154–155
  Lincoln Park, 132, 139–148
    alfresco, 145
  Little Italy, 114
  The Loop, 111–122
  The Magnificent Mile and The Gold Coast, 123–130
  The North Side, 132–133, 148–150
  Pilsen, 115
  pizza, 154

Polish, 123
price categories, 107
River North, 130–139, 145
suburban, 121
Taste of Chicago, 22, 218
Taste of Lincoln Avenue, 23
tipping, 294
tips for dining out in (relative) peace, 124–125
Wicker Park/Bucktown, 133, 145, 150–154
Wrigleyville, 148–150
  alfresco, 145
Economy class syndrome, 42
Ecotourism, 43
Eileen Fisher, 234
The El (elevated train), 59, 62
Electricity, 290
1154 Lill Studio, 241
Embassies and consulates, 290–291
Emerald City Theatre Company, 268
Emergencies, 290–291
Entertainment, 253–281
  arcades, 280–281
  big venues, 259–265
  comedy clubs, 272–273
  current listings, 253
  dance performances, 275–276
  finding better seats, 261
  movies, 274–275
  puppet shows, 276
  seasonal events, 265–267
  spectator sports, 277–280
  story hours, 280
  theater, 267–270
  tickets, 258
Entry requirements, 15–17
E-Passport, 16
ESPN Zone, 280–281
Ethel's Chocolate Lounge, 250
Ethical tourism, 43
Expedia, 29

Facets Multi-Media, 274
Family Travel & Resorts, **34**
Family Travel Times, **34**
Fantasy Costumes, 247
Farmers markets, 23
Farm-in-the-Zoo, 197, 220
Far Out Fridays, 160
Fashions (clothing), 244–246
Fax machines, 294
Ferris Wheel (Navy Pier), 20–21

The Field Museum of Natural History, 162–165, 167
  classes and field trips, 230
  story hours, 280
57th Street Art Fair, 21
Film, flying with, 38
Fine Arts Building, 210
Fishing, 226
Flash Cab, 63
Fleet Feet Sports, 249
Flights.com, 28
FlyCheap, 28
Folk music, 274
Food. *See also* **Restaurants**
  aboard planes, 36–38
  Taste of Chicago, 22, 218
  Taste of Lincoln Avenue, 23
Foodlife, 234
Ford Center for the Performing Arts, 260–261
Fox River Trolley Museum, 188
Frank Lloyd Wright by Bus tour, 203
The Frank Lloyd Wright Home & Studio (Oak Park), 194
Frank Lloyd Wright Neighborhoods by Bus tour, 203
French Connection, 234
Frequent-flier clubs, 29
Fresh, 239
Frommers.com, 46
Frommer's favorite experiences, 54–55
Frommer's Fly Safe, Fly Smart, **15**
Frontier Airlines, 26
Fullerton Avenue bridge, 177, 220

Gallery 37 Store, 237
Galt Toys, 252
Gamers Paradise, 236
Games and hobby shops, 247
Gangster tours, 206
GapKids and babyGap, 244
Gardens and conservatories, 199–200
  Chicago Botanic Garden (Glencoe), 285
Garfield Park Conservatory, 199
Garrett Popcorn Shop, 249
Gasoline, 291
Gay & Lesbian Pride Parade, 22–23
Gays and lesbians, 22–23

Ghirardelli Chocolate Shop & Soda Fountain, 250
Ghost tours, 206
Gilson Park, 284
Ginkgo Tree Bookshop, 192
Glessner House, 196
Glove Me Tender, 236
The Gold Coast
  accommodations, 100–101
  brief description of, 54
  restaurants, 123–130
    alfresco, 144
  tours, 205–206
  walking tour, 211
Goodman Theatre, 260, 261
Google, 48
Go! The Game Store, 236
Graceland, 206–207
Grant Park, 217–218
Grant Park Music Festival, 22, 265–266
Gray Line, 202
Great Games for Kids on the Go, 36
Greektown, restaurants, 115
Green Dolphin Street, 263
Green Mill, 263
Greyhound Bus Station, 39
Grow, 245
GSM (Global System for Mobile Communications), 48
Guitar Center, 247
Gymboree, 229, 245

Halsted Street, 239
Hamill Family Play Zoo, 165, 197
The Hancock Observatory, 175–176
Harold Washington Library Center, 181
  Internet access, 291
Health concerns, 41–42
  economy class syndrome, 42
  jet lag, 28
Heller House, 195
Henry Crown Space Center, 171
Highlights by Bus, 203
Historic houses, 191–196
Historic Pullman, 182–183
Holidays, 291
Hollywood-Ardmore Beach (Kathy Osterman Beach), 216
Horseback riding, 227
Horse racing, 279

Hospitals, 291
Hot dogs, 154–155
Hotels, 73–106. See also Accommodations Index
  best, 6–8
  concierges, 87
  convention dates and, 75
  The Gold Coast, 100–101
  green-friendly, 45
  landing the best room, 74
  Lincoln Park and The North Side, 101–106
  The Loop, 75–82
  Near North and The Magnificent Mile, 84–97
  price categories, 74
  reservations, 73–74
  River North, 97–100
  tipping, 294
Hot Rooms, 74
Hot Tix, 258
House of Blues, 262, 272
How to Take Great Trips with Your Kids, 34
Hubbard Street Dance Chicago, 275–276
Hyde Park, brief description of, 58

Ice-skating, 227–228
Illinois Bureau of Tourism, 12, 49, 74
Illinois Railway Museum, 188–189
IMAX Theater, Navy Pier, 174, 274
Immigration and customs clearance, 26
ImprovOlympic, 273
Independence Day Celebration, 23
Independence Park, 224
Indiana Dunes State Park, 282–283
In-line skating, 228
International Cluster of Dog Shows, 20
The International Ecotourism Society (TIES), 43
International Museum of Surgical Science, 183
Internet access, 48, 291
Intuit: The Center for Intuitive and Outsider Art, 183
Ireland
  embassy and consulates, 290
  passports, 293
  visas, 295

Irish-American Heritage Festival, 23
Italian ices, 116
The Italian Village, 117
Itineraries, suggested, 66–72

Jammin' at the Zoo, 22
Jane Addams Hull-House Museum, 184
Jazz and blues
  Chicago Jazz Festival, 24
  concerts, 270, 272–273
  venues and clubs, 262–263
Jazz Record Mart, 247
Jazz Showcase, 263, 272
J. Crew, 236
Jet lag, 28
Jewelers' Row, 238
Joe's Be-bop Cafe and Jazz Emporium, 273
Joffrey Ballet of Chicago, 276
John G. Shedd Aquarium, 165–167

Kathy Osterman Beach (Hollywood-Ardmore Beach), 216
Kingston Mines, 262–263
Kohl Children's Museum (Glenview), 283
Kozy's Cyclery, 249
Kraft Kids Concerts, 266–267

Lake and river cruises, 204–205
The Lakefront, 167–168
Lakeshore Academy, 225–226
Lakeshore Athletic Club–Illinois Center, 225
Lake Shore Drive, 63, 211
  warning for walkers, 176
Lake Shore Park, 218
Lakeview
  brief description of, 56
  shopping, 239–240
LaSalle Bank Theatre, 260, 261
Legal aid, 291
LEGOLAND Discovery Centre, 281
LEGO Store, 236, 252
Lifeline Theatre KidSeries, 270
Lightology, 238
Lill Street Art Center, 230

Lincoln, Abraham, statues
The Seated Lincoln, 218
standing (Lincoln Park), 220
Lincoln Park, 211, 218, 220, 223
accommodations, 101–106
brief description of, 55–56
restaurants, 132, 139–148
alfresco, 145
shopping, 239
tours, 205–206
walking tour, 214
Lincoln Park Conservatory, 199–200
Lincoln Park Pritzker Children's Zoo & Farm-in-the-Zoo, 197, 220
Lincoln Park Zoo, 197
Spooky Zoo Spectacular, 25
Zoo Lights Festival, 25
Lincoln Square, 56
Liquor laws, 291
Little Italy, restaurants, 114
Little League, 223
Little Strummer, 248
LMNOP, 245
Lodging, 73–106. *See also* Accommodations Index
best, 6–8
concierges, 87
convention dates and, 75
The Gold Coast, 100–101
green-friendly, 45
landing the best room, 74
Lincoln Park and The North Side, 101–106
The Loop, 75–82
Near North and The Magnificent Mile, 84–97
price categories, 74
reservations, 73–74
River North, 97–100
tipping, 294
Lookingglass Theatre Company, 262–264
The Loop. *See also* South Loop; West Loop
accommodations, 75–82
Pedway, 209
restaurants, 111–122
alfresco, 144
breakfast and brunch, 132
shopping, 237
walking tour, 209–211
The Loop Sculpture Tour, 168
The Loop Tour Train, 168
Lost and found, 41, 291–292

Lost children, 44–45
Luggage Express, 27
Lush, 239
Luxe Home, 238–239
Lyric Opera of Chicago, 260, 273

McArthur House, 195
McCormick Place Parking, 64
McCormick Tribune Freedom Museum, 184
McCormick Tribune Ice Rink, 227
McFetridge Sports Complex, 227, 229
Macy's, 234, 243
Macy's at State Street, 237
Madison and Friends, 245
The Magnificent Mile
accommodations, 84–97
brief description of, 52, 54
restaurants, 123
alfresco, 144
breakfast and brunch, 132
shopping, 232–236
walking tour, 208–209
Magnificent Mile Lights Festival, 25
Mail, 292
Manifesto, 238
Marathon, Chicago, 25
Margie's Candies, 250–251
Mario's Italian Lemonade, 116
MasterCard
emergency number, 41
traveler's checks, 40
Mayor's Office of Special Events, 19, 49
Medical requirements for entry, 17
Medieval Times, 270
Merchandise Mart, 238
Messiah, Do-It-Yourself, 266
Metra commuter railroad, 60
Metra Electric, 61
Mexican Independence Day Parade, 24
Michigan, Lake, 228–229
Midcontinental Plaza Garage, 64
Midway, 29
Mig & Tig, 238
Millennium Park, 168, 170, 210, 220, 222
mp3 audio tour, 167
Mini Me, 245

Mity Nice Grill, 234
Moment's Notice, 29
Momentum, 249
Money and costs, 39–41
Montrose Beach, 216
Morton Arboretum, 200
Movies, 274–275
about Chicago, 65
Chicago-based, 275
Muntu Dance Theatre of Chicago, 276
Museum Campus, 170
Museum of Contemporary Art, 184–185
Museum of Contemporary Photography, 185
Museum of Science and Industry, 167, 170–174
hands-on science and technology activities, 230
Museums, 55. *See also* Art museums and exhibits
Adler Planetarium and Astronomy Museum, 157, 160
Chicago Archicenter, 179–180
Chicago Cultural Center, 49, 180, 210, 259
Chicago Fed Money Museum, 180
Chicago History Museum, 180–181, 214
children's
Chicago Children's Museum, 160, 162
Children's Museum of Immigration, 190
Dupage Children's Museum (Naperville), 286–287
Kohl Children's Museum (Glenview), 283
Smith Museum of Stained Glass Windows, 174
Wonder Works (Oak Park), 287–288
Cuneo Museum & Gardens (Vernon Hills), 288
DuSable Museum of African-American History, 182
Field Museum of Natural History, 162–165, 167
classes and field trips, 230
story hours, 280

304 Museums *(cont.)*
Fox River Trolley Museum, 188
Frank Lloyd Wright Home & Studio (Oak Park), 194
free days, 175
Historic Pullman, 182–183
Illinois Railway Museum, 188–189
International Museum of Surgical Science, 183
Jane Addams Hull-House Museum, 184
McCormick Tribune Freedom Museum, 184
Museum of Science and Industry, 167, 170–174
  hands-on science and technology activities, 230
Oriental Institute Museum, 187–188
Peggy Notebaert Nature Museum, 200–201
Polish Museum of America, 188–189
Spertus Museum, 190
Swedish-American Museum Center, 190
Music
classical, 270–271
concerts, 270–274
folk, 274
jazz and blues
  Chicago Jazz Festival, 24
  concerts, 270, 272–273
  venues and clubs, 262–263
opera, 271, 273
Music Box Theater, 240
Music stores, 247–248

Naperville, 286–287
National Museum of Mexican Art, 185–186
National Passport Information Center, 293
National Vietnam Veterans Art Museum, 186
Natural History, Field Museum of, 162–165, 167
classes and field trips, 230
story hours, 280
Nature centers, 200–201
Navy Pier, 174–176, 228
Navy Pier IMAX Theater, 274
Navy Pier Parking, 64

Near North and The Magnificent Mile
accommodations, 84–97
brief description of, 52, 54
restaurants, 123
  alfresco, 144
  breakfast and brunch, 132
shopping, 232–236
walking tour, 208
Near West Side (West Loop), 56–57
Neighborhoods, tours, 204, 205–206. *See also* **Walking tours, self-guided**
Neiman Marcus, 243
Newberry Library, 186–187
Newberry Library Book Fair and Bughouse Square Debates, 24
***New City,* 50**
New Sound Gospel, 248
Newspapers and magazines, 13, 49–50, 292
New Zealand
customs regulations, 18
embassy and consulates, 290
passports, 293
visas, 295
Niketown, 249
900 North Michigan Ave., 236
Noble Horse, 202, 227
Nordstrom, 236, 243–244
North Avenue, 211
North Avenue Beach, 168, 214, 216, 229
biking, 64
Chicago Air & Water Show, 24
sightseeing, 177
North Michigan Avenue, 50
shopping, 234, 236
North Shore Center for the Performing Arts in Skokie, 264
The North Side
accommodations, 101–106
restaurants, 132–133, 148–150
Northwest Airlines, 26
economy-class meal policy, 38
Northwestern Memorial Hospital, 42, 291
Physician Referral Service, 290
Northwestern Wildcats, 279

Novelty Golf and Games, 227
Nursing moms and infants, 47
The *Nutcracker,* 25, 266

Oak Park, 191–196
Oak Park Visitor Center, 191
Oak Street Beach, 168, 216, 229
in-line skating, 228
Oak Woods, 207
Odyssey Fun World, 229–230
O'Hare International Airport, 29, 31
Ohio Street Beach, 216
swimming, 229
Oilily Kids, 245
Old Navy, 245
Old Town
brief description of, 55
tours, 205
walking tour, 211–213
Old Town Aquarium, 212–213
Old Town Art Fair, 21–22
Old Town School of Folk Music, 230–231, 274
Olive Park, 174
OMNIMAX Theater (Museum of Science and Industry), 171, 275
Opening Day, baseball, 20
Opera, 271, 273
Orbitz, 29
Oriental Institute Museum, 187–188
Oriental Theatre, 260–261
Orientation tours, 202
Outdoor activities, 216–231. *See also specific activities*
beaches, 216–217
classes and workshops, 230–231
parks, 217–222
playgrounds, 222–223
sports and games, 223–229
Oz Park, 224

Pablo Picasso's *Untitled,* 168
Pace buses, 60
Pacifiers, 37
Packing tips, 14–15
Parking, 63
Parks, 217–222. *See also specific parks*
Passports, 15–16, 292–293
Pearl Art and Craft Supplies, 241
Pedway, 209

Peggy Notebaert Nature Museum, 200–201
Petrillo Music Shell, 260
Petrol, 291
Pharmacies, 293
Picasso, Pablo, *Untitled,* 168
Piggy Toes, 248
Pilsen, 57
  restaurants, 115
Ping Tom Memorial Park, 222
Pipers Alley, 211
Pizzerias, 154
Planning your outings, 46
Planning your trip, 12–65
  calendar of events, 19–25
  customs regulations, 17–18
  entry requirements, 15–17
  finding an address, 51–52
  finding restrooms, 46–47
  getting around, 58–65
  getting kids interested in Chicago, 65
  getting to know Chicago, 48–58
  health concerns, 41–42
  Internet access, 48
  layout of Chicago, 50–51
  money and costs, 39–41
  neighborhoods in brief, 52–58
  nursing moms and infants, 47
  packing tips, 14–15
  planning your outings, 46
  red alert checklist, 13
  safety concerns, 42–43
  sustainable tourism, 43–44
  telephones and cellphones, 47–48
  traveling to Chicago. *See* Traveling to Chicago
  visitor information, 12–13, 49–50
  when to go, 18–19
Playgrounds
  indoor, 229–230
  outdoor, 222–223
Police, 293
Polish Museum of America, 188–189
Pools, 228–229
Pops for Champagne, 263
Portage Park, 224, 228
Porte Rouge, 241
Post office, 293
Precipitation, average, 19
Printers Row Book Fair, 21
Psycho Baby, 245

Public transportation, 58–65
  to entertainment venues, 260
  green-friendly, 45
Puerto Rican Fest, 22
Pullman district, 182–183
Puppet shows, 276

Qixo, 29

Radio stations, 293
Ravinia Festival, 21, 266–267
Reckless Records, 248
The Red Balloon Company, 240, 248–249
Redmoon Theater, 276
Reservations, for accommodations, 73–74
Restaurants, 107–155. *See also* Restaurants Index
  alfresco, 144–145
  best, 8–11
  breakfast and brunch, 132–133
  Chinatown, 114
  by cuisine, 108–111
  Greektown, 115
  green-friendly, 45
  hot dogs, 154–155
  Lincoln Park, 132, 139–148
    alfresco, 145
  Little Italy, 114
  The Loop, 111–122
  The Magnificent Mile and The Gold Coast, 123–130
  The North Side, 132–133, 148–150
  Pilsen, 115
  pizza, 154
  Polish, 123
  price categories, 107
  River North, 130–139, 145
  suburban, 121
  tipping, 294
  tips for dining out in (relative) peace, 124–125
  Wicker Park/Bucktown, 133, 145, 150–154
  Wrigleyville, 148–150
    alfresco, 145
Restrooms, finding, 46–47
The Right Start, 250
Ringling Bros. and Barnum & Bailey Circus, 267
River North
  accommodations, 97–100
  brief description of, 54–55

  restaurants, 130–139, 145
  shopping, 237–239
River North Dance Company, 276
Robie House (Oak Park), 194–195
Rogers Park, 56
Rosemont Theatre, 264

Safety concerns, 42–45
Sailing, 228
St. Patrick's Day Parade, 20
Saks Fifth Avenue, 236, 244
Sales taxes, 232
The Savvy Traveller, 246
Schiller Street, 211
Science and Industry, Museum of, 171, 275
Sculpture Tour, The Loop, 168
Sears, 237
Sears Tower Skydeck, 177–178
Seasons, 18–19
Seat belts, on planes, 35
The *Seated Lincoln,* 218
Seats, airline, 31–32
  bulkhead, 34
The Second Child, 245–246
Second City, 272–273
Seneca Playlot Park, 222–223
Shedd Aquarium, 165–167
Sheffield Garden Walk, 23
Shipping your luggage, 27
Shoes, 248
Shopping, 232–252
  districts, 232–241
  hours, 232
  sales taxes, 232
The Shops at North Bridge, 236
Shoreline Sightseeing, 64
Shower and baby gifts, 248–249
Sights and attractions, 156–207
  best rides, 190–191
  best views, 175–178
  do-it-yourself sightseeing, 166
  gardens and conservatories, 199
  historic houses, 191–196
  nature centers, 200–201
  by neighborhood, 156–157
  top 10 attractions, 157–175
  tours, 201–207
  zoos, 196–199
Six Flags Great America, 191

306

Skokie Sports Park, 223, 227
SkyCap International, 27
Skyscrapers tours, 203–204
Sky Theater, 157, 160
Sluggers Sports Bar, 223
The Smart Museum of Art, 189–190
Smith Museum of Stained Glass Windows, 174
Snacks, for air travel, 36
South Loop
    accommodations, 82–83
    brief description of, 57
Southport Avenue, shopping, 240
Southwest Airlines, 26
Souvenirs, only-in-Chicago, 246
The *Spearman and the Bowman,* 218
Spectator sports, 277–280
Spertus Museum, 190
Spooky Zoo Spectacular, 25
Sports and games, 223–229
Sports Authority, 246, 250
Sports Express, 27
Sports stuff, 249
Spring Flower Shows, 20
StarRider Theater, 157
State Street, shopping, 237
State Street Thanksgiving Parade, 25
STA Travel, 28
Steppenwolf Theatre Company, 260
Steve Madden, 248
Storefront Theater, 264
Story hours, 280
Street maps, 52
Strollers, cribs and furniture, 250
Strolls, neighborhood. *See* Walking tours, self-guided
Studio Theater, 264
Subway, 59–60
SummerDance, 267
Sustainable tourism, 43–45
Swedish-American Museum Center, 190
Sweets, 250–251
Sweet Thang, 251
Swimming, 228
Symphony Center, 260, 264

T aste of Chicago, 22, 218
Taste of Lincoln Avenue, 23
Taxes, 294
    sales, 232

Taxis, 62–63
    tipping, 294
Ted, 26
Telegraph and telex services, 294
Telephones, 47–48
Temperatures, average, 19
Tennis, 229
10pin, 225
Thanksgiving Parade, State Street, 25
Theater, 267–270
    etiquette for kids, 269
Theater on the Lake, 220
Think Small, 244
Thomas Hughes Children's Library at Harold Washington Library Center, 181
    story hours, 280
Thoroughbred racing, 279
TIES (The International Ecotourism Society), 43
Timeless Toys, 252
Time Out Chicago, 50
Time zones, 294
Tipping, 294
Toilets, 294
Tour Black Chicago, 206
Tourist information, 12–13, 49–50
Tours, 201–207
    bike, 224
    cemetery, 206–207
    Chicago Architecture Foundation, 202–204
    gangster, 206
    ghost, 206
    neighborhoods, 204–206
    walking (*See* Walking tours)
Toys, 252
    for air travel, 35–36
Toys Et Cetera, 252
Tragically Hip, 240
Train travel, 39
    attractions for train lovers, 188–189
    commuter trains, 60–61
Transit info, 59, 294
Transportation, 58–65. *See also* Taxis; Train travel
    bus travel, 58–60
    car travel, 63–64
    The El (elevated train), 59, 62
    to entertainment venues, 260
    green-friendly, 45
    subway, 59–60
Transportation Security Administration (TSA), 17, 30

Travelers Advantage, 29
Traveler's checks, 40
Traveling to Chicago, 26–39
    by bus, 39
    by car, 38–39
    by plane, 26–38
        arriving at the airport, 26
        children traveling solo, 32–34
        documents needed by minors, 32
        fun for kids, 36
        green-friendly, 44
        jet lag, 28
        long-haul flights, 26–27
        packing tips, 15
        safe seats for kids, 31–32
        safety instructions, 35
        security measures, 30
    by train, 39
Travelocity, 29
Tribune Tower, 185, 208
Trolleys, free, 60
The T-Shirt Deli, 240
Twisted Sister Bakery, 213

U nabridged Books, 242
Uncle Fun, 247
Union Pacific North Line, 61
Union Station, 39
United Airlines, 26
    economy-class meal policy, 38
United Kingdom
    customs regulations, 18
    embassy and consulates, 290
    passports, 293
    visas, 295
Unity Temple, 195–196
Untitled, Pablo Picasso's, 168
Untouchable Tours, 206
The UPS Store, 294
Uptown, brief description of, 56
Urban Outfitters, 246
US Airways, 26, 38
U.S. Cellular Field, 223, 279
US-VISIT, 16

V acation Fun Mad Libs, 36
Vandenberg Ambulance, 291
Venetian Night, 23
Victory Gardens Theater, 264–265

Videotape, flying with, 38
Virtual Bellhop, 27
Visa, traveler's checks, 40
Visas, 16, 294–295
Visa Waiver Program
(VWP), 16
Vision, 238
Visitor information, 12–13,
49–50
Visitor Pass, 59
Viva! Chicago Latin Music
Festival, 24
Volunteer travel, 43–44
Vosges Haut-Chocolat, 251

Walgreens, 293
Walking tours
guided
Chicago Architecture
Foundation, 202–204,
207
Chicago History
Museum, 205–206
Oak Park, 192
self-guided, 208–215
Bucktown/Wicker Park,
215
The Gold Coast, 211
Lincoln Park, 214
The Loop, 209–211
Near North/Magnifi-
cent Mile, 208
Old Town, 211–213
Wallet, lost or stolen, 41
Washington Square Park,
222
Water park, 201
Water taxis, 64
Water Tower Place, 234
Waveland Bowl, 225
Waveland Courts, 229
Weather, 18–19
Weather reports and
forecasts, 295
Websites, 12–13
best, 7
of museums and other
attractions, 167
on travel with kids, 45–46
Wells Street Art Festival, 22
Wendella Commuter
Boats, 64
Wendella Sightseeing Boats,
205
West Division Street,
shopping, 240–241
Western Union, 292

West Loop (Near West Side),
56–57
restaurants, 122–123
Wheelchair accessibility, 73
White Sox, 20, 279
Wicker Park/Bucktown
brief description of, 57
restaurants, 133, 145,
150–154
shopping, 240
walking tour, 215
Wi-Fi access, 48
Windy, 205
Windy City Sports, 216
Winter Delights, 19–20
Women & Children First, 242
story hours, 280
Wonder Works (Oak Park),
287–288
World Music Festival
Chicago, 24
Wright, Frank Lloyd
The Frank Lloyd Wright
Home & Studio (Oak
Park), 194
tours, 21, 203
Wright Plus Tour (Oak
Park), 21, 194
Wrigleyville
brief description of, 56
restaurants, 148–150
alfresco, 145

Yellow Cab, 63
YMCA of Metropolitan
Chicago, 224

Zoo Lights Festival, 25
Zoos, 196–199
Hamill Family Play Zoo, 165

ACCOMMODATIONS
Ambassador East, 100
The Belden-Stratford, 101,
104
Best Western Hawthorne
Terrace, 104
Best Western River North
Hotel, 99
City Suites Hotel, 105
Conrad Chicago, 84
Courtyard by Marriott
Chicago Downtown, 94
Courtyard by Marriott
Chicago Downtown/
Magnificent Mile, 94

Doubletree Chicago—
Magnificent Mile, 94–95
The Drake Hotel, 89–90
Embassy Suites Hotel Chi-
cago—Downtown, 97–98
Fairmont Hotel, 78
Four Points by Sheraton—
Chicago Downtown/
Magnificent Mile, 95
Four Seasons Hotel Chicago,
84, 86
Hampton Inn & Suites
(Wilmette), 284
Hampton Inn & Suites Chi-
cago—Downtown, 99–100
Hard Rock Hotel Chicago,
78–79
Hilton Chicago, 82–83
Hilton Garden Inn, 95–96
Hilton Suites Chicago/
Magnificent Mile, 90
Homewood Suites, 96
Hotel Allegro, 82
Hotel Burnham, 79
Hotel Indigo, 100–101
Hotel Monaco, 79–80
Hotel Sax Chicago, 98
InterContinental Chicago,
90–91
The James Hotel, 91–92
Majestic Hotel, 105–106
Millennium Knickerbocker
Hotel, 92
Park Hyatt Chicago, 86–87
The Peninsula Chicago, 88
Red Roof Inn Chicago
Downtown, 97
Renaissance Chicago Hotel,
80–81
The Ritz-Carlton Chicago,
88–89
Sheraton Chicago Hotel &
Towers, 92–93
The Silversmith Hotel &
Suites, 81
Sofitel Chicago Water
Tower, 89
Swissôtel Chicago, 81
Talbott Hotel, 93
Travelodge Chicago
Downtown, 83
Tremont Hotel, 93
Westin Chicago Michigan
Avenue, 96–97
Westin Chicago River North,
98–99
Windy City Urban Inn,
104–105

American Girl Place Cafe, 123
Ann Sather, 132, 149
Arco de Cuchilleros, 145
Artopolis, 115
Athena, 115, 144
Atwood Cafe, 111
Bandera, 123–124
Big Bowl, 128
Billy Goat Tavern, 128
Bistro 110, 126
Bongo Room, 133
Bourgeois Pig, 143
Brasserie Jo, 130–131
Buca di Beppo, 131
Café Brauer, 143, 220
Cafe Iberico, 135
Café Jumping Bean, 115
Café Mestizo, 115
California Pizza Kitchen, 128–129
Carson's, 131–132
Castaways Bar & Grill, 216
Charlie's Ale House, 145
Charlie's Ale House at Navy Pier, 129, 144
Cheesecake Factory, 126–127
Chicago Pizza & Oven Grinder, 154
Club Lucky, 152
Coco Pazzo Café, 127
Corner Bakery, 129
Costas, 115
Dave & Buster's, 135
The Drake Hotel, 132
Earwax Café, 241
Ed Debevic's, 135–136
Edwardo's, 154
El Jardin, 143
ESPN Zone, 127
Filter, 241
Flat Top Grill, 146
Fluky's, 155
foodlife, 129–130
Four Seasons Hotel, 132
Francesca's Bryn Mawr, 149
Francesca's Forno, 149
Francesca's on Taylor, 114, 149
Frontera Grill & Topolobampo, 136
Garden Café (Glencoe), 286
Geja's Café, 139
Gino's East, 136–137
Gold Coast Dogs, 155
Goose Island Brewing Company, 148

Greek Islands, 115
Green Door Tavern, 137
Hard Rock Cafe, 137
Harry Caray's, 131
Hawthorne Center Mall (Vernon Hills), 288
Heaven on Seven, 119, 132
Hecky's Barbecue (Evanston), 121
Homer's Ice Cream (Wilmette), 121
Hot Chocolate, 152–153
Hot Doug's, 155
House of Blues, 132
The Italian Village, 117
Jack Melnick's Corner Tap, 127–128
Jane's, 152
John Barleycorn, 146
John's Place, 146
Kabuki, 142
Kitsch'n River North, 137–138
La Cantina Enoteca, 117–118
La Creperie, 146–147
Le Colonial, 144
Leona's Pizzeria, 142, 154
Lou Malnati's (Naperville), 287
Lou Malnati's Pizzeria, 154
Lou Mitchell's, 120, 132
McDonald's, 138
Maggiano's, 133–134
Manny's Coffee Shop & Deli, 120
Mia Francesca, 149
Mike Ditka's Restaurant, 124
Mirai Sushi, 151–152
Moody's, 145
Mr. Beef, 138
Murphy's Red Hots, 155
Nookies, 132–133, 147
North Pond, 145
Northside Café, 145, 153
Nuevo Leon, 115
Oak Street Beachstro, 125–126, 144
Oak Tree, 130
O'Brien's Restaurant, 139, 142, 145
O'Donovan's, 149
Orange, 133
Osteria Via Stato, 134
Park Grill, 111, 116, 144, 170
Parthenon, 115
Pegasus, 115
Penang, 114
Penny's Noodle Shop, 149–150

Petersen's (Oak Park), 287–288
Petterino's, 116
Phil Smidt's (Hammond, IN), 121
Phoenix, 114
Piece, 153
Pizzeria Uno, 138
Pizzeria Uno (Vernon Hills), 288
Playa Azul, 115
Portillo's, 155
Potbelly Sandwich Works, 120
Puck's at the MCA, 144
Rainforest Café, 139
Ranalli and Ryan's, 154
Red Apple, 123
Reza's, 134
Rhapsody, 144
Robinson's No. 1 Ribs (Oak Park), 121
Ron of Japan, 126
Room 12, 133
The Rosebud, 118
Rosebud on Taylor, 114
Russian Tea Time, 116–117
Sai Café, 142–143
Saint's Alp Teahouse, 114
Santorini, 115
Scoozi, 134–135
The Signature Room at the 95th, 176
Silver Cloud Bar & Grill, 153–154
South Water Kitchen, 118
Stanley's, 147
Superdawg Drive-In, 155
SushiSamba Rio, 145
Toast, 133, 147
Tufano's Vernon Park Tap, 121–122
Tuscany, 115, 117
Twin Anchors, 148
Uncommon Ground, 150
The Village, 118–119
Vivere, 119
Walker Bros. Original Pancake House (Wilmette), 284–285
White Fence Farm (Romeoville), 121
The Wieners Circle, 155
Wishbone, 122, 132
Won Kow, 114

FROMMER'S® COMPLETE TRAVEL GUIDES

Alaska
Amalfi Coast
American Southwest
Amsterdam
Argentina
Arizona
Atlanta
Australia
Austria
Bahamas
Barcelona
Beijing
Belgium, Holland & Luxembourg
Belize
Bermuda
Boston
Brazil
British Columbia & the Canadian
  Rockies
Brussels & Bruges
Budapest & the Best of Hungary
Buenos Aires
Calgary
California
Canada
Cancún, Cozumel & the Yucatán
Cape Cod, Nantucket & Martha's
  Vineyard
Caribbean
Caribbean Ports of Call
Carolinas & Georgia
Chicago
Chile & Easter Island
China
Colorado
Costa Rica
Croatia
Cuba
Denmark
Denver, Boulder & Colorado Springs
Eastern Europe
Ecuador & the Galapagos Islands
Edinburgh & Glasgow
England
Europe
Europe by Rail

Florence, Tuscany & Umbria
Florida
France
Germany
Greece
Greek Islands
Guatemala
Hawaii
Hong Kong
Honolulu, Waikiki & Oahu
India
Ireland
Israel
Italy
Jamaica
Japan
Kauai
Las Vegas
London
Los Angeles
Los Cabos & Baja
Madrid
Maine Coast
Maryland & Delaware
Maui
Mexico
Montana & Wyoming
Montréal & Québec City
Morocco
Moscow & St. Petersburg
Munich & the Bavarian Alps
Nashville & Memphis
New England
Newfoundland & Labrador
New Mexico
New Orleans
New York City
New York State
New Zealand
Northern Italy
Norway
Nova Scotia, New Brunswick &
  Prince Edward Island
Oregon
Paris
Peru

Philadelphia & the Amish Country
Portugal
Prague & the Best of the Czech
  Republic
Provence & the Riviera
Puerto Rico
Rome
San Antonio & Austin
San Diego
San Francisco
Santa Fe, Taos & Albuquerque
Scandinavia
Scotland
Seattle
Seville, Granada & the Best of
  Andalusia
Shanghai
Sicily
Singapore & Malaysia
South Africa
South America
South Florida
South Korea
South Pacific
Southeast Asia
Spain
Sweden
Switzerland
Tahiti & French Polynesia
Texas
Thailand
Tokyo
Toronto
Turkey
USA
Utah
Vancouver & Victoria
Vermont, New Hampshire & Maine
Vienna & the Danube Valley
Vietnam
Virgin Islands
Virginia
Walt Disney World® & Orlando
Washington, D.C.
Washington State

FROMMER'S® DAY BY DAY GUIDES

Amsterdam
Barcelona
Beijing
Boston
Cancun & the Yucatan
Chicago
Florence & Tuscany

Hong Kong
Honolulu & Oahu
London
Maui
Montréal
Napa & Sonoma
New York City

Paris
Provence & the Riviera
Rome
San Francisco
Venice
Washington D.C.

PAULINE FROMMER'S GUIDES: SEE MORE. SPEND LESS.

Alaska
Hawaii
Italy

Las Vegas
London
New York City

Paris
Walt Disney World®
Washington D.C.

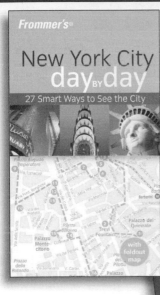

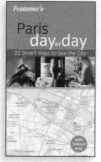

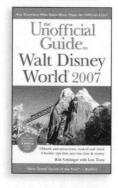